Digital Telephony
Over Cable

Digital Telephony Over Cable

The PacketCable™ Network

D.R. Evans

Addison-Wesley

Boston • San Francisco • New York • Toronto
Montreal • London • Munich • Paris • Madrid • Capetown
Sydney • Tokyo • Singapore • Mexico City

The publisher offers discounts on this book when ordered in quantity for special sales. For more information, please contact:

Pearson Education Corporate Sales Division
One Lake Street
Upper Saddle River, NJ 07458
(800) 382-3419
corpsales@pearsontechgroup.com

Visit AW on the Web: www.awl.com/cseng/

Library of Congress Cataloging-in-Publication Data

Evans, D. R.
   Digital telephony over cable / D. R. Evans
      p. cm.
   Includes bibliographical references and index.
   ISBN 0-201-72827-3
      1. Digital telephone systems.   I. Title.

TK5103.7 .E98 2001
   621.385—dc21   2001018887

OpenCable™, PacketCable™, DOCSIS™, CABLENET®, Go2Broadband^SM, "Revolutionizing Cable Technology™" and CableLabs® and the "CableLabs Certified™" logo are trademarks of Cable Television Laboratories, Inc. and are used with permission.

ISBN 0-201-72827-3

Text printed on recycled paper
1 2 3 4 5 6 7 8 9—PH—05 04 03 02 01
First printing, May 2001

3 3001 00854 8249

CONTENTS

List of Tables

List of Figures

Foreword

In 1998, North American cable operators started researching technologies that would enable the cable television network to deliver advanced real-time multimedia services to subscribers. Although several solutions existed at that time, none provided the integrated end-to-end solution required to maximize the service-delivery potential inherent in the broadband capabilities of the cable television network. Those involved in the PacketCable™ project set out to identify existing or develop new mechanisms that would work in concert with the cable television network to deliver compelling new services to subscribers.

PacketCable recognized the emergence of the Internet Protocol (IP) as the technology of choice for delivery of services over packet data networks. The Internet Protocol is the foundation of the many protocols and interfaces that make the World Wide Web a viable delivery mechanism for entertainment, information exchange and online commerce. The PacketCable objective became clear: develop a suite of protocols and interface specifications based on IP that enable the delivery of voice, video and other multimedia services over the cable television network.

The PacketCable interface specifications were developed through the collaborative effort of North American cable operators and forward-looking product development vendors for the cable industry. Based on open industry standards, these specifications were designed to promote multivendor product interoperability. Thanks to the dedicated effort of this talented group of individuals, we'll be seeing services such as Voice over IP, multimedia conferencing and interactive gaming delivered over the cable network.

As an industry consultant, Doc Evans has been a key technical contributor to many areas of the PacketCable project. Doc's breadth of knowledge on the PacketCable project coupled with his technical background gave him the insight necessary to describe the technology from multiple perspectives, as he has done with this book.

Digital Telephony Over Cable chronicles the development of PacketCable. It describes the design of the architecture in ways that are practical and entertaining. General technical concepts are introduced in a straightforward manner and often described using interesting and tangible real-world examples. As expected, technical details are also presented thoroughly.

As a companion document to the PacketCable specifications, this book provides real value to the reader by adding explanation and insight that is not typically found in technical interface specifications. We anticipate finding dog-eared copies of this book on desktops and lab benches for quite some time.

Glenn Russell
    Director, Multimedia Architectures, CableLabs®

Maria Stachelek
    Director, Business Development and Standards, CableLabs®

Preface

We live in interesting times, especially in the telecommunications industry. The ubiquity of cellphones, deregulation, voice mail (a double-edged sword if ever there was one), cheap long-distance phone service, direct international dialing, broadband access, always-on access to the Internet—the list of recent fundamental changes in the way that telecommunications impact ordinary consumers could probably extend over several paragraphs. Despite the many changes that have occurred, there seems no reason to believe that the flood of new services will not continue for at least the next half decade, and probably longer.

This book describes a brand new communications technology that is in the process of moving from small-scale trials to full national deployment.

Starting in the late 1990s, consumers have become acquainted with the notion of broadband access to the Internet. The two principal methods used to provide this high-speed access are cable modems, which send their traffic through the same cable as is used to supply cable television, and variants of a technology known as DSL (Digital Subscriber Line), which works over ordinary telephone lines.

The cable and telephone companies are in a race to provide the dominant technology (either cable modem or DSL, respectively) that will provide broadband Internet access to homes. Especially in the United States, cable modem technology has maintained an early lead over DSL, in part because most cable modems use standardized technology whereas DSL technology has (so far) been hampered by the lack of a single, pervasive standard.

DSL does have one tremendous advantage, though. A DSL line can be used simultaneously to provide broadband Internet access and to place (and receive) ordinary phone calls. Until now, cable modems have provided only the first of these features. This book addresses the mechanism by which the cable companies have chosen to provide true digital telephony over the cable access network using ordinary cable modems.

The technology is known generically as Packet Cable Telephony. The particular implementation that we discuss is the result of several years of cooperative effort by cable television operators and vendors of networking and telephony equipment. Known as PacketCable™, all of the major cable companies have stated that they intend to deploy large-scale PacketCable networks in the course of the next few years.

In this book, we provide a detailed explanation of how PacketCable works. The author's intention is to provide a "one-stop" book on PacketCable for graduate students, implementers, managers and anyone else interested in understanding how a complete, functional telephony network can be built from scratch using IP (Internet Protocol) technology running over a shared access medium. This (unfortunately for the author) is a nontrivial task.

The PacketCable specifications alone run close to a thousand pages. The specifications for other technologies that are required in the network (such as the various Internet Protocol standards and the cable modem DOCSIS standards) are roughly the same length. The problem then is obvious: How can one summarize a couple of thousand pages of dense, technical documentation in a way that is simultaneously accurate, thorough and comprehensible? Clearly, something has to give.

The author has attempted to explain in some detail each of the important parts of the technology. Individual chapters are dedicated to the various principles on which PacketCable is built. The intention is that a reader with little background in either networking or telephony should be able to read a chapter—possibly in conjunction with Chapter 1 or Chapter 2—and come away with a solid understanding of exactly how PacketCable handles the particular issues discussed in that chapter.

What we do not discuss are many of the extreme cases, exceptions and detailed requirements placed on equipment by the specifications. The specifications expend a lot of effort ensuring that PacketCable equipment manufactured by vendor A is guaranteed to interoperate correctly with similar equipment manufactured by vendor B. And, in a few cases (although as infrequently as possible), we simply punt: If a feature is particularly complicated and not sufficiently central to the basic theme of explaining PacketCable, we sometimes either avoid it completely or mention it and refer the reader directly to the specifications. Usually only an implementor would be interested in such details, and an implementor should be reading the original specifications in conjunction with this book anyway.

Which brings us to the subject of the market for this book. We just mentioned three likely markets: graduate students, managers and implementors.

We anticipate that graduates working in the fields of advanced networking and telecommunications will find here a thorough explanation of the many issues (and the chosen solutions) facing anyone wishing to design a large-scale, commercially deployable digital telephony network using modern technology and protocols. Managers in the telecommunications industry will find the book useful because it encompasses the entire network. Managers need to understand the "big picture," which is provided in the first couple of chapters of the book, as well as the beginning portions of each of the remaining chapters.

For the implementor, this book is intended to provide an in-depth contextual reference for the PacketCable and other specifications. Implementors are usually concerned with the "small picture," and often this is at the expense of a good understanding of the context in which the implementor is working. Before plunging into the details of one or other of the specifications, this book is useful for providing an explanation of the specifications in ordinary words (well, mostly ordinary words), as well as providing a picture of how all the specifications fit together to define a functioning network.

I recommend reading Chapter 1 even if you have acquired this book for some of the technical material in one of the later chapters. Chapter 1 provides, among other things, an overview of the PacketCable architecture and an introduction to most of the common PacketCable devices. Also, if when skipping around you come across a term that you do not recognize, don't forget that there's a comprehensive glossary in Appendix A.

The organization of most of the chapters follows a model in which detailed information about the format of messages is provided before the higher-level picture that shows how the messages fit together to perform a useful purpose. Although this is an order of presentation that this author prefers, some people may feel uncomfortable with this approach and may prefer to skip forward to obtain a good grasp of the message flows before returning to understand exactly what is in the various messages. Feel free to skip around: It's your book, and you're entitled to use it in whatever way works for you.

The author would like to express his thanks to all who helped this book come to fruition. The author had the pleasure of working with many intelligent and knowledgeable technical architects in various PacketCable Focus Teams. Any list would be bound to miss someone, so I simply say a big "Thank you" to all.

A few people responded to specific questions while the book was being written. I would particularly like to thank Bill Marshall of AT&T Research and Flemming Andreasen, orginally of Telcordia and now with Cisco Systems, both of whom have probably forgotten more about PacketCable than any other person will ever know. Bill Kostka of CableLabs responded promptly and effectively to my DOCSIS questions, and Sasha Medvinsky of General Instruments (now Motorola) clarified several issues related to security.

CableLabs supplies liaison members to the PacketCable Focus Teams, and I would like to explicitly thank those people who fulfilled that role on the teams of which I was a member in the period that the PacketCable 1.0 specifications were being written: Ed Miller (Distributed Call Signaling), Andrew Sundelin (Dynamic Quality of Service), Glenn Russell (Dynamic Quality of Service), Chet Birger (Security), Jean Chess (Security) and Nancy Davoust (PacketCable Electronic Surveillance Protocol).

Thank you to Lucent Cable Communications in general and Jane Gambill, Marty Glapa and Rich Gitlin in particular for allowing me to represent Lucent at CableLabs. Thank you also to SecureCable, Inc. for allowing me the time to complete this book while representing them on PacketCable 1.x Focus Teams.

I wish to thank the various people at Addison-Wesley who helped make this book possible. The technical reviewers were Paul Obeda, Neil Olsen, Khaled Amer,

Andrew Valentine, Don Stanwyck, Al Vonkeman, Laura Knapp, Dan Pitt and John J. Brassil. To them go my thanks for pointing out many places where the original text left something to be desired (including, sometimes, accuracy). Special thanks go to my editor, Stephane Thomas, for being such a pleasant person to communicate with on the phone and via e-mail. Thanks also to the people behind the scenes at the production department who had a hand in turning this from a word-processed document into a real book.

Thank you especially to the cable companies for seeing the need for, and supporting, PacketCable.

And, finally, a few words of blatant self-promotion. Writing a technical book is interesting, but hardly fun. One day I hope to escape the hurly-burly of real life and "retire" to write novels full-time instead of merely as time allows. In the Bad Old Days of last year, getting a novel published was much harder than publishing a technical book. After many "very-nearly-almost" acceptances by big New York publishers, I became disenchanted with the whole idea of spending several months writing a novel only to discover that every publisher had a different reason for rejecting it.

With the advent of Print-On-Demand technology, which allows publishers to print books one at a time as orders come in, my novels are now being made available. Please check out *http://www.sff.net/people/N7DR/drevans.htp* for details.

D. R. Evans
    President, D. R. Evans Consulting, Inc.
    September, 2000
    N7DR@arrl.net

Chapter

1

Background

The PacketCable architecture is designed to be a robust, complete, end-end
broadband architecture that supports voice, video, and other multimedia
services. The architecture is capable of supporting millions of subscribers over
multiple cable operator networks.

PKT-TR-ARCH-V01-991201[1]

As a reminder that not all the important technological changes affecting consumers are driven by the creation of ever-faster, ever-smarter hardware and software, the technology used to deliver digital telephony over cable television systems has been driven into existence as much by the U.S. government's 1974 antitrust suit against AT&T as for any immediate technological reason.

After several years of legal maneuvering surrounding the antitrust suit, the government and AT&T agreed to the terms of a consent decree, called the "Modified Final Judgement", which was finalized in 1982.[2] The terms of the Modified Final Judgement came into effect on January 1, 1984, and resulted in what has come to be known as "the breakup of AT&T". By the terms of the agreement, the once-monolithic monopoly was broken into many pieces, including several large **Regional Bell Operating Companies** (**RBOC**s) that would be responsible for carrying local telephone calls, as well as a much-reduced AT&T responsible for carrying long-distance traffic.

Unfortunately for the new, long-distance-only AT&T, any long-distance call also has to traverse local lines at the ends of the call, and those local lines were now owned and managed by RBOCs. Thus the RBOCs were entitled to receive an access charge for the use of their local lines every time a long-distance call was made. These access charges were typically a few cents per minute and resulted in an annual cost

---

1. This, like most of the chapter epigraphs, is taken directly from a PacketCable™ document.
2. United States v. AT&T Co., 552 F. Suppl. 131.

to AT&T of roughly $17 billion, paid to the RBOCs, many of which used that money to begin construction of long-distance networks to compete directly with AT&T.[3]

In 1996, Congress passed a new Telecommunications Act, which did away with many of the restrictions that had been emplaced by the Modified Final Judgement. Broadly speaking, all companies were now free to compete with one another on a more or less equal footing, whether in the local or long-distance markets.

However, the fact remained that local access was still in the hands of the RBOCs, and AT&T began to seek a way to build a local-access network that would bypass the RBOCs—and, not incidentally, the $17 billion annual bill for access.

At about the same time, cable TV companies were beginning to upgrade their aging equipment to allow them to carry two-way digital traffic, with the intention of allowing high-speed access to the Internet from the home. But if the cable companies' networks could carry high-speed two-way digital traffic, there was no reason to confine that traffic to e-mail and Web browsing. The traffic could just as easily be voice traffic, or, in a word, telephony.

AT&T saw its opportunity and began investing heavily in the cable TV industry. In the year 1999 alone, it invested more than $110 billion buying cable companies outright, upgrading plants, and entering into service agreements. And packet cable telephony was born.

The Residential Broadband Pipe

For most of the twentieth century, homes had two sets of utility wires connecting them to the outside world: One set carried voice telephony (commonly called "twisted pair"), and the second was a connection to the local electrical utility to deliver power to the home. During the past 30 years, a third connection has become commonplace: As of 1997, approximately 67% of American homes were subscribed to a coax-based cable television service, and nearly 97% of all homes were passed by cable.[4]

At the same time that America was being wired for cable television, another phenomenon swept the country. Thirty years ago, most computers were large machines maintained by universities and corporations in vast air-conditioned rooms, of interest only to a tiny minority. Gradually, though, computers moved into the home, first merely as interesting toys for tinkerers and hobbyists but, quite quickly, as truly useful tools. And then the Web arrived.

The World Wide Web was a byproduct of an invention by Tim Berners-Lee, at the time a high-energy physicist working at the **European Organization for Nuclear Research**, **CERN**. Dr. Berners-Lee invented a document management system that

---

3. It is also worth noting that this sum is greater than the total profit of the RBOCs.
4. "Cable Television Developments", Fall, 1997, NCTA, Washington, D.C.

not only displayed the text of research papers, but also allowed the reader to jump immediately to a paper referenced within the text. This mechanism is called hyperlinking, and the language that Berners-Lee invented to perform this magic became the basis for **Hypertext Markup Language**, **HTML**, which remains even today the basic building block out of which most pages on the World Wide Web are constructed. The small web of hyperlinked physics research papers that Berners-Lee envisaged grew at a rate and in ways that no one could have foreseen. HTML version 0 was invented in 1989. Ten years later there were an estimated 800 million pages on the Web, with no end in sight.

But it wasn't just the invention of HTML that brought computers out of the universities and into the home. Until the mid-1990s, the Internet was run under a strict policy that allowed no commercial traffic. (Think about that the next time you are waiting for a Web page full of advertisements to download.)

Originally, the Internet was a research network, run for the benefit of universities, and no traffic pertaining to the exchange of money was permitted by the U.S. government. In the early 1990s, the Internet was run under the auspices of the National Science Foundation and was a place of (mostly) amiable academic discussion and collaboration and a mechanism that permitted a slow but on the whole reliable method of moving files (often of arcane scientific data) around the country. Although, toward the end of this period, ordinary citizens were allowed to use the Internet for other purposes, anyone wishing access to the Internet for personal use had to sign an agreement, called an Acceptable Use Policy, that she would send no messages with commercial content.

In 1994 the funding model for the Internet changed. Instead of being funded as a research project of the U.S. government, the Internet was essentially privatized. The government became only one of many possible sources of revenue for the operators of the various equipment and services that constituted the Internet. Since the government became only one of many entities paying for the Internet, the ban on commercial content was unsustainable. And as soon as commercial interests were let loose, the Internet—and the world—was changed forever.

The near-simultaneous commercialization of the Internet, the invention of the Web, and the steady decline in the price of reasonably powerful computers, as well as the increase in the speed of analog modems to the point where entire Web pages could be downloaded in a matter of seconds, drove an unprecedented explosion in the availability of information online and the ability of ordinary people to access that information.

People flocked to the Internet and, particularly, the relatively bandwidth-hungry Web. Prior to the emergence of the Web, the main use of the Internet was for non-real-time electronic mail. To someone sending or receiving e-mail, a slow modem was a minor annoyance but little more. But to someone browsing a Web site, delays of even a few seconds while downloading a page quickly become irritating.

Modem speeds increased, eventually reaching a maximum of more than 50 kilobits per second (which still seems astonishing to those of us who once edited documents remotely over 110-baud links). However, even as modem speeds were increasing, the Web, now that it was open to commercial interests, became a place of eye-catching, moving, full-color advertisements and (often even more annoying to users) trite jingles.

The transformation of the typical Web page from a static representation of text to a multimedia "experience" caused the bandwidth requirements for Web pages to download in anything close to "real-time" to escalate astronomically. The 1996 corporate home page comprising a few tens of lines of text by 1999 might sport several full-color images of several tens of kilobytes each, to say nothing of hundreds of lines of JavaScript and one or more Java applets. Analog modems could not keep up with this need for speed, and, as is often the case, new technologies appeared to meet the need.

ISDN and DSL

For many years, most telephone companies have made available a digital alternative to ordinary analog phone lines. These lines are called **Integrated Services Digital Network** (**ISDN**) lines, and they typically provide a data bandwidth of 128 kbps to the end user. This is more than twice the bandwidth of the fastest analog modems.

However, ISDN, especially in the United States, is not cheap, since it was intended for business rather than residential use. Start-up costs typically exceed $500, and per-month fees approach $100 per month in many parts of the country. Not surprisingly, it never became popular for residential use.

More recently, a group of alternative methods for providing digital services over ordinary twisted pair copper wires has surfaced. These methods are usually known as **xDSL**, or **Digital Subscriber Line**, technologies. The most common variant of DSL offered to residential users is known as **ADSL**, or **Asymmetric Digital Subscriber Line** service. ADSL offerings vary greatly from locale to locale, but a typical residential ADSL service allows 128 kbps upstream (from the house) and 256 kbps downstream (to the house) for a cost of around $30 per month. In some competitive markets, although the price is usually not lowered, the bandwidth provided may be substantially higher.

There are, however, considerable technical difficulties that hinder the widespread adoption of ADSL. The principal obstacle is that a user's telephone lines have to meet stringent quality criteria before the service can be supported. The telephone companies, content to milk businesses for ISDN subscription fees, have been caught off-guard by the sudden demand for residential and home-office ADSL, and they did not upgrade their lines in time to meet the unexpected surge in demand. However,

ADSL and its variants have emerged as the only currently viable alternative to what is presently the most common method of obtaining high-speed Internet access in the home: the cable modem.

Cable Access to the Internet

As the pressure for increased bandwidth—particularly in the downstream direction—intensified, it was not long before cable television companies realized that this represented an opportunity to tap a new—and possibly quite considerable—source of income.

The cable that delivers television is called coaxial because it is constructed from cylinders that share a common axis (see Figure 1-1). Generally, its name is shortened simply to "coax"—pronounced "co-ax".

Signals are transmitted on the so-called "inner" of the coax, which is simply a copper wire. The "outer", which is constructed of a flexible braid, screens the signals from the outside world. This prevents the signals from radiating into space and also blocks ingress of interfering signals from the outside world. Although signal strength is not reduced by radiation, it does become attenuated through losses in the coax. The signal strength can be increased in long runs of coax by amplifiers, but each amplifier introduces some noise, so that although the signal strength is increased, its quality is slightly degraded.

Separating the inner wire from the outer braid is a flexible plastic insulating material called a **dielectric**. Coax with a high-quality dielectric has a greater bandwidth than coax with a lower-quality dielectric. A typical high-quality coax has a bandwidth of 700 MHz or more. Very high-quality (and therefore expensive) coax may have a bandwidth as high as 1 GHz. High-quality coax also allows for greater separation between amplifiers.

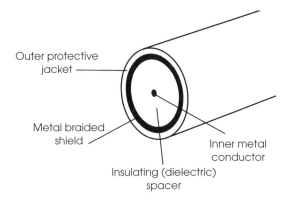

Figure 1-1 Cutaway Picture of Coaxial Cable (coax)

The coax that provides cable television to a home represents an extraordinarily wide pipe for information delivery. A single analog television signal encoded to North American standards occupies 6 MHz of bandwidth. If, instead of filling that bandwidth with an analog television signal, the 6 MHz is used to carry digital data, rates of 30 to 40 Mbps are realizable (see the "Downstream Data Flow Through a Cable Modem" section in Chapter 3). A single coax cable can carry *simultaneously* a hundred or more analog television channels. If one were to take an extreme case and dedicate the entire cable to digital transmissions, it could theoretically deliver something in excess of 4 Gbps to the home.

Users accustomed to analog modem downstream speeds of 50 kbps (on a good day), or even ADSL users operating with downstream speeds of 256 kbps, quite reasonably find the thought of speeds measured in the tens of millions of bits per second fairly mind-boggling. Unfortunately, life isn't quite this simple; users of cable-based systems cannot expect to receive bandwidths even close to these numbers. To understand why not, we need to take a closer look at how cable television systems work.

Hybrid Fiber Coax Networks

No two cable television companies are alike. They range in size from the minuscule, serving perhaps only a thousand or so subscribers in a single rural county, to the enormous, serving millions of people in several major metropolitan areas. A cable television company may offer half a dozen channels or more than a hundred. The network used to deliver programming into the home might have been laid 30 years ago or just last week. There is no "typical" cable operator; every cable company will have idiosyncrasies in its operation. However, for our purposes, we will invent a cable company, the Really Astounding Television Company—RATCo for short—with characteristics that approximate those of many real companies.

RATCo is a so-called **Multiple Systems Operator**, or **MSO**. Technically, an MSO must operate *multiple* cable TV systems, but the term has now become synonymous with "cable TV operator", regardless of the size of the operator's network. As in common usage, we will use a number of terms to describe a cable TV company: MSO, network operator and service provider. All these are, for our purpose, synonymous.

RATCo serves a single large metropolitan area. Its coax passes half a million homes, two-thirds of which subscribe to some form of cable programming. Its distribution plant comprises an efficient **Hybrid Fiber Coax** (**HFC**) network—a network that carries signals over both coax and fiber links. In an HFC network, the signal path passes through three hierarchical systems: the trunk system, the distribution system and the subscriber drop.

Figure 1-2 shows an overview of the RATCo distribution system. Signals are injected into the trunk system at the headend. These signals are typically received

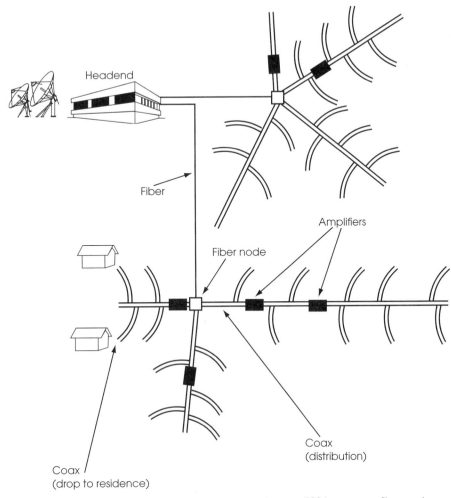

Headend

Fiber

Amplifiers

Fiber node

Coax
(distribution)

Coax
(drop to residence)

Approx. 500 homes per fiber node
Approx. 20,000 homes per headend

Figure 1-2 RATCo Distribution System

from a geostationary satellite orbiting above Earth's equator, although sometimes they are locally generated programs. Less frequently, they are backhauled from over landline networks from some other broadcast or cable television system.

Originally, cable TV systems were constructed using only coax as the distribution medium. However, signals in reasonably priced coax are attenuated relatively quickly. In order to provide a sufficient signal level at the television, long chains of amplifiers are needed in coax-only systems. Each amplifier introduces a small but measurable loss of signal quality, so that after a long chain of perhaps as many as

40 or more amplifiers, picture quality can be severely degraded to the point where it might be unacceptable to the consumer.

In addition, amplifiers are relatively expensive and often require maintenance, since their performance tends to deteriorate over time as components age and are exposed to extremes of temperature.

The solution to these problems is to change the topology of the cable system into a tree-and-branch configuration, as shown in Figure 1-2. In the trunk, fiber is used to carry the signals. Fiber has much better attenuation characteristics than coax, especially at high frequencies, and allows for the reduction, or even the elimination, of amplifiers over the long distance between the headend and neighborhoods.

The fiber is terminated in a **fiber node** (sometimes called a **distribution node**), out of which extends a coax distribution system, usually in a star configuration. The distribution system contains amplifiers as needed, and from it occur the actual coax drops, typically 150 feet in length, that deliver the television signals to the homes. In this architecture, the signal typically passes through only a few amplifiers (less than ten, often less than five) between headend and the home. A typical fiber node serves around 500 homes, using four legs of roughly 125 homes apiece.

The useful bandwidth of this system, depending on the quality and number of the amplifiers installed as well as the quality of the coax itself, generally extends to at least 750 MHz. As we have mentioned, in some areas bandwidth is as high as 1 GHz. Figure 1-3 shows how this bandwidth is allocated according to the most common frequency plan. This frequency plan, commonly known as a **bandplan**, is not compulsory. A cable distribution plant is not subject to mandatory frequency restrictions like the ones imposed on ordinary broadcast signals.

For electromagnetic broadcast radiation, the spectrum is strictly regulated within the United States by the FCC, which operates in concert with similar authorities in

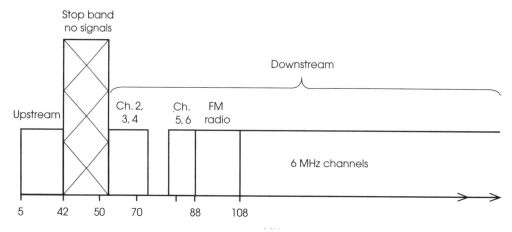

Figure 1-3   Frequency Use Inside a Cable Distribution System

other countries when necessary in order to ensure that each user of the spectrum can operate without interference to or from other users.[5] However, this kind of regulation is unnecessary for cable systems, since the signals are confined to the transmission medium (fiber or coax) and do not escape into the surrounding environment. Consequently, an MSO is free to adopt any frequency bandplan that suits its purpose.

Most of the frequency spectrum is allocated to downstream signals (signals travelling from the headend to the home). Only a relatively small portion of the available bandwidth, in the range 5 to 42 MHz, is allocated for upstream traffic. Since cable television systems are predominantly a one-way medium, the upstream/downstream allocation is highly asymmetric, and the upstream portion is in the noisiest, lower-frequency part of the spectrum. The amplifiers in many older cable television systems operate only in one direction (downstream) and contain filters to prevent unwanted noise in the lower part of the spectrum from being carried upstream and interfering with the television signals.

Before a cable network can carry two-way traffic, whether voice or data, it must be upgraded, which is often an expensive operation. Special two-way amplifiers called **diplexers** must be installed. These amplify one frequency band in the upstream direction and another band in the downstream direction. In addition, the quality of the connectors and terminators in the system must often be improved to minimize noise ingress and generation in the spectrum below 42 MHz.

Even when the plant has been upgraded, it is often the case that only a small portion of the theoretical upstream bandwidth is actually available, since it is almost impossible to eliminate all ingress noise. In a typical environment, only between 10 and 20 MHz of upstream bandwidth will be sufficiently noise-free to be usable.

Even with such a limitation, the available upstream bandwidth would seem to be much higher than for other systems such as ADSL or ISDN. There is, however, a fundamental difference between cable systems and those based on telephony lines: A subscriber has full, exclusive use of a leased telephony line, but the cable plant is a resource that must be shared with other users in the neighborhood. This difference, as we shall see, has pervasive repercussions that drive most of the differences between cable-based and wire-line telephony systems.

One important but perhaps non-obvious fact should be stressed. Cable networks are principally a *residential* phenomenon. Relatively few businesses have ready access to cable HFC networks; therefore, the cable companies see residential customers, telecommuters and Small Office/Home Office (SOHO) users as the principal early market for telephony over cable services.

---

5. The list of such users is long. They included entities such as amateur radio operators, the military, direction finding and navigation services, civil aviation, emergency services, cellphones, Bluetooth devices and others.

Customer Premise Equipment

Most of this book is concerned with what happens outside the customer's home, inside the cable network. However, since this particular chapter is intended to provide background information to provide a context for what follows, we will digress briefly to examine some of the equipment that a customer might have in his home and which the customer might wish to integrate with the network outside that home.

Home Networks

Although they have been predicted for many years, true home networks—several electronic devices communicating quickly and easily—are only just beginning to appear. Until recently, home networks were largely the plaything of technogeeks with too much time on their hands. They were complicated to install, difficult to debug, and, in an era when few houses had more than one computer, ultimately rather pointless.

The convergence of several technologies, combined with an unforeseen need, has acted to change this situation. The unexpected demand for functional home networks has, like so many things in recent years, been driven by the advent of the World Wide Web. Many schools now expect students to be able to perform research for homework assignments over the Web. Parents want to analyze investments at home, kids want to play games and talk to one another in chat rooms, and everyone wants to simply browse the Web.

The oft-repeated paradigm of "one person, one computer" is no longer sufficient. Those computers must have access to the Internet if they are to be useful. The most common way of arranging for all computers in a home to have Internet access is to configure one machine as a gateway, with a connection, typically through a broadband "always-on" medium such as ADSL or cable, to an ISP. The remaining machines then connect to the gateway through a home network.

Other devices may be connected to the network as well as computers, allowing all the users in the house to share them. Some resources, such as disk drives, may be local to one of the computers but made accessible through the network to the other computers. Figure 1-4 shows the kind of home network that is becoming increasingly common.

At the time of this writing, several competing technologies exist for supplying the connections among devices on a home network, and it is impossible to guess which (or which combination) will eventually become dominant.

Although each of the technologies is initially being deployed with only data networking in mind, all can be adapted to support real-time, two-way, packetized telephony traffic. Hence it is likely that as home networks become more widely deployed,

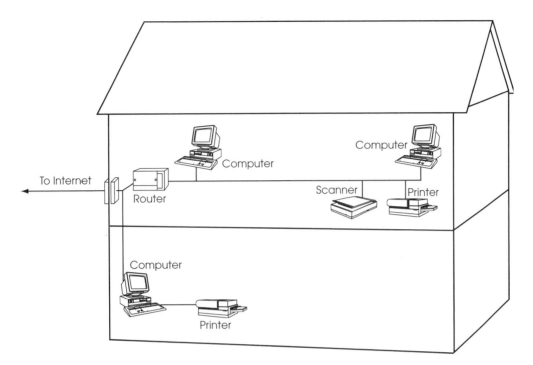

Figure 1-4 Home Network

and as telephony changes from being a circuit-switched to a packetized medium, telephones will become an increasingly common peripheral on home networks.[6]

Ethernet

Traditional home networks have used the **Ethernet** standard (specified in IEEE standard 802.3) running over cables specifically installed for the purpose. Ethernet is fast (typically 10 Mbit per second[7] but sometimes ten times faster). It is also cheap, with network cards typically costing less than $50 in the retail market. However, it is relatively complicated to install, and the inconvenience of running new wires through a home has led to only limited acceptance. Nevertheless, as of this writing the majority of home networks use standard Ethernet technology.

---

6. As the term is used in this book, a *packet* network is a network that carries digital data that are clumped together for transmission into small units called packets.

7. The actual throughput of a high-speed shared network (for example, during a file transfer) is typically about 10% of the theoretical maximum, although this number varies greatly as a function of network load. It may reach around 50% or even higher on a home network, which is often rather lightly loaded.

The other technologies are more experimental, and all are undergoing rapid change. New standards are published frequently, and new equipment comes to market every few months. Prices for all of these technologies are at least several times the cost of Ethernet but dropping rapidly.

Power Line

The electrical wiring within a home can be used to carry digital data. This has the advantage of ubiquity: Every room has one or more power outlets. However, as of this writing, the current state of the technology allows only relatively low-speed networks. In-home power wiring is inherently noisy (every time an electrical device turns on or off, a noise spike is generated, which briefly halts the network); there are also difficulties associated with ensuring that data carried on power lines remain private.

Wireless

Wireless is relatively expensive and currently quite slow (1 to 2 Mbps for typical low-end systems available in retail stores). As with power line networks, there are concerns about ensuring that data carried on wireless networks remain private. However, the chances are good that the sheer convenience of wireless networks, as well as standards that are currently being developed to support higher bandwidth, increased convenience and strong security, will eventually outweigh any increased expense.

Phone Wiring

Home networks based on the HomePNA specifications are probably the most common type of home network after Ethernet. Several large companies have introduced products based on these specifications. Although network speeds and cost are reasonable, phone outlets are far from ubiquitous, and the wiring in some houses (especially older houses with multiple phone lines) does not easily support networking. Any of these technologies may be easily interfaced to a coaxial cable access network provided by a cable company, through a device called a **Network Interface Unit**, or **NIU** (see Figure 1-5, which shows one of many possible configurations).

The NIU is typically located on the side of the home, mounted in a manner similar to the traditional telephony **Network Interface Device** (**NID**). Like an NID, it serves as the demarcation point between the user's in-home wiring and the larger network to which it is attached. It also provides electrical isolation from the larger network, so that electrical surges (induced, for example, by lightning strikes) do not raise voltages in the home to dangerous levels.

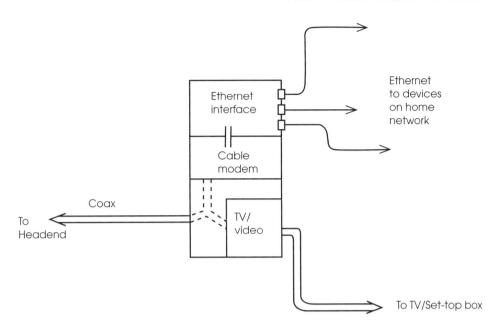

Figure 1-5 Home Network Connecting to a Cable Through a Network Interface Unit

The cable provided by the cable company allows the user high-speed access to the cable company's network and through that to services and applications supplied by the cable company and by other providers. One such major application is the subject of this book: high-quality digital telephony.

The PacketCable™ Project

In the early days of the telephone and railroad networks, many small companies sprang up, installing the new technology in different parts of the country. However, there was no incentive for these companies to build networks that interoperated with each other, and the result was a plethora of incompatible systems (utilizing different voltage and impedance characteristics in the case of the telephone networks and different gauges of track in the case of the railroads). Each of these systems worked well enough in themselves, but they were for the most part incapable of easily interoperating with a competitor's system—or even a noncompeting system in a neighboring state.

In order to ensure that a similar situation did not arise with the new networks designed to deliver packetized telephony over cable systems, a consortium of cable companies initiated the PacketCable™ project under the auspices of Cable Laboratories, Inc. (usually referred to simply as CableLabs®), with the goal of precisely specifying the interface and behavior of all the elements within such a network, so that interoperability would be possible even in the early stages of deployment.[8] This book describes the resulting version 1.0 PacketCable network, which is now being deployed to deliver digital telephony over cable to residences throughout the country.[9]

There is an interesting twist to the PacketCable specifications. In order to participate in the process of generating the specifications, a vendor must give up the right to require a fee of any kind for intellectual property that is incorporated into the specification, so long as the specification is being used to implement a product for the cable industry. In other words, if the SuperCableTelephone Corporation holds a patent on some particularly nifty piece of technology that it would like to see incorporated into a specification (so that all its competitors would be forced to use that technology in creating a PacketCable-compliant product), the SuperCableTelephone Corporation can only do so if it is prepared to allow its competitors to use that technology at no charge in products destined for the cable market. This is a very different approach from the more formal standards-making bodies such as the **IETF** and the ITU, which normally require only that intellectual property be made available on a nondiscriminatory basis and at a reasonable price.

Table 1-1 lists the complete set of PacketCable specifications that are the subject of this book. These specifications run to several thousand pages of detailed technical material and are available at *www.packetcable.com* for those who have trouble sleeping at night. Note that **Distributed Call Signaling** (**DCS**) is not part of the official release of PacketCable 1.0. However, its likely future importance is such that we will include it as if it were a fully fledged member of this release. The DCS specification can be found at *ftp://ftp.cablelabs.com/pub/ietfdocs/dcsdraft.pdf*.[10]

A word of caution is in order here. The PacketCable specifications are not as stable as ITU standards; they are not even as stable as IETF ones. Version 1.0 of the specifications will be followed by later versions, which will address areas left unspecified by the version 1.0 documents. In addition, minor changes to the version 1.0 specifications

---

8. The original constituent companies were Comcast Cable Communications, Inc., Cogeco, Cox Communications, Tele-Communications, Inc., Time Warner Cable, MediaOne, Inc., Rogers Cablesystems Limited, Le Groupe Vidéotron, and CableLabs, acting on behalf of its member companies.

9. PacketCable was specifically a North American project. Undoubtedly a large portion of the PacketCable specifications will be used by overseas cable operators in designing similar systems. However, international interoperability was never a stated goal of the PacketCable project. As of this writing, CableLabs is in the process of submitting many of the specifications for approval by the ITU and the IETF. The PacketCable project will thus benefit both from the rapid development provided by an industry-based consortium and from the wide acceptance that is accorded ITU and IETF standards.

10. Note added in proof: Subsequent to writing this book, the electronic surveillance specification was recategorized as a version 1.1 specification. The author treats it herein as a version 1.0 specification, as it was originally intended.

Table 1-1 PacketCable 1.0 Documents

Specifications	
Area Covered	*Document*
Network-Based Call Signaling (NCS)	PKT-SP-EC-MGCP-I02-991201
Security	PKT-SP-SEC-I01-991201
NCS MIB	PKT-SP-MIB-NCS-I01-991201
MIB Framework	PKT-SP-MIBS-I01-991201
MTA MIB	PKT-SP-MIB-MTA-I01-991201
Internet Signaling Transport Protocol (ISTP)	PKT-SP-ISTP-I01-991201
PSTN Gateway Call Signaling (TGCP)	PKT-SP-TGCP-I01-991201
Dynamic Quality of Service	PKT-SP-DQOS-I01-991201
Event Messaging	PKT-SP-EM-I01-991201
Codecs	PKT-SP-CODEC-I01-991201
Provisioning	PKT-SP-PROV-I01-991201
Electronic Surveillance	PKT-SP-ESP-I01-991229
Distributed Call Signaling (DCS)	PKT-SP-DCS-D02-991007
Technical Reports	
Area Covered	*Document*
Electronic Surveillance Call Flows	PKT-TR-ESCF-V01-991229
On-Net MTA to On-Net MTA Call Flow	PKT-TR-CF-ON-ON-V01-991201
On-Net MTA to PSTN Call Flow	PKT-TR-CF-ON-PSTN-V01-991201
Architectural Framework	PKT-TR-ARCH-V01-991201
PSTN to On-Net MTA Call Flow	PKT-TR-CF-PSTN-ON-V01-991201
Operations Support System Overview	PKT-TR-OSSI-V01-991201

are made on an ongoing basis.[11] If you are an implementor writing code that is meant to comply with the specifications, you should check the current version of the specifications to see if they contain any changes from the versions we describe in this book. Every specification contains within its name the date on which it was released; the current versions will always be available at *www.packetcable.com.*

---

11. These, however, are mostly either clarifications or corrections to remove inconsistencies.

Table 1-1 also lists several "Technical Reports". These augment the specifications by providing useful background material and describing assumptions that might not be discussed in the specifications themselves. Although they include no requirements that describe PacketCable operation in detail, the Technical Reports are useful for providing high-level overviews of much of the network, and they also provide useful insights into the reasons for some of the decisions that were made as the project developed.

As if that were not enough, PacketCable makes a fundamental assumption about the connection between a home and the operator's network: It assumes that the access protocols are those defined by version 1.1 (or later) of **DOCSIS** (the **Data-Over-Cable Service Interface Specifications**). This set of specifications, which are only marginally less soporific than the PacketCable ones, can be found at *www.cablemodem.com*.

PacketCable Architecture

Figure 1-6 shows the basic architecture of a PacketCable telephony network. The **MTA** (**Multimedia Terminal Adapter**) is a device in the home that performs all the control functions for PacketCable telephony calls. On one side, the MTA accepts input from telephones or telephone-like devices (called endpoints), and on the other side the MTA connects to a cable modem. The MTA could be a dedicated device, but the architecture also allows it to be a personal computer running an MTA program, in which case the computer might combine the functions of the MTA and a multimedia endpoint.

Although the PacketCable network was designed initially for telephony, the designers recognized from the beginning that this was a chance to not only duplicate the ordinary telephone network, but to provide an infrastructure capable of handling demands such as real-time, video-conferencing, interactive gaming and other applications that no one has yet thought of. The emphasis of this book is on telephony, but the reader should not lose sight of the fact that the PacketCable architecture is also suited to providing these other services—a topic to which we will return in our final chapter.

In the current release of the PacketCable specifications, it is assumed that the MTA is tightly coupled to a **cable modem** (**CM**). In other words, the MTA and the CM will most likely be provided in the same box and the MTA will be a specialized device rather than software running on a general-purpose computer. This requirement—that the MTA be "embedded" rather than "standalone"—is a temporary technical requirement, not a fundamental architectural one, and it will be relaxed in future releases of the specifications.

For most purposes the difference between an embedded MTA and a standalone MTA, and the difference between a dedicated MTA device and MTA software running on a general-purpose computer, may be safely ignored.

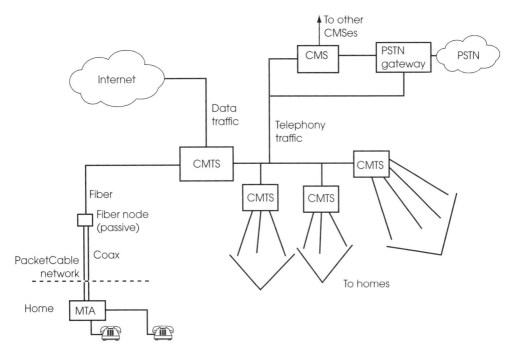

Figure 1-6 Basic PacketCable Telephony Network Architecture

The CM is the device that actually generates and places upstream signals on the coaxial cable and decodes the raw downstream signals coming from the network so that they can be interpreted by the MTA.

In the MSO's headend, the access network is terminated in a **Cable Modem Termination System** (**CMTS**). The CMTS is a somewhat complex device responsible for ensuring that all the CMs on the network remain synchronized and have fair access to the telephony network. This is necessary because, unlike the PSTN, in which each subscriber has a pair of wires dedicated to carrying that subscriber's traffic, the cable that connects a subscriber to the MSO is a shared resource. The CMTS has to manage this resource efficiently, fairly and with a very rapid response to changing requests for access from cable modems. Unlike analog modem systems, where the two ends of the link are peers, CMs act as clients to CMTSes, which instruct them exactly how to operate (see Chapter 3). The fact that the cable portion of the HFC network is a relatively low bandwidth resource that must be shared among many users is at the root of many of the difficulties in deploying digital telephony over such networks. Beyond the CMTS is the service provider's telephony network. Figure 1-5 shows a few of the more important devices in that network.

The **Call Management Server** (**CMS**) is responsible for initiating, processing and forwarding call signaling information. For example, when a subscriber wishes to place a call, the identity of the destination party—in the form of the digits dialed by the subscriber—is passed to the CMS. The CMS verifies that the subscriber is permitted to place this call and then initiates and processes signals related to the call as it proceeds. Each MTA will generally interact only with one (local) CMS, which may, depending on the manner in which the network is deployed, serve as many as 100,000 subscribers.

The PacketCable network must be able to send calls to, and receive calls from, the **Public Switched Telephone Network** (the **PSTN**)—that is, the ordinary telephone network. It does this by utilizing a PSTN gateway, which performs the necessary interface functions between the two networks for both call signaling and so-called "bearer traffic" (the actual contents of calls).

The mechanisms by which a PacketCable network operates are quite different from those that underpin the PSTN. In particular, there are two fundamental differences that pervade the PacketCable architecture and cause it to operate quite differently from the PSTN.

1. In the PSTN, each subscriber leases dedicated lines that connect the subscriber to the service provider's central office. Only the subscriber has access to the information flowing on his lines.

   In a PacketCable network the access network is a shared resource. As many as several hundred nearby homes have access to the cable that carries a particular subscriber's phone conversations.

2. The PSTN is based on **circuit-switched** technology. Originally, circuit-switched technology required wires to be physically linked to form a pathway for voice signals. Nowadays hardware switching devices simulate the same behavior.

   PacketCable networks are based on packet technology. Voice is sampled and digitized and then assembled into packets. These packets contain additional information, such as the address of the destination. The packets are transmitted to the PacketCable network, which takes responsibility for delivering them to their destination via a process called packet switching.

Both of these differences have serious ramifications for the delivery of a reliable, robust and inexpensive telephony service with adequate quality and that provides a "user experience" similar to that of the PSTN. It is the second—the change from circuit switched to packet switched technology—whose consequences are the more pervasive.

By the way, the issue of "user experience and expectation" is an important one. If one were to design a telephony network from scratch using modern technology, it is highly unlikely that the user interface would bear much resemblance to the handsets, star codes, pulse/tone signaling and so forth that we are used to. The PacketCable project set out to design a system that could closely emulate the user's experience with the PSTN, even in cases where it would be rather easy to improve on that experience.

Packet Technology

The principal building block of a packet network is, as might be guessed, a packet. A packet is a small quantity of digital information that includes both the user data to be transported and routing information that allows the network to transport that information to its correct destination. The format of packets used in PacketCable is identical to that used in the Internet and is specified in RFC 760.[12] Such packets are termed "IP" (for Internet Protocol) packets. The format of an IP packet is shown in Figure 1-7.

In an IP packet, a 24-octet[13] header occurs at the start of the packet; user data fills out the rest of the packet. The most important header fields are the following.

- Version

    The standard version number is 4. There is also a version 6 protocol, but that has not been widely adopted and PacketCable does not support it.

- Type of Service

    A field used to prioritize traffic

- Protocol

    Defines a higher-level protocol (see the section "Protocol Stacks" that follows)

- Source and Destination IP addresses

    Identifies the sending and receiving devices

Not all of the fields in an IP packet header are important in a PacketCable network, but the ones defined above are used extensively. Note in particular the fields Source IP address and Destination IP address. Every device on an IP network has a unique 32-bit address, and every packet traversing such a network must contain the address of both the sender and the ultimate destination. Packets wend their way through the network in a process called routing that is performed by devices known

---

12. **RFC**s are numbered documents issued by the Internet Engineering Task Force and are available at *www.ietf.org*. RFC stands for "Request For Comments", reflecting the relatively unstructured nature of the early days of the Internet.

13. An octet is a group of eight digital bits, each of which has the value zero or one.

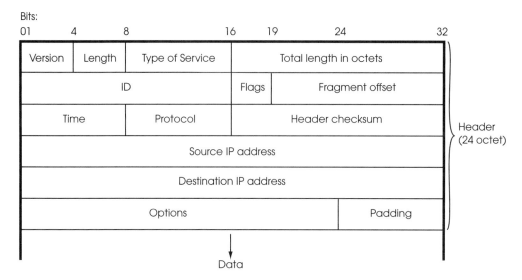

Figure 1-7 Format of an IP Packet

as **routers**. The job of a router is to examine the destination IP address of a packet and send it either directly to that destination or to another router that is closer (topologically, not necessarily physically) to the destination. This process takes place extremely rapidly; modern routers can redirect many millions of packets per second. Every single piece of information that flows on a PacketCable network, be it call signaling, instructions to allocate bandwidth to a call, an endpoint's request for configuration information, or Aunt Agatha's phone call about her recent operation, is transported inside IP packets that are handled in this manner.

Protocol Stacks

Useful information is rarely embedded directly into an IP packet. Instead, IP is used as the mechanism for transporting higher-level protocols that may provide more useful properties and features than does IP itself.

To understand why this is so, consider what IP actually does: It merely places routing information into a packet along with data, and the packet is then transmitted. If the packet is received properly at the other end, the header is removed and the data recovered. But note the following difficulties.

- There is no guarantee that the receiver will actually receive the packet or, if it does, that it wasn't corrupted in transit.

- There is no guarantee that the receiver will receive packets in the order in which they were transmitted. Since there may have been several routers between the transmitter and the receiver, there is no guarantee that every packet is routed over exactly the same path or that every path will take exactly the same amount of time to traverse.

- The transmitter has no way of knowing that the receiver ever received (or did not receive) the packet correctly.

To resolve these difficulties, other protocols have been designed that run *on top of* IP. For example, we can design a simple protocol that requires the receiver to transmit an acknowledgement packet every time it receives an IP packet. The acknowledgement could itself be an IP packet but with a special bit pattern in the data portion (perhaps the ASCII characters "ACK", followed by the contents of the Identification field of the IP packet that is being acknowledged).

Using this protocol, a transmitter wanting to send a string of packets might send them one at a time, waiting for an ACK to each transmitted packet. If after some reasonable period of time it does not receive an ACK for the most recently transmitted packet, it could resend that packet.[14] If we call our protocol SAP—the Simple Acknowledgement Protocol—then when we want to transmit information from point A to point B, we might well decide to use SAP instead of plain IP, since SAP has the advantage of informing the transmitter that the receiver received the packets and in the correct order.

When our transmitter sends information, he will talk about "sending it over SAP", and he does not care that underneath SAP lies a different protocol, IP, with quite different properties than SAP.

We have just built a two-layer **protocol stack**, with IP on the bottom and SAP on the top. In real networks, there are usually several layers of protocols. In IP networks, IP is near the bottom of the stack (but even IP usually runs above one or more lower-layer protocols that are adapted to the physical characteristics of the particular transmission medium). At intermediate layers are protocols such as the **Transmission Control Protocol** (**TCP**) or the **User Datagram Protocol** (**UDP**) that correspond to our SAP.[15] At the top of the stack is an alphabet soup of high-level protocols implemented by application programs (such as IKE, used for security key exchange, or COPS, used for Quality of Service communication).

Throughout the PacketCable network, even though all data is passed as IP packets, those packets are always part of a protocol stack that may contain any one

---

14. Note that if the transmitter is also using our protocol, we have to include a condition that ACKs are not ACKed; otherwise the very first packet will spawn a never-ending sequence of ACK, ACK of ACK, ACK of ACK of ACK, and so on ad infinitum.

15. Common protocols such as UDP and TCP are assigned a unique number, which is placed in the Protocol field of the IP header. This turns out to be important when securing communications using mechanisms such as IPsec, which is discussed in the next chapter.

of a large number of possible protocols, depending on which two devices are communicating and exactly what it is that they are trying to communicate. It is a wonderful feature of a layered network that the routers have no interest in what kind of higher-level protocol to which a particular packet belongs. They simply look at the destination IP address of the packet and route it accordingly. Thus any number of different protocols may run simultaneously over the network.

It is even possible (and frequently happens) that two devices are exchanging multiple sets of information simultaneously. For example device A may be transmitting information about a particular telephone call to device B at the same time as it is transporting the contents of a conversation to the same device. None of this matters. The routers will route the IP packets correctly, and the protocol stacks in the two devices will correlate the various streams of packets with the higher-level programs so that they all exchange information correctly. It is this magic that allows IP packet networks to function properly.

Placing a Call in a Packet Network

Let's examine the process of making an ordinary telephone call on a packet-based network. We will keep the example simple and gloss over (or even completely ignore) some of the details for now. There will be plenty of scope for complications later (call forwarding, placing calls to the PSTN or the Internet, three-way calls, security associations, wiretapping and so on). Figure 1-8 provides a summary of this simple example.

Assume that our friendly cable TV company, RATCo, has decided to get into the telephony business and, after upgrading its network so that it can handle two-way traffic (and changing its name to the Really Astounding *Telephone* Company), it has begun to offer PacketCable telephony to its subscribers.

Alice and her friend Bob, being progressive people, are both subscribers to RATCo's telephony service. After a couple of weeks, Alice, not unreasonably, decides to place a call to Bob to tell him how pleased she is with the quality of RATCo's service.

Alice's phone is connected to a small box near her television. Although she doesn't realize it, this box contains an embedded MTA—in other words, inside it is a cable modem and a Multimedia Terminal Adapter. The phone she is about to use is simply the input/output portion of the MTA. Also connected to the box is the same coax that feeds her cable television—although the television plays no part in the telephony network. It merely obtains its programs from the same cable as the one over which Alice places her phone calls.

When Alice lifts the phone, she hears a dial tone. Unlike a regular PSTN phone, this dial tone comes not from the phone company's central office but from the MTA itself. Alice dials Bob's number.

On a regular PSTN phone line, each digit is sent as it is dialed to the central office, where a switch collects the digits, checking after each one to see whether an

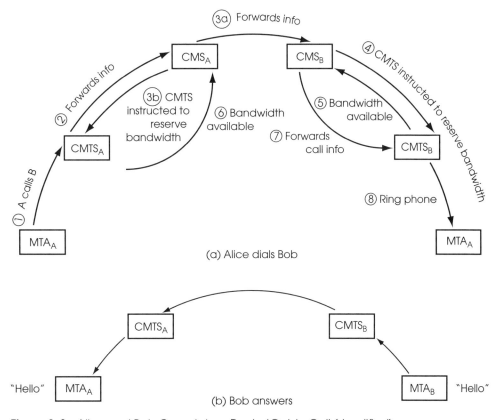

Figure 1-8 Alice and Bob Complete a PacketCable Call (simplified)

entire phone number has been dialed. On the RATCo network, things are different. The MTA itself collects the digits. Until the moment when Alice presses the last digit of Bob's number, the MTA has sent no signal to the network to indicate that Alice is placing a call. Alice presses the final digit, and things begin to happen—a lot of things, and very quickly.

Alice's MTA (we'll call it MTA_A), has an internal **digit map** that tells it when she has completed dialing a call. As she presses the final digit, the MTA realizes that she has completed a valid number. MTA_A now builds a UDP[16] packet that contains information about itself and the number that Alice has dialed and places it on the coax. In the field corresponding to the destination IP address, the MTA places the address of its local Call Management Server (CMS_A).

---

16. UDP, the User Datagram Protocol, is a very simple protocol (in some ways even more primitive than our Simple Acknowledgement Protocol) that runs on top of IP. Most messages in a PacketCable network use UDP.

The packet travels up the coax to Alice's $CMTS_A$, which acts as a router and forwards it to CMS_A. When the packet reaches CMS_A, the Call Management Server decodes the data and checks that Alice is a paid-up subscriber to RATCo's telephone service. Once it has assured itself that the caller is legitimate, it performs a **database dip**—that is, it consults a database—to determine the identity of the CMS, CMS_B, that serves Bob's telephone.

CMS_A now contacts CMS_B, informing it that Bob has an incoming call from Alice. At the same time, it sends a message to $CMTS_A$, telling it to reserve enough bandwidth on the HFC network to ensure that the call will be of sufficient quality. (This step is unnecessary on calls placed on ordinary lines, since each subscriber has exclusive use of his line. On a shared and extremely limited resource such as an HFC network, the MSO has to be certain that sufficient bandwidth is available before the call can be allowed to go through.)

While $CMTS_A$ is reserving bandwidth for the call in the coax between Alice and $CMTS_A$, CMS_B receives from CMS_A the news that Bob has an incoming call. CMS_B contacts $CMTS_B$ and instructs it to reserve bandwidth for the incoming call on the coax leading to Bob's phone. Once this has been done, $CMTS_B$ informs CMS_B that the bandwidth is available. (At about the same time, $CMTS_A$ is telling CMS_A that resources have been reserved on Alice's coax.)

Now, at last, CMS_B sends a signal to Bob's MTA that Bob has an incoming call. This signal is routed by $CMTS_B$ to MTA_B, which recognizes that there is an incoming call and begins to ring the phone.

Included in the signals that pass between the two CMSes and their corresponding MTAs are the destination IP addresses of the far end. That is, MTA_A is told the address of MTA_B, and MTA_B is told the address of MTA_A. This means that, from this point on, they can place each other's IP addresses in the destination fields, and the network will route the packets directly between the MTAs instead of forcing the packets to travel through the CMSes.

And this is exactly what happens when Bob picks up the phone and says, "Hello". His voice is digitized and packetized by MTA_B, and the packets are transmitted with the address of MTA_A in the destination field. The opposite occurs at Alice's end, and the two are now talking. It would be impolite to listen to what they actually say, so we will jump directly to the end of their conversation.

When one of them puts down the phone, the MTA signals the far end and also its local CMTS that the call is completed. The CMTS recovers the bandwidth resources used by the call so that they may be used for a new call, sending instructions to the far-end CMTS that cause it also to release the HFC bandwidth at that end of the call. Finally, several kinds of billing and logging messages are sent to RATCo's billing and event databases to ensure that Alice is properly billed for the extremely high-quality call she has just enjoyed. All calls on PacketCable networks are variants of this basic flow.

PacketCable and the Internet

The question naturally arises: If PacketCable networks use the same protocols as the Internet, do the two networks communicate with one another? Simple question, not-quite-so-simple answer.

Most subscribers to RATCo's telephony service probably also want to use the cable for ordinary access to the Internet—quite possibly at the same time that they are using the cable for a phone conversation. Can this be done? The answer is Yes.

There are several ways in which this could be managed. One of the easiest works like this: Remember that all IP packets look the same—they have a header followed by data. Included in the header is information about the destination of the packet. The CMTS can use the destination address to decide whether a packet is a telephony packet or an ordinary Internet packet. If the packet contains an address of a device on the PacketCable network, then the packet goes one way; if it contains some other address, it goes another way: into the Internet (see Figure 1-9).

In practice, the situation is somewhat more complicated than this. For example, what about packets coming in from the Internet? RATCo would not want its equipment to be vulnerable to an anonymous attack from the Internet. Therefore it protects its PacketCable network by placing routers and firewalls at the edges of its network so as to ensure that traffic from the Internet has no access to the devices in the core of the PacketCable network.

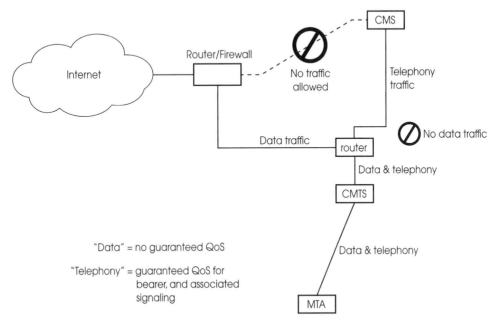

Figure 1-9 PacketCable and the Internet

In this way, Internet traffic can skirt the edges of the PacketCable network (this also allows certain kinds of phone calls to be made to phones on the Internet), but access to the devices and features at the core of the PacketCable network is limited to entities that require such access to place calls.

While we are on the subject of the Internet, we should mention the difference between "conventional" voice-over-IP (**VoIP**) technology and what the author calls "telephony over IP". Many VoIP architectures exist. In general the term *VoIP* carries no promise of Quality of Service, that any particular services or feature sets are supported, that calls might be billed, that the system interoperates with the PSTN and so forth. True telephony-over-IP attempts to closely simulate the PSTN and promises a user experience as close to that of the ordinary PSTN user as possible—and also interoperates seamlessly with the PSTN. PacketCable is a true telephony-over-IP architecture.

The Rest of the Book

So now that we know basically what PacketCable Telephony is and have a basic idea of how it works, we're going to spend the next several hundred pages trying to follow in detail exactly how the various devices in a PacketCable network communicate so as to allow calls to be placed, features to be invoked and (oh-so-important for the network operator) the details of all the activity to be recorded for billing purposes.

In the next chapter, we'll take a brief detour to cover the subject of security, followed in Chapter 3 by a fairly detailed look at how cable modems communicate in a cooperative manner over the shared coax.

Chapter 4 begins a discussion of call signaling, focusing on the Network-based Call Signaling protocol, followed in Chapter 5 with a similar discussion of Distributed Call Signaling.

Chapter 6 examines how PacketCable builds on the Quality of Service hooks provided by the DOCSIS 1.1 specifications to ensure that sufficient bandwidth is made available to phone calls.

In Chapter 7 we look at how MTAs are provisioned and also at how billing information is transmitted to a Record Keeping Server that acts as an interface between the PacketCable network and the billing services.

Chapter 8 briefly discusses how PacketCable interoperates with the PSTN, and we conclude with a short chapter on the likely future of the PacketCable specifications and the networks they describe.

Chapter

2
Security

Good random number generation is vital to most cryptographic mechanisms.
PKT-SP-SEC-I01-991201

Addressing security issues in PacketCable networks is somewhat problemmatical. Although security has been designed to be pervasive in the PacketCable architecture, there is a sense in which the various security mechanisms merely obscure the manner in which the network accomplishes any particular task. Moreover, the security mechanisms themselves are some of the most complicated features in the network, so that one cannot simply describe them in a brief aside when dealing with some other issue.

The approach we have taken is to dedicate a full chapter (this one) to fundamental security concepts and functions viewed more or less in isolation. Then, at the appropriate time in later chapters, particular security mechanisms described in this chapter are discussed in the context of PacketCable.

This chapter is quite complex and may be skipped on first reading or unless one needs to understand some particular aspect of security in more detail. However, when security issues are discussed in later chapters, reference will be made back to the contents of this chapter as necessary. So, lets begin by looking at the security needs of a network that is designed to carry the private conversations of fee-paying subscribers.

Classes of Attack

Broadly speaking, there are two major categories of possible attack against a system: theft of service and denial of service. In a telephony network there is a third possible category, which we might label invasion of privacy. People expect their phone conversations to be private, and they would be dismayed (to put it mildly) to have a phone conversation broadcast on the evening news or the World Wide Web.

We will briefly examine a few examples of the various kinds of attacks that might be mounted against a telephony network.

Theft of Service

Theft of service attacks have little or no effect on the operation of the network. If successful theft of service attacks are common on a network, usually the only discernible effect to the average consumer is that his monthly bill may increase, since that consumer is effectively subsidizing the customers who are stealing service. If a sufficiently large quantity of resources are being misappropriated, it is possible that the network may become so busy that calls from bona-fide, fee-paying customers cannot be completed, thus turning a major theft of service attack into a double loss to the service provider. One subscriber is using resources for which he has not paid; a second subscriber might be willing to pay for a service, but because the network is overloaded, the opportunity to provide that service is denied.[1]

The principal target of theft of service attacks is the network provider: The attacker simply wants to use a service without paying for it. The most common form of this kind of attack in the PSTN is called subscriber fraud, in which a consumer sets up an account with the service provider but gives false billing information (using a stolen credit card, for example). Other forms of classical theft of service attacks are more technical, often utilizing devices such as red boxes, black boxes and so forth.

In a PacketCable network, a new kind of theft of service attack is possible: stealing bandwidth. As we shall see in Chapter 3, the scarcest resource in a telephony-over-cable network is upstream bandwidth. In order to ensure that subscribers enjoy telephone conversations of a quality at least equal to the PSTN, the upstream bandwidth resources must be carefully managed to provide a guaranteed Quality of Service (QoS). Billing for calls is closely tied to granting QoS, so if someone were to find a way to allocate herself QoS for a call while at the same time circumventing the billing mechanisms, she thereby mounts a successful theft of service attack against the network.

Denial of Service

A denial of service attack is one in which one or more legitimate users of a network are denied access to the features and services offered by that network. A denial of service attack may be mounted against specific users (such as, for example, a next-door neighbor), or it may be mounted against a larger area (those subscribers served by a single CMTS or CMS, or even against the entire network).

---

1. Any provider that permits theft of service attacks to reach this level will obviously not remain in business very long.

In a complicated network, there is a vast number of possible denial of service attacks. Typical examples might be bombarding devices with pings so frequently that the device has no spare processing power to respond to legitimate requests for service;[2] subtle attacks involving injected packets that cause encryption engines to thrash wildly; or sending false signaling messages so that as soon as a conversation begins, an MTA is fooled into believing that the other party has gone on-hook.

It is often impossible to think of all the possible denial of service attacks when designing a network. Although network designers will try to thwart all the specific attacks that they can think of, often the safest defense is simply to be cautious and to include as many sanity checks as possible in the system to thwart the attacks that the designers didn't think of.

Invasion of Privacy

Traffic crossing a telephony network is expected, with few exceptions, to be private. By this we mean that at a minimum no one should be able to monitor a conversation without a government warrant authorizing them to do so. Included in the general heading of invasion of privacy are other, more subtle, expectations such as that no third party will be able to change the communication—an expectation that is particularly important for fax communications. In addition the mere fact that Alice has made 15 calls to Bob in the past week is usually regarded as private information: No one monitoring the network should be able to determine who has called whom and how often.

It is impossible to guarantee that a network will never be breached, and it would be foolish to presume that PacketCable telephony networks are immune to successful attacks. The designers of the security features concentrated on ensuring that when someone successfully infiltrates a PacketCable network, he will be able to learn nothing useful about any of the conversations taking place on the network. For the sake of completeness, we should mention that the PacketCable security specification does not address issues relating to operational or physical security. That is, it does not, for example, specify how to protect private keys nor how network devices are to be protected from attacks instigated by employees colocated with the devices.

The PacketCable system has been designed from the beginning to embrace state-of-the-art defenses against attacks of all kinds: theft of service, denial of service and invasion of privacy. In this chapter we will examine these defenses in detail.

---

2. A "ping", named after the SONAR echo-location mechanism, is a low-level probe to detect whether a particular computer is running on a network. A single ping consumes negligible resources, but a bombardment of pings from multiple sources can effectively bring even a powerful machine to a halt.

Security and Conventional Telephony

When you place a telephone call from a handset physically connected to the telephone wires in your house, you generally assume that, unless a law enforcement agency such as the FBI has obtained a warrant to tap your phone, no one is eavesdropping on the call.[3] This is not an unreasonable assumption.

Apart from the fact that it's illegal to tap phone calls (unless, of course, you are the government), the physical activity needed to do so is a reasonably effective deterrent. It's disconcerting to have to go outside in the dead of night to physically attach wires to your neighbor's phone lines, especially since a telephone repairman might happen along the next day and wonder what exactly those extra wires are doing there. And if you happen to want to tap the phone of someone who isn't your immediate neighbor, or if you live in an area where the phone lines are buried, life becomes even more difficult.

This is not to say that no one can listen to conversations on the PSTN. Apart from the possibility of the repairman up the pole (or down the manhole) connecting his eavesdropping equipment to your line, there are places inside the telephone central office where it is at least theoretically possible to listen to an individual's conversations. Generally, however, we rely on the telephone company's physical security to ensure that our conversations are private. Whether it is reasonable to expect the PSTN telephone companies to keep our conversations private is a matter outside the scope of this book.

The story is clearly quite different when we consider a digital network in which packetized voice travels through a system in which hundreds or thousands of conversations are passing simultaneously over the same connection—and unscrupulous crackers are at the same time using the same connection to probe the network for weaknesses. Physical security and a vague expectation that the telephony company is "secure" are no longer enough, since the packetized data are subject to a wide variety of possible attacks (for example, from misconfigured routers) as they traverse the network.

Other attacks that are either impossible or extremely difficult on the PSTN are much easier to mount on a packetized network. In particular, generalized denial of service attacks are extremely difficult to mount on the PSTN but can be quite easy on packetized networks.

---

3. In fact, you probably make this assumption even if the call is from a cordless phone, a car phone, or a cellphone. You might be in error. If you want your call to be private, don't broadcast it.

Security in Digital Networks

Consider again the PacketCable network. This time, we add more detail than we presented in the high-level view depicted in Figure 1-6. For now, we don't need to worry about the exact purposes of all the boxes (see Figure 2-1). The important point to note is that any of the interfaces between network elements may be compromised, as may the network elements themselves. One hopes, of course, that in practice this is both difficult and time-consuming, but the goal of the security system is to ensure that even if such compromises take place, the malfeasant responsible for the break-in can do no damage and, in particular, can learn nothing of value.[4]

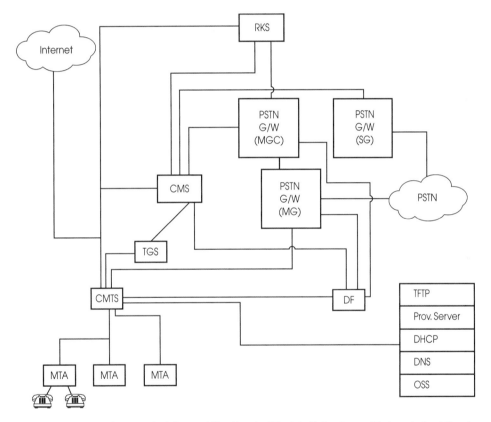

Figure 2-1   More Complete View of the PacketCable Telephony Network Architecture

---

4. In many cases, the most dangerous breaches of security are not the ones where a system is shut down but those in which an intruder silently reads the traffic on the network. A clever intruder might watch a packet network indefinitely without being detected.

This is quite a different approach than is used in many networks, especially, for example, those used by businesses. In such networks, dedicated firewalls are placed at every point of entry into the network that is to be protected. These firewalls are programmed to allow packets that meet only particular criteria to pass into the network; all other packets are (usually) silently dropped. This strategy allows the traffic within the network to flow without the need for encryption or other protection.

The problem with this approach is that its strength rests entirely on the supposition that the firewalls will keep out all attempts to break in. Should such an attempt somehow succeed, the network is at the mercy of the interloper. The PacketCable network assumes that at some point an interloper *will* gain access to the network, no matter how many hurdles are put in his way. The trick is to maintain the security of the network even after the interloper has gained access.

The strength of the firewall-based approach rests substantially in the integrity of the software running on the firewalls; the strength of the PacketCable design lies in the strength of the cryptographic algorithms used to protect the traffic flowing in the network.

The PacketCable security architecture is not uncontroversial. The author is aware of several vendors who, at least privately, believe that the classical firewall approcach would be sufficient to protect the network. After all, the argument goes, if this is enough to safeguard their own businesses, surely it should be enough to safeguard telephone conversations as well. The problem with this is that experiments have shown that firewall-based so-called "managed networks" are usually not very secure against a determined attack. The PacketCable architecture does not preclude the use of some anti-intruder techniques—but it is designed to assure that these are not the last line of defense.[5]

Security Concepts

When looking at an interface between two devices in a network, it is useful to determine exactly what kind of security is desired for that interface. It is tempting to say that all interfaces must be as secure as possible; however, not all interfaces require the same level of security, and security is often expensive to add to an interface. (The cost may be in terms of memory, CPU cycles, additional complexity, loss of stability, bandwidth or man-hours to implement, as well as simply in cost to purchase.) It is worth remembering that security is essentially a form of insurance, and there is no point in paying for insurance that one will never need.

---

5. For example, the October 2000 issue of *Dr. Dobbs Journal* reports that the Information Design Assurance Red Team at the Sandia National Laboratories has successfully penetrated all 35 of the systems that it has been invited to attack.

The following five general concepts are useful when trying to make decisions about the kind of security to be applied to a particular interface.

Authentication   Does either side really care about the identity of the element at the other end of the connection? If my phone rings and my Caller ID says that the call is from my bowling buddy, Ed, I will be annoyed if, when I pick up the phone, the call turns out to be from a telemarketer wanting me to switch from RATCo to the Fly-By-Night CablePhone Company. However, a free Speaking Clock service probably doesn't care about the identity of the person calling to find out the time, although RATCo will still want to be sure that its bill for the call goes to the correct subscriber.

Access Control   If I am a network element that provides a service, do I allow anyone to use the service, or is it reserved only for particular people (for example, subscribers who have actually paid their bill)?

Integrity   When sending information, do I care whether it might be intercepted and changed before it arrives at its destination? If I send you a fax, I might care if someone intercepts it and changes the word "Do" to "Don't".

Confidentiality   Is what I am sending private? I probably care that no one should be able to listen to my conversations, but perhaps I don't care if someone obtains the IP address of my MTA.

Nonrepudiation   Is it important that, having sent information, the transmitter later be able to deny sending it? When Fred sends me a faxed contract, does it matter if he can later deny doing so, claiming that the fax must have been sent by someone else instead?

PacketCable security is built around testing every interface in the network against each of these concepts and then applying sufficient security to the interface to ensure that the appropriate requirements are met. We will look first at some general security and cryptographic concepts and then examine in detail how these concepts are applied to PacketCable networks.

Cryptographic Security

Most security in digital networks is based on cryptography. Cryptography is the science of encoding messages in such a way that only the intended recipient can decode them correctly. This is accomplished by encoding a message in such a way that only the possessor of a particular **key** may decode it correctly. Note that cryptographically based security does not (usually) attempt to hide the fact that a message has been sent, nor does it make any attempt to stop a third party from reading the message (although other noncryptographic security measures may do so). It simply makes it very, very difficult for a third party to extract any useful information out of the message.

More generally, we can say that the possessor of a key uses that key in conjunction with some algorithm to convert one message into another. The typical manner in which this process is used is shown in Figure 2-2.

Let us walk through a simple example. (Don't worry if this seems trivial; things will quickly get more complicated.) Alice, who wishes to send a message to Bob, first writes down the message M. This message is comprehensible to anyone (perhaps it says something like "Meet me for dinner at 6 o'clock") and is known as plaintext.

Alice now applies an encryption algorithm (sometimes loosely called a "cipher", a term that originally was applied to the output of an encryption algorithm), A_1, and a key, K_1, to M. This results in an encrypted message, M'. This message looks like gibberish (perhaps something like "Qwjjo 87 lkeH,,;)LGHtfk" and is called ciphertext.

Alice now transmits the ciphertext to Bob via whatever mechanism she sees fit: e-mail, telephone, carrier pigeon, classified advertisement, inside IP packets or whatever. The route may be relatively public (classified advertisement) or it may be relatively secret (buried inside an IP packet on a network); Alice simply uses some convenient delivery mechanism, since she doesn't really care how many people see the message, as it looks like gibberish.

Bob receives the message M'. He then applies a decryption algorithm, A_2, and a key, K_2, to M'. If Alice and Bob have arranged things correctly, this results in a copy of the plaintext, M, which he may now read, secure in the knowledge that no one else knows that Alice wants to meet him for dinner at 6 o'clock.

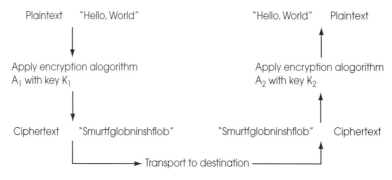

Figure 2-2 Encrypting and Decrypting with Keys

There are several things to note about this simple example.

1. The key that Alice used (K_1) was not necessarily the same as the one that Bob used (K_2). Although the decryption key may be identical to the encryption key, it is not always the case.

2. Alice and Bob must have had some prior communication. If you unwound a piece of paper from a carrier pigeon's leg and read "Qwjjo 87 lkeH,,;)LGHtfk", you would have no way of knowing whether the message contained directions for a date or a recipe for rice pudding. (Although it would have to be a very brief recipe for rice pudding—maybe just the name of the cookbook and a page number.) Therefore Alice and Bob must agree on the encryption and decryption algorithms they will use before they can begin to communicate securely.

3. Even if Alice and Bob agree on the algorithms, they also need to be sure that when Bob applies K_2, it is the correct key (that is, the one that will correctly decode messages encrypted with K_1). This also implies that there must have been prior communication between the parties. Note, however, that it is not necessary that both parties know both keys. All that is necessary is that they be certain that the pair of keys {K_1, K_2} are correctly matched for encoding and decoding messages according to the chosen encryption and decryption algorithms.

4. Although in theory Alice may not care whether the transmission mechanism used to deliver the message is relatively public or relatively private, in practice she may do so. There are at least three reasons for this.

   a. She may be transmitting particularly sensitive information and may therefore hope that no one will even notice that the message has been sent, since the message certainly can't be decrypted if no one possesses a copy ("The treasure is buried six steps north of the palm tree").

   b. She may be suspicious that the decryption algorithm is particularly weak. ("If the key is the number N, subtract N from each character's position in the alphabet to recover the plaintext" is a weak decryption algorithm, even though the range of choices for N is effectively infinite.)

   c. She may believe that there is a good chance that Bob is not the only person who holds the key or that the key might be easily guessed (the key might be the name of Bob's dog, for example).

   It is often not a good idea to rely solely on cryptographic security, even when it is thought to be strong. If a malfeasant has only a small probability of intercepting a message, then he is less likely to be able to decrypt it properly, since he is unlikely to possess the ciphertext in the first place.

Cryptographic Algorithms

The science of cryptography has made great advances in the last three decades. It used to be believed that a secure algorithm was necessarily a secret one. In other words, Alice and Bob decided on an algorithm, preferably one as esoteric and complicated as possible and then kept the algorithm as secure as their keys.

However, this notion has changed completely in recent decades. It has proven ridiculously easy for cryptography experts with high-powered computers to recover the plaintext from ciphertext whose principal strength was the secrecy of the algorithm. Nowadays, the opposite belief holds true: The best algorithms for cryptography are those that are public and have been attacked by specialists and have still failed to reveal any weaknesses (a strong cryptographic algorithm is one that appears to be difficult to break under all reasonable circumstances, given a key of appropriate length). Few of the recognized cryptography algorithms are secret; true security is now generally believed to lie in a combination of a good algorithm and a strong key.

Not all cryptographic algorithms are equally appropriate in all circumstances. At least partly for this reason PacketCable networks use several algorithms. The other good reason for choosing a particular algorithm is typically to make some aspect of the network compatible with another specification or standard, especially if there are off-the-shelf implementations available. We examine the various algorithms used by PacketCable below.

Cryptographic Hashes

It is not always necessary to encrypt information. Sometimes it is necessary only to ensure that information has not been altered by a malfeasant in transit (this is the difference between confidentiality and integrity) or that the transmitter of a message is indeed who he or she claims to be (which is the difference between confidentiality and authentication).

Integrity and authentication can be combined by the process of including a **Message Integrity Check** (**MIC**) or a **Message Authentication Check** (**MAC**) as an integral part of the message. (Typically, this is simply referred to as "including a MAC", since the same mechanism is often used to guarantee both integrity and identity simultaneously.) A particularly strong mechanism for ensuring both integrity and identity is the **Hashed Message Authentication Check** (**HMAC**, pronounced "aitch-mac").

A **hash** is an algorithm for converting a variable-length bitstream into a fixed-length string, typically much shorter than the length of the original bitstream. A hash may or may not use a key; if it does not, then generally it can act only as an integrity check. More typically, keyed hashes are used to ensure both integrity of the data and identity of the transmitting party. When a hash is calculated and appended to a message, it becomes an HMAC.

When the recipient receives a packet containing an HMAC, it first recalculates the value of the HMAC from the contents of the rest of the packet. If the result does not match the value of the HMAC contained in the received packet, this implies that the packet is invalid—either because it was generated by a device with an incorrect key or was somehow corrupted in transit. In either case, the packet should not be processed. Typically, the recipient device simply throws the packet away without transferring it to higher-level protocols. In the alternative, it may be prudent to log the event, especially if a large number of such packets are received, since it might indicate that an attack is under way.

Nonces

One common method of authenticating messages is to use a **nonce**. A nonce is simply a number that is sent from one device to another in an encrypted form and is then returned to the originator along with other information. Since only the original destination had the correct key to decrypt the nonce, the fact that the second message contains the correct nonce authenticates the message.

Nonces are also used to foil *replay attacks,* in which a third party captures and stores a valid message and replays it at a later time, so that to the recipient it looks as if the original source of the message has just (re-)transmitted it. This is how it works: Suppose that A and B are exchanging information. Unknown to them, E is eavesdropping on their conversation; E also has the ability to inject packets into the network.

If A includes a nonce, N_1, in a message M_1 to B, B then returns the value N_1 inside the response to M_1, which we will call R_1. E takes a copy of R_1 as it goes past. Assume that all these communications are encrypted, so that E cannot decrypt the information in any of the messages.

Some time later, A sends another message, M_2, to B, this time including another nonce, N_2. Now, in order to confuse A, E floods the network with copies of R_1. These are perfectly legitimate messages, correctly encrypted, but the nonce value they contain is incorrect. A can detect this and treat the packets appropriately.

Keys

The strength of the encryption of a particular message is a function of both the strength of the underlying algorithm and the secrecy of the key. Assuming that the key is generated reasonably randomly (it is not some simple password generated by a human), the secrecy of the key is a direct function of its length. The more bits contained in the key, the harder it will be to guess and the longer it will take for any potential eavesdropper to search through all possible keys to find the one that correctly decrypts the message.

No algorithm is secure if the length of the key is too short. (How long would it take to find the correct key if its length was only 1 bit? Not very long!) While it is generally true that longer keys are stronger, the actual length at which a key becomes "strong" is a function of the underlying algorithm. Some algorithms may require key lengths of only a few tens of bits to be reasonably secure; others may require thousands of bits. This does not necessarily mean that algorithms that require longer keys are "worse" than those that require shorter keys; the environment or purpose for which the algorithms were designed might be quite different.[6]

No matter how strong the key appears to be, devices that are sharing encrypted data over an extended length of time should periodically change keys (sometimes called **periodic re-keying**). Changing keys periodically means that even if one key is compromised, then only a fraction of the exchanged information can be decrypted. In addition, changing keys reasonably often means that an eavesdropper has much less ciphertext with which to work for any given key. Thus, periodic rekeying makes a cracker's job harder by decreasing the amount of ciphertext available, and also by limiting his success should he happen to break a key.

Key Management

PacketCable relies on strong cryptographic methods to maintain the security of the network. It utilizes a number of different encryption, decryption, and HMAC algorithms, attempting to match the strengths of the various algorithms to the different environments within the network.

One (perhaps *the*) principal difficulty in a network that makes wide use of a cryptographic security is the issue of key management. We just saw that in order for cryptographic security to work, both parties (the devices at the two ends of an interface) need to agree on two things: the algorithm and the key.

The algorithm can easily be settled. Either the interface specification mandates a particular algorithm, or a simple, well-defined automatic negotiation can take place between the two devices. However, the whole point of a key is that it must remain a secret. Therefore a key cannot appear in a specification document. (Actually, as we are about to see, there is a certain kind of key called a public key that may appear in a specification document.) Also, a key cannot be negotiated, except over a channel that is known to be secure, since otherwise the packets containing the negotiation may be silently monitored (or even changed) by an eavesdropper.

In the past, the best hope two parties had to exchange shared secrets was to do so by some **out-of-band** mechanism. Typically this involved one device generating a key, which was then physically copied to a floppy disk and transferred to a second

---

6. For example, the keys used in public key cryptography are typically an order of magnitude longer than those used in stream ciphers. Public key ciphers, however, are used for quite different purposes (typically related to authentication) than are stream ciphers.

device. There are still occasions when such a mechanism is practical. In fact, several of the interfaces in PacketCable 1.0 require the use of such **pre-shared** keys. However, advances in cryptography have provided a mechanism for key exchange over network interfaces that, for practical purposes, is often just as secure, albeit slower. This mechanism uses Public Key Cryptography.

Public Key Cryptography

Public Key Cryptography was a milestone in cryptographic science. First published by Whitfield Diffie and Martin Hellman in the academic press in 1976,[7] it has transformed the ease with which cryptography can be used by nonspecialists. In particular, it has changed forever the problem of how to manage keys securely.

In a **public key** system, there are two keys, one used for encryption and one used for decryption.[8] In other words, the keys K_1 and K_2 are different—but the real advance made by Diffie and Hellman is that *only one of the keys needs to be kept secret*.

If Alice wants to send a message to Bob using public key cryptography, she uses Bob's so-called public key to encrypt the message. How does she obtain Bob's public key? Simple! The reason it's called a public key is that Bob makes the key known to anyone. Indeed, in the big, wide world (not just inside a PacketCable network) there exist public key servers whose purpose it is to store people's keys and make them freely available to anyone who wants to locate a particular person's public key.

If Alice can't find Bob's key on a server, she can simply ask Bob for it, and he will happily transmit it over an insecure link, not caring who might be eavesdropping on the network traffic as it passes by. A public key is truly public.

So Alice encrypts her message using one of the well-known public key algorithms (such as the RSA algorithm, which is the one used by PacketCable) and Bob's public key. The message is now ciphertext, but it's a particular kind of ciphertext: As we have discussed, it's a ciphertext that requires a *different* key to decrypt it. In fact, it needs a particular key known as Bob's **private** (or **secret**) **key**. Bob knows this key, but, unlike the public key, he keeps it very, very secret. The strength of the security provided by a public key cryptographic system lies in the difficulty of deducing Bob's private key, even though one possesses his public key.

The RSA public key cryptographic system relies on the ease with which two numbers may be multiplied as compared to the difficulty with which the factors of a

---

7. The NSA has claimed to have recognized the concept of public key cryptography in the mid-1960s. However, being the NSA, they have never offered proof of this claim. It does seem clear, however, that the basic mechanisms of public key cryptography were known to at least one major government prior to their publication in the academic press (see *http://www.cesg.gov.uk/about/nsecret/home.htm*).

8. Alternatively, one key is used for signing a document and one to validate the signature. One of the strengths of some public key systems is that they allow the same pairs of keys to be used for both encryption/decryption and signing/verification.

large number can be calculated. To give a simple example: If I give you the prime numbers 541 and 1223, it is an essentially trivial problem to calculate that their product is 661643. However, if I gave you the number 661643, it would be much more difficult for you to give me its prime factors.

The details of the RSA system are rather complex for a book whose purpose is to describe telephony rather than cryptography, but they may easily be found in many cryptography books or Web sites that specialize in such matters.[9] The upshot, however, is that RSA satisfies the basic requirement of a public key system: The private key is difficult to guess from the public key. For keys in excess of 1,024 bits, private keys will probably remain unguessable even with state-of-the-art computer technology for the next decade or so.[10]

Digital Signatures

As well as using public key cryptography systems for encrypting data, they may also be used to sign data digitally. The term *digital signature* is somewhat misleading. It is true that in some ways a digital signature is similar to an ordinary signature on a paper document, but a digital signature (apart from being unforgeable) accomplishes rather more than an ordinary signature.

If Bob receives a digitally signed document from Alice, he can check the validity of the signature, and, if it passes the check, he can be certain that (1) the document he received was exactly the same as the document that Alice signed, and (2) it really was Alice who signed it. Actually, to be thoroughly pedantic, he can actually only be sure that the document was signed by an entity with access to Alice's private key. He has to trust Alice to be diligent about keeping that key secure (from programs as well as people).

So how does this work? Digitally signing a "document" (which is merely a collection of bits that may represent a letter, an image or simply a data packet) is, in some sense, the inverse of encryption. To sign a message comprising a sequence of bits, Alice calculates the value of some function that takes as its parameters the message and her private key. She then appends the result of her calculation to the package. To verify the signature, Bob applies a different algorithm that takes as its input the message as received (including the digital signature) and Alice's public key. This algorithm is constructed in such a way that only the correct digital signature (that

---

9. In fact, it has not been mathematically proven that it is intrinsically difficult to factor large numbers. However, there are good reasons for believing that the problem is indeed a "difficult" one, in the strictly mathematical sense that it seems likely no algorithm will ever be found for rapidly factoring large numbers of general form.

10. It is said that only a fool makes predictions concerning the security of cryptographic algorithms. You will note the word "probably", which is my attempt to avoid being foolish in public. See, however, Chapter 9.

is, one produced from Alice's private key) produces a result that Bob will accept. Any other digital signature applied to the original package of bits will cause the received document to fail the verification test.

It is important to note the following.

1. To encrypt a message, Alice uses the public key of the recipient. To sign a message, she uses her own private key.

2. To decrypt a message, Bob uses his own private key. To verify a signature, he uses the public key of the sender.

3. A single message may be both signed and encrypted (this is usually called a signed and sealed message).

4. When she signs a message, Alice does not need to know who the recipient will be. This is analogous to a signature on a paper document, where one need not know who will later read the document. However, a digital signature is *much* harder to forge than a paper signature, assuming that the signer takes good care to prevent his or her private key from becoming known.

In practice, the scheme for signing messages is slightly different from the one we have just described, although it is conceptually equivalent. The reason that a different scheme is needed is that public key cryptography algorithms are relatively complex and require relatively large amounts of computational power per octet of message secured compared to the computational requirements of conventional symmetric key cryptography.

In order to avoid most of this computational requirement, a typical public key scheme will first compress the message efficiently, then apply a symmetric key encryption algorithm to the message, and then use public key cryptography only to encrypt the value of the symmetric key and the encryption and compression algorithms.

Certificates

Certificates (sometimes called **digital certificates**) are a method of encapsulating information so that it may easily be passed from one device to another. Typically, certificates are digitally signed by an entity who is trusted by the recipient and who guarantees that the information contained in the certificate is accurate.

A manufacturer might place a certificate into a device at the time of manufacture. This certificate might contain, for example, the serial number and Media Access Control (MAC; not to be confused with a Message Authentication Check) address of the device, as well as a string identifying the manufacturer. The certificate would be signed by the manufacturer, using his private key. When the certificate is presented to a server, the server authenticates the certificate by checking the validity of the signature (using the manufacturer's public key). This assures him that the information contained in the certificate has not been tampered with.

Often, an individual certificate is one of many in a hierarchy of certificates. A good example of this is the certificates that are placed inside DOCSIS-compliant cable modems at manufacture. Certificate hierarchies are frequently used in cases where there is a single, ultimate entity whom everyone trusts.

Hierarchies work like this. At the root is a single trusted entity, known as the Root Certificate Authority. This root has a widely known public key and an extremely carefully guarded private key. The root generates a (primary) certificate for each (primary) entity whom it serves (for example, the DOCSIS Root Certificate Authority may choose to generate a certificate for each manufacturer of DOCSIS modems). Each of these contains the public key of the particular primary entity, signed by the root.

So, for example, the MagicModem Company, a manufacturer of DOCSIS-compliant cable modems, hands its public key to the DOCSIS Root Certificate Authority. The Root Certificate Authority generates a digital certificate that contains, among other things, MagicModem's public key. The certificate is signed by the Root Certificate Authority's private key. Each primary entity then generates secondary certificates as needed. The secondary certificates contain the primary certificate as well as the public key of the secondary entity, all signed by the primary entity.

So, in our example, when MagicModem builds a cable modem, it might choose to place a unique certificate within the modem. This certificate might contain information such as the public key of the modem, the modem's MAC address, its serial number, and any other information that MagicModem feels might be useful. The certificate also contains a copy of the certificate that the DOCSIS Root Certificate Authority gave to MagicModem. Finally, the certificate in the modem is signed by MagicModem's private key. This whole process is shown in Figure 2-3.

When presented with a secondary certificate, a device authenticates it as follows.

1. It extracts the primary certificate and authenticates the root's signature. This gives it the primary entity's public key.

2. It authenticates the secondary certificate by checking the signature with the primary public key that it has just obtained. If the certificate passes this authentication step, then the recipient can trust all the information contained in the certificate.

Theoretically, certificate hierarchies may extend many levels deep. However, because of the comparative expense of public key operations (in terms of CPU load), generally the hierarchies are limited to a small number of levels. There is an international standard for the format of certificates, promulgated by the **International Telecommunications Union** (**ITU**). This standard, the X.509 standard, is used by all certificates within PacketCable.

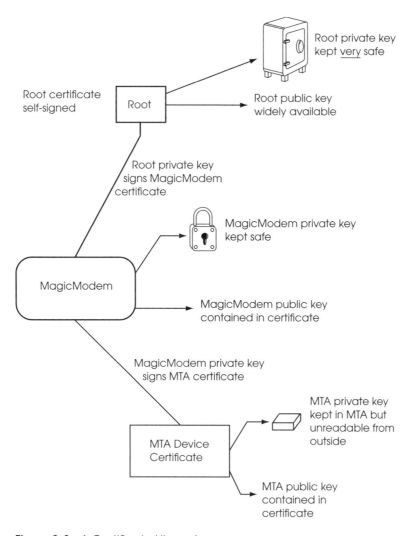

Figure 2-3 A Certificate Hierarchy

It is important to recognize that a certificate hierachy is relatively fragile. The integrity of the hierarchy is maintained only as long as all the private keys are truly secret. If any private key is compromised, all the certificates below that key are immediately suspect. (That is, the certificates signed by that key, and all the certificates below those.) For a certificate hierarchy containing millions of certificates, the private key of the Root Certificate Authority must be guarded by extreme measures. In addition, there should be some mechanism that allows compromised certificates to be revoked and replaced by new ones, signed by keys that have not been compromised.

Conventional Cryptography

Although public key cryptography is very powerful, it turns out that, as we have already mentioned, it is also computationally expensive. In a real-time system with a restricted delay budget, it is sometimes impossible to use public key cryptography even though it is otherwise desirable. PacketCable networks therefore are forced to resort to conventional cryptography when the time constraints are such that public key cryptography would be too slow.

In conventional cryptography, sender and receiver use the same key for encryption and decryption. This key, which is sometimes called a **symmetric key**, is a shared secret that must be distributed either out-of-band or, more often, through some secure mechanism based on some other preexisting shared secret, often one established through public key cryptography.

To give a somewhat concrete example: Suppose that two devices, A and B, need to pass several messages between themselves securely. Also suppose that this communication has to take place during the time that a phone call is being set up between Alice and Bob (that is, the communication between A and B occurs between the time that Alice finishes dialing Bob's number and the moment when Bob's phone begins to ring). Usually, the network provider would want there to be as little delay as possible before Bob's phone starts ringing; therefore there is not enough time for A and B to encrypt each message passing between them using the public key of the other device.

Instead of using public key cryptography to encrypt each message, A and B might choose to do something like the following: A will send B its certificate, which B will use to authenticate A's public key. (This step is relatively slow; it might be done before A and B have to carry Alice's call, maybe at system initialization time.) B then generates a pseudorandom key; it encrypts this key with A's public key and sends it to A. (This step is also rather slow, but again it could be done in advance. More likely, it will be done periodically, completely independently of any calls that are being made through A and B.) Now A and B share a secret, and they use this secret symmetrically to secure the messages passing between them—and this can be done very quickly, since no slow public key operations are needed.

PacketCable networks must manage both conventional symmetric and also public key cryptography keys in a secure manner. We now turn to the mechanisms for performing this key management, but before we do so, honesty compels us to issue a warning: We are going to gloss over a lot of the details. Key management protocols tend to be extremely complex because they are designed to be secure against a wide range of possible attacks. This complexity results in specifications that are long and arcane, full of specialized terms that require a course in cryptography to fully appreciate. This is supposed to be a book about digital telephony, not about the intricacies of key exchange algorithms. Therefore we suggest that if the reader is interested in learning more of the details, he or she should take a course in cryptography and then settle down for a few evenings with the RFCs, which document the algorithms in excruciating detail.

Kerberos

Kerberos is a protocol described in RFC 1510. The purpose of Kerberos is to allow clients to authenticate themselves to servers so that servers are assured that they are granting services only to clients that are permitted to use those services (typically, this mechanism can be used to ensure that services are granted only to paying customers). The mechanism by which this is done involves the use of Kerberos **tickets**.

PacketCable uses only a small subset of the entire Kerberos protocol, and we will describe only that subset. Those interested in the entire Kerberos suite and with several hours to kill should settle down in a comfortable chair with the RFC.

As used by PacketCable, a Kerberos ticket is essentially a *cookie* provided by a **Ticket Granting Server** (**TGS**) to an MTA and that the MTA passes to a CMS to allow it access to telephony services. Figure 2-4 shows this process.

The flow of information is as follows.

1. During the initialization process, an MTA is provided a certificate by the telephony service provider. One of the items within this certificate (called the **MTA Telephony Certificate**) is a public key unique to that MTA. The certificate is signed by the service provider.

2. The MTA presents its MTA Telephony Certificate to the TGS, requesting access to a particular CMS.

3. The TGS verifies the MTA Telephony Certificate and returns to the MTA a Kerberos ticket valid for that MTA and the requested CMS. The ticket includes the following.

   - The MTA name

   - The MTA network address

   - The server name

   - A timestamp

   - A symmetric session key, S, which will become a shared secret between the MTA and the CMS

   The reply also includes a copy of S encrypted in a key negotiated by the MTA and the TGS. This allows the MTA to prove knowledge of S to the CMS.

4. The MTA passes the ticket to the CMS. The session key S is used to derive a set of keys that are used to construct an IPsec Security Association between the CMS and the MTA.

PKINIT

Kerberos as originally envisioned did not use public key cryptography. However, PacketCable networks use a variant of Kerberos known as **PKINIT**, which does use public key cryptography, to authenticate the MTA and the TGS to each other. PKINIT is an Internet Draft.

The details of the contents of PKINIT messages are complicated (like many cryptographic messages), and it is perhaps not too useful to dwell on the detailed format, especially since much of the information is encoded deeply in a hierarchical tree of fields. On the other hand, it is probably a good idea to have at least a basic understanding of what is involved in the exchange.

The MTA sends a KRB_AS_REQ message to the TGS, as specified in RFC 1510. The PKINIT message, known as a PA_PK_AS_REQ and defined in the PKINIT draft, is carried within the preauthenticator field of the message. The PA_PK_AS_REQ contains only a single field:[11] signedAuthPack.

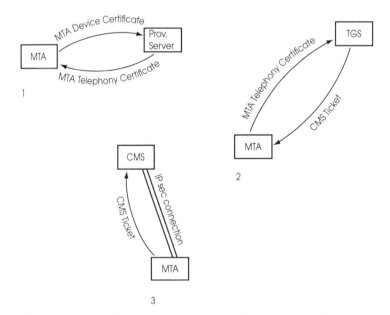

Figure 2-4 Obtaining and Presenting a Kerberos Ticket

---

11. Other optional fields are specified in the PKINIT draft; these are not used in PacketCable.

The field signedAuthPack is an object of type SignedData, which is part of the **Cryptographic Message Syntax** (**CMS**[12]), specified in RFC 2630. The object contains the following.

- version

  The version number of Cryptographic Message Syntax being used

- digestAlgorithms

  An identifier for the SHA-1 cryptographic hash function

- encapContentInfo

  This provides encapsulation in CMS format for further data. It contains two fields.

  - eContentType

    Set to the value id-data,[13] as defined in RFC 2630

  - eContent

    A data structure of type PKAuthenticator

- certificates

  Contains the X.509 telephony certificate of the MTA, which in turn contains the device's RSA public key

- signerInfos

  Contains the MTA signature, using the RSA algorithm operating on a SHA-1 digest of the eContent field

Essentially this provides a rather complex mechanism for passing the MTA's Telephony certificate to the TGS. Figure 2-5 attempts to show the various levels of encapsulation of this information.

After authenticating the MTA (by checking the certificate the MTA has just handed it inside the KRB_AS_REQ) the TGS responds with a KRB_AS_REP that contains a ticket, valid for a period not to exceed one week, that the MTA can present to its CMS. Since the ticket has a limited lifetime, the PKINIT sequence must be repeated periodically. This happens asynchronously to any phone calls. The MTA

---

12. The overloading of the abbreviation CMS (Call Management Server; Cryptographic Message Syntax) more than once led to confusion during meetings of the PacketCable Security Focus Team—as if cryptography weren't confusing enough!

13. id-data is a so-called ASN.1 object identifier. For a discussion of ASN.1, see the section "Format of X.509 Certificates" and, for more detail, Chapter 7.

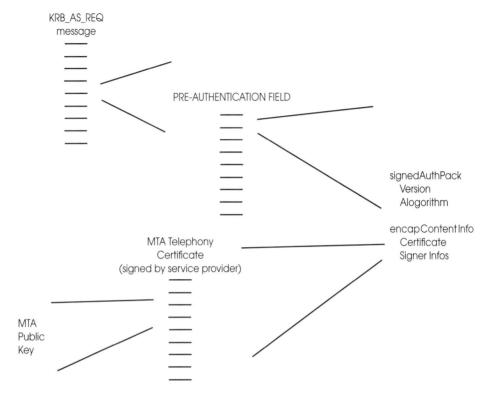

Figure 2-5 Encapsulated PKINIT Information

simply requests a new ticket from the TGS before the old one expires, and it uses the new ticket to maintain or regenerate its security association with the Call Management Server.

Internet Key Exchange (IKE)

Internet Key Exchange (**IKE**, typically pronounced like the name, Ike) is specified in RFC 2409. IKE is a two-phase peer-to-peer key management protocol, typically used to generate keys for IPsec connections (see the section "IPsec" for more details on IPsec).

In phase 1 of an IKE exchange, a shared secret is generated. The second phase negotiates a secret, which is used to derive further keys used for IPsec encryption, decryption and authentication.

The IKE RFC allows three different forms of phase 1 negotiation but only one of these ("IKE with preshared keys") is supported in PacketCable version 1.0. This method requires that the two devices be provided with the initial shared secret by some unspecified out-of-band mechanism.

The two devices authenticate one another by assuring themselves that they share a secret. They then move directly to the second part of the negotiation. This is a primitive solution to key management, and it scales poorly (since every pair of devices that will ever have to communicate must be provisioned with a shared secret). In future versions of PacketCable this will be replaced by a more robust solution—probably by using X.509 certificates to authenticate the devices in the first phase.

In the second phase, a new shared secret is established using nonces that are exchanged between the two devices. All the keying material needed to construct the IPsec Security Association is derived from this secret using the mechanisms described in RFC 2409.

Specific Security Mechanisms and Algorithms

PacketCable uses several mechanisms and algorithms for securing the network. All the algorithms are readily available, and all are believed to be unbreakable (as long as they are used with keys of sufficient length) with technology that is currently available or that is likely to become available in the foreseeable future.

In this section we shall discuss the algorithms used by PacketCable. For the most part, we shall defer discussion of the particular manner in which these algorithms are actually used until later chapters.

IPsec

Encryption security may be applied at many levels in a packetized network. Most frequently, encryption is supplied under the direct control of an application at the application layer. For example, an e-mail application that allows users to send secure e-mail might offer the user a choice of using either Pretty Good Privacy (PGP) or Secure MIME (S/MIME). The user will select one of these mechanisms, and the application will then take care of the details of encrypting the message correctly according to which choice the user made.

However, in an IP network, it is also possible to encrypt data at a much lower level in the protocol stack—even at the IP layer itself. The advantage of doing this is that the applications need not (in fact, usually they *cannot*) know anything about the encryption that is taking place. As far as the application is concerned, all communication is "in the clear"; however, any eavesdropper sitting on the network and watching the traffic will see only encrypted packets.

The usual method of supplying security at the IP layer is to use "secure IP", more commonly known as **IPsec**. IPsec is fully specified in a series of RFCs: 2401, 2402 and 2406. The RFCs specify two varieties of IPsec: tunnel mode and transport mode. PacketCable networks use only the latter. This is important because many implementations of IPsec are geared toward providing Virtual Private Network support, which uses the former. Therefore not all stacks that claim to support IPsec can be used in PacketCable applications. Data flow through a typical IPsec system is shown in Figure 2-6.

Unlike ordinary IP, which is a connectionless protocol, IPsec provides a secure connection between known endpoints. This connection is known as a **Security Association**, or **SA**, sometimes more colloquially referred to as a secure pipe. IPsec security associations are unidirectional; in order to provide for bidirectional communication, two security associations must be generated, one for communication in each direction.

The process is conceptually easy. Two devices that wish to establish an IPsec association first agree on a secret key. This key is passed to the IPsec program, along with the identity of the distant endpoint, the direction of this particular association and details of the cryptographic algorithms that are going to be used on this particular pipe. The algorithms specify how the data flowing in the pipe will be encrypted and whether authentication is required.

Suppose that network device A has set up an IPsec pipe with device B, where A and B have agreed on all the cryptographic details and the key to be used. The IPsec program inserts itself into the protocol stack in A and B in such a way that it is

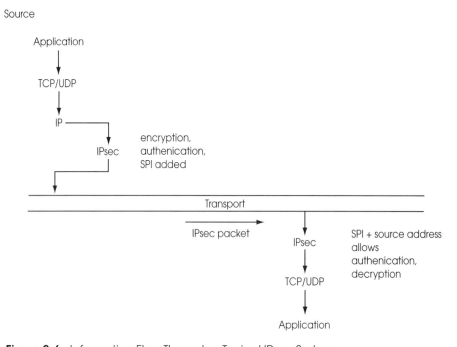

Figure 2-6 Information Flow Through a Typical IPsec System

transparent to all network communication except when packets between A and B are involved.

Assume that A wishes to send a packet to B. As the IP packet is being assembled, the IPsec program sees that the destination address shows that B is the recipient. It looks up its list of IPsec pipes and determines that there is an IPsec association between A and B—in particular, it sees that all packets from A to B are to be transmitted through that pipe.

IPsec now takes the untransmitted packet and applies the agreed algorithms to the packet. This process is designed to leave the important routing information in the packet untouched. The data contents of the packet are encrypted (and/or authenticated). The encrypted packet is then transmitted.

Even though the data are encrypted, the packet is still a valid IP packet, with routing information unchanged. The network is unconcerned with the encrypted portion. The various routing devices simply use the routing information to route the packet correctly to its destination, B.

When the packet arrives at B, the inverse process takes place. B recognizes from the source address that the packet has arrived from a secure pipe. It applies the correct decryption (and/or authentication) to the packet, which converts it back to an ordinary unencrypted IP packet, which it then reinserts into the protocol stack for it to be handled in the usual manner.

The way in which IPsec is usually implemented has several consequences.

1. IPsec security associations are generated pair-wise between IP addresses.

2. Any given pair of IP addresses may have only one valid pair of unidirectional IPsec security associations extant at any one time, and these unidirectional associations must flow in opposite directions.

3. A bidirectional pipe is easily constructed from a pair of unidirectional ones.

4. It takes longer for a packet to traverse an IPsec stack than a stack without IPsec (the security association has to be detected, and then the correct cryptographic algorithms must be applied).

5. A device may have numerous independent coexisting IPsec associations, as long as each is with a different IP address.

6. The IPsec pipe has no knowledge of higher layers. The packets from all applications that communicate over the pipe will be secured.

7. Similarly, the applications have no knowledge of the existence of the pipe. The encryption/decryption process is completely invisible to the application.

IPsec pipes are typically used between devices that need to exchange secure information from a number of different applications, and over a relatively long period of time. The key management process, and occasionally the delay caused traversing the stack, makes IPsec more useful for carrying signaling and control information than telephony voice traffic.

The Security Parameter Index (SPI)

When a secured packet is received by the destination, there has to be some way for the destination to know what keying material it should apply to the packet. The mechanism for ensuring that the destination applies the correct keying material (and encryption and authentication algorithm) is the **Security Parameter Index**, or **SPI**.

During the key management phase for an IPsec Security Association, the two devices agree on a 32-bit number, the SPI. Usually, since the SPI must uniquely identify the correct Security Association at the recipient's end, the receiving device chooses the SPI and forwards its choice to the transmitter.

Every packet transmitted through the negotiated Security Association includes the SPI in an unencrypted portion of the packet. The destination then uses the SPI as an index into a table of active Security Associations, which then allows it to apply the correct keying material, and the correct algorithms, to the received packet.

IPsec Internals

The use of IPsec affects the operations that may be performed on IP packets as they traverse the network. For this reason, we will briefly examine exactly how IPsec modifies packets before it injects them into the network.

We saw in Chapter 1 that an ordinary IP packet can be divided into two sections: an IP header (containing routing information), followed by data. The header includes a one-octet field indicating the next higher protocol in the protocol stack, which is typically either TCP or UDP.

The data portion of the packet then includes a protocol header for the higher-level protocol. This header includes routing and control information pertaining to that protocol; specifically it includes items such as the port number on the destination device. A port is a conceptual destination within the destination device. It is a number that serves the same purpose as a maildrop in an ordinary mailing address and is frequently associated with a particular kind of service. For example, when an e-mail client wishes to transmit a piece of e-mail to an e-mail server, it does so by addressing TCP messages to port number 25. The port number is carried within the TCP header, not the IP header (since IP has no concept of ports). The higher-level header is then followed by data that will be passed up to a higher level application for its use. Figure 2-7 shows an example IP packet carrying TCP.

Most IP networks contain devices such as routers, filters and firewalls that perform certain actions on packets, depending on their contents. Typically, these

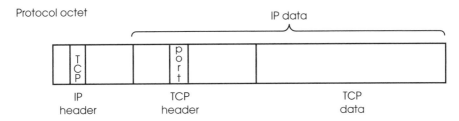

Figure 2-7 An IP Packet Carrying TCP

devices are interested not only in the IP header, but also the higher-level protocol information. For example, a firewall may be configured in such a way that it will permit UDP traffic only to certain ports. It will examine every incoming packet, and, if it is a UDP packet addressed to a disallowed port, it will "drop the packet on the floor" (simply throw it away). Alternatively, a router might be configured to route TCP traffic differently from UDP traffic. In these and other scenarios, it is important for the device to be able to examine the protocol octet in the IP header and also the data portion of the IP packet, which is where the higher-level protocol information is stored. IPsec makes this impossible.

Figure 2-7 shows a "normal" IP packet containing TCP information. Figure 2-8 shows an equivalent IPsec packet. IPsec changes the protocol octet in the IP header from whatever it was before (for example, 6, in the case of TCP) to the value 50, indicating "this is an IPsec packet with an encrypted payload". Immediately following the IP header a new IPsec protocol header is added. And after that the original data portion of the IP packet is encrypted according to information contained in the new IPsec header. The original protocol identifier is placed at the end of the original data *and is encrypted*.

This means that the information that indicates the identity of the higher-level protocol, as well as all the information pertaining to that protocol (for example, the

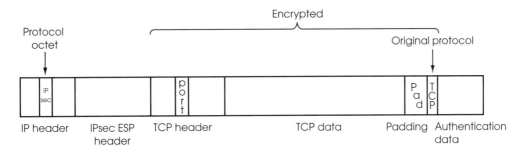

Figure 2-8 An IPsec Packet Carrying TCP

destination port number), is encrypted before transmission. Therefore it is impossible for any intervening device such as a filter or firewall to take any action based on those values. Consequently, the PacketCable architecture does not include firewalls or other devices of the kind typically deployed within data-only networks to route or block IP packets based on the data they carry.

This does not mean that a real-life network cannot include such devices. In fact, typically they do. But the job they perform is to segregate data traffic from telephony traffic so that only telephony packets reach the core PacketCable network. Throughout this book, we will assume that the PacketCable devices need deal only with telephony traffic; data traffic is assumed to be handled by a separate network. In practice, the two networks may overlay one another to a greater or lesser extent. After all, most network operators will want to deploy only a single high-speed backbone for all their traffic. Conceptually, however, the data and the telephony networks are quite distinct, and we will concern ourselves only with the latter.

Ciphers

There are two fundamental types of ciphers: **block ciphers**, which operate on short units of plaintext of fixed size, and **stream ciphers**, which operate on a stream of data one bit or one octet at a time. PacketCable networks use both types of ciphers.

DES and 3DES

The canonical block cipher is **DES**, the Data Encryption Standard cipher. DES is a product of what was then the National Bureau of Standards (now the National Institute of Standards and Technology) and was adopted as a federal standard in November 1976, when it was authorized for use on all unclassified government communications.

No one knows whether DES is truly secure. The National Security Agency (NSA), an agency so secret that in 1976 it still did not officially exist, made some changes to DES prior to its release, although they have claimed that these did not impact the algorithm's security. For more than 20 years, academic cryptographic experts have attacked DES, and no serious weaknesses have been detected other than those revealed by the ever-increasing speed of computers. However, some people still worry that the NSA installed a "trapdoor" in DES, which allows them to decrypt DES-encrypted messages more easily than other people can. (Most cryptographers believe that the fundamental DES algorithm is probably secure— but one does wonder why its use is authorized only for *un*classified government documents.)

DES is a block cipher that acts on blocks of 8 octets of data at a time. Eight octets of plaintext produce 8 octets of ciphertext (which means that it is often a good idea to disguise the length of the original plaintext using either padding or compression). It is also a symmetric algorithm: Unlike the case in public key cryptography, the same algorithm and key are used for both encryption and decryption.

The major problem with DES is not the algorithm per se but its key length, which is fixed at 56 bits. Although cracking DES is still well beyond the capability of most individuals, it is equally within the capability of even quite small companies. The Electronic Frontier Foundation has built a machine that cracks DES in an average of about four days, at a total cost of $200,000.[14] By the year 2010, it is entirely conceivable that individuals will be able to purchase by mail-order a PC board for $1,000 that will crack DES in a few hours.

Details of the DES algorithm are outside the scope of this book, but they are readily available in standard cryptographic texts and on the Internet. It is important to recognize that DES was designed to run efficiently in hardware, not necessarily in software. A stronger variant of DES, **3DES**, that uses triple encryption, requires even more powerful hardware to perform well in situations where encryption or decryption must be performed rapidly. Consequently, DES and/or 3DES is usually used only in cases where the added cost of the additional cryptographic hardware is justified or in cases where it can be implemented in software but the slowness of the algorithm is unimportant.

PacketCable does not use ordinary DES, except in the access link between the cable modem and the Cable Modem Termination System (CMTS)—and the only reason that DES is used there is because it is mandated by the DOCSIS specifications. PacketCable does, however, use 3DES.

There are two major variants of 3DES. The weaker variant is triple encryption with two keys (which is used in the BPKM protocol, used for key management between a DOCSIS cable modem and its CMTS), in which the following operations are performed in order to encrypt a block.

1. Encrypt with the first key

2. Decrypt with the second key

3. Encrypt with the first key

The recipient performs these operations.

1. Decrypt with the first key

2. Encrypt with the second key

3. Decrypt with the first key

---

14. The Electronic Frontier Foundation has made the entire project—including schematics—public in *Cracking DES; Secrets of Encryption Research, Wiretap Politics & Chip Design,* published by O'Reilly.

This encrypt-decrypt-encrypt/decrypt-encrypt-decrypt sequence is known as the **EDE** mode of 3DES.

A more powerful technique is to use the same encrypt-decrypt-encrypt sequence for encryption (and the inverse for decryption) but with three different keys. Three-key EDE mode 3DES is equivalent in strength to using ordinary DES with a 112-bit key. This cipher is likely to remain secure for the foreseeable future.

Block ciphers may be converted into an equivalent stream cipher by adding a feedback loop. The most common way to do this is to operate the cipher in **Cipher Block Chaining** (**CBC**) mode. The "ordinary" way of using a block cipher, in which a blocks of n octets are encrypted independently of one another and in which the same block of n plaintext octets will always encrypt to the same block of n ciphertext octets (if the key is unchanged), is known as **Electronic Codebook** mode, or **ECB**.

In CBC mode, plaintext is bitwise XORed with the immediately preceding ciphertext block prior to encryption. XORing is a simple (and very fast) operation whose input is two bits and whose output is a single bit. If the two input bits are the same, the output is zero; otherwise it is one. The XOR operator is written thusly: $\oplus$.

Thus:

$$0 \oplus 0 = 0$$
$$1 \oplus 0 = 1$$
$$0 \oplus 1 = 1$$
$$1 \oplus 1 = 0$$
$$x \oplus y = y \oplus x$$
$$x \oplus y \oplus y = x$$

The last property is particularly useful in cryptography. It tells us that XORing a message twice against the same bit string is a null operation. The application is very simple: The transmitter can XOR plaintext against a key to produce ciphertext. The recipient can recover the plaintext merely by XORing the received ciphertext against the same key.

By introducing a CBC feedback loop, the output of any encryption operation is dependent, not just on the block of data being encrypted, but also on all the preceding data as well. The entire operation is depicted in Figure 2-9.

Decryption in CBC mode is just as simple: A block of ciphertext is decrypted, and then bitwise XORed with the result of the prior decryption. The result is the original plaintext. This is how it works. If P_n is the nth block of plaintext, C_n is the nth block of ciphertext, E is the encryption operation, and D is the decryption operation, then:

$$D(E(P_n)) = P_n \text{ (by definition)};$$

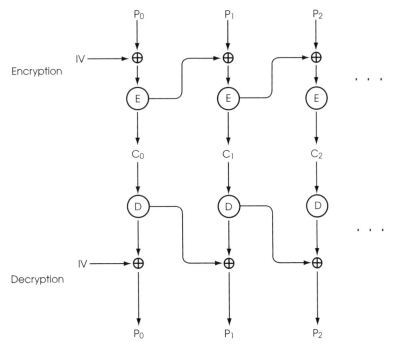

Figure 2-9 Cipher Block Chaining Mode

and

$$C_n = E(P_n \oplus C_{n-1})$$
$$P_n = C_{n-1} \oplus D(C_n) \text{ (because } D(C_n) = D(E(P_n \oplus C_{n-1})))$$
$$P_n = C_{n-1} \oplus P_n \oplus C_{n-1}$$

In order to prime the algorithm (that is, to provide a "prior" block for the first block in the message), an **Initialization Vector** (**IV**) is used. The value of the IV is usually part of the negotiation that occurs when the key is being shared. Sometimes the value of the IV is publicly specified, since knowing the value of the IV is usually of little help to a cracker attempting to decrypt the traffic. (Knowing the IV means that the cracker knows one of the components of the first XOR, but it does not help him with any of the subsequent XORs.)

RSA

RSA (named after its inventors, Rivest, Shamir and Adleman) is one of the most widely used public key algorithms and is used throughout PacketCable. Since it is a public key algorithm, it is computationally intensive. It typically operates at between 0.1% and 1% the speed of DES.

Like all public key algorithms, RSA requires two keys, one public and one private. The key pair is generated as follows.

1. Generate two large pseudo-random prime numbers, p and q, each containing the same number of bits.[15] (RSA does not require that each number be the same length, but the algorithm is most secure when this condition is met.)

2. Calculate the product.

   $$n = p * q$$

3. Choose an encryption key, e, such that e and the product (p–1)(q–1) are relatively prime. (Two numbers are relatively prime if their greatest common divisor is 1.) For reasons of computational efficiency, e is usually given the value 65537. This, however, is merely a convenience and is not necessary.

   In the case that e is a particular fixed value (such as 65537), it may sometimes be necessary to try several values of p and q before the requirement of relative primacy is met. Typically, however, the requirement is quickly met.

4. The decryption key, d, is given by solving this formula.

   $$d * e = 1 \bmod (p–1)(q–1)^{16}$$

The number pair (e, n) constitutes the public key; d is the private key. Encryption and decryption proceed as follows.

Suppose that we wish to encrypt a message M using the public key derived above. Divide M into blocks such that the numerical value of the block is less than n. (For example, if p and q are each 1,024 bits long, n will be about 2048 bits long, and each block of M should be about 2,048 bits long but always numerically less than n.) Call the ith block M_i. Each block of plaintext encrypts directly to a block of ciphertext, C_i, by this formula.

   $$C_i = M_i^e \bmod n$$

---

15. There are efficient algorithms for generating prime numbers of any length. The algorithms are quite interesting in that all of the ones in widespread use do not absolutely guarantee that a particular number *n* is prime; they merely aver its primacy to a particular (but arbitrarily high) degree of confidence. See, for example, Bruce Schneier's *Applied Cryptography* for more details on this or almost any other subject related to cryptography.

16. Using the extended Euclidean algorithm, also described in *Applied Cryptography*.

To decrypt a block, calculate:

$$M'_i = C^d_i \bmod n$$

$$\text{Now } C^d_i = (M^e_i)^d$$

$$= M_i^{(e*d)}$$

$$= M_i^{(k(p-1)(q-1)+1)}$$

$$= M_i M_i^{(k(p-1)(q-1))}$$

$$= M_i \text{ (all calculations mod n)}$$

Therefore $M'_i = M_i$ and the plaintext of the block has been recovered.

Encrypting a message of any reasonable length with RSA requires a large number of calculations that operate quite slowly in software. A more common method of encrypting long messages is to encrypt the message using an efficient symmetric algorithm and a secret key and then to use RSA to encrypt the (much shorter) key and to include the encrypted key as part of the message.

RC4

RC4 is a proprietary variable-key-length stream cipher claimed as a trade secret by RSA Data Security, Inc. It runs extremely efficiently in software and appears to be sufficiently strong that much of the electronic commerce that takes place on the Internet is secured by RC4.

RC4 has a particularly interesting history. In 1994, a piece of source code claiming to be an implementation of the (unknown) RC4 algorithm was posted anonymously to an Internet reflector. Whether the code is or is not an implementation of RC4 has never been confirmed by RSA Data Securities, which continues to maintain that RC4 is a trade secret. What is known is that the posted code appears to be completely interoperable with RC4—that is, plaintext encrypted by a particular key in RC4 can be decrypted with the same key by the posted code, and vice versa.

This places RSA Data Securities in an odd position. RC4 has never been patented (presumably because patents expire, and RSA Data Securities would like to earn licensing fees on RC4 for longer than the lifetime of a patent). Therefore their only grounds for suing someone who uses the public algorithm is that a trade secret has been violated. In that case, however, RC4 would definitely no longer be a secret, since a successful lawsuit would merely confirm that the published code is indeed an implementation of RC4! The obvious thing to do, of course, is for RSA Data Securities to concede that the published code implements RC4 (if indeed it does so) and to effectively give the algorithm away. However, there is no sign that they intend to do so, so for now, anyone using the published code instead of licensing RC4 from

RSA Data Securities runs a risk (small, but non-zero) of being sued. The code is not included in this book, but it is readily available on the Internet.

The algorithm underlying the posted code has been extensively studied and has no relevant known weaknesses when used with keys of reasonable length (128 bits or longer). It consists of a very simple state machine with a large number of possible states that evolve randomly. To encrypt a single octet takes of the order of 30 CPU cycles, depending on the details of the CPU architecture, which is why it runs so quickly. In most practical applications, the overhead associated with encrypting and decrypting a data stream with RC4 is negligible (in terms of both time and CPU cycles).

Message Authentication Codes

PacketCable allows the use of optional Message Authentication Codes (MACs) in bearer-channel communication between MTAs. The particular algorithm used is a variant of the **Multilinear Modular Hash** (**MMH**). Several other MACs are implicit in PacketCable, used within protocols that mandate their use. Calculations using these MACs are typically performed within libraries designed to implement the protocol in question. MMH, however, is not normally available as part of an off-the-shelf protocol library.

Multilinear Modular Hash (MMH)

Unlike other cryptographic algorithms such as RSA and RC4, MMH is not widely used. In addition, the algorithm as used in PacketCable is slightly changed from the published version. For these reasons we will examine MMH in rather more detail than would otherwise be necessary. For a detailed explanation of how MMH is used in PacketCable, see Chapter 4.

The MMH function takes three parameters: the size of a word, σ; the number of input words, N_i; and the number of output words N_O. In PacketCable, the word size s is fixed at 16 bits. The number of output words may be either 1 or 2. (That is, the output may be either two or four octets.)

We will first discuss the algorithm when $N_O = 1$ (that is, output is two octets). We denote this version of MMH (with $\sigma = 16$, and $N_O = 1$) by H. To calculate the MMH of an input containing N_i words, the algorithm uses a key of length N_i. We denote this key by k, and the jth word of k by k_j. We denote the message whose hash we are seeking as M and the jth word of the message as M_j.

Define the set S_n as the set of n integers.

$$\{ -n/2, -n/2 \div 1, \ldots, 0, \ldots n/2 - 2, n/2 - 1 \}$$

Now define the operator *smod* such that for any integer z, z *smod* n is the element α of S_n such that z mod n $\equiv \alpha$ mod n.

For example, suppose that $n = 2^{16}$. Then S_n is the set of integers $\{ -32768, \ldots 0, \ldots 32767 \}$ Now if $z = 233408036$, $z \bmod n = 34340$. The member of S_2^{16} with the value 34340 (mod n) is -31196. Hence, $\alpha = -31196$.

Finally, for any *positive* integer p, let Z_p denote the set of integers.

$$\{ 0, 1, \ldots p - 1 \}$$

Now consider the key k of N_i words. Each word is interpreted as a signed 16-bit integer, which corresponds to a member of S_2^{16}. The input stream, M, also contains N_i words; these words are also interpreted as signed 16-bit integers.

The MAC *H* is defined by the following steps.

1. Calculate the number H_1 as follows.

$$H_1 = (\sum_{i=1}^{n} N_i (k_i * m_i)) \, smod \, 2^{32}$$

2. Calculate the number H_2 as follows.

$$H_2 = H_1 \bmod \Pi, \text{ where } \Pi \text{ is the prime number } \Pi = 2^{16} + 1$$

3. Calculate *H* as follows.

$$H = H_2 \bmod 2^{16}$$

Or in a single line.

$$H(k, M) = (((\sum_{i=1}^{Ni} (k_i * m_i)) \, smod \, 2^{32}) \bmod \Pi) \bmod 2^{16}$$

The case where $N_O = 2$ is a simple extension of the case when $N_O = 1$. Call the new algorithm H'. The length of the key is now one greater than for *H;* that is, the length of k is $(N_i + 1)$.

Define k^1 to be the N_i words of k beginning with k_1. Similarly, k^2 are the N_i words of k beginning with k_2.

H' is then given by:

$$H' = H(k^1, M) + H(k^2, M)$$

where the + operator is understood to mean simple bitwise concatenation of two 16-bit quantities to yield a 32-bit result.

To use MMH to generate a usable MAC, the receiver and the sender must share knowledge of the keystream used to generate the hash. In PacketCable, a shared secret is distributed through the call signaling, and this secret is used to derive a keystream. The details of this derivation are given in the section "Key Derivation Function" in Chapter 4. The message, which is being authenticated, is typically a single packet of RTP bearer-channel data. The MMH-MAC is calculated over the header and the encrypted payload and then appended to the packet.

To calculate the PacketCable MMH-MAC of an arbitrary message M, the MMH-MAC is given by:

$$MMH\text{-}MAC = H(k, m) + [key]$$

where [key] is either 16 bits (for $N_O = 1$) or 32 bits (for $N_O = 2$) of keystream information, and the addition is performed mod 16. The exact bits of keystream information used to calculate the MMH-MAC are discussed in the section "Procedure for Encrypting and Decrypting" in Chapter 4. At this point, maybe it's a good idea to look at a brief example.

First of all, the reason for adding a MAC is so that an MTA that receives a bearer-channel packet can be sure that it came from the MTA with which it is in communication. As part of the call signaling used to set up the call, the two MTAs shared a secret. The MTAs then applied an algorithm to the secret, giving them identical pseudo-random streams of octets that can be used as a keystream for the MAC.

PacketCable does not require the use of MACs on bearer-channel data. The reason that MACs are optional is that they add overhead to each transmitted packet, and upstream bandwidth is often at a premium on cable access networks. Each network operator can decide whether MACs should be used and, if so, whether a two-octet or a four-octet MAC best serves his purposes. Use of MACs is controlled within the signaling, so an operator may dynamically change whether MACs are used; he can even target specific MTAs to produce MACs if they have been the subject of attack in the past.

The example we will use is based on the implementation provided in Appendix E of the PacketCable security specification. We will generate the 16bit MMH-MAC for a short message.[17] In practice, of course, the MAC would be calculated over a series of octets that comprise an RTP packet. Table 2-1 shows the parameters for the example. Using these values gives us (all results are in hex):

$$H_1 = 663aa46d$$
$$H_2 = 00003e33$$
$$H = 3e33$$

Adding this to the additional keystream octets, mod 2^{16}, gives the final result.

$$MMH\text{-}MAC = ec3a$$

HMACs

RFC 2104 describes a general method for including cryptographic hash functions in the calculation of a Message Authentication Code; it coins the abbreviation **HMAC** to refer to such a code.

---

17. Thanks to Mike Sabin for generating the reference code on which this example is based.

Table 2-1 Parameters for MMH-MAC Example Calculation

Description	Value (hex)	Comment
Message	4e 6f 77 20 69 73 20 74 68 65 20 74 69 6d 65 2e	Equivalent to ASCII text: Now is the time.
Keystream	35 2c cf 84 95 ef d7 df b8 f5 74 05 95 eb 98 d6	Same length as Message
Additional keystream	ae 07	Two additional octets for 16-bit MMH-MAC

The general mechanism for calculating an HMAC as described in RFC 2104 is presented below. In PacketCable, the SHA-1 cryptographic hash function is used as the basis for HMAC calculations.

Denote the specific cryptographic hash to be used as H, and the key (normally based on a shared secret, so that the recipient can authenticate the HMAC) as K. The block-length of H we denote by B (B is typically 64 octets), and the output length of H by L (for example, $L = 20$ for the SHA-1 cryptographic hash). K may be any length less than or equal to B.

Two binary strings are defined.

1. *ipad* is a string B octets in length, with all octets equal to the value 0×36.[18]

2. *opad* is a string B octets in length, with all octets equal to the length 0×56.

To calculate the HMAC, the following algorithm is used.[19]

1. If necessary, pad K with zeros to create a string of length B; call this K'.

2. Calculate $K' \oplus ipad$; call this K''.

3. Append the data over which the HMAC is to be calculated to K''; call this D.

4. Calculate $H(D)$; call this D'.

5. Calculate $K' \oplus opad$; call this K'''.

6. Append D' to K'''; call this D''.

7. Calculate $H(D'')$; this is the HMAC.

---

18. Numbers expressed in the form *0xnn* are hexadecimal (base 16) numbers; this notation is taken from the C programming language.

19. A slightly more complex algorithm is given in RFC 2104 for the case when the length of K is greater than B.

The HMAC algorithm is used in MTAs to derive keying material from shared secrets, as described in the section "Key Derivation" of Chapter 4 and in Appendix D.

X.509 Certificates

We talked briefly earlier about digital certificates. Since they are at the root of security in PacketCable networks (pun intended) and also are used in the DOCSIS access network that we will discuss in the next chapter, this is probably a good time to look at them in a little more depth. Note, however, that a thorough description of X.509 certificates would require a book approximately as long as this one already is. All we will attempt to do here is to give a reasonable (and accurate) explanation of the features of X.509 certificates that are important to PacketCable.

Recommendation **X.509** of the ITU-T, entitled *Information Technology—Open Systems Interconnection—The Directory:Authentication framework,* defines a certificate-based method of authentication. A certificate is a binary object that encapsulates information (typically, at a minimum, a public key) that is signed by a third party whose signature is trusted by the certificate's recipient, and ultimately, the reason for a certificate's existence is to authenticate the bearer to a third party.

Suppose that Bob has agreed to meet Charlie, whom he has never met before, in a certain place at a certain time. Bob arrives, and a few moments later a man walks up to him, thrusts out his hand and says, "Hello, Bob. I'm Charlie". If Bob and Charlie are simply meeting for lunch, perhaps this is good enough for Bob (especially if Charlie will be paying). But if Bob intends to hand Charlie several thousand dollars in unmarked bills (not that *our* Bob and Charlie would ever be involved in such suspicious dealings), he is likely to demand something more than Charlie's assurance that he really is who he says he is.

One way that Charlie might be able to convince Bob is to produce a letter that says, "This is my good friend Charlie", signed by Bob's good friend Alice. And that's what a certificate does. The strength of the guarantee that the information it contains is correct comes not from the entity that presents the certificate but from the fact that it has been signed by a trusted third party. That trusted third party, of course, must be careful to sign only certificates whose contents it can itself authenticate; otherwise the trust placed in the signer by the certificate's recipient will be sorely misplaced.

Format of X.509 Certificates

A certificate is used to encapsulate several important pieces of authentication information, including the certified data, the name of a signature algorithm, the name and digital signature of the certifying entity and the lifetime for which the certificate should be deemed valid. The format of these is specified by the X.509 standard using ASN.1 notation. ASN.1 is a notation for defining the precise format of general objects. It is described in recommendation X.680 of ITU-T and an overview is provided in Chapter 7 of this book. Although designed to be precise and to be parsed by a computer, it is sufficiently readable that the casual reader can usually gain a general understanding of the data encapsulated by an object by examining the ASN.1 encoding for that object. The ASN.1 definition of an X.509 certificate is as follows.

```
Certificate                           ::=     SIGNED { SEQUENCE {
    version                    [0]    Version DEFAULT v1,
    serialNumber                      CertificateSerialNumber,
    signature                         AlgorithmIdentifier,
    issuer                            Name,
    validity                          Validity,
    subject                           Name,
    subjectPublicKeyInfo              SubjectPublicKeyInfo,
    issuerUniqueIdentifier     [1]    IMPLICIT UniqueIdentifier OPTIONAL,
                               -- if present, version must be v2 or v3
    subjectUniqueIdentifier    [2]    IMPLICIT UniqueIdentifier OPTIONAL,
                               -- if present, version must be v2 or v3
    extensions                 [3]    Extensions OPTIONAL
                               -- If present, version must be v3 - }  }
Version                               ::=     INTEGER { v1(0), v2(1), v3(2) }
CertificateSerialNumber               ::=     INTEGER
AlgorithmIdentifier                   ::=     SEQUENCE {
    algorithm                         ALGORITHM.&id ({SupportedAlgorithms} ),
    parameters                        ALGORITHM.&Type ({SupportedAlgorithms} {
@algorithm} ) OPTIONAL }
-- Definition of the following information object set is deferred, perhaps to
-- standardized
-- profiles or to protocol implementation conformance statements. The set is
-- required to
-- specify a table constraint on the parameters component of AlgorithmIdentifier

-- SupportedAlgorithms          ALGORITHM               ::=     { ... }
  Validity                              ::=     SEQUENCE {
      notBefore                         Time,
      notAfter                          Time }
  SubjectPublicKeyInfo         ::=     SEQUENCE {
      algorithm                         AlgorithmIdentifier,
      subjectPublicKey             BIT STRING }
```

```
Time   ::=   CHOICE {
    utcTime                               UTCTime,
    generalizedTime                GeneralizedTime }
Extensions                                 ::= SEQUENCE OF Extension
Extension                          ::= SEQUENCE {
    extnId                         EXTENSION.&id ({ExtensionSet} ),
    critical                             BOOLEAN DEFAULT FALSE,
    extnValue                            OCTET STRING
                        -- contains a DER encoding of a value of type &ExtnType
                        -- for the extension object identified by extnId — }
ExtensionSet      EXTENSION      ::=    { ... }
```

There are currently three versions of X.509 certificates. PacketCable certificates are version 3 certificates and conform to RFC 2459 as well as to the more generic X.509 specification. In practice, a digital certificate looks like a (fairly lengthy) string of binary characters. The ASN.1 description can be used to decompose the string into the various component fields, which can then be passed to an application for its use.

PacketCable Certificate Hierarchies

As we discussed earlier, certificates may be chained to form a certificate hierarchy. In PacketCable, there are two such hierarchies, one for devices and one for network operators. Figure 2-10 shows the device certificate hierarchy. At the top of the hierarchy is the PacketCable Root Certification Authority. This is an entity operating under contract to CableLabs and that signs certificates containing the public keys of individual MTA manufacturers.

MTA Root Certificate

There is a single PacketCable root certificate with the characteristics given in Table 2-2. Note that this certificate is expected to be valid for a very long time (more than 40 years). The key is very long in order to provide some level of protection against the advances in cryptography and computing power that will occur over the lifetime of the key.

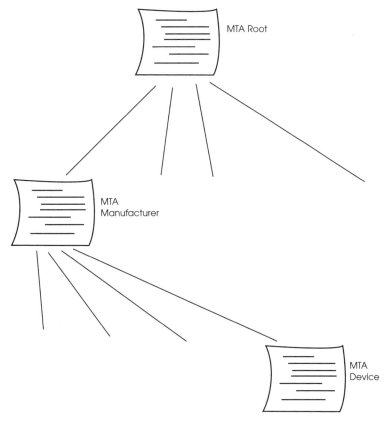

Figure 2-10 MTA Device Certificate Hierarchy

Table 2-2 Characteristics of PacketCable Root Certificate

Subject / Name	C=US, O=CableLabs, OU=PacketCable, CN= PacketCable Root Device Certificate Authority
Use	This certificate is used to sign MTA Manufacturer Certificates and is used by the Provisioning Server. This certificate is not used by the MTAs and thus does not appear in the MTA MIB.
Signed by	Self-signed
Validity Period	40+ Years. It is intended that the validity period is long enough that a new MTA Root Certificate will never have to be reissued.
Length of Encapsulated Key	2048

By way of example, here is a legal Root Certificate, preceded by its contents in human-readable form.[20]

```
Certificate #1:
    Certificate:
        Data:
            Version: v3 (0x2)
            Serial Number: 1 (0x1)
            Signature Algorithm: PKCS #1 SHA-1 With RSA Encryption
            Issuer: C=US, O=CableLabs, OU=PacketCable,
            CN=PacketCable Root Device Certificate Authority
            Validity:
                Not Before: Wed Jan  5 12:51:40 2000
                Not  After: Tue Jan  5 12:51:40 2010
            Subject: C=US, O=CableLabs, OU=PacketCable,
           CN=PacketCable Root Device Certificate Authority
            Subject Public Key Info:
                Algorithm: PKCS #1 RSA Encryption
                Public Key:
                    Modulus:


00:d8:db:f7:00:bf:fb:70:24:4d:57:12:1f:09:79:78:3c:b6:
62:cb:9c:ec:83:f5:28:68:a5:b6:11:99:a1:2e:68:47:86:a9:
d3:17:9f:29:03:83:01:42:78:23:38:84:0c:7d:0c:99:8d:54:
e9:d5:0d:de:8a:64:6e:de:32:a2:08:f2:47:63:87:af:97:16:
23:f0:3b:f4:12:8d:84:9d:67:ce:67:5b:80:c7:07:20:21:0f:
9c:f6:a1:9b:73:70:26:5c:87:ad:eb:1b:78:4d:f0:8b:06:aa:
3c:93:a6:7b:c0:93:fa:47:e2:8b:72:0e:7c:1a:cb:fd:2e:9d:
68:75:30:d3:26:3b:e0:7b:eb:f0:0a:2d:2d:02:95:8f:9e:80:
83:cf:02:ee:b5:64:21:e3:6f:0e:c4:72:35:47:3b:69:57:bf:
9a:44:56:9a:f7:e1:64:17:19:65:85:b7:0d:dc:be:43:e9:29:
c5:92:c5:6b:ad:73:dd:1a:21:73:e0:f6:c6:52:1c:d5:bd:ad:
f0:06:f4:44:ca:b8:4d:43:10:35:fa:06:cf:79:66:b7:1d:8f:
bd:4c:5f:06:f5:3c:46:22:f1:33:7a:f1:1f:8f:aa:f1:81:07:
4d:49:44:cb:55:75:31:bb:86:94:64:15:50:e4:6d:32:31:a3:
a0:5f:fc:e1:ff
                    Public Exponent: 65537 (0x10001)
            Extensions:
                Identifier: UNKNOWN OBJECT IDENTIFIER
                oid contents:
                    55:1d:13 -- 2.5.29.19 basicConstraints
                    Critical: yes
```

---

20. The author is indebted to Mike St. Johns for the example certificates.

```
            DER Value:
                30:06:01:01:ff:02:01:00
         -- cA True, pathLen 0
        Identifier: UNKNOWN OBJECT IDENTIFIER
        oid contents:
            55:1d:0f -- 2.5.29.15  keyUsage
        Critical: yes
        DER Value:
            03:02:02:04
     -- BITSTRING keyCertSign
      Identifier: Subject Key Identifier
        Critical: no
        Value:
        25:84:13:d3:91:18:1b:7c:ca:e3:7c:fc:d3:67:9c:c9:3d:3a:17:04
    Signature:
        Algorithm: PKCS #1 SHA-1 With RSA Encryption
        Signature:
15:28:7e:a1:7e:1a:2d:ed:f3:f5:76:80:a3:bd:f1:35:f0:4e:54:eb:31:
9c:48:7c:46:fa:e2:ad:4c:29:b9:f0:91:a2:5c:89:c8:9e:5b:2e:3e:99:
70:ba:1f:f0:50:8a:1a:07:d5:bf:6d:fa:f2:49:52:f9:10:78:86:2a:84:
8e:83:ae:e5:52:36:c8:82:db:20:87:1f:af:5c:20:7a:cc:3b:ba:46:95:
0b:53:a6:9d:df:6b:50:9d:85:33:8d:fb:4a:18:b5:d8:16:64:d5:6a:d6:
9f:4e:4e:83:42:08:6b:73:7f:b8:09:70:35:11:19:69:26:a9:a7:0e:b9:
41:f6:11:96:53:d0:f0:44:2e:05:bd:76:9d:3b:13:6a:17:7f:70:83:cd:
ad:b7:31:75:3f:7b:af:be:d7:b1:4b:58:12:47:a0:2e:12:77:73:21:d1:
28:1b:00:81:9e:f5:31:7f:9d:ba:11:2c:20:f7:5f:41:53:73:63:89:95:
46:85:c6:3e:d5:29:f7:36:af:24:07:a2:cd:7f:f9:cb:21:b4:14:54:3d:
ae:76:3b:7f:a1:8c:e1:c1:85:0d:d3:cb:b9:b7:ad:0e:9f:ad:b4:98:5e:
71:84:0b:94:23:2b:32:62:eb:99:d7:15:75:cd:2c:e0:e6:7f:bf:c4:79:
06:8f:f5:41
```

```
-----BEGIN CERTIFICATE-----
MIIDnjCCAoagAwIBAgIBATANBgkqhkiG9w0BAQUFADBvMTYwNAYDVQQDEy1QYWNr
ZXRDYWJsZSBSb290IERldmljZSBDZXJ0aWZpY2F0ZSBBdXRob3JpdHkxFDASBgNV
BAsTC1BhY2tldENhYmxlMRIwEAYDVQQKEwlDYWJsZUxhYnMxCzAJBgNVBAYTAlVT
MB4XDTAwMDEwNTIwNTE0MFoXDTEwMDEwNTIwNTE0MFowbzE2MDQGA1UEAxMtUGFj
a2V0Q2FibGUgUm9vdCBEZXZpY2UgQ2VydGlmaWNhdGUgQXV0aG9yaXR5MRQwEgYD
VQQLEwtQYWNrZXRDYWJsZTESMBAGA1UEChMJQ2FibGVMYWJzMQswCQYDVQQGEwJV
UzCCASIwDQYJKoZIhvcNAQEBBQADggEPADCCAQoCggEBANjb9wC/+3AkTVcSHwl5
eDy2Ysuc7IP1KGilthGZoS5oR4ap0xefKQODAUJ4IziEDH0MmY1U6dUN3opkbt4y
ogjyR2OHr5cWI/A79BKNhJ1nzmdbgMcHICEPnPahm3NwJlyHresbeE3wiwaqPJOm
e8CT+kfii3IOfBrL/S6daHUw0yY74Hvr8AotLQKVj56Ag88C7rVkIeNvDsRyNUc7
aVe/mkRWmvfhZBcZZYW3Ddy+Q+kpxZLFa61z3Rohc+D2xlIc1b2t8Ab0RMq4TUMQ
NfoGz3lmtx2PvUxfBvU8RiLxM3rxH4+q8YEHTUlEy1V1MbuGlGQVUORtMjGjoF/8
```

4f8CAwEAAaNFMEMwEgYDVR0TAQH/BAgwBgEB/wIBADAOBgNVHQ8BAf8EBAMCAgQw
HQYDVR0OBBYEFCWEE9ORGBt8yuN8/NNnnMk9OhcEMA0GCSqGSIb3DQEBBQUAA4IB
AQAVKH6hfhot7fPldoCjvfE18E5U6zGcSHxG+uKtTCm58JGiXInInlsuPplwuh/w
UIoaB9W/bfrySVL5EHiGKoSOg67lUjbIgtsghx+vXCB6zDu6RpULU6ad32tQnYUz
jftKGLXYFmTVatafTk6DQghrc3+4CXA1ER1pJqmnDr1B9hGWU9DwRC4FvXadOxNq
F39wg82ttzF1P3uvvtexS1gSR6AuEndzIdEoGwCBnvUxf526ESwg919BU3NjiZVG
hcY+1Sn3Nq8kB6LNf/nLIbQUVD2udjt/oYzhwYUN08u5t60On620mF5xhAuUIysy
YuuZ1xV1zSzg5n+/xHkGj/VB
-----END CERTIFICATE-----

MTA Manufacturer Certificate

The MTA Root certificate is used to sign MTA Manufacturer certificates. Every bona fide manufacturer of MTAs is provided with one or more such certificates, with the properties shown in Table 2-3.

MTA Device Certificate

The **MTA Device Certificate** identifies the particular MTA (see Table 2-4). That is, each MTA contains a globally unique certificate. This uniqueness is guaranteed by the fact that the certificate contains the MAC address of the device in the CN field.

Table 2-3   Characteristics of PacketCable MTA Manufacturer Certificate

Subject / Name	C=<country>, O=<CompanyName>, [S=<state/province>], [L=<city>], OU=PacketCable, [OU=<Manufacturer's Facility>], CN=<CompanyName> PacketCable CA
Use	This certificate is issued to each MTA manufacturer and is installed into each MTA, either in the factory or at the time of a code download. The provisioning server cannot update this certificate. This certificate appears as a read-only parameter in the MTA MIB. This certificate, along with the MTA Device Certificate, is used to authenticate the MTA device identity (its MAC address) during provisioning.
Signed by	MTA Root Certificate
Validity Period	5 Years. Reissued biannually
Length of Encapsulated Key	1024, 1536, 2048

Table 2-4 Characteristics of PacketCable MTA Device Certificate

Subject / Name	C=<country>, O=<Company Name>, [S=<state/province>,] [L=<city>], OU=PacketCable, [OU=<Product Name>,] [OU=<Manufacturer's Facility>,] CN=<MAC Address>
Use	This certificate is issued by the MTA manufacturer and is installed in the MTA at the factory. The provisioning server cannot update this certificate. This certificate appears as a read-only parameter in the MTA MIB.
	This certificate is used to authenticate the MTA device identity (its MAC address) during provisioning.
Signed by	MTA Manufacturer Certificate
Validity Period	20 Years+
Length of Encapsulated Key	1024

MTA Device Certificates are not normally renewable; therefore the validity period of the certificate should exceed the expected lifetime of the device in which it is installed. Here is an example Device Certificate.

```
Certificate:
     Data:
          Version: v3 (0x2)
          Serial Number: 1 (0x1)
          Signature Algorithm: PKCS #1 SHA-1 With RSA Encryption
          Issuer: C=US, O=Mike's Modems, OU=PacketCable,
     OU=Redwood City Manufacturing Plant,
     CN=Mike's Modems PacketCable CA
          Validity:
               Not Before: Wed Jan  5 12:51:42 2000
               Not  After: Sun Jan  5 12:51:42 2020
          Subject: C=US, O=Mike's Modems, OU=PacketCable,
     OU=Redwood City Manufacturing Plant, CN=00:80:00:AB:CF:D0
          Subject Public Key Info:
               Algorithm: PKCS #1 RSA Encryption
               Public Key:
               Modulus:
00:cc:69:cf:c9:64:5a:51:19:b6:28:08:e4:5e:aa:ff:8d:31:
2d:6c:1b:66:cc:6a:a7:7d:f9:5d:38:07:14:84:06:5a:1a:f6:
04:bc:01:06:98:05:3c:0e:30:3e:ed:5b:bc:44:76:4c:a9:cb:
a8:b9:7f:31:77:3b:57:46:58:1c:d4:f2:92:ab:f1:c2:0c:40:
51:9c:c6:1e:a3:e4:0c:5f:5b:d7:95:df:ed:2c:7d:ae:a1:19:
```

```
88:a5:07:18:b8:5c:69:d3:7c:6a:28:0c:ce:10:53:83:4f:ef:
36:4f:d5:42:8f:44:64:8f:26:e0:d6:93:95:7d:4d:7c:99:ba:
45:b0:9d
                    Public Exponent: 65537 (0x10001)
         Extensions:
              Identifier: Authority Key Identifier
                   Critical: no
                   Key Identifier:
79:97:12:7d:4c:3d:ce:36:db:9e:bf:19:6a:51:7c:54:ec:9f:
ca:9e
              Identifier: UNKNOWN OBJECT IDENTIFIER
              oid contents:
                   55:1d:0f — 2.5.29.15 keyUsage
                   Critical: no
                   DER Value:
                        03:02:03:a8
              -- BITSTRING digitalSignature, keyEncipherment,
              --     keyAgreement
        Signature:
             Algorithm: PKCS #1 SHA-1 With RSA Encryption
             Signature:
2c:57:91:af:56:c2:40:e7:a3:73:fc:11:99:ea:33:5c:6e:ef:6e:6a:04:
7c:e5:88:07:69:24:09:cd:f7:6f:40:fc:83:e0:44:31:87:7e:4e:37:d9:
55:aa:53:0d:c5:0d:4e:8e:b6:65:a7:c4:b9:7a:f6:9a:f0:61:b4:d0:a2:
2a:74:a8:64:4e:18:d7:8e:d9:f0:9a:5c:7b:19:0d:db:6a:af:3e:b3:11:
e7:ab:6d:b5:6f:41:62:e8:16:87:09:30:dd:66:6c:da:09:e7:06:7b:3b:
42:ea:b3:b9:af:39:3f:ba:57:09:1e:e1:5c:1a:4f:6c:25:b3:a5:a8:3c:
90:fe:1a:e7:0e:e2:e0:30:f8:c8:0b:55:6e:b5:6c:f5:45:11:34:09:c8:
1c:a8:b2:4d:d3:55:d1:63:c8:7b:8f:5d:92:c7:62:52:ce:a0:1b:36:03:
e7:c0:8f:0e:71:a1:93:80:8d:30:48:82:5f:96:fa:5c:fd:2c:a9:1f:cf:
86:34:d2
```

```
-----BEGIN CERTIFICATE-----
MIIC9zCCAiCgAwIBAgIBATANBgkqhkiG9w0BAQUFADCBjTElMCMGA1UEAxMcTWlr
ZSdzIE1vZGVtcyBQYWNrZXRDYWJsZSBDQTEpMCcGA1UECxMgUmVkd29vZCBDaXR5
IE1hbnVmYWN0dXJpbmcgUGxhbnQxFDASBgNVBAsTC1BhY2tldENhYmxlMRYwFAYD
VQQKEw1NaWtlJ3MgTW9kZW1zMQswCQYDVQQGEwJVUzAeFw0wMDAxMDUyMDUxNDJa
Fw0yMDAxMDUyMDUxNDJaMIGCMRowGAYDVQQDExEwDo4MDowMDpBQjpDRjpEMDEp
MCcGA1UECxMgUmVkd29vZCBDaXR5IE1hbnVmYWN0dXJpbmcgUGxhbnQxFDASBgNV
BAsTC1BhY2tldENhYmxlMRYwFAYDVQQKEw1NaWtlJ3MgTW9kZW1zMQswCQYDVQQG
EwJVUzCBnzANBgkqhkiG9w0BAQEFAAOBjQAwgYkCgYEAzGnPyWRaURm2KAjkXqr/
jTEtbBtmzGqnffldOAcUhAZaGvYEvAEGmAU8DjA+7Vu8RHZMqcuouX8xdztXRlgc
1PKSq/HCDEBRnMYeo+QMX1vXld/tLH2uoRmIpQcYuFxp03xqKAzOEFODT+82T9VC
j0Rkjybg1pOVfU18mbpFsJ0CAwEAAaMwMC4wHwYDVR0jBBgwFoAUeZcSfUw9zjbb
```

nr8ZalF8VOyfyp4wCwYDVR0PBAQDAgOoMA0GCSqGSIb3DQEBBQUAA4HBACxXka9W
wkDno3P8EZnqM1xu725qBHzliAdpJAnN929A/IPgRDGHfk432VWqUw3FDU6OtmWn
xLl69prwYbTQoip0qGROGNeO2fCaXHsZDdtqrz6zEeerbbVvQWLoFocJMN1mbNoJ
5wZ7O0Lqs7mvOT+6Vwke4VwaT2wls6WoPJD+GucO4uAw+MgLVW61bPVFETQJyByo
sk3TVdFjyHuPXZLHYlLOoBs2A+fAjw5xoZOAjTBIgl+W+lz9LKkfz4Y00g==
-----END CERTIFICATE-----

IP Telephony Root Certificate

In addition to the device certificate hierarchy, there is an independent hierarchy of certificates tied to the notion of service rather than the notion of hardware devices. This hierarchy is known as the Service Provider hierarchy, and it is shown in Figure 2-11.

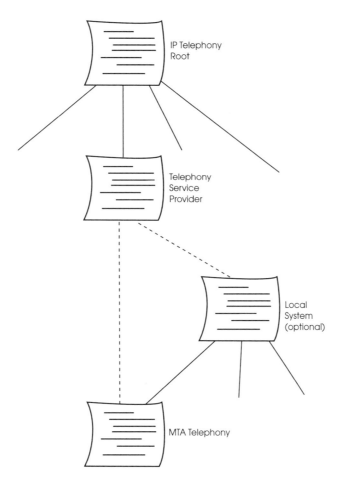

Figure 2-11 Service Provider Hierarchy

Table 2-5 Characteristics of PacketCable IP Telephony Root Certificate

Subject / Name	C=US, O=CableLabs, OU=PacketCable, CN=PacketCable Root IP Telephony Certificate Authority
Use	This certificate is used to sign Telephony Service Provider certificates. It is used by an MTA to verify a Provisioning Server certificate chain associated with a signature on a configuration file. This certificate (or the corresponding public key) is installed into each MTA in the factory and cannot be updated. Neither this root certificate nor the corresponding public key appears in the MTA MIB.
Signed by	Self-signed
Validity Period	40+ Years. It is intended that the validity period is long enough that this certificate is never reissued.
Length of Encapsulated Key	2048

Just as for the device certificate hierarchy, the root certification authority is an entity operating under contract to CableLabs. There is a single IP Telephony Root Certificate, with characteristics summarized in Table 2-5.

During manufacture, the MTA is provided with a copy of the public key of the root certification authority of the operator certificate authority. This allows it to authenticate a certificate hierarchy rooted at the root of the operator certificate hierarchy.

During customer enrollment, a certificate is issued to the enrolling MTA, either by the local system certification authority or by the central service provider certification authority. The public key encapsulated within this certificate is the same key that is contained in the MTA Device Certificate. (In other words, the telephony operator is certifying that the device with this public key is permitted service on the operator's network.)

Telephony Service Provider Certificate

This is the MSO's certificate, signed by the IP Telephony Root Certification Authority (see Table 2-6).

Local System Certificate

There may or may not exist Local System Certificates, depending on the hierarchy preferred by the MSO. If the MSO uses Local System Certificates, the private key

Table 2-6 Characteristics of PacketCable Telephony Service Provider Certificate

Subject / Name	C=<country>, O=<Company>, OU=PacketCable, CN=<Company> PacketCable System Operator CA
Use	This certificate serves as the local root of the intradomain trust hierarchy for the network operator. Each network element is configured with this certificate so that all intradomain communication is limited to this one service provider. This certificate appears as a read-write parameter in the MTA MIB. The provisioning server needs the ability to update this certificate in the MTAs via both SNMP and configuration files. Since each MTA port may be configured with a different telephony service provider, this certificate is associated with an MTA port, rather than with the MTA as a whole.
Signed by	IP Telephony Root Certificate
Validity Period	10 Years. Reissued every 5 years
Length of Encapsulated Key	2048

corresponding to the public key encapsulated by the Local System Certificate is used to issue individual MTA Telephony Certificates. If the MSO does not use Local System Certificates, then the private key corresponding to the public key encapsulated by the Telephony Service Provider is used to issue the MTA Telephony Certificates instead (see Table 2-7).

MTA Telephony Certificate

The **MTA Telephony Certificate** is the certificate issued by the service provider directly to the MTA. It is held by the MTA and allows it access to the services offered by the service operator. Most importantly, it contains the FQDN (Fully Qualified Domain Name) of the MTA—that is, the string by which the MTA is known to the network. It also contains the same public key as the MTA Device Certificate, encapsulating both of these identifying pieces of information in a single certificate.

As discussed above, the MTA Telephony Certificate is signed either by the Local System Certification Authority or by the Telephony Service Provider Certification Authority, depending on the topology favored by the particular MSO (see Table 2-8).

Table 2-7 Characteristics of PacketCable Local System Certificate

Subject / Name	C=<Country>, O=<Company>, OU=PacketCable, OU=<Local System Name>, CN=<Company> PacketCable Local System CA
Use	This certificate appears as a read-write parameter in the MTA MIB (possibly with length zero if the certificate does not exist). The provisioning server needs the ability to update this certificate in the MTAs via both SNMP and configuration files. Since each MTA port may be configured with a different telephony service provider, this certificate is associated with an MTA port rather than with an MTA device as a whole.
Signed by	Telephony Service Provider Certificate
Validity Period	5 Years. Reissued biannually
Length of Encapsulated Key	1024, 1536, or 2048 bits

Table 2-8 Characteristics of PacketCable MTA Telephony Certificate

Subject / Name	C=<Country>, O=<Company>, OU=PacketCable, [OU=<Local System Name>,] CN=<MTA FQDN>
Use	This certificate is used to authenticate the identity of the MTA to the TGS (as described in Chapter 7). This certificate appears as a read-write parameter in the MTA MIB. The provisioning server needs the ability to update this certificate in the MTAs via both SNMP and configuration files. Since each MTA port may be configured with a different telephony service provider, this certificate is associated with an MTA port, rather than with the MTA device as a whole.
Signed by	Telephony Service Provider Certificate or Local System Certificate
Validity Period	45 days, reissued monthly, or 13 months, reissued annually.
Length of Encapsulated Key	Same as MTA Device Certificate (shares same public key)

Certificate Revocation

In general, there should be a mechanism for *revoking* certificates. In other words, the system must have a mechanism by which one or more certificates can be rendered operationally ineffective, even though they are otherwise valid. The need for this usually occurs if a private key somewhere in the chain is compromised (stolen).

When a private key is compromised, all certificates signed by that key (and all certificates signed by entities whose public keys are certified by the stolen key, and all certificates signed by entities whose public key was signed by an entity whose key was stolen, and so on ad infinitum) should immediately be revoked.

Unfortunately, revocation mechanisms in practice are typically complicated and often not very effective. Usually, the operators of certificate based trust hierarchies simply try to make sure that private keys cannot be stolen in the first place. Currently, there is no defined mechanism for revoking any of the certificates in a PacketCable telephony network, although that may change in the future.[21]

Other Certificates

In addition to the certificates that are part of a recognized chain, there is a small number of so-called operational ancillary certificates that are used within the network to assure that devices are authenticated appropriately. We will include a brief discussion of those certificates here, even though we have not yet examined the devices that use them.

Ticket Granting Server Certificate

In the PKINIT exchange between an MTA and a TGS, both sides authenticate themselves to the other. We have already seen that the MTA uses an MTA Telephony Certificate to authenticate itself to the TGS in the initial KRB_AS_REQ message. The TGS authenticates itself by including a TGS certificate in the corresponding KRB_AS_REP.

The TGS certificate is signed by the MSO, either by the Local System Certificate, if the MSO uses them, or by the Telephony Service Provider certificate, if the MSO does not use Local System Certificates. The MSO Certificate is in a hierarchy rooted by the IP Telephony Root certificate, for which the MTA has the corresponding public key, allowing it to authenticate the TGS certificate (see Table 2-9).

Provisioning Server Certificate

During the power-on initialization sequence, the MTA downloads a configuration file from a Provisioning Server (Chapter 7). Included in the configuration file is a Provisioning Server Certificate. Like the TGS, this certificate is signed by the MSO, either with the Local System Certificate or the Telephony Service Provider Certificate, whichever the MSO chooses to use (see Table 2-10).

Enough about security. It's time to start looking at how digital telephony over cable actually works.

---

21. One hopes it does change before any of the private keys is stolen. In PacketCable's defense, however, revoking certificates and replacing them in a secure manner is a rather complex problem.

Table 2-9 Characteristics of PacketCable TGS Certificate

Subject / Name	C=<Country>, O=<Company>, OU=PacketCable, OU=[<Local System Name>], OU=Ticket Granting Servers, CN=<DNS Name>
Use	Authenticates the identity of the TGS server to the MTA during PKINIT exchanges. This certificate is passed to the MTA inside the PKINIT replies. It is not included in the MTA MIB and cannot be updated or queried by the Provisioning Server.
Signed by	Telephony Service Provider Certificate or Local System Certificate
Validity Period	5 years, reissued annually
Length of Encapsulated Key	1024

Table 2-10 Characteristics of PacketCable Provisioning Server Certificate

Subject / Name	C=<Country>, O=<Company>, OU=PacketCable, OU=[<Local System Name>], OU=Provisioning Servers, CN=<DNS Name>
Use	Authenticate the identity of the Provisioning Server to the MTA when it receives a signed configuration file. This certificate is passed to the MTA with the signed configuration file and is therefore not included in the MTA MIB and cannot be updated or queried by the Provisioning Server using SNMP.
	At the time that the MTA receives the configuration file it does not know the identities of either the provisioning server or the service provider. Therefore, the MTA will accept any provisioning server certificate—as long as the corresponding certificate chain is rooted at the IP Telephony Root Certificate.
Signed by	Telephony Service Provider Certificate or Local System Certificate
Validity Period	5 years, reissued annually
Length of Encapsulated Key	1024

Chapter
3
The Access Link

The KEK is a two-key triple DES encryption key that the CMTS uses to encrypt Traffic Encryption Keys (TEKs) it sends to the modem. Traffic encryption keys are used for encrypting user data traffic. CM and CMTS use message authentication keys to authenticate, via a keyed message digest, the key requests and responses they exchange.

SP-BPI+-I02-990731

In order for a user to access a service offered by a provider—whether that service is telephony or simple data access—there must be a communications link between that user and the service provider's facilities. On a cable network, that link is implemented through the cable modem, or CM, located in the user's residence, and the Cable Modem Termination System, or CMTS, located in the headend. All traffic between the user and the network travels over this CM-CMTS link.

The CM-CMTS link is not symmetric. Cable modems are not at all like the ordinary analog modems commonly used for low-speed access over analog telephone lines. Rather, they are complex devices that act as clients to the CMTS, which in turn directs in real-time exactly how the each CM on the access network is to behave.

The DOCSIS Specifications

Early cable modems were designed according to specifications developed by individual manufacturers using proprietary protocols. Although many of these modems worked well, because each manufacturer adopted a different protocol it was impossible for them to interoperate. Since the cable modem communicates with a CMTS, this meant that once a service provider decided on a particular vendor's CMTS, its customers were immediately locked into using only cable modems from the same vendor. Because several vendors were competing to produce CM-CMTS pairs, the market was fragmented and the hardware was relatively expensive.

In order to standardize the CM-CMTS protocols, a consortium of cable operators was formed. This consortium was called the **Multimedia Cable Network System**, or **MCNS**,[1] and its stated goal was to prepare "a series of interface specifications that will permit the early definition, design, development and deployment of data-over-cable systems on an [sic] uniform, consistent, open, non-proprietary, multi-vendor interoperable basis". These specifications are collectively referred to as the **Data-Over-Cable Service Interface Specifications** or "**DOCSIS**".

Note that the original emphasis was on *data* over cable. The first version of DOCSIS was designed to support only ordinary data communication. Telephony

Table 3-1   DOCSIS Specifications

SP-BPI+-I02-990731
Baseline Privacy Plus Interface Specification—Specifies security over the cable access network.
SP-CMTRI-I01-970804
Cable Modem Telephony Return Interface Specification—Specifies the use of telephone lines for upstream information flow.
SP-CMTS-NSII01-960702
Cable Modem Termination System–Network Side Interface Specification—Specifies how the network interfaces with HFC.
TR-DOCS-OSSIW08-961016
Operations Support System Framework for Data Over Cable Services—Specifies a high-level framework for OSS for data services over cable.
SP-RFIv1.1-I02-990731
Radio Frequency Interface Specification—Provides a low-level description of communication between a cable modem and the Cable Modem Termination System.
SP-OSSI-RFI-I03-990113
Operations Support System Interface Specification Radio Frequency Interface— RF Interface MIBs
SP-OSSI-BPI-I01-980331
Operations Support System Interface Specification Baseline Privacy Interface MIB–Privacy MIBs

---

1. The original members of MCNS were Comcast Cable Communications, Inc., Cox Communications, Tele-Communications, Inc., Time Warner Cable, MediaOne, Inc., Rogers Cablesystems Limited, and Cable Television Laboratories, Inc. (acting on behalf of the CableLabs member companies).

communication has requirements over and above those needed for data (in particular, telephony requires guaranteed Quality of Service and enhanced privacy); support for these requirements was added in version 1.1 of the DOCSIS specifications.

The current version of the DOCSIS specifications may be downloaded from *www.cablemodem.com*. Table 3-1 lists the versions that were current at the time this book was written. The DOCSIS specifications are intended to define the behavior of Cable Modem and Cable Modem Termination System devices in sufficient detail that products conforming to the specifications will be interoperable. The specifications are not designed to imply any particular method of implementing these devices.

PacketCable telephony is designed to run over DOCSIS version 1.1 or later. Theoretically, the entire PacketCable network is independent of the underlying layers and infrastructure. In theory, PacketCable could be implemented to run over a completely different technology such as DSL or wireless. However, when the PacketCable telephony network was being designed, the strengths and weaknesses of DOCSIS 1.1 were taken into account, so that many of the design decisions reflect the assumption that DOCSIS 1.1 is being used over the access network.

The relationship between PacketCable and DOCSIS is shown in Figure 3-1. All current implementations of PacketCable use the Quality of Service "hooks" provided by DOCSIS and discussed later in this chapter. In principle, DOCSIS and PacketCable can be completely decoupled: PacketCable could be built on a completely different access technology. Similarly, a totally different telephony architecture could be constructed on top of DOCSIS. However, as of this writing, there is no

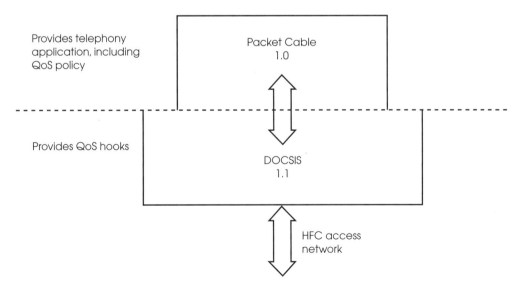

Figure 3-1 DOCSIS and PacketCable

indication that any vendor intends to separate the PacketCable telephony "application" from the underlying DOCSIS transport.

Note that in this chapter, we will be discussing the behavior of cable modems, not of MTAs. In the current release of PacketCable, these are intended to be embedded in the same device, since there is no standard API that allows a cable modem to be driven by an external MTA. This sometimes leads to a certain level of sloppiness when referring to CMs and MTAs. However, in the future MTAs and CMs will migrate to become physically distinct entities and a clear distinction will have to be made. The cable modem will remain the point where the home network interfaces to the cable, and it will continue to function as described in this chapter.

Overview of the Cable Access Network

Before we examine in detail the workings of DOCSIS modems and their corresponding CMTSes, we will look briefly, at a high level, how a DOCSIS access network operates.

DOCSIS cable modems located in homes are clients of Cable Modem Termination Systems, which are located at the other end of the coax/fiber access link, at the MSO's headend. In order that the CMTS is properly able to manage the access network, on which there may be several hundred cable modems all competing for the available upstream and downstream bandwidth, DOCSIS cable modems are required to obtain and obey instructions from the CMTS. This ensures that the resources are allocated fairly and efficiently among the active cable modems on the network.

Initialization

When a cable modem is first connected to the cable and powered up, a complex series of transactions takes place between the modem and its CMTS. The modem is at all times unaware (at least directly) of the presence of other modems on the network; the modem communicates *only* with the CMTS. This is true even if two modems on the same access network wish to communicate—all traffic passes through the CMTS.

The cable modem initialization sequence is as follows.

1. Locate a downstream channel and synchronize operation with the CMTS.

2. Obtain upstream transmit parameters from the CMTS.

3. Perform a ranging operation.

4. Confirm that IP connectivity exists.

5. Synchronize time of day with the CMTS.

6. Transfer operational parameters between CM and CMTS.

7. Register.

8. Initialize Baseline Privacy Plus.

In order to perform this sequence in a reliable and secure manner, two items are placed in the cable modem at the time of manufacture. These items are in non-volatile memory and should never be changed.

- A unique 48-bit MAC address (equivalent to the MAC address in an ordinary Ethernet network interface card)

- An X.509 digital certificate, which is used to authenticate the modem to the CMTS. Typically, this certificate is signed by the modem manufacturer, whose public key the service provider has obtained through other means and that is loaded into the CMTS software so that it can authenticate modems as they attempt to initialize and obtain service.

Downstream Synchronization

The cable modem begins to scan the 6 MHz downstream video channels, looking for a CMTS signal. If the modem has previously been used and is simply restarting after a temporary failure—for example, power-down—the modem first tries to lock on to a CMTS signal in the most recently used downstream channel. It continues to scan until it finds a signal that it can properly detect and with which it can properly synchronize.

Obtaining Upstream Parameters

The CMTS periodically transmits messages called **Upstream Channel Descriptors** (**UCD**s) on all downstream channels. Nominally, UCDs are broadcast every two seconds. UCDs describe the correct parameters that a modem must use to transmit on the various upstream channels to which the CMTS is currently listening.

When the modem receives a UCD containing parameters for a channel that it can use, it stores this information and uses it to determine the transmit parameters for future upstream transmissions.

As well as UCDs, the CMTS periodically transmits **SYNC** messages (nominally every 200 milliseconds). These contain information about the CMTS's notion of time and allow the modem to synchronize properly with the CMTS and the other modems on the network.

Ranging

A number of operational parameters within the modem may need to be adjusted slightly in order to guarantee that all modems on the access link are operating cooperatively. For example, the transmit power level or the center frequency of the upstream channel might need to be adjusted slightly if the modem is out of alignment. In addition, since cable modems are not all at the same distance from the CMTS, it is insufficient for a CM merely to synchronize its clock with the CMTS. It must also have some notion of the transmission delay between itself and the CMTS, otherwise the transmissions from two modems, one told to transmit at time t and another told to transmit at time t', might overlap.[2]

In order to make these adjustments, the cable modem must actively exchange information with the CMTS. It does this through a process known as **ranging**. Cable modem transmissions are sent in one of two modes: contention or noncontention. In the cable system, time is divided into short intervals known as minislots, which are a small multiple of 6.25 microseconds in length. (The precise duration of a minislot depends on the modulation scheme in use. Basically, a minislot is usually the time taken to transmit 16 octets.) Noncontention minislots are allocated by the CMTS in such a way that only one CM is permitted to transmit within the minislot. Transmissions occurring in noncontention minislots have a high probability of being received correctly at the CMTS, since it is guaranteed that there will be no other signal on the line in the same upstream channel at the same time. Contention minislots (which are typically about 25% of the available total) are unallocated, and any CM is permitted to transmit during them. These transmissions may have a low probability of being received correctly if there are many active devices on the access network.

The CMTS manages the ratio of contention to noncontention minislots, just as it manages exactly which modem may transmit during a noncontention minislot. In fact, at the risk of digressing from the point at hand, calculating optimum ratio of noncontention to contention minislots is an interesting problem in network bandwidth management, since it depends on the kind of data that is passing across the network. If most of the traffic flows at relatively constant rates (for example, when the network is handling principally telephony traffic), then there are fewer ad hoc requests for upstream bandwidth, and the need for contention minislots decreases. This in turn allows the CMTS to allocate more bandwidth to noncontention minislots, and thus even more telephony-like traffic may be permitted to flow. If, on the other hand, the traffic is "bursty", such as occurs with Web browsing, then the number of contention minislots typically needs to be increased and the usable bandwidth

---

2. Upstream bandwidth is an extremely scarce resource on the access network. The modems and the CMTS go to great lengths to use the available bandwidth as efficiently as possible. Part of this process is to ensure that all the devices on the network maintain very closely synchronized clocks to reduce packet collisions on the network.

of the system decreases. A good working average of noncontention:contention mode slots for "typical" traffic is roughly 3:1.

Except for informational messages, transmissions sent in contention mode usually demand an explicit response from the CMTS. If the expected response is not received, the CM will usually retransmit the transmission in another contention-mode minislot, and will continue to do so until a response is received.

Ranging requests are sent in contention mode and so may need to be repeated a number of times before the CM receives the information it desires from the CMTS. In response to a ranging request, the CMTS will instruct the CM to adjust parameters such as clock skew, carrier frequency and transmit power so that they are within acceptable limits.

In addition to the ranging performed during initialization, the CMTS provides specific opportunities for each attached CM to perform subsequent ranging operations to ensure that slight adjustments to the operational parameters may be made as necessary, so that the entire system stays acceptably synchronized.

Establishing IP Connectivity

Once the low-level transmission parameters are properly set, the CM should be able to communicate correctly with the CMTS (and, through it, to the MSO's network on the far side of the CMTS). It now begins communication by transmitting a **Dynamic Host Configuration Protocol** (**DHCP**) "discover" request. In response, a DHCP server provides the modem with an assigned IP address, as well as the address of another DHCP server (possibly the same one) that can provide the modem with more parameters. The initial DHCP response also contains name of a file that contains further, network-specific configuration parameters for the CM. The CM issues a DHCP request to the second server and obtains whatever additional parameters are needed to establish IP connectivity with the network. Note that it does not yet download the configuration file.

Synchronizing Time of Day

As well as a low-level shared notion of time (for the correct synchronization of packet transmissions), the CM and the CMTS need to share a common notion of the approximate time of day, which may be used for logging abnormal events and for key management by the security system (which will typically require that keys be changed periodically).

One of the parameters obtained from the DHCP server is the address of a Time Server (which may be the DHCP server itself). The modem connects to this server on port 37 and obtains the time, using the Time Protocol specified in RFC 868.

Transferring Operational Parameters

The CM now downloads the configuration file whose name was provided by the original DHCP server. This download uses the Trivial File Transfer Protocol specified in RFC 1350. The operational parameters overwrite any default values configured into the modem during manufacture.

A large number of parameters may (but need not) be present in the configuration file. These parameters provide values used by the low-level system, such as upstream and downstream channel frequencies and data rates, as well the addresses of various network servers, timer values, and so on. If explicit values are not provided, the modem adopts sensible default values provided at the time of manufacture.

The configuration file may direct the modem to use an upstream or downstream channel different from the one it is already using, in which case the modem switches to the new channel(s) and performs a new Ranging request.

Registering

Once the modem has obtained and processed the configuration file, it informs its CMTS of the values of its operational parameters in a Registration Request message. The CMTS assigns Service IDs (SIDs), which will be used to identify the various classes of service flowing through this particular modem and informs the modem of the SID values that have been assigned to it.

Initializing Baseline Privacy Plus

A security association between a cable modem and its CMTS allows information to flow between the two without fear that the data can be read or manipulated by a third party. This is an important requirement on a cable access network, since there is at least a theoretical possibility that a neighbor may be eavesdropping on the CM-CMTS communication.

In order to create a security association, the modem now initializes its Baseline Privacy Plus (BPI+) configuration, which effectively secures the link from casual eavesdroppers. (BPI+, however, uses only 56-bit DES to secure the link, which is insufficient to deter a determined attempt to decrypt the traffic.) Once BPI+ is correctly initialized, the modem is a fully fledged member of the network, operating completely under the control of the CMTS.

DOCSIS Protocol Layers

Figure 3-2 shows the protocol layers included in the DOCSIS specifications. They range from the Physical Media Dependent sublayer, which carries modulated **RF** (**Radio Frequency**) energy, to a layer carrying some of the network administration

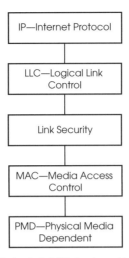

Figure 3-2 DOCSIS Protocol Layers

protocols used in an IP network. In this chapter we will concentrate on discussing the lower layers, since these are specific to cable and adequate descriptions cannot easily be found elsewhere.

Physical Media Dependent Sublayer

At the bottom of the DOCSIS stack is the **Physical Media Dependent** (**PMD**) sublayer. Communications textbooks describe many ways to modulate waveforms to allow information to be transmitted from a source to a destination. Common modulation methods, with which you are probably familiar, include **Amplitude Modulation** (**AM**) and **Frequency Modulation** (**FM**), which are used for ordinary broadcast radio transmission, but there are also many other modulation schemes used for other purposes. Each scheme has characteristics that may make it useful in one set of circumstances, whereas another scheme may be better suited to different circumstances.

Some modulation schemes, for example, are relatively immune to extraneous noise, whereas others may work rather badly in the presence of noise. Others allow for very rapid information flow, whereas some may operate relatively slowly. The schemes used in cable systems are well adapted to that particular environment, and allow relatively high rates of information flow in the cable access network.

Modulation Schemes

All modulation schemes begin with the notion of a pure monochromatic (single frequency) sine wave such as the one depicted in Figure 3-3.

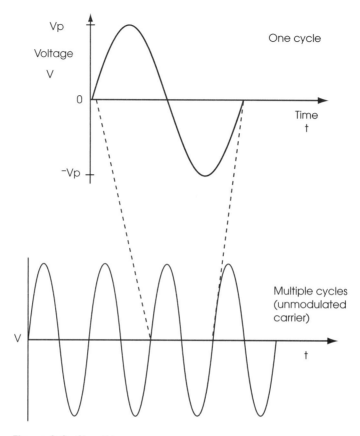

Figure 3-3 Sine Wave

The amplitude of a sine wave (typically measured in volts or millivolts) varies smoothly in time: It starts from zero, crests at a value V_p, decreases again to zero, continues decreasing until it reaches a peak negative value, $-V_p$, and then returns again to zero. This cycle is repeated many times, as shown in Figure 3-3.

The number of complete cycles that occurs in a second is called the frequency of the wave. For the kinds of waves that we will be talking about in this book, the frequency ranges from a few million per second to a few hundreds of million per second. Each cycle per second is called a Hertz, abbreviated as Hz; millions of cycles per second are called megahertz, abbreviated as MHz.[3]

3. The frequency range of naturally occurring waves is extremely wide: Micropulsations, which have their origin in the Earth's magnetosphere, have frequencies below 1 Hz. Ordinary light ranges in frequency from 1.4×10^{14} Hz (red) to 2.5×10^{14} Hz (blue); gamma rays have frequencies as high as 10^{34} Hz. Isn't it wonderful what subjects can turn up in a book about telephony?

A sine wave of a particular frequency carries no information, but it can be modified by a process called **modulation**: The information transmitted is used to deform it from a pure sine wave so that once the wave reaches a distant receiver, the amount of deformation can be measured, and the sender's information can be recovered through **demodulation**. This is shown in Figure 3-4. Because the original sine wave, although it contains no information, is used to *carry* information, it is called a carrier, and the frequency of the carrier is called the carrier frequency.

Most services that utilise carrier waves adopt a channelized bandplan, in which a range of frequencies is broken up into a number of channels, and each channel contains exactly one carrier frequency. For example, the domestic AM broadcast band is

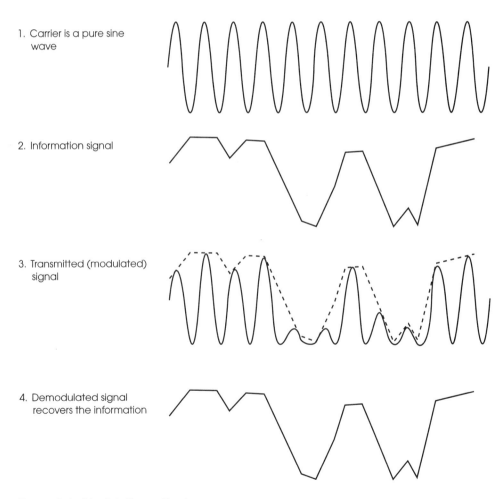

1. Carrier is a pure sine wave

2. Information signal

3. Transmitted (modulated) signal

4. Demodulated signal recovers the information

Figure 3-4 Modulating a Carrier

assigned by the **Federal Communications Commission** (**FCC**) to frequencies between 535 and 1605 kHz. However, if stations were to place their carrier frequencies wherever they desired in this range, they would interfere with one another. To prevent this, the FCC mandates a bandplan of fixed channels spaced by 10 kHz and ensures through a licensing system that no two stations in the same geographical area are assigned the same carrier frequency. So, for example, an AM broadcast station may be assigned to the 590 kHz channel (imagine an ugly jingle here, followed by a cheery voice announcing, "KQIQ AM 590"), but, since channels are separated by multiples of 10 kHz, there cannot be a station on 595 kHz.[4]

The FM broadcast band operates under a similar scheme, although in that case the band edges lie at 88 and 108 MHz, and the channels are spaced by 200 kHz. The reason for the greater separation between carrier frequencies is that frequency modulation, although it is more immune to noise than AM—which is why most stations broadcasting music use FM—it also occupies much greater bandwidth than AM. This is an example of different modulation schemes being used for different purposes in different environments.

Broadcast radio is, clearly, quite different from two-way digital data communication over a cable. Although the two share the fundamental characteristic of modulating a carrier wave to transmit information, the two services have different requirements: Broadcast is analog. It is relatively unconcerned with noise and reliability, and information is transmitted at a relatively low rate. By contrast, data communication is digital. It is important that the transmissions be reliable and untainted by errors induced by noise, and the information flow may be quite high-speed. Therefore it is unsurprising that different (and more complicated) modulation techniques are used to transfer data than the relatively simple techniques used in broadcast radio.

The greatest single difference lies in the digital nature of the information. Digital data may always be reduced to a stream of zeros and ones. Therefore it is necessary to modulate the carrier only in such a way as to be able to distinguish between the "zero" state and the "one" state, and then to be able to switch quickly between these states.

Simple modulation schemes such as AM can be operated in this way. For example, in standard ASCII computer code, the uppercase letter A is represented by the 8-bit string 01000001. In a simple digital amplitude modulated system, the waveform corresponding to the letter A might look as in Figure 3-5.

A more common modulation method used for transmission of digital data is **Phase Shift Keying**, or **PSK**. Instead of varying the amplitude of the frequency or the carrier, its phase is shifted according to some well-defined scheme. Figure 3-6

---

4. The channel spacing in other countries may be different. Since signals in the so-called "medium wave" broadcast band—535 to 1605 kHz—typically do not travel very far, it is not necessary for every country to adopt the same channelized bandplan. This is not true for all frequencies.

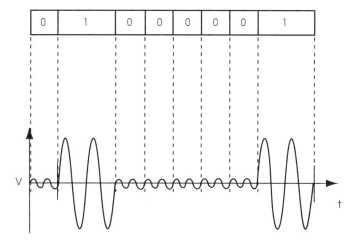

Figure 3-5   Representation of the ASCII Character "A" in Digital AM

shows the letter A in a PSK scheme in which a phase shift of 180° represents a binary one and a phase shift of 0° represents a zero.

A relatively simple variant of ordinary PSK, called **Quadrature Phase Shift Keying** or **QPSK**, is often used in modems. QPSK is a modulation scheme that, although rather inefficient, is also more robust (that is, less prone to errors on noisy channels) than more complicated schemes.

In QPSK, a single carrier is split into two components phased 90° apart. (Two signals with the same frequency but 90° apart in phase are said to be *in quadrature*.) The two components are known as the I-channel and the Q-channel. Dividing the carrier in this way allows us to send twice as much information in the same amount of time, since the two channels are independent of each other.

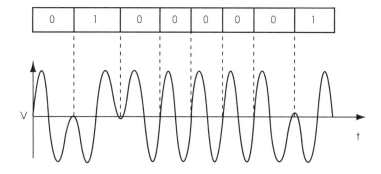

Figure 3-6   Representation of the ASCII Character "A" in Digital PSK

Consider first just the I-channel. We can modulate this exactly the same way as we did in ordinary PSK: A phase shift of 180° represents a binary 1, and a phase shift of 0° represents a binary 0. But we can also do the same for the Q-channel: Adding a phase shift of 180° to the Q-channel (which is already shifted +90° relative to the I-channel) represents a binary 1, and a phase shift of 0° represents a binary 0.

Thus we can transmit bits in pairs, allowing the first bit of the pair (for example) to modulate the I-channel, and the second (for example) to modulate the Q-channel. The I-channel and the Q-channel signals are combined before transmission and are transmitted simultaneously. At the receiving end, a demodulator splits the incoming signal into I-channel and Q-channel, and then examines each channel to determine whether it is at phase 0° or phase 180°. From this measurement, the original pair of bits may be recovered.

QPSK demonstrates an important point about digital transmission systems that is often not clearly understood—that is, that the bit rate of a communication is not always equal to the baud rate. The baud rate is defined as the rate at which individual symbols are transmitted. In QPSK, the carrier may be in one of four states, corresponding to the waveform for 00, 01, 10 and 11, respectively; each state is referred to as a symbol. The baud rate in a QPSK system is therefore the number of (00, 01, 10, 11) symbols transmitted per second. Since each symbol represents two independent bits, the bit rate of a QPSK transmission is twice the symbol, or baud, rate.

The different states in QPSK (as well as other quadrature modulation schemes) are often shown in what is called a constellation diagram, in which each possible symbol is marked with a dot (see Figure 3-7).

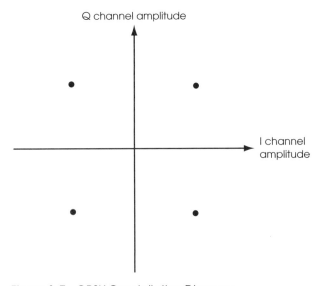

Figure 3-7 QPSK Constellation Diagram

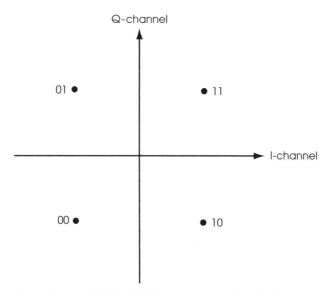

Figure 3-8 DOCSIS QPSK Symbol Mapping (I, Q)

Naturally, both the transmitter and the receiver must agree on the meaning of each symbol. DOCSIS mandates the symbol mapping shown in Figure 3-8, where the I-channel bit precedes the Q-channel bit.

Another common modulation scheme is known as 16-QAM. (**QAM**, as you may be able to guess, stands for **Quadrature Amplitude Modulation**.) This uses the same basic mechanism of splitting the carrier into an I-channel and a Q-channel and shifting the phase of the two channels, but in addition it applies amplitude modulation independently to the two channels. Suppose that the channel is such that we can reliably detect two different levels of amplitude, then the corresponding constellation diagram looks like Figure 3-9.

The total number of different symbols in this system, N, is given by:

```
N = number of phase axes *
      number of distinguishable phases per axis *
      (number of amplitude states)²
```

or, putting in the numbers:

```
N = 2 * 2 * 2²
  = 16; hence, 16-QAM.
```

Even more efficient modulation schemes are possible if the communication channel is noise-free and the modulator and demodulator are capable of reliably

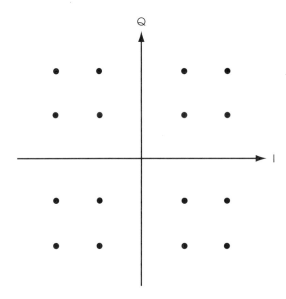

Figure 3-9 Constellation Diagram for Two-Amplitude Quadrature PSK (16-QAM)

distinguishing a greater number of amplitude levels. Both 64-QAM (four amplitude states) and 256-QAM (eight amplitude states) are commonly used where circumstances permit.

Just as the bit rate is twice the baud rate in ordinary QPSK (which is sometimes called 4-QAM), the following relationships hold for the more efficient modulation schemes in Table 3-2.

On most cable systems, upstream communication takes place in the frequency range between 5 and 40 MHz. This tends to be a rather noisy part of the electromagnetic spectrum.[5] Because of the relatively noisy nature of the upstream channel, cable modems must be capable of transmitting only QPSK and 16-QAM. The noise level in the range 5 to 40 MHz is generally too great for 64-QAM and 256-QAM to be useful. 64-QAM and 256-QAM are, however, used in the higher-frequency downstream direction, where the noise is typically much less. When operating in 16-QAM mode, DOCSIS-compliant modems are required to follow the symbol diagram given in Figure 3-10.

The 16-QAM mode of DOCSIS modems can also be programmed to operate according to a symbol mapping in which the transmitted symbol depends on the

---

5. Theoretically, the cable is sufficiently isolated by the braiding that no noise can enter. In practice a small amount of noise does enter, and the amount that enters increases with decreasing frequency.

Table 3-2 Bits per Symbol for Various Modulation Schemes

Modulation Scheme	Bits per Symbol (Bit Rate ÷ Baud Rate)
16-QAM	4
64-QAM	6
256-QAM	8

previously transmitted symbol, a method that is called differential symbol mapping, or differential coding. The constellation diagram for DOCSIS 16-QAM differential coding is shown in Figure 3-11.

Table 3-3 shows how the quadrant of the about-to-be-transmitted symbol is derived from the current bits. (The abbreviation **MSB** in the table stands for **Most Significant Bit**; similarly the abbreviation **LSB** is commonly used to mean **Least Significant Bit**.) The combination of Figure 3-11 and Table 3-3 tells us what symbols must be transmitted and how much phase change to apply to the transmission. Note that Table 3-3 shows us that the prior symbol does not affect the phase (although it does affect which bits are transmitted, as Figure 3-11 tells us).

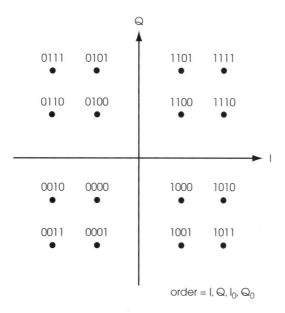

order = I, Q, I_0, Q_0

Figure 3-10 16-QAM DOCSIS Symbol Mapping
(I_1, Q_1, I_0, Q_0)

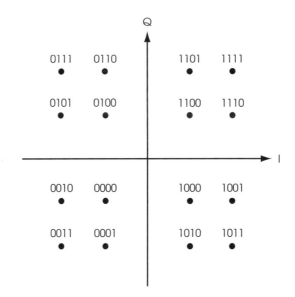

Figure 3-11   16-QAM DOCSIS Differential Symbol
Mapping (I_1, Q_1, I_0, Q_0)

As an example, suppose that the last symbol that the modem transmitted was
the one marked $(1, 0, 1, 0)$ in Figure 3-11 and that the next symbol will represent the
four bits 1110. The current input bits (I_1, Q_1) are 11. The MSBs of the prior symbol
were 10. Then Figure 3-11 and Table 3-3 tell us that the MSBs for the currently
transmitted symbol must be 01 and the quadrant must change phase by 180°. The
LSBs for the currently transmitted symbol are identical to the LSBs of the input
signal (that is, differential encoding is used only for the MSBs).

Time Slices

Data transmission in a cable system is synchronous. This means that events are
linked to carefully synchronized clocks running within the cable modem and its corresponding cable modem termination system. Time slices are allocated to one or more
transmitting modems in a process called **Time Division Multiple Access** (**TDMA**).
The unit of temporal granularity in a DOCSIS cable system is 6.25 microseconds.

Data are transmitted and received in indivisible time slices called **minislots**,
each of which is an integral power-of-two multiple of 6.25 microseconds (1×6.25
microseconds, 2×6.25 microseconds, 4×6.25 microseconds, 8×6.25 microseconds
and so on). If the data do not exactly fit within a minislot, the time up to the next
available minislot boundary is effectively wasted, since minislots are always synchronized across the network. A single packet of data may occupy several contiguous
minislots, depending on its length.

Table 3-3 Derivation of Quadrant in DOCSIS Differential 16-QAM

Input Bits I_1Q_1	MSBs of Prior Symbol	Phase Change
00	11	0°
00	01	0°
00	00	0°
00	10	0°
01	11	90°
01	01	90°
01	00	90°
01	10	90°
11	11	180°
11	01	180°
11	00	180°
11	10	180°
10	11	270°
10	01	270°
10	00	270°
10	10	270°

When the modem is using QPSK modulation, a total of 64 symbols (corresponding to 16 octets, or 128 bits) can be transmitted in a single minislot.[6] The duration of a minislot on a particular channel, expressed as a multiple of 6.25 microseconds, is present in Upstream Channel Descriptors transmitted periodically by the CMTS.

The CMTS keeps track of time with an internal 32-bit counter (which wraps silently back to zero after reaching $2^{32} - 1$) synchronized to a 10.24 MHz clock. The value of this counter is used to synchronize transmissions by modems throughout the access network.

Both QPSK and 16-QAM are supported on the upstream channel, with symbol rates of 160, 320, 640, 1,280 and 2,560 kilosymbols per second. The highest upstream bit rate that a DOCSIS modem can support is therefore 2,560 kilosymbols times 4 bits per symbol (16-QAM modulation), for a total of 10.24 megabits per second.

---

6. In the less common case where the modem is using 16-QAM, the modem may transmit 32 octets in a single minislot.

Upstream Transmission

The actual procedure of transmitting a data packet is quite complicated; it is diagrammed in Figure 3-12. We will briefly look at the various values and steps shown in Figure 3-12.

1. Data to be transmitted

   This is simply the string of zeros and ones that the CM wishes to transmit at this time.

2. Block the data

   The data are divided into smaller units called Information Blocks.

3. Apply optional FEC

   In any transmission medium, there is a possibility that bits may be lost or recovered incorrectly in the receiver. To guard against this, CMs may use a system called **Reed-Solomon Forward Error Correction**. This process takes an Information Block and adds bits to it in such a way that if a few consecutive bits are lost or scrambled in transmission, they can be recovered at the receiver.[7] These bits are sometimes called FEC Parity bits. The Information Block plus the FEC Parity is called a codeword.

4. Scramble

   Many electronic circuits at the receiver assume that all DC bias (that is, a "long-term" non-zero voltage) has been removed from a signal. Long strings of zeros or ones in the data stream may result in a short-term apparent DC bias, which can cause receiver circuitry to misinterpret the data. To prevent this, each codeword is scrambled prior to transmission by XORing it with a pseudorandom sequence of bits. The receiver XORs the received data with the same

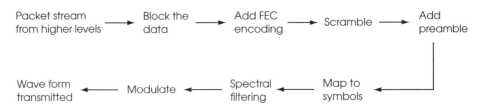

Figure 3-12 Upstream Data Flow Through a Cable Modem

---

7. The number of bits added and the amount of protection afforded by FEC encoding at the CM are ordered by the CMTS during the initialization sequence. Remember that once it is on the network, the CM can do nothing unless it is explicitly ordered to do so by the CMTS.

pseudorandom sequence, effectively recovering the original codeword. (See Chapter 2 for more details about the XOR operation.)

5. Preamble prepend

A preamble is placed at the beginning of the packet. This is a sequence that will help the CMTS synchronize correctly so that it recognizes that data are about to be received. The length and contents of the preamble are sent to the CM by the CMTS during initialization.

6. Symbol map

The bitstream is converted by the process described in Modulation Schemes into the corresponding stream of symbols.

7. Filter

A stream of bits that changes too rapidly between the zero and one states can cause the bandwidth of the transmitted signal to increase beyond that allocated to the upstream channel. (It is a fundamental law of physics that the more abruptly a signal changes state, the wider the bandwidth that it occupies. To a good approximation, if a signal changes state in n microseconds, it will occupy a bandwidth of $1/n$ MHz.) Before transmission, the cable modem smooths the modulating signal so that the transmitted signal will fit within a channel width no greater than 1.25 times the symbol rate.

8. Modulate

The carrier is modulated with the filtered signal and placed on the coax.

The process is arranged so that the final step, modulation, begins precisely at the start of a minislot.

Downstream Data Flow Through a Cable Modem

Downstream flow is essentially the inverse of the upstream process: The incoming data are demodulated; the bitstream is recovered by applying an inverse symbol map; the preamble is removed; the bits are unscrambled; the FEC encoding is removed (or, if necessary, the information in the FEC parity bits is used to correct for erroneous bits in the data); and finally, the actual data are extracted.

Because the downstream data travel in a less noisy part of the spectrum, they are not subject to the same bandwidth and noise constraints as the upstream data and can be transmitted using more efficient modulation schemes. On the downstream link, a DOCSIS cable modem is required to support 64-QAM with a symbol rate of 5.056941 megasymbols per second (corresponding to 30.341646 megabits per second) and 256-QAM with a rate of 5.360537 megasymbols per second (corresponding to

42.884296 megabits per second). These two rates are often referred to as "30 megabits" and "40 megabits", respectively. Note, however, that these numbers refer to total raw downlink capacity and make no allowance for the overhead that is added to each data packet, nor to the fact that many modems are probably sharing the same downstream channel.

The packet format for downstream data is formatted quite differently from that used for upstream traffic. Instead of using Ethernet-based formatting, the downstream packets are formatted as a continuous stream of 188-octet MPEG[8] packets, each packet comprising a four-octet header followed by 184 octets of data. The MPEG format was chosen for the downstream data because this particular format is well adapted to carrying real-time video data, and the format is already used to deliver certain kinds of digital television down the cable. The details of the MPEG formatting used to carry data packets are provided in the DOCSIS RF specification.

Media Access Control Layer

Above the PMD layer lies the **Media Access Control** (**MAC**) protocol layer. This layer supports the following key properties and features.

- Bandwidth allocation

- Providing upstream minislots

- Contention-based and reservation-based upstream transmission

- Variable-length packets

- Quality of Service, providing bandwidth and latency guarantees and creation, management and deletion of dynamic flows

- Range of data rates

The MAC layer network topology is not confined to a single CM/CMTS pair. Rather it comprises a CMTS and a suite of managed CMs. As we have discussed, the CM-CMTS relationship is not peer-to-peer. CMs act as clients of a CMTS, which instructs them exactly how they are to behave in order that fairness is ensured for all the CMs for which the CMTS is responsible.

---

8. **MPEG** stands for **Moving Picture Experts Group**. The MPEG format, which was originally defined by this group, has been adopted by ITU as recommendation H.222.0.

All transmitted data obey the following rules of ordering.

1. Within an octet, the least significant bit is transmitted first.

2. When the value being transmitted spans more than one octet, the octets are transmitted in order of most significant to least significant. This way of ordering values that span multiple octets is known as **network order**. In the absence of an explicit directive to the contrary, all such values used in all the protocols in this book are transmitted in network order.

3. Signed integer values are transmitted in two's complement format.

   In two's complement format, negative values are transmitted as follows: In order to transmit the negative number –N (where N is positive), calculate +N-1, then invert all the bits in the binary representation of this number. This is the value to be transmitted.

   For example, to transmit a single octet representing the value –15, the octet that is transmitted has the form 11110001 (but remember that the bits are actually transmitted in reverse order, per the first rule).

Figure 3-13 shows the relationship between the MAC layer and the PMD layer.

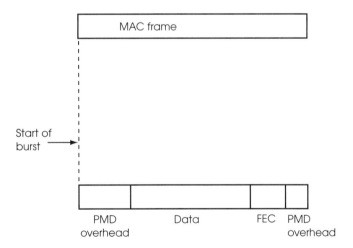

Figure 3-13 Relationship Between MAC Layer and PMD Layer

MAC Header Format

DOCSIS MAC headers have the format shown in Figure 3-14. The Extended Header field, EHDR, is optional. (The DOCSIS security mechanism, Baseline Privacy Interface Plus, requires this field. For details, see the section "BPI + MAC Extended Header".)

The fields in the MAC header are as follows.

- FC

  Frame Control; an octet that identifies the type of the header. The octet is broken down as follows.

  - FC TYPE

    2 bits used to define the type of the rest of the packet

  - FC PARM

    5 bits set to 0; other values are reserved for future use and are currently ignored

  - EHDR_ON

    1 bit, set to 1 if an Extended Header field is present; otherwise set to 0

- MAC_PARM

  Parameters; an octet whose meaning depends on FC

  If EHDR_ON is 1, then MAC_PARM contains the length of the EHDR field.

  Else, if this is part of a concatenated frame, contains the MAC frame count.

  Else indicates the number of minislots requested.

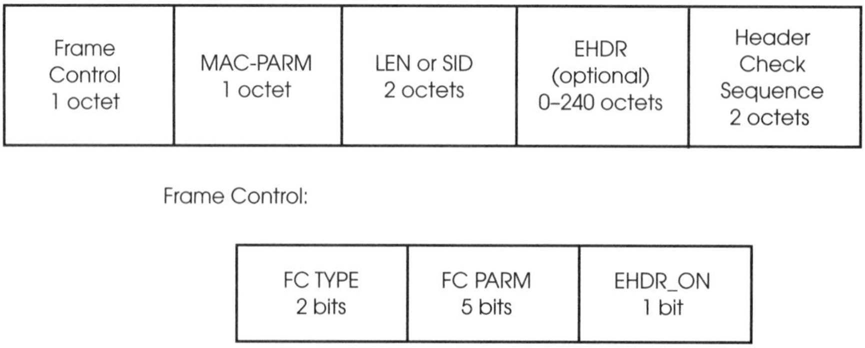

Frame Control 1 octet	MAC-PARM 1 octet	LEN or SID 2 octets	EHDR (optional) 0–240 octets	Header Check Sequence 2 octets

Frame Control:

FC TYPE 2 bits	FC PARM 5 bits	EHDR_ON 1 bit

Figure 3-14 DOCSIS MAC Header Format

- LEN (SID[9])

  Length of the MAC frame, or the SID; 2 octets

  If this is a Request header, contains the SID for which the request is being made in the bottom 14 bits.

  Else, contains the length of the MAC frame, defined as the sum of the number of octets in the extended header (which may be zero) and the number of octets following the HCS field.

- EHDR

  Extended header; optional, length 0 to 240 octets

- HCS

  Header Check Sequence; 2 octets. Used to ensure the integrity of the MAC header, this is a 16-bit Cyclic Redundancy Check (CRC) calculated over the rest of the MAC header (including the EHDR, if present). The method of calculating the HCS is CRC-CCITT($x^{16} + x^{12} + x^5 + 1$), described in ISO recommendation 8802-3. See also Appendix B, where the CRC calculation is presented in some detail.

MAC Packet Protocol Data Unit (PDU) Format

DOCSIS modems support variable-length packets that may contain up to 1,500 user octets per packet. The format of DOCSIS MAC data packets is the same as is used in Ethernet, described in ISO 8802-3.

Each data packet begins with a six-octet header as defined in the section "MAC Header Format", with FC TYPE and EHDR_ON both set to 0.

The **Packet Protocol Data Unit** (**PDU**) immediately follows the header and has the format shown in Figure 3-15.

The octets of user data are embedded in the PDU, following 14 octets of routing information and preceding 4 octets of CRC checking, as follows.

- DA

  Destination Address. A 48-bit (6-octet) destination address that identifies the intended recipient.

- SA

  Source Address. A 48-bit (6-octet) source address that identifies the originator of the packet.

---

9. SID is a DOCSIS term for a Service ID, a concept discussed more fully in the section "MAC Management".

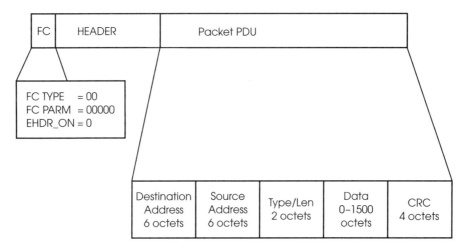

Figure 3-15 DOCSIS MAC Packet PDU Format

- Type/Len

  A 16-bit (2-octet) field that defines either the Ethernet Type or the Length of the data, in conformance with ISO 8802-3.

- CRC

  A 32-bit (4-octet) CRC calculated over the rest of the packet PDU, as specified in ISO 8802-3 and in Appendix B.

Specialized MAC Headers

There are also many specialized MAC headers that are used for specific management functions that maintain synchronization between the CM and the CMTS. These are the headers.

- Timing Header
- MAC Management Header
- Request Frame
- Fragmentation Header
- Concatenation Header
- Fragmentation Extended Header
- Service Flow Extended Header

- Payload Header Suppression Header
- Unsolicited Grant Synchronization Header

For the most part, the details of these headers are beyond the scope of this book. However, the MAC Management header and the Request frame are of interest, since they are used to request and deliver guaranteed Quality of Service for telephony on the upstream link.

The MAC Management header supports MAC management messages (unsurprisingly). It has the following fields.

- FC
  - FC TYPE

    11
  - FC PARM

    00001
  - EHDR_ON

    0
- MAC_PARM

  Reserved for future use
- LEN

  Length of the packet PDU, in octets
- HCS

  Header Check Sequence.

The header is followed by a specific MAC management message.

The request frame is used by the cable modem to request upstream bandwidth for sending information packets. The header is transmitted "bare", without any subsequent PDU. Since it is only 6 octets long, it fits in a single minislot. Here is its format.

- FC
  - FC TYPE

    11

- FC PARM

  0001x

  x = 0 for a minislot request

  (x = 1 for an ATM cell request)

- EHDR_ON

  0

- MAC_PARM

  Total number of minislots requested; this is the actual number of minislots needed to transmit the desired data, including any PMD overhead.

- SID

  The Service ID for the flow requesting bandwidth

- Header Check Sequence

Format of MAC Management Messages

There are 255 possible different types of MAC Management message; of these, 22 are currently defined, as shown in Table 3-4.

The format of MAC Management messages is as shown in Figure 3-16. MAC management messages are encapsulated within an LLC unnumbered information frame, described in ISO 8802-2. The MAC Management Message is preceded by an ordinary MAC header that indicates that the PDU contains a MAC Management Message, formatted according to the section "Specialized MAC Headers".

The fields in the MAC Management Message Header (that is, the header contained in the PDU, not the one that preceeds the Management Message) are as follows.

- DA

  Destination Address (48 bits)

- SA

  Source Address (48 bits)

- msgLen

  The length, in octets, of the MAC message, starting at DSAP and ending at the end of the payload. (This does not include the CRC check.) 2 octets.

- DSAP (Destination Service Access Point)

  Defined to be 0; 1 octet

Table 3-4 MAC Management Messages

Message Type Value	Message Name	Message Description
1	SYNC	Timing Synchronization
2	UCD	Upstream Channel Descriptor
3	MAP	Upstream Bandwidth Allocation
4	RNG-REQ	Ranging Request
5	RNG-RSP	Ranging Response
6	REG-REQ	Registration Request
7	REG-RSP	Registration Response
8	UCC-REQ	Upstream Channel Change Request
9	UCC-RSP	Upstream Channel Change Response
10	TRI-TCD	Telephony Channel Descriptor
11	TRI-TSI	Termination System Information
12	BPKM-REQ	Privacy Key Management Request
13	BPKM-RSP	Privacy Key Management Response
14	REG-ACK	Registration Acknowledgement
15	DSA-REQ	Dynamic Service Addition Request
16	DSA-RSP	Dynamic Service Addition Response
17	DSA-ACK	Dynamic Service Addition Acknowledgement
18	DSC-REQ	Dynamic Service Change Request
19	DSC-RSP	Dynamic Service Change Response
20	DSC-ACK	Dynamic Service Change Acknowledgement
21	DSD-REQ	Dynamic Service Deletion Request
22	DSD-RSP	Dynamic Service Deletion Response

- SSAP (Source Service Access Point)

  Defined to be 0; 1 octet

- Control

  Defined to be 3 (which marks this as an Ethernet unnumbered information frame); 1 octet

- Version

  Defined to be either 1 or 2, depending on the Type field; 1 octet

- Type

  The type of the message, taken from Table 3-4; version = 1 for messages 1 to 13; version = 2 for messages 14 to 22; 1 octet

- RSVD (reserved, used only for alignment)

  Defined to be 0; 1 octet

The header is followed by the management message payload. Following the payload is a 4-octet CRC check calculated as specified by ISO 8802-3 and Appendix B, which covers the message, beginning with DA and ending at the end of the payload.

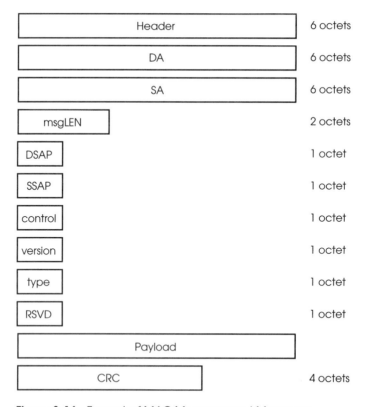

Figure 3-16 Format of MAC Management Messages

MAC Management

We have referred several times to the fact that, unlike on a peer-to-peer analog modem system, a cable modem acts as a client of its termination system. This is necessary for efficient operation in a shared environment where multiple modems are contending for limited bandwidth resources. In order for a CMTS to manage its client modems effectively, DOCSIS defines a number of MAC management messages, which are used to ensure that all the modems served by a single CMTS act in a fair and reasonable manner.

Not all of the MAC management messages listed in Table 3-4 are of equal importance to telephony applications. We will describe only the most important ones, which are useful to understanding how a cable modem establishes its place in the access network and recognizes when it is permitted to transmit upstream data.

Service Identifiers and Service Flow Identifiers

The CMTS manages CM data flows by assigning to each modem two or more 32-bit **Service Flow Identifiers** (**Service Flow IDs**, or **SFIDs**), each of which is unique within the set of cable modems for which the CMTS is responsible. At least one SFID represents a data flow in the upstream direction, and at least one represents flow downstream.

In addition to the SFIDs, **upstream** flows are assigned 14-bit **Service IDs** (**SIDs**), which the modem uses to request, and the CMTS to grant, upstream bandwidth. SFIDs are explored in greater detail in the section "Quality of Service (QoS)".

Within a cable modem, SFIDs are treated independently and may have different priorities. Call signaling traffic, for example, might be deemed more important than bearer data and so be assigned to a SFID with a higher priority. Similarly, voice conversation may be allocated to a SFID with a guaranteed upstream bandwidth, whereas an e-mail application would more likely be transmitted via an SFID associated with a low-priority, "best-effort" stream.[10]

Time Synchronization Message (SYNC)

It is vital that all the modems in a system (those sharing a common CMTS) have a closely aligned notion of the time. This is accomplished through the periodic transmission of SYNC messages by the CMTS. Nominally, SYNC messages are transmitted every 200 milliseconds.

The CMTS contains a master clock, running at precisely 10.24 MHz. Every time this clock ticks (every 0.09765625 microseconds) a 32-bit counter inside the CMTS

---

10. A "best effort" channel is one that does not provide a guaranteed amount of bandwidth.

increments. In order to bypass the (perhaps variable) delay in the CMTS protocol stack, the current value of the clock is inserted into the SYNC message at the moment that the message is handed to the PMD Sublayer, so that the most accurate value possible is transmitted.

Note that the resolution of the master clock is such that 64 counts correspond to 6.25 microseconds. Since the minimum duration of a minislot is 12.5 microseconds, the resolution of the time in the SYNC message is sufficient to enable the CM/CMTS combination to synchronize clocks within a tiny fraction of a minislot.

Because electrical signals travel at a finite speed, there is a correspondence between time and distance. Since signals travel through the access network rather more slowly than they do in air, a single tick of the 10.24 MHz clock, or 0.09765625 microseconds, corresponds to a distance of approximately 80 feet. This is the ultimate spatial resolution of the access network.

Upstream Channel Descriptor (UCD)

Upstream Channel Descriptors are transmitted periodically by the CMTS (nominally once every two seconds). Their purpose is to define the characteristics of each upstream channel. Because of the many parameters that may be required to completely define the characteristics of a particular upstream channel, UCDs require on an extensible mechanism for encoding parameters. The mechanism used is known as **TLV** encoding (from "Type-Length-Value") and is used frequently throughout DOCSIS and PacketCable when a protocol calls for passing variable amounts of information.

In TLV encoding, the value of a parameter is encoded using the following.

1. A Type field, of length one octet, which represents the parameter being encoded
2. A Length field, of length one octet, which gives the length, in octets, of the value of the parameter
3. The Value of the parameter

The length of a TLV-encoded parameter is therefore equal to the length of the value of the parameter, plus two. The entire UCD is shown in Figure 3-17.

The non-TLV-encoded fields are interpreted as follows.

- Upstream Channel ID

  Value used to identify the particular upstream channel to which this message refers
- Configuration Change Count

  This value is incremented by one whenever there is a change in any parameter encoded in the UCD. This allows a modem to disregard the rest of the message if

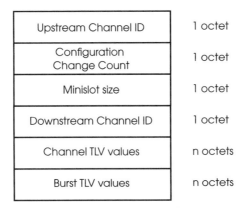

Figure 3-17 Upstream Channel Descriptor

the Configuration Change Count is the same as for a message that has already been processed.

• Minislot size

The duration of the minislot for this upstream channel, given in units of 6.25 microseconds. Allowable values are: 2, 4, 8, 16, 32, 64, 128.

• Downstream Channel ID

Value used to identify the downstream channel on which this message is being transmitted.

DOCSIS defines four different allowable TLV parameters for the channel.

• Symbol Rate

Type = 1; Length = 1. Gives the symbol rate, in units of the base rate of 160 kilo-symbols per second. Allowable values are: 1, 2, 4, 8, 16.

• Frequency

Type = 2; Length = 4. Gives the carrier frequency of the upstream channel, in Hertz.

• Preamble Pattern

Type = 3; Length = 1 to 128. Preamble superstring. See below.

• Burst Descriptor

Type = 4; Length = total length of descriptor.

The last two of these require further explanation.

Preambles are required in DOCSIS in order to help the receiver synchronize properly (see Upstream Transmission). A Type 3 TLV parameter provides a "super" preamble bit stream, from which actual preambles are chosen (in the burst descriptor).

Burst Descriptors are unordered compound encodings of further TLV-encoded quantities that may be used to define a number of physical-layer characteristics. For further details of these, consult the DOCSIS specifications.

Ranging

The ranging process was briefly described in Initialization. Cable modems need to perform ranging during initialization and periodically during operation, in order to ensure that power levels, carrier frequencies and clocks do not drift out of alignment with the other CMs on the network. The mechanism for this is the Ranging Request (RNG-REQ) and Ranging Response (RNG-RSP) pair of messages.

The most difficult adjustment to understand concerns clock synchronization. Because of the finite speed at which information flows in the cable network, it is not trivial to maintain highly accurate clock synchronization.[11] Depending on the ratio of fiber to coax in the access network, as well as the number and quality of the amplifiers, the speed at which information flows between a modem and its CMTS is typically between 67% and 80% of the speed of light in vacuo (which is approximately 186,000 miles per second or roughly 1 foot per nanosecond).

Since an access network may cover distances of several tens of miles, and cable modems must cooperate in transmitting data within an accuracy of a few microseconds, each modem must establish quite accurately its location within the network. This makes it possible to time its transmissions so that they do not collide with transmissions from other modems and so that they arrive at the CMTS at the correct time.

The CMTS defines both the master time and the master location within the network. All timing is performed on the basis of the 10.24 MHz clock located within the CMTS. If the CMTS instructs a modem to transmit at a particular time t, t references the arrival time of the information at the CMTS. In other words, all time corrections must be performed by the individual modems on the network. The CMTS itself makes no allowances for transmission delays.

Ranging Request (RNG-REQ)

Ranging Requests are transmitted by cable modems at initialization and thereafter when requested to do so by the CMTS. Ranging requests are used to determine the

---

11. Deviating slightly from the subject at hand, the difficulty of synchronizing clocks at a distance was one of the problems that led to Einstein's Special Theory of Relativity.

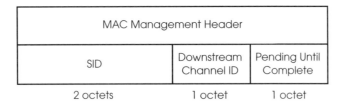

Figure 3-18 Format of a CM Ranging Request
(RNG-REQ) Message

packet-delay time on the network between the CM and the CMTS, as well as to ensure that the carrier frequency and power levels are within reasonable limits. The format of an RNG-REQ is given in Figure 3-18.

- SID

  An Initialization SID, a Temporary SID, or a Registration SID if this is an "Initial Maintenance" Request. If this is a "Station Maintenance" request, then an Assigned SID.

  The SID is transmitted in the lower 14 bits.

- Downstream Channel ID

  Identifier of the downstream channel on which the CM received the UCD that provided the parameters for this upstream channel. This allows the CMTS to know on which downstream channel the CM is listening for a response.

- Pending Till Complete

  Indicates whether all received Ranging Responses have been processed. If zero, processing is complete; if non-zero then this field contains an estimate of the amount of time needed (in hundredths of a second) by the CM to complete processing of a received Ranging Response.

Ranging Response (RNG-RSP)

Unsurprisingly, Ranging Responses are transmitted to cable modems in response to Ranging Request messages. However, they may also be transmitted at other times, and a cable modem must be prepared to receive and process a Ranging Response message at any time. (For example, a CMTS may notice that the transmissions from a particular CM are in danger of exceeding tolerable limits in regards to power, frequency or time, and may choose to unilaterally transmit an RNG-RSP rather than requesting a CM to perform an explicit ranging operation.) The format of an RNG-RSP message is given in Figure 3-19.

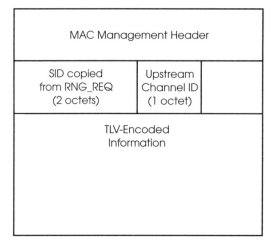

Figure 3-19 Format of a CMTS Ranging
Response (RNG-RSP) Message

- SID

  Either an initialization SID, if this response is instructing the CM to change
  channels, or the SID contained in the corresponding RNG-REQ, or the temporary SID if the RNG-REQ was part of the initialization sequence.

- Upstream Channel ID

  Identifier of the channel on which the CMTS received the RNG-REQ.

- Ranging Status

  Indicates whether the received messages from the CM are within tolerable limits. (If they are not, the CM should perform ranging until they do fall within the
  correct limits, or, if that does not happen after several attempts, the modem
  should shut itself down and indicate a fault.)

Other values are TLV-encoded, according to Table 3-5. *Note*: The decibel is a unit that
measures the ratio of two power levels, P_1 and P_2. P_1 and P_2 are separated by N db
where $N = 10 \log_{10}(P_2/P_1)$. If P_2 is twice P_1, then the signals are separated by almost
exactly 3 dB. If P_2 is ten times P_1, then the signals are separated by precisely 10 dB.

Upstream Bandwidth Allocation Map (MAP)

Upstream data may be transmitted in either contention minislots or noncontention
minislots. Generally, user data—especially telephony data—are sent in noncontention

Table 3-5 TLV-Encoded Ranging Response Parameters

Adjustment	Type (1 octet)	Length (1 octet)	Meaning
Timing	1	4	Signed transmission timing offset; units of 6.25/64 microseconds (that is, units of the number of ticks of the 10.24 MHz clock)
Power	2	1	Signed power offset; units of 1/4 dB
Frequency	3	2	Signed frequency offset, units of Hz
Equalization	4	n	Equalization data; see DOCSIS specifications for details.
Ranging Status	5	1	1 = continue; 2 = abort; 3 = success
Downstream Frequency	6	4	Center frequency of new downstream channel (Hz)
Upstream Channel ID	7	1	ID of new upstream channel

minislots. The CMTS periodically broadcasts Upstream Bandwidth Allocation Map (**MAP**) messages, which describe the detailed allocation of upcoming timeslots for each upstream channel. The format of a MAP message is shown in Figure 3-20 and described below.

The measurement of time as used in MAP messages can be somewhat confusing. MAP messsages measure time in units of minislots, using a 32-bit counter that wraps silently at $2^{32}-1$. This is akin to the counter in the SYNC messages broadcast by the CMTS, but the unit of time is different in the two cases.

In the SYNC message, the unit is the number of ticks of the 10.24 MHz clock, which ticks many times per minislot. The number of ticks per minislot is given in the UCD message and is always a power of two. Time as measured in the MAP message must agree with time as measured in the SYNC messages, except that the latter is more accurate. The least-significant bits in the MAP message must match the corresponding (more significant) bits in the SYNC message.

For example, if the time as measured in the SYNC message has the value 1234567890, which corresponds to the bit pattern 01001001 10010110 00000010 11010010, and if there are 128 ticks per minislot, then the corresponding time in the MAP message must have the lowest 25 bits equal to 0 10010011 00101100 00000101. See Figure 3-20.

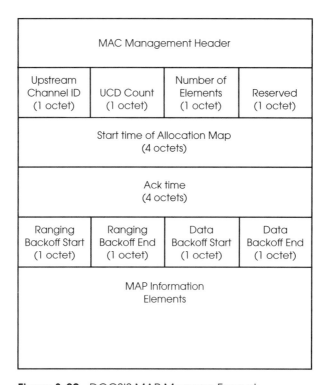

Figure 3-20 DOCSIS MAP Message Format

- Upstream Channel ID

  Value used to identify the particular upstream channel to which this message refers

- UCD Count

  Matches the value of the Configuration Change Count field of the UCD, which contains the Burst Descriptor that applies to this map. This ensures that any modem transmitting data according to this map will do so with the correct physical parameters.

- Number Elements

  Number of information elements that appear in the map

- Reserved

  Used for alignment

- Alloc Start Time

  Effective start time, in minislots, of assignments within this map

- Ack Time

  Latest time, in minislots, that was processed in the upstream direction before this map was generated. That is, requests or other upstream signals from cable modems timestamped with values subsequent to this time were unprocessed by the CMTS when this map was generated.

- Ranging Backoff Start

  Initial backoff window, used for ranging contention, expressed as a power of two. Possible values range from zero to 15.

- Ranging Backoff End

  Final backoff window, used for ranging contention, expressed as a power of two. Possible values range from zero to 15.

- Data Backoff Start

  Initial backoff window, used for contention data and requests, expressed as a power of two. Possible values range from zero to 15.

- Data Backoff End

  Final backoff window, used for contention data and requests, expressed as a power of two. Possible values range from zero to 15.

- MAP Information Elements

MAP Information Elements

When providing an upstream bandwidth allocation map, the CMTS uses Information Elements (IEs) to encode the details of the allocation. For each granted interval described in a MAP, the CMTS transmits a 32-bit quantity, divided into three fields that encode the upstream SID, the precise time of the minislots granted, and the use to which these minislots are to be put. For more details, see the next section.

Example Upstream Bandwidth Allocation

As we have seen, the process by which a cable modem obtains permission to transmit data upstream is far from trivial. In this section we will attempt to walk through the process slowly to be sure that we understand how the mechanism works.

The essential problem is that a number of modems share a single upstream channel (there are a number of upstream channels, and each channel can be treated independently, but even so, each upstream channel is shared by several modems). Therefore there has to be an arbitrated mechanism by which each modem can be assured of opportunities to transmit. The fact that all the modems share a notion of time, with themselves and their controlling CMTS, makes cooperation possible.

The upstream channel is treated as a sequence of contiguous minislots. The CMTS transmits (on the downstream channel) a MAC management message, the MAP message, that describes exactly how an upcoming series of minislots is to be used. Note that a malfunctioning cable modem that does not honor these commands will be quickly discovered and will be effectively shut down by the CMTS. (Unless, of course, the malfunction is so great that it fails to obey these commands as well. In such a circumstance, the CMTS should recognize what has happened and move traffic on to other channels; it should also notify the network operator of the problem so that, if nothing else can be done, the malfunctioning CM can be shut down manually.) However, it is possible for an individual to create a CM-like device that, when connected to a cable, either renders the cable useless or at least severely degrades performance (for example, by rapidly sweeping a powerful carrier in the frequency domain). This is a consequence of a shared pipe, and there is little that can be done to prevent such attacks.[12]

A typical MAP might grant some minislots for the exclusive use of particular modems that have indicated in prior Request frames that they have data ready to transmit requiring a number of minislots to transmit. It might also set aside some minislots for modems to use in contention mode and yet others that may be used only by new modems signaling that they wish to join the network. The scheduling algorithm is controlled entirely by the CMTS, and, in most cases, the CMTS will contain intelligence that allows the detailed scheduling to change as a function of the kind of traffic currently on the network. The exchange that occurs between modem and CMTS is shown in Figure 3-21. Figure 3-22 shows an example of how a MAP might allocate an upcoming series of minislots.

Contention Resolution

The timing of all upstream signaling is under the control of the CMTS. In particular, the CMTS decides which minislots are allocated to a particular CM and which are subject to contention.

Data transmitted in a contention minislot are not guaranteed to arrive at the CMTS, since several CMs may simultaneously transmit within the minislot, in which case all their data will be lost. Data transmitted in a noncontention minislot are almost certain to arrive at the CM (barring problems with the low-level link), since only one CM is permitted to transmit in a noncontention minislot.

---

12. How an MSO might go about detecting the source of such attacks in a timely manner is an interesting problem that we leave as an exercise for the reader.

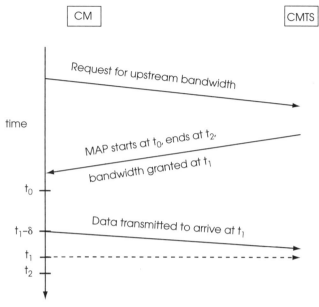

Figure 3-21 CM-CMTS Interaction Granting Upstream
Bandwidth

Contention minislots are, in a sense, "wasted" upstream bandwidth, since they (generally) are not used to send useful data. However, they are necessary since the only way of reserving guaranteed bandwidth for user data is by requesting noncontention minislots—and the mechanism for doing this is via messaging that is carried in contention minislots.

The optimum ratio of contention minislots to noncontention minislots is a function of the type of traffic being carried. If the upstream flows on a cable are mostly carrying telephony traffic, then the number of contention minislots may be decreased

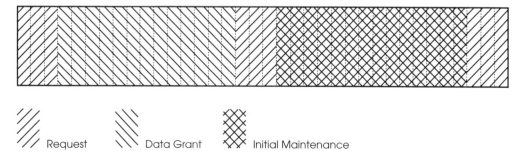

Figure 3-22 Minislot Allocation in a DOCSIS MAP Message

because the CMTS typically allocates fixed-bandwidth flows using an Unsolicited Grant mechanism, which requires very few contention minislots to operate (see Quality of Service).

On the other hand, if the flows are mostly best-effort data flows, then a relatively large number of contention minislots are needed because a relatively larger number of requests for upstream bandwidth need to be made because of the unpredictable nature of the traffic. The shorter and more bursty the data, the more contention mode minislots are needed. A well-designed CMTS will monitor the upstream traffic flow and frequently adjust the percentage of contention minislots so as to optimize the way that the upstream bandwidth is being used.

Since there is no guarantee that transmissions made in a contention minislot will be received (because of collisions), there has to be some mechanism to allow for CMs to retransmit contention data. The mechanism must also ensure that any two CMs, once they have transmitted into the same minislot and caused a collision, do not continue to do so. This is called contention resolution.

In every MAP message, the CMTS supplies a pair of values corresponding to an initial back-off window and a maximum back-off window to be used for contention resolution in the time period covered by the MAP (see Upstream Bandwidth Allocation Map). The values are presented as powers of two, such that a value of 5, for example, would indicate a back-off window of width 32.

When a CM transmits a packet in a contention minislot, it sets the width of a window to the value corresponding to the value of Data Backoff Start in the current MAP. At some time later it receives a MAP message from the CMTS (see the section "The MAP Message" for more details about this exchange). If the MAP indicates that the CMTS did not receive the modem's packet, the modem assumes that the packet was lost and begins its retransmission strategy.

The modem selects a random value in the range (0, window width − 1). It then allows this number of retransmission opportunities to pass before it retransmits its request. For example, suppose that a CM has a current value for Data Backoff Start of 5. This means that the back-off window runs from zero to 31. It transmits a request, but suppose that the CM receives no response. The CM now randomly selects a number in the range (0, 31). Suppose that it selects 13. This means that the CM must allow 13 retransmission opportunities to pass before it retransmits its request. Assume that the first Request IE[13] in the MAP is for 5 requests. It must allow these to pass, and it still has 8 more to go. The next Request IE might be for 7 requests. It must allow these to pass as well. The next Request IE might be for 2 requests. It must remain silent for the first but will retransmit on the second.

---

13. A "Request IE" is a list of opportunities provided by the CMTS in which requests for upstream bandwidth may be made. For details of this and other Information Elements (IEs) see the next section.

If this transmission also fails to elicit a response, the CM doubles the length of the back-off window (to a maximum value controlled by the maximum back-off window allowed in the currently applicable MAP), generates a new random number within this window, lets that number of opportunities pass, and then retransmits.

The MAP Message

A MAP message contains an ordinary MAC management header, followed by a variable number of **Information Elements** (**IEs**) in the format given in Figure 3-23. IEs within a MAP message are ordered strictly according to time, as decribed by the time counter in the CMTS. Except for the first IE, the start time of an IE is (usually) inferred from the start time and duration of the prior IE. A null IE terminates the list of IEs.

Each IE contains a 14-bit SID, a 4-bit type code and a 14-bit time offset. A SID of 0x3FFF indicates a broadcast intended for all CMs. Ordinary unicast SIDs are in the range 0x0001 to 0x1FFF and are used to describe a particular CM or a particular service within a particular CM. SIDs in the range 0x2000 to 0x3FF0 are used for multicast messages, which are used only for administrative purposes. SIDs in the range 0x3FF1 to 0x3FFE are used to describe contention minislots of various lengths, as shown in Table 3-6. The transmissions sent in a single contention-mode burst may not exceed 14 minislots in length. Therefore if a modem desires to transmit information that exceeds 14 minislots, it must do so in noncontention mode.

Note that the there is no practical difference between a "broadcast" message and a "multicast" message in this context. We preserve the difference in terminology merely because the DOCSIS specification does so. The basic idea is simple: The

SID (14 bits)	Interval Usage code (4 bits)	Time offset (14 bits)

Interval Usage Code	Information Element
1	Request
2	Request/Data
3	Initial Maintenance
4	Station Maintenance
5	Short Data Grant
6	Long Data Grant
7	Null
8	Data Acknowledgement
9–14	Reserved
15	Expansion

Figure 3-23 MAP Information Elements

CMTS makes the list of available minislots known to all the cable modems. The following IEs are defined:

Request IE   Corresponds to intervals in which CMs may make requests for upstream bandwidth. The Request IE is usually broadcast, indicating that the marked minislots are considered to be contention minislots. If it is unicast to a particular modem, then only that modem may use the marked minislots to request upstream bandwidth.

Request/Data IE   Marks minislots that may be used either for requests for upstream bandwidth or to transmit short data packets that fit entirely within the allocated minislots. The value of the SID, which is typically a multicast SID, indicates exactly how the data may be sent, according to Table 3-6.

Since these minislots are contention minislots available for any CM to use, if a CM uses them to transmit data (as opposed to Requests), the transmitted data packets should request a data acknowledgement; otherwise the CM has no way to determine whether the information reached the CMTS.

Initial Maintenance IE   Provides an opportunity for new devices to join the network. Initial Maintenance grants are for relatively large numbers of minislots, as

Table 3-6 Mapping of Multicast SIDs to Data Transmission Algorithms

SID	*Meaning*
0x0000	Broadcast
0x3FFF	Broadcast
0x3FF1	Multicast; a CM may transmit at any minislot, but the transmission must fit entirely within a single minislot.
0x3FF2	Multicast; a CM may start to transmit at minislot number 1, 3, 5 and so on, and the transmission must fit entirely within two minislots.
0x3FF3	Multicast; a CM may start to transmit at minislot number 1, 4, 7 and so on, and the transmission must fit entirely within three minislots.
...	...
0x3FFE	Multicast; a CM may start to transmit at minislot number 1, 15, 29 and so on, and the transmission must fit entirely within 14 minislots.

they must allow for the maximum possible round-trip delay, plus the time to transmit a Ranging Request message.

Station Maintenance IE Allows CMs to perform periodic station maintenance, such as ranging or adjustments to power or frequency. Station Maintenance IEs may be either broadcast or unicast, depending on the policy of the network operator.

Null IE The Null IE is used to mark the end of the list of allocated minislots.

Data Grant IEs There are two kinds of Data Grant IEs: the Short Data Grant IE and, as you might guess, the Long Data Grant IE. Both of these IEs are used to allocate minislots for a CM to transmit data for which it has indicated (via a Request) a desire to transmit. The difference between a Short Data Grant and a Long Data Grant pertains to the physical layer: Short Data Grants are used for bursts whose length is less than the maximum burst size indicated in the Upstream Channel Descriptor (UCD); Long Data Grants are used for data that will exceed this length. Short Data Grants and Long Data Grants are effectively identical insofar as allocating upstream bandwidth is concerned.

A Data Grant IE may allocate a length of zero minislots, in which case it is a Data Grant Pending IE, and indicates to the CM that its request has been received but that no minislots have yet been allocated to it. Reception of a Data Grant Pending IE informs the CM that there is no need to repeat its request for upstream bandwidth. (Data Grant Pending IEs are placed after the Null IE that indicates the end of the allocated minislots.)

The Data Grant Pending IE is obviously useful when a large number of modems make more or less simultaneous requests for upstream bandwidth; the CMTS can acknowledge receipt of the requests without actually granting bandwidth.

Data Acknowledge IE This simply indicates that a particular data PDU was received from a CM. Typically, this is issued in response to a request for acknowledgement that was contained in an upstream packet, and upstream packets typically only request acknowledgements when they are transmitted in contention minislots. Like Data Grant Pending IEs, Data Acknowledge IEs are placed after the Null IE.

Expansion IE This is currently unused and is present merely to allow for extensibility.

A CM may make a request for upstream bandwidth during a minislot associated in the MAP with any one of the following: Request IE, Request/Data IE, Data Grant IE. The request indicates the SID for the flow that desires to transmit and the number or minislots being requested.

When a CMTS transmits a MAP containing upcoming minislot usage, it must do so sufficiently in advance of the first minislot mapped in the message to allow for the most distant CM in the network to receive and process the message before the map becomes operative. Typically, this requirement means that the CMTS must allow something of the order of a millisecond between the MAP transmission and the earliest minislot mapped in the message. Figure 3-24 shows the process of obtaining upstream bandwidth.

Suppose that a CMTS transmits, at time T_1, a MAP whose first minislot is for time T_2 and whose last minislot is at time T_3. A particular CM whose propagation delay from the CMTS is δ, receives this MAP message at some time T_1' ($= T_1 + \delta$), prior to T_2. Suppose now that sometime shortly after T_2 the CM assembles a packet that it wishes to transmit. The CM does not immediately transmit the Request. In order to decrease the probability of collisions, it uses a strategy similar to that used for contention resolution. Using the value of the Data Backoff Start in the MAP, it generates a random number, n, of transmit opportunities that it must let pass (see Contention Resolution). It then scans the currently applicable MAP, looking for minislots in which it is permitted to transmit a request for sufficient upstream bandwidth to transmit the data packet. It allows n of them to pass and settles on the $n+1$th, for time T_5 in which to transmit its request.

The CM issues a request for the number of minislots needed to transmit the data at T_4, where $T_4 = T_5 - \delta$. However, since the Request IE was not directed at a particular CM, other modems may also transmit during the same minislot. Therefore our CM calculates a back-off timer as described in Contention Resolution, in case the CMTS does not receive the request.

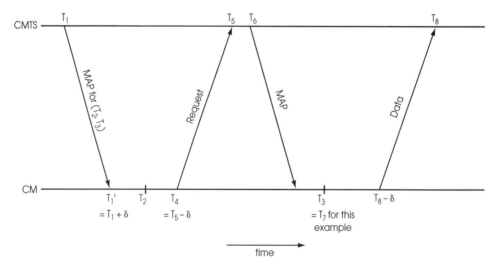

Figure 3-24 Example of a CM Obtaining Upstream Bandwidth

To keep things simple, we will assume that the CMTS receives the request at T_5 (the section "Contention Resolution" describes the back-off strategy if the CMTS does not receive it). The CMTS processes the request and (normally) will find time in the next MAP to schedule our CM's transmission. It allocates the correct number of minislots in the next MAP, whose starting time is T_7; it transmits the map at time T_6. Our CM receives the MAP at $T_6 + \delta$, scans it, and determines that it has been granted a transmit opportunity at T_8. At $T_8 - \delta$, it transmits the data, which is received at the CMTS exactly at time T_8.

Quality of Service (QoS)

In a telephony network, it is vital that users be guaranteed access to sufficient bandwidth in both upstream and downstream directions to ensure that their conversations will not be interrupted by pauses, gaps or other annoying artifacts caused by a lack of necessary bandwidth. Because of the nature of the HFC network, bandwidth management is especially important in the upstream direction, where noise is greater and available bandwidth much less than in the downstream direction.

DOCSIS contains mechanisms designed to provide CMs with guaranteed bandwidth. If the bandwidth cannot be guaranteed, a signal may be passed to higher level protocols so that they may take appropriate action (which may be, for example, to deny setup for the call). The guarantee is made *at the beginning of the call,* so that once a call has been allowed to start the users can be sure that the needed bandwidth will be available for the duration of the call.

DOCSIS modems provide QoS through the notion of Service Flows: A **Service Flow** is a unidirectional flow of packets that are guaranteed a particular bandwidth, which the flow requested at the time it was set up. Service Flows are identified by a 32-bit Service Flow Identifier (SFID) assigned by the CMTS. Each active *upstream* Service Flow also has a unique 14-bit SID.

At least two Service Flows are defined in the configuration file that the modem downloads during initialization: a Primary Upstream Service Flow and a Primary Downstream Service Flow. These flows are used for subsequent unclassified traffic and all MAC messages.

Conceptually, the resources[14] required by Service Flows belong to a three-level hierarchy. When a CM attempts to create a Service Flow, the requested resources are tested (by the CMTS) against a provisioned authorization envelope to ensure that the request can be allowed. If so, the Service Flow is *authorized*.

The CMTS then checks to ensure that sufficient resources are actually available to grant the request. If so, the Service Flow is *admitted*. Admission ensures that the

---

14. The resources may not be limited to bandwidth: Memory, DSP processing power or other resources may be involved. However, in practice, bandwidth is almost always the resource in shortest supply.

resources are available for use, and it reserves the necessary resources. It does not yet, however, grant the CM the right to use them. To do so, the Service Flow must be *activated*.

This notion of three levels of envelopes of resource control is an important one that we shall examine in more detail when we discuss PacketCable QoS in Chapter 6.

The particular QoS attributes of a Service Flow may be specified either by an explicit definition or by using a Service Class Name in a request. A Service Class Name is a string that the CMTS recognizes as a shorthand to refer to a particular set of QoS parameters. Service Class Names provide a useful level of indirection. For example, they allow higher-level applications to construct flows with sensible QoS values simply by using a particular name. Also, the set of QoS parameters to which a name refers may change dynamically in response to traffic patterns, allowing the CMTS to more effectively manage the various traffic flows passing through it.

Using Service Flows frees higher-level applications from the need to manage the Request frames and MAP messages we have discussed earlier. In particular, depending on the kind of flow granted, transmission opportunities may be presented to a CM without an explicit packet-by-packet request from the modem. Conceptually, a higher-level application may simply request bandwidth for a particular codec without worrying about any of the low-level details about how the packets are actually transmitted from the modem to its CMTS.

The creation of a Service Flow may be initiated either by the CM or by the CMTS. The mechanism used is a three-way handshake of MAC messages known as a Dynamic Service Addition: DSA-Request, DSA-Response and DSA-Acknowledge. Changes to an existing Service Flow are made through a similar series of Dynamic Service Change messages, and deletions of Service Flows occur through a two-way handshake of DSD-Request and DSD-Response.

The DSA and DSC messages allow for very fine-grained control of the bandwidth allocated to a Service Flow. We will talk in rather more detail about these messages in the section "Dynamic Service Flows."

When upstream bandwidth is requested, there are several mechanisms that may be used to fulfil the request. Which mechanism is chosen depends on the policy of the network operator, as well as the amount of intelligence in the CMTS and the traffic load on the upstream access network.

Unsolicited Grant Service (UGS)

An **Unsolicited Grant Service** Flow (**UGS**) is a flow to which the CMTS allocates a fixed number of minislots periodically to allow for a constant-bit-rate flow of information. If the packetized output from a voice codec consists of constant-sized packets, produced at a constant rate (as is usually the case), UGS is a very efficient method of allocating upstream bandwidth. Typically, UGS is used for telephony traffic because it incurs very little maintenance traffic. Essentially, the CM says, "Give me n minislots every m milliseconds", and the CMTS then grants these minislots (they appear in the MAP messages) without the need for the CM to explicitly request them.

Real-Time Polling Service

Real-Time Polling is similar to UGS, except that the CMTS periodically gives the modem an opportunity to request upstream minislots to transmit queued data. If the CM has no data to transmit, it issues no request and therefore the CMTS is free to reallocate those minislots to another modem.

UGS with Activity Detection (AD)

Combining elements of UGS and real-time polling, a Service Flow operating under UGS/AD is monitored by the CMTS. When the CMTS detects a number of unused minislots, it reverts to real-time polling until such time as the CM begins transmitting traffic on the flow; at that time the Service Flow reverts to UGS.

Non-Real-Time Polling Service

A Service Flow operating under non-real-time polling is guaranteed some transmit opportunities even when the network is congested. This service is of limited use in telephony systems. Essentially, this is a means to ensure that even in a congested network each modem is sure of at least some transmission opportunities.

Best Effort Service

In Best Effort Service Flows, the modem and CMTS simply do their best to send data when possible, with no guaranteed noncontention minislots. In a highly congested network, effective data rates may be very low in Best Effort service flows. Typically, data services use Best Effort Service Flows; unless the access network is very lightly loaded, it is not useful for transporting telephony packets.

Committed Information Rate

A Committed Information Rate Service Flow is usually configured as one that is delivered Best Effort but with some reserved non-real-time polling to ensure that at least some information will flow, even on a fully loaded network. Typically, current telephony services use the UGS mechanism to provide upstream bandwidth, although there is no specific requirement that they do so. With the deployment of more advanced non-constant-bit-rate codecs, Real-Time Polling or UGS/AD will likely become more widespread. The way in which PacketCable networks use the hooks provided by DOCSIS Dynamic Service Flows is more fully described in Chapter 6.

Dynamic Service Flows

Because of their importance to providing real-time telephony, it is worthwhile spending some time examining DOCSIS Dynamic Service Flows. Dynamic Service Flows are Service Flows that can be created, modified or deleted at will. In a typical implementation, each telephone conversation will be assigned to two Service Flows, one in the upstream direction and one downstream. We will look at how Dynamic Service Flows are created; the process for modifying (through DSC messages) and deleting (through DSD messages) Service Flows is very similar.

A Dynamic Service Flow is created by a Dynamic Service Add Request (DSA-Req); either the CM or the CMTS may initiate creation of a Dynamic Service Flow by transmitting a DSA-Req to the other device. A single DSA-Req can create at most two Service Flows, one in each direction. Whichever side initiates the request, a three way handshake takes place before the Dynamic Service Flow is in place and usable (see Figure 3-25).

A Service Flow has associated with it as many as three so-called QosParameterSets, each of which defines characteristics such as jitter, latency and details of the bandwidth allocation for the Service Flow. These are known as the ProvisionedQosParameterSet, the AdmittedQosParameterSet and the ActiveQosParameterSet.

ProvisionedQosParameterSet   This is a static set of QoS parameters obtained during initialization. The parameters represent a maximal set of resources that the modem may consume for a single Service Flow. For example, if the subscriber pays only for low-bandwidth access using low-bit-rate codecs, that fact will be reflected in the values in the ProvisionedQosParameterSet.

AdmittedQosParameterSet   This represents a set of QoS parameters for which the CM and/or CMTS has reserved resources. However, although the resources are guaranteed to be made available immediately on request, they cannot actually be used.

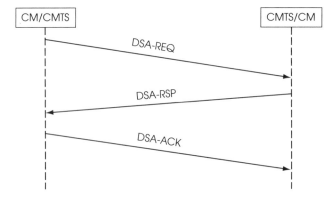

Figure 3-25   Three-Way DSA Handshake

ActiveQosParameterSet This set of parameters represents resources that are available for use. Only a Service Flow with a non-null ActiveQosParameterSet may actually carry packets.

When a DSA-Req is made, the CMTS will check that the requested resources do not exceed the ProvisionedQosParameterSet. Assuming that they lie within these boundaries, the CMTS will then check whether sufficient resources exist to admit the Service Flow and, if possible, it will do so. Typically, a DSA-Req contains a null ActiveQosParameterSet, so the Service Flow is merely admitted, not made active. A subsequent DSC command is used to convert the AdmittedQosParameterSet to an ActiveQosParameterSet—and hence to allow traffic to be carried on the Service Flow. Sometimes, however, the DSA-Req specifies that the flow is to be made immediately active (it does this by containing a non-null ActiveQosParameterSet), in which case traffic is immediately permitted to pass through the new Service Flow.

The flows for CM-initiated and CMTS-initiated Dynamic Service Additions are shown in Figures 3-26 and 3-27. As always, it is the CMTS that does the bulk of the work. The CM's role is limited to confirming that it can support the new Service Flow, configuring itself to do so and signaling that it is ready to use the new flow.

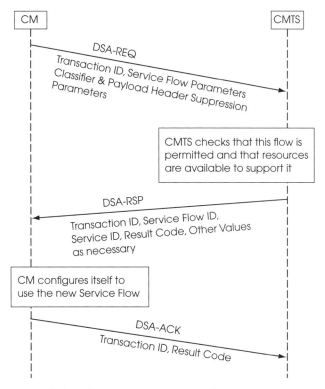

Figure 3-26 CM-Initiated Dynamic Service Addition

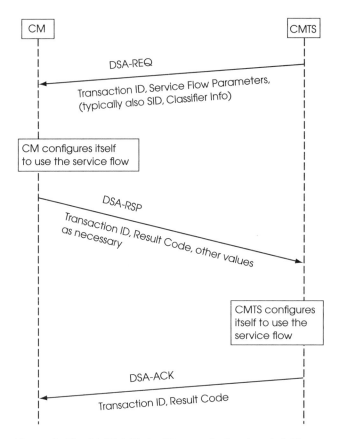

Figure 3-27 CMTS-Initiated Dynamic Service Addition

Baseline Privacy Interface Plus

On a shared-access medium such as the one provided by cable companies, it is important that each user's data—both upstream and downstream—be protected from eavesdropping and alteration by other users of the same cable. In principle, there is nothing to stop a device attached to cable from eavesdropping on, and potentially capturing, passing traffic. At least in theory, it is possible for a malfeasant to attach a device to the cable in his own home and capture the digital traffic being transmitted and received by cable modems in nearby houses.[15]

---

15. In practice, and as of this writing, this is quite hard because of the limited number of DOCSIS chip sets available for interfacing to cable systems, none of which were designed to support such monitoring. This situation, however, is likely to change in the near future. Earlier schemes were typically much simpler than DOCSIS and were therefore prone to being monitored.

In early, proprietary cable-based data systems there was sometimes no protection against such eavesdropping, leaving sophisticated computer users free to access information on other users' machines and also to examine the traffic passing along the coax. The current version of DOCSIS prevents this by implementing a mechanism called **Baseline Privacy Interface Plus**, **BPI+**. (An earlier incarnation was called the Baseline Privacy Interface. BPI+ is considerably more secure than BPI. It is mandatory to implement BPI+ on DOCSIS 1.1 compliant modems.)

BPI+ does not discriminate among the types of data flowing over the cable. All packets of user data transmitted over the cable are protected equally by the BPI+ security protocols. The mechanism used to secure communications between a CM and its corresponding CMTS is encryption of the traffic flows between the two devices.

BPI+ comprises two protocols.

- An encapsulation protocol, used for encrypting and decrypting the packets. This protocol defines the format for encrypted packets, the set of supported ciphersuites and the rules for applying the cryptographic algorithms to the packetized data.

- A key management protocol (Baseline Privacy Key Management, BPKM) that provides a secure method for distributing keying material between the cable modem and its CMTS.

The only encryption/decryption algorithm supported by the current version of BPI+ is the CBC mode of DES (see Chapter 2). Note that this is ordinary DES, not 3DES, and so is restricted to a 56-bit key.[16] While adequate for ordinary use, this is insufficient to confound a well-funded, determined attacker. For this reason (as well as others) PacketCable does not rely merely on BPI+ to ensure the security of telephone conversations. Instead, PacketCable places another layer of stronger encryption on top of the BPI+ encryption.

BPI+ provides only encryption; it does not use any authentication algorithms. While this may be adequate for some services, it may not be so for a telephony service. Consequently PacketCable also adds authentication (as needed) to some of the flows associated with telephony traffic.

BPI+ encrypts only MAC frame data (user data). It does not encrypt MAC frame headers. Also, it is not used to protect MAC management messages; these always travel in the clear.

---

16. An even weaker variant, with a 40-bit key, is also supported. The United States government for many years allowed automatic export of devices only if the device supported a maximum key length of 40 bits. Since any company that deploys a system whose security is based on 40-bit DES does not deserve to remain in business very long—and possibly because it finally dawned on the governmental authorities that the only people being penalized were those who chose to comply with the law—the government finally eased these restrictions early in 2000.

Security Associations in BPI+

BPI+ recognizes three kinds of **security associations** (**SA**s) that may exist between a CM and its CMTS.

- A Primary SA is established during MAC registration. It is an association that remains in place between the CM and the CMTS as long as the CM retains power and is unique to the CM/CMTS pair.

- Static SAs are preprovisioned within the CMTS. Multiple CMs may share the same static SA with a single CMTS.

- Dynamic SAs are created and destroyed on the fly in response to the creation and termination of specific *downstream* traffic flows. Multiple CMs may share the same dynamic SA with a single CMTS.

At any given time, apart from the single primary SA, a modem may share several static and dynamic SAs with its CMTS, each pertaining to a particular traffic flow. Each security association is identified by a 14-bit **Security Association Identifier** (**SAID**) that is unique within the universe of SAs maintained by a single CMTS. The SAID for a modem's Primary SA is numerically equal to the value of its Primary Service ID (SID).

An SA has associated with it three parameters: traffic encryption keys, CBC initialization vectors and a **ciphersuite** identifier (currently limited to whether the encryption/decryption algorithm is 40-bit or 56-bit DES).

The Primary SA is used to carry all upstream traffic. Downstream flows may use any of the three types of security association. Typically, however, telephony traffic is also carried over the Primary SA, since it would defeat the purpose of encrypting the traffic if multiple CMs had access to the keying material.

Baseline Privacy Key Management (BPKM)

In most cryptographically based security systems, key management is the most complicated part of the system. Ensuring that keys are generated randomly and shared in a secure manner is usually a complex problem, and the solutions are likewise complicated. Key management in BPI+ is no exception.

Baseline Privacy Key Management (**BPKM**) uses X.509 certificates, the RSA public key encryption algorithm, and two-key 3DES to secure the exchange of keys between a CM and its CMTS.

BPKM uses a two-tiered approach to key management, in which computationally intensive public key cryptography is used to establish a shared secret, the **Authorization Key** (**AK**), between the devices. The Authorization Key is then used to secure the exchange of the keys used for securing traffic, which are known as **Traffic**

Encryption Keys (**TEK**s). This allows the TEKs to be changed frequently without the need for expensive public key operations. Figure 3-28 shows this diagramatically.

Each modem contains an X.509 certificate, emplaced at the time of manufacture. The certificate contains the modem's public key, its 48-bit address, a manufacturer ID, and a device serial number. The certificate is signed by the modem manufacturer. This allows the CMTS, when it is presented with the certificate, to authenticate the modem. The initialization process is reasonably straightforward:

1. The CM sends the certificate to the CMTS, and the CMTS authenticates the CM.

2. The CMTS generates an Authorization Key and returns it to the CM, encrypted by the CM's public key (which was obtained from the X.509 certificate).

3. In addition to the Authorization Key, the CMTS identifies the SAID and the corresponding properties of the primary SA shared by the CM and the CMTS.

4. The CM and CMTS jointly derive a Key Encryption Key (KEK) and authentication keys from the Authorization Key.

5. The CM requests Traffic Encryption Keys for its traffic flows; the CMTS responds, encrypting the TEKs with the KEK.

The rest of this section discusses this exchange in more detail.

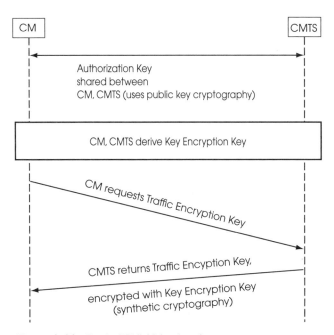

Figure 3-28 Basic BPKM Mechanism

Authenticating the CM

The BPI+ initialization sequence begins when a CM sends an Authentication Information message to the CMTS. The detailed format of this message is contained in the DOCSIS specifications. For our purposes, the important thing to know is that the message contains the modem's X.509 certificate.

The CMTS does not respond to the Authentication Information message, which is purely informative. It does, however, allow the CMTS to authenticate the modem in advance of an explicit request for security information.

Immediately after sending the Authentication Information message, the CM transmits an Authorization Request. This, as its name suggests, is an explicit request to generate security parameters for communication between the modem and the CMTS. The Authorization Request message contains the following.

- A CM-Identification attribute, which itself contains, at a minimum the following

  —The modem's manufacturer and its serial number

  —The modem's 48-bit address

  —The modem's public key

- The modem's X.509 certificate

- The list of ciphersuites supported by the modem

- The modem's Primary SID (which was the first static SID assigned to the modem during MAC registration). The value of a cable modem's Primary SAID is always equal to the value of its Primary SID, so this implicitly generates the first SAID value for this CM at the CMTS.

If it has not already done so, the CMTS authenticates the X.509 certificate. It then returns an Authorization Reply message, containing the following.

- An Authorization Key (of length 160 bits) encrypted with the modem's RSA public key as obtained from the X.509 certificate. The public key must be 1,024 bits in length.[17] The AK is used to derive two message authentication keys (one each for upstream and downstream messages) and a **Key Encryption Key** (**KEK**). The algorithm used to derive these keys is described later, in Key Derivation.

---

17. Earlier versions of DOCSIS specified a key length of 768 bits. The CMTS must be able to process public keys of both lengths.

- A 4-bit value that acts as a sequence number to distinguish among generations of Authorization Keys
- The lifetime of the Authorization Key
- The SAID of the CM's Primary SA, as well as the SAIDs of any Static SAs for which the modem is authorized to obtain keying information

The Authorization Key

The Authorization Key is a 160-bit key that is encrypted by the CM's 1,024-bit public RSA key. The precise algorithm used for this encryption is the RSAES-OAEP encryption scheme described in version 2 of the PKCS#1 standard, obtainable from *http://www.rsasecurity.com/rsalabs/pkcs/*.

Obtaining TEKs

Each SAID in a cable modem is independent of any other SAIDs that the modem might have. Whenever a key is needed for a particular SAID, the modem sends a Key Request for that SAID to the CMTS. The purpose of a Key Request is to obtain a TEK. The TEK, as the name Traffic Encryption Key implies, is the key that is actually used to encrypt traffic flowing through this SAID. The Key Request contains the following.

- A CM-Identification attribute
- The value of the SAID for which the request is being made
- An HMAC, allowing the CMTS to authenticate the Key Request message. The key for this HMAC is derived from the Authorization Key, using the algorithm described in Key Derivation.

The keying material for the referenced SAID is returned in a Key Reply message containing the following.

- The TEK for this SAID; the key is 3DES EDE encrypted, using a two-key 3DES Key Encryption Key derived from the Authorization Key.
- A CBC initialization vector
- A sequence number for this key
- The remaining lifetime for this key
- An HMAC, which allows the CM to authenticate this message

Figure 3-29 shows this diagrammatically.

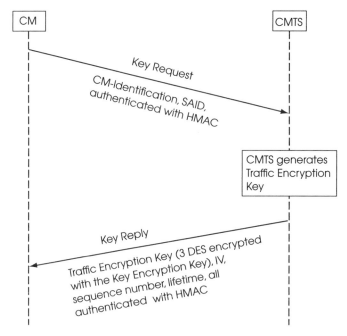

Figure 3-29 Keying Messages in BPKM

So we can summarize the process as follows.

1. The modem authenticates itself to the CMTS and asks for an Authorization Key.

2. The CMTS returns the Authorization Key, encrypted by the modem's public key.

3. Both the modem and the CMTS derive two authentication keys and a single Key Encryption Key from the Authorization Key.

4. The modem requests a Traffic Encryption Key for a particular SAID.

5. The CMTS returns the TEK, encrypted with the KEK, along with other keying material.

6. The TEK is used to encrypt traffic flowing through this SAID.

Key Derivation

The various keys used in BPI+ are derived from a 160-bit Authorization Key (AK) that is generated by the CMTS and passed to the CM, encrypted by the CM's public key. Three keys are derived from AK: the KEK, used to encrypt TEKs as they are passed from the CMTS to the CM; HMAC_KEY_U, the message authentication key used in upstream Key Requests and HMAC_KEY_D, the message authentication key used in downstream Key Replies and error messages.

The keys are generated as follows.

```
KEK = Truncate(SHA1(K_PAD + AK), 128)
HMAC_KEY_U = SHA1(H_PAD_U + AK)
HMAC_KEY_D = SHA1(H_PAD_D + AK)
```

where:

Truncate(x, n) means to truncate x to its left-most n bits;

$x + y$ means to concatenate x and y (in that order)

SHA1(x) means to calculate the SHA-1 hash of x

K_PAD is a 512-bit string formed by repeating the value 0x53 63 times.

H_PAD_U is a 512-bit string formed by repeating the value 0x5C 63 times.

H_PAD_D is a 512-bit string formed by repeating the value 0x3A 63 times.

TEK Encryption

The TEK that is passed in a Key Reply message is encrypted with the KEK. Traffic is encrypted using 56-bit DES, so a 56-bit TEK is necessary. The CMTS actually generates a 64-bit TEK. The least significant bit of each octet in the generated TEK is ignored, resulting in a 56-bit key suitable for encrypting the traffic.[18]

The mechanism used to encrypt the TEK as it is passed from CMTS to the modem is two-key EDE ECB 3DES, applied as follows.

```
C = Ek₁[Dk₂[Ek₁[P]]]
P = Dk₁[Ek₂[Dk₁[C]]]
```

where:

P = plaintext 64-bit TEK

C = ciphertext 64-bit TEK

k_1 = 64 leftmost bits of KEK

---

18. This behavior is nonstandard. Normally, the least significant bit of each octet in a 64-bit DES key is a parity bit, and each octet of the key must be of odd parity. In DOCSIS, the least significant bit is simply ignored.

$k_2 = 64$ rightmost bits of KEK

$E[M] = 56$-bit DES encryption of M in ECB mode

$D[M'] = 56$-bit DES decryption of M′ in ECB mode

Lifetime of Keying Material

In practice, a CMTS maintains two valid sets of keying material for each SAID, staggered so that the lifetime of one set expires midway through the life of the other set. It places both sets into a single Key Reply whenever a modem sends a Key Request for that SAID. This ensures that there is always at least one valid set of keying material for the SAID. Since the CM knows when the keys expire, it can schedule Key Requests appropriately.

As well as periodic Key Requests, the CM also sends periodic (but much less frequent) Authorization Requests. The CMTS generates Authorization Keys with overlapping lifetimes, so that at least one Authorization Key is always valid.

Packet Formats

BPKM messages are carried in the Management Message Payload Field of DOCSIS MAC management messages. The details of the many different kinds of messages are beyond our scope, but they are readily available in the DOCSIS documentation. The generic format of a BPKM message is shown in Figure 3-30. The meanings of the various fields are as follows.

- Code—One octet. Identifies the type of the BPKM packet according to Table 3-7.

- Identifier—One octet. The CM increments the Identifier field whenever it transmits a new BPKM message. When sending a response, the CMTS places the value of the Identifier field in the matching request into its response.

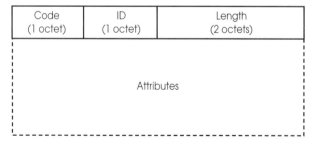

Figure 3-30   BPKM Message Format

Table 3-7 BPKM Message Codes

BPKM Code Octet	BPKM Message Name	MAC Management Equivalent Message Name
0–3	Reserved	
4	Auth Request	BPKM-REQ
5	Auth Reply	BPKM-RSP
6	Auth Reject	BPKM-RSP
7	Key Request	BPKM-REQ
8	Key Reply	BPKM-RSP
9	Key Reject	BPKM-RSP
10	Auth Invalid	BPKM-RSP
11	TEK Invalid	BPKM-RSP
12	Authent Info	BPKM-REQ
13	Map Request	BPKM-REQ
14	Map Reply	BPKM-RSP
15	Map Reject	BPKM-RSP
16–255	Reserved	

- Length—Two octets. Gives the number of octets in the Attribute field.

- Attributes—Variable length. Carries the specific request or response information as defined by the DOCSIS specifications. Attributes are TLV encoded.

The CM's X.509 Certificate

Ultimately, the security of BPI+ rests in the X.509 certificate inserted into the modem during manufacture. If a CMTS is presented with what it believes to be a valid certificate, it will proceed with BPI+ initialization. In order to authenticate the validity of a CM certificate, BPI+ utilizes the hierarchy shown in Figure 3-31 (see Chapter 2 for more about certificate hierarchies).

The CMTS is preprovisioned with the DOCSIS root RSA public key. This enables it to authenticate certificates claiming to be signed by the DOCSIS root. Manufacturer certificates are such certificates. A manufacturer certificate contains the manufacturer's RSA public key. Since it is signed by the DOCSIS root, which the CMTS

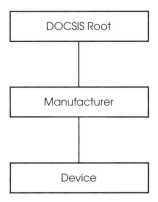

Figure 3-31 DOCSIS Certificate Hierarchy

can verify, then the CMTS can trust that the manufacturer's public key as handed to it by the CM is indeed correct.

The CM certificate, which contains the modem's RSA public key, is signed by the manufacturer. Since the CMTS now has the manufacturer's public key, it can validate this certificate in turn, thereby authenticating the cable modem's public key.

Once it is certain that it has the cable modem's public key, BPI+ initialization can continue with the generation of an Authorization Key on request, and the AK can be delivered securely, encrypted with the modem's public key.

BPI+ MAC Extended Header

BPI+ operates to encrypt the data PDU portion of MAC frames. It signals this by using the Extended Header (EHDR) field of the MAC header.

As we saw earlier, the Extended Header is an optional, variable length field that occurs in the MAC header, immediately following the LEN field. The BPI+ Extended Header is five octets in length, divided as in Figure 3-32.

Type

A 4-bit field that defines the direction of flow of the frame. The value may be either BPI_UP (defined to be 3) or BPI_DOWN (defined to be 4).

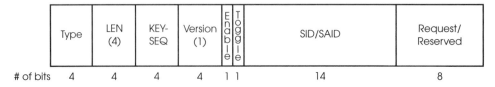

Figure 3-32 DOCSIS BPI+ Extended Header Format

LEN

A 4-bit field containing the value 4

KEY_SEQ

A 4-bit field. This field contains the number of the key that is currently in use for the Security Association ID associated with this frame, starting with zero and incrementing by one every time that the CMTS generates new keying material for this SAID. The value in the field wraps around with every nth key generation, where n mod 16 is zero.

Version

A 4-bit field containing the value 1

ENABLE

A 1-bit field identifying whether the PDU is actually encrypted. A one indicates encryption, a zero indicates no encryption.

TOGGLE

A 1-bit field that matches the LSB of the KEY_SEQ field

SID/SAID

A 14-bit field. In the upstream, this field contains the SID of the frame; in the downstream, it contains the Security Association ID.

REQUEST/Reserved

A 1-octet field. In the upstream, this field contains a number of minislots that may optionally be requested for upstream bandwidth. In the downstream, the field is set to zero and is ignored.

Where Do We Go from Here?

In this chapter we have looked at the essential facilities provided by DOCSIS modems operating on an HFC access network.

These facilities are available to all the traffic being handled by the modems. You have probably noticed that there was little specific mention of telephony in this chapter. However, most of the concepts we have examined—in particular the difficulty of obtaining guaranteed upstream bandwidth and the security applied to DOCSIS transmissions—are important grounding for understanding the design of the PacketCable telephony network.

In the next several chapters we will examine how the facilities provided by DOCSIS modems are used as an integral part of a fully fledged telephony network capable of providing high quality and advanced services to large numbers of subscribers.

Network-Based Call Signaling

Although MGCP is not NCS, and NCS is not MGCP, the names MGCP and NCS will be used interchangeably in this document. . . .

PKT-SP-EC-MGCP-I02-991201

Although most people associate telephony systems simply with the audio traffic that flows between the parties in a call, practical telephony networks require a tremendous amount of **call signaling** to occur before the audio traffic associated with a call can begin to flow. Call signaling is control information that the network must process in order to manage the flows of audio data correctly. Signaling occurs before and after every call, and, for calls that invoke certain features such as call waiting, signaling also occurs during the call when the feature is invoked.

In the Public Switched Telephone Network, the conventional "circuit-switched" telephone network that operates by creating circuits between subscribers, merely taking a telephone off-hook initiates call signaling. (The first and most important feature of the PacketCable network is that it closely emulates the behavior—as perceived by the end user—of the PSTN.) When a user lifts a handset, the LEC's central office sees a change in the impedance of the line to the user's home, and it transmits a dial tone to the user.[1] Every digit that the user dials is recorded at the central office, in a process called **digit collection**, and checked against a **digit map** to determine whether the user has dialed a complete number.

When the user has finished dialing, the central office processes the information and passes information about the call to the central office at the far end. More signaling takes place, resulting in the circuit between the two phones being established,

---

1. The LEC (pronounced "lek"), or Local Exchange Carrier, is the subscriber's local telephone company. The central office is what is often known colloquially as "the telephone exchange".

ringing at the far end telephone, and **ringback** in the calling party's phone. Yet more signaling occurs when the call is answered, as well as when the initiating party goes on hook to terminate the call.

In the PSTN, the local signaling that occurs between a telephone and the local central office is of a very elementary kind, since it was originally designed to be used with a simple analog telephone. The only input signals that a telephone can produce are those reflecting its on-hook/off-hook state and the dialing of individual digits. Similarly, the only signals to which a simple telephone can respond are those associated with ringing the phone when it is on hook.

Because of the basic lack of capability of a simple analog phone, many events are signaled by transmitting in-band audio tones, which a subscriber interprets according to local custom. For example, there is no direct way to signal that the phone at the far end is ringing; instead a ringback tone is generated and transmitted to the user's handset. Usually, the ringback tone that the user hears is generated at the far end of the connection, which can lead to confusion if the call is an international one and the user is not familiar with the tones that are customary in the destination country.

Between central offices, a much richer set of signaling is possible. These signals are specified by the **Signaling System 7 (SS7)** standard. The telephony SS7 network runs in parallel with, but is distinct from, the network that carries telephone conversations. Lines between central offices are designated as either "signaling trunks" or "bearer trunks," depending on whether they carry signaling or voice traffic.

PacketCable systems must also provide call signaling, but the signals that they produce and manage may be far more complex than those used in the PSTN, since they are intended to support complex multimedia services. Because PacketCable networks are based on IP, the signaling and bearer networks are not differentiated: Both signaling and bearer travel across the same network. It is the format of a particular packet that identifies the kind of traffic it contains.

In the PSTN, all "knowledge" of a call resides within the network itself. If Zoe tries to place a call to Yvonne, who is already in a call with Xavier, the network is aware of the fact that Yvonne is already engaged in a call and will signal the fact to Zoe with a special tone that Zoe interprets as "busy" or "engaged".

It is possible to architect a packet-based telephony network in a similar way, wherein *call state* is maintained within the network itself. It is also possible to architect the network in quite a different manner, in which the endpoint devices are presumed to contain intelligence and to have the ability to maintain call state within themselves. In such a network, for example, rather than the network signaling to Zoe that Yvonne's phone was busy, Zoe's incoming request would be forwarded to Yvonne's endpoint, and the endpoint itself would signal to Zoe that there was already a call in progress.

The power of this method of signaling might already be obvious: Yvonne's endpoint would generally know the identity of both Zoe and Xavier. If Zoe was, for example, Yvonne's daughter, it could alert Yvonne to the incoming call and at the same time send a signal to Zoe's endpoint that Yvonne is currently on another call but is being informed of Zoe's attempted call. Such features are possible with PSTN-like signaling, but the mechanisms are complex and depend on the service provider's ability to support them.

PacketCable specifically supports both kinds of signaling. The former, which is similar to the current PSTN signaling method, is called **Network-Based Call Signaling**, or **NCS**. The latter, which is more similar to the signaling used on computer networks, is called Distributed Call Signaling, or DCS. The remainder of this chapter will discuss NCS. DCS will be the subject of the next chapter.

Media Gateway Control Protocol (MGCP)

NCS is a **profile** (a particular instantiation) of the **Media Gateway Control Protocol** (**MGCP**) described in RFC 2705, with a small number of extensions. MGCP is a protocol designed for networks in which the "intelligence" (and more precisely the state) associated with call management lies in devices within the core network. This closely mirrors the architecture of the PSTN, in which calls are controlled by "switches", which are complex devices that reside in the local central office.

The basic constructs in MGCP, and therefore also in NCS, are endpoints, gateways and connections. These entities are grouped together dynamically to create calls. A gateway is responsible for controlling endpoints. You can think of endpoints as physical handsets and gateways as base stations (actually MTAs) responsible for a small number of handsets. However, sometimes the terminology blurs the distinction between an endpoint and a gateway, since, in terms of the basic protocol, the network does not care how well separated these are in a particular implementation. For example, sometimes we may speak of an endpoint accumulating events, but in practice this accumulation is more likely to occur in the MTA than the handset. The important point from the protocol's point of view is that they must be accumulated somewhere at the "client" end of the system.

The topology of a PacketCable phone system at the subscriber's premises is slightly different from an ordinary PSTN system. A single PacketCable MTA may control several physical endpoints, even if they are associated with different phone numbers (see Figure 4-1).

The gateways and endpoints have no call intelligence. They can produce and react to a strictly limited set of simple messages. Incoming messages may produce results known as signals. Gateways may also produce outgoing messages in response to external or internal events. For example, when an MTA receives a message indicating that there is an incoming call on a certain line, it will send a signal to the corresponding handset to cause that handset to start ringing or otherwise alert the

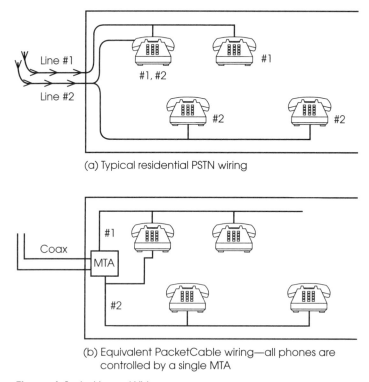

(a) Typical residential PSTN wiring

(b) Equivalent PacketCable wiring—all phones are controlled by a single MTA

Figure 4-1 In-Home Wiring

subscriber of the incoming call. When the subscriber takes the handset off-hook, that action generates an event, which causes the handset to send a message to the MTA (and the MTA to send a message to the network) that the endpoint has gone off-hook.

PacketCable does not specify the details of the messaging between the MTA and the handset. The PacketCable specifications control behavior only out to the MTA. How the MTA communicates with the endpoints under its control is left up to the various vendors. However, the intention is that, at least with the earliest deployments, a phone attached to a PacketCable network will function essentially identically to a phone connected to the conventional PSTN.

As well as endpoints and gateways, NCS uses the notion of connections, which are manipulated by a device in the core of the network (that is, on the far side of the CMTS) known as a **Call Agent** (**CA**). The CA is also sometimes identified as the **Call Management Server** (**CMS**). To be technically accurate, the CMS comprises the combination of the NCS Call Agent *and* the DQoS Gate Controller that we shall discuss in detail in Chapter 6. In practice, however, both of these functions are almost always performed by a single device, so we will generally follow the usual practice and use the terms CA and CMS as synonyms.

NCS gateways (which, in the PacketCable network, are the devices known as MTAs) have the following simple characteristics.

1. When certain events occur, they can signal the occurrence of that event to the Call Agent. Typical events that would produce signals are activities such as going off-hook and dialing digits.

2. They can produce signals in response to messages received from the Call Agent. These signals are simple actions such as producing dial tone, providing audible ringback, lighting a message-waiting indicator, and so forth.

An NCS gateway generally does not perform actions of its own volition. Its activities occur as a result of receiving instructions from the network. Typically, when an event occurs on an endpoint, the endpoint notifies the gateway of the fact. The gateway then examines a list of so-called "RequestedEvents" that it has received from the Call Agent in a REQUEST-NOTIFICATION message, and if the event is found in the list, then the gateway sends a NOTIFY message to the Call Agent to inform it that the event has occurred. Typically, the Call Agent will then instruct the gateway to cause the endpoint to behave in some appropriate manner.

In addition to this "normal" behavior, there are some events known as "persistent" events that are processed in this way regardless of whether they appear in the list of RequestedEvents. Persistent events can be regarded as implicitly included in the list of RequestedEvents.

NCS is a rich protocol that allows for many ways of implementing telephony networks. The PacketCable specification defines the protocol messages and the manner in which they interact. It does *not* specify a particular implementation of the protocol in a real network.[2] The PacketCable project team, however, has produced a series of Technical Reports providing examples of call flow sequences that have to be supported by any implementation of NCS, and we will use flows based on the ones in the Technical Reports whenever it is necessary to discuss examples of particular interactions within NCS.

NCS defines a total of eight commands, as shown in Table 4-1. In NCS, every command requires a response. The names of the commands are reasonably self-explanatory. For completeness though, here is a brief description of what each command does.

---

2. This is an important distinction. It means, for example, that it is very difficult to talk about the way things *must* work in a PacketCable NCS network. Theoretically, two vendors may use quite different message flows to produce the same result. The only guarantees are the format of messages and the effect the messages must have on various devices. Not only does this make it difficult to write about NCS networks, it also makes it difficult to test them for conformance to the specifications.

Table 4-1 NCS Commands

Command Name	Abbreviation	Direction
CreateConnection	CRCX	From CA
ModifyConnection	MDCX	From CA
DeleteConnection	DLCX	From CA, To CA
NotificationRequest	RQNT	From CA
Notify	NTFY	To CA
AuditEndpoint	AUEP	From CA
AuditConnection	AUCX	From CA
RestartInProgress	RSIP	To CA

CreateConnection (CRCX)

Creates a connection. The command includes parameters to describe the connection to be created.

ModifyConnection (MDCX)

Modifies an extant connection. The command includes parameters to describe the modified connection.

DeleteConnection (DLCX)

Deletes an extant connection.

NotificationRequest (RQNT)

Requests an endpoint to notify the Call Agent when certain events (specified in the parameter list) occur.

Notify (NTFY)

Notifies the Call Agent that an event that was previously specified in an RQNT has occurred.

AuditEndpoint (AUEP)

Used to interrogate an endpoint about its current state.

AuditConnection (AUCX)

Used to interrogate an endpoint about the state of a connection.

RestartInProgress (RSIP)

Used to indicate to a Call Agent that the endpoint is in the process of rebooting.

Later in this chapter (in the section "Basic NCS Call Flow") we will give a detailed call flow showing exactly how a simple call might be signaled. However, it's probably a good idea for us to take a quick look at the outline of a call flow now, so we can get a basic feel for how NCS works. Ignoring much of the detail then, Figure 4-2 shows the essentials of one way of placing a call via NCS signaling.[3]

1. The CA sends an RQNT. This "clears" the originating MTA, MTA_O so that it is ready for the next call and instructs MTA_O to inform the CA when it goes off-hook.

2. MTA_O sends an NTFY. The notify may contain information about the digits dialed by the user, or it may initiate a digit-by-digit transfer to the CA as the user dials the digits. For the sake of simplicity in this example, we will assume that the NTFY contains all the dialed digits.

3. The CA sends a CRCX to MTA_O. This creates a connection, but neither transmission nor reception may occur on that connection. (This is called an inactive connection.)

4. The CA sends a CRCX to MTA_T. This also creates an inactive connection.

5. The CA sends a MDCX to MTA_O. This informs the MTA about the detailed bandwidth requirements for the call, as determined by MTA_T.

6. Sometime later, the network is sure that sufficient bandwidth is available in both directions for the call to take place. It sends RQNTs to both MTAs. The RQNT to MTA_O tells it to play ringback; the RQNT to MTA_T tells it to start ringing.

7. When MTA_T goes off-hook, it sends an NTFY to the CA.

8. The CA sends MDCX commands to both MTAs, converting the connections to full duplex send/receive connections.

At this point, the parties may converse. So that's basically how NCS sets up a call. Now we'll take a look at exactly how NCS messages are formatted.

Format

Commands and responses are encoded as a series of human-readable ASCII-encoded lines of text, separated either by a CRLF pair (a 0x0D followed by a 0x0A) or by a single LF character (a single 0x0A). Each command consists of one or more header

---

3. As we shall see, there are many ways in which the various NCS messages may be strung together to create a valid call flow, even for a simple call. This is merely one such way.

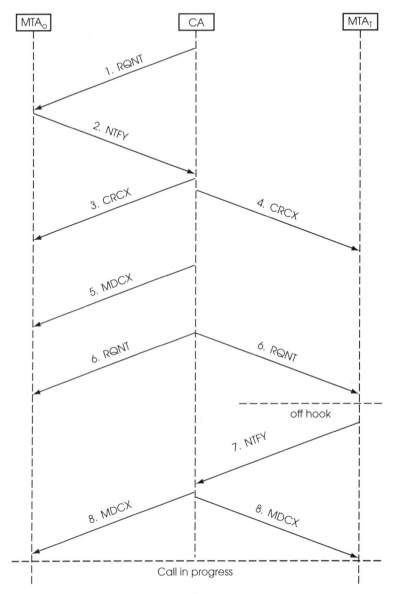

Figure 4-2 Overview of an NCS Call

lines, possibly followed by one or more body lines. A single empty line separates the body from the header. NCS uses a transaction identifier carried in the header so that responses can be matched to the command that generated them. Unless otherwise specified, all the material in a command header is case-insensitive. Material in the body may be case-sensitive, depending on the application. In PacketCable, the body usually comprises lines that conform to the Session Description Protocol, which in general *is* case-sensitive (see section 6 of RFC 2327 for more details).

Command Header

The command header begins with a single line that identifies the command, the transaction identifier, the destination for the command and the protocol version numbers for both MGCP and NCS. For example,

```
DLCX 63991 aaln/1@flemmingsMTA.nj.ratco.com MGCP 1.0 NCS 1.0
```

is a valid NCS command header line.

We see from the first two parameters that this is a DeleteConnection command, transaction number 63991. The response to this message will also contain the number 63991, so that it can be identified as a response to this command.

The third parameter requires some explanation. A particular endpoint is associated with a line that is attached to an MTA. Endpoints are referenced by a syntax similar to that used for e-mail. To the right of the "@" is the Fully Qualified Domain Name (FQDN) of the MTA that controls the endpoint—in this case flemmingsMTA. nj.ratco.com. To the left of the "@" is the identifier for the particular line. "Analog access lines" such as would be used for an ordinary telephony handset are identified as such by the sequence "aaln".[4] The particular number of the line, starting from 1 for each MTA, follows the aaln identifier and a slash. Hence, in the above example, "aaln/1" indicates that the destination for the message is the first analog access line attached to the MTA. All devices (not just MTAs and endpoints) are denoted by an address in a similar format. For example, a particular Call Agent might be identified as CA.Missouri.1@callagents.ratco.com

The default port number for MGCP connections is number 2427. This, or any other port number, may be explicitly encoded by appending it, following a colon, to the FQDN of the destination device.

```
CA1@callagents.telephony.net:7752
```

The last two parameters indicate that what follows conforms to MGCP version 1.0 and NCS version 1.0.

Most commands require considerably more than a single header line. The parameters for a command are placed on header lines (before the blank line that separates the header from the body).

---

4. aaln lines are the only ones currently supported by PacketCable.

```
DLCX 63991 aaln/1@flemmingsMTA.nj.ratco.com MGCP 1.0 NCS 1.0
C: FFEE12A087EE5390
I: DF2E438C
```

NCS supports a total of 25 different parameter types in its commands and responses. Each parameter type is represented by a short code (typically one or two letters), to conserve space in the signaling packets. These codes are given in Table 4-2. The table also identifies whether a particular parameter is mandatory (M), optional (O) or forbidden (F) in each possible command message. Some parameters, such as the Capabilities parameter, are marked as being Forbidden in all commands. Such parameters can never be part of a command message but may only be included in a response.

Note: A RemoteConnectionDescriptor is not a parameter in the same sense as the other entries. A RemoteConnectionDescription is a part of the message body and contains a **Session Description Protocol (SDP)** description of a remote connection. This is described in greater detail later in the chapter.

Tedious though it is, we are about to provide a list of the meanings of each of these parameters. This is intended mostly as reference material to provide some of the material in the PacketCable specifications in a more accessible form. Unless you are interested in the details of a specific parameter, you would probably be better served by skipping forward a few sections to "Basic NCS Call Flow", where we look at how NCS messages can actually be strung together to perform useful functions.

So, with that warning, we will proceed to the details of the parameters.

CallId (C)

A string of hexadecimal characters (that is, any of the digits or a character in the range A to F). The length of a CallId is limited to a maximum of 32 characters. Since it takes two hexadecimal characters to encode a single binary octet, a CallId can be viewed internally as a 16-octet binary value. Every connection has an associated CallId (as well as an associated ConnectionId). An example of how a CallId parameter might appear in an NCS message is:

```
C: 17AF930EDC20006777FFB1059B29A010
```

Capabilities (A)

Capabilities are textual encodings of an endpoint's abilities, designed to be returned when the endpoint is audited by the network (that is, if the network needs to know whether an endpoint supports a particular capability).

Table 4-2 NCS Command Parameters

Parameter Name	Code	AUCX	AUEP	CRCX	DLCX	MDCX	NTFY	RQNT	RSIP
CallId	C	F	F	M	O	M	F	F	F
Capabilities	A	F	F	F	F	F	F	F	F
ConnectionId	I	M	F	F	O	M	F	F	F
ConnectionMode	M	F	F	M	F	O	F	F	F
ConnectionParameters	P	F	F	F	O	F	F	F	F
DetectEvents	T	F	F	O	O	O	F	O	F
DigitMap	D	F	F	O	O	O	F	O	F
LocalConnectionOptions	L	F	F	M	F	O	F	F	F
MaxEndPointIds	ZM	F	O	F	F	F	F	F	F
NotifiedEntity	N	F	F	O	O	O	O	O	F
ObservedEvents	O	F	F	F	F	F	M	F	F
QuarantineHandling	Q	F	F	O	O	O	F	O	F
ReasonCode	E	F	F	F	O	F	F	F	F
RemoteConnectionDescriptor		F	F	O	O	F	F	F	F
RequestedEvents	R	F	F	O	O	O	F	O	F
RequestedInfo	F	O	O	F	F	F	F	F	F
RequestIdentifier	X	F	F	O	O	O	M	M	F
ResponseAck	K	O	O	O	O	O	O	O	O
RestartDelay	RD	F	F	F	F	F	F	F	O
RestartMethod	RM	F	F	F	F	F	F	F	M
SignalRequests	S	F	F	O	O	O	F	O	F
SpecificEndPointId	Z	F	O	F	F	F	F	F	F

The encodings are similar (but not quite identical) to those used in the LocalConnectionOptions parameter that we shall meet a little later in this list. The options may be in any order. Multiple options are separated by commas, and multiple values of the same option are separated by semi-colons. The possible encodings are:

- Name of the supported compression algorithm, encoded by the string "a:", followed by a character string. For example, the standard 64 kilobits-per-second G.711 encoding is encoded as:

```
A: a:G711
```

- Packetization interval in milliseconds, encoded by the string "p:", followed by a decimal number. A range may be specified by two decimal numbers separated by a dash. For example, if the endpoint supports only a codec that produces a packet every 10 milliseconds, the capability would be encoded:

```
A: p:10
```

- Bandwidth in thousands of bits per second, encoded by the string "b:", followed by a decimal number. A range may be specified by two decimal numbers separated by a dash. It is important to realize that this is the *total* bandwidth needed to carry the digitized flow. This is not the same as the rate at which bits are produced by the codec. The number encoded here must always be greater than the output rate from the codec so as to allow for the overhead of the various protocol layers that are used to carry the codec output. In practice, for 64-kilobit G.711, the actual bandwidth on a cable access system is likely to be close to 120 kilobits per second. So the bandwidth of the G.711 64-kilobit-per-second codec might in practice be encoded as:

```
A: b:120
```

If the codecs are well known (as in the case of G.711), this line may not be strictly necessary, since the names of the codecs contained in the a: parameter may be sufficient to define the necessary bandwidth. However, it is wise to include this line even when the codec is a well-known one.

- Echo cancellation flag, encoded as one of the strings e:on or e:off.
- "Type of Service" support. The IP header includes a "Type of Service" field that can be used to prioritize packets. If the device supports this field, then the capability is encoded by the non-zero value of the t: parameter. If it does not support the Type of Service field, this is indicated by the encoding t:0.
- Silence suppression flag, encoded as one of the strings s:on or s:off.
- Supported event packages, encoded by the string v:, followed by a semicolon-separated list of supported package names. The first value is taken to be the default. Event packages are a means of encapsulating a

large number of events and signals under a single name. They are important enough that we have dedicated a section to them later in this chapter (called, oddly enough, "Event Packages").

A typical list of event packages looks like this:

```
A: v:L;S
```

where L indicates support for the ordinary analog line package, and S indicates support for the Analog Display Services Interface (ADSI) package; these are the only two packages defined in PacketCable 1.0.

- Supported connection modes as specified in Table 4-3, encoded by the string m:, followed by a semicolon-separated list of supported connection modes. A typical example would be:

```
A: m:sendonly;recvonly;sendrecv;inactive
```

- The string dq-gi if the device supports Dynamic Quality of Service.
- The string sc-st if PacketCable Security is supported. If sc-st appears, one or both of the following two parameters also appear.
- Supported RTP ciphersuites are encoded by the string sc-rtp:, followed by a semicolon-separated list of supported RTP authentication algorithms. Following this list is the single character "/", followed by a semicolon-separated list of supported RTP encryption algorithms. The encoding used for both the authentication and the encryption algorithms is described in the section "Attributes".
- Supported RTCP ciphersuites are encoded by the string sc-rtcp:, followed by a semicolon-separated list of supported RTCP authentication algorithms. Following this list is the single character "/", followed by a semicolon-separated list of supported RTP encryption algorithms. The encoding used for both the authentication and the encryption algorithms is described in the section "Attributes".

A couple of example encodings of capabilities follow. (Note that in practice each example would be transmitted as a single line. The constraints of formatting on the page of a book requires us to split the examples across multiple lines.)

The first example is for a device that supports only the G.729A codec, with packetization periods of between 30 and 90 milliseconds, with support for echo cancellation and silence suppression. The device supports unidirectional, bidirectional and conference connections, the PacketCable analog line and ADSI packages, PacketCable QoS and encryption and authentication of the RTP stream.

```
A: a:G729A; p:30-90, e:on, s:on, v:L;S,
m:sendonly;recvonly;sendrecv;inactive;confrnce, dg-qi, sc-st, sc-
rtp:00/51;03
```

The second example is for a simple device that supports only 12 millisecond packetization of G.711, the analog line package, unidirectional streams and PacketCable DQoS:

```
A: a:G711; p:12, e:off, s:off, v:L, m:sendonly;recvonly; inactive, dg-qi
```

ConnectionId (I)

A string of hexadecimal characters (that is, any of the digits, or a character in the range A to F). The length of a ConnectionId is limited to a maximum of 32 characters. Since it takes two hexadecimal characters to encode a single binary octet, a ConnectionId can be viewed internally as a 16-octet binary value. Every connection has an associated ConnectionId.

ConnectionMode (M)

This is used to describe the mode of operation of a connection. Possible values are given in Table 4-3.

Table 4-3 Permitted Connection Modes

Mode Name	Meaning
confrnce	Sending and receiving packets in conference mode
inactive	Neither sending nor receiving packets
netwloop	Endpoint in Network Loopback mode
netwtest	Endpoint in Network Continuity Test mode
recvonly	Receiving packets only
replcate	Sending packets in replicate mode
sendonly	Sending packets only
sendrecv	Sending and receiving packets

In general use, connections are usually in the inactive, recvonly, sendonly or sendrecv mode.

Example:

```
M: sendrecv
```

ConnectionParameters (P)

The ConnectionParameters parameter is used to provide statistics regarding the quality of a connection. The statistics are presented as a comma-separated series of values, in any order. Each value is encoded as a two-character identifier, followed by an equals sign and a decimal value. Legal two-character identifiers are given in Table 4-4.

Usually, the network should not trust these values, since they are returned by a device outside the control of the network operator. However, taken in the aggregate (over many devices), the values returned may be useful in a statistical sense to gauge the quality of the operator's network.

Table 4-4 Observed QoS Parameters on a Connection

Name	*Two-Character Identifier*	*Meaning*
Jitter	JI	The mean interpacket jitter of received packets, in milliseconds
Latency	LA	Mean latency in milliseconds. ("Latency" is essentially the mean travel time between transmitter and receiver.)
Octets received	OR	Number of octets received on a connection
Octets sent	OS	Number of octets transmitted on a connection
Packets lost	PL	Number of packets that have not been received, as deduced by gaps in the RTP sequence number in the received packets
Packets received	PR	Number of packets received on the connection
Packets sent	PS	Number of packets transmitted on the connection

For example:

```
P: PS=5531, OS=553100, PR=412, OR=20500, PL=1, JI=15, LA=51
```

DetectEvents (T)

Specifies a comma-separated list of events from the package in use. See the section "Event Packages" for a more detailed discussion of packages and events. The device continuously monitors its state, and, when an event in the list occurs, it remembers that fact but it otherwise performs no action. The CMS can interrogate the MTA for a list of ObservedEvents to determine whether a particular event has occurred.

For example, to require that the MTA record the fact that hangup occured, the CA would send:

```
T: hu
```

DigitMap (D)

A digit map is a textual encoding of the rules for determining when a complete, valid telephone number has been dialed. See the section "Digit Maps" for a detailed discussion of digit maps. An example of a basic digit map might look like this:

```
D: (0T|00T|#xxxxxxx|*xx|91xxxxxxxxxx|9011x.T)
```

LocalConnectionOptions (L)

The LocalConnectionOptions parameter is used to encode the parameters of a particular connection. The options may be in any order. They correspond closely to the possible values of the Capabilities parameter, except that they refer to the characteristics of a particular connection rather than to the fundamental capabilities of a device. The permitted encodings are the following.

- Packetization interval in milliseconds, encoded by the string `p:`, followed by a decimal number.

- Name of the compression algorithm, encoded by the string `a:`, followed by a character string.

- Echo cancellation flag, encoded as one of the strings `e:on` or `e:off`.

- The Type of Service, encoded by the string `t:`, followed by two hexadecimal characters. If the Type of Service field in the IP header is not supported, then the parameter has the value `t:0`. If the value is non-zero, then the corresponding IP Type of Service value can be obtained by taking the left-most hexadecimal character of the pair and dividing that value by 2. For example, the encoding `t:A0` corresponds to an IP Type of Service value of 5.

Several LocalConnectionOptions parameters are associated with PacketCable Dynamic Quality of Service (DQoS), which we shall explore in depth in Chapter 6. Since DQoS is protocol-neutral, it would not be appropriate to discuss NCS-specific issues in that chapter. So for a discussion of how DQoS is related to NCS signaling, see the section "NCS and DQoS" later in this chapter, where we shall explore the meaning of the additional LocalConnectionOptions parameters: `dq-gi:`, `dq-rr:`, `dq-ri:`, and `dq-rd:`.

- The string `sc-st:` if PacketCable Security is supported (as it should be; PacketCable security is a requirement for PacketCable networks), followed by a shared secret. For more details of the shared secret and the way that it is used, see the section "Encrypting RTP Packets". If PacketCable Security is supported, one or both of the following parameters also appear.

- Supported RTP ciphersuites are encoded by the string `sc-rtp:`, followed by a semicolon-separated list of supported RTP authentication algorithms. Following this list is the single character "/", followed by a semicolon-separated list of supported RTP encryption algorithms. The encoding used for these algorithms is described in the section "Attributes".

- Supported RTCP ciphersuites are encoded by the string `sc-rtcp:`, followed by a semicolon-separated list of supported RTCP authentication algorithms. Following this list is the single character "/", followed by a semicolon-separated list of supported RTP encryption algorithms. The encoding used for these algorithms is described in the section "Attributes".

The items in a LocalConnectionOptions line may appear in any order and are separated by commas.

For example, a simple QoS-enabled bidirectional connection that supports the G.729A codec with a packetization interval of 30 milliseconds, with echo cancellation but without silence suppression and for which the IP Type of Service field is set to 5 could be encoded:

```
L: p:30, a:G729A, e:on, t:A0, s:off, dq-gi:00FEA831
```

MaxEndPointIds (ZM)

A string of decimal digits whose length does not exceed 16 characters. This parameter can be used to limit the number of endpoints whose audit information is returned by an MTA. In practice, MaxEndPointIDs is most likely to be equal to the number of endpoints currently managed by the MTA, so that all its endpoints are audited by a single command.

NotifiedEntity (N)

An e-mail-like string, optionally followed by a colon and a port number. This is used to inform the MTA which device should be notified when one of the events in the DetectEvents list occurs. Typically, the NotifiedEntity is the Call Agent responsible for the MTA:

```
N: CA.Missouri.1@callagents.ratco.com
```

ObservedEvents (O)

This parameter provides a list of events that have been observed, using the same encoding as used by the DetectEvents parameter. For example, suppose that an MTA has been commanded to detect a hangup event; when the hangup occurs, the MTA will transmit a NTFY message containing the line:

```
O: hu
```

If the detected event occurs on a connection (as opposed to being the result of user input), the connection ID is included on the line. For example, the code ma corresponds to the start of media flow on a connection, so to signal the start of media flow on the connection identified by the value 4AA0EF, an MTA would send:

```
O:ma@4AA0EF
```

QuarantineHandling (Q)

This parameter is either Q:process or Q:discard, and instructs the MTA how to handle quarantined events as they occur. For more details about quarantined events, see the section "Quarantine".

For example, if the MTA is to ignore quarantined events, it would be sent the following line:

```
Q: discard
```

Table 4-5 Reason Codes

Code	Meaning
900	Endpoint malfunctioning
901	Endpoint taken out of service
902	Loss of lower layer connectivity
903	QoS resource reservation was lost

ReasonCode (E)

Reason codes are three-digit codes, optionally followed by white space and a textual explanation. They are used by the MTA to inform the Call Agent for the reason why a connection has been deleted. The allowable codes are shown in Table 4-5.

For example, if the QoS system somehow lost a resource reservation for a call in progress, the following line would be included in the DeleteConnection:

```
E: 903 QoS resource reservation was lost
```

The textual information is ignored by the protocol (which uses only the Reason Code), but it can be useful when humans are required to debug a problem.

RequestedEvents (R)

This parameter provides a list of events about which the Call Agent wishes to be notified, should they occur on the MTA. The event encoding is discussed in detail in the section "Event Packages".

The parameter also instructs the MTA about the action or actions it is to perform when each event occurs by providing a list of coded actions in parentheses immediately after the event code. Table 4-6 lists the valid actions.

If no explicit action is attached to an event, the default is N; in other words, the Call Agent is to be notified as soon as the event occurs. For example, to inform the MTA that it is interested in a hangup and wants to be notified as soon as the hangup occurs, the Call Agent might include a line like this:

```
R: hu(N)
```

Table 4-6 RequestedEvents Action Codes

Code	Action to perform
A	Accumulate
C	Embedded MDCX
D	Accumulate according to digit map
E	Embedded RQNT
I	Ignore
K	Keep signal(s) active
N	Notify immediately

NCS allows the RequestedEvents parameter to contain an embedded MDCX or RQNT command. If such a command is present in the RequestedEvents line, it is interpreted to mean "when this particular event occurs, act as if you have just received the following command".

An embedded RQNT has the format:

```
E(R(requested events), D(digit map), S(signal requests))
```

where each of the three elements R, D, and S is optional and may be specified in any order.

For example, suppose that the MTA receives the following R line:

```
R:hd(A, E(S(dl), R(oc(N), [0-9#T](D)), D((1xxxxxxxxxx|9011x.T))))
```

What does this mean?

Section "Event Packages" tells us that the events encoded in the command are: hd (off-hook), dl (dial tone) and oc (operation complete). The entire activity can be broken down into two actions, both associated with the single event hd. The first activity is an A (which Table 4-6 tells us means to accumulate events); the second is an embedded RQNT.

So when an offhook event occurs, the MTA will accumulate the fact (that is, store it in an internal event accumulator), it will then act as if it had immediately received a RQNT containing the instructions encoded in the E() portion of the R line.

The S(dl) instructs the MTA to provide dial tone. The R([0-9#T](D)) tells it to accumulate the dialed digits according to the digit map provided in the D() parameter. Once the operation is complete, the R(oc(N)) instructs the MTA to notify the Call Agent immediately.

Embedded MDCX commands have the format:

```
M(connection mode 1(connection ID 1)), connection mode 2(connection ID 2))
... )
```

The current connection is encoded as a dollar sign, $.

Suppose that the MTA receives the following R line:

```
R: hf(A, C(M(inactive($)), M(sendrecv(AA00)))), oc(N), of(N)
```

This tells the MTA that when it receives a hookflash (a brief on-hook period), it is to force the current connection to be inactive and set connection AA00 to sendrecv mode. The MTA then instructs the CA that it has done so successfully (oc(N)) or has failed in the attempt (of(N)).

This particular example is a RequestedEvents line that might be sent by a Call Agent to implement call waiting on an NCS endpoint, since it performs exactly the actions needed to toggle between two calls on the same endpoint when a hookflash occurs.

RequestedInfo (F)

This parameter contains a comma-separated list of items that the Call Agent wishes to audit. The items use the same letter-encoding as in Table 4-2. The list may contain any of the following: Capabilities (A), ConnectionIdentifier (I), DetectEvents (T), DigitMap (D), EventStates (ES), NotifiedEntity (N), ObservedEvents (O), RequestedEvents (R), RequestIdentifier (X) or SignalRequests (S). It may also contain either or both of LocalConnection-Descriptor(LC) and RemoteConnectionDescriptor(RC).

For example, the line:

```
F: D, A
```

tells the MTA to return its digit map and the MTA capabilities to the Call Agent.

RequestIdentifier (X)

The RequestIdentifier is contained in an NTFY message and identifies the particular RQNT to which the device is responding. The string containing the single digit "0" is used to report a persistent event for which no RQNT has been received.[5]

The format is a string of hexadecimal characters, not to exceed 32 characters in length.

ResponseAck (K)

A comma-separated series of Transaction IDs, or ranges of Transaction IDs. An example would be:

```
K: 663-671, 677, 690-705
```

This parameter is used to confirm to a gateway that a previously transmitted response has been received by the Call Agent. For example, the K: line above informs the gateway that the Call Agent has received transactions numbered 663 through 671, 677 and 690 through 705.

RestartDelay (RD)

A decimal number representing the number of seconds before a restart is going to occur.

For example, to inform the Call Agent that an endpoint is going to reboot in one minute's time:

```
RD: 60
```

RestartMethod (RM)

One of the following words indicating the kind of restart that is going to occur: graceful, forced, restart or disconnected. For example:

```
RM: forced
```

---

5. We have noted before that a persistent event is one whose occurrence is signaled even if it does not occur in the list of RequestedEvents. Typically, and as the name implies, a persistent event extends for a period of time rather than occurring at a single specific moment. For example, "off-hook" is a persistent event. (One can think of a persistent event as a particular kind of change of state in the endpoint.) MGCP per se offers little support for persistent events. The mechanism described in the text ensures that the Call Agent receives notification of persistent events even when it has not specifically requested notification.

SignalRequests (S)

This parameter contains a comma-separated list of signals that the MTA is instructed to perform. The complete list of defined signals for the analog access line package is provided in Table 4-7.

Table 4-7 Encoding for NCS SignalRequests

Signal Encoding	Meaning	Type	Comments
0,1,2,3,4,5,6,7,8,9,A,B,C,D,*,#	DTMF tones	BR	
bz	Busy (or "engaged") tone	TO	Default time-out 30 seconds
cf	Confirmation tone	BR	Typically used to indicate successful activation of a pay-per-use feature (often three brief tones in rapid succession)
ci(ti, nu, na)	Caller ID	BR	ti = time in the format "month/day/hour/minute" nu = number na = name
dl	Dial tone	TO	Default time-out 16 seconds
mwi	Message waiting indicator	TO	Default time-out 16 seconds
ot	Off-hook warning tone	TO	Never times out
r0, r1, r2, r3, r4, r5, r6, r7	Distinctive ringing	TO	Default time-out 3 minutes
rg	Ringing	TO	Default time-out 3 minutes
ro	Reorder tone	TO	Default time-out 30 seconds
rs	Ringsplash	BR	
rt	Ringback tone	C, TO	Default time-out 3 minutes
sl	Stutter dial tone	TO	Default time-out 16 seconds
vmwi	Visual message waiting indicator	OO	
wt1, wt2, wt3, wt4	Call waiting tones	BR	

Some signals can be qualified by one or more modifiers. Every signal has an associated signal type, which must be one of these.

- Brief (BR)
- On/Off (OO)
- Time-out (TO)

A plus sign (+) turns an On/Off signal on, and a minus sign (−) turns it off. An On/Off signal with no associated explicit plus or minus sign is assumed to have an implicit plus sign. For example, to signal an incoming call on the Caller-ID, the CA may include the following line.

```
S: ci(04/10/08/57, "303 123 4567", Addison-Wesley)
```

SpecificEndPointId (Z)

An e-mail-like string (that is, a string in RFC 821 format) comprising a sequence of characters, the "@" sign, the FQDN of the requesting entity, optionally followed by a colon and a port number. For example:

```
Z: aaln/1@MTA.subscriber.0123456789.co.ratco.com
```

Digit Maps

In any telephony system there has to be a device somewhere that has access to the digits as they are dialed by a subscriber and that can tell when the dialed digits constitute a completed phone number. In the PSTN, this device is the switch that is located at the phone company's central office. In an NCS network, the device that performs this task may be either the CMS or the MTA itself.

If the PacketCable network is configured in such a way that the CMS decides when a user has dialed a valid phone number, the CMS instructs the MTA to send an NTFY message every time that a digit is dialed (once the phone is off-hook and assuming that a call is not already in progress). Alternatively, the CMS may instruct the MTA to perform digit collection locally and send only a single Notify message containing the entire string of digits when the MTA itself has determined that the subscriber has finished dialing.

Regardless of which device actually performs this function, the mechanism is essentially the same in the two cases. The device (either CMS or MTA) contains a digit map, which is a pattern that represents all possible phone numbers. The idea is that all possible valid phone numbers match the pattern, but nothing that is not a phone number matches it. In other words, in order for a sequence of digits to be a valid phone number, it is both necessary and sufficient that it match the digit map.

In operation, dialed digits are matched, one at a time, as they are dialed, against the digit map until the device determines that a valid phone number has been dialed (typically, any additional dialed digits are simply ignored). Once the device has detected a complete match, appropriate action is taken. For example, if the dialed digits represent a destination phone number and the device is a CMS, the CMS will begin the process of setting up the call. If instead the device is an MTA, it will send an NTFY with the dialed-digit string to the CMS. The process is shown diagramatically in Figure 4-3.[6]

When the digit map is contained in a core network device such as a CMS, the details of the process by which the device examines the string of dialed digits for a match is usually a matter for the device manufacturer. When digit collection occurs

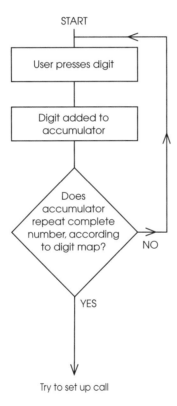

Figure 4-3 A Digit Map in Action

---

6. To be strictly accurate, the MTA might also contain a digit map designed to match only partially dialed numbers. It might, for example, look for a match to the U.S. international direct-dial prefix "011" and, when one occurs, send a NOTIFY containing this string to the Call Agent, which would then request further digits one at a time.

in an MTA, however, the manner in which a digit map is used has to be carefully specified, so that MTAs from different vendors behave identically.

In a PacketCable network, digit maps are expressed in a pattern-matching syntax derived from—but not quite identical to, although the differences are small—the UNIX **egrep** command. The *egrep*—"extended global regular expression pattern"—command is used to test a string of characters to see whether it matches a particular pattern. The syntax of the PacketCable MTA digit map can be described in the following BNF-like notation.

```
Digit ::= "0" | "1" | "2" | "3" | "4" | "5" | "6" | "7" | "8" | "9"
Timer ::= "T" | "t"
```

(used to detect a timer that has timed-out)

```
Letter ::= Digit | Timer | "#" | "*" | "A" | "a" | "B" | "b" | "C" | "c" |
"D" | "d"
Range ::= "X" | "x" (matches any digit) | "[" Letters "]"
```

(matches any of the letters specified in "Letters")

```
Subrange ::= Letter | Digit "-" Digit
```

(matches the specified letter or any digit between the first and last)

```
Letters ::= Subrange | Subrange Letters
Position ::= Letter | Range
StringElement ::= Position | Position "."
String ::= StringElement | StringElement String
StringList ::= String | String "|" StringList
DigitMap ::= String | "(" StringList ")"
```

When the user dials a number on an MTA that is collecting digits, the MTA processes each digit as follows.

1. Add the just-dialed digit to the internal "dialed number" string.

2. Attempt to match the "dialed number" string to the digit map.

3. If the result partially matches at least one entry in the digit map, do nothing.

4. If the result exactly matches an entry in the digit map, or if the "dialed number" string cannot possibly match any entry in the digit map no matter what digits are subsequently dialed, then the list of digits is sent to the Call Agent and the "dialed number" string is cleared.

By way of example, suppose that an MTA can dial the various kinds of numbers specified in Table 4-8.

The digit map for such an MTA could be encoded as:

```
(0T | 00T |  8xxxxx | *xx | 9303xxxxxxx | 9720xxxxxxx | 91xxxxxxxxx |
9011x.T)
```

Note the last entry, for international numbers. Different countries use different numbers of digits for telephone numbers. Furthermore, inside a single country, not all publicly accessible phone numbers necessarily have the same number of digits.[7] It is not possible to program an MTA with knowledge of all the various quirky international dialing plans in existence. Therefore, in this example, the MTA "cheats" by using a timer to recognize that the user has completed dialing the number. When the subscriber dials an international number, as long as she leaves only a relatively short period between digits, the MTA will continue to accumulate digits. When several seconds elapse without the subscriber dialing any more digits, the MTA assumes that he has finished dialing and sends the complete string to the CMS. Note, however, that the MTA might be provided with some additional information in the digit map. For example, it might be told that numbers beginning with 9011441, which correspond to numbers in the United Kingdom, must have at least six more digits to be considered a valid phone number.

Table 4-8 Example List of Possible Valid Phone Numbers

Dialed String	Connects with
0	Local operator
00	Long distance operator
8xxxx	Local extension number
*xx	Various "star" services
9303xxxxxxx or 9720xxxxxxx	Local number
91xxxxxxxxx	Long distance
9011 + many digits	International number

---

7. In the United States, all numbers follow the same basic format: three-digit area code, three-digit local exchange identifier, four-digit number, so that all numbers contain ten digits. In some countries the number of digits in a phone number may vary, depending on location (for example, in the United Kingdom).

Quarantine

In ordinary operation, an MTA will receive a list of events in which the CMS is interested. The CMS will send it a list of DetectEvents for events whose occurrence the MTA is simply to note and a list of RequestedEvents, which are to produce a specific action when they occur.

At some point, an event will occur that will cause the MTA to send a Notify message to the CMS indicating that fact. When the Notify is transmitted, the MTA begins to accumulate events for the endpoint in a quarantine buffer, which is a storage area in which it can queue outstanding events that have occurred but that the CMS is not yet prepared to process.

The MTA continues to accumulate events in the quarantine buffer until it receives a new RequestNotify command from the CMS. The RequestNotify will include a QuarantineHandling parameter, which has one of the two possible values `discard` or `process`. These perform the actions that you would expect of them. The contents of the quarantine buffer are either silently discarded or they are processed in accordance with the just-received RequestNotify message.

While processing a quarantine buffer, the MTA may reach a condition where it needs to send another Notify. It does so, and further events are accumulated in the quarantine buffer until a new RequestNotify is received. This is shown diagrammatically in Figure 4-4.

NCS and DQoS

Dynamic Quality of Service (**DQoS**) is the mechanism by which PacketCable networks assure subscribers of guaranteed quality on bearer-channel virtual circuits. The DQoS mechanism, which we will discuss at length in Chapter 6, is signaling-protocol-neutral. That is, it was designed to be usable with any reasonable signaling protocol. It does, however, require support from that protocol, since some DQoS-related information needs to be carried in various call signaling messages.

In **NCS**, the necessary information is carried to the MTA in the LocalConnection Options parameter. Four fields carry the DQoS-related information.

DQoS instantiates resource **gates** on the local CMTS. Each two-way call will typically have two gates allocated, one upstream and one downstream. Both gates share a single 32-bit identifier known as a GateID. The value of this GateID is contained in the `dq-gi:` field, as a string of at most 8 hexadecimal characters. For example:

```
dq-gi: 0FE357AC
```

Mimicking the two-stage process by which DOCSIS resources are made available, DQoS does likewise. DQoS resources may be either merely reserved (corresponding to the DOCSIS admitted state), or they may be committed (corresponding

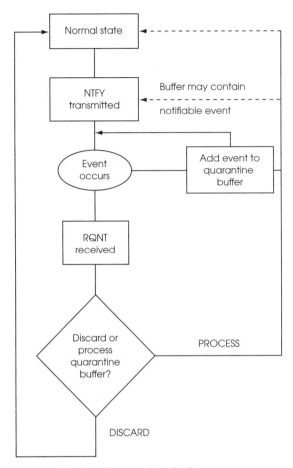

Figure 4-4 The Quarantine Buffer

to the DOCSIS active state). In addition, the resources may be allocated in either the upstream or downstream direction, or in both directions. Each of these possibilities is encoded within the dq-rr: field, according to Table 4-9.

A normal two-way connection with guaranteed quality committed in both directions is therefore encoded as:

```
dq-rr: snrccomt
```

In addition to the GateID, the CMTS maintains a ResourceID that uniquely identifies the actual set of resources in use. The ResourceID is encoded within a dq-ri: field; like the GateID it is a 32-bit value encoded as a hexadecimal string.

In simple calls, neither the GateID nor the ResourceID will change for the lifetime of the call. However, for calls that use some features (such as call waiting, three-way

Table 4-9 Encoding of `dq-rr:` Parameter

Field value	Meaning
sendresv	Reserved, upstream only
recvresv	Reserved, downstream only
snrcresv	Reserved, bidirectional
sendcomt	Committed, upstream only
recvcomt	Committed, downstream only
snrccomt	Committed, bidirectional

calling, or mid-call codec changes) the identity of one or both of these fields might change as the feature is invoked. A typical example ResourceID looks like this.

```
dq-ri: AC 0FE357
```

The final field is the ReserveDestination field, `dq-rd:`. This contains the IP address, along with an optional port number, of the device (typically an MTA or MG) at the far end of the virtual circuit. For example:

```
dq-rd: 10.10.10.1:54321
```

Event Packages

Event packages are used to (gasp!) package events. A package is a collection of events (or signals—the nomenclature is rather sloppy in that sometimes the term *event package* is used to include signals as well as events) that may be used by a particular type of endpoint. The package defines shorthand codes for all the events and/or signals that it contains. PacketCable version 1.0 defines two packages, both used for analog access lines: the "Line" package (abbreviated by the letter L) and the "ADSI" package (abbreviated by the letter S). The Line Package is the default; ADSI is used only for textual display of short messages.

An event or signal is fully described by using the abbreviation for the package, followed by a slash and then the code defined by the package for the event in question. For example, in the Line package, the dialtone signal has the abbreviation "dl". The correct abbreviation for "dialtone in the Line package" is therefore L/dl. However, since the Line package is the default for analog access lines, the package can be elided, and the signal may be referenced simply as "dl".

Table 4-7 gives a list of all the signals in the Line package; Table 4-10 provides a similar listing of the events in the Line package.

Table 4-10 Events Defined by the Line Package

Event Encoding	Meaning	Comments
0,1,2,3,4,5,6,7,8,9,A,B,C,D,*,#	DTMF tones	
aw	Answer tone	2100 Hz tone for answer by modem or fax
ft	Fax tone	Generated when a fax call is detected
hd	Off-hook	
hf	Hook flash	A hook flash is a quick on-hook/ off-hook sequence
hu	On-hook	
L	Long-duration DTMF tones	Generated when a DTMF tone has continued for two seconds
ld	Long-duration connection	Generated when a connection has been in existence for one hour
ma	Media start	Generated when the first valid RTP packet is detected on a connection
mt	Modem tones	Generated when a modem call is detected
oc	Operation complete	Generated when one or more TO signals was completed without detection of a requested event
of	Operation failure	Generated when one or more TO signals failed before timing out
t	Timer	A timer that is cancelled by DTMF input; generally used during digit accumulation
TDD	TDD tones	Generated when a TDD (Telecommunications Devices for the Deaf) call is detected
X	Wildcard for DTMF tones	Matches any digit

Responses

In NCS, it is mandatory for any device receiving a command to return a response. Since NCS messages travel over UDP, receipt of a response is the originating device's assurance that the original command was received correctly (as well as possibly returning useful information to the originating device).

Just like commands, responses contain human-readable headers. They may also have a body, separated from the headers by an empty line. Response headers contain a single "response line", which may be followed by further lines that encode response parameters. Like commands, responses are formatted as plain ASCII strings, delimited by either CRLF pairs or by single LFs.

The response line, which is always the first line in a response, begins with a three-digit response code, followed by white space and then the transaction number of the command to which the response applies. The transaction number is optionally followed by further white space and human-readable commentary or explanation.

For example:

```
200 1201 OK
```

is a valid single-line response. The response code is 200, the transaction number is 1201, and the human-readable explanation is OK. This is a typical response to a command that has been successfully executed and which requires no returned parameter values.

Figure 4-5 shows the structure of a valid response. Table 4-11 provides a list of all the defined response codes. The general rules are as follows.

000

> This is a special code used to acknowledge a final response. It is typically used as a response to a 2xx code when an earlier 1xx code was received, thereby indicating receipt of the final (2xx) response.

1xx

> A provisional response.

2xx

> The command has completed successfully.

4xx

> The command has encountered a transient error.

5xx

> The command cannot be executed because of a permanent error.

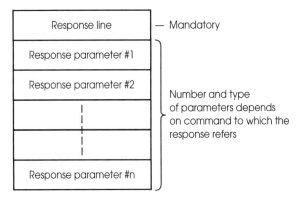

Figure 4-5 NCS Command Response Structure

Table 4-11 NCS Response Codes

Code	Meaning
000	Response acknowledgement
100	Transaction is being executed. A final response will follow later.
200	The requested transaction was completed without error.
250	The connection(s) was/were deleted.
400	The transaction could not be completed due to a transient error.
401	The phone is off-hook.
402	The phone is on-hook.
500	Endpoint is unknown.
501	Endpoint is not ready.
502	Endpoint has insufficient resources.
510	Protocol error
511	Command contains an unrecognized extension.
512	Gateway is not equipped to detect one of the requested events.
513	Gateway is not equipped to generate one of the requested signals.
514	Gateway cannot send the specified announcement.
515	Invalid connection ID (may have already been deleted)
516	Unknown call ID

(continued)

Table 4-11 NCS Response Codes (*cont.*)

Code	Meaning
517	Unsupported or invalid mode
518	Unsupported or invalid package
519	Endpoint does not have a digit map.
520	Endpoint is restarting (rebooting).
521	Endpoint redirected to another Call Agent.
522	No such event or signal
523	Unknown action, or illegal combination of actions
524	Internal inconsistency in LocalConnectionOptions
525	Unknown extension in LocalConnectionOptions
526	Insufficient bandwidth
527	Missing RemoteConnectionDescriptor
528	Incompatible protocol version
529	Internal hardware failure
532	Unsupported value(s) in LocalConnectionOptions
533	Response too large

Response Parameters

NCS recognizes a total of 21 different response parameters. Like command parameters, each of these has its own short code. Table 4-12 lists all of the allowed parameters along with their shortened code. The table also indicates whether each parameter is Mandatory, Optional or Forbidden in a response to every possible command. The LocalConnectionDescriptor and the RemoteConnectionDescriptor are not parameters in the same sense as all the other entries in the table. Instead, they are part of the message body, and contain a Session Description Protocol (SDP) description of either the local or the remote connection. For more details on encoding session descriptions, see later in the chapter.

Many of these parameters are identical to a parameter that may be present in a command. We will not repeat an explanation of the meaning of these parameters here. Some parameters, however, may appear only in a response. These parameters are the following.

Table 4-12 NCS Response Parameters

Parameter Name	Code	AUCX	AUEP	CRCX	DLCX	MDCX	NTFY	RQNT	RSIP
CallId	C	O	F	F	F	F	F	F	F
Capabilities	A	F	O	F	F	F	F	F	F
ConnectionId	I	F	O	M	F	F	F	F	F
ConnectionMode	M	O	F	F	F	F	F	F	F
ConnectionParameters	P	O	F	F	O	F	F	F	F
DetectEvents	T	F	O	F	F	F	F	F	F
DigitMap	D	F	O	F	F	F	F	F	F
EventStates	ES	F	O	F	F	F	F	F	F
LocalConnectionDescriptor		O	F	M	F	O	F	F	F
LocalConnectionOptions	L	O	O	F	F	F	F	F	F
NotifiedEntity	N	O	O	F	F	F	F	F	O
NumEndPoints	ZN	F	O	F	F	F	F	F	F
ObservedEvents	O	F	O	F	F	F	F	F	F
RemoteConnectionDescriptor		O	F	F	F	F	F	F	F
RequestedEvents	R	F	O	F	F	F	F	F	F
RequestIdentifier	X	F	O	F	F	F	F	F	F
ResourceId	DQ-RI	F	F	O	F	O	F	F	F
ResponseAck	K	O	O	O	O	O	O	O	O
SignalRequests	S	F	O	F	F	F	F	F	F
SpecificEndPointId	Z	F	O	O	F	F	F	F	F
VersionSupported	VS	F	O	F	F	F	F	F	O

EventStates (ES)

This is a comma-separated list of events and is used only in the response to an AUEP command. The events correspond to the current state of the end-point. For example, if the endpoint is in the off-hook state, then the list will include the off-hook event. For example:

```
ES: hd
```

NumEndPoints (ZN)

> A string of decimal digits whose length does not exceed 16 characters. This is the number of endpoints currently supported by the MTA.

ResourceId (DQ-RI)

> The ResourceID is used by PacketCable DQoS signaling. It represents the resource ID of the DQoS gate in question. It is a 32-bit quantity, encoded as a series of hex characters.

VersionSupported (VS)

> A comma-separated list of the protocol version supported. For example, an endpoint that can support both plain MGCP and the NCS profile of MGCP might return the following:

```
VS: MGCP 1.0 NCS 1.0, MGCP 1.0
```

The ResponseAck parameter has special behavior: It is used only to indicate a final response after a provisional response has already been issued for the transaction in question. The ResponseAck triggers transmission of a special Response Acknowledgement message, and any values provided in the ResponseAck are ignored.

The LocalConnectionDescriptor and RemoteConnectionDescriptor are transmitted as the body of the message, using the Session Description Protocol encoding as described in the section "Encoding Session Descriptions". We will now briefly look at the allowed responses to each of the various possible command messages.

Response to CRCX

The response header to a CreateConnection message contains the ConnectionID of the connection that was created. The body of the response contains a LocalConnection-Descriptor that fully describes the parameters associated with the connection. If there has been a prior provisional response, the final response may contain a ResponseAck. If DQoS has been allocated for this connection, the ResourceID of the DQoS gate is also contained in the message.

For example:

```
200 3433 OK
K:
I: AA02FE56
DQ-RI: 0012FFBC
```

```
v=0
o=- 25678 753849 IN IP4 128.96.4.1
s=-
c=IN IP4 128.96.41.1
t=0 0
m=audio 3456 RTP/AVP 96
a=rtpmap:96 G726-32/8000
```

This header of this response contains a ResponseAck (the K: line), indicating that there was an earlier provisional response. It also contains the necessary ConnectionID and a DQoS ResourceID. The SDP in the body of the message contains the parameters for the connection identified by the ConnectionID.[8]

Since the example contains a ResponseAck, it will be acknowledged by a Response Acknowledgement message, which is a simple message containing a single line with a response code of 000, followed by white space and the transaction ID.

```
000 3433
```

Response to MDCX

The Response Line of a response to an MDCX is the only mandatory header line. If the connection is associated with a DQoS gate (as is usually the case), the ResourceID must also be included. In the body of the response, the LocalConnectionDescriptor is included, but only if the MDCX resulted in a change of the SDP parameters. Note, however, that merely changing the mode of a connection (for example, from sendonly to sendrecv) does not cause any change in the SDP parameters, and therefore the LocalConnectionDescriptor would not be included in such a response. The following example is a valid response to an MDCX.

```
200 5433 OK
DQ-RI: 668901AE

v=0
o=- 25678 753849 IN IP4 128.96.4.1
s=-
c=IN IP4 128.96.41.1
t=0 0
m=audio 3456 RTP/AVP 96
a=rtpmap:96 G726-32/8000
```

---

8. See the section "Encoding Session Descriptions" for a more detailed discussion of SDP.

As before, if the response is a final response containing a ResponseAck, the response will be acknowledged by a Response Acknowledgement message from the Call Agent.

Response to DLCX

The response to a DLCX contains only header lines. It may contain a single response line, or if the command requested them, it may also contain a ConnectionParameters line giving the values pertaining to the connection that has just been deleted, as in the following example.

```
250 2862 OK
P: PS=1234, OS=62345, PR=780, OR=45123, PL=10, JI=27, LA=48
```

Note, however, that MTAs are always untrusted devices (an MTA could, for example, be implemented as easily hacked software running on a PC, at least theoretically). As such, it is important that information about the quality of a connection as returned by an MTA not be relied upon. A good rule of thumb is to regard the MTA as a hacked piece of software that will always act in its own best interest, regardless of the requirements of the PacketCable specifications. The PacketCable security team did a good job of ensuring that even hacked MTAs cannot subvert the network in any meaningful way.

Suppose, for example, that Agatha places a billable call to Bertram, and, as soon as the call is over, she calls the operator to complain about the quality of the connection. The operator should not rely only on the ConnectionParameters returned by the MTA when the DLCX was issued to determine whether the connection was really flawed, since Agatha might have altered her MTA to return incorrect values. In the aggregate, however (that is, when data from many hundreds or thousands of MTAs are available), such data may be useful to the network operator as he tries to optimize his network.

Response to RQNT

The response to a NotificationRequest contains only this response line.

```
200 6088 OK
```

Response to NTFY

The response to a Notify contains only this response line.

```
200 9524 OK
```

Response to AUEP

The response to an AuditEndPoint command (which may be for a specific endpoint or for a number of—usually all—endpoints) is followed by the requested information for each of the parameters of the AUEP. Each parameter appears on a separate line. If the endpoint receives a request for a parameter that currently has no assigned value, a line containing simply the code for the parameter is returned. For example, the following indicates an unassigned digit map.

```
D:
```

If a parameter has multiple values (for example, the endpoint may have multiple sets of Capabilities), multiple lines are returned, each with the same parameter code. For example (note that each response would be transmitted on a single line, but the constraints of formatting on the page requires us to split each response over two lines):

```
A: a:PCMU;G728, p:10-100, e:on, s:off, t:1,
          v:L, m:sendonly;recvonly;sebdrecv;inactive
A: a:G729A; p:30-90, e:on, s:on, t:1,
          v:L, m:sendonly;recvonly;sendrecv;inactive;confrnce
```

Response to AUCX

The response to an AuditConnection command is followed by the requested information for each of the parameters in the AUCX. Each parameter appears on a separate line. If the endpoint receives a request for a parameter that currently has no assigned value, a line containing simply the code for the parameter is returned.

If both local and remote connection information is returned, the local information appears first. If a connection descriptor is requested but does not exist, the returned SDP contains only the single line showing the SDP version number (the v= line).

For example:

```
200 5747 OK
C: 75AF8EB4C10AA5F
N: [128.96.41.12]
L: p:10, a:PCMU;G728
M: sendrecv
P: PS=622, OS=311172, PR=390, OR=22561, PL=5, JI=29, LA=50

v=0
o=- 4723891 7428910 IN IP4
128.96.63.25
```

```
s=-c=
IN IP4 128.96.63.25
t=0 0
m=audio 1296 RTP/AVP 96
a=rtpmap:96 G726-32/8000
```

Response to RSIP

The response to a RestartInProgress may include the name of another Call Agent that the endpoint may contact. This allows the call to proceed when the primary Call Agent is unavailable. For example:

```
521 666 Redirect
N: CA2@ratco.net
```

Encoding Session Descriptions

Session description information (that is, the high-level operational parameters for a connection) is encoded in a simplified version of the Session Description Protocol as defined in RFC 2327. As in RFC 2327, session descriptions are case sensitive, unlike the NCS headers.

In NCS, only the parameters specified in this section are used (RFC 2327 itself describes many other parameters; these are unused in NCS). No other parameters are transmitted, and if received, they are ignored. The parameters must be present in the order in which they are described below, although not all parameters are present in every session description.

Permitted Session Description Parameters

Table 4-13 provides a complete list of NCS Session Description parameters. Note that according to RFC 2327, no whitespace may surround the equals sign. They are described more fully in the following subsections.

Protocol Version

The protocol version is zero (0).
Example:

```
v=0
```

Origin

The Origin field comprises six subfields separated by white space.

Table 4-13 SDP Parameter Encodings

Parameter Name	SDP Encoding
Protocol Version	v=
Origin	o=
Session Name	s=
Connection Data	c=
Bandwidth	b=
Time	t=
Encryption Keys	k=
Attributes	a=
Media Announcements	m=

username

In NCS, the username is always a hyphen (-) to protect the privacy of the calling party

session-ID

Usually a timestamp (to ensure uniqueness) but may be any value.

version

Usually a timestamp (to ensure uniqueness) but may be any value.

network-type

Always IN (meaning "Internet").

address-type

Always IP4.

address

Either the FQDN or the address of device in dotted decimal representation.

On receipt all of the fields are ignored. This is an example of a not infrequent occurrence in PacketCable. Many times the messages contain information that is redundant, unused or occasionally even plain silly. This is not because the designers were either incompetent or inebriated, but is instead an unfortunate consequence of the decision to use standard preexisting protocols wherever possible. Many times, these protocols require that certain messages, parameters or fields be sent, even when they make little or no sense in PacketCable. In this particular case, RFC 2327 requires that the o= line be present with the designated fields. Therefore it is included in PacketCable transmissions, even though PacketCable devices ignore the information when it is received.

Example:

```
o=- 15463295 15463295 IN IP4 192.10.20.30
```

Session Name

In order to protect the privacy of the calling party, the Session Name must always be encoded as a hyphen (-).

```
s=-
```

Connection Data

The Connection Data field comprises three subfields, separated by white space.

network-type

> Always IN (meaning "Internet").

address-type

> Always IP4.

connection-address

> The connection-address is an IP address at which the endpoint is prepared to receive media traffic. In NCS, an MTA must use the same address for both sending and receiving, so this is also the address from which the MTA will transmit media packets.

So, for example:

```
c=IN IP4 192.30.40.50
```

Bandwidth

Bandwidth data are required so that the PacketCable DQoS mechanisms can allocate bandwidth resources correctly. If the Attributes line includes either an rtpmap or the name of a PacketCable-defined codec, the bandwidth data do not have to be included in a separate b= line. However, for ease of implementation it is recommended that the bandwidth requirement is explicitly defined in a Bandwidth line.

The Bandwidth parameter is given as the string "AS:" followed by an integer representing the maximum bandwidth requirement of the media stream in kilobits per second, for example:

```
b=AS:120
```

The value specified is the application's notion of the maximum bandwidth required. In other words, it includes all the additional low-level packetization and link-layer overhead, as well as the basic output from the codec.

Time

The Time field comprises two subfields, separated by white space.

```
start-time stop-time
```

The start time should be the current time (although it may also be given as zero, which is interpreted as "now"). The stop time is zero (which is interpreted as "at infinity"). The times are encoded as decimal representations of Network Time Protocol (NTP) time values in seconds. NTP time values correspond to UNIX time values plus 2208988800. NTP time is the number of seconds since zero hours UTC on January 1, 1900. Details of NTP are in RFC 1129.

For example:

```
t=2219289835 0
```

Encryption Keys

Encryption keys and security algorithm information for securing bearer traffic are normally passed in the k= line of SDP in networks that are compliant with RFC 1889, 1890 and 2327. However, NCS does not support passing keys through this mechanism. No PacketCable NCS SDP encoding should ever include a k= line, because PacketCable uses a completely different mechanism to pass security information. PacketCable relies on special extension attributes (an extension attribute is an attribute whose name begins with the string x-) to pass the necessary security information, as we discuss in the following section.

Attributes

The attributes associated with a connection are listed on a= lines. An SDP description may, and usually does, contain more than one such line, each specifying a different attribute. Attributes may be either *property attributes* or *value attributes*.

Property attributes are used to indicate that the session has a particular property. Value attributes are used to associate a value with a property.

A property attribute for the property PROP is encoded by the following.

```
a=PROP
```

A value attribute for the property PROP with the value VAL is encoded by the following.

```
a=PROP:VAL
```

The property attributes recognized by NCS are sendonly, recvonly and sendrecv, and are used to indicate whether a flow is unidirectional or bidirectional. For example,

```
a=sendrecv
```

indicates that the session described by this SDP is bidirectional.

NCS also recognizes several value attributes. The most important of these are used to convey information about the codec in use. This information is encoded using the rtpmap mechanism discussed in the section "RTPMAPs." A typical example of an rtpmap attribute is:

```
a=rtpmap:96 PCMU/8000
```

This example indicates that RTP packets of type 96 are associated with the PCMU codec (which is another name for G.711) sampled 8,000 times per second.

Several extension attributes (attributes whose names begin with X-) are also used by NCS. Extensions used by PacketCable begin with the string X-pc-.

X-pc-codecs

In future versions of PacketCable, a robust mechanism will be specified to allow two endpoints to negotiate among the set of codecs that they have in common.[9] At present, endpoints merely select the first codec that they have in common. The X-pc-codecs attribute line is used to provide a list of supported codecs, in order of decreasing preference.

---

9. This, like most things in telephony once you start thinking about them, is not a trivial task. The person who pays for the call is the one who should make the final decision as to which codec to use. Trying to perform this negotiation without several round-trip messages—which would add an unacceptable delay—is not easy and was deferred to a later version of PacketCable.

For example, an endpoint that can support G711 digitized at either 8,000, 10,000 or 12,000 times per second, with a preference for the first of these, would signal those capabilities through.

```
a=X-pc-codecs: PCMU/8000 PCMU/10000 PCMU/12000
```

X-pc-secret

Security for the RTP and RTCP traffic between PacketCable MTAs is based on a shared secret, from which the necessary keying material is derived (see the section "Encrypting RTP Packets" for complete details). The value of this secret, which is the same for both the RTP and the RTCP streams in both directions (that is, all four streams use the same secret), is placed on the X-pc-secret line. The encoding is of the form <method>:<value>, where <method> describes the method of encoding the secret, and <value> is the value of the secret.

<method> may be either "clear" or "BASE64". BASE64 encoding is a method for converting arbitrary binary strings into a format that contains only ASCII printable characters. Details of the encoding are provided in Appendix C.

Since only printable characters are valid in NCS messages, it is unlikely that any reasonable implementation would choose to use the "clear:" encoding, since that can be used only with keys that themselves contain only ASCII printable characters—highly unlikely if the keys are being generated by a good pseudorandom generator (as they should be).

An example line for transmitting a shared secret is (in practice, this would be transmitted on a single line):

```
a= X-pc-secret: base64:pV6BIIHWt+
        0gDkpgnuxgTfROxYAemhYJTHWgHNt1crTtEUKFatJfSdEFVQuueo==
```

X-pc-csuites-rtp and X-pc-csuites-rtcp

These fields are used to list the ciphersuites that the endpoint is capable of using in a manner similar to that used for codecs in the X-pc-codecs field. The first ciphersuite in the list is the one that the endpoint is expecting to use, with alternatives listed in decreasing order of preference.

A ciphersuite is encoded as a pair of ASCII-encoded single hexadecimal digits, separated by a slash ("/").

```
Authentication_algorithm/Encryption_algorithm
```

Values for which support is guaranteed are given in Tables 4-14 through 4-17.

So, for example, if the endpoint supports RC4 with any authentication mechanism on RTP, but with a preference for the 4-octet MMH HMAC authentication, and 3DES CBC encryption with SHA-1 authentication on RTCP, it would indicate this by sending this.

```
a=X-pc-csuites-rtp: 64/51 62/51 0/51
a=X-pc-csuites-rtcp: 02/03
```

Table 4-14 IPsec Authentication Algorithm Codes (Used for RTCP)

Algorithm Description	Key Length (Bits)	Code
MD5 HMAC	128	01
SHA-1 HMAC	160	02

Table 4-15 IPsec Authentication Algorithm Codes (Used for RTCP)

Algorithm Description	Key Length (Bits)	Code
3DES CBC	192	03
No Encryption	0	11

Table 4-16 Bearer Authentication Algorithm Codes (Used for RTP)

Algorithm Description	Key Length (Bits)	Code
No Authentication	0	0
2-octet MMH HMAC	Variable (same as message length, see section "Procedure for Encrypting and Decrypting")	62
4-octet MMH HMAC	Variable (same as message length, see section "Procedure for Encrypting and Decrypting")	64

Table 4-17 Bearer Encryption Algorithm Codes (Used for RTP)

Algorithm Description	Key Length (Bits)	Code
RC4 stream cipher	128	51

X-pc-spi-rtcp

> IPsec connections require a Security Parameter Index (SPI) to identify the precise parameters to be used on the connection (see the section "Security Parameter Index (SPI)" in Chapter 2). The RTCP connection between endpoints is secured by IPsec, and the X-pc-spi-rtcp field of the SDP is used to pass the value of the SPI to be used for this connection. It is a 32-bit number that is transmitted as a series of up to 8 ASCII-encoded hex characters.

Media Announcements

The final parameter carried by the SDP is the Media Announcements field, which comprises four subfields separated by white space.

```
m=<media> <port> <transport> <format>
```

The <media> value is always "audio" in a pure telephony network.

The port is the number of the port on which the MTA will receive data. The number of the transmitting port may or may not be the same, but in either case it is not specified in the SDP description of the connection.

The transport type always has the value "RTP/AVP", which corresponds to the Real-time Transport Protocol (RFC 1889) using the Audio/Video profile carried over UDP (RFC 1890).

The format is one of the format numbers defined in RFC 1890. Usually, the format number is 0, which corresponds to μ-law PCM encoded single-channel audio sampled at 8 kHz. The format number is inserted into RTP packets and the m= line tells the receiving device what codec to use to correctly decode a packet with a particular format number. See the next section for more details.

So, for example, the Media Announcements line for an audio stream of RTP packets of μ-law PCM encoded single-channel audio sampled at 8 kHz that will be received on port 22954 would look like this.

```
m=audio 22954 RTP/AVP 0
```

RTPMAPs

Bearer-channel packets (such as voice conversations) are formatted according to the specifications in RFCs 1889 and 1890, which specify the format for the Real-Time Transport Protocol, RTP. An RTP packet header includes a 7-bit payload type field, which informs the recipient of the codec format of the data in the packet. The RFCs define a number of static mappings between the value in the payload field and the codec used to generate the packet. For example, the payload type 0 corresponds to

8000-sample-per-second μ-law PCM encoding (in other words, G.711 with 0.125 milli-second samples, which is a very common sample rate in telephony networks).

However, there may be occasions when a pair of endpoints wish to communicate using a nonstandard codec or a packetization interval that is not explicitly included in the RFCs. This need is accommodated by using *dynamic* payload mappings.

Dynamic payload mappings are signaled in the m= and a= lines of the SDP. The a= line is used to define the mapping between a codec and a payload type as signaled in the RTP header. Payload types in the range from 96 to 127 are allocated to dynamic mappings. The format is:

```
a=rtpmap:<payload type> <encoding type>/<packetization rate>
```

The string rtpmap: indicates that what follows is a mapping between the number contained in the RTP header and the type of payload carried by the packet.

So, for example, let's suppose that the endpoints want to use G711 encoding, but with 10,000 instead of 8,000 samples per second. They would signal this by the following a= line.

```
a=rtpmap:96 PCMU/10000
```

Now the recipient knows that when it sees an RTP packet with the payload type 96, it is to be interpreted as a 10,000-sample-per-second μ-law PCM encoded packet.

Before the media can actually be sent, the SDP also associates a media type with the connection, via the m= line. So, if the port number associated with the connection is 24680, the SDP would also include the following line.

```
m=audio 24680 RTP/AVP 96
```

This tells the recipient to prepare itself to handle RTP packets with payload type 96 on port number 24680. Payload type 96, as we have just seen, has been dynamically assigned to correspond to 10,000 samples-per-second μ-law PCM encoded information.

Message Transmission

As we mentioned earlier, all NCS signaling messages travel over UDP, which provides no automatic mechanism to allow the transmitter to know that the receiver actually receives packets that have been sent to it. In order to be certain that transmitted messages have actually been received, all commands require that a response be sent in the opposite direction. The lack of a response in a reasonable time indicates to the transmitter that either the original message was not received or that the response was lost. When this occurs, the transmitter must retransmit the command, and it must continue to do so either until it receives a response or until so many attempts have been made that it is reasonable to conclude that the link has been lost and an appropriate error should be flagged.

Since its response may be lost, if a network entity receives a command that is an exact duplicate of one that it has already completed, it should send the response as usual but must not take any further action in addition to that which it already took when it processed the original command. In other words, it should simply repeat the prior response without performing any associated action. A transaction ID is included in all commands so that the recipient will be able to determine whether a received command is a duplicate (that is, a retransmission) of a previously sent command or a new command to be acted on as normal. For example, in the command

```
DLCX 63991 aaln/1@flemmingsMTA.nj.ratco.com MGCP 1.0 NCS 1.0
```

the number immediately following the command name is the transaction ID (63991 in this example).

One twist to PacketCable networks lies in the fact that some network entities may be implemented as clusters of devices that may not all share the same transmit IP address. A good example is a *clustered NCS Call Agent,* wherein a Call Agent is implemented as a cluster of small computers, each of which may have its own IP address.

The endpoint may send a command to the IP address of a "controller" computer in a cluster. The controller will pass the message to another computer in the cluster for processing and response. Alternatively, the recipient computer might be heavily loaded and might in real-time determine that another computer in the cluster has more processing power available to deal with the command, and so it might hand off the command to the lightly loaded computer for processing and response.

In either case, the response to a Notify (for example) might come from a different IP address than the one to which it was sent, as shown in Figure 4-6. Since the MTA must be able to accommodate such a situation, it must use the transaction ID contained in the response—*not the IP address from which the response came*—to match responses with transmitted commands.

The retransmission strategy used to resend commands to which no response is received is similar to that used by the Transmission Control Protocol, TCP. TCP is not used directly, however, because an application has little control over the parameters that control the TCP retransmission strategy. By using a similar mechanism within the NCS application itself, a network operator can more easily adapt the retransmission timers to the needs of his particular network.

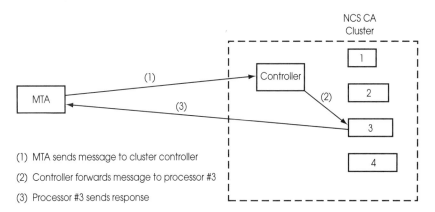

Figure 4-6 Messaging and Clustered NCS Call Agents

Two variables control the retransmission rate.

- AAD—The average acknowledgement delay, AAD, which is estimated through an exponentially smoothed average of the observed delays.

- ADEV—The average deviation, estimated through an exponentially smoothed average of the absolute value of the difference between the observed delay and the current average.

The retransmission timer T_r (measured in seconds) is set to the sum (AAD + N * ADEV), where N is a constant, at the time that a command is transmitted.

If T_r expires without receipt of the corresponding response, the command is retransmitted, and a new value of T_r calculated as follows.

1. The value of AAD is doubled.

2. A pseudorandom number, P, uniformly distributed on (0.5, AAD) is calculated.

3. T_r is set to the minumum of either (P + N * ADEV) or some maximum provisioned value, typically 4 seconds.

In the absence of a good estimate of AAD (such as when the connection is newly established), the initial value of T_r is set to some preprovisioned value, typically 200 milliseconds.

Piggybacking Messages

Several NCS messages may be concatenated into a single UDP packet in a process called "piggybacking". Piggybacked messages are separated from one another by a line with the single character "." (ASCII character 46). If a piggybacked message needs to be retransmitted because a response was not received, the entire original message is retransmitted, not just the command(s) for which no response was received.

Provisional Responses

There are occasions when a command may take a significant amount of time to process, with the result that there may be a considerable delay before the correct response can be returned. When this happens, the retransmission timer T_r is likely to expire, causing an already-received command to be unnecessarily retransmitted. To prevent this waste of bandwidth, PacketCable uses *provisional responses*.

Theoretically, a provisional response might be an appropriate mechanism whenever a network entity responsible for performing some action in response to a command has reason to believe that the action may take more than some small amount of time to complete. Also theoretically, a provisional response need contain no information other than the fact that the command or request was received and is being acted on. However, NCS PacketCable networks violate these theoretical dicta in two ways.

1. Provisional responses are sent only in response to CRCX and MDCX commands.

2. A connection identifier and the SDP for the connection (if any, in the case of an MDCX) is included in the provisional response.

When the command finally completes successfully and the final response is sent, the SDP information is also included in the final response. The SDP in the final response must be identical to that in the provisional response. If the command fails, then a normal error response is sent, containing no SDP.

It is mandatory for the final response to a request or command for which a provisional response has been sent to include a ResponseAck (a request that the response be acknowledged). The reason for this is as follows.

Ordinarily, the failure to receive a response quickly will cause retransmission of the original command. Once a provisional response has been received, however, the originator of the command knows that the command was received correctly, and it has no need to retransmit it. Suppose, however, that the final response is lost. There needs to be a mechanism that can cause the final response to be retransmitted, and the ResponseAck provides that mechanism. Figure 4-7 shows an example of provisional and final responses in an NCS network.

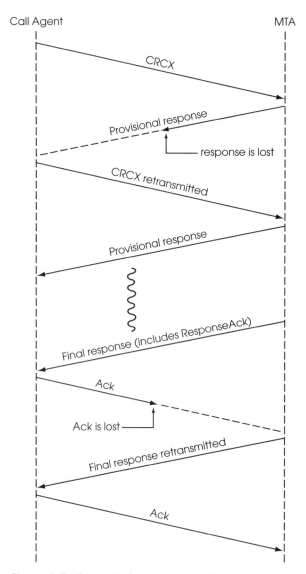

Figure 4-7 Example Provisional and Final Responses in an NCS network

Security

NCS provides no security in and of itself. The messages are all plain ASCII text and therefore easily readable, and even subject to change, by an intruder. This is, of course, an unacceptable risk in a network carrying telephony signaling. Therefore, in PacketCable networks, all NCS signaling is carried over IPsec connections. As well as being itself secured, NCS signaling is used to carry additional security information needed to secure the actual bearer traffic (the phone conversations).

IPsec is discussed in Chapter 2. The essential notion is that an IPsec connection (or "pipe") connects two IP addresses in such a way that IP traffic traveling through the pipe cannot be read or undetectably altered by a malicious third party. The IPsec pipes used to carry NCS call signaling are set up asynchronously—that is, apart from the fact that a pipe has to exist before a message can pass through it, the creation, deletion and control of pipes happens without reference to the messaging that is happening in the network. For this reason, whenever we present a call flow in this book, the security messaging is not included; the security mechanisms are not directly associated with the progress of a call.

Before we can see how NCS carries the security information needed to ensure that phone conversations are private, we need to look in some detail at the kinds of security that PacketCable applies to the bearer channel (the actual voice traffic).

Bearer-Channel Security

IPsec connections generally take several hundred milliseconds to initialize correctly—or even longer if the network path taken by the setup messages is not very reliable. In addition, IPsec connections require several end-to-end messages be passed between the devices that will communicate via the pipe. In a real-time telephony network with limited access bandwidth, a better alternative is to use application-level security for the end-to-end voice communications. In other words, the voice information travels over ordinary unsecured IP, but higher-level mechanisms are used to assure privacy and message integrity (see Figure 4-8).

It almost goes without saying that it is of paramount importance that the contents of communications traveling through a (nonwireless) telephony network are expected to remain private. Any network operator who provided a system that did not meet this basic need would surely not remain in business for long after the first

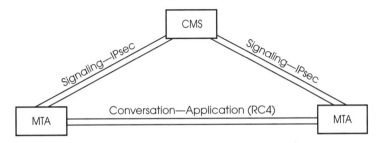

Figure 4-8 IPsec and Application-Level Security in a PacketCable Telephone Conversation

intercepted conversation between private individuals was replayed on the evening news (or, more likely these days, on a Web site in streaming audio).

The method used to ensure that this cannot happen to conversations carried over PacketCable networks is to encrypt all packets carrying audio with the RC4 stream cipher. RC4 is covered in some detail in Chapter 2. Here we will describe its implementation and use in PacketCable.

Almost as important as privacy in telephony communications is an assurance that packets cannot be manipulated undetectably en route from transmitter to receiver. In ordinary audio person-to-person conversations, this is not generally a great threat (imagine the sophistication it would require for a malicious third party to change my "Yes, of course that's OK" to a "No way" in such a manner that you might be fooled by it).

However, not all "conversations" occurring over an audio path are person-to-person. A fax call might be more easily manipulated by an intervening entity, changing black pixels to white, and vice versa, and thereby changing the meaning of a transmission.

In general, unless the intervening entity knows the RC4 key that the two conversing parties share, he cannot make changes in a coordinated manner (in other words, he can insert packets that are meaningless when decrypted, but he cannot in general insert a packet with specific meaning without knowing the RC4 key). What he *can* do without knowing the key is to insert packets that consume decryption resources at the recipient MTA: RC4 is a stream cipher that has to be synchronized with every packet. By inserting packets with incorrect synchronization information, a malicious third party can send packets to an MTA that will cause its RC4 engine to thrash interminably, consuming considerable processing resources.

For this reason, PacketCable allows the inclusion of an optional Message Authentication Check on every audio packet. The first thing that a recipient MTA does when it receives an incoming audio packet from the IP stack is to check the value of the Media Authentication Code (the MAC), if one is present. If the check fails, the packet is ignored and no further processing takes place.

The particular MAC used in PacketCable is the MMH algorithm, twinned with RC4. Two points are worth noting in connection with the MAC.

1. The MMH algorithm was chosen because it was specifically designed to be lightweight to implement and execute in software. It adds little delay to the overall end-to-end communication.

2. Its use is optional, and when it is used, either a 2-octet or a 4-octet version may be used. The reason that its use is specifically not mandatory is because bandwidth on the upstream access network is a precious resource, and a network

operator has to balance the cost of adding the MAC (which requires extra bandwidth) with the cost of an interloper being able to alter packets en route.[10] The presence and size of the MAC is signaled within the NCS messages, as the one-hexadecimal-digit authentication code exchanged between endpoints during call setup (in the `X-pc-csuites-rtp:` attribute in the SDP; see the section "Attributes" earlier in this chapter).

RTP

All bearer traffic is transmitted in RTP packets, as defined RFCs 1889 and 1890. The format of an RTP header is shown in Figure 4-9. The meaning of the various fields is as follows.

V (2-bit field)

The version number, defined to be 2

P (1-bit field)

If 1, then padding is present at the end of the payload. The final octet in the packet contains the number of padding octets added. This final octet is included in the number of octets of padding. If 0, then there is no padding added to the data.

X (1-bit field)

If 1, then the header is followed by a header extension as defined within RFC 1889.

CSRC count (4-bit field)

The number of 32-bit Contributing Source (CSRC) identifiers included in the header. A Contributing Source is a source that has contributed to a mixed output. In ordinary point-to-point communication, there are no Contributing Sources.

M (1-bit field)

The interpretation of the marker bit is a function of the profile of RTP used. Ordinarily, the value of this bit may be safely ignored in a PacketCable telephony network.

---

10. The situation is, as usual, rather more complicated than this. Depending on the codec in use, it might be possible to accommodate a two- or even a four-octet MAC on the audio packets without the transmission spilling over into an extra DOCSIS upstream minislot. In such circumstances, adding the MAC consumes no extra bandwidth.

PT (7-bit field)

> The payload type, which determines the interpretation of the payload data. See the section "RTPMAPs" earlier in this chapter for a discussion of payload types.

Sequence number (16-bit field)

> The sequence number increments by one every time that an RTP packet is sent within a session. In PacketCable, the initial sequence number *must be zero*. This is a violation of RFC 1889, which specifies that the initial sequence number be a random 16-bit quantity. There is no good reason for this violation. It is a consequence of a decision that was made early in the design process and was later rescinded. However, the final specification mistakenly left the (now unnecessary) requirement in place. It is likely that a future revision of the PacketCable specifications will remove this unnecessary divergence.

Timestamp (32-bit field)

> This field is used in PacketCable as a surrogate sequence number, which drives the RC4 engine. The initial value of the field is derived from the secret shared between the two MTAs, by a process described in the section "Encrypting RTP Packets".

SSRC (32-bit field)

> Synchronization source; a 32-bit randomly-chosen value that identifies the source of the packet.[11]

Encoded RTP Format

PacketCable MTAs encrypt the payload carried in RTP packets. If a MAC is added to a packet, the authentication hash is calculated over the entire packet subsequent

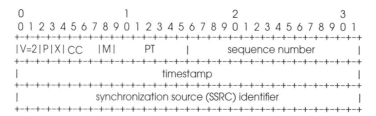

Figure 4-9   RTP Header Format

---

11. RFC 1889 describes mechanisms intended to resolve collisions of SSRC identifiers within a single RTP session (that is, when two RTP sources happen to select the same value of SSRC).

to encryption, and the result is appended to the end. The MAC is not encrypted. Figure 4-10 shows this diagrammatically.

Encrypting RTP Packets

NCS signaling includes a secret that the two endpoint MTAs share, carried on the `X-pc-secret:` line of the SDP. This secret is the basis of the bearer channel security. The two MTAs independently calculate a set of keys from this shared secret. The keys are then used to secure the end-to-end communications between the MTAs. At no time do the keys themselves travel across the network. The end-to-end secret does travel across the network, of course (within the NCS signaling). However, all the channels through which it passes are secured by IPsec and are therefore protected from eavesdropping.

The shared secret is exactly 46 octets in length, and in the current version of PacketCable it is provided by the Call Agent at the initiating end of the call. Presumably, the secret is a pseudorandom binary number although the way that the secret is generated is an implementation detail left to the vendor of the Call Agent equipment. Note that one or more Call Agents involved in the call must maintain a copy of the secret in case the phone conversation is subject to interception by a lawfully authorized surveillance agency. (A law enforcement agency with a court

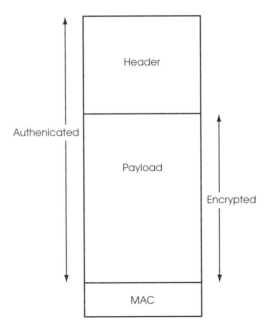

Figure 4-10 Format of Encoded RTP Packet
(with Optional MAC)

order authorizing interception of a call is legally entitled to any encryption keys which are "reasonably available" to the network operator. See Chapter 7 for more details about lawfully authorized electronic surveillance.)

All encryption and authentication is applied to unidirectional streams. Therefore keys are derived in pairs, one for sending and one for receiving. The initiating MTA derives the "send" values first, followed by the matching "receive" value in each pair. The destination MTA derives the values in the opposite order, so that the originator's "send" key matches the destination's "receive" key, and so on. The next section will discuss the Key Derivation Function, $\mathcal{F}$, used to actually generate the keys from the shared secret.

In order for the originating and destination MTAs to generate the same keys, the sequence of key generation must be the same on both devices. The following sequence is used.

1. Bearer-Channel Security

   The Key Derivation Function used is $\mathcal{F}$(S, "End-End RTP Security Association"), where S is the shared secret and the ASCII string does not include the quotation marks. The following keys are calculated from this function, in order.

   a. The RC4 key, which is 128 bits in length

   b. The initial value of the RTP timestamp, which is 32 bits in length; the 4 octets are generated in Big Endian octet order

   c. If the RTP packets are to have an HMAC, the value of the HMAC key the size of the HMAC key is calculated as follows.

   ```
   key size = N_h + N_e + N_m - 1
   ```

   where:

   $N_h = 72$

   N_e is the maximum number of octets in a packet payload, which is defined to be the number of octets in a single frame of audio as produced by the codec. In the case that the codec encodes silence in special short frames, N_e is the number of octets in a nonsilent frame

   N_m is the number of octets in the HMAC (which may be either 2 or 4)

2. IPsec keys for the RTCP Security Association

   The Key Derivation Function used is $\mathcal{F}$ (S, "End-End RTP Control Protocol Security Association"), where S is the shared secret and the ASCII string does not include the quotation marks. The following keys are calculated from this function, in order.

a. HMAC key

b. Encryption key

The legal authentication and encryption algorithms, together with the length of the associated keys, are given in Tables 4-14 and 4-15.

Key Derivation Function

The PacketCable Key Derivation Function, $\mathscr{F}$, is a function of two values.

1. S, a secret of arbitrary length

2. Δ, a seed comprising a string of ASCII-encoded characters (*not* terminating in a NULL character)[12]

$\mathscr{F}$ is based on the HMAC algorithm described in Chapter 2, using the SHA-1 cryptographic hash function, which produces a 160-bit (20-octet) output.

The process for deriving a key is as follows. We denote the SHA-1 HMAC of Δ with the key k by HMAC_SHA-1(k, Δ).

First we define a function A(n) where:

```
A_0 = Δ
A_i = HMAC_SHA-1(S, A_{i-1})
```

Now $\mathscr{F}$ (S, Δ) is calculated as:

```
𝓕(S, Δ)  = HMAC_SHA-1(S, A_1 + Δ) +
           HMAC_SHA-1(S, A_2 + Δ) +
           HMAC_SHA-1(S, A_3 + Δ) + . . . .
```

where "+" implies concatenation.

This algorithm proceeds until a key of the correct length has been derived.

A complete example is provided in Appendix D.

---

12. This caution is included for the benefit of C programmers; C strings are ordinarily terminated with a NULL character.

Procedure for Encrypting and Decrypting

To encrypt a single RTP bearer-channel packet, the transmitting MTA uses several quantities in addition to the keys derived from the shared secret.

- N_c—The number of octets in a frame of audio; each codec has a well-defined value of N_c, given in Table 4-18.

Table 4-18   Octets per Audio Frame

Codec	N_c
G.711 (10 ms)	120
G.711 (20 ms)	100
G.711 (30 ms)	93.3
G.726.16 (10 ms)	60
G.726.16 (20 ms)	40
G.726.16 (30 ms)	33.3
G.726.24 (10 ms)	70
G.726.24 (20 ms)	50
G.726.24 (30 ms)	43.3
G.726.32 (10 ms)	80
G.726.32 (20 ms)	60
G.726.32 (30 ms)	53.3
G.726.40 (10 ms)	90
G.726.40 (20 ms)	70
G.726.40 (30 ms)	63.3
G.728 (10 ms)	60
G.728 (20 ms)	40
G.728 (30 ms)	33.3
G.729A (10 ms)	50
G.729A (20 ms)	30
G.729A (30 ms)	23.2

- N_u—The number of distinct speech samples in a single frame. There may be more than one frame in a single RTP packet, so the number of distinct speech samples in a packet is always an integral multiple of N_u.

- N_f—The number of the frame. The first frame produced by the sender's codec is number zero. Subsequent frame numbers increase by one per frame generated by the codec.

- M_f—The maximum number of frames per packet

For example, suppose that a codec samples speech at the rate of 12,000 frames per second, the frame duration is 8 milliseconds (there are 125 frames per second), there are 50 packets per second, and the audio output from the codec is 16,000 bits per second (2,000 octets per second). Then $N_c = 16$; $N_u = 96$; $M_f = 3$.

Ignoring wraparound when the 32-bit counter is filled, the timestamp contained in the packet must then be equal to the value of the initial RTP timestamp (as derived from the shared secret), plus $(N_f * N_u)$, where N_f is the frame number of the first frame in the packet, counting from zero.

Other quantities are also defined.

- N_m—The number of MMH-MAC octets, which may be 0, 2, or 4.[13]

- N_e—The maximum number of octets that might be sent in an "event" packet. Event packets are those that contain information about events such as DTMF signaling, rather than audio. In PacketCable version 1.0 there is no special support for event packets, so N_e is defined to be identically equal to N_c.

- N_k—The position in the RC4 keystream, measured in octets. N_k is defined to be zero when the RC4 engine has been initialized but before any keystream octets have been generated. Note that N_k is not the same as the number of octets of the keystream that have been generated, since if a packet arrives out of order, the RC4 engine may have to be run backwards. This increases the number of keystream octets that have been generated but causes N_k to decrease (probably only temporarily, though).

---

13. We discussed the MMH-MAC algorithm in Chapter 2. The basic notion here is that the key used for the MMH-MAC calculation is the same length as the message. The MMH-MAC algorithm also requires either 2 or 4 octets of material from the RC4 key stream—the trickery is that the RC4 keystream from which these octets are taken is the *same* keystream as is used to encrypt the RTP packet. In other words, only a single RC4 engine needs to be running.

Before the first packet is encrypted, the MTA performs the following actions.

1. The RC4 encryption engine is initialized with the key for the "sending" channel. The key used to define the initial state of the RC4 encryption engine is derived from the shared secret by the mechanism given in Appendix D.

2. N_k is set to 0.

3. N_f is set to 0.

Each subsequent packet is then encoded as follows.

1. The timestamp is set equal to the value of the initial RTP timestamp, plus $(N_f * N_u)$, modulo 2^{32}.

2. The other fields in the header are calculated in accordance with RFC 1889.

3. The state of the RC4 engine is set to: $N_k = N_f * (N_e + N_m) + N_m$.

4. The octets of the packet payload are encrypted serially; N_k is incremented by one for every octet encrypted.

If N_m is non-zero, the MTA performs two additional steps.

5. The encryption state is set to $N_k = N_f * (N_e + N_m)$.

6. The MMH-MAC is calculated, beginning with the first octet of the unencrypted header and ending with the last octet of the encrypted payload, and is keyed with the RTP MAC key. The digest calculation requires N_m keystream consecutive octets, beginning with octet number N_k.

Note that with this algorithm not every octet of the keystream is necessarily used. Unused keystream octets are simply ignored. Note also the nonobvious order in which the keystream octets are used. Even though the MMH-MAC is calculated after encryption has occurred, the keystream octets used in the MMH-MAC calculation appear earlier in the keystream than the octets used in the encryption. The reason for this apparently peculiar order is that it makes it generally faster to check the MMH-MAC at the destination—which is important since one of the purposes of the MMH-MAC is to allow the recipient of invalid packets to discover that they are invalid without expending too much processing power. The algorithm used for packet decryption is similar to the encryption algorithm, but with the additional complication that the decryption algorithm must take into account the fact that packets may arrive out of order, or may be lost entirely.

Before the first packet is decrypted, the MTA initializes the RC4 decryption engine with the key for the "receiving" channel. The key used to define the initial

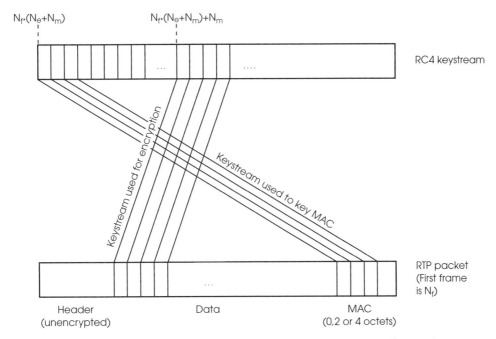

Figure 4-11 Relationship Between RC4 Keystream and RTP Packet Contents

state of the RC4 decryption engine is derived from the shared secret by the mechanism given in Appendix D.

When a packet is received, prior to any attempt at authentication or decryption, the value of the timestamp is subjected to a sanity check. The nature of this check is left to the vendor, but it is important that some reasonable check be applied, otherwise it is possible for a malicious entity to flood the MTA with packets that will cause the MTA to expend many cycles running the RC4 decryption engine unnecessarily. Packets carrying unreasonable timestamps are discarded without further processing. Once the timestamp passes the sanity check, the MTA performs the following actions.

1. N_f is calculated from the timestamp. N_f = (Timestamp – RTP Initial Timestamp) / N_u. If N_f is non-integral, the packet is discarded without further processing.

2. The state of the RC4 decryption engine is set to $N_k = N_f * (N_e + N_m)$.

If N_m is non-zero:

3. The HMAC is calculated, beginning with the first octet of the unencrypted header and ending with the last octet of the encrypted payload, and is keyed

with the RTP HMAC key. The digest calculation requires N_m keystream consecutive octets, beginning with octet number N_k.

If the computed value of the HMAC does not match the value carried in the packet, the packet is discarded without further processing. If the HMAC does match, then:

4. The payload octets are decrypted, using the contiguous keystream octets, starting from the current state of the RC4 decryption engine.

5. The remaining header fields are processed.

Key Management in NCS

Figure 4-12 shows a simplified NCS call flow that shows the messages used to convey keying information to devices in a telephone call. Remember that all of the signaling messages travel along channels asynchronously secured by IPsec, and so are resistant to tampering or eavesdropping. The messages are numbered and an explanation of each message follows the figure.

The call begins following an RQNT from the Call Agent to the originating MTA, MTA_O, informing it that it is to be notified when the MTA has collected a sequence of digits that matches a downloaded digit map. When this occurs, MTA_O sends the Call Agent an NTFY message.

Note that there are several different ways in which security information can flow within the NCS messages, depending on where the network operator places responsibility for various decisions (for example, the initial list of ciphersuites may be generated by the Call Agent or by the MTA, although ultimate control lies in the Call Agent). The flow in Figure 4-12 shows just one of many plausible scenarios.

1. The Call Agent resolves the collected digits and sends a CRCX to MTA_O. The Call Agent generates and includes an end-to-end secret, κ, in the CRCX. It also includes two lists of ciphersuites, one for RTP bearer-channel security, and one for the IPsec channel that will be established between the endpoints for RTCP. All this information goes inside the LocalConnectionOptions parameter.

   For example, the CRCX might contain the following lines.

```
a=X-pc-csuites-rtp: 62/51
a=X-pc-csuites-rtcp: 02/03 01/03
a=X-pc-secret: base64:
        U2VjdXJlQ2FibGUgbWFrZXMgdGhlIGJlc3Qgc2VjdXJpdHkgcHJvZHVjdHMuIA==
```

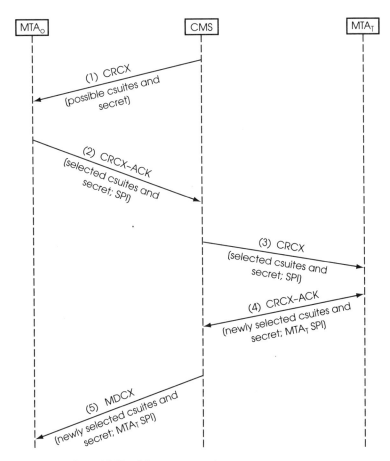

Figure 4-12 NCS Key Management

With the help of Tables 4-14 through 4-17, we can interpret the codes. The RTP will be encrypted using RC4 (which is the only possibility in version 1.0 of PacketCable) with a 2-octet HMAC.

The IPsec encryption algorithm will be 3DES CBC (again, this is the only possibility in PacketCable 1.0). Both of the permitted authentication algorithms are offered—SHA-1 and MD5—with a preference for SHA-1.

2. MTA_O generates a ConnectionID to identify the connection and internally associates κ with the connection. It selects one or more of the ciphersuites that it is prepared to support from each of the RTP and RTCP lists and returns them in the CRCX acknowledgement. The selected ciphersuites, if more than one of each type, are presented in order of preference. MTA_O is also permitted to generate its own value of κ and return that value in the acknowledgement.

MTA$_O$ also generates a 32-bit number to be used as the Security Parameter Index (SPI) for the inbound RTCP IPsec connection.

All these items, except the ConnectionID, are placed in the LocalConnection-Descriptor of the acknowledgement. The ConnectionID is returned on a separate I: header line.

For example:

```
200 3433 OK
I:FDE234C8

v=0
[other lines elided]
a=X-pc-csuites-rtp: 62/51
a=X-pc-csuites-rtcp: 02/03 01/03
a=X-pc-spi-rtcp: A7843B2
a=X-pc-secret: base64:
        U2VjdXJlQ2FibGUgbWFrZXMgdGhlIGJlc3Qgc2VjdXJpdHkgcHJvdHVjdHMuIA==
```

As soon as the 200 OK acknowledgement has been transmitted, MTA$_O$ configures itself to be ready to receive RTP and RTCP according to the parameters it sent in the acknowledgement. In the case that more than one ciphersuite is listed, it configures itself according to the first ciphersuite on the list.

3. The CRCX command sent to MTA$_T$ includes the ciphersuite lists, the end-to-end secret, and the SPI within the LocalConnectionOptions parameter:

```
a=X-pc-csuites-rtp: 62/51
a=X-pc-csuites-rtcp: 02/03 01/03
a=X-pc-spi-rtcp: A7843B2
a=X-pc-secret: base64:
        U2VjdXJlQ2FibGUgbWFrZXMgdGhlIGJlc3Qgc2VjdXJpdHkgcHJvdHVjdHMuIA==
```

4. MTA$_T$ generates a ConnectionID for this connection. Normally, MTA$_T$ will select the first ciphersuite in the RTP and RTCP lists, in which case it may configure itself accordingly and transmit packets immediately. If, however, it cannot support one of the first-listed suites, it cannot send packets until the originating MTA has been informed of the fact that it must change its default configuration.

The acknowledgement sent back to the Call Agent includes the selected ciphersuites in the LocalConnectionDescriptor parameter. It may select more than one ciphersuite for RTP and/or RTCP, but if it does so, the first-listed ciphersuite is the one to which it has configured itself. Any ciphersuites listed must be ones that were contained in the original list received from the Call Agent. (If any alternative ciphersuites are listed, the MTAs may initiate a change to one of the listed alternatives later in the call, but a new key negotiation must occur at the same time as the switch to a new ciphersuite.)

MTA_T also generates a 32-bit number to be used as the Security Parameters Index (SPI) for the inbound RTCP IPsec connection. As we discussed in Chapter 2, IPsec Security Associations are unidirectional, and the recipient is responsible for informing the source of the correct SPI value that the receiver is using on a particular inbound connection. Thus, both MTAs must generate an SPI and each must inform the other of the chosen value.

All these items, except the ConnectionID, are placed in the LocalConnection-Descriptor of the acknowledgement. The ConnectionID is returned on a separate I: header line.

For example:

```
200 3511 OK
I:C834E2ED

v=0
[other lines elided]
a=X-pc-csuites-rtp: 62/51
a=X-pc-csuites-rtcp: 02/03
a=X-pc-spi-rtcp: 66FF4231
```

MTA_T now configures itself to receive RTP and RTCP according to the information it transmitted in the acknowledgement.

5. The Call Agent sends an MDCX to MTA_O. The MDCX contains a copy of the security information from the SDP in MTA_T's acknowledgement.

MTA_O now configures itself according to the security values contained in the MDCX (if the MDCX indicates that a change is necessary). From this point on, all the security information is in place for the call to proceed.

Basic NCS Call Flow

Now we have covered the security and the NCS messages themselves in some detail, we are ready to begin to put them together to place real calls. Remember the caveat from earlier in the chapter, though: The NCS specification defines messages, it does not define call flows. So what we will talk about in this section is not the only way that a call might be placed. It is, however, the generally accepted way that the

PacketCable project uses for its internal testing procedures, and all conformant implementations of NCS are guaranteed to be able to place a call according to the scheme we are about to discuss.

The basic flow of signaling within an ordinary NCS call is quite simple. The same call flow is used for both direct on-net to on-net calls (calls from one MTA to another) and for calls in which one party is connected to the PSTN. In the latter case, the Call Agent routes the call to a PSTN gateway, which acts as a proxy MTA, so that the signaling remains essentially unchanged.

Figure 4-13 shows a basic call. In practice, some equipment may be designed to perform actions in parallel in order to reduce delays. Note one other important item that we have so far glossed over: This call contains only a single Call Agent. In other words, this is essentially a local call. In order to place a long-distance call over a PacketCable network, there has to be a mechanism by which Call Agents can pass the correct information between themselves. In version 1.0 of the specifications, this need is recognized *but is not addressed*. Vendors are free to provide proprietary interfaces to carry the messaging between Call Agents. This glaring gap in the specifications is the subject of intense activity at the time of this writing and will be filled in an upcoming release of the specifications, probably late in the year 2000. For now, however, since the protocol between Call Agents is unspecified, we will confine ourselves to discussing only local calls.[14]

Let's walk through the messages, one at a time.

1. At the end of the prior call, the Call Agent sends an RQNT to MTA_O. As well as telling the MTA to provide dial tone when the endpoint goes off-hook, this RQNT either tells the MTA to collect digits when the endpoint goes off-hook and to transmit the digit sequence when the dialed digits match a downloaded digit map, or it tells the MTA to inform the Call Agent when an off-hook event occurs (in which case, digits will be passed one at a time to the Call Agent, which will collect the digits itself).

2. MTA_O notifies the Call Agent that the requested event(s) have occurred. If the notified event is merely an off-hook, the Call Agent will request that the MTA transmit digit events until a match with the Call Agent's digit map occurs.

3. Once a valid sequence of digits has been dialed, the Call Agent transmits a CRCX to the MTA. This creates a connection in the inactive state.

4. Resource authorization occurs (see Chapter 6).

---

14. In all likelihood, the protocol used to pass messages between NCS Call Agents will be very similar to the protocol that performs the same function in DCS—that is, it will be SIP.

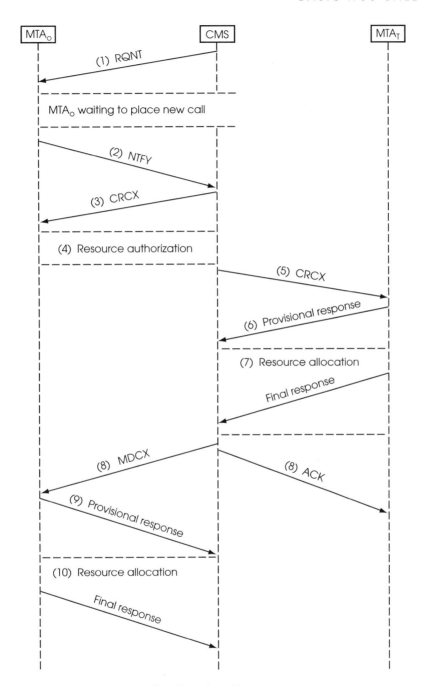

Figure 4-13 Basic NCS Call Flow (*cont.*)

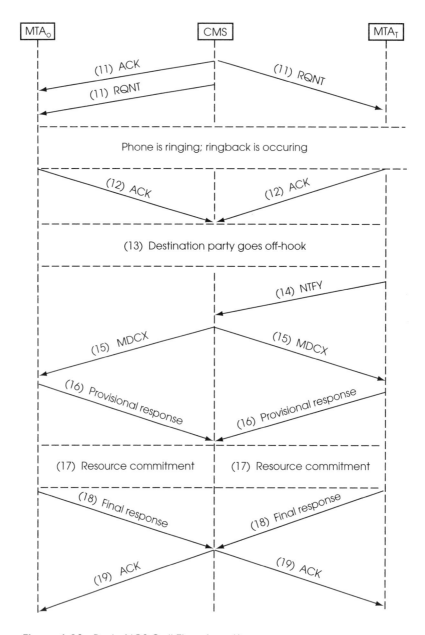

Figure 4-13 Basic NCS Call Flow (*cont.*)

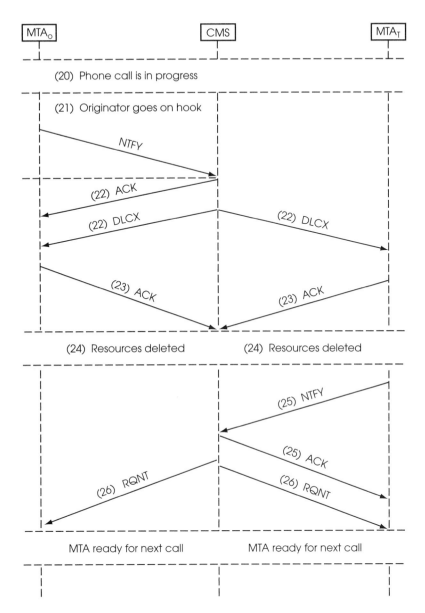

Figure 4-13 Basic NCS Call Flow

5. The Call Agent transmits a CRCX to MTA_T. This connection is also created in the inactive mode, so that the phone *does not* ring.

6. Since resource allocation may take a significant period of time (possibly hundreds of milliseconds), MTA_T returns a provisional response to stop the Call Agent from retransmitting the CRCX request.

7. Resource allocation on MTA_T's local access network occurs (see Chapter 6), and MTA_T sends a final response to the Call Agent.

8. The Call Agent sends an MDCX containing the final SDP to MTA_O. It also sends an acknowledgement to MTA_T's final response. (Remember that final responses request an acknowledgement if an earlier provisional response has been transmitted.)

9. MTA_O returns a provisional response to the CA.

10. Resource allocation on MTA_O's local access network occurs (see Chapter 6), and MTA_O sends a final response to the CA.

11. The Call Agent sends messages to both endpoints. To MTA_O it sends an acknowledgement of the MTA's final response. It also sends a RQNT to command the MTA to play ringback to the user. To MTA_T it sends a RQNT telling the phone to start ringing.

12. Both MTAs acknowledge their respective RQNTs.

At this point, the destination phone is ringing, and the calling party can hear that it is doing so because of the locally provided ringback.

13. At some time, the destination party picks up the phone.

14. MTA_T sends an NTFY to the Call Agent, to tell it that the phone has gone off-hook.

15. The Call Agent sends an MDCX to both MTAs, converting the connection from inactive to sendrecv mode.

16. Both MTAs respond with a provisional response.

17. Both MTAs commit resources on the access network (see Chapter 6).

18. Both MTAs send a final response to the Call Agent, to indicate that resources are committed.

19. The Call Agent sends a 000 acknowledgement to both MTAs.

20. As soon as resources are available in both directions, the phone conversation may begin. Voice packets may have been transmitted prior to this, but there is

no guarantee that they will receive adequate bandwidth until the DQoS resources have been committed.

21. At some time, one of the parties puts the phone down. For the purpose of the example, we assume it is the originating party.[15] MTA_O transmits to the Call Agent an NTFY containing the on-hook event.

22. The Call Agent sends a DLCX to both MTAs, as well as an acknowledgement to MTA_O.

23. Both MTAs acknowledge the DLCX, and also send back statistics about the just-completed call. (As we have noted, however, the network operator should not assume that these statistics are valid since MTAs are untrusted devices.)

24. Both MTAs delete the resource allocations on the local access networks.

25. Typically, the other party puts the phone on the hook, causing an NTFY and acknowledgement to be exchanged with the Call Agent.

26. The Call Agent sends RQNTs to both MTAs, preparing them for the next call.

Whew! You probably never guessed that signaling a simple call could be so complicated. And remember that this description is only of the PacketCable signaling. Many more low-level messages have to pass between the cable modems and the CMTSes involved in order to configure the bandwidth allocation appropriately. But, amazingly enough, it all works, and it does so quickly enough that the users are completely unaware of any of the complexity involved.

Call Features

A wide range of call features may be implemented using NCS. Just as for the basic call flow, there is often more than one possible signaling mechanism that could be used to produce the desired result. Individual network operators or vendors may choose slightly different methods of implementing some call features. In this section we look at some workable mechanisms for implementing the most common call features in NCS. Space precludes us from examining in detail every one of the enormous range of possible features. However, what follows should be enough to give a flavor of how to go about designing a workable implementation of most of the commonly used features.

---

15. If the operator has configured the PacketCable network to emulate the PSTN, then the situation is more complex if the destination party goes on-hook. In this case the call does not terminate (the connections are not torn down) until a timer has expired. This gives the called party an opportunity to put a phone on-hook, move to another room, and pick up another extension without losing the call.

One of the goals of the PacketCable project was that the experience of the end-user should be as similar as possible to that of the end-user on the PSTN. In a way this is an unfortunate requirement. If the designers had been building a telephony network from scratch, many features would have been designed to work in ways that can be more efficiently implemented in NCS signaling. However, subscribers have certain expectations about the way features on their telephones work, and it would be pointless to try to change those expectations. So we have to put up with the inefficiencies in the name of consistency. This is a good general design point to remember: Inconveniencing system designers is always preferable to inconveniencing system users.

Caller ID

In the PSTN, information identifying the calling party is transmitted on the line between the first and second rings. Usually, there is an ongoing subscription fee for this service and the information is not transmitted if the called party does not subscribe to the service.

In PacketCable, the information has to be carried within ordinary signaling messages, and so it is delivered to the destination MTA within the MDCX message that instructs the phone to ring. The MTA could, of course, delay posting the information until after the first ring so as to perfectly imitate the user experience with ordinary phones, but it seems unlikely that any vendor would seriously consider emulating what amounts to a bug in the PSTN. Consequently, the Caller ID in PacketCable systems becomes available immediately when the phone begins to ring. Indeed, an MTA could be designed to examine the Caller ID information before it begins to ring—and possibly, depending on the information, it might decide not to interrupt the subscriber's supper with a call from an unknown source.

The mechanism for delivering the Caller ID information is very simple. (Well, as simple as anything ever gets in PacketCable.) There is a specific signal in the analog access line package that carries Caller ID information. The `ci` signal has the form `ci(ti, nu, na)`, where `ti` is the date and time in the format month/day/hour/minute, `nu` is the calling party number, and `na` is the calling party name.

Signal requests are carried in the SignalRequests (`S:`) header line. So an example Caller ID line would look like this.

```
S: ci(04/17/11/24, 303-123-4567, Fred Bloggs)
```

This would cause the MTA to display the information in some reasonable format on a display device associated with the endpoint receiving the call.

The user must not be permitted to declare his own identity, of course. The information seen by the called party must have been provided by the network itself. This is most easily accomplished by obtaining the correct name associated with the calling number at the time when the Call Agent checks to make sure that the calling subscriber is permitted to make this phone call. The Call Agent then simply inserts the appropriate S: line at the time when it tells the destination phone to begin to ring.

Anonymity

Sometimes the calling party wishes to remain anonymous, even if the called party has Caller ID. In NCS, this is handled in exactly the same way as in the PSTN: as a feature implemented within the network. As part of the database lookup performed by the Call Agent when the dialed digits have been collected, the Call Agent determines whether the subscriber prefers to remain anonymous. The feature can also be invoked on a per-call basis by including the correct sequence of digits at the start of the dialed digit string.

If the subscriber wishes to remain anonymous, then the Caller ID information transmitted to the destination MTA in the S: line is changed to reflect this fact. The name and number are replaced by strings that cannot be used to identify the calling party, typically the word "Private".

A party requesting anonymity is not the same as a party whose identity is unknown. If MTA_T's Call Agent does not know the identity of the calling party—for example, if the call was placed on the PSTN and the identifying information hasn't been transmitted to the Call Agent—then the name and number are replaced by strings that indicate that the identity of the calling party is unknown (typically, the word "Unknown"). There is a twist to anonymity on an IP-based network such as PacketCable: The IP address itself may convey useful location and/or identifying information. For a discussion of this, see the section "IP-Anonymity" in Chapter 5.

Call Waiting

We now turn to a more complicated example. Call Waiting is a feature that allows a subscriber to receive a second call even if he or she is already participating in a call. When the second call comes in, the subscriber is notified and is free to switch between calls by performing a **hookflash** (by going on hook momentarily).

In our example, Alice will be in conversation with Bob when she receives an incoming call from Carol. The initial call, between Alice and Bob, was set up as usual (since of course the network had no way of knowing that Carol was going to phone Alice at the time it set up the call between Alice and Bob).

The initial part of Carol's call looks normal. When the Call Agent checks the state of Alice's line, though, it sees that she is already involved in a call. It then checks to see whether Alice subscribes to Call Waiting. If she didn't subscribe, the Call Agent would instruct MTA_C (Carol's MTA) to play the busy tone for Carol. However, since Alice does subscribe to Call Waiting (and since she hasn't already invoked the feature), the Call Agent forwards the call to Alice, instructing the endpoint to signal the presence of a second incoming call.

Note that a lot of things might happen at this point, depending on how the network operator has configured the network. Carol's identity might or might not be passed to Alice. The Call Agent might compare the bandwidth needs for the call from Carol to the ones of the call already under way; it might decide that extra bandwidth needs to be reserved for the new call; or, more likely, it will use the same resources as the call between Alice and Bob (since the Call Waiting feature allows Alice to speak with either Bob or Carol, but not with both simultaneously).

For the sake of simplicity, we will assume that no new resources are needed. The call is not signaled, though, until the network is sure that bandwidth is also available on Carol's access network (see Figure 4-14). When it is sure that there are sufficient resources at both ends of the call, the Call Agent sends an appropriate alerting signal to Alice and at the same time instructs MTA_A to notify it of a flashhook event. Carol's MTA is commanded to provide ringback, just as for a normal call.

When Alice flashes the hook, several things happen. The Call Agent is notified that the hook has been flashed. It immediately transmits a MDCX to MTA_A, instructing it to modify the connection so that instead of pointing at Bob, it now points at Carol. (If Carol's call used more resources than Bob's, separate messaging would also cause the GateID associated with the call to change, so that a different set of resources is used on the CMTS.) Carol's MTA is sent an MDCX that places the connection with Alice into the sendrecv state (just as in a normal call). And although not strictly necessary, the network operator will probably also send an MDCX to Bob's MTA to place the connection into the inactive state.

If Carol were to perform another hookflash, each MTA would receive an MDCX such that Alice's connection with Bob would be restored, and Carol's connection would be placed in the inactive state.

There is one bit of bookkeeping that we haven't mentioned. Remember that MTAs are untrusted devices and may not always behave as the network would like. What if Bob's MTA were to ignore the MDCX that places the connection in the inactive state? Then he could continue to talk and his MTA would send the RTP packets to Alice's MTA. Even though Alice can transmit to only one destination (Carol), we are still left with the situation where a one-way talk-path exists with guaranteed Quality of Service between Bob and Alice. In order to prevent this, the DQoS gate in Bob's CMTS will close, so that even if he does transmit the packets, they will not be permitted to reach Alice. The DQoS protocols described in Chapter 6 manage this automatically—Alice's call with Bob will have a different gate than her call with Carol, even if the same resources are used for both calls. When she flashes the hook to talk to Carol, her gate with Bob will close, and this automatically causes Bob's gate to Alice also to close. Although the gates close, they are not deleted; they can be reactivated at a moment's notice should Alice perform another hookflash.

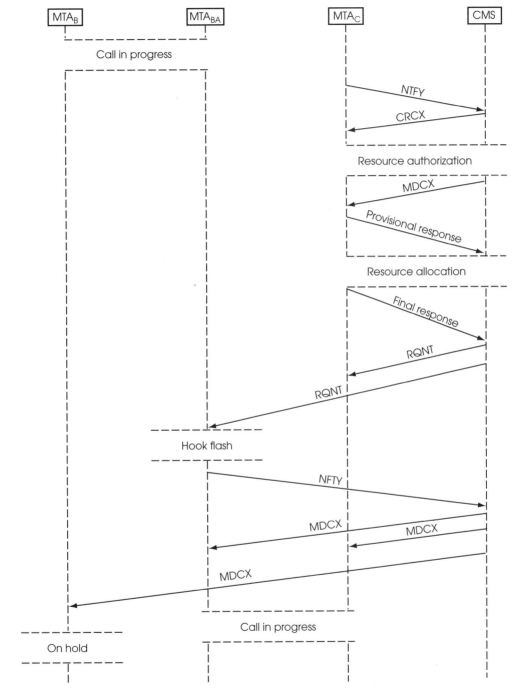

Figure 4-14   One Way to Implement NCS Call Waiting

Three-Way Calling

Three-way calling is the most complicated of the "normal" residential features. Not only is it complicated, but there are several ways in which it might be implemented. For example, the calls might be treated as independent connections, but the audio from the two connections might be mixed within the MTA. More commonly, a device called a network bridge is used. In a bridge, several audio streams, A, B, C, D, and so on are mixed. Each party hears the sum of the audio from all the other parties in the call. That is, if S is the sum of all the audio, A hears S-A, B hears S-B, and so on.

Providing three-way calling by mixing audio within the MTA is much simpler than doing so via a bridge. However, it consumes more of the precious upstream bandwidth on the HFC access network, since two sets of upstream packets must be transmitted from the MTA performing the mixing instead of just one. For this reason, MSOs strongly discourage implementing three-way calling in this manner.

The subscriber uses three-way calling like this: Alice first places a call to Bob. When that call is established, she uses some mechanism (such as a hookflash) to put

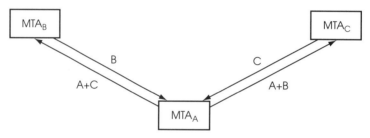

Figure 4-15 Local Mixing to Provide Three-Way Calling

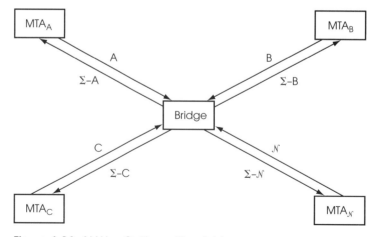

Figure 4-16 N-Way Calling with a Bridge

Bob on hold while she places a second simultaneous call to Carol on the same line. After Carol answers, she joins both calls together by using some well-defined signal (such as a double hookflash) on her phone. Now all three parties can hear the other two. If one of the other parties hangs up, then the call reverts to an ordinary two-person call again. If Alice hangs up, however, all the connections are torn down, effectively ending the call for all three parties. So that's what Alice experiences. How can we signal this in NCS, assuming that a bridge is available to perform the necessary audio mixing?

The call from Alice to Bob is signaled like any other call. The only difference is that because the CA knows that Alice has subscribed to three-way calling, it must be prepared to initiate this feature should it receive a hookflash during a call. Therefore, when Bob answers the phone and the CA modifies Alice's connection, putting it into sendrecv mode, in addition to requesting notification of a hang-up event, it also requests notification of a hookflash event.

So we begin with Alice in conversation with Bob. She now performs a hookflash. (Remember the usual caveat with NCS signaling that what follows is just one way in which the signaling might be arranged to create the desired result. Many other call flows would effectively achieve the same result.)

1. The MTA sends an NTFY(hookflash) to the CA. (A hookflash is an event coded as "hf" in the NCS Line Package.)

2. The CA recognizes that Alice is invoking the three-way calling feature. It sends an MDCX to Alice's MTA, placing the connection with Bob into the inactive state. It also tells the MTA to provide dial tone and to start collecting digits until it finds a match with the digit map.

3. A new call is set up with Carol, just as if the call with Bob did not exist. The connection with Bob remains in the inactive state during this process.

   Just as with the call to Bob, when the CA sends the MDCX command that places the connection with Carol into sendrecv mode, it also tells the MTA that it wishes to be informed should Alice issue a hookflash.

   One important issue surrounds the question of upstream bandwidth. To simplify matters so that we can concentrate purely on the call signaling, we will assume that the codecs in use on the call from Alice to Carol is identical as the codec used between Alice and Bob. Theoretically, however, this may not necessarily be so. For early deployments of PacketCable 1.0 networks, it is reasonable to assume that all conversations use the G.711 codec, which allows the Alice/Carol conversation to reuse the same upstream bandwidth that had been used for the Alice/Bob conversation. In future releases of PacketCable this may not be a safe assumption, and two separate flows might have to be committed, even though only one will be in use at any one time.

4. After beginning her conversation with Carol, Alice decides to conference the Bob and Carol into a single conversation, so she performs a "double hook-flash": two hookflashes in a brief space of time.

   The NCS Line Package does not include a "double hookflash" event. Therefore it is encumbant on the CA to recognize that a double hookflash is signaled by a pair of hookflash events occurring in a short span of time.

   The MTA signals the two hookflash events, and the CA recognizes this as the signal to initiate three-way calling.

5. The CA examines its internal state regarding Alice's MTA and recognizes that she wishes to hold a three-way conversation with Bob and Carol. This sets in motion a complex set of events, which, since they must occur as quickly as possible, are signaled as much as possible in parallel.

   As was the case when Alice initiated the second call, there will in the future be issues to do with bandwidth reservation, since the audio bridge might require different codecs than an end-to-end communication. This is actually fairly likely, at least with audio bridges from some vendors, since the task of seamlessly mixing audio from several different audio codecs is very CPU-intensive and also tends to give rather poor results, so at least some audio bridges will probably require that all input be presented as G.711-encoded packets. This raises the possibility that a call from Alice to Bob (and/or Carol) may have been initiated with a low bit rate codec, which will switch to G.711 when the call is switched to the bridge. This in turn allows the possibility that the increased upstream bandwidth will be unavailable and the attempt to bridge the call will fail. In the future, then, quite complicated signaling will be necessary to ensure that Alice's experience is reasonable under all possible circumstances.

   However, in PacketCable 1.0, it is reasonable to assume that G.711 is the universal codec, so the signaling is greatly simplified.

   a. The CA checks that an audio bridge with sufficient ports is available. The signaling for this is out of scope of the current version of PacketCable, and so the function is performed with proprietary signaling. The CA will be provided with the correct IP address and port numbers for the conversation that is going to be bridged (a total of three ports will be required, one for each participant).

   b. The CA sets all currently active connections on the call (the connections between Alice and Carol) to the inactive state.

   c. The CA creates a series of new active sendrecv connections: one on each of the MTAs, connecting the MTA to the bridge, and three on the bridge, one to each MTA. The upstream resources at each of the MTAs are simply reallocated to the new call to the bridge. The CA must be careful to ensure that each connection is created with compatible codecs and security algorithms at both ends.

In order to meet this criterion in future versions of PacketCable, the CA would in all likelihood not be able to assume that the audio bridge can support all possible codecs and and possible security algorithms. Under these circumstances, the CA cannot merely issue a series of active CRCX connections to the various devices. Instead, it would first create the connections in the inactive state and then issue MDCX commands to bring the connections into compatible active states. In PacketCable 1.0, though, it is reasonable to assume that all devices are sufficiently compatible that the CA can create the connections immediately in sendrecv mode.

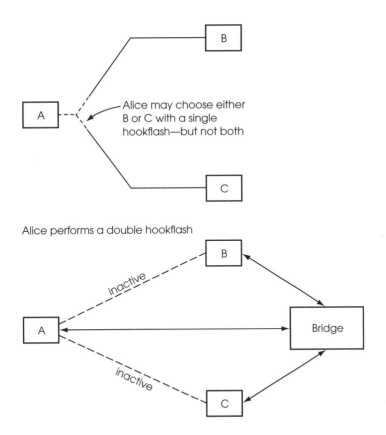

Figure 4-17 Initiating a Three-Way Call

Note that the CA would also (most likely) be designed to provide new security keys for each of these connections, and that from a security standpoint the MTAs would treat each connection as if it were a new call, initializing the RC4 engine for the new connection.

If Alice now goes on hook, the CA issues a series of DLCX commands to delete all the connections. If, instead, one of the other parties goes on hook (say Carol) then either the CA signals the connections with Carol to be deleted (including the inactive connection on Alice's MTA), and the call continues as a two-party call routed through the bridge, or after deleting the connections involving Carol, the CA deletes all the connections to the bridge and sets the two remaining connections—one on Alice's MTA with Bob and the reciprocal connection on Bob's MTA with Alice—back to the active sendrecv state.

Chapter
5

Distributed
Call Signaling

Network-based call signaling mimics a traditional telephony network. The endpoints are assumed to be relatively unintelligent devices capable only of responding to simple signals and notifying a controlling entity when simple events occur. Since the endpoints are regarded as simple devices, all the information pertaining to a call resides not in the endpoint (or even in the MTA, which in a sense is merely part of the endpoint) but within entities in the core network itself. The endpoint itself does not even "know" that it is taking part in a call—only the network knows that. So, for example, if an incoming call comes in to a phone number serviced by an NCS device, it is the network that is responsible for realizing that a call is under way on that line and doing the appropriate thing (which would normally be to tell the calling party that the line is busy, without signaling the destination that a second call was incoming).

Such an approach has definite advantages. The PSTN is constructed on a similar model—telephones do not need to "know" that they are busy—and therefore a vast body of knowledge and experience concerned with the control and management of such a network has been accumulated. The large vendors to the circuit-switched network know how to design and build products that function well in an NCS-like environment, and telephone companies such as AT&T that now have a presence in the cable market similarly understand the network-based paradigm very well.

In addition, the fact that endpoints are simple tends to keep their cost down (although most reasonable people would admit that a PacketCable MTA, even one that uses NCS signaling, could not honestly be described as "simple"), which can be an important attribute in a new technology as it begins to face wide deployment.

However, the network-centric approach also has disadvantages. Core network elements must maintain an intimate knowledge of call state, burdening them with demands that are only tangentially associated with their principal task of expediting call signaling. Most features must be implemented within the network itself, relying only on the primitive signal/event handshake mechanism to communicate with endpoints. Perhaps more importantly, the network-centric model flies in the face of a new model that has to a large extent displaced the telephone network as the paradigm for mass communications in the last few years: the Internet.

The Internet (and in particular the part of it known as the World Wide Web) operates in a manner quite different from the telephony network. The network itself plays little role in communication, apart from providing the pipe that allows two endpoints to communicate. The state of a communication is maintained within the endpoints themselves and adding a new feature to, for example, a Web browser does not require any changes in an ISP's software or hardware infrastructure. It merely requires that the user download a new version of the browser (or perhaps merely a new plug-in for his current browser).

While traditional telephony vendors and operators have a wealth of experience with NCS-like signaling, newer companies are more likely to wish for a less network-centric, and more Internet-like, model.

While it is too early to say which of these two paradigms is likely to "win out" eventually, it is clear from the speed with which it has been adopted that the distributed Internet model is a powerful challenger to the network-centric telephony model. With this in mind, the PacketCable project has prudently chosen to specify two different models for call signaling. We have already examined the Network-based Call Signaling model. In this chapter we will look at the Distributed Call Signaling model, which is based on concepts more akin to those used for intercomputer communication on the Internet. Note that we will briefly return to the topic of NCS and DCS in Chapter 9, when we attempt to discern the future.

We do, however, note that only NCS is an official part of the PacketCable 1.0 specification suite. Partly this was to allow vendors to concentrate on building, and MSOs on deploying, only a single version of a product. Partly this was probably a short-term business decision, driven by large companies with more experience in traditional rather than IP telephony. The DCS specification, however, is a publicly available document (you may download it from *ftp://ftp.cablelabs.com/pub/ietfdocs/dcsdraft.pdf*) and, oddly enough, became public before any of the official PacketCable 1.0 specifications. It is currently scheduled to become an official PacketCable 1.x specification sometime within 2001. At the time of writing, at least one major vendor has publicly demonstrated product built to the DCS specification, and several other vendors are in the process of building similar products.

Because of its likely importance in the long term, and because it represents a very different paradigm than does NCS, we will devote a full chapter to DCS. DCS evolved from an AT&T project known as the **Distributed Open Systems Architecture (DOSA)**. It is somewhat ironic that the same company that invented what eventually became DCS has chosen to favor initial deployment of NCS because it has such a vast body of experience operating traditional telephony networks, to which NCS bears a reasonable resemblance—unlike DCS, which looks much more like a data-network protocol than a telephony-network one. DOSA as it was originally presented to CableLabs was deemed unusable, since it relied on elegant but proprietary messaging, and one of the stated goals of the PacketCable project was to use open, existing, standard protocols wherever possible. (DOSA was also the parent of DQoS, which was originally part of DCS before being redesigned to be signaling-neutral.)

Over the course of several months, the AT&T team modified the DOSA signaling messages to use a slightly enhanced version of the standard SIP protocol as defined in RFC 2543.[1] The result was DCS.

The essential network elements used in a DCS architecture are the same as those in NCS. The only essential change, from the point of view of nomenclature, is that the NCS Call Agent (CA) is replaced by a DCS-Proxy (DP). A CMS is therefore a joint DP and Gate Controller (GC), rather than a joint CA and Gate Controller as in NCS.

The DP does not maintain state. It necessarily is involved in call setup, but as soon as an end-to-end connection is established between the participating MTAs, the DP no longer participates in a call. Indeed, it loses all knowledge that the call exists. This means that a DP may reasonably be expected to handle call signaling for many more calls than may a CA (perhaps as many as ten times as many calls for a computing platform with equivalent power).

The fact that a DP does not maintain call state also places a much lower reliability requirement on a DP than is on a CA. If a CA crashes, unless the network has been specifically designed to allow for the possibility by using redundant devices, calls currently in progress through that CA are in jeopardy, since any attempt to invoke a feature will necessarily fail. In DCS, since calls once they are initiated are

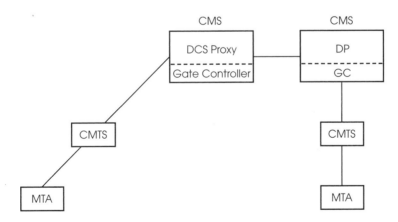

Figure 5-1   Basic DCS Architecture

---

1. The extensions that were introduced in DCS are now before the IETF for possible integration into the definition of "standard SIP".

no longer associated with a DP, the loss of a DP causes no loss of ongoing calls (although of course no new calls can be placed through the DP until it comes back into service). The basic architecture of a DCS network is shown in Figure 5-1.

Basic Call Flow

A simple call is shown in Figure 5-2, and proceeds as follows.

1. MTAs are responsible for providing dial tone and all digit collection automatically—unlike NCS, where an MTA, operating under orders from the CA may send each digit to the CA for processing. No message is sent from the MTA to the DP until the user has gone off-hook and dialed a complete digit string that matches a preprovisioned digit map. Once it has such a string, the MTA, MTA_O, sends a SIP INVITE(stage1) message containing the dialed digits to the originating DP, DP_O.

2. Like NCS, all DCS signaling travels over connections secured by IPsec, so authentication of DCS messaging is automatic. There is no need for DP_O to authenticate that the incoming message actually came from MTA_O; IPsec performs this authentication check automatically.

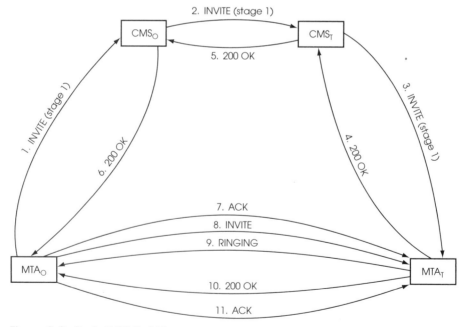

Figure 5-2 Basic DCS Call Flow

DP_O receives the authenticated INVITE, checks that the call is permitted, and determines the correct destination DP,[2] DP_T, for the phone number. It forwards the INVITE(stage1) to DP_T.

3. DP_T checks that the call is permitted, determines which MTA (MTA_T) is associated with the destination phone number and forwards the INVITE(stage1) to MTA_T.

4. MTA_T checks that it can accept the call and sends a 200 ACK back to DP_T.

5. The 200 ACK is forwarded from DP_T to DP_O . . .

6. . . . and from DP_O to MTA_O.

The acknowledgement contains the IP address of MTA_T. From this point on, messaging is end-to-end, and neither of the DCS-Proxies is involved further in the call.

7. MTA_O sends an ACK to MTA_T, acknowledging the 200 OK.

At this point, QoS resources are reserved (but not committed). The destination phone has not yet begun to ring, nor has ringback been provided to the originating user.

8. Once QoS resources are reserved at the originating side, MTA_O sends an INVITE to MTA_T. This is an ordinary SIP INVITE, not an INVITE(stage1).

9. When MTA_T receives the INVITE and has reserved resources for the call, the destination phone begins to ring.

10. MTA_T sends a 180 RINGING to MTA_O. When it receives this message, MTA_O supplies local ringback to the user.

11. When the destination party goes off-hook, MTA_T sends a 200 OK to MTA_O. This is a final response (as opposed to the 180 provisional response) to the second INVITE. MTA_T also commits the resources.

12. When it receives the 200 OK, MTA_O sends an ACK to MTA_T and simultaneously commits its network resources.

The call is now in progress.

Call termination is simple: When MTA_O goes on-hook, it sends a BYE to MTA_T. In response, MTA_T sends a 200 OK to MTA_O. At this point the call is over.

---

2. In NCS, the protocol used to pass information between Call Agents is unspecified in PacketCable 1.0, and therefore each vendor can choose a proprietary mechanism. In DCS, the protocol between DCS-Proxies is fully defined.

Trust

A PacketCable network may be divided into two domains: a trusted domain, which includes the CMTSes and all the devices on the "core" side of the CMTSes, and an untrusted domain, which constitutes everything "outside" the CMTSes—in particular MTAs.

MTAs are always treated as untrusted elements since the network operator has no control over their operation. An MTA, especially if it is a PC rather than a sealed box, may be arbitrarily hacked, so that there is never any guarantee that a particular MTA is telling the truth in any message that it might send. Nor is there any guarantee that its messages will arrive in the expected order, especially if the MTA owner believes that by altering the message sequence he might be able to steal service from the operator.

However, this poses a special problem for DCS, since call state is not maintained within DPs. Some state for calls in progress is stored in the MTA's local CMTS. Some state, however, including long-lived state such as the identity of the last party to call the MTA, must be stored on the MTA itself. State stored on the MTA is encrypted into a **state blob** by the network before storage. When it needs access to the state maintained on the MTA, the network retrieves the state blob and decrypts it.

The encryption/decryption process includes an authentication check so that the network can be sure that the MTA has not tampered with the state blob while it was in the MTA's possession. The nature of the state information in the blob is such that, if the network detects that it has been tampered with, the blob can be ignored, and the only consequence is that a requested feature will not be invoked.

To give a trivial example, one of the items stored in the state blob is the phone number of the party that most recently placed an incoming call. If, for some reason, the MTA attempts to change this number and then to invoke a Call Return feature, the network would detect that the blob has been compromised and discard its contents. It would then be unable to implement the Call Return feature.

In other words, it is to the MTA's benefit not to tamper with stored encrypted state blobs. If it does tamper with such a blob, a service normally offered by the network provider may become temporarily unavailable.

Intelligent MTAs

DCS is designed to permit many features that are commonly implemented in the PSTN to be implemented within the endpoint instead of being provided by the network operator.

At first sight, this might seem (if you are a network operator) to be a disadvantage: Features for which you might be accustomed to charging a monthly fee are no longer a source of revenue. However, if one looks at many (although not all) of these features, there is no reason why they cannot be implemented on intelligent endpoints even within the PSTN. The principal reason that most of them are not commonly implemented on today's phones is a matter of cost and administration, rather than one of feasibility.[3]

The geometry of in-home wiring is quite different for a PacketCable network and for an ordinary twisted-pair home served by the PSTN. In a PacketCable network, the MTA can act as a single centralized intelligence for controlling features. In a house wired for ordinary telephony, there is no single place where intelligence can be concentrated. Consequently, each separate telephone has to be intelligent, which is expensive and a waste of resources, and therefore something that is infrequent (although becoming less so) in the common PSTN topology.

Once a home has an MTA, however, that MTA can emulate many of the features provided by today's central offices, regardless of whether that MTA uses DCS or

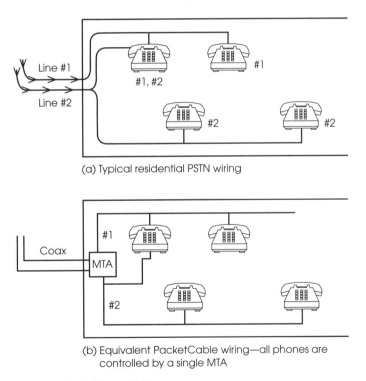

(a) Typical residential PSTN wiring

(b) Equivalent PacketCable wiring—all phones are controlled by a single MTA

Figure 5-3 In-Home Wiring

---

3. Examples of features that can be implemented on ordinary phones are local conferencing, speed dial, last call return (if the subscriber has Caller ID) and automatic call blocking (both incoming and outgoing). There are many others.

NCS signaling. In fact, the MTA, if it has sufficient intelligence, can act as a kind of mini-PBX. It seems clear, then, operators of PacketCable networks will have to accustom themselves to the fact that subscribers will provide some features for themselves and will no longer look to the network to provide those services, regardless of whether the operator chooses to deploy an NCS or a DCS network.

However, there are still many features that can be controlled by the network operator (regardless of whether DCS or NCS is used), and these will continue to provide a revenue stream for those operators that desire it. There is a distinct possibility, however, that a new kind of telephony service provider will emerge as PacketCable and other Voice-over-IP (VoIP) networks become widely deployed: one that simply charges for access bandwidth and that obtains only a very small portion of its income from providing services and implementing features. Accounting and billing for services and features can be expensive, and at least in some cases it might make more sense to provide some features without cost rather than to try to keep track of which features a subscriber has used in any particular month.

In any case, part of the design goal of DCS is to support and encourage the use of intelligence outside the core network. These are a few of the features that are likely to be implemented *within the MTA*.

Distinctive ringing

> The MTA examines the phone number associated with an incoming call and rings the phone in a distinctive manner (perhaps using a voice synthesizer) to announce the identity of the caller.

Anonymous call reject

> Incoming calls whose Dcs-Anonymity: header is not OFF can be treated specially. Either they could be rejected outright, or they could be automatically forwarded to a recording device (which may be integrated into the MTA itself), or a special less-intrusive ringing cadence could be used to alert the user.

Answering machine and features

> The MTA may function as a complete answering machine, with voice mailboxes, message waiting indicators and the full complement of answering machine features.

Multiple simultaneous calls

> If a party is already using a particular line, a second party can use another endpoint associated with the same phone number to place a second, simultaneous outgoing call.

In-home conferencing and PBX

An MTA to which multiple phones are attached can act as a simple in-home PBX, allowing phones to ring one another and bridging multiple conversations or sets of conversations simultaneously.

Local bridging

The MTA can perform local bridging, so that (for example) a three-way calling feature can be implemented entirely within the MTA.

Call queuing and other features

If a line is busy, instead of another incoming call receiving an automatic "busy" indication, the MTA could play a message (perhaps depending on the identity of the calling party) and then place it on hold. The thought is repulsive, but one could even (shudder!) implement one of those awful tree-based voicemail systems entirely within an MTA.

Call interrupt

If a call comes in from an important party, any current call could be automatically dropped or placed on hold to make way for the new call.

Call blocking

An MTA could be programmed to disallow certain types of calls (long distance, international, 1-900, and so on). Even particular destinations could be disallowed.

Speed dial; N-call return

It is simple to implement speed dialing or N-call return on an MTA. In the case of N-call return, support from the network is needed if the caller whose call is being returned did not reveal his phone number. The MTA would then return the state blob corresponding to the call to the local DP, rather than the state blob for the most recent call.

Intelligent call forwarding

Calls may be forwarded to a destination that could depend on the identity of the calling party, the time of day, and so forth.

Disable call waiting

Call waiting could be disabled entirely within the MTA, rather than requiring that a network feature be invoked (typically, this feature is currently invoked on the PSTN by dialing *70).

Warm-line and hot-line

> An MTA could be programmed so that it automatically dials a particular number as soon as and endpoint goes off-hook, or it could maintain a connection regardless of whether the endpoint is on-hook or off-hook.

Doubtless there are many other candidate features that could be implemented on an MTA. In any case, the point is that DCS envisages an MTA being able to do all these things and probably considerably more.

Although first-generation MTAs are relatively simple devices embedded in the same package as a cable modem, it will not be long before the MTA becomes a separate device running software—in other words, a computer. It is quite possible, and the author believes likely, that within a few years MTA software will be downloadable from the Internet and will run on an ordinary personal computer. For more discussion of this, see Chapter 9.

SIP Messaging

SIP messages follow a simple, line-based, human-readable ASCII format. A header, which typically contains several lines, is separated from any body by a blank line (CRLF pair).

DCS extends the messages defined in RFC 2543 with the addition of several new header lines, which are used to support several features required by a telephony network. Standard SIP, for example, does not easily support the two-stage INVITE used in PacketCable to thwart Theft of Service attacks. Other header extensions are necessary to support various flavors of privacy and anonymity.

SIP Header Extensions

Before examining the details of the messaging that flows in the network, let's look at the DCS extensions to the standard SIP header set defined by RFC 2543. In order to use any of these extensions, devices must use the standard SIP headers Require: and Proxy-Require:.

When a device receives a SIP message, it is normally expected to understand only the headers defined in the base RFC. However, if the message contains one or more Require: headers, these indicate that the message has headers that require additional knowledge (over and above that defined in the RFC) for them to be handled correctly. DCS messages containing such headers should contain this line.

```
Require: DCS
```

In addition, some headers may be present for the benefit of intermediate DPs rather than the final destination of the message. If a message contains such headers, it must also contain this line.

```
Proxy-Require: DCS
```

INVITE(stage1)

Because of the two-stage commit mechanism used for DQoS resources, DCS requires two different kinds of INVITE message. The first, called an INVITE(stage1), is used to initiate resource reservation and does not cause the terminating phone to ring. The second is used after resources have been successfully committed, and does cause the terminating phone to ring.

An INVITE is marked as an INVITE(stage1) by inclusion of this header line.

```
Dcs-Stage1:
```

Note that there is no equivalent INVITE(stage2) or Dcs-Stage2: header. The second stage INVITE is an ordinary SIP INVITE message with no additional header used to distinguish it.

This allows a "standard SIP" client (as opposed to a DCS MTA) to place a call to a PacketCable MTA. The lack of an INVITE(stage1) means that no DQoS resource reservation occurs, so there is no guaranteed Quality of Service for such calls. The first incoming INVITE is an ordinary SIP INVITE, which causes the recipient MTA to ring the phone immediately (assuming it is configured to allow incoming calls from non-DCS-compliant devices).

DCS-CALLER

In SIP, there is a mandatory From: header, which is used to identify the calling party. In a telephony network, however, sometimes the identity of the calling party should be hidden from the destination party. DCS encrypts the information in the ordinary From: header, so that even though it may be delivered to the destination, that destination can glean no useful information from it.

However, it is still necessary for the network (as opposed to the destination endpoint) to be able to identify the caller. For example, suppose that the destination receives an anonymous call and then activates a Return Call feature. Even though the destination party does not know the identity (or phone number) of the calling party, it should still be possible for him to return a call to that person.

In order to provide for this capability, DCS defines a Dcs-Caller: header. The definition of this header is:

```
Dcs-Caller = "Dcs-Caller" ":" [display-name ";"] Caller-Number ["/" Caller-
Type] [ "<" addr-spec ">"]
```

where

Caller-Number = phone-number | "private" | "not-subscribed" | "not-available"

Display-name, if present, is a string that identifies the account name of the calling party (often, this is the name under which the phone number is listed in the telephone directory). If it has the value "private", then this indicates that, for this call, the originator has requested caller-name privacy (his name is not to be sent to the destination). As you can tell from the name of this field, the intention is that if the destination party subscribes to Caller-ID, this will be the name that appears on the Caller-ID display (and hence will always be a string that is supplied, or at least verified, by the network).

The Dcs-Caller: header is passed to the destination MTA only if the originating party did not request privacy and the destination MTA is subscribed to a Caller-ID service.

The phone number in the Caller-Number field is the phone number of the originator. If this field contains the string "private", then the originating MTA has requested calling-number privacy for this call. Note that to ensure that both name and number are hidden from the destination, both the display-name and Caller-Number must be set to "private".

The Caller-Type field is used to signal that the originator may require special privileges. The word "Operator" is reserved, and can be issued only by certain devices inside the trust domain of the network.

DCS-ANONYMITY

Regardless of the values in the Dcs-Caller: header, the Dcs-Anonymity: header is used to provide control over what identifying information is to be provided to the other party. It may be, for example, that even though the originator requests anonymity, the Dcs-Caller: is populated with identifying information so that the call may be properly accounted. In this case, the contents of the Dcs-Anonymity: header will determine what (if any) caller-identifying material is passed to the destination MTA.

The format of the header is:

```
Dcs-Anonymity: <tag>
```

where <tag> is one of: Off, Full, Caller-Num, Caller-Name or IPAddr.

Off

> The party requests no particular privacy. Any available identifying information may be freely passed to the other party.

Full

> The party requests complete anonymity. No information that might be used to identify name, number or location may be passed to the other party.

Caller-Num or Caller-Name

> Number or name information respectively are to be withheld from the other party.

IPAddr

> The actual IP address being used must not be forwarded to the other party. In DCS, hiding the IP address from the other party has interesting ramifications, since both bearer and signaling go end-to-end. We will look at the repercussions of this later, in "Anonymity".

DCS-GATE

The Quality of Service (QoS) mechanism in PacketCable networks is based on the concept of gates, which are logical entities that exist in a CMTS but are controlled by the MTA and the CMS. A special header is needed to carry information about the QoS gate(s) associated with a call. The format of the header is:

```
Dcs-Gate = "Dcs-Gate" ":" [hostport "/"] Gate-ID [";" Gate-Key ";" Gate-
Cipher-Suite]
```

Gate-ID is a token used at the system named in the hostport parameter to identify the particular session. For DCS systems, it is a 32-bit quantity encoded as an 8-character string of the digits 0–9 and the letters a–f. The Gate-Key and the Gate-Cipher-Suite are the security parameters associated with the gate, identifying the key and the algorithms used to secure QoS gate coordination messages. "hostport" gives the IP address or FQDN of the CMTS on which the gate lies.

DCS-STATE

As we discussed earlier, because MTAs are untrusted devices and because long-lived state (as well as some state necessary to implement mid-call features) must be stored outside the core network, DCS stores call state in MTAs in the form of encrypted state blobs. The blobs are passed into and out of MTAs with the Dcs-State: header.

The information contained within a blob is, at a minimum the following:

- The identity of the calling party
- The level of privacy requested
- The location of the local QoS gate, and the Gate-ID
- A series of SIP routing Via: headers that indicate the route taken by signaling

Other information may be contained in the blob as deemed necessary by the network. Often, for example, billing information is present. Particular features may require additional information be added to the blob.

The exact method of encrypting the state blob is unspecified, since it is generally assumed that only the device that initially encrypted the blob will need to decrypt it. It is expected that a proven, strong encryption algorithm will be used, and also that part of the blob encryption/decryption process will include authentication measures to assure that the blob has not been tampered with during the time it resides on the untrusted MTA.

The format of the Dcs-State: header is simple:

```
Dcs-State: <token>
```

where <token> is simply an opaque ASCII string beginning with an alphabetic character.

DCS-ALSO:

Suppose that Bob has instituted a Call Forward No Answer (CFNA) feature, such that if he does not answer an incoming call, the call is automatically sent to Carol's number instead. When Alice calls Bob, and Bob does not answer, a mechanism has to be in place for Bob's MTA to instruct Alice's MTA to initiate a call to Carol. The Dcs-Also: header is that mechanism. The Dcs-Also: header takes a single value, the identity of the party to which the INVITE is to be issued.

```
Dcs-Also: sip:555-3333@dp.provider
```

The identity of the new destination party is formatted as a DCS URL (see DCS URLs for more details).

Just a note: Typically, the messaging will also cause Bob to pay for the new call leg. This can actually become quite complex, since although the call actually contains a single leg from Alice to Carol, it should be billed, following the PSTN model, as two separate calls: one from Alice to Bob, and one from Bob to Carol. The packet-network topology is very different from the case on the conventional PSTN, where the forwarded call would still pass through Bob's central office. A call that passes through an apparently unnecessary location (such as Bob's central office in this example) is said to be **hairpinned**.

DCS-REPLACES:

It is sometimes necessary to replace one call leg with another. Continuing the example of the CFNA feature, when Bob's MTA instructs Alice's MTA to issue an INVITE to Carol's MTA, it must also instruct Alice's MTA to drop the connection to itself. The Dcs-Replaces: header instructs the recipient to issue a BYE for the call leg identified in the message, which has the effect of tearing down that leg. The format is the same as the Dcs-Also: header, except that multiple legs may be replaced simultaneously by providing a comma-separated list of DCS-URLs.

```
Dcs-Replaces: <DCS-URL> [, <DCS-URL>]
```

Usually, the Dcs-Also: and Dcs-Replaces: headers occur together (see Figure 5-4). For example,

```
Dcs-Also: sip:303-123-3333@dp.provider
Dcs-Replaces: sip:303-123-2222@dp.provider
```

would forward an incoming call whose original destination was 303-123-2222 to the new destination 303-123-3333.

DCS-OSPS:

A special header is necessary for the operator to perform Busy Line Verify (BLV) and Emergency Interrupt (EI) services. This is the Dcs-OSPS: header:

```
Dcs-OSPS: <tag>
```

where <tag> is either "BLV" or "EI". See the section "BLV and EI" for more details on these services.

DCS-BILLING-INFO:

A header is needed to allow billing information associated with a call to be passed around the core network. The Dcs-Billing-Header: is used for this purpose. This header is never sent outside the trusted domain, although information it contains may be stored in a state blob carried by a Dcs-State: header.

```
Dcs-Billing-Info  = "Dcs-Billing-Info" ":" [hostport] "<" Acct-Data ">"
```

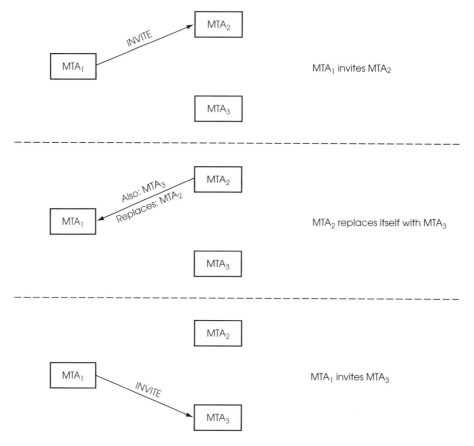

Figure 5-4 Example of Dcs-Also: and Dcs-Replaces: Headers in Use

The hostport specifies a Record Keeping Server (RKS) for event messages relating to this call.

The Acct-data field carries accounting information for the call. The format is:

```
Acct-Charge-Number "/" Acct-Calling-Number  "/" Acct-Called-Number
  ["/" Acct-Routing-Number "/" Acct-Location-Routing-Number]
```

where Acct-Charge-Number, Acct-Calling-Number, Acct-Called-Number, Acct-Routing-Number and Acct-Location-Routing-Number are defined as 20-octet E.164 formatted addresses (see also Chapter 7 for more information about billing).

So, for example, the Dcs-Billing-Info: header

```
Dcs-Billing-Info: RKS1@ratco.com
        <5123-0123-4567-8900/303-123-1111/303-123-2222>
```

specifies that the Record Keeping Server that is handling this call is RKS1@ratco.com, the account number responsible for payment is 5123-0123-4567-8900, the calling party is 303-123-1111, and the destination party is 303-123-2222.

DCS-BILLING-ID:

Like Dcs-Billing-Info: this header is transmitted only between trusted entities. It carries a globally unique identifier that allows the RKS to correlate items from multiple entities associated with the call, so that the call may be billed correctly.

```
Dcs-Billing-ID     = "Dcs-Billing-ID" ":" Billing-Correlation-ID
```

The Billing-Correlation-ID is discussed in Chapter 7. It is a 32-octet hexadecimal string of 16 octets of encoded identifying information (address of the device; timestamp; sequence number) that is designed to be globally unique.

SIP Response Extensions

In addition to the new headers, DCS defines a single new response over and above those defined in RFC 2543.

183 SESSION PROGRESS

DCS allows a 183 provisional response to be sent in answer to an INVITE *by trusted network devices only*. The response indicates that the destination will provide an audible ringback stream of RTP packets. Typically, this response would come from a PSTN gateway involved in an on-net to off-net call.

The MTA is, of course, free to ignore both the response and the stream of ringback packets that follow and instead to generate the ringback locally. However, it is more user-friendly for it to play back the packets, since ringback cadences vary from country to country, and the user would typically expect (for example) that a call placed to the United Kingdom would generate the U.K. ringback cadence while he is waiting for the call to be answered.

SIP and DCS

DCS clients are designed to be a kind of "super-SIP" client. The SIP RFC, RFC 2543, defines the behavior of DCS entities, except where the behavior is explicitly overridden by statements in the DCS specification. DCS clients should be able to interoperate with SIP clients (for example, a standard SIP client should be able to place a call to a DCS client), although when they do so, the available feature set becomes the lowest common denominator of the two protocols—that is, SIP, since DCS is a superset of SIP.

The interoperability is therefore limited from the point of view of the DCS client. The features supported by the DCS extensions cannot be supported in a call that has a standard SIP client as one of the parties. Since one of the extensions is designed to support the needs of PacketCable Quality of Service, QoS is not granted to calls (or call legs) to which a standard SIP client is a party. Thus, although communication can still occur, it will not be true telephony communication, since there are no guarantees that the resources necessary are in fact available.[4]

The SIP RFC emplaces requirements that are not fundamentally necessary in a pure DCS environment dedicated to placing calls over a PacketCable network. However, in order to ease interoperability, and in the interest of allowing code-reuse, DCS still mandates that these requirements be met, even though in the context of DCS they are redundant, meaningless, and/or unnecessary. In other words, DCS *extends* SIP, it does not change it.

DCS URLs

SIP uses **Uniform Resource Locators** (**URL**s) to identify entities such as users. In particular, as we shall see, URLs are used in INVITE messages to identify the far end of a connection.

DCS uses the (complicated) syntax of a SIP URL in a manner that permits a large amount of information to be included in a field in such a way that a standard SIP parser will accept it as a valid username, and a DCS parser can interpret meaningfully the contents of what, to SIP, is merely an opaque blob.

A URL that conforms to this syntax is referred to as a DCS-URL.

```
User⁵ = telephone-subscriber *("," dcs-user-param) | dcs-user-param *(","
dcs-user-param) | *(unreserved | escaped | "&" | "=" | "+" | "$" ",")
```

where

telephone-subscriber = global-phone-number | local-phone-number | special-service-name

dcs-user-param = lnp-param | private-param | other-param

lnp-param = "lnp=" token

private-param = "private=" token

special-service-name = "return-call" | "call-trace" | "bridge"

---

4. It is sometimes useful to distinguish between *Voice*-over-IP (which is the domain of standard SIP) and *Telephony*-over-IP (which is the domain of PacketCable). The latter has more stringent requirements.

5. Elements that are undefined in this and other BNF descriptions in this chapter assume the definitions in RFC 2543. Space precludes us repeating the (sometimes lengthy) definitions given therein.

What does all this mumbo-jumbo mean in practice? Well, an ordinary SIP URL identifying a user by telephone number looks like this.

```
sip:303-123-1111:1234@ratco.com;user=phone
```

DCS extends this syntax to allow, for example, something along the lines of:

```
sip:303-123-1111,lnp=720-123@ratco.com;user=phone
```

in which a Local Number Portability (LNP) database has been consulted to resolve the correct destination for the original phone number.

It also allows for URLs like this:

```
sip: return-call,private=x419d2b70a3@dcs-proxy.ratco.com
```

in which a phone number has been encrypted by a private key.

More generally, it allows for arbitrary information to be included in the URL in a private field.

```
sip:private=Encrypted-state-blob-in-hexadecimal-encoding
                        @host.ratco.com;user=phone
```

Thus, an entire encrypted state blob can be included in a URL. The DP to which the URL is sent can then decrypt the blob and extract from it whatever information it desires.

Supported Headers

SIP defines a large number of headers, only a small subset of which are necessary for DCS to operate correctly. A DCS-compliant application must support the following headers (in addition to the header extensions we have already discussed).

```
Call-ID:
Contact:
Content-Length:
Content-Type:
CSeq:
Expires:
From:
Proxy-Require:
Record-Route:
```

```
Require:
Route:
To:
Via:
```

A DCS application may also respond to other SIP headers as defined by RFC 2543; it should silently ignore any headers that it does not implement.

SDP

Like NCS, DCS uses the Session Description Protocol, SDP, to describe the parameters of the bearer channel.[6] SDP is fully defined in RFC 2327. Table 5-1 provides a complete list of DCS Session Description parameters. They are described more fully in the following subsections.

Protocol Version (v=)

Example:

```
v=0
```

Table 5-1 SDP Parameters

Parameter Name	SDP Encoding
Protocol Version	v=
Origin	o=
Session Name	s=
Connection Data	c=
Bandwidth	b=
Time	t=
Encryption Keys	k=
Attributes	a=
Media Announcements	m=

---

6. The use of SDP in DCS is *almost* the same as in NCS. The differences are just enough to be dangerous.

Origin (o=)

The Origin field comprises six subfields separated by whitespace.

username

> In DCS, the username is always a hyphen (-) to protect the privacy of the calling party

session-ID

> Usually a timestamp (to ensure uniqueness) but may be any value.

version

> Usually a timestamp (to ensure uniqueness) but may be any value.

network-type

> Always IN (meaning "Internet").

address-type

> Always IP4.

address

> A unique value is used. In order not to reveal any identifying information, the Call-ID is a good choice.

Example:

```
o=- 15463295 15463295 IN IP4 1FECA3958A728B
```

None of these subfields is used by a receiving MTA. They are, however, required by SIP.

Session Name (s=)

In order to protect the privacy of the calling party, the Session Name must always be encoded as a hyphen (-).

```
s=-
```

Connection Data (c=)

The Connection Data field comprises three subfields, separated by whitespace.

network-type

> Always IN (meaning "Internet").

address-type

> Always IP4.

connection-address

> The connection-address is an IP address at which the endpoint is prepared to receive media traffic. In DCS, an MTA must use the same address for both sending and receiving, so this is also the address from which the MTA will transmit media packets.

So, for example:

```
c=IN IP4 192.30.40.50
```

Bandwidth (b=)

Although this line is theoretically optional, in order for the PacketCable DQoS mechanism to function correctly, its use is highly recommended. The Bandwidth parameter is given as the string "AS:" followed by an integer representing the maximum bandwidth requirement of the media stream in kilobits per second, for example:

```
b=AS:120
```

The value specified is the application's notion of the maximum bandwidth required. In other words, it includes all the additional low-level packetization and link-layer overhead, as well as the basic output from the codec.

Time (t=)

The Time field comprises two subfields, separated by whitespace.

```
t=start-time stop-time
```

The start time should be the current time (although it may also be given as zero, which is interpreted as "now"). The stop time is zero (which is interpreted as "at infinity"). The times are encoded as decimal representations of Network Time Protocol (NTP) time values in seconds. NTP time values correspond to UNIX time values plus 2208988800. NTP time is the number of seconds since zero hours UTC on 1 January, 1900. Details of NTP are in RFC 1129.

For example:

```
t=2219289835 0
```

Encryption Keys (k=)

PacketCable does require that encryption keys be associated with every RTP and RTCP stream. However, the mechanism used is quite different from the mechanism described in RFCs 1889, 1890, 2327 and 2543, which require the use of the k= line of the SDP to pass encryption information. Therefore the k= line of the SDP is not used, and must be ignored if it is present.

Attributes (a=)

The attributes associated with a connection are listed on a= lines. An SDP description may, and usually does, contain more than one such line, each specifying a different attribute. Attributes may be either property attributes or value attributes. Property attributes are used to indicate that the session has a particular property; value attributes are used to associate a value with a property.

A property attribute for the property PROP is encoded by:

```
a=PROP
```

A value attribute for the property PROP with the value VAL is encoded by:

```
a=PROP:VAL
```

The property attributes recognized by DCS are sendonly, recvonly and sendrecv, and are used to indicate whether a flow is unidirectional or bidirectional. For example,

```
a=sendrecv
```

indicates that the session described by this SDP is bidirectional.

DCS also recognizes several value attributes. The most important of these are used to convey information about the codec in use. This information is encoded using the rtpmap mechanism discussed in the section "RTPMAPs" in Chapter 4. A typical example of an rtpmap attribute is:

```
a=rtpmap:96 PCMU/8000
```

This example indicates that RTP packets of type 96 are associated with the PCMU codec (which is another name for G.711) sampled 8,000 times per second.

The ptime value attribute is used by an MTA to calculate the correct QoS reservations necessary to carry the media flow. If the rtpmap contains a "well-known" codec (that is, one specified in RFC 2327), then the ptime does not have to be explicitly declared in the SDP, and the MTA uses a reasonable value associated with the name of the well-known codec.

```
a=ptime:<packet time>
```

The "packet time" is the duration in milliseconds of the media contained in a packet. So, for example, if the codec produces 100 packets per second, the corresponding SDP line would be:

```
a=ptime:10
```

Several extension attributes (attributes whose names begin with x-) are also used by DCS. Extensions used by PacketCable begin with the string x-pc-.

X-pc-bridge

> This attribute takes a single numeric value, which corresponds to the maximum number of participants that may be attached simultaneously to a bridge. This number is used by a bridge to determine how to allocate its resources to the call.

X-pc-codecs

> This attribute contains an ordered list of codecs that the endpoint is willing to use for this connection. The list is ordered in decreasing order of preference. A codec cannot actually be used to encode information until its use has been signaled on an SDP m= line.

X-pc-csuites-rtp, X-pc-csuites-rtcp

> This attribute (one for RTP, one for RTCP) contains an ordered list of ciphersuites (pairs of encryption and authentication algorithms) that the endpoint is willing to use on this connection. The list is ordered in decreasing order of preference.

> A ciphersuite is encoded as a string of four hexadecimal characters where the first pair denotes the authentication algorithm and the second pair the encryption algorithm. The list of permitted ciphersuites is the same as for NCS. See Tables 4-14 through 4-17.

X-pc-secret

> Security for the RTP and RTCP traffic between PacketCable MTAs is based on a shared secret, from which the necessary keying material is derived (see the section "Encrypting RTP Packets" in Chapter 4 for complete details). The value of this secret, which is the same for both the RTP and the RTCP streams in both directions (that is, all four streams use the same secret) is

placed on the X-pc-secret line. The encoding is of the form <method>:<value>, where <method> describes the method of encoding the secret, and <value> is the value of the secret.

<method> may be either "clear" or "BASE64". BASE64 encoding is a method for converting arbitrary binary strings into a format that contains only ASCII printable characters. Details of the encoding are provided in Appendix C.

Since only printable characters are valid in DCS messages, it is unlikely that any reasonable implementation would choose to use the "clear:" encoding, since that can be used only with keys that themselves contain only ASCII printable characters—highly unlikely if the keys are being generated by a good pseudorandom generator (as they should be).

An example line for transmitting a shared secret is (in practice, this would be transmitted on a single line)

```
a= X-pc-secret: base64:pV6BIIHWt+
          0gDkpgnuxgTfROxYAemhYJTHWgHNt1crTtEUKFatJfSdEFVQuueo==
```

Media Announcements (m=)

The media announcement line contains four subfields.

```
m=<media> <port> <transport> <format>
```

The <media> value is always "audio" in a pure telephony network.

The port is the number of the port on which the MTA will receive data. The number of the transmitting port may or may not be the same, but in either case it is not specified in the SDP description of the connection.

The transport type always has the value "RTP/AVP", which corresponds to the Real-time Transport Protocol (RFC 1889) using the Audio/Video profile carried over UDP (RFC 1890).

The format is one of the format numbers defined in RFC 1890. Usually, the format number is 0, which corresponds to μ-law PCM encoded single-channel audio sampled at 8 kHz. The format number is inserted into RTP packets. The m= line instructs the device what codec to use to correctly decode the packet. See the section "RTPMAPs" in Chapter 4 for more details.

So, for example, the Media Announcements line for an audio stream of RTP packets of μ-law PCM encoded single-channel audio sampled at 8 kHz that will be received on port 22954 would look like this.

```
m=audio 22945 RTP/AVP 0
```

Details of DCS Signaling

Most of the protocols used in PacketCable are specified in such a way that only the messages themselves and the way in which they interact are described. Detailed call flows that use the messages are generally taken to be illustrative only. Even though most implementations follow closely the example call flows provided in the specifications, a vendor is free to construct quite different call flows there appears to be a competitive advantage in doing so. As long as the individual messages conform to the PacketCable specifications, the resultant system is still regarded as compliant.

DCS, however, is an exception. Its call flows are much more tightly defined. This makes it easier to construct a DCS system that is guaranteed to interoperate correctly with devices from other vendors. The cost, of course, is that a vendor is not free to implement a different call flow, even if it appears to be more efficient. Therefore, with minor exceptions, any implementation of DCS will implement the basic call flow contained in this chapter.

Basic Messaging—INVITE and Its Variants

A standard SIP session begins with a three-way handshake: INVITE; 200 OK; ACK. As we mentioned at the beginning of this chapter, DCS extends this to allow for various features needed to implement telephony-grade service.

As well as the simple basic SIP INVITE (which is still used, to ring the phone at the far end), there are a number of varieties of extended versions of INVITE in DCS, as follows.

INVITE(stage1)

Used for an exchange of information between endpoints prior to ringing the phone. The INVITE(stage1) is always proxied, as is its response.[7]

INVITE(replace) and INVITE(also)

These invitations are used to change the topology of a call by replacing call legs within an existing call. These invitations also pass through proxies, so that resource gates are controlled correctly, and billing records sent to the

---

7. It is generally true in SIP that whatever route a request takes, the response should traverse the same route in opposite order. Thus the INVITE(stage1), being proxied, causes the response to pass through the same proxies (in reverse order).

Record Keeping Server using the Event Messaging mechanism described in Chapter 7.

INVITE(hold) and INVITE(resume)

These messages are used to place a call on and off hold. There is no need for call legs to change or for billing messages to be associated with these messages, and so they are sent end-to-end, without the knowledge or participation of core network devices.

INVITE(return-call) and INVITE(call-trace)

These are special invitations used to implement specific features. Since the call state needed to implement these features is not maintained within the network, these invitations must carry with them an encrypted state blob associated with a prior call. The invitations must be sent to a DCS Proxy, which is the only entity that has the knowledge to decrypt the state blob. Once it has decrypted the state blob, the DCS Proxy has sufficient information to implement the requested feature.

INVITE(BLV) and INVITE(EI)

These messages are initiated on a PSTN gateway and are associated with incoming requests on a special operator trunk on the PSTN. The messages are used to implement Busy Line Verify and Emergency Interrupt on the MTA to which these messages are sent.

The presence of a special header (Dcs-OSPS:) in the message signals that the message is an INVITE(BLV) or an INVITE(EI) and causes the MTA to act differently than if it were to receive an ordinary INVITE(stage1) while the line is in use. Instead of returning a response that indicates that the line is busy, the MTA either makes a copy of the media stream and sends it to the operator (for an INVITE(BLV)) or immediately switches the active call leg to the incoming operator call (for an INVITE(EI)).

You may be wondering how this behavior can be guaranteed. After all, an MTA is an untrusted device that may act in ways contrary to the behavior defined in the specifications. This is true. There is, in fact, no guarantee that the MTA will behave as we have described. However, there is no obvious gain in causing it to behave differently, although a perverse MTA could certainly do so (for example, by playing a recording audio stream to the operator regardless of whether the line was or was not busy, when it sees an incoming INVITE(BLV)).

Retransmission Strategy

DCS messages travel over UDP.[8] Since UDP does not guarantee message delivery, there has to be a well-defined mechanism to deal with the case of lost messages. DCS messaging uses three timers—T_1, T_2 and T_3—to control the retransmission strategy. During the provisioning process values for several timers are provided to the DCS MTA (or, if not, they assume default values), as shown in Table 5-2. The timers T1 and T3 assume these values as appropriate for the message and transaction currently under way.

Timers T_1 and T_2 are similar to those described in the SIP RFC. T_1 is the initial value of the retransmission timer; T_2 is the maximum value that the timer will be permitted to reach if several messages are sent without an acknowledgement being received. The mechanism is a simple exponential doubling: If a response to a request has not been received within T_1, the request is retransmitted. The value of T_1 is then doubled (or set to T_2, if the value of T_2 is less than $2 \times T_1$). If no response has been received within the new value of T_1, then the request is transmitted again.

This continues until some maximum number of retransmissions has occurred. (The maximum number is either 7 or 11, depending on the type of request. See RFC 2543 for details.)

In addition to the two standard SIP timers, DCS introduces a third timer, T3, which is a transaction timer associated with initial call setup. This timer starts when a provisional response has been received to an INVITE(stage1) request. If the timer expires without a final response being received, the MTA returns to the idle state (and possibly flags the error to the user, if such a mechanism exists). T_3 is set to the value T-session in Table 5-2. Default values to which DCS timers may reasonably be set are shown in Table 5-2. These values may be changed during provisioning.

Table 5-2   DCS Timer Values

Timer Label	Default Duration	Description
T-proxy-request	500 ms	Timer between an MTA sending a request to a Dcs-Proxy (for example, an INVITE (stage1)) and receiving a valid response. If T-proxy-request expires before receiving a response, the MTA resends the request.
T-proxy-response	500 ms	Timer between an MTA sending a response to a Dcs-Proxy (for example, 200-OK to an INVITE(stage1)) and receiving a valid

---

8. By default, the DCS Proxy listens for connections on UDP port 5060.

Timer Label	Default Duration	Description
		response. If T-proxy-response expires before receiving a response, the MTA resends the response.
T-direct-request	500 ms	Timer between an MTA sending request directly to another MTA (for example, an INVITE) and receiving a valid response. If T-direct-request expires before receiving a response, the MTA resends the request.
T-direct-response	500 ms	Timer between an MTA sending a response directly to another MTA (for example, a 200-OK message) and receiving a valid response. If T-direct-response expires before receiving a response, the MTA resends the response.
T-ringing	3 to 4 minutes	Timer between beginning to ring the phone and connect. If T-ringing expires before connect, the MTA sends a BYE message and releases the reserved resources, or invokes a feature such as Call Forward No Answer.
T-ringback	5 to 6 minutes	Timer between beginning ringback and receiving a connect. If T-ringback expires before connect, the MTA sends a BYE message and releases the reserved resources. T-ringback should be sufficiently larger than T-ringing to allow for clock skew.
T-session	30 seconds	Timer between receiving a provisional response to an INVITE(stage1) and receiving a final response. If T-session expires before receiving the final response, the MTA or proxy aborts the call attempt.
T-stage1	10 seconds	Timer between receiving an INVITE(stage1) request and receiving a second stage INVITE request. If T-stage1 expires before receiving the second stage INVITE, the MTA aborts the incoming call attempt.

Occasionally, perhaps because of the failure of a DCS Proxy, an MTA might receive no response to an INVITE(stage1) even after all the permitted retransmissions have occurred. During provisioning, the MTA should have been provided with a list of reserve DPs. If no response is received to its INVITE(stage1) requests, the MTA tries another DP in the list (after first setting up an IPsec security association with the new proxy, assuming one does not already exist). If it reaches the end of its list without a response, then the MTA returns to the idle state, flagging the error to the user if a mechanism for doing so exists. Note that failure to be able to communicate with a DP means that the MTA is unable to place any calls until the situation is corrected.

MTAs do not ordinarily return provisional responses. However, if they do so (for example, if resource reservation is likely to take more than 100 milliseconds), then they may transmit a *single* provisional response (generally a "100 Trying") to an INVITE. This allows the originating MTA to start its T_3 transaction timer and to time-out cleanly if, for some reason, the destination MTA never completes the request (for example, if the coax is cut while the call is in the process of being set up).

Establishing a Connection

The basic message flow for establishing a two-way connection is as we depicted in Figure 5-2. Table 5-3 shows the same information in a different format.

We will walk through an example call flow in some detail. In this example, Alice places an ordinary call to Bob. Alice is placing the call from 303-123-1111, and Bob's number is 303-456-2222.

Although this, like any single example, cannot hope to address all the issues involved in DCS call signaling, we will attempt to address many of the issues as we

Table 5-3 Establishing a Connection Between MTAs in DCS

Message #	Message Type	Source	Destination
1	INVITE(stage1)	MTA_O	DP_O
2	INVITE(stage1)	DP_O	DP_T
3	INVITE(stage1)	DP_T	MTA_T
4	OK	MTA_T	DP_T
5	OK	DP_T	DP_O
6	OK	DP_O	MTA_O
7	ACK	MTA_O	MTA_T
8	INVITE	MTA_O	MTA_T
9	Provisional Response	MTA_T	MTA_O
10	OK	MTA_T	MTA_O
11	ACK	MTA_O	MTA_T

discuss the various operations that occur as the call progresses. Details of how special features are implemented are discussed in later sections.

For this example call, we will assume the set of parameters given in Tables 5-4 and 5-5. The Call Sequence Number has not been mentioned before. It serves a similar function to the Transaction-ID in NCS signaling, allowing the recipient of a response or an acknowledgement to match the response or acknowledgement with the request that generated it.

Message Number 1—INVITE(stage1)

MTA_O begins the process of setting up a call by sending an INVITE(stage1) to DP_O. (As we have mentioned, DCS, unlike NCS, has specified the protocol that allows CMSes to forward information between themselves. Therefore there is no requirement that MTA_O be served by the same DP as MTA_T. In this example, Alice and Bob are served by different DCS Proxies.) This occurs after Alice has dialed Bob's phone number. The MTA recognizes that the sequence of digits represents a completed phone number, and transmits the INVITE(stage1) to Alice's DCS Proxy.

Table 5-4 Example Attributes (1)

Attributes Associated with End-Points	Origination	Destination	Example
Name	$User_O$	$User_T$	Alice Abernathy
Hostname	$Host_O$	$Host_T$	alice.abernathy.mta.ratco.com
MTA IP address	$IP(MTA_O)$	$IP(MTA_T)$	44.20.0.3
MTA port number	$Port(MTA_O)$	$Port(MTA_T)$	24680
DP address	$Host(DP_O)$	$Host(DP_T)$	192.136.26.6
Telephone number	$E.164_O$	$E.164_T$	303-538-0145
CMTS address	$Host(CMTS_O)$	$Host(CMTS_T)$	192.136.26.1
CMTS port number	$Port(CMTS_O)$	$Port(CMTS_T)$	24000
Gate ID at CMTS	GID_O	GID_T	0x2354fab5
Gate Key	GK_O	GK_T	0x00112233445566778899aabbccddeeff
Dcs state	DS_O	DS_T	Encrypted blob

Table 5-5   Example Attributes (2)

Attribute Associated with Calls	Notation	Comments
Call-ID	ID	Random string, unique within a call. The specification suggests that it should be implemented as a base64 encoding of a SHA-1 or MD5 cryptographic hash of local provisioned parameters (for example, the phone number) combined with a timestamp and a sequence number.
Call Sequence Number	n_0	Unique within SIP handshake with same call ID within a single client. n_0 is the sequence number generated by MTA_O.
	n_0+1	Increment in the sequence number for a subsequent request message sent by the same client. Each client has an independently managed call sequence number for each call instance at that client.

The format of the INVITE(stage1) is:

```
INVITE sip:303-456-2222@dp0.ratco.com;user=phone SIP/2.0
```

Contains dialed string and name of local DP

```
Via: SIP/2.0/UDP mta.abernathy.aa.widget.ratco.com
```

Contains FQDN of MTA_O

```
Dcs-Caller: Alice Abernathy; 303-123-1111
```

Contains the identity of the caller. However, note that this is untrusted information.

```
Dcs-Anonymity: Off
```

Details the level of anonymity. For this call we will assume that no anonymity is requested.

```
Require:DCS
```

Necessary because the message contains DCS extensions

```
Proxy-Require: DCS
```

Necessary because the proxy must process DCS extensions

```
From: "Alice Abernathy" <sip:BASE64(SHA-1(303-123-1111; time=36123E5B;
seq=127))>
```

Call legs are identified by a triple of header lines: From:, To: and Call-ID:. The set of these three values is sufficient to uniquely identify a leg within a call.

However, the From: header is problematical, since the identifying information that a normal SIP From: header carries should not be automatically passed to the destination MTA.

This problem is circumvented by encoding the identifying information in a one-way encoding that is guaranteed to be unique (with high probability), but from which no useful information can be extracted. A suggested encoding is to take the triplet: phone number+time+sequence number (in some unspecified format), and then to calculate the SHA-1 hash of the triplet, encoding the 20-octet result in BASE64 and using this BASE64 string as the identifying information.

The From: header may include a so-called "display name" in quotation marks. There is no guarantee that this display name is meaningful, nor that it have any relationship whatsoever to the actual identity of the originating party. The intention of the display name is to permit people to use pseudonyms that may be displayed in some manner by a recipient MTA. *This should not be displayed by the Caller-ID mechanism.* The Caller-ID display is for a *trusted* representation of the caller's identity. What is carried in the From: header is *untrusted* information.

There is no guarantee that a display name on the From: line will be passed unchanged by intervening DPs. The display name allows an originator to pass useful information to a destination before a call acquires QoS and could conceivably be used in such a way as to provide a quick messaging service to recipient phone numbers without any party being billed for the service. Not all network operators might be willing to allow this, and such operators might choose to strip the display name from any INVITE(stage1) passing through their networks.

```
To: sip:BASE64(SHA-1(303-456-2222; time=36123E5B; seq=127))
```

Like the From: header, the To: header does not look much like a real destination, does it? There are a couple of reasons for this.

Firstly, SIP does not require that the To: header contain meaningful information. As far as DCS is concerned, the To: header is merely one part of a triple (From:,

To:, Call-ID:) that is used to identify a particular call leg. The contents of the To: header are never used by DCS to determine the destination of the call. Instead, the first line in the INVITE contains the dialed digits, and it is this line that is used to derive the identity of the party whom the user is trying to reach.

The second reason for the rather obscure format of the To: header is that it must look syntactically exactly like the From: header. This is because DCS allows end-point to end-point signaling to perform certain features, such as three-way calling and Call Forward No Answer, in which the contents of a From: header are moved into a To: header.

Hence, the To: header, like the From: header, is a BASE64 encoding of a SHA-1 MAC.

```
Call-ID: BASE64(random number)
```

The Call-ID is designed to identify the call uniquely within the system over a period of at least several months (since this number is used to identify calls within the billing system). One suggested implementation is to set the Call-ID to exactly the same as the contents of the From: header, which has the desired properties.[9]

```
CSeq: 127 INVITE
```

The sequence number is generated by the MTA and is designed to identify the particular "SIP handshake" (typically a three-way handshake comprising an INVITE, a response and an acknowledgement) within a call. The purpose of this is so that if messages are lost within the intervening network, the correct acknowledgements and responses can be matched with the INVITE with which they are associated.

```
Dcs-Stage1:
```

Informs the far end that this is a DCS stage1 INVITE, not a normal SIP INVITE.

```
Contact: sip:192.10.20.10
```

Contains the IP address of the originating MTA. Since the MTA is untrusted, the contents may be a lie, but DP_O will check the value to make sure that it is correct before allowing the call to proceed.

```
Content-type: application/sdp
```

---

9. The SHA-1 hash contains 160 bits, which are essentially randomly distributed. The probability of a collision in N calls is therefore roughly $(1 - ((2^{160} - 1) / 2^{160})^N)$. In a system that handles 100 million calls per month, the probability of a collision in a three-month period is therefore negligible.

This line must be present.

```
Content-length: 221
```

This line must be present. The value of the field is the length, in octets, of the message body (including any nonprinting characters, such as the end-of-line markers). In this example, the body is 221 octets in length.

```
<blank line>
```

An empty line separates the message headers from the message body. The latter contains the SDP description associated with the call, as we discussed in the section SDP earlier in this chapter. For example:

```
v=0
o=- 2987933615 2987933615  IN IP4 A3C47F2146789D0
s=-
c=IN IP4 192.30.40.1
b=AS:64000
t=907165275 0
a=X-pc-suite:312F
a=rtpmap:0 PCMU/8000
a=rtpmap:96 G726-32/8000
m=audio 3456 RTP/AVP 0
a=X-pc-codecs:0 96
```

This concludes the INVITE(stage1) that is sent from MTA_O to DP_O.

Message Number 2—INVITE(stage1)

A SIP proxy (or, in our case, a DCS Proxy, which is merely a specialized form of SIP Proxy) is designed to service requests on behalf of clients, either by handling them internally or by forwarding the request, possibly with modifications, to a client or to another SIP proxy.

SIP defines *stateful* and *stateless* proxies. A DCS Proxy is a stateful proxy (which perhaps seems counterintuitive given that DCS purposefully does not maintain state within the network). During the brief period that a DP is involved in call setup, it maintains a sense of the state associated with that call. However, as soon as the end-to-end connection is made, all the state is pushed to the endpoints and the DP loses, not just the state, but even any memory of the fact that the call has ever existed.

A DCS Proxy contains a large number of functions over and above those needed simply to act as a SIP proxy for DCS calls. Not only must it support call signaling, but it must contain functions for handling issues such as number translation, call routing, support of telephony features and admission control through the DQoS mechanism. Architecturally, a DP is combined with a Gate Controller (GC), which controls the DQoS gates located on CMTSes. The DP/GC combination is a full Call Management System (CMS). Just as NCS blurs the distinction between a Call Agent and a CMS, DCS tends to blur the distinction between a DP and a CMS. Theoretically, a DP is but one component of a CMS, but in practice the two terms are often used as synonyms.

Let's continue with our example of Alice's call to Bob. Alice's INVITE(stage1) has arrived at DP_O. DP_O checks the format of the INVITE(stage1). If any of the required fields is missing, it responds to MTA_O with an appropriate error code (4xx, 5xx, or 6xx), and the message is ignored.

Before the DP begins to process the INVITE(stage1), it performs several authentication steps. The mere fact that the DP has received the message means that the IP address of the source is guaranteed to be known and authenticated, since the message has been received over an IPsec connection that was set up via a process that included authentication (see Chapter 2). Therefore the DP has certain knowledge of the sending party's IP address. This allows it to be sure of other parameters that identify Alice (probably by looking them up in a database).

The DP examines the Dcs-Caller: header and checks that the originating phone number contained in the Dcs-Caller: header is indeed associated with this MTA. It also checks that the number is permitted to invoke whatever service the INVITE is attempting (in our example, the DP would check that Alice's line is permitted to make outgoing calls).

If there is a calling name in the Dcs-Caller: header, the DP checks that the name corresponds to the identity of the party responsible for the originating phone number. It also checks that the values in the Via: and Contact: headers match the entries in its database for that phone number. If the message fails any of these checks, the DP returns an appropriate 4xx, 5xx, or 6xx error code and the message undergoes no further processing. This was a conscious design decision. Theoretically, the DCS could ignore most of these errors and simply overwrite the erroneous parameters. However, since an MTA should never send incorrect values, it was deemed better to fail the call and to inform the MTA of the reason than to correct the errors silently and to allow the call to proceed.

If there is no name in the Dcs-Caller: header (which is legal; only the phone number is required), the DP inserts the name from its database. This allows DP_T to forward the authenticated name of the caller to MTA_T for display on a Caller-ID device, if the destination party has subscribed to a Caller-ID feature.

Once DP_O has authenticated the fields in the received INVITE(stage1), it begins to process the message. It checks that the URL in the first header is valid. In our simple example, the URL contains a plaintext phone number. However, this may not always be the case. The call may contain an encrypted state blob as the URL, signaled by the presence of a user=private field.

If the URL is a state blob, then the DP must attempt to decrypt it. This may fail for any one of a number of reasons. For example, the user may have tried to hack her MTA and in the process altered the values in the state blob in an attempt to obtain access to features for which she has not paid or to obtain free service. The state blob should fail to decrypt correctly in this case.

Perhaps more likely are two scenarios involving the DP: If a reasonably long period of time has elapsed since the state blob was stored on the MTA, the original DP might have failed and its place might have been taken by another machine, which could (depending on the way in which the network operator manages his equipment) have no knowledge of the key used to encode the blob. Alternatively, even on a single DP, the keys should change from time to time, and the DP might have no knowledge of the key that it used to encrypt the blob if the time of that encryption lay sufficiently far in the past.

If the information does not decrypt correctly, for whatever reason, the DP responds to the originating MTA with an appropriate 4xx, 5xx, or 6xx error message and ceases its attempt to process the message.

Now the DP must examine the URL in the first line to see whether the user is attempting to invoke a network-based call feature provided by the network (for example, return-call or call-trace). Typically, such features are invoked by dialing special codes, usually of the form *nn, at the originating handset. If the subscriber is not permitted access to the requested service, a 4xx, 5xx, or 6xx error is generated; otherwise the DP acts on the service request.

Eventually, the DP resolves the contents of the URL into a valid phone number. The DP determines whether the destination number is serviced by itself or by some other CMS or MGC (if the call is going to go off-net, then the call will be routed to an MGC, which acts as if it were the destination DP).

It is possible that during the process of trying to resolve the destination number, the "dialed string" might be modified. That is, the real destination phone number might be different from the string that was dialed. If so, the DP replaces the actual dialed string in the URL with the replacement "dialed" string. There is no need for subsequent devices that handle the message to know that the destination string is different from the one that was actually dialed.

The DP now proceeds to modify the INVITE(stage1) message. When it has finished modifying it, the DCS Proxy will then forward the message to DP_T, the DP that is responsible for handling signaling associated with MTA_T.[10] DP_O also creates a temporary state blob that it stores so that it can refer to the parameters associated with the call later in the set-up process if necessary.

---

10. In a large network, DP_O might not communicate directly with DP_T. Instead, this and subsequent proxied messages might pass through a chain of DCS proxies.

DP_O adds several headers to the INVITE(stage1) before forwarding it to DP_T.

1. A new Via: header containing DP_O's own IP address or FQDN is added in front of the first Via: header. Via: headers trace the route that a particular message has taken through a network. When a response passes through the network, it does so in the reverse order, stripping the Via: headers as it goes. This allows the proxies to delete any state associated with the initial message cleanly instead of relying on a time-out mechanism.

   The Via: header added by DP_O includes a branch=n parameter, to support forking proxies (proxies that are implemented in such a way that they submit multiple requests in parallel). Most proxies, though, generate only a single branch.

```
Via: SIP/2.0/UDP dp0.ratco.com; branch=1
```

2. A Dcs-Billing-Info: header is added. This header contains the hostname and port number of the RKS that will collate billing information for this call. It also contains necessary account information for the call: the account number responsible for payment, the originating number and the destination number.

```
Dcs-Billing-Info: 192.23.34.56:7632<AC#153-96847-264850/
            303-123-1111/303-456-2222>
```

3. A Dcs-Billing-ID: header is added. This is a unique string obtained from the IP address of DP_O, a timestamp, and a sequence number that identified the transaction on the DP, like this.

```
Dcs-Billing-ID: 36123E5C01520F15EC001950B5AF0001
```

4. A Dcs-Gate: header is added. This header contains the IP address and port of the originating CMTS, an identifier that will be used to label the gate on the originating CMTS, and a key that will be used for gate coordination. In order to get this information, the DP interrogates CMTSO, using the DQoS messaging described in the next chapter.

```
Dcs-Gate: 192.11.22.33:3612/17S30124/37FA1948
```

This completes the modifications made to the INVITE(stage1). The complete message now looks like this.

```
INVITE sip:303-456-2222@dp0.ratco.com;user=phone SIP/2.0
Via: SIP/2.0/UDP dp0.ratco.com; branch=1
Via: SIP/2.0/UDP mta.abernathy.aa.widget.ratco.com
Dcs-Caller: Alice Abernathy; 303-123-1111
```

```
Dcs-Anonymity: Off
Dcs-Gate: 192.11.22.33:3612/17S30124/37FA1948
Dcs-Billing-Info: 192.23.34.56:7632
         303-123-1111/303-456-2222>
Dcs-Billing-ID: 36123E5C01520F15EC001950B5AF0001
Require:DCS
Proxy-Require: DCS
From: "Alice Abernathy" <sip:BASE64(SHA-1(303-123-1111; time=36123E5B;
seq=127))>
To: sip:BASE64(SHA-1(303-456-2222; time=36123E5B; seq=127))
Call-ID: BASE64(random number)
CSeq: 127 INVITE
Dcs-Stage1:
Contact: sip:192.10.20.10
Content-type: application/sdp
Content-length: 221

v=0
o=- 2987933615 2987933615  IN IP4 A3C47F2146789D0
s=-
c=IN IP4 192.30.40.1
b=AS:64000
t=907165275 0
a=X-pc-suite:312F
a=rtpmap:0 PCMU/8000
a=rtpmap:96 G726-32/8000
m=audio 3456 RTP/AVP 0
a=X-pc-codecs:0 96
```

DP_O now transmits this message to DP_T.

Message Number 3—INVITE(stage1)

DP_T does not need to authenticate the message explicitly, since the connection between DP_O and DP_T is secured by IPsec. Therefore it is assured that DP_O is indeed the source, although it should check that DP_O is identified correctly in the topmost Via: header.

DP_T consults a database to determine the destination MTA responsible for handling the phone number indicated in the URL in the first line of the header, which should be an MTA that is directly managed by DP_T.[11] It then checks that the MTA_T is authorized to receive this call. (Not all phone numbers accept incoming calls.)

---

11. Depending on the manner in which the network is deployed, it is possible that the database instead returns the address of another DCS Proxy, to which the INVITE should be forwarded, with the caution that DP_T should ensure (by examining the Via: headers) that a forwarding circle has not been generated.

DP$_T$ strips the Dcs-Billing-Info:, Dcs-Billing-ID: and Dcs-Gate: headers and stores them locally, since the information contained in these headers should not be forwarded to the destination MTA.

DP$_T$ also saves the Via: headers for future use. The response from MTA$_T$ must traverse the same path as the original INVITE(stage1), in the reverse order, but since the MTA is untrusted, there is no guarantee that the list of Via: headers that MTA$_T$ will eventually return will match the list that it receives.

However, it is also important that, if the originator has requested anonymity, the routing information contained in the Via: headers must not be passed to MTA$_T$. To ensure that this information doesn't reach the MTA, the headers are encrypted. This may be done by a "one-way super-encryption algorithm". In other words, by encrypting them to something like the letter "a", SIP requires that the Via: header reflect the fact that DP$_T$ was not the origination point for the message but not that the routing be interpretable by the destination MTA. PacketCable makes no use of this information, so it can safely be compressed and one-way super-encrypted.

DP$_T$ generates a state blob, which it signs and encrypts. It then adds a Dcs-state: header containing the encrypted blob to the INVITE(stage1) message. DP$_T$ communicates with CMTS$_T$, obtaining gate information that it inserts into a Dcs-Gate: header in the INVITE(stage1).

If the caller has requested anonymity, DP$_T$ replaces the Dcs-Caller: header with one that contains the string "private". If the destination party has not subscribed to a Caller-ID feature, the Dcs-Caller: header is removed from the message. In all cases, DP$_T$ deletes the Dcs-Anonymity: header from the message.

The INVITE(stage1) now looks like this.

```
INVITE sip:303-456-2222@dp0.ratco.com;user=phone SIP/2.0
Via: SIP/2.0/UDP dpt.ratco.com, a
Dcs-Caller: Alice Abernathy; 303-123-1111
Dcs-Gate: 192.11.22.33:3612/17S30124/37FA1948
Dcs-state: <encrypted state blob>
Require:DCS
From: "Alice Abernathy" <sip:BASE64(SHA-1(303-123-1111; time=36123E5B;
seq=127))>
To: sip:BASE64(SHA-1(303-456-2222; time=36123E5B; seq=127))
Call-ID: BASE64(random number)
CSeq: 127 INVITE
Dcs-Stage1:
Contact: sip:192.10.20.10
Content-type: application/sdp
```

```
Content-length: 221

v=0
o=- 2987933615 2987933615  IN IP4 A3C47F2146789D0
s=-
c=IN IP4 192.30.40.1
b=AS:64000
t=907165275 0
a=X-pc-suite:312F
a=rtpmap:0 PCMU/8000
a=rtpmap:96 G726-32/8000
m=audio 3456 RTP/AVP 0
a=X-pc-codecs:0 96
```

The INVITE(stage1) is now forwarded to MTA$_T$.

Message Number 4—200 OK

If the message contains a Dcs-Caller: header, then the contents of that header are used to display the identity of the caller (rather than any untrusted "display name" inserted by the originating MTA). Note that the destination phone number might be in use (DP$_T$ has no way of knowing this). Therefore if the destination subscriber has subscribed to a Caller-ID feature, then he can be informed of the identity of a calling party, even when the line is already in use. This feature is available in the PSTN but usually at extra cost to the subscriber. It is not possible (as DCS is currently designed) for a service provider to charge extra for this feature in a DCS network.

As we have hinted earlier, one can imagine that MTA$_T$ could maintain a list of "important callers". If one of these parties calls when the line is in use, the MTA could summarily drop the existing connection (perhaps with a warning tone) to make itself available for the incoming call. One of the interesting things about DCS is that it allows MTA designers to permit their imaginations to run rampant. This will be especially true when Open Source standalone MTAs become available for download from the Internet.

For the purpose of our example, we will assume that Bob's line is available for the incoming call. Remember that the MTA does *not* ring the phone when it receives an INVITE(stage1), since at this point it has no way of knowing whether sufficient resources are available for the call. When it receives the INVITE(stage1), MTA$_T$ first examines the m= and a= lines of the SDP to determine whether it has the capability to accept audio encoded by any of the means allowed by the SDP.

Assuming that it determines to accept the call, MTA$_T$ stores the entire INVITE(stage1) for (at least) the duration of the call. The state blob from the message is explicitly stored in long-term storage, so that the MTA can hand it back to

DP_T at a later time if necessary—for example, to utilize a Last Call Return or some other feature that requires the state blob. The entire INVITE(stage1), or important parts of it, may also be stored in long-term storage to allow the intelligent MTA to provide some features.[12]

If MTA_T receives a malformed INVITE(stage1), then it generates a 4xx response and discards any information contained in the message. At this point, the MTA attempts to reserve resources for the call, using the DQoS mechanism described in Chapter 7.

If this might take more than approximately 100 milliseconds—which would typically be the case—the MTA is permitted to return a 100 Trying provisional response to DP_T, which will return the provisional response through the proxy chain to MTA_O. This will cause the originating MTA to recognize that INVITE(stage1) has reached its destination, and so it will not retransmit the message. (It also begins the T_3 transaction timer, as described earlier in the chapter.)

Assuming that $CMTS_T$ confirms that DQoS resources are available for the call, then MTA_T reserves the resources and transmits a 200 OK status response to DP_T. The 200 OK is a simple message that looks like this.

```
SIP/2.0 200 OK
```

Indicates that this is a 200 OK message

```
Via: SIP/2.0/UDP dpt.ratco.com, a
```

This is a copy of the topmost Via: header from the INVITE(stage1). If more than one Via: header was present in the INVITE(stage1), they should be included as well (although no harm will be done if they are absent).

```
Dcs-Anonymity: OFF
```

In PacketCable, *both* parties may independently request a degree of anonymity. A calling party may not always know the precise identity of the destination (for example, if a last-call-return feature was invoked to place the call), and so the destination party might reasonably request a degree of anonymity.

```
From: "Alice Abernathy" <sip:BASE64(SHA-1(303-123-1111; time=36123E5B;
seq=127))>
To: sip:BASE64(SHA-1(303-456-2222; time=36123E5B; seq=127))
```

---

12. The long-term storage may accommodate more than one state blob, so that the MTA might implement "Trace the nth last call" and other similar features that are not currently available on the PSTN.

```
Call-ID: BASE64(random number)
CSeq: 127 INVITE
```

These four headers are copied directly from the INVITE(stage1).

```
Contact: sip:192.10.20.2
```

MTA_T inserts its IP address here, so that future signaling messages can go end-to-end.

```
Content-Type: application/sdp
Content-Length: yyy
```

Must be present to indicate that SDP follows in the body of the message.

```
<blank line>
```

A blank line separates the headers from the body.

The body of the message contains an SDP description defining media flow parameters that are acceptable to MTA_T (from the list of possibilities provided in the INVITE(stage1)). For example:

```
v=0
o=- 2987933615 2987933615  IN IP4 A3C47F2146789D0
s=-
c=IN IP4 192.10.20.2
b=AS:64000
t=907165275 0
a=X-pc-suite:312F
a=rtpmap:0 PCMU/8000
m=audio 3456 RTP/AVP 0
a=X-pc-codecs:0
```

Message Number 5—200 OK

DP_T forwards the SDP (via an undefined mechanism) contained in the 200 OK to the DQoS Gate Controller responsible for controlling $CMTS_T$. The mechanism for this is undefined because PacketCable assumes that the DCS Proxy and the Gate Controller are actually two different processes running on the same computer (or are so tightly coupled that they can be treated as if they were doing so). Communication can be via any interprocess mechanism defined for the operating system in use—a couple of reasonable examples are shared memory and internal sockets. In any case, the PacketCable project has not defined this interface nor placed any specific security requirements on it.

The way in which the Gate Controller converts the SDP into a real reservation of resources on the HFC access network is covered in some detail in Chapters 3 and 6. Before DP_T forwards the 200 OK back to DP_O, it makes some changes to the headers.

1. It removes any Via: headers and replaces them with the cached series from the original INVITE(stage1). This allows any intervening DPs between DP_O and DP_T to route the 200 OK correctly.

2. It adds a Dcs-Gate: header containing the information for the gate that has been established on $CMTS_T$. This header contains the IP address and port number for $CMTS_T$, that Gate-ID of the established gate, and the security key that will be used to authenticate DQoS messages travelling directly between $CMTS_O$ and $CMTS_T$.

3. It adds a Record-Route: header that contains the IP address or FQDN of both DP_T and MTA_T. This is needed so that if a feature is invoked later in the call and that feature needs to issue an INVITE that follows the same route as the initial INVITE, then a record exists of the route that was taken.

4. Normally no other changes are necessary. However, it may also be necessary to write a Dcs-Billing-Info: header into the message if the calling party will not be responsible for paying for this call.

So the response now looks like this.

```
SIP/2.0 200 OK
Via: SIP/2.0/UDP dp0.ratco.com; branch=1
Via: SIP/2.0/UDP mta.abernathy.aa.widget.ratco.com
Record-Route: DP_T-IP-Address, MTA_T-IP-Address
Dcs-Anonymity: OFF
Dcs-gate: CMTS_T-IP-Address:CMTS_T-Port/Gate-ID/Gate-Key
From: "Alice Abernathy" <sip:BASE64(SHA-1(303-123-1111; time=36123E5B;
seq=127))>
To: sip:BASE64(SHA-1(303-456-2222; time=36123E5B; seq=127))
Call-ID: BASE64(random number)
CSeq: 127 INVITE
Contact: sip:192.10.20.2
Content-Type: application/sdp
Content-Length: 192

v=0
o=- 2987933615 2987933615  IN IP4 A3C47F2146789D0
```

```
s=-
c=IN IP4 192.10.20.2
b=AS:64000
t=907165275 0
a=X-pc-suite:312F
a=rtpmap:0 PCMU/8000
m=audio 3456 RTP/AVP 0
a=X-pc-codecs:0
```

The 200 OK is now forwarded to DP_O, or it traverses a series of DCS Proxies until it reaches DP_O. Each intervening DCS Proxy strips its own Via: from the list, adds itself to the Record-Route: header, and forwards the message to the DP identified in the highest remaining Via: header.

In a perfect network, each DP would be able to delete all information about the call as soon as it has transmitted the 200 OK. However, the signaling is being carried via UDP and hence has a non-zero probability of being lost, and the 200 OK is unacknowledged by the recipient DP. Therefore a DP cannot immediately jettison all the call state information. Retransmission is forced, not on a hop-by-hop basis but end-to-end.

MTA_T begins a timer when it transmits the 200 OK. If it does not receive an ACK from MTA_O in a timely manner, then it will retransmit the 200 OK to DP_T. (Because the ACK to the 200 OK is going to travel end-to-end, and not via the DPs, its absence cannot be detected by the DPs.) Figure 5-5 shows this.

The DP must maintain the call state for a period sufficiently long to ensure that there is no possibility of it being required to retransmit the 200 OK. (It could, in theory, jettison all the state and simply cache the transmitted 200 OK for a while. That, however, is called Living Dangerously.) The definition of "sufficiently long" is left to the vendor (which is called Passing the Buck).

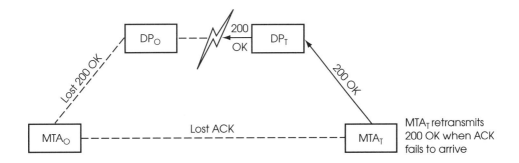

Figure 5-5 Retransmission After a Lost 200 OK

Message Number 6—200 OK

The 200 OK arrives at DP_O, which strips the topmost remaining Via: (which refers to DP_O itself). It removes the Record-Route: header and adds the information contained therein to the state blob associated with this transaction. It signs and encrypts the state blob and adds it to the 200 OK as a Dcs-State: header. The only entity expected to be able to decrypt the state blob is DP_O itself. Therefore the key used for this encryption does not have to be shared with any other entity. The blob is signed before encryption so that any tampering with the encrypted blob by MTA_O can be detected.

The Dcs-Gate: header is replaced by the corresponding information for the local gate. As at the terminating DCS Proxy, the SDP contained in the 200 OK is forwarded to the local Gate Controller, which instructs $CMTS_O$ to create a gate with sufficient resources to allow the call to proceed.

DP_O also adds an X-pc-secret: parameter to the SDP. This will be the secret shared between the two endpoints and from which will be derived all the necessary keying information to ensure that the ensuing conversation is private. (See the section "Encrypting RTP Packets" in Chapter 4 for details.) The resulting message looks something like this.

```
SIP/2.0 200 OK
Via: SIP/2.0/UDP mta.abernathy.aa.widget.ratco.com
From: "Alice Abernathy" <sip:BASE64(SHA-1(303-123-1111; time=36123E5B;
seq=127))>
To: sip:BASE64(SHA-1(303-456-2222; time=36123E5B; seq=127))
Call-ID: BASE64(random number)
CSeq: 127 INVITE
Contact: sip:192.10.20.2
Dcs-gate: CMTS_O-IP-Address:CMTS_O-Port/Gate-ID/Gate-Key
Dcs-State: <encrypted state blob>
Content-Type: application/sdp
Content-Length: 280

v=0
o=- 2987933615 2987933615  IN IP4 A3C47F2146789D0
s=-
c=IN IP4 192.10.20.2
b=AS:64000
t=907165275 0
a=X-pc-suite:312F
a=rtpmap:0 PCMU/8000
m=audio 3456 RTP/AVP 0
a=X-pc-codecs:0
```

```
a=X-pc-secret: base64:pV6BIIHWt+
            0gDkpgnuxgTfROxYAemhYJTHWgHNt1crTtEUKFatJfSdEFVQuueo==
```

Just as in NCS, the shared secret that will be used to derive the keys for the bearer-channel encryption is known by the network. Note that the shared secret that is carried in X-pc-secret is *not* the key that is used to encrypt the bearer-channel traffic. Rather, it is the secret that is used to derive the keys that are actually used (one in each direction). This mechanism means that only one cryptographic value needs to be shared between the two end-points. All keys are then derived from that single value. This has important repercussions for the actual amount of privacy that the network guarantees. (See section "DCS and Privacy" for a detailed discussion.)

Message Number 7—ACK

MTA_O finally receives the 200 OK response to the original INVITE(stage1). It stops the T_1 and T_3 timers, and saves the Dcs-Gate:, Dcs-State: and Contact: headers, as well as the SDP description.

Both MTAs now have the IP address of the MTA at the other end of the connection. All further communication on this phone call is end-to-end, unless call features that require the intrusion of DCS Proxies are invoked. MTA_O transmits an acknowledgement directly to MTA_T.

```
ACK sip: 192.10.20.2 SIP/2.0
Via: SIP/2.0/UDP 192.10.20.10
From: "Alice Abernathy" <sip:BASE64(SHA-1(303-123-1111; time=36123E5B;
seq=127))>
To: sip:BASE64(SHA-1(303-456-2222; time=36123E5B; seq=127))
Call-ID: BASE64(random number)
CSeq: 127 ACK
```

The number in the CSeq is the same as the one in the 200 OK that is being acknowledged (which in turn is the same as the one in the original INVITE(stage1)). As we have discussed, the sequence number is used to identify the particular transaction. The INVITE(stage1)/200 OK/ACK form a single complete transaction.

```
Content-Type: application/sdp
Content-length: <length of body>

<SDP follows in message body>
```

As soon as the ACK is transmitted, MTA_O reserves the network resources for the call, in conformance with the SDP contained in the ACK. The SDP in the ACK is optional, but for efficiency reasons it should be sent, unless the original INVITE(stage1) did not allow for any negotiation (only one codec and one ciphersuite were specified). This SDP is the final agreed-on description for the session that is being started.

When MTA_T receives the ACK, it also has a copy of the final SDP (normally this would be identical to the SDP it transmitted in the 200 OK), and can reserve the necessary resources.

Message Number 8—INVITE

When it has confirmed that local resources are available to carry the session, MTA_O transmits an INVITE directly to MTA_T.

```
INVITE sip: 192.10.20.2 SIP/2.0
Via: SIP/2.0/UDP 192.10.20.1
From: "Alice Abernathy" <sip:BASE64(SHA-1(303-123-1111; time=36123E5B;
seq=127))>
To: sip:BASE64(SHA-1(303-456-2222; time=36123E5B; seq=127))
Call-ID: BASE64(random number)
Cseq: 128 INVITE
```

This is a new transaction, so the sequence number increments.

```
Content-Type: application/sdp
Content-length: <length of body>


<SDP follows in message body>
```

If present, the SDP contained in the INVITE must be identical to the SDP contained in the ACK. Remember that there is a possibility that MTA_T never received the ACK, so the SDP should normally also be carried in the INVITE. As before, there is one case in which this is not necessary: when the SDP in the original INVITE(stage1) allowed for no choices of codec and ciphersuite.

Note that this INVITE is quite short compared to the original INVITE(stage1). All the parameters needed to describe the call have already been carried to the appropriate parties, so it is unnecessary to carry much information in this second INVITE (especially if there was no SDP to be negotiated).

The retransmission timer on this message should be set to T-direct-request, and retransmissions are made as necessary. Once MTA_O has transmitted this INVITE, it should be prepared to receive bearer packets that comply with the SDP at any time. This is because signaling associated with the other end going off-hook may be temporarily lost or delayed in the network, so there is a non-zero probability that the first indication MTA_O will have that a conversation has started is when it begins to receive bearer channel packets.

Similar activity occurs at MTA_T when it receives either the ACK or the INVITE, if the ACK is lost. It begins by attempting to reserve network resources. Optionally, it may send a 100 Trying message in response to the INVITE, to indicate to MTA_O that it has received the INVITE and is attempting to reserve the requested resources. If resource reservation fails, it sends a BYE directly to MTA_O, which tears down the call.[13]

Message Number 9—18x

Assuming, however, that the resource reservation at MTA_T succeeds, it transmits either a 180 Ringing or 183 Session Progress message to MTA_O. Simultaneously it begins alerting the user that an incoming call has arrived (by ringing the phone). The arrival of any 1xx message at MTA_O causes MTA_O to stop retransmitting the INVITE, since the MTA now knows that the INVITE arrived at its destination.

Message Number 10—200 OK

When MTA_T goes off-hook, it commits the local resources and sends a 200 OK to MTA_O.

```
SIP/2.0 200 OK
Via: SIP/2.0/UDP 192.10.20.1
From: "Alice Abernathy" <sip:BASE64(SHA-1(303-123-1111; time=36123E5B;
seq=127))>
To: sip:BASE64(SHA-1(303-456-2222; time=36123E5B; seq=127))
Call-ID: BASE64(random number)
Cseq: 128 INVITE
Content-Type: application/sdp
Content-Length: <length of body>


<SDP follows in message body>
```

The SDP is present only if there was SDP in the second INVITE from MTA_O. MTA_T should be prepared to receive bearer channel packets as soon as it has transmitted this 200 OK (since it signals an "off-hook" condition, and the far end may begin to send bearer packets at any time after it knows that MTA_T has gone off-hook).

---

13. Part of tearing down a call is to delete the Dynamic Service Flow between MTA_O and $CMTS_O$. Deleting this flow causes the CMTS to transmit an event message to the RKS so that the correct billing occurs.

Message Number 11—ACK

When it receives this 200 OK, MTA_O completes the SIP three-way handshake for this transaction by sending an ACK back to MTA_T.

```
ACK sip: 192.10.20.2 SIP/2.0
Via: SIP/2.0/UDP 192.10.20.1
From: "Alice Abernathy" <sip:BASE64(SHA-1(303-123-1111; time=36123E5B;
seq=127))>
To: sip:BASE64(SHA-1(303-456-2222; time=36123E5B; seq=127))
Call-ID: BASE64(random number)
Cseq: 128 INVITE
```

If it hasn't done so already, MTA_O commits the resources for the call, and at this point, the call is under way.

Tearing Down a Call

Call teardown is much simpler: The MTAs perform a simple two-way handshake. Suppose that the endpoint on MTA_1 has gone on-hook. (In practice, if MTA_1 is MTA_T, then the exchange will occur only after it has gone on-hook *and* a timer with a value of around ten seconds has expired. This gives Bob the opportunity to go on-hook, move to another room, and pick up another phone on the same line without losing the call. For the sake of determining the values carried in our example messages, we will assume that MTA_1 is MTA_O—Alice terminates the call.) The other MTA is MTA_2. MTA_1 releases the network resources and sends a BYE.

```
BYE sip:Host(mta2) SIP/2.0
From: "Alice Abernathy" <sip:BASE64(SHA-1(303-123-1111; time=36123E5B;
seq=127))>
To: sip:BASE64(SHA-1(303-456-2222; time=36123E5B; seq=127))
Call-ID: BASE64(random number)
Cseq: 129 BYE
```

The sequence number is incremented by one from the prior SIP transaction (which would normally be the second INVITE).

MTA_2 also releases the resources, and responds with a 200 OK.

```
SIP/2.0 200 OK
From: "Alice Abernathy" <sip:BASE64(SHA-1(303-123-1111; time=36123E5B;
seq=127))>
To: sip:BASE64(SHA-1(303-456-2222; time=36123E5B; seq=127))
Call-ID: BASE64(random number)
Cseq: 129 BYE
```

And that's it. Both MTAs return to their basic "idle" state, ready either to place outgoing calls or receive incoming ones.

Implementing Features

As a rule, it is generally much easier to implement the signaling messages for call features in DCS than it is in NCS. It is easy to see why this should be so. Consider the analogy of surfing the Web with an ordinary browser. The client (the browser) can interact with extremely complex pages located on the server without the intervening ISP needing to be aware of anything that is happening at the two ends of the connection. The browser might even receive a software "update" in real-time (by downloading a plug-in), allowing it to implement a feature that it could not implement at the start of the session. This is the DCS paradigm. If the Web were to follow the NCS paradigm, the Internet would have to be aware of every change in state on the browser and the server. The Internet itself would have to provide the new feature—so that new features could not be deployed without the explicit agreement of the ISP, who would doubtless charge the end-user every time a feature was used. And every software writer who wanted to deploy a feature would have to take into account all possible states of the browser/server "call" to be sure that the new feature did not interact in some unforeseen manner with all the other features that have been deployed by that ISP.

The NCS model is fine for an environment in which relatively few features are offered, and the feature set rarely changes. It breaks down horribly when one wants to deploy a large number of features rather quickly.

Some features do require that DCS Proxies become involved, sometimes because they involve managing call legs, sometimes because they must be reflected in the billing records. When a DCS Proxy has to be involved in a feature invocation, the MTA requesting the feature sends an INVITE to its DP. The INVITE contains no Dcs-Stage1: header, which tells the DP that the message concerns an existing call (about which, of course, it has no prior knowledge, since it does not maintain call state).

A typical INVITE to request a change in the call has the following form (we assume that the change is being requested at DP_O).

```
INVITE sip:private=DState@Host(dpo); user=phone SIP/2.0
```

The private-param must be present. The format looks like a particularly obscure e-mail address. The portion before the "@" sign is the encrypted state blob that has been held on MTA_O, represented in BASE64 encoding. The portion following the "@" sign identifies the DP that originally encrypted the blob. Normally this would be DP_O. If, for some reason, the encryption was performed by some other DP (for example, perhaps this is a long call, and the original DP_O that set up the call has crashed while the call has been under way), then either the current DP_O signals an error or it obtains the correct key to decrypt the state blob via some undefined mechanism.

The DCS specification requires that state blob contain, at a minimum originating and terminating phone numbers; address and port number of the local CMTS; the Gate-ID and shared secret for the gates; the identity of the terminating DP; and the identity of the terminating MTA.

```
Via: SIP/2.0/UDP 192.10.20.2
```

IP address or FQDN of originating MTA

```
Require:DCS
Proxy-Require: DCS
```

These are needed to permit the DP and the other MTA to process the DCS extension headers correctly.

```
From: <value from original INVITE>
To: <value from original INVITE>
Call-ID: <value from original INVITE>
```

These values of the fields in this triple are the same as in the original INVITE(stage1).

```
Cseq: 129 INVITE
```

The transaction number must increment by one from the most recent transaction number.

Depending on the feature being requested, other fields may also be present. For example, if anonymity is desired, a Dcs-Anonymity: header will be present. If the feature requests some sort of redirection, a Dcs-Also: and a Dcs-Replaces: header will be present, indicating the identity of the new destination and the current destination, respectively.

Most of the features that are signaled in this manner are simple analogs of features that are commonly present in the PSTN. One particular "feature", however, is not necessary in the PSTN but is needed in a PacketCable network that supports multiple codecs: the mid-call codec change.

Mid-Call Codec Changes

Since all communication in a PacketCable network comprises streams of digital RTP packets, the two sides have to agree at all times on the algorithms used to encode and decode the traffic.[14] In addition, the CMTSes that house the DQoS gates must also be aware of the traffic requirements for the codec in use, so that sufficient resources are available.

Initially, these coordinations are achieved during the initial call setup by the exchange of SDP. Most of the time, this should be sufficient. There are some cases, however, in which users might wish to signal a change in codec in a call that is already under way.

The most common reason for doing this is a situation in which a call has begun with a relatively low bit-rate codec (for example, an ordinary voice call using compression), but the need becomes apparent after the call is under way to switch to a higher bit rate (for example, the parties decide to exchange a fax[15]). Another situation might be where a call has begun as a fax call but then later turns into an ordinary voice call. The parties might wish to switch to a low bit-rate codec for the latter part of the call in order to save money—assuming that the service provider charges differently for high-bandwidth and low-bandwidth calls.

First, let's consider the case where the change in codecs will lead to a change in billing rate. It doesn't matter whether the new codec consumes fewer or more resources than the old one. The important fact is that the service provider is going to alter the marginal billing rate once the codec has been changed. Therefore the service provider has to be given enough information for the billing change to take place correctly. In order to keep the messaging down to a reasonable length, we will assume that the newer codec fits within the envelope of the older one. If this is not the case, then additional DQoS message exchanges (typically GATE-SETs) are necessary between the CMSes and the respective CMTSes, as well as DOCSIS messaging (to allocate the correct Dynamic Service Flow) between the MTAs and the CMTSes.

MTA_O sends an INVITE;[16] the INVITE is similar to the one we discussed in the last section, except that it also contains the SDP associated with the new codec.

```
INVITE sip:private=DState@Host(dpo); user=phone SIP/2.0
Via: SIP/2.0/UDP Host(mtao)
Require:DCS
Proxy-Require: DCS
From: <value from original INVITE>
```

---

14. This is not the same agreement as the agreement on the algorithms and keys used to secure the connection.

15. Faxes cannot be communicated reliably with low bit-rate codecs. Typically, fax transmissions require full G.711 capability. Analogue modems (sending analog modem transmission on top of the digital PacketCable audio) have a similar requirement.

16. Although it may be obvious, it bears emphasizing that such a statement underscores one of the principal differences between IP telephony and the conventional PSTN. In PacketCable, signaling messages can be sent over the access network regardless of whether audio is being transmitted concurrently.

```
To: <value from original INVITE>
Call-ID: <value from original INVITE>
Cseq: n+1 INVITE
Content-Type: application/sdp
Content-Length: <length of body>

<SDP for new codec goes here>
```

DP_O decodes the state blob and sends an INVITE based on the received INVITE but with some additions and changes using the data contained in the state blob, to DP_T.

```
INVITE sip: dest-phone-number@Host(dpt); user=phone SIP/2.0
        The destination has been extracted from the state blob; the
        destination now gives the phone number of the other party
        and the terminatin DCS Proxy
Via: SIP/2.0/UDP Host(dpo); branch=1
        Identifies the originating DCS Proxy
Via: SIP/2.0/UDP Host(mtao)
Route: Host(mtat)
        This tells the destination DP where to send this INVITE
Dcs-Gate: Host(cmtst):port#/Gate-ID/Gate-coord key
        Identifies the address and port of the destination CMTS, the
        Gate-ID and the key used to authenticate the gate coordination
        messages
Dcs-Billing-Info: Host(rkso):port#<account information>
        Identifies the RKS for this call, and provides billing
        information
Dcs-Billing-ID: Billing Correlation ID
Require: DCS
Proxy-Require: DCS
From: <value from original INVITE>
To: <value from original INVITE>
Call-ID: <value from original INVITE>
CSeq: n+1 INVITE
Content-Type: application/sdp
Content-Length: <length of body>

<SDP for new codec; DP_O adds a new shared secret, for example:
a=X-pc-secret:clear:ThisIsAKey>
```

Most of what follows is similar to the process for a new call. CMS_T authorizes the resources on $CMTS_T$ and generates a new INVITE for MTA_T.

```
INVITE sip: dest-phone-number@Host(dpt); user=phone SIP/2.0
Via: SIP/2.0/UDP Host(dpt), a
            The Via: headers are, as usual, removed and cached.
            Since SIP requires that the Via: headers must be present
            but may be encrypted, they are replaced by the single
            letter "a", thus meeting the letter (but not the spirit)
            of the SIP requirement.
Dcs-Gate: Gate-ID
            MTA_T knows the identity of the controlling CMTS, so that
            does not need to be passed; MTA_T does not need to know the
            value of the encryption key for gate coordination messages.
Require: DCS
From: <value from original INVITE>
To: <value from original INVITE>
Call-ID: <value from original INVITE>
CSeq: n+1 INVITE
Content-Type: application/sdp
Content-Length: <length of body>

<new SDP goes here, as received from DP_O>
```

When it receives this message, MTA_T looks at the triple (From:, To:, Call-ID:) to determine the call for which the change is being requested. It checks that it can indeed accommodate the requested SDP and issues a normal 200 OK back to DP_T. The rest of the signaling proceeds as for initial call setup: The 200 OK is passed back along the chain of DPs to MTA_O. Each DP drops the call state, just as in an ordinary INVITE(stage1).

When MTA_O receives the 200 OK, it sends an ACK directly to MTA_T to signal that the transaction is complete. At this point, both MTAs are free to begin transmitting RTP encoded with the new codec.

Theoretically, it is possible that a user would request a change to a new codec whose envelope fits entirely within the envelope of the current codec and for which no change in billing is requested. The DCS specification actually includes a call flow for such a circumstance. However, it is hard to see why this flow would ever occur in practice. The only reason for switching to a lower-quality codec would be if there was some financial gain in doing so. In other words, one would do so only if it would materially affect the billing for the call, but if it does that, then the relevant flow is the one that we have just discussed.

The DCS specification includes many example call flows showing feature-invocation. Rather than merely duplicate this information, which in any case adds little to what we have already discussed, we will show a couple of sample flows with annotations to describe particularly novel or tricky messaging sequences.

BLV and EI

There are several points worth noting about the Busy Line Verify (BLV) and Emergency Interrupt (EI) operations.

1. Only an operator may issue BLV and EI requests.

2. An MTA must cooperate in order for these features to function correctly. A hacked MTA (or MTA software downloaded from an untrusted source; such as a binary downloaded from the Internet) may not cooperate properly and may result in a line that cannot support the BLV and EI features.

3. An EI is assumed to require a prior BLV. That is, the EI feature cannot be invoked alone; the operator must first perform a BLV.

Figure 5-6 shows the basic BLV call flow. In initial PacketCable deployments, there are no operator services available within the IP network. Therefore any interaction with an operator requires that signaling and bearer traffic pass through a PacketCable PSTN gateway.

Part of the PSTN gateway is connected to PSTN operator signaling trunks, which are used for signaling special operator services such as BLV and EI. The on-net signaling begins when the PSTN gateway receives such a signal from the PSTN operator. The gateway generates a special INVITE(BLV) for the destination MTA.

An INVITE(BLV) is a stage1 INVITE (that is, it contains a Dcs-Stage1: header). It also contains the special header.

```
Dcs-OSPS:BLV
```

Apart from this special header, the message looks just like an ordinary DCS stage1 INVITE.

The PSTN gateway passed the INVITE(BLV) to DP_T, which processes it and forwards it to MTA_T as usual. MTA_T, however, does respond differently to the INVITE(BLV). Regardless of whether the phone is on-hook or off-hook, the MTA proceeds to set up a call. If the phone was on-hook, then, once call setup is complete, it transmits silence packets. If the phone was off-hook and therefore already engaged in a conversation, it duplicates the audio packets generated at MTA_T and sends the duplicate stream to the operator.

The audio will be decrypted as it passes through the PSTN gateway, but the operator's console "scrambles" it so that although the operator can tell whether the line is in use (silence scrambles to silence, and nonsilence scrambles to non-silence), he or she cannot tell what is being said.

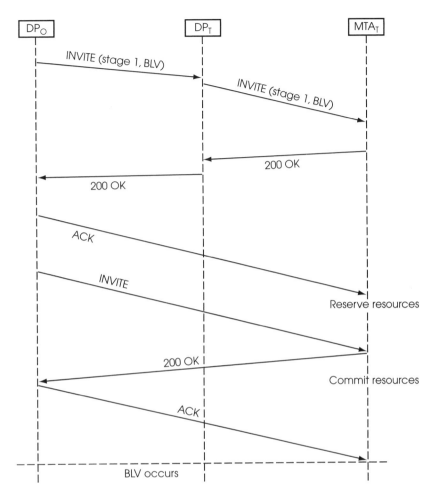

Figure 5-6 Busy Line Verification

Only the operator may terminate a BLV call. Termination occurs when the operator signals a logical "hang-up" at the console, which causes a BYE to be sent from the PSTN gateway, tearing down the call.

If the operator wants to break in on the call, he or she generates an alerting tone at the operator console. This causes the Media Gateway Controller portion of the PSTN gateway to generate an INVITE(EI), which is transmitted directly to MTA_T. Since it travels directly, this is an ordinary INVITE, not an INVITE(stage1). It does, however, carry a special header to identify it as an Emergency Interrupt.

```
Dcs-OSPS: EI
```

The MTA responds with a 200 OK, and the Media Gateway Controller responds in turn with an ACK to complete the three-way handshake.[17]

The MTA is free to implement the break-in function in a number of ways. For example, it could put the current call on hold, allowing the subscriber to talk to the operator, or it could mix the audio from the two calls locally. There are other possibilities, but the important point is that it should open a talk path between the subscriber and the operator.

There is an issue of trust here: How does the MTA know that a request for a BLV or EI is indeed from an operator? The answer is that the network itself ensures this. The originating DCS Proxy, or the originating Media Gateway Controller in the PSTN gateway, will check that any INVITE containing a reserved "operator-only" header does indeed come from an operator before passing the message.

IP-Anonymity

On a circuit-switched network, once the circuit has been established the data (the conversation) flows end-to-end without the need for routing or addressing information. As we saw in Chapter 1, this is not true on a packet-switched network. Every packet on a PacketCable network carries both an origination IP address and a destination IP address.

This means that if a user truly wants to be anonymous, it is not enough to suppress delivery of the usual name/number information to the destination MTA. Even when these are suppressed, the IP address of the originator is available: either in the SIP that is part of the signaling messages or in the IP packets themselves that flow from end to end, carrying the conversation.

Although the PacketCable 1.0 specifications do not mandate any particular mechanism to assure IP-address anonymity, the DCS specification includes an informative[18] appendix that describes one method for implementing IP-address anonymity. A future release of the specifications will establish a PacketCable-sanctioned mechanism, but it is worthwhile taking a brief look at the issues even in the absence of a definitive specification that provides this feature.

Many networks provide a form of IP-address anonymity through a technique known as Network Address Translation (NAT). In NAT, one of the devices through which the packet passes (typically a router) changes the source and/or destination address of the packet, according to some set of operator-defined rules. By changing

---

17. See Chapter 8 for a detailed discussion of the PSTN gateway.

18. The word *informative* is used in its technical sense. In a specification, a section is normative if it contains specific requirements that must be met. It is informative if it is intended merely to provide background information or an example.

the source address of the packet in this way, the true source address of a packet can be hidden from the destination.

Usually, NAT is implemented so that it is bidirectional, as shown in Figure 5-7. This allows the destination to route packets back to the source, even though it does not know the real IP address of the source. Unfortunately, simple NAT does not work in a PacketCable architecture. The reason for this is that IP addresses are carried within the signaling messages themselves (in particular, in the origin and connection parameters of the SDP in both DCS and NCS messages).

One solution to this is to require that the network operator provide a special device called an Anonymizer, whose job is to "anonymize" calls. An Anonymizer is a special kind of proxy MTA that can convert IP addresses like a NAT device but is also aware of the call signaling protocol so that it can change the contents of SDP. Figure 5-8 shows one particular architecture that demonstrates how an anonymizer functions in the network. It intercepts the call signaling packets pertaining to calls originating on MTA_O and changes the embedded IP address to match the address of the anonymizer. In this way both MTA_O and MTA_T believe that the anonymizer is actually the MTA at the far end of the call. Thus instead of sending bearer-channel (and DCS signaling) packets directly end-to-end, all end-to-end packets are passed to the anonymizer, which can perform the NAT function on the packets before handing them on to the true destination device.

Other architectures may perform the same job more effciently in practice, but since the anonymizer function is not yet part of PacketCable, there is little point in discussing the topic in detail. Appendix AA of the DCS specification details a different architecture in rather more depth and includes a sample DCS call flow with bidirectional anonymity.

DCS and Personal Privacy

The original purpose of encrypting bearer traffic on the PacketCable network was not to ensure that conversations are truly completely private. Rather, the intent was to guard against the possibility of a malfeasant somehow gaining access to the traffic passing through the network and listening to conversations in real-time. (In fact, the

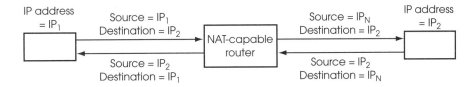

Figure 5-7 Network Address Translation

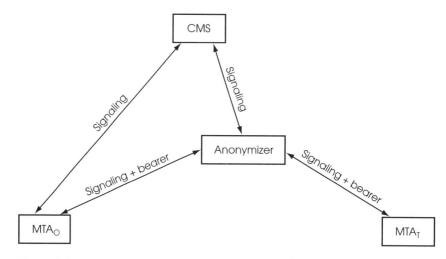

Figure 5-8 An Anonymizer

only encryption algorithm currently supported, RC4, is believed to be sufficiently strong that it also guards against the possibility of offline decryption as well.)

As we discussed in Chapter 4, the keys that the two endpoints use to encrypt their traffic (one key in each direction) are derived from a shared secret that has been handed to them by the local CMS in the call signaling. Since the signaling travels over connections secured by IPsec, the shared secret is never exposed. Therefore, even if an interloper does gain access to all the traffic traveling to/from an MTA (for example, by changing the routing tables in the MTA's CMTS in such a way that all packets are silently routed through a device that sniffs every packet), it still cannot decrypt the conversation correctly.

So conversations are secured against third-party snooping, but they are *not* secured against snooping by the network operator himself or by an agency that acts in collusion with the network operator and to which the network operator has handed the shared secret that unlocks a particular conversation. The principal example of this is when a court-ordered wiretap takes place.

Section 103 (b) (3) of the Communications Assistance for Law Enforcement Act, 1994 (known as "CALEA") states the following.

> Encryption—A telecommunications carrier shall not be responsible for decrypting, or ensuring the government's ability to decrypt, any communication encrypted by a subscriber or customer, unless the encryption was provided by the carrier and the carrier possesses the information necessary to decrypt the communication.

Despite the "and" joining the clauses in the last sentence, it is likely that a court would rule that the intention of the statute is that the government must be given the shared secret if the network operator possesses it. In any case, the shared secret is probably "reasonably available call identifying information" and therefore must be handed to the government under other terms contained in the statute. As of this writing, these issues have not been tested in the courts and as yet there is no case law interpreting the details of the statute's wording.

So PacketCable encryption does not guarantee that the government (or the service provider) is not able to decode the conversation. In order to provide such a guarantee, the MTAs would have to engage in an end-to-end negotiation that does not form part of the PacketCable specifications—although manufacturers, of course, are free to design such a mechanism independently of the base specifications. Such an exchange would likely impact call set-up time, but it could result in truly private communications.

For the sake of completeness, we should mention that a truly paranoid user might be concerned about the network operator mounting a man-in-the-middle-attack against the exchange (perhaps because a court has ordered it as a last-ditch attempt to intercept communications). There are ways to detect and/or thwart this attack as well, resulting in communications that appear to be immune to interception using current technology, but they are beyond the scope of this book. Ultimately, and as long as encryption is legal, it seems that the knowledgeable crook can always outwit law enforcement. Fortunately, most crooks do not have sufficient technical competence to thwart the measures taken to intercept their communications. Almost certainly, however, at least some drug cartels routinely communicate using techniques that are immune to eavesdropping.

Chapter
6

Quality of Service

It is anticipated that, from a billing perspective, one of the resources that will
need to be accounted for is the use of QoS in the DOCSIS network.

PKT-SP-DQOS-I01-991201

Apart from security, ensuring Quality of Service is probably the most complex aspect of PacketCable networks. With that daunting thought, let's try to sneak up on the subject so that at least we understand *why* it is so complicated.

In a general-purpose IP network, there must be some way for the system to guarantee that packets carrying time-sensitive information are handled expeditiously. In particular, the network must be able to ensure that packets containing encoded voice data are not unduly delayed as they cross the network.

In PacketCable networks, the access to the core network is through an HFC medium whose upstream bandwidth (that is bandwidth from the customer to the cable company) is usually tightly constrained (see Chapter 1 and especially Chapter 3 for more details). The packets flowing through this medium are not limited to packets containing encoded voice: call signaling, general data and other types of packets flow simultaneously through the HFC access network, and all want their "fair share" of the upstream bandwidth.

The process of ensuring that telephony and other time-sensitive packets are handled expeditiously in these circumstances is known as guaranteeing **Quality of Service**, often abbreviated to **QoS** (and sometimes pronounced "kwos" or "kwoz"). The mechanism by which QoS is guaranteed in PacketCable networks is called **Dynamic Quality of Service**, or **DQoS**, usually pronounced "Dee-kwoz".

Packets may be divided into (at least) two kinds: those requiring guaranteed bandwidth (that is, the network must be prepared to accept packets of this type at a guaranteed rate) and those that may be handled according to the network's notion of "best effort" delivery (that is, the network may delay the packet or may even drop it entirely). DQoS ensures that time-sensitive packets, such as those carrying voice data, are assured guaranteed bandwidth in the upstream access network. (Actually,

287

it may also assure downstream bandwidth as well, but that resource is typically relatively unconstrained in a cable-based access network.)

PacketCable DQoS allows QoS to be guaranteed on a call-by-call basis, using parameters matched to the requirements of the call. For example, a voice call requires considerably less upstream bandwidth than a video call. A fax call typically requires greater bandwidth than an ordinary voice call. By allocating bandwidth resources on a dynamic, call-by-call basis, the network can maximize its use of the available resources.

QoS is intimately associated with the concept of billing for a call. Indeed, it is tightly coupled to the notion of a call itself.

There was a time, not so long ago, when the precise meaning of a "telephone call" was reasonably clear. A user picked up a telephone, dialed a number and was connected to the party to whom he or she wished to speak. As soon as the destination party picked up the phone, a "telephone call" was in progress (and, usually, someone started being billed for the call). However, widespread access to the Internet has considerably undermined the usefulness of this definition.

Inexpensive software, often called "IP telephony" programs, are available that enable suitably equipped personal computers to act as if they were telephones, using the Internet as the transport to carry the voice signals between them. The method used to do this is conceptually simple. The voice input is digitized within the computer and then placed into ordinary IP packets. These packets are sent to the user's ISP just like any other IP packet. Once forwarded into the Internet, they are indistinguishable from other traffic: They are routed by exactly the same mechanisms as would apply to packets created by other applications such as e-mail, Web browsing or file transfer.

Once they reach their destination, the packets are passed to the recipient's IP telephony program, which unpacks the packet, converts the digitized voice back to analog signals and plays the resultant waveform through speakers or a headset.

Unfortunately, most users of IP telephony programs find the results disappointing. The quality of the "phone calls" varies widely and is often so poor as to be unusable, with frequent pauses and breaks in the conversation that manifest themselves as an unacceptable choppiness. The principal reason for this is the lack of bandwidth dedicated to carrying the "call". The voice packets, since they are treated no differently from (for example) e-mail, may be delayed or even dropped entirely in the journey from speaker to listener. In the case of e-mail, packet loss does not matter: A higher-level protocol[1] detects the loss of the packet and, after a pause of typically a few seconds, causes any lost packets to be retransmitted. However, there is no point in retransmitting a voice packet: By the time the transmitting computer could detect

---

1. Actually, TCP.

that the packet has failed to reach its destination and cause the packet to be retransmitted, too much time will have elapsed, and the played-back audio will be well past the audio contained in the dropped packet.[2] This behavior is typical of "calls" that have no Quality of Service associated with them.

Generally, any IP-based network can handle voice-based traffic in a manner similar to the Internet-based IP telephony programs we described above. Unless bandwidth is dedicated to the call, however, the results will usually be similar to those just described, unless the network is so overengineered that there is enough excess bandwidth to cause very few packets to be dropped (either during transmission or at the receiver because of unacceptable latency/jitter). In order to provide true telephone calls of acceptable quality on ordinary IP networks, a QoS mechanism has to be used. In PacketCable networks—which are especially troubled by bandwidth issues in the upstream direction on the HFC access network—this mechanism is DQoS.

In general, a service provider bills customers only for those calls that use the services provided by DQoS. In a PacketCable network, a user may place free "calls", but when he does so, he receives no guarantees concerning the quality of the "call", just as a user of an IP telephony program on other networks receives no such guarantees.

One other difference between calls that use the DQoS mechanism and those that do not is that the PacketCable "wiretapping" specification requires that only the former be tappable by law enforcement agencies under normal circumstances. See Chapter 7.

Figure 6-1 shows the three parts of an on-net to on-net PacketCable call. The first part is the upstream access link over the HFC network between the MTA and the CMTS. The second part is called the "backbone" and represents the inner "core" portion of the network, utilizing high-bandwidth links between network devices. The final portion is the downstream HFC link to the destination MTA.

The current PacketCable specifications do not cover the backbone portion of the network. It is assumed, for the present, to be of effectively infinite capacity. This, of course, is not true, and later versions of the DQoS specification will describe in detail how backbone traffic is to be managed. For the present, however, any prioritization or other management of traffic passing over the backbone is handled by proprietary, vendor-specific mechanisms.

The current version of the DQoS specification does address the other two portions of the network—the upstream and downstream access links. Typically, the downstream portion has adequate bandwidth available. We should not forget that the principal use of the cable over which calls are being made is to provide a downstream television service comprising a large number of broadband signals. The HFC

---

2. These "calls" therefore use UDP, which provides no automatic recovery of lost packets.

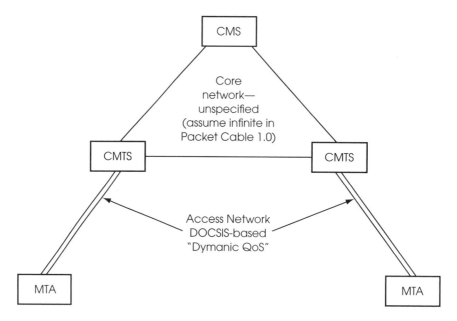

Figure 6-1 Different QoS Portions of a PacketCable Call

networks are engineered in such a way that downstream signals travel in a low-noise portion of the spectrum, which allows for more efficient modulation schemes. In addition, the downstream frequency band is far wider than that available for upstream traffic (typically more than ten times as wide). Further details are in Chapters 1 and 3, but the important point to remember is that downstream bandwidth is a much less scarce resource than upstream bandwidth.

DQoS does provide mechanisms to manage downstream bandwidth. In fact, it uses the same mechanisms as those used to manage upstream bandwidth. However, it is the scarcity of upstream bandwidth that makes management techniques absolutely necessary in that direction, rather than merely useful.

PacketCable assumes that traffic on the HFC is managed in accordance with the DOCSIS 1.1 (or later) specifications. DOCSIS provides a method whereby a Service Flow (a unidirectional voice stream belonging to a particular telephone call) can be guaranteed bandwidth. The method utilizes the creation, modification and deletion of Service Flows using the DSA, DSC and DSD MAC-layer commands that are more fully described in Chapter 3. The PacketCable DQoS mechanism provides a way to manage these Service Flows in such a way that telephone calls can be guaranteed the necessary bandwidth. If the bandwidth is not available (typically because of congestion in the upstream access network) the call will be **blocked**—that is, it will fail to complete, and a signal will be sent to the MTA indicating the reason why the call has not been completed. Once a PacketCable call begins, it is guaranteed that the necessary bandwidth will remain available to it for the duration of the call.[3]

DQoS and RSVP

We mentioned above that the PacketCable DQoS architecture assumes that the access portion of the network is compliant with version 1.1 or later of the DOCSIS specifications. This is not strictly true. One chapter of the DQoS specification is devoted to a generalized mechanism based on the Resource Reservation Protocol, RSVP, which is defined in RFC 2205. That chapter of the specification, however, is designed to "future-proof" the DQoS architecture against the day when MTAs are no longer embedded with a cable modem.

Therefore, although the specification supports the use of DQoS with RSVP messaging instead of merely using DOCSIS messaging, the intention is that in early PacketCable networks all MTAs will be embedded with cable modems and will use only the DOCSIS portions of the DQoS specification.

So, although the DQoS specification supports the use of RSVP, we will discuss only the DOCSIS portion in this book, since this is the mechanism supported by current PacketCable products. As we shall discover, DQoS is a sufficiently complex specification that even omitting the RSVP support we are in for an interesting time in this chapter.

Customer and Operator Expectations

When a paying customer places a phone call on whatever network, she has certain expectations about what will happen when she finishes dialing the digits. In particular, she generally expects the following.

- The call has a high probability of ringing the phone at the other end.

- Unanswered calls will not be billed.

- The party who answers the call is the same as the one dialed (unless some sort of call forwarding mechanism is in place).

- The delay from when she dials the last digit to when she hears the phone at the far end beginning to ring will be no more than a few seconds.

---

3. This is the case unless the bandwidth requirements change during the call. The most common example of this is a call that begins as a voice call but then changes to a fax call. The fax requires more bandwidth than ordinary voice (because the human voice carries more redundancy in its frequency information than does a fax, so audio codecs designed to carry human conversation generally require less bandwidth than codecs that carry fax information well).

- When the party at the other end picks up the phone, communication can begin instantly.

- Once a call has begun, communication can continue indefinitely until one party hangs up.

- The quality of audio delivered on the call will be reasonable.

- Both parties can speak at the same time, and both will still be heard at the far end.[4]

PacketCable DQoS explicitly addresses the last five of these expectations. It also addresses one of the chief expectations of the network operator: that it should be impossible for a customer to place a high-quality call without paying for it. Typically, an operator links the granting of QoS to the billing mechanism, so that per-second billing begins as soon as QoS resources are committed to the call and stops as soon as they are released. (See Chapter 7 for more details about record keeping and billing.)

Quality of Service is a *two-way* operation. A call that has guaranteed bandwidth in only one direction is generally considered unacceptable. From an operator's perspective, such a call is unbillable (unless the operator has no particular desire to stay in business for long). This caveat, however, opens the possibility of a method for a cooperating pair of users to steal service from the operator: User A places a call to user B but arranges the signaling (perhaps by hacking his MTA) so that the call is provided with QoS only in the direction from A to B. This results in a usable talk-path from A to B, but as far as the network operator is concerned the call is unbillable because there is no QoS in the reverse direction. Simultaneously, however, B can place a similar call to A. The result is a pair of usable one-way talk-paths, each of which A and B can use to communicate without paying the operator for the service. This theft of service technique is known as placing two **half-calls**. DQoS ensures that half-calls cannot exist in a PacketCable network (except under special circumstances) by ensuring that QoS resources in the two directions at both ends of the call are simultaneously coordinated.

Gates

The fundamental logical construct in DQoS is the **gate**. A gate is a logical entity that resides in a CMTS and is under the control of a portion of a CMS known as the Gate Controller (GC). Every gate has an identifier, a Gate-ID, which is assigned at its

---

4. This expectation might not be obvious. Indeed there are now some digital networks deployed that do not automatically meet this expectation—voice calls carried over such networks can be very annoying, since it is no longer easy to interrupt the other party. Worse, such networks cannot carry data efficiently, since data connections typically require simultaneous transmit and receive capability.

creation by the CMTS and is used to identify it in subsequent operations. Gates are unidirectional; when a gate is open, it allows packets to flow with guaranteed quality of service in one direction.

Theoretically, Gate-IDs and gates share a one-to-one mapping. However, there is an exception: The gates associated with the upstream and downstream flow in a single call in either an originating or terminating CMTS may share a common Gate-ID. In other words, although the upstream and downstream traffic pass through two different gates, the two gates share a common Gate-ID. Gates that share a common Gate-ID are called a **gate pair**.

Gates are created during call setup in the closed state. Gates are destroyed during call teardown. Gate pairs themselves exist in cooperating pairs called **gate quartets**, with one pair in the source CMTS and one pair in the destination CMTS. This is shown diagrammatically in Figure 6-2.

A gate, even though it resides on a CMTS, is controlled only by a GC (or, to a lesser extent, by an MTA or another CMTS). If a gate pair is opened (for example, because the CMTS receives a GATE-OPEN(REQ) message), it will stay open only for a brief period, typically a few hundred milliseconds, unless the other gates in the quartet are also opened. This process, called **gate coordination**, ensures that a half-call cannot exist within the network. When a call is completed, the associated gates are closed and immediately destroyed.

DQoS uses signaling messages between a CMTS and its GC, and between CMTSes, to ensure that the gate coordination mechanism works correctly. There is one important complication regarding DQoS and the gate coordination messages. DQoS was designed to be a signaling-protocol-neutral mechanism to assure Quality of Service. However, it was originally designed in the context of DCS, and the manner in which gate coordination occurs in NCS and DCS is slightly different in the two signaling schemes. DQoS remains signaling-protocol-neutral in that the messages themselves are independent of the signaling protocol chosen by the network operator. However, the way in which those messages are used to ensure that the gates at the two ends of a call remain coordinated varies between NCS and DCS.

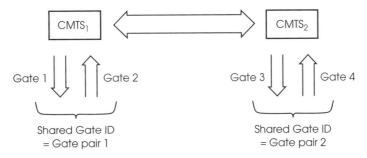

Figure 6-2 A Gate Quartet

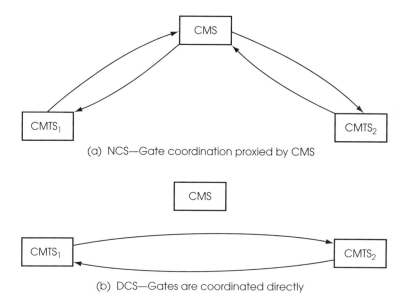

(a) NCS—Gate coordination proxied by CMS

(b) DCS—Gates are coordinated directly

Figure 6-3   Gate Coordination in DCS and NCS

Simply put, in DCS gate coordination messages are passed directly between the CMTSes. In NCS the messages are proxied by each CMTS's controlling CMS. This is shown in Figure 6-3.

Resources

The term **resources** is used to refer to services available to a network or to a device that are sufficiently scarce that they may not be freely made available for use and must therefore be managed. The most important managed resource in a PacketCable network is upstream bandwidth, and the word *resources* is sometimes loosely used as a synonym for *upstream bandwidth*. However, it is good to remember that other kinds of limited resources also occur in various devices in the network. Typical examples are memory, DSP processing power, jitter buffer sizes and so forth.

Authorization, Reservation and Commitment

PacketCable uses a similar mechanism to that used in DOCSIS to categorize resources, marking them as being in one of three states: *authorized, reserved* or *committed.*[5]

---

5. These three states correspond closely to the provisioned, admitted and active states of DOCSIS QoS resources.

Authorized resources are those for which a user is allowed by the network to make a request. The authorized resources are typically a set of pre-provisioned values associated with a phone number, the values having a lifetime greatly in excess of the lifetime of a single call. For example, an operator may choose to configure his system in such a way that the monthly fee paid by a subscriber determines the particular set of codecs available to that subscriber. In such a network, the subscriber's monthly payment will determine the set of provisioned and hence the set of authorized resources available to that subscriber when he places a call.

When a user makes a request for resources, assuming that they do not exceed those for which the user is authorized, the system checks to make sure that the resources are actually available at that moment. If so, they are **reserved** for use by the requesting party and marked as unavailable for guaranteed use by anyone else. Although the resources are reserved for use by one person at this time (perhaps by Alice), this does not necessarily mean that they are completely unavailable for use by another party (perhaps Carol).

Suppose, for example, that Alice is in the process of placing a fax call to Bob. As part of the call setup process, Alice will reserve the necessary bandwidth for the G.711 encoded RTP traffic that she will use once the call completes. However, the network operator may have configured the low-level DOCSIS system to use Unsolicited Grant Service with Activity Detection (UGS/AD), or Real-time Polling. These allow Alice's DOCSIS minislots to be used by Carol on a best-effort basis—in other words, for data traffic but not voice traffic—until Alice actually begins to use the resources.

Once a user decides to actually use a set of reserved resources, the system **commits** them to that user. Committing resources makes them immediately available for use without any further action on the user's part.

In general, the resources to which a user commits must be less than or equal to the resources that were reserved. The resources that are reserved for a user must be less than or equal to those for which he is authorized. This is depicted diagrammatically in Figure 6-4, which shows a two-dimensional representation of the n-dimensional resource space comprising bandwidth, memory, DSP CPU cycles and so on.

Two-Stage Commitment

You may have noticed that, from the system's point of view, there is no substantive difference between resources that are reserved and those that are committed: In neither case may those resources be reassigned for guaranteed use by someone else. Why, then, do these two categories exist?

The answer lies in the fact that there are two parties involved in the call, and the system must be sure that sufficient resources are available to both parties before the call can be allowed to go through. Furthermore, once the destination party

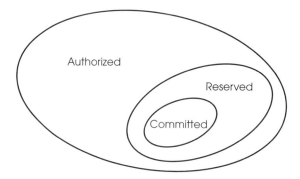

Figure 6-4 Relationship Among Authorized,
Reserved and Committed Resources

answers the call, the resources must be usable almost immediately; otherwise the greeting (or the synchronization tones in the case that one electronic device is calling another) would be clipped. (This is often called "clipping the Hello", the process of allowing the audio to flow between the parties is called "cutting through" the audio. The process of committing reserved resources "cuts-through" the audio.)

Suppose that Alice places a call to Bob. During the time that the call is being set up, *before Bob's phone rings,* the requested resources at both ends of the call are checked to ensure that they do not exceed the authorization limits, and, assuming that Alice and Bob are authorized to use the requested resources (and also assuming that they are available), the resources are marked as reserved. Only when all the necessary resources have been reserved does Bob's phone begin to ring because it is not until then that the system is assured that sufficient bandwidth is available for audio to flow in both directions—and clearly it would be a mistake to allow the phone to ring before the system is sure that a conversation will be possible.

However, resources that are merely reserved are not available for use.[6] When Bob picks up the phone, the reserved resources are marked as committed. Committing resources is an easy operation for the network to perform (unlike reservation, which may take several hundred milliseconds or even longer) and hence can be performed very quickly. This ensures that when Bob says "Hello" his greeting is not clipped. This is shown in Figure 6-5.

Suppose, however, that the system provided for no distinction between reserved and committed resources, so that resources were simply *acquired* and could immediately be used. Several problems exist with this scenario.

First, the QoS mechanism can no longer be used to determine billing, since the resources have to be acquired before the destination phone is allowed to ring

---

6. Actually, as we shall see, they may sometimes be used to carry ringback. They cannot, however, be used to carry useful information from another party.

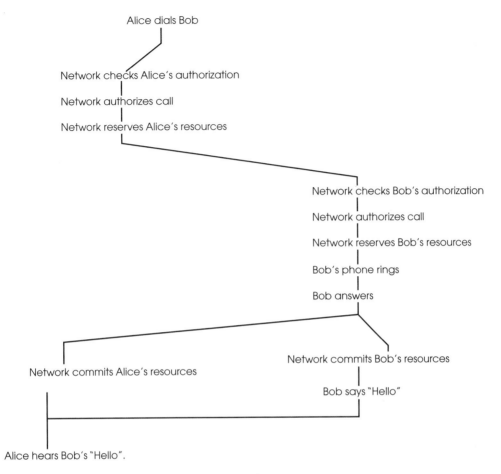

Figure 6-5 DQoS and the Two-Stage Commit

(otherwise there is a possibility that the phone will ring and then the network's attempt to acquire resources will fail because there are none available, meaning that the call cannot go through, even though the phone has already started to ring).

Second, either side could begin to transmit bearer packets as soon as its (local) resources are available. This is an instance of the half-call theft of service mechanism mentioned earlier. Suppose that Amanda and Bill (who are Alice's and Bob's evil twins) each have two phone lines. Amanda uses her first line to call Bill's first line. Simultaneously, Bill uses his second line to call Amanda's second line. At each end, as soon as local resources are acquired, the respective user can transmit bearer packets, even though the phone at the far end has not been taken off-hook. A hacked MTA could easily arrange to play the audio contained in the packets. In this way Amanda and Bill can have a free call with QoS in both directions.

The two-stage commit mechanism adopted by PacketCable avoids these pitfalls. It also has the merit of meeting the design requirement that DQoS be *signaling protocol neutral,* by which we mean that it can be used regardless of the protocol used to signal the progress of a call (which may be NCS or DCS, or even some as-yet-unspecified protocol). The detailed implementation of the two-stage process will vary with the choice of call signal protocol, but any reasonable call signaling protocol should be able to support DQoS signaling.

Security and DQoS

The DQoS mechanism causes signaling traffic to flow between the following pairs of entities.

- MTA and CMTS
- GC and CMTS
- CMS and CMTS (NCS)
- CMTS and CMTS (DCS)
- CMS and CMS (NCS)

PacketCable ensures that all the DQoS messages passing between the entities within the first three pairs in this list are authenticated and confidential. The last two pairs are special cases.

The inter-CMS signaling protocol used by NCS is undefined in PacketCable 1.0. The assumption is made, however, that whatever protocol is used, it will be properly secured.

If DCS call signaling is used, then gate coordination messages flow between CMTSes, rather than between a CMTS and its CMS. However, the 1.0 version of the PacketCable security specifications does not address this interface because DCS is not officially part of the 1.0 bundle of specifications. Therefore any vendor implementing DCS is free to secure the DQoS messages passing between the CMTSes in any manner the vendor feels appropriate. However, one simple way to implement security on this interface is to use a preshared key carried in signaling messages, and in Chapter 5 we saw that DCS messages indeed carry a key especially for this purpose. Because of the large number of calls occurring simultaneously in a PacketCable network, the key would be used to encrypt the DQoS messages at the application layer, rather than being used to drive a low-level security mechanism such as IPsec, which can be slow to set up and incurs relatively large memory and management overhead for a device such as a CMTS. Let's take a look at each of the communicating pairs of devices in turn.

MTA and CMTS

This interface lies completely within the HFC access portion of the network, in which all traffic is protected by the DOCSIS BPI+ security mechanisms described in Chapter 3. This is deemed sufficient protection for DQoS messages, so no additional security is added for DQoS messages passing between the MTA and the CMTS.

GC and CMTS

This is a particularly sensitive interface, since some of the DQoS messages travelling over it contain billing information. Because the association between a GC and a CMTS is long-lived (all the gates within a CMTS are generally controlled by a single GC), this interface is authenticated and encrypted by IPsec, with key management performed by IKE using preshared keys.

CMS and CMTS

Gate coordination messages are used to ensure that service cannot be stolen by maintaining two half-calls in opposite directions. As we have mentioned, in NCS these messages pass between the CMTS and its CMS, whereas in DCS these messages travel directly between CMTSes.

The gate coordination messages are formatted according to the RADIUS specification (RFCs 2138, 2139), which includes an authenticator. The authenticator is used to assure message integrity. Since no sensitive billing information is carried in the messages, they travel without encryption. The key is 16 octets in length and is included in a Gate Authorization message sent from the CMS to the CMTS.

DQoS and DOCSIS

It is useful to keep in mind the fact that, logically, DQoS and DOCSIS are independent in the sense that (at least theoretically) DQoS could run over non-DOCSIS networks, and DOCSIS networks could be used to provide Quality of Service using mechanisms other than DQoS. In practice, at least in cable networks, the two are closely linked, but it is a good idea to remember that this is not a requirement.

A good way to think of this independence is to regard DQoS purely as a *policy* layer. In other words, when a DQoS gate is created and opened, it does not, in and of itself, allow traffic to flow. Rather, it tells the CMTS what to do when it receives a subsequent DOCSIS request to instantiate a particular service flow.[7] Before traffic

---

7. One can imagine a super-broadband access network with effectively infinite bandwidth in which only policy needs to be dictated, without the corresponding low-level service flows needing to be explicitly created. However, in all current access networks something equivalent to the DOCSIS Dynamic Service Flow commands must be present to ensure that bandwidth is available.

can flow, the access network must be physically capable of supporting the flow (that is, DOCSIS must be able to support the Dynamic Service Flow), *and* the policy obtained from the Gate Controller must agree that the traffic is permitted to obtain QoS (that is, DQoS must create a gate for the flow).

The access portion of a PacketCable network (the portion that operates over the HFC fabric between the residence and the headend) is assumed to use DOCSIS version 1.1 or later. DOCSIS provides hooks that allow for the creation of traffic flows with guaranteed upstream bandwidth. These hooks are the DSA-REQ, DSC-REQ and DSD-REQ MAC messages, which are used for the creation, modification and deletion of DOCSIS Dynamic Service Flows, respectively. Dynamic Service Flows are more fully described in Chapter 3. In the following sections, we will examine how DQoS uses these hooks to provide guaranteed bandwidth for telephony.

Codecs

The amount of bandwidth required by a call is largely determined by the codec used. A **codec** (a neologism coined from "coder/decoder") is a pair of algorithms, one of which takes analog input and delivers digital output, and the other of which does the opposite, as in Figure 6-6.

There are many codec algorithms, with widely varying properties. Codecs may be used to transfer audio, video, gaming and other analog information across a digital network. Typically, each particular kind of data may be most efficiently transported by using a codec especially designed for handling that particular kind of data. Thus there are audio codecs, video codecs and many other kinds of codecs. PacketCable 1.0 specifies support for only audio codecs.

Even in the limited realm of audio, there is a wide variety of codecs. Different codecs are designed with different purposes in mind. These are typical design criteria when constructing codecs.

- Providing high fidelity
- Occupying minimal bandwidth
- Minimizing CPU memory
- Minimizing CPU computations
- Decoding efficiently at the cost of increased complexity while encoding
- Providing low latency (sampling frequently and constructing small packets)

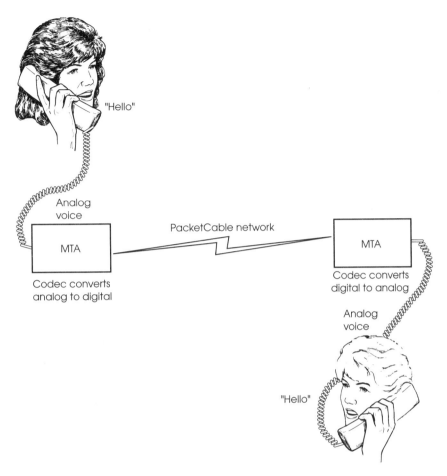

Figure 6-6 A Codec at Work

Often, these objectives are more or less mutually exclusive (for example, producing a high-fidelity, low-bandwidth audio codec is not possible[8]).

Not all audio codecs can be relied upon to pass the audio information with sufficient fidelity for any particular purpose. In other words, the audio codec chosen for a telephony connection is dependent on the kind of information that is going to be carried over that connection. This restriction is especially true for low bit-rate codecs, where some of the desired signal may be irretrievably lost during the compression process that is required to assure that the signal can travel through a low bit-rate channel.

8. By "low bandwidth" here we mean a channel that can carry a maximum of only a few thousand bits per second.

The PacketCable codec specification requires that MTAs provide support for only one audio codec: G.711. It also recommends support for G.728 and G.729E. All of these are codecs defined by the ITU. Support for other codecs is not prohibited by the specification, but because in general one cannot guarantee that a particular codec will be understood at the far end unless it is a mandatory codec, there is little to be gained by implementing any codecs other than the ones recommended by the specification. Indeed, a strong argument can be made that since G.711 is the only mandated codec in PacketCable version 1.0, a vendor should include support only for that codec because there is no guarantee that the MTA at the far end will support any other codecs.[9]

A major weakness of PacketCable 1.0 is that the only codecs for which support is discussed are in-band audio codecs. In particular, no support is offered for signaling out-of-band events. What this means in practice is that all bearer-channel information has to be encapsulated within the bearer-to-bearer audio stream; it also means that the codec in use on that stream must be capable of representing all such information faithfully.

This becomes a problem with, for example, some DTMF tone generators. It is usually much more efficient to pass these with a specialized codec (called a "relay" codec). These codecs, instead of attempting to represent the waveform digitally, effectively capture a specific event such as "the digit 2 was pressed" and transmit the event in a manner that uses bandwidth very efficiently. It is highly likely that the next release of PacketCable will include at least some support for relay codecs.

The basic idea is similar to that used to represent MIDI music. With MIDI, no attempt is made to capture and transport true waveforms. Instead "events" such as "the instrument on channel 1 plays an F for a quarter measure" are captured. MIDI files are only a tiny fraction of the size of the comparable waveform files. But we digress. . . .

It is possible to insert information from relay codecs within the audio flow by marking the packets as being associated with non-audio information. (RFC 2833 specifies the usual way in which this is implemented.) However, this approach suffers from (at least) two limitations. First, in a severely bandwidth-restricted environment such as cable, it is not possible merely to add packets to the stream. The non-audio information can only be carried by dropping audio packets. Second, it is very difficult to use such a system when all packets are subject to a stream cipher that must remain properly synchronized. Future PacketCable support for RFC 2833 will therefore require a fundamental change in the way in which media streams are encrypted.

---

9. Unless the PacketCable network operator also supplies all the MTAs used on the network. See Chapter 9 for a discussion of the viability of this possibility in the long term.

The mandatory and recommended audio codecs were chosen to provide reasonable audio in high, medium and low bit-rate environments.

G.711

This codec is widely used in non-PacketCable IP audio networks. It provides audio equivalent to so-called "toll quality" in the PSTN. G.711 is an uncompressed codec that produces 64,000 bits per second of output. (Usually referred to as "64 kilobits", in most computer-related fields the term "kilo" usually means 1,024, but in codec work it typically means 1,000.) G.711 will accurately pass specialized audio such as DTMF and fax tones and the tones used to provide support for the hearing impaired. There are no license fees and it requires minimal computation resources.

G.728

This codec produces good quality and uses 16 kbps of bandwidth. Although not as faithful as G.711, it has good characteristics for suppressing background noise and can be used to carry low-fidelity music. The fidelity is insufficient to pass fax messages or high-speed analog modem signals or to guarantee capture and correct interpretation of DTMF tones.

G.729E

G.729E provides relatively high-quality output at the rate of 11.8 kbps. The quality is sufficient for voice conversations and can also carry medium-quality music. Like G.728, the fidelity of G.729E is insufficient to pass fax messages or high-speed analog modem signals, or to guarantee capture and correct interpretation of DTMF tones.

All of these codecs are Constant Bit Rate (CBR) codecs. That is, they produce digital output at a rate that is independent of analog input. In particular, they transmit packets even during periods of silence.

Although the bandwidth requirement of each codec is well defined, merely knowing the bandwidth tells us nothing about how, in detail, that bandwidth must be made available to carry the digitized traffic through the network. For example, merely knowing that G.711 requires 64 kbps does not tell us whether to reserve a 64-bit slot every millisecond or whether to reserve 100-bit slots every sixty-fourth of a second (or any other combination of size and frequency that results in a bandwidth utilization of 64 kbps).

In order to provide this additional detail, PacketCable uses the notion of flowspecs, as defined in RFC 1363. Flowspecs provide a method to describe the way in which a codec produces packets in enough detail that transmission slots of the correct size and periodicity can be reserved to carry the flow. But before we can discuss flowspecs, we must first delve into the workings of buckets and jitter buffers.

Buckets and Jitter Buffers

In most networks, there are mechanisms in place to permit a user to reserve a constant amount of bandwidth to carry a particular flow of information. However, traffic to be injected into the flow may not become available at a precisely constant rate. Even more likely, because of variable delays in the network, traffic may not leave the flow and become available for playback at the destination at precisely equal intervals. Buckets and jitter buffers are used to regulate the traffic rate into and out of a flow.

Buckets

A **bucket** is a logical entity that is associated with a flow and holds items called credits, which are placed into the bucket at a constant rate. A *credit* is simply a number of octets, so you can think of a bucket simply as a place to accumulate octets at a constant rate. Whenever a packet is assembled and injected into the bucket's associated flow, a number of credits equal to the size of the packet is removed from the bucket.

A good analogy is provided by those buckets that one often sees in water amusement parks.[10] These overlarge buckets are typically mounted high over a walkway and are filled at a constant rate from a pipe. They are designed so that they periodically tip and pour water over the unsuspecting people beneath (see Figure 6-7). The analogy is not perfect: In the amusement park, the bucket tips and releases water because the water reaches a certain level; in networks, typically the flow *requests* a packet of octets from the bucket.

Three parameters determine the rate at which traffic enters the flow: Token Bucket Rate; Token Bucket Size and Maximum Transmission Rate.

Token Bucket Rate (R)

One can think of a single credit as the right to inject a single octet into the bucket's associated flow. The Token Bucket Rate, R, is the rate at which credits are placed into the bucket. For example, a video flow that can carry 800 kbps will need to have a credit placed into its associated bucket every hundred-thousandth of a second (because each octet contains eight bits).

---

10. The model we are about to describe is sometimes called the "leaky bucket admission control scheme" in computer science texts.

In a water amusement park

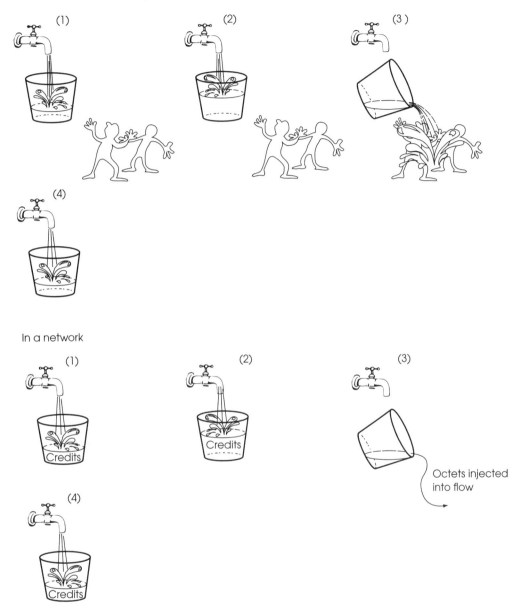

In a network

Figure 6-7 A Bucket's Relationship to a Flow

Token Bucket Size (B)

The token bucket size represents the maximum number of credits that the bucket can hold. Once the bucket is full (that is, it contains a number of credits equal to the token bucket size), no additional credits may be added. The token bucket size can be thought of as representing the maximum size of a burst of data that may be injected into the flow: If the bucket is full, then an additional B octets may be injected into the flow, thereby emptying the bucket. In an arbitrary time t, the maximum amount of data that can be removed from the bucket is therefore $R \times t + B$ octets.

Maximum Transmission Rate (p)

The Maximum Transmission Rate is simply the maximum rate at which octets may be injected into the flow, which is identical to the maximum rate at which credits may be removed from the bucket. Conceptually, the Maximum Transmission Rate represents a secondary, leaky bucket: When a packet is transmitted, a number of credits equal to the size of the packet is removed from the primary bucket and placed into a secondary bucket. The secondary bucket leaks at a rate equal to the maximum transmission rate, and no more packets may be sent until the secondary bucket is empty.

Even if one attempts to empty the primary bucket and transmit the entire B octets, the Maximum Transmission Rate forces one to limit the rate at which the secondary bucket can be emptied. The maximum amount of information that can be injected into a flow in time t is therefore the minimum of $p \times t$ and $R \times t + B$.

Jitter Buffers

The nature of IP networks is that consecutive packets are not guaranteed to experience the same amount of delay as they cross the network. Indeed, there is no guarantee that packets will even arrive at the destination in the same order as that in which they were transmitted. In fact, there is not even a guarantee that all the transmitted packets will *ever* reach their destination.

For many applications, higher-level protocols such as TCP can be used to implement a retransmission and/or reordering strategy. For real-time telephony applications, there is not enough time to signal the need for retransmission. It is possible, however, to implement a primitive reordering strategy to control packets that arrive out of order, providing that packets are not delayed too long while crossing the network.

Suppose that packets containing digitized voice information are transmitted at the rate of one packet every hundredth of a second. When these packets arrive at their destination, they are unlikely to do so at a constant rate. Instead, each packet is likely to arrive at some time δt offset from a clock that ticks every hundredth of a second (see Figure 6-8).

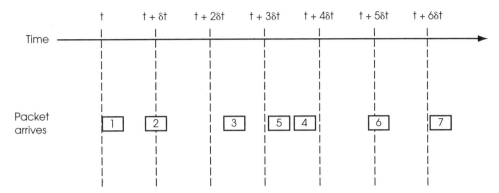

Figure 6-8 Variable Rate of Arrival of Voice Packets

If the recipient device was simply to play back each packet as it is received, the resultant audio would likely be of unacceptable quality because some packets would arrive while an earlier packet was still playing, and others would arrive too late, leaving a gap in the audio output. In order to circumvent these problems, most audio playback devices incorporate a **jitter buffer**.

Implementations of jitter buffers vary, but the essential purpose of a jitter buffer is to smooth the flow of packets so that playback occurs in the correct order and at a regular rate. Like most things, the increased quality provided by a jitter buffer comes at a cost, in this case the addition of delay into the end-to-end flow of audio packets. Figure 6-9 shows the action of a jitter buffer in the receiver.

A jitter buffer has a certain duration, usually of the order of a few tens of milliseconds, and a size usually sufficient to hold some small number of samples of the codec in use. Packets may be inserted anywhere within the jitter buffer, but they are played out in a steady stream at a rate determined by the parameters of the codec in use and in an order that is determined by the timestamp associated with each packet of audio information. A single output from a codec is called a **frame**. One or more frames are then placed into a packet, which also contains a timestamp. Usually (although not necessarily) each packet contains a single frame, so as to reduce latency in the system. (The packet containing the single frame can be transmitted before the next frame is available.)

A jitter buffer may be thought of as a floating window on to a timeline, so that it has a beginning time, a duration and an ending time. The absolute position of the jitter buffer moves along the timeline in step with real-time (as determined by the clock on the receiver).

Suppose that a device implements a jitter buffer of duration T_j, and the most recently played packet contained a timestamp of time t_1, which contained t_{packet} milliseconds of data.

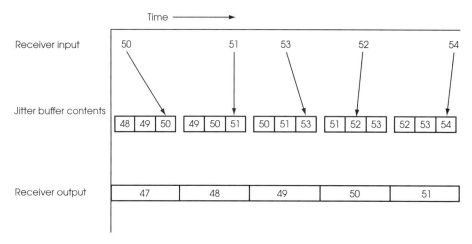

Figure 6-9 Flow of Packets in a Receiver

In PacketCable, audio packets are formatted according to the requirements of the **Real-time Transport Protocol** (**RTP**) as defined in RFC 1889. When a new audio packet is received, the application first examines the timestamp that is contained in the header portion of the RTP packet. The next packet to be played must contain a timestamp greater than or equal to $t_1 + t_{packet}$. This represents the time at the starting end of the jitter buffer. The time at the other end is $t_1 + t_{packet} + T_j$. If the timestamp on the packet is outside this range, it is discarded. Otherwise, it is placed into the jitter buffer at a time corresponding to the value of its timestamp. This algorithm is followed for all incoming packets.

When time advances to time $t_1 + t_{packet}$, the audio from the most recently played packet has been completely played. The application examines the jitter buffer to determine the packet with the earliest timestamp contained in the buffer. In the normal case, the buffer will contain a packet with a timestamp value exactly equal to $t_1 + t_{packet}$. In this case, the packet is extracted and sent to the codec algorithm for conversion and playback.

If there is no such packet, the application may choose to replay the most recently played packet, or to deliver a period of silence, or fill in the time until the start of the next available packet through some other mechanism. At the appropriate time, the packet with the earliest timestamp is removed from the buffer and played back.

The jitter buffer serves to ensure that all packets *appear* to be delayed by the same amount, T_j as they cross the network. In practice, some of that delay is caused by network transmission delay and some by the time it takes for a packet to reach the front of the jitter buffer. A packet that arrives relatively early (compared to a steadily ticking clock) is placed further back in the jitter buffer, and a packet that arrives relatively late (compared to a steadily ticking clock) is placed closer to the beginning of the jitter buffer. In the end (assuming no packets are actually lost in transmission) each packet will be played back in order and at the right time.

Flowspecs

Now we can return to the main thread of the discussion. As we have mentioned, flowspecs, which are described in detail in RFC 1363, are a method of describing the precise bandwidth characteristics of an information flow.

A **flowspec** is a combination of two descriptions of flows: a traffic flow specification, known as a **T-spec**, and a resource requirement specification, known as an **R-spec**. The T-spec contains values that describe the actual traffic carried by the flow. The R-spec describes the resources needed to carry that traffic.

In PacketCable, a T-spec contains five values.

Bucket Depth (b)

> A value in octets representing the size of a single sample.

Bucket Rate (r)

> A value in octets per second representing the total amount of information in the flow.

Peak Rate (p)

> A value in octets per second representing the peak rate of the flow. For a constant bit rate flow (as in all the currently defined PacketCable codecs), $p \equiv r$.

Minimum Policed Unit (m)

> A value in octets that represents the minimum size of packet in the flow. If a packet smaller than this appears in the flow, it is treated as a packet of size m in the flow calculations.

> Suppose, for example, that a T-spec contains a value m of 256, but in fact the packets entering the flow are all of size 128 octets. Then any device policing the flow (such as, for example, a CMTS) will treat all the packets as if they were of size 256 octets, and it would be legitimate for the device to throttle the flow by dropping half of the packets presented to it.

Maximum Datagram Size (M)

> A value in octets that represents the largest packet that will be produced by the source. The values of M and m include all the overhead added by the IP and higher layers. (In other words, they include the RTP headers and even the IP header. If the media were passing through an IPsec pipe, the IPsec

header would also be included. However, in PacketCable the media are secured by a stream cipher—RC4—rather than IPsec.)

A PacketCable R-spec contains two values.

Reserved Rate (R)

This is the amount of bandwidth actually allocated to the flow. One might believe that setting $R \geq r$ would be sufficient to ensure that enough bandwidth has been allocated to the flow. Unfortunately, this turns out not to be enough to guarantee adequate quality. The reason for this lies in the fact that the delay experienced by packets as they traverse the network will not (in general) be the same for all packets, and sometimes a burst of several packets will arrive in a relatively short period of time (that is, there will be jitter in the flow). Such a burst will, for a brief period, require increased bandwidth to be available. The maximum amount of jitter is the difference between the maximum possible delay and the minimum possible delay. We can model these values as follows.

If we pretend that all the devices in the network work infinitely quickly, and the speed at which signals traverse the medium between devices is also infinite, then the only delay is introduced by the fact that emptying the primary bucket may cause the transmitting device to wish to inject B octets into the flow at once, which it is prohibited from doing by the leaky secondary bucket. This introduces a delay, D_1, where:

$$D_1 \leq B / R$$

Two kinds of additional delay may be introduced by network elements. The first, D_2, is caused by queuing delays and is inversely proportional to R:

$$D_2 = \delta_1 / R$$

The second kind of additional delay is simply due to the time taken to process and move the data and is (more or less) constant.

$$D_3 = \delta_2$$

Assuming that $R \geq r$ (that is, that the channel is not filled beyond capacity), then the total delay, D, is given by:

$$D = D_1 + D_2 + D_3; \text{ or}$$
$$D \leq b / R + \delta_1 / R + \delta_2$$

The maximum delay, D_{max}, is therefore given by:

$$D_{max} = (b + \delta_1) / R + \delta_2$$

The maximum jitter in the flow is the difference between the maximum delay, D_{max}, and the minimum possible delay. There are several ways of estimating the latter. One could simply set it equal to D_3 or to the speed of light delay, or even to zero. We will simply suppose that some defensible estimate is available and call this D_{min}.

The maximum jitter, J_{max}, is, by definition:

$$J_{max} = D_{max} - D_{min}$$

A playback device is likely to contain an internal jitter buffer of the sort we have discussed, specifically designed to remove jitter up to some value J_{buffer}. If $J_{buffer} > J_{max}$, then it is possible to introduce a non-zero "slack" term, S, into the R-spec, where S is interpreted to mean an additional amount of jitter that may be introduced in the flow without adversely affecting the quality of the final output (since the jitter buffer can correct for it). The value of S is simply bound by the condition:

$$S \leq J_{buffer} - J_{max}$$

To put it another way, the slack term is the amount by which the receiver's jitter buffer is "overdesigned", given the actual variation in delays that packets will experience as they traverse this particular network.

This leads us to the second term in the PacketCable R-spec.

Slack Term (S)

> This is a value, in microseconds, corresponding to an additional maximum delay that may be applied to packets in the flow, as derived above.

Flowspecs, DOCSIS and SDP

There are three mechanisms used to define bandwidth requirements in PacketCable, and the system must be sure that all three are in agreement as necessary. The three mechanisms are the flowspecs we have just described, the Service Flow parameters used in DOCSIS and the SDP descriptions used in call signaling. Any failure of these three descriptions to agree with one another will likely result in a call with unacceptable quality.

Table 6-1 shows the flowspecs defined by PacketCable for carrying the mandatory and recommended codecs. The table includes the corresponding values carried in the SDP portion of the call signaling.

Table 6-1 PacketCable Flowspecs

SDP RTP/AVP Code	SDP rtpmap	SDP ptime (Milliseconds)	Codec	Flowspec Value of B, m, or M (Octets)	Flowspec Value of R and p (Octets per Second)	Comment
0	<none>	10	G.711	120	12000	G.711 with RTP
0	<none>	20	G.711	200	10000	payload type 0
0	<none>	30	G.711	280	9333	(assigned by IETF)
96–127	PCMU/8000	10	G.711	120	12000	G.711 64 kbps. This
96–127	PCMU/8000	20	G.711	200	10000	is the default codec.
96–127	PCMU/8000	30	G.711	280	9333	
15	<none>	10	G.728	60	6000	G.728 with RTP
15	<none>	20	G.728	80	4000	payload type 15
15	<none>	30	G.728	100	3333	(assigned by IETF)
96–127	G728/8000	10	G.728	60	6000	G.728 16 kbps
96–127	G728/8000	20	G.728	80	4000	
96–127	G728/8000	30	G.728	100	3333	
96–127	G729E/8000	10	G.729E	55	5500	G.729E 11.8 kbps
96-127	G729E/8000	20	G.729E	70	3500	10 millisec frame
96-127	G729E/8000	30	G.729E	85	2833	size with 5 millisec
						look-ahead

In order to manage the upstream data flow correctly, it is the MTA's job to map the values in the flowspec (as derived from the codec) into equivalent DOCSIS Service Flow parameters. The precise mechanism by which this happens is currently undefined—since PacketCable 1.0 supports only MTAs that contain an embedded Cable Modem, and there is as yet no public API to control the Cable Modem independently, PacketCable merely requires that the MTA/CM combination be able to map a flowspec into a Dynamic Service flow that is capable of supporting the flowspec.

Constant Bit Rate (CBR) codecs can obtain upstream bandwidth with very little overhead on the DOCSIS link by using the DOCSIS Unsolicited Grant Service, and this is the usual mechanism by which bandwidth is guaranteed in current technology MTA/CMs, since all the current codecs in PacketCable are CBR. In the future, when PacketCable supports non-CBR codecs,[11] upstream bandwidth may be best provided using the DOCSIS Real-Time Polling.

Consider an example in which Alice uses G.711 as her audio codec. G.711 produces output at the rate of 64 kbps. This is the raw output rate from the codec; to it must be added all the overhead necessary to form the output into valid RTP packets that must travel over the DOCSIS link between the CM and the CMTS.

Suppose that Alice's MTA is configured to produce packets every 10 milliseconds. According to Table 6-1, this corresponds to 120 octets of data per packet (of which 80 octets are audio data, and 40 octets are header information).

The DOCSIS MAC layer overhead is a number that depends on the precise configuration of Alice's modem. A reasonable number is 29 octets: 11 octets for the MAC header, which includes 5 octets of BPI+ keying information; 6 octets for the destination address; 6 octets for the source address; 2 octets for the length; 4 octets for the CRC (see Chapter 3 for more details about DOCSIS), so that the modem must reserve a total of 149 octets of upstream bandwidth every 10 milliseconds. Since G.711 is a CBR codec, the reservation is most efficiently made using a DOCSIS Unsolicited Grant Service request.

As we saw in Chapter 3, a DOCSIS Service Flow has three sets of associated QoS parameters: Authorized (or Provisioned), Admitted and Active. These correspond closely to the PacketCable DQoS states of Authorized, Reserved and Committed resources. DQoS reservation and commitment are most easily implemented by using DOCSIS Dynamic Service messages, changing the AdmittedQoSParameterSet and ActiveQoSParameterSet parameters of the Service Flow.

Resource reservation can occur in a DSA-REQ or DSC-REQ message by setting QoSParameterSetType to the value 2, which corresponds to the value "Admitted". Similarly, resource commitment occurs by setting QoSParameterSetType to 4 ("Active") or to its functional equivalent, 6 ("Admitted + Active").

Continuing the example of Alice using G.711, the DSA-REQ message sent by her modem to reserve the bandwidth could look like Table 6-2.

Table 6-3 shows the DSC-REQ message that Alice's modem could send to commit the resources.

The values of parameters such as ToleratedGrantJitter, TrafficPriority and so on may be preprovisioned or may be calculated on the fly by the CM.

---

11. Not all audio codecs are CBR. In addition, many non-audio codecs (codecs used for video) are also non-CBR.

Table 6-2 Example DSA-REQ

TransactionID		1
UpstreamServiceFlow	ServiceFlowReference	1
	QoSParameterSetType	Admitted (2)
	ServiceFlowScheduling	UGS (6)
	NominalGrantInterval	10ms
	ToleratedGrantJitter	2ms
	GrantsPerInterval	1
	UnsolicitedGrantSize	149
DownstreamServiceFlow	ServiceFlowReference	2
	QoSParameterSetType	Admitted (2)
	TrafficPriority	3
	MaximumSustainedRate	12,000

Table 6-3 Example DSC-REQ

TransactionID		1
UpstreamServiceFlow	ServiceFlowID	10288
	QoSParameterSetType	Admitted 1 Active(6)
	ServiceFlowScheduling	UGS (6)
	NominalGrantInterval	10ms
	ToleratedGrantJitter	2ms
	GrantsPerInterval	1
	UnsolicitedGrantSize	149
DownstreamServiceFlow	ServiceFlowID	10289
	QoSParameterSetType	Admitted 1 Active(6)
	TrafficPriority	3
	MaximumSustainedRate	12,000

A Note About RTCP

The RFC that describes the Real-Time Transport Protocol, RTP (RFC 1889), also defines a control protocol to manage session containing streams of RTP packets. This is the **Real-Time Control Protocol**, **RTCP**. We have seen in earlier chapters how the authentication and encryption keying material for the RTCP messages is passed in a manner very similar to that for RTP. However, we have had almost nothing to say about the RTCP messaging itself.

Partly this is because the PacketCable specifications themselves have little to say on the subject. Support for RTCP is mandatory because RFC 1889 requires it, and therefore, in order to follow the standard PacketCable operating procedure, RTCP must be supported to the extent necessary within PacketCable. However, RTCP is not very useful in the context of PacketCable, since the protocol is designed to transfer control and information between the endpoints—which in this case are *untrusted* MTAs. In other words, MTAs cannot be trusted to report valid RTCP information, nor to act correctly on received RTCP information.

In addition, there is one area in which PacketCable violates the spirit of RFC 1889 because the mechaism used to transfer RTCP is not the same as that used to transfer the RTP on which the reports are based. RFC 1889 states the following.

> The control traffic should be limited to a small and known fraction of the session bandwidth: small so that the primary function of the transport protocol to carry data is not impaired; known so that the control traffic can be included in the bandwidth specification given to a resource reservation protocol, and so that each participant can independently calculate its share.

In other words, the RTCP and the RTP are expected to share the bandwidth in a conceptual "channel". This is not what happens in PacketCable. In PacketCable, QoS-enabled bandwidth is allocated (via the gate mechanism) *only* for the RTP stream(s). The RTCP packets are left to take their chance in parallel "best-effort" streams.

Consequently, in all the bandwidth calculations for QoS-enabled flows, we need concern ourselves only with the bandwidth needed to carry the RTP packets, and the RTCP packets are left to fend for themselves. This is hardly what the authors of RFC 1889 had in mind, but given the untrusted nature of MTAs and the scarcity of upstream bandwidth on HFC networks, the PacketCable architects had little choice in the matter.

More About Gates

We have examined in some detail the underlying DOCSIS mechanism used by DQoS to provide upstream bandwidth. The question naturally arises: "All this is well and good, but when exactly does the MTA command the CM to make the various DSA, DSC and DSD requests to create, modify and delete the DOCSIS Service Flows"?

To answer this question we must look at the concept of resource management in a PacketCable network at a higher level. Earlier, we looked briefly at the concept of a *gate,* which is a logical entity residing on a CMTS and controlled by a GC. Gates are created, opened, closed and destroyed by commands originating outside the CMTS on which the gate resides (except that a CMTS is permitted unilaterally to close a gate if it detects a long period of inactivity on the flow associated with that gate).

When a CM sends a DSA-REQ, the CMTS should not grant the request unless an associated gate has already been called into existence by a command from its GC. Typically, a telephone call utilizes two unidirectional gates on a CMTS, both associated with a single GateID in a gate pair.

A gate encapsulates the following values.

- GateID

  A Gate-ID is a 32-bit quantity allocated by the CMTS on which the gate resides. A maximum of two gates (a gate pair) may share a single Gate-ID. In a gate pair, one gate must control the upstream flow, and the other the downstream flow.

  A Gate-ID is associated with various coordination and billing information. Coordination information is used to ensure that the gates at the two ends of the phone call remain synchronized. Billing information is sent to the system Record Keeping Server (RKS) for the backoffice to process and possibly add a charge for the call to the subscriber's bill.

- Gate coordination information

  — Address and port of the remote entity with which coordination has to occur

  — Gate-ID for the gate or gate pair on the remote entity

  — Security Key for communication with the remote entity

  — No-Gate-Coordination flag. If set, it does not require receipt of a Gate-Open to keep the local gate open. Normally, a gate will remain open only if it receives notification in a short period of time that the corresponding gate on the remote entity is also open. We will see shortly how this is managed. This flag is very poorly named. One could be forgiven for thinking that setting this flag turns off all gate coordination messaging. However, that is not the case. The only effect of this flag is to cause the gate not to look for an incoming Gate-Open message.

— No-Gate-Open flag. If set, it does not send a Gate-Open. Normally, when a gate is opened, it will send a notification to the corresponding gate on the remote entity informing it of the fact that the gate has just opened.

- Billing information

  — Address and port of the primary Record Keeping Server (RKS).

  — Address and port of the secondary RKS (in case the primary RKS is unreachable)

  — Flag indicating whether events are transmitted to the RKS in real-time or whether they are batched. The CMTS may send billing information at the same time that events occur, or it may store them locally and send a (perhaps large) batch of event records later at a time when the network is likely to be less heavily loaded.

  — Billing-Correlation-ID, which is used by the backoffice to collate event messages and to manage billing for the call

  — Possible additional billing information

- Prototype Classifier

  A Prototype Classifier is a 6-tuple that itself encapsulates a number of parameters to manage service flows within a CMTS. It is not necessary for us to go into details, but essentially a Prototype Classifier is a template against which packets are matched, and allows the CMTS to identify with which Service Flow a particular packet is associated.

  The precise encoding of a Prototype Classifier is unspecified, since it is used entirely within a CMTS and does not appear in any PacketCable DQoS messages and is therefore implementation dependent. A Prototype Classifier contains the following elements.

  - Direction

    May be either upstream or downstream

  - Protocol

  - Source IP address

    IP address of the originator of the flow; typically the address of the local MTA for an upstream flow, or of the remote MTA for a downstream flow

  - Destination IP address

    IP address of the destination of the flow

  - Destination port

  - Source port

- Auto-Commit flag

  If set, this signals that the resources should be committed immediately subsequent to reservation without any further high-level signaling. This might be used, for example, when a call is being placed to a network device such as a voicemail system, which does not require a two-phase commit mechanism. For ordinary user-to-user calls, the auto-commit flag is always unset. See the discussion in the next section for more details concerning this flag.

- Commit-Not-Allowed flag

  If set, instructs the CMTS to ignore any requests for the resources associated with this gate to be committed. In ordinary use, this flag is never set. See the discussion in the next section for more details concerning this flag.

- Authorized envelope

  The flowspec describing the authorized resources associated with this gate

- Reserved envelope

  The flowspec describing the reserved resources associated with this gate

- Resource-ID

  A 32-bit quantity allocated by the CMTS on which the gate resides, and which identifies a set of resources.

  It is tempting to identify the GateID with a Resource-ID, and in many simple implementations this turns out to be a reasonable thing to do. However, a more complicated CMTS may be able to manage its resources more efficiently than a simple CMTS, by using a single set of resources for multiple gates if it knows that there is no possibility of multiple gates needing to access the resources simultaneously. In this case, the Resource-ID must be understood to be distinct from the GateID.

  Any number of gates may share a single Resource-ID. This means that they are sharing *a single set of resources*. It follows that only one of the set of gates that share a single Resource-ID may have the resources committed at any one time (see Figure 6-10). This might be used, for example, for call waiting, in which the same set of resources may be used for the two calls, switching between them as the user toggles between the calls.

There is one situation when more than one gate may access the resources simultaneously: Remember that even though a gate is associated with a unidirectional flow, the GateID may refer to a gate pair corresponding to *two* flows, one in each direction. The resources identified by a particular Resource-ID, however, may contain both upstream and downstream resources. PacketCable assumes that the upstream

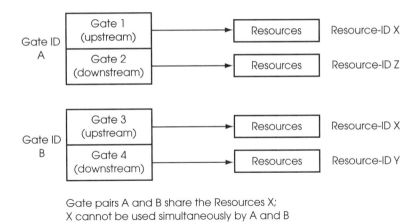

Gate pairs A and B share the Resources X;
X cannot be used simultaneously by A and B

Figure 6-10 Multiple Gates Sharing the Same Resources

and downstream resources are completely independent of one another and therefore, in a set of gates that share a Resource-ID, one upstream gate and one downstream gate are permitted to commit their associated resources at any one time.

Auto-Commit and Commit-Not-Allowed Flags

As we saw above, a gate encapsulates two flags that may be used to control the way in which a gate commits resources. The Auto-Commit flag causes the resources to be committed as soon as they are reserved by the MTA. The Commit-Not-Allowed unsurprisingly causes the gate to ignore any explicit requests to commit the resources. The need for these flags, as well as the way in which they are used, can be illustrated with a couple of examples.

Auto-Commit Flag

The Auto-Commit flag causes an additional DOCSIS exchange to occur once a gate has been created and a Dynamic Service Flow granted. If the CM creates the Dynamic Service Flow with only the Admitted state (that is, the flow is not Active, so that traffic cannot flow), then as soon as the three-way DSA-REQ/DSA-RSP/DSA-ACK handshake is completed, the CMTS transmits a DSC-REQ, changing the state of the Service Flow to Active. The CM will respond with a DSC-RSP, and the CMTS will further respond with a DSC-ACK reflecting the active state of the service flow.

The Auto-Commit flag is often set when the far end of the call is off-net and the PSTN gateway will be used to provide audible ringback. In this case the downstream resources must be committed in order to allow the ringback audio to reach the MTA.

The Auto-Commit flag may also be used to save time when the network can guarantee that resources will be available at the far end of the call. Typically, this is the case when a user is placing an On-net to Off-net call or if the call is to a device within the network, such as a voicemail device. A good rule of thumb is that if the far end of the call requires that packets pass through a CMTS, then the Auto-Commit flag should not be set. If, on the other hand, the far-end packets do not pass through a CMTS, then the call may be a candidate to have the gate Auto-Commit its resources, since it is reasonable to expect that "upstream" bandwidth (at the far end) will be available. Note, however, that setting the Auto-Commit flag does allow audio to flow to the subscriber without that subscriber having to commit resources in the upstream direction, and it is the latter that is often used as a signal to start billing.

Whether using the Auto-Commit flag for this purpose is a good idea therefore depends on the nature of the device being called and the exact mechanism used for billing calls to that device.

Commit-Not-Allowed Flag

The Commit-Not-Allowed flag causes the CMTS to ignore any requests to commit resources for this gate. This may be desirable in certain situations where the flow of signaling messages is such that a gate is created before the identity of the far endpoint is known. In these cases, the gate can still be created, but the operator might not want the CMTS to respond to a received request to commit the resources, since it makes no sense to commit resources on a flow until the identity of both ends is known.[12] Therefore if the identity of the far end is unknown (which will be only a temporary situation), then the gate may be created with the Commit-Not-Allowed flag set.

As soon as the Gate Controller becomes aware of the identity of the far end, it can send a GATE-SET message that identifies the far endpoint (in the Gate-Spec record) and simultaneously unsets the Commit-Not-Allowed flag, so that the resources may be committed as usual.

Gate States

Gates are always in one of the following states.

Allocated

> The gate exists, but nothing more.

---

12. The MTA needs to know the identity of the far end in order to transmit bearer-channel packets. The CMTS needs to know it in order to set up an internal packet classifier to manage the flow properly.

Authorized

The gate exists, and the resources associated with it do not exceed those that the subscriber is permitted to use.

Reserved

The resources have been reserved, but they cannot yet be used by the gate.

Committed

The gate is open; the resources associated with the gate are in use by the gate.

Remote-Committed

The remote gate is open, but the local gate is not.

Local-Committed

The local gate is open, but the remote gate is not.

A gate is created in the Allocated state. The Authorized, Reserved and Committed states correspond to the state of the resources associated with the gate. The last two states, Remote-Committed and Local-Committed, are transient states through which a gate may pass while coordinating call setup with another gate.

Having mentioned the various states in which a gate may be, we must come clean and mention that the DQoS specification contains an interesting twist: State is associated not with a gate but with a Gate-ID (which, in practice means that state is associated with a gate pair, not with a single gate). Usually, this does not complicate matters, since both gates tend to move in synchronicity. But there is no requirement for them to do so, and sometimes it is not clear what state the gate pair is in.

The most common occurrence of a pair of gates in which one gate is allowing information to flow and the other is not is following an Auto-Commit. In this case, the MTA has requested that the gate pair go into the Reserved state, but has not committed resources. The Auto-Commit flag, however, causes downstream resources to be committed. This does *not* change the state of the gate pair, which remains in the Reserved state.

Although the specification does not explicitly state this, the following general rule applies and can be used to determine whether the gate pair is in a committed state. The trigger to move from the Reserved to the Committed or Local-Committed states is a request *from the MTA* for upstream resources to be committed.

Gates can be influenced by two different kinds of messages: direct control from a GC or MTA, and gate coordination messages that pass between CMTSes, either directly or via proxying CMSes. We will now proceed to examine these two kinds of messages in some detail.

Common Open Policy Service (COPS)

DQoS messaging between a Gate Controller and its CMTSes uses the **Common Open Policy Service** (**COPS**) protocol,[13] described in detail in RFC 2748. We will first briefly examine some of the concepts embodied in COPS and then look at how they are implemented in a PacketCable network.

COPS is a client/server protocol designed to be used for admission control to QoS networks. COPS runs over TCP, using port number 3288. Logical COPS entities reside in network edge devices, which are typically COPS clients, and a central policy server. Three logical entities are defined.

Policy Decision Point (PDP)

> The COPS server. The **PDP** is the entity that decides whether to admit or reject a session into the network, based on policy to which it has access.

Policy Enforcement Point (PEP)

> The COPS client. The **PEP** may either ask the PDP to make the decision to allow or deny a session access to the network, or it may ask the PDP for policy information that allows the PEP itself to make such a decision.
>
> The PEP may receive a session's request for access and then query the PDP for a response to the request, or it may signal the PDP that it wishes to receive decisions and policy information on an unsolicited basis.

Local Decision Point (LDP)

> A variant of the COPS client, in which local information (which might include information gleaned from a prior interaction with a **PDP**) is used to inform decisions as to whether a request should be granted. A decision from a PDP always takes precedence over a decision based on local information.

The usual implementation of COPS is conceptually simple. The PEP, which lies at the edge of the core network, receives a request for access from an entity such as an end-user device. The PEP then consults the PDP either for a decision as to whether the entity should be admitted or for information that will permit the PEP itself to make that decision. This is shown digrammatically in Figure 6-11.

---

13. At this point you are probably thinking, "Oh no! Not another protocol". That's understandable, but I'm afraid it's not the last one. Perhaps one good thing about COPS is its name: Apart from the play on the word "cop" (as a synonym for "policeman", this is rather appropriate for a protocol designed to transfer policy), the word "policy" itself serves to remind us that DQoS gates really describe policy to be applied to requests for Dynamic Service Flows, rather than actually creating such flows themselves.

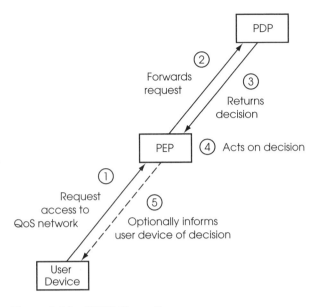

Figure 6-11   COPS Operation

Intserv and Diffserv Networks

QoS networks may be divided into two types, known as Intserv and Diffserv networks, as follows.

In an **Intserv** ("Integrated services") network, there is no distinction between traffic flows. Intserv connections conceptually resemble fat pipes into which flows are injected. All traffic in the pipe is treated identically.

In a **Diffserv** ("Differentiated services") network, individual traffic flows (or bundles of flows) are tagged so that they retain their identity within the network. This allows the network to treat different flows differently. For example, in a Diffserv network, audio streams might receive a different priority from signaling streams.

The usual implementation architectures of COPS vary slightly depending on whether the QoS network to which access is being controlled is an Intserv or a Diffserv network. In most Intserv implementations, the PDP makes the decision and transmits that decision to the PEP. In most Diffserv networks, the PDP sends the policy information to the PEP and allows the PEP to determine whether to permit access. In this regard, PacketCable functions similarly to a Diffserv network, with the Gate Controller acting as the PDP and the CMTS taking the part of the PEP.

COPS in PacketCable Networks

Figure 6-12 shows the COPS architecture as it is implemented in PacketCable networks. The (local) GC acts as the COPS PDP for a particular MTA, and the (local)

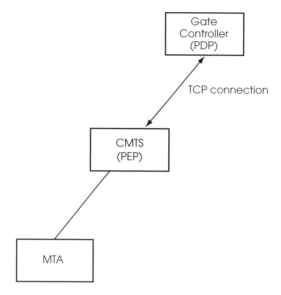

Figure 6-12 COPS Architecture in a PacketCable Network

CMTS acts as the corresponding PEP. The PacketCable specifications permit the CMTS to cache policy information provided by the PDP, allowing the CMTS to act as a quasi-independent COPS LDP should the service provider so wish.

The COPS RFC defines a specialized protocol (unsurprisingly termed *the COPS protocol*) to perform the required signaling between the PDP and the PEP. In PacketCable, the COPS messages are treated as a kind of signaling, and travel over an IPsec connection, so that the protocol stack is as shown in Figure 6-13.[14]

In the next few sections we will see how COPS messages are encoded. Then we will look at some practical examples of how the protocol actually works in a PacketCable network.

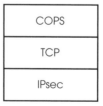

Figure 6-13 PacketCable COPS Protocol Stack

---

14. Ordinary call signaling messages use UDP rather than TCP, as described in the chapters on NCS and DCS.

COPS Messages

COPS messages share a common format, in which the message data are appended to an 8-octet COPS Message Header, as depicted in Figure 6-14. COPS messages in PacketCable networks are either commands (called Decisions by COPS) or responses (called Reports by COPS). In each case, the high-level structure is the same: A COPS header is followed by one or more COPS objects, the first of which is a type of COPS object called a Handle. In PacketCable, although the Handle object must be present (to satisfy the demands of the COPS protocol) and must be used in accordance with the COPS protocol, it serves no useful purpose. The value of the Handle is determined by the CMTS during initialization of the COPS connection (see "Initialization of the COPS Connection"). We will first look at the format of COPS messages and objects. Then we will discuss how PacketCable COPS messages are actually constructed.

The COPS Message Header fields are as follows.

Version

> A 4-bit field giving the COPS version number. In PacketCable this must be set to 1.

Flags

> A 4-bit field. Only the LSB is used by PacketCable; all other bits must be zero. The LSB is the "solicited message" flag. This flag must be set to 1 if the message is a response to an earlier COPS message. Otherwise, it must be set to 0.

Op-code

> A 1-octet field that defines the operation to be performed. Table 6-4 shows the mapping between op-codes and COPS Messages.

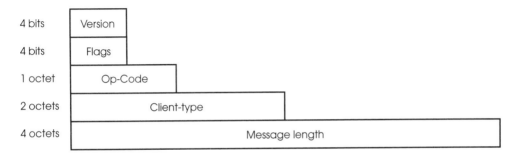

Figure 6-14 COPS Message Header Format

Table 6-4 COPS Op-Codes

Op-Code	Meaning
1	Request (REQ)
2	Decision (DEC)
3	Report-State (RPT)
6	Client-Open (OPN)
7	Client-Accept (CAT)
9	Keep-Alive (KA)

Client-type

> A 2-octet field. If the message is a Keep-Alive, then the Client-type is zero. Otherwise it has the value 0x8005, which indicates a PacketCable client.

Message-length

> A 4-octet field giving the total length of the message, including the header, in octets. COPS messages are always a multiple of 4 octets in length.

Following the header is a variable number of COPS objects. Each object has the format shown in Figure 6-15. The COPS object fields are as follows.

Length

> A 2-octet field. This is the total length of the object, in octets. COPS objects are always a multiple of 4 octets in length.

> (Actually, this is not quite true. It is good practice to make COPS objects a multiple of 4 octets in length. If the length is not a multiple of 4 octets, then padding must be added to make the number of octets transmitted a multiple of 4, but the actual length specified in the header does not have to be a multiple of 4. Typically, though, the length is defined to be a multiple of 4 octets by adding sufficient "Reserved" fields so the object (including the Reserved fields) is a multiple of 4 octets in length.)

C-Num

> A 1-octet field. C-Num identifies the COPS class of the information contained within the object. Allowable values are shown in Table 6-5.

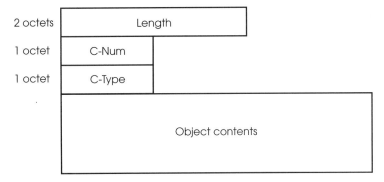

Figure 6-15   Format of COPS Objects

Table 6-5   Allowed COPS Information Classes

C-Num	COPS Information Class
1	Handle
6	Decision
8	Error
9	Client Specific Information
10	Keep Alive Timer
11	PEP Identification

C-Type

A 1-octet field. Identifies the subtype or version of the information in the object.

The remainder of the object follows the 4-octet COPS object header.

PacketCable clients can use several specialized COPS objects that are defined especially for PacketCable networks. Each specialized COPS object contains a pair of 1-octet values called S-Num and S-Type, respectively, which together uniquely identify the type of the specialized COPS object.

Figure 6-16 gives a high-level view of the structure of a COPS message that contains two PacketCable COPS objects. All of the specialized PacketCable COPS objects begin with a 4-octet object header containing the following information.

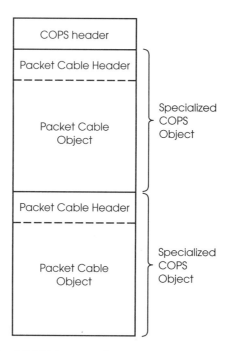

Figure 6-16 COPS Message Containing Two Specialized
PacketCable COPS Objects

Length

A 2-octet field. This gives the total length, in octets, of the specialized
PacketCable COPS object.

S-Num

A 1-octet field. This field gives the S-Num of the specialized COPS object,
that, together with the S-Type, uniquely identifies the type of the object.

S-Type

A 1-octet field. This field gives the S-Type of the specialized COPS object
that, together with the S-Num, uniquely identifies the type of the object.

The rest of the specialized COPS object follows this 4-octet header. Table 6-6
gives the values of Length, S-Num and S-Type for all the defined specialized
PacketCable COPS objects. The following sections describe the specialized
PacketCable COPS objects in more detail.

Table 6-6 Length, S-Num and S-Type of Specialized PacketCable COPS Objects

Object Name	Length (Octets)	S-Num	S-Type
Transaction-ID	8	1	1
Subscriber-ID	8	2	1
Gate-ID	8	3	1
Activity-Count	8	4	1
Gate-spec	60 + n ´ 28	5	1
Remote-Gate-Info	variable	6	1
Event-Generation-Info	36	7	1
Media-Connection-Event-Info	36	8	1
PacketCable-Error	8	9	1
Electronic-Surveillance-Parameters	20	10	1
Session-Description-Parameters	variable	11	1

Transaction-ID

As in many places in PacketCable, a Transaction-ID is used to match a response to the request that generated it. However, the Transaction-ID is not, as in other places in PacketCable, merely a number. Instead, it is broken into two constituent parts that identify both the number and the type of the transaction. Following the specialized header are two 2-octet fields, the Transaction Identifier and the Gate Command Type.

The Transaction Identifier is the number used by the Gate Controller to match responses returning from the CMTS with commands issued by the GC.

The Gate Command Type contains a value that is used to identify a particular command issued by the GC. The possible values of Gate Command Type are given in Table 6-7.

We will often talk about (for example) a GATE-SET message. This is a short-hand description for a COPS message containing a specialized PacketCable COPS object with the Gate Command Type set to the value 4 (in the case of a GATE-SET message).

So, for example, when a GC wishes to allocate a particular gate, the COPS message that it sends to the CMTS will include a Transaction-ID object with the Gate Command Type set to the value 1 and the Transaction Identifier set to some unique 16-bit value. This is often referred to as a GATE-ALLOC message. The corresponding response from the CMTS will contain a Transaction-ID object with an identical

Table 6-7 DQoS Gate Commands

Gate Command	Corresponding Value of Gate Command Type
GATE-ALLOC	1
GATE-ALLOC-ACK	2
GATE-ALLOC-ERR	3
GATE-SET	4
GATE-SET-ACK	5
GATE-SET-ERR	6
GATE-INFO	7
GATE-INFO-ACK	8
GATE-INFO-ERR	9

Transaction Identifier and a Gate Command Type with the value either 2 (if the transaction was successful—a GATE-ALLOC-ACK) or 3 (if the transaction was not successful—a GATE-ALLOC-ERR).

Subscriber-ID

The Subscriber-ID contains the IP address of the line on behalf of which this request is being made. For example, if Alice places a call to Bob, messages pertaining to the gate on the originating CMTS will contain a Subscriber-ID that identifies the line that Alice is using. Messages on the terminating CMTS will contain a Subscriber-ID that identifies Bob's line.

There is an important issue surrounding the Subscriber-ID. The PacketCable 1.0 Dynamic Quality of Service specification says (section 5.3.2.2), "The Subscriber-ID identifies the subscriber for this service request". *This is not true.* Since the value of the Subscriber is merely an IP address, it actually identifies merely the MTA that is placing the request. The difference can, in some instances, be important. Suppose, for example, that the MTA is a 100-line device serving an apartment building. The DQoS mechanism uses the value of the Subscriber-ID to ensure that a device is not attempting to allocate too many gates simultaneously. Since all the inhabitants of the apartment complex effectively share a single Subscriber-ID, then one person can, by bombarding the network with spurious requests for service, effectively deny service to the others. Presumably, this potential Denial of Service attack will be eliminated in some future version of PacketCable.

Gate-ID

The Gate-ID identifies the gate (or the gate pair comprising one upstream gate and one downstream gate) to which this message applies. Gate-IDs are assigned by CMTSes and are unique within the universe of a single CMTS. Note that this means that Gate-IDs are not necessarily unique within the universe of a CMS, since two CMTSes with which it communicates might happen to assign the same Gate-ID at the same time (to completely different calls).

Activity-Count

This is a 4-octet value that is returned by a CMTS to a CMS and contains the number of gates currently assigned to the line identified by Subscriber-ID. In general, a service provider would probably want to limit the number of simultaneous gates that a line may have open to some small number (quite possibly one).

Gate-Spec

A Gate-Spec is a complex object that defines the QoS flow characteristics of a gate. It contains the following fields, in order, after the specialized PacketCable COPS object 4-octet header.

Direction

A 1-octet field. The value 0 represents a downstream flow; the value 1 represents an upstream flow.

Protocol ID

A 1-octet field that identifies the protocol for the flow. This number matches the Protocol ID octet in the IP header (see Chapter 1). If zero, then any value of the protocol ID in the IP header is permitted in the flow. In general, for telephony flows the Protocol ID has a value of 17, corresponding to UDP.

Flags

A 1-octet (8-bit) field of eight independent flags. Currently only two flags are defined.

0x01: Auto-Commit. If set, resources are committed immediately following a successful reservation.

0x02: Commit-Not-Allowed. If set, any subsequent COMMIT message for this gate is ignored.

Session Class

A 1-octet field that allows the gate to be marked as a special kind of gate, with particular properties that may be defined by the network operator. These are the permitted values.

1: Normal priority

2: High priority (911 call)

The actual behavior of the network for the two permitted service classes is unspecified and depends on the policy of the individual network operator. For example, an operator may choose to operate a policy whereby a high-priority call can cause other calls to be summarily dropped if the high-priority call is unable to obtain bandwidth by any other means.

Source IP Address

Destination IP address

The Source and Destination IP addresses are 4-octet values of the source and destination MTA, respectively. A value of zero in either of these fields acts as a wildcard, meaning that the respective address will not be policed by the CMTS.

Source Port

Destination Port

The Source and Destination IP ports are 2-octet values of the ports on the source and destination MTA, respectively. A value of zero in either of these fields acts as a wildcard, meaning that the respective port number will not be policed by the CMTS.

Reserved

A four-octet value reserved for use in later versions of PacketCable.

Timer value (T_1 timer)

Timer value (T_2 timer)

Coordination between the gates on the CMTSes at the two ends of a call depends on the values of two timers, T_1 and T_2. The values of these timers are 4-octet values, representing times in milliseconds. For more details of the gate coordination mechanism, see the section "Gate Coordination".

Following these fields are one or more sets of 28-octet flowspecs, however many are necessary to describe the flow. Each flowspec is encoded as follows.

Token Bucket Rate

> A 4-octet field containing a single number in IEEE floating point format, representing the number of octets per second in the flow.

Token Bucket Size

> A 4-octet field containing a single number in IEEE floating point format, representing the size, in octets, of a single bucket in the flow.

Peak Data Rate

> A 4-octet field containing a single number in IEEE floating point format, representing the peak rate, in octets per second, in the flow.

Minimum Policed Unit

> A 4-octet field containing a 32-bit integer. This is the minimum size of packet that will enter the flow (including all the headers from the IP and higher layers). If a packet smaller than this is injected into the flow, it will be treated as a packet of this size for QoS purposes.

Maximum Packet Size

> A 4-octet field containing a 32-bit integer. This is that maximum size of packet that will enter the flow (including all the headers from the IP and higher layers).

Rate

> A 4-octet field containing a single number in IEEE floating point format. This is the actual bandwidth, in octets per second, allocated to the flow.

Slack Term

> A 4-octet field containing a 32-bit integer. This is a value, in microseconds, designed to bound the amount of jitter in the flow. See the section "Flowspecs" for details.

Remote-Gate-Info

In order to coordinate the gates at both ends of a call, each gate must know something about its peer at the other end of the call. This information is passed in a Remote-Gate-Info object, which contains the following fields, in order, after the specialized PacketCable COPS object 4-octet header:

CMTS IP address

> A 4-octet field containing the IP address of the CMTS that hosts the remote gate.

CMTS-Port

A 2-octet field containing the port number on the remote CMTS to which gate coordination messages are to be sent.

Flags

A 2-octet (16-bit) field of 16 independent flags. Currently only two flags are defined.

0x0001: No-Gate-Coordination. If set, gate coordination does not occur; the CMTS will not require receipt of a Gate-Open from the remote CMTS in order to keep the local gate open.

0x0002: No-Gate-Open. If set, the remote CMTS will not send a Gate-Open message when it commits its resources.

Remote-Gate-ID

A 4-octet field containing the value of the Gate-ID for the remote gate, as generated by the remote CMTS.

Algorithm

A 1-octet field that has the decimal value 100 (which corresponds to the hexadecimal value 0x64). This specifies that the Message Authenticator Code algorithm is MD5, following the specification in the RADIUS RFC, RFC 2139.

Security Key

A variable-length field used to authenticate gate coordination messages (see the section "Format of Gate Coordination Messages"). In PacketCable, the length of the security key is always 16 octets.

Event-Generation-Info

As we will see in Chapter 7, a CMTS generates specific Event Messages at the start and completion of a call, and possibly at other times as well. Specifically, the QoS-Start and QoS-Stop event messages are used for billing purposes and also by the wiretap system if a subject is under surveillance. The Event-Generation-Info object carries information informing the CMTS how to manage the billing event messages.

Primary-Record-Keeping-Server-IP-Address

A 4-octet field containing the IP address of the RKS to which events are to be sent.

Primary-Record-Keeping-Server-Port

> A 2-octet field containing the port number to which events are to be sent.

Flags

> A 1-octet (8-bit) field of eight independent flags. Currently only one flag is defined.

> *0x01: Batch Processing.* If this flag is set, the CMTS accumulates events and sends them in a batch transmitted at periodic intervals. If this flag is not set, the CMTS forwards the events in real time. (Note that the CMTS *always* forwards events to wiretap servers in real time.)

Reserved

> A 1-octet field used for alignment purposes.

Secondary-Record-Keeping-Server-IP-Address

> A 4-octet field containing the IP address of the RKS to which events are to be sent if the primary RKS is unavailable.

Secondary-Record-Keeping-Server-Port

> A 2-octet field containing the port number to which events are to be sent if the primary RKS is unavailable.

Reserved

> A 2-octet field used for alignment purposes.

Billing-Correlation-ID

> A 16-octet field assigned by a CMS and used to correlate all the events and records pertaining to this call.

Media-Connection-Event-Info

This object contains information encapsulated by Call-Answer and Call-Disconnect event messages. If a Media-Connection-Event-Info object is contained in a DQoS GATE-SET message, then the CMTS generates the Call-Answer and Call-Disconnect event messages for the RKS (and possibly an electronic surveillance DF) at the appropriate time.

Called-Party-Number

> A 20-octet field containing the E.164 formatted telephone number of the called party in ASCII. The string is not null terminated; it is *right* justified, with unused fields set to spaces (ASCII value 32 decimal).

Routing-Number

A 20-octet field containing the E.164 formatted telephone number of the called party in ASCII. The string is not null terminated; it is *right* justified, with unused fields set to spaces (ASCII value 32 decimal). In the current release of PacketCable, this field contains exactly the same information as the Called-Party-Number field.

Charged-Number

A 20-octet field containing the E.164 formatted telephone number of the billable party in ASCII. The string is not null terminated; it is *right* justified, with unused fields set to spaces (ASCII value 32 decimal).

Location-Routing-Number

A 20-octet field containing the E.164 formatted telephone number of the called party in ASCII. The string is not null terminated; it is *right* justified, with unused fields set to spaces (ASCII value 32 decimal). In the current release of PacketCable, this field contains exactly the same information as the Called-Party-Number and Routing-Number fields.

PacketCable-Error

This object is used to pass error information.

Error-code

A 2-octet field containing an error code according to Table 6-8.

Error-sub-code

A 2-octet field that is currently unused.

Table 6-8   DQoS Error Codes

Error-Code Value	Meaning
1	No gates currently available
2	Illegal Gate-ID
3	Illegal Session Class value
127	Unspecified Error

Electronic-Surveillance-Parameters

When a call is under electronic surveillance (see Chapter 7), certain event messages must be sent to a Delivery Function (DF), which is responsible for collating, reformatting and forwarding messages as appropriate to one or more Law Enforcement Agencies. The Electronic-Surveillance-Parameters object tells the CMTS how to manage these event messages.

DF-IP-Address-for-CDC

A 4-octet field containing the IP address of the DF to which the event messages are to be sent. Note that there is no option to batch these messages; they must be sent in real-time.

DF-Port-for-CDC

A 2-octet field containing the port number on the DF for the event messages.

Flags

A 16-bit field containing 16 independent flags. Currently only two flags are defined.

0x0001: DUP-EVENT. If set, the CMTS sends a copy of all the event messages related to this gate to the address and port specified in the DF-IP-Address-for-CDC and DF-Port-for-CDC fields. If not set, the CMTS does not transmit the event messages.

0x0002: DUP-CONTENT. If set, the CMTS sends a copy of all the packets carried in the flow controlled by this gate to the address and port specified in the DF-IP-Address-for-CCC and DF-Port-for-CCC fields. If not set, the CMTS does not transmit the packets.

In order for electronic surveillance to occur, at least one of the flags must be set.

DF-IP-Address-for-CDC

A 4-octet field containing the IP address of the DF to which the duplicated call content packets are to be sent. The packets must be sent in real-time.

DF-Port-for-CDC

A 2-octet field containing the port number on the DF for the call content packets.

Reserved

A 2-octet field used for alignment.

Session-Description-Parameters

This is a special object, used to convey information to electronic surveillance equipment to ensure that a Law Enforcement Agency has sufficient information to correctly decode the stream of packets that it receives.

Following the four-octet header field, the object contains ASCII-encoded SDP strings. The first such string contains the SDP for the upstream flow. This is followed by a NULL octet, which is followed in turn by the SDP for the downstream flow. One or more NULL octets are appended to the downstream flow such that the total length of the object is a multiple of four octets, as required by COPS. At least one NULL octet must be appended to signal the end of the downstream SDP.

The Session-Description-Parameter may only appear in a GATE-SET message, and if it does so, then the CMTS must include the SDP information in the corresponding QoS-Start event message that is generated when the resources are committed.

Example PacketCable COPS Object

At this point it's probably a good idea to take a breather and take a look at an example of a plausible PacketCable COPS object. Some objects are very simple (like the Subscriber-ID object) and some are quite complex (like the Gate-Spec object). We will choose for our example an object with middling complexity, the Remote-Gate-Info object. An example complete Remote-Gate-Info object might look like this.

Octet 1	Octet 2	Octet 3	Octet 4	Description
Length: 36		S-Num: 6	S-Type:1	Object length and type information
IP address: 0x0a010203				IP address of the remote CMTS, represented as a 32-bit number
Port: 12749		Flags: 0		Port for gate coordination messages on the remote CMTS; value of the No-Gate-Coordination and No-Gate-Open flags (in this example, neither is set)
Gate-ID: 0x9f532bcd				The value of the Gate-ID on the remote CMTS
Algorithm: 0x64	Security Key:			Algorithm corresponds to MD5-based MAC, as specified in RFC 2138. Security Key is 16 octets in length.
Security Key (continued)				

Octet 1	Octet 2	Octet 3	Octet 4	Description
Security Key (continued)				
Security Key (continued)				
Security Key Padding (continued)				Padding must be added so that the length of the entire object is a multiple of four octets.

These are important things to remember.

- The length is measured in octets and must be a multiple of four octets.
- The S-Num and S-Type are used to identify this as a Remote-Gate-Info object.
- The value for the algorithm field must be 0x64, since MD5 is the only supported value in PacketCable.
- The length of the security key in PacketCable is always 16 octets.
- The padding is necessary because COPS requires that objects be a mulitple of four octets in length.

Other COPS objects are structured similarly.

Protocol Operation

DQoS messages used to control gates pass between a Gate Controller and a CMTS. All messages flowing from GC to CMTS are COPS Decision messages. These messages contain an object with a C-Num of 6 and a C-Type of 2, which is defined to mean "Client-specific Decision data" by the COPS specification.

Note that in the released RFC, the meaning of C-type with a value 2 was changed to mean "Stateless Data". The PacketCable specification was written at a time when the COPS protocol was merely an Internet Draft, not a published RFC. (The IETF warns against using Internet Drafts in long-lived specifications; however, PacketCable chose in several instances to ignore this warning.) As a result, there is a conflict between the wording of the published COPS RFC, number 2748, and the wording of the PacketCable specification. Since the subject of this book is PacketCable, we will adhere to the conventions in the published PacketCable 1.0 specification. Later versions of the specifications are likely to remove the discrepancies (in the instant case, probably by changing C-Type to the value 4).

All messages flowing in the reverse direction are COPS Report messages. These messages contain an object with a C-Num of 9 and a C-Type of 2, which is defined to mean "Client-specific data" by the COPS specification. Objects with this particular combination of C-Num and C-Type are sometimes referred to as "ClientSI objects".

A total of 13 different messages are defined. The contents of each message are defined below, where optional fields are enclosed in square brackets ([like this]) and choices are separated by a vertical bar (like this: <choice a> | <choice b> | <choice c>).

Gate Control Messages

The following messages are used to control gates.

GATE-ALLOC

Travels from GC to CMTS and contains:

```
Decision Header
Transaction-ID
Subscriber-ID
```

GATE-ALLOC-ACK

Travels from CMTS to GC and contains:

```
ClientSI-Header
Transaction-ID
Subscriber-ID
Gate-ID
Activity-Count
```

GATE-ALLOC-ERROR

Travels from CMTS to GC and contains:

```
ClientSI-Header
Transaction-ID
Subscriber-ID
PacketCable-Error
```

GATE-SET

Travels from GC to CMTS and contains:

```
Decision-Header
Transaction-ID
```

```
Subscriber-ID
[Gate-ID]
[Remote-Gate-Info]
[Event-Generation-Info]
[Media-Connection-Event-Info]
[Electronic-Surveillance-Parameters]
[Session-Description-Parameters]15
Gate-Spec
[Gate-Spec]
```

GATE-SET-ACK

Travels from CMTS to GC and contains:

```
ClientSI-Header
Transaction-ID
Subscriber-ID
Gate-ID
Activity-Count
```

GATE-SET-ERR

Travels from CMTS to GC and contains:

```
ClientSI-Header
Transaction-ID
Subscriber-ID
PacketCable-Error
```

GATE-INFO

Travels from GC to CMTS and contains:

```
Decision-Header
Transaction-ID
Gate-ID
```

GATE-INFO-ACK

Travels from CMTS to GC and contains:

```
ClientSI-Header
Transaction-ID
```

---

15. If present, then the CMTS must place the information in the ensuing Qos-Start event message. See Chapter 7 for details.

```
Subscriber-ID
Gate-ID
[Remote-Gate-Info]
[Event-Generation-Info]
[Media-Connection-Event-Info]
Gate-Spec
[Gate-Spec]
```

GATE-INFO-ERR

Travels from CMTS to GC and contains:

```
ClientSI-Header
Transaction-ID
Gate-ID
PacketCable-Error
```

Examples of COPS Messages

Before we go any further, let's briefly look at a couple of simple example messages to be sure that we understand how they are constructed. The more complex messages are very similar, except more lengthy.

Our first example will be a GATE-ALLOC message, which is sent by the GC to the CMTS, to check the number of gates that a particular endpoint is already using. Note that the CMS at this point is interested only in the *number* of gates, not the amount of resources that they consume. The major purpose of the GATE-ALLOC message (and its response) is to enable the system to respond efficiently in the event that an MTA attempts to mount a Denial of Service Attack by requesting a large number of gates to be opened—a simple check of the number of gates that the device already has open allows the network to return an error quickly, without having to have the CMTS check whether the specific resources requested are available.

The GATE-ALLOC contains three specialized COPS objects: Decision Header, Transaction-ID and Subscriber-ID. All COPS messages begin with the 8-octet COPS header.

Version

> 4 bits, with the value 0001

Flags

> The 4-bit "solicited message" flag. Since this is an unsolicited Decision message, it has the value 0000.

Op-code

> The 1-octet field that determines the type of the message. This is a Decision message, so it has the value 2.

Client-type

> The 2-octet field that determines the type of the client for which the message is intended (and therefore indicates the kinds of specialized COPS objects that the message contains). Since the CMTS is a PacketCable client, the field has the value 0x8005, which corresponds to "PacketCable client".

Message length

> The 4-octet field giving the total length of the message. At the moment, we don't know what the length is, so we leave this to be filled in later.

Following the COPS Header is the first COPS object, which is the Handle. As a reminder, the Handle object is required by the COPS protocol, but it serves no useful purpose in PacketCable. The Handle object looks just like any other COPS object.

Length

> A 2-octet field giving the length of the object in octets. In this case the length reflects whatever the CMTS uses as a Handle. For the purposes of our example, let's assume that the CMTS issues 4-octet Handles (which is slight overkill since normally the CMTS is involved in only a single COPS session, with its Gate Controller). In this case, the length will have the value 8.

C-Num

> This 1-octet field always has the value 1 for a Handle.

C-Type

> This 1-octet field always has the value 1 for a Handle.

Contents

> This is where the Handle goes. We have already agreed that its length in this example will be four octets. We will give it the arbitrary value 2.

The GATE-ALLOC is a Decision[16] and therefore the next item in the message is the Decision header.

---

16. The manner in which PacketCable uses COPS is rather unconventional. As you may have noticed, in PacketCable the COPS server (the Gate Controller) has a habit of sending unsolicited "decision" messages to the COPS client. The standard COPS nomenclature does not fit well with the PacketCable architecture, although it is arguably a valid use of the protocol.

Length

The 2-octet field giving the length of the COPS object. At the moment, we don't know how long it will be, so leave this to be filled in later.

C-Num

This has the value 6 for a Decision object.

C-Type

This has the value 2, since the message is going to contain client-specific (PacketCable) decision data.

There are two specialized COPS objects inside the message. The first is the Transaction-ID.

Length

The Transaction-ID has a length of 8 octets.

S-Num

This has the value 1 for a Transaction-ID.

S-Type

This has the value 1 for a Transaction-ID.

Transaction Identifier

This 2-octet field contains a numeric identifier for the transaction. Let's arbitrarily give it the value 1111.

Gate Command Type

This 2-octet field identifies this as a GATE-ALLOC. The correct entry for a GATE-ALLOC is the value 1 (see Table 6-7).

The second object is the Subscriber-ID.

Length

The Subscriber-ID has a length of 8 octets.

S-Num

This has the value 2 for a Subscriber-ID.

S-Type

This has the value 1 for a Subscriber-ID.

IP address

> This is a 4-octet field containing the IP address of the MTA for this subscriber. Suppose for the sake of our example that the MTA's IP address is the value 0x0A2538F1 (that is, equivalent to the dotted address 10.37.56.241).

Now we can go back and fill in the values of any unknown length fields. The length of the complete Decision object is now known to be 20 octets. The Message Length in the COPS header contains the length of the entire message which we now know to be 36 octets.

The complete GATE-ALLOC message looks like this.

Octet 1	Octet 2	Octet 3	Octet 4	Description
Version:1;	Op-code:3	Client-type: 0x8005		COPS header
Message Length: 36				
Length: 8		C-Num: 1	C-Type: 1	Handle
Handle: 2				
Length: 20		C-Num: 6	C-Type: 2	Decision header
Length: 8		S-Num: 1	S-Type: 1	Transaction-ID
Transaction Identifier: 1111		Gate Command Type: 1		
Length: 8		S-Num: 2	S-Type: 1	Subscriber-ID
IP address: 0x0A2538F1				

Our second example is of a GATE-INFO-ERR Response from a CMTS to the GC. We will go through this example rather more quickly. As before, we start with the COPS header.

Version

> 4 bits, with the value 0001

Flags

> The 4-bit "solicited message" flag. Since this is a solicited Response message (even though it contains an error indication), it has the value 0x0001.

Op-code

> The 1-octet field that determines the type of the message. This is a Report message, so it has the value 3.

Client-type

> The 2-octet field that contains the PacketCable client code, 0x8005.

Message length

> The 4-octet field giving the total length of the message. As usual, we don't know what the length is, so we leave this to be filled in later.

Next comes the Handle.

Length

> As before, we will assume that handles are 4 octets long, so the value of the length field is 8.

C-Num

> This 1-octet field always has the value 1 for a Handle.

C-Type

> This 1-octet field always has the value 1 for a Handle.

Contents

> As before, we will give it the handle the arbitrary value of 2.

The ClientSI header follows.

Length

> The 2-octet field giving the length of the COPS object. At the moment, we don't know how long it will be, so leave this to be filled in later.

C-Num

> This has the value 9 for an object containing client-specific information.

C-Type

> This has the value 2, since the message is going to contain client-specific (PacketCable) data.

There are three specialized COPS objects inside the message. The first is the Transaction-ID.

Length

> The Transaction-ID has a length of 8 octets.

S-Num

> This has the value 1 for a Transaction-ID.

S-Type

> This has the value 1 for a Transaction-ID.

Transaction Identifier

> This 2-octet field contains a numeric identifier for the transaction. We'll arbitrarily give it the value 2222 (0x8ae).

Gate Command Type

> This 2-octet field identifies this as a GATE-INFO-ERR; the correct entry for a GATE-INFO-ERR is the value 9 (see Table 6-7).

The next object is the Gate-ID.

Length

> The Gate-ID has a length of 8 octets.

S-Num

> This has the value 3 for a Gate-ID.

S-Type

> This has the value 1 for a Gate-ID.

Gate ID

> The 32-bit value of the Gate ID to which this message refers. We will give it the value 0x12345678.

The final object in the message is a PacketCable-Error.

Length

> A PacketCable-Error has a length of 8 octets.

S-Num

> This has the value 9 for a PacketCable-Error.

S-Type

> This has the value 1 for a PacketCable-Error.

Error-code

This 2-octet field contains the error code as in Table 6-8. Let us suppose that the error is that the Gate-ID is illegal—that is, the error code is 2.

Error-sub-code

This 2-octet field is currently unused. We'll just give it the value 0.

We can go back and fill in the missing lengths. The length in the ClientSI header will be 28, and the Message Length in the COPS header will be 44. The entire message looks like this.

Octet 1	Octet 2	Octet 3	Octet 4	Description
Version:1; Flags: 0	Op-code:3	Client-type: 0x8005		COPS header
Message Length: 44				
Length: 8		C-Num: 1	C-Type: 1	Handle
Handle: 2				
Length: 28		C-Num: 9	C-Type: 2	ClientSI header
Length: 8		S-Num: 1	S-Type: 1	Transaction-ID
Transaction Identifier: 2222		Gate Command Type: 9		
Length: 8		S-Num: 3	S-Type: 1	Gate-ID
Gate ID: 0x12345678				
Length: 8		S-Num: 9	S-Type: 1	PacketCable-Error
Error-code: 2		Error-sub-code: 0		

All the other COPS messages are generated by a similar process.

Initialization of the COPS Connection

The CMTS listens on port number 3288 for incoming TCP connections from a GC. When such a connection occurs, the CMTS sends a COPS CLIENT-OPEN message to the GC.[17] In response, the GC returns a COPS CLIENT-ACCEPT message. Note that, although the CMTS is the COPS client, it is the GC that initiates the sequence that causes the CMTS to register itself as a client with the GC.

---

17. For details of the format of ordinary COPS messages, as well as a detailed explanation of the protocol, see RFC 2748.

The connection is maintained by periodic COPS Keep-Alive messages, transmitted by the CMTS. The initial CLIENT-ACCEPT instructs the CMTS how frequently these messages are to be transmitted. (The frequency of the Keep-Alive messages is determined by the network operator; a value of a few tens of seconds to a few minutes is typical.)

To complete the initialization sequence, the CMTS transmits a COPS REQUEST message containing a Handle object to the GC. This Handle is used in the subsequent Decision and Response messages to identify the COPS connection over which the messages are flowing. COPS requires this so that a client can keep track of multiple connections that may be simultaneously open. In PacketCable, however, usually a CMTS is controlled by only a single GC and therefore it has only one COPS connection open at any given time.

Operation

As we have discussed, although gates exist on CMTSes, they are controlled by messages arriving from a GC. Attempts to control the gate by any other entity are ignored by the CMTS (and possibly logged, since they could indicate an attack on the system). All messages sent by the GC that controls a particular gate are formatted as COPS DECISION messages; responses are formatted as COPS REPORT-STATE messages. Messages contain the Handle that the CMTS assigned during the initialization sequence.

Allocating a Gate

A GATE-ALLOC message is transmitted by the GC when it receives notification from an MTA that a new call has been placed. This message is poorly named, since it does not instruct the CMTS to create a gate. Rather, it asks the CMTS, "How many gates are already allocated to this MTA"?

The purpose of the GATE-ALLOC is to allow the network to police the number of connections that a user has available at one time.[18] In response to the GATE-ALLOC, the CMTS informs the GC of the number of gates currently allocated to that MTA. The GC can then consult a database of provisioning information so that it can determine whether it is reasonable for the MTA to desire to open another gate.

Setting (Creating) a Gate

If the GC determines that it is permissible for the subscriber to create a gate, it sends a GATE-SET message to the CMTS. (GATE-SET messages may also be used

---

18. As we have noted, it actually polices the number of gates currently open on an MTA basis, not on a subscriber basis.

to modify the parameters of a gate that already exists. In such a case, the GATE-SET contains the Gate-ID of the gate being modified.)

The GATE-SET message contains either one or two Gate-Spec objects: These describe either a single unidirectional gate (either upstream or downstream) or an upstream/downstream gate pair that will be allocated a single Gate-ID by the CMTS.

When it receives a GATE-SET message, the CMTS does not attempt to reserve the resources on the corresponding HFC network. The GATE-SET message merely indicates the policy to be applied to incoming requests from the MTA. If the reservation is successful, it returns a GATE-SET-ACK to the GC. This GATE-SET-ACK contains a Gate-ID assigned by the CMTS and that will be used to refer to this gate (or gate pair) in future transactions.

Multiple GATE-SET messages may be transmitted as more information about a call becomes available to a GC. For example, when the originating Gate Controller, GC_O initially sends a GATE-SET to $CMTS_O$, it has no information available about the destination CMTS. Later, the call signaling will deliver this information to CMS_O, which can then, through its Gate Controller interface, send a new GATE-SET containing the additional information to $CMTS_O$.

The message flow showing a typical sequence is shown in Figure 6-17. The created gate is associated with *authorized* resources, but not with *committed* resources. In other words, the gate is created in the closed state. The gate is *not* opened by a putative GATE-OPEN COPS message from the GC. As we shall shortly see, there is a GATE-OPEN message, but it is not a COPS message, and the way in which gates are opened is quite different from the way a naïve user might expect.

Querying a Gate

A GC may query a CMTS to determine the parameters assigned to a particular gate (this saves the GC from having to store this information itself). It does this by sending a GATE-INFO message containing the Gate-ID of the gate being queried. The CMTS responds with a GATE-INFO-ACK message containing the parameters of the pertinent gate.

Closing and Deleting a Gate

There are no specific messages to close or delete a gate. This is because they are not needed. On ordinary calls, when the originator hangs up the phone, the associated DOCSIS Service Flow is deleted (via a DOCSIS DSD-REQ message). Deletion of the DOCSIS flow at the CMTS in turn causes the associated gate pair to be deleted. Gate Coordination messages then cause the corresponding gate pair in the remote CMTS to be deleted.

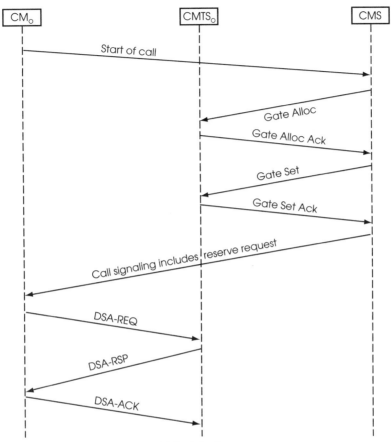

Figure 6-17 Allocating and Setting a DQoS Gate

Gate Coordination

In order to thwart several theft of service scenarios, the gates at both ends of a connection must ensure that they open and close in a coordinated manner. To enable this, the CMTSes exchange GATE-OPEN and GATE-CLOSE messages, along with their respective acknowledgement messages. Note that gate coordination messages are exchanged even in the case when both parties to the call are using the same CMTS.

Gate coordination messages may be transmitted directly between CMTSes (as in DCS), or they may be proxied by the corresponding CMSes (as in NCS). In fact, in NCS the CMS does not merely proxy the gate coordination messages. It may actually "fake" such messages so as to cause the correct things to happen at the gates at the two ends of the calls.[19] GATE-OPEN messages are sent when resources are committed; GATE-CLOSE messages are sent when the resources are released.

Gate-to-Gate protocol messages are sent as UDP packets. They use the RADIUS format that is also used for event messages sent to the Record Keeping Server and for wiretap messages sent to the Delivery Function. (RADIUS is specified by RFC 2138 and is discussed in more detail in Chapter 7. It is important to note, however, that the Gate Coordination messages do not use the RADIUS protocol per se, they merely use the same format as RADIUS messages.) The destination address and port for Gate-to-Gate messages is provided in a GATE-SET command as soon as the information is available to the CMTS's Gate Controller. As usual, we'll first look at how Gate Coordination messages are formatted, and then we'll proceed to trying to understand how they are actually used.

Format of Gate Coordination Messages

Gate Coordination messages share a common header that is identical to the RADIUS format, as follows.

Message Type

> A 1-octet field used to identify the type of the message. Allowable type codes are given in Table 6-9.

Message Length

> A 2-octet field that indicates the total length of the message, in octets.

Table 6-9 Message Type Codes for the Gate Coordination Protocol

Message Type Value	*Meaning*
48	GATE-OPEN
49	GATE-OPEN-ACK
50	GATE-OPEN-ERR
51	GATE-CLOSE
52	GATE-CLOSE-ACK
53	GATE-CLOSE-ERR

---

19. In DCS all gate coordination messages are exchanged directly between the CMTSes involved. The author carefully refrains from commenting on the relative elegance of the coordination mechanisms in the two call signaling protocols.

Message Authenticator

For GATE-OPEN and GATE-CLOSE messages: a 16-octet field containing an MD5 hash[20] calculated over the following fields, in order.

Message-Type; Transaction-ID; Message-Length; 16 octets filled with zeros; the message parameters; a shared secret.

For GATE-OPEN-ACK, GATE-OPEN-ERR and GATE-CLOSE-ACK messages: a 16-octet field containing an MD5 hash calculated over the following fields, in order.

Message-Type; Transaction-ID; Message-Length; Message Authenticator from the corresponding request; the response parameters (if any); a shared secret.

Following the header are the message parameters, encoded in RADIUS TLV format. The RADIUS TLV format is a slightly modified version of ordinary TLV: It requires that the Value field commence at a 4-octet boundary, so a zero-filled Reserved field occurs immediately before the Value, as described below.

Type

A 1-octet field containing a value from Table 6-10

Length

A 1-octet field containing the length in octets of the parameter. The length must be a multiple of 4.

Reserved

A 2-octet field, zero-filled (unless the Type corresponds to Error-Code, in which case, see below)

Table 6-10 RADIUS TLV Encoding Types for Gate Coordination Messages

RADIUS Type Value	*Meaning*
224	Gate-ID
225	T-spec
226	Reverse-T-spec
227	Error-code

---

20. The MD5 algorithm is contained in RFC 1321. It is too complicated to include here.

Value

As specified in the Type field, the encoded value is one of the following: Gate-ID, T-spec, Reverse-T-spec, or Error-code. These are encoded as follows.

Gate-ID

A 4-octet field containing the 32-bit Gate-ID

T-spec

The T-spec is encoded in complex RADIUS structure laid out as in Figure 6-18.

The structure is a 32-octet object containing the following items, in order.

a. A 4-bit field containing the version number, which is currently zero

b. A 12-bit field that is reserved and ignored (but that should be zero)

c. A 2-octet field containing the size of the object, measured in 4-octet words. This value does not include the size of the header. T-specs are seven 4-octet words in length.

d. A 1-octet RADIUS "service 1" header, defined to be 1. The RADIUS "service 1" header includes this field and the three octets immediately following.

e. A 1-bit field defined to be zero

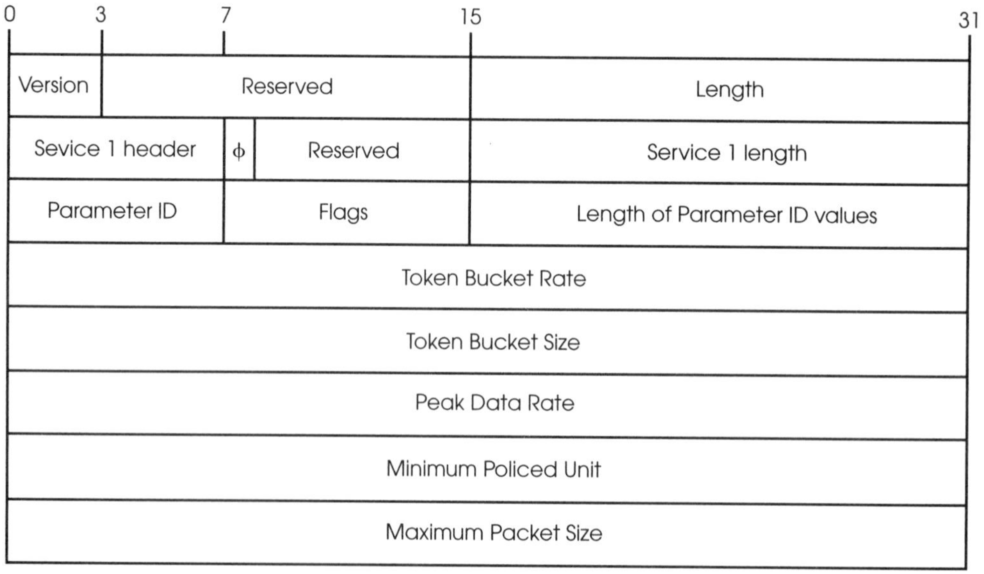

Figure 6-18 Structure of T-Spec Value

f. A 7-bit field that is reserved and ignored (but that should be zero)

g. A 2-octet field containing the length of the RADIUS "service 1" data, in 4-octet words. For a T-spec, this has the value 6.

The rest of the fields hold the RADIUS "service 1" data.

h. A 1-octet field containing the RADIUS Parameter ID, which has the value 127

i. A 1-octet field containing the flags for this Parameter ID, which are all zero

j. A 2-octet field containing the length of the values of this Parameter ID in four-octet words. For a T-spec this is the value 5.

k. A 4-octet field containing the Token Bucket Rate (r) formatted as a 32-bit IEEE floating point number

l. A 4-octet field containing the Token Bucket Size (b) formatted as a 32-bit IEEE floating point number

m. A 4-octet field containing the Peak Data Rate (p) formatted as a 32-bit IEEE floating point number

n. A 4-octet field containing the Minimum Policed Unit (m)

o. A 4-octet field containing the Maximum Packet Size (M)

An example later in the chapter shows what an encoded T-spec might actually look like.[21]

Reverse-T-spec

This Value is encoded identically to the T-spec Value and describes the T-spec for the flow in the reverse (received) direction.

Error-code

The error-code returned in GATE-ALLOC-ERR, GATE-SET-ERR and GATE-INFO-ERR messages is a 1-octet field that immediately follows the 1-octet Length field. It is followed by a 1-octet Reserved field. (That is, in place of the usual 2-octet Reserved field, there is a 1-octet Error-code, followed by a 1-octet Reserved field, as shown in Figure 6-19.)

The possible error codes are given in Table 6-11.

---

21. The flow parameters included in Gate Coordination messages are, confusingly, not exactly the same as those included in DQoS gate control messages. In particular, the rate (R) and slack term (S) are present in the latter but absent in the former.

Figure 6-19 Encoding an Error-Code Value

Gate Coordination Message Contents

In this section we will describe what the various Gate-to-Gate Protocol messages contain. In the next section we will discuss how they are actually used.

The contents of each message is defined below, where optional fields are enclosed in square brackets ([like this]) and choices are separated by a vertical bar (like this: <choice a> | <choice b> | <choice c>).

Table 6-11 Error-Code Values

Error-Code	Meaning
0	A release of resources was initiated by the MTA (informational)
1	Close initiated by CMTS due to lack of signals maintaining a granted reservation
2	Close initiated by CMTS due to lack of DOCSIS MAC-layer signaling
3	No COMMIT was received from the MTA before a timer expired (timer typically in the range of a few tens of seconds; the specification recommends 200 to 300 seconds, but this seems to be rather long for a practical network)
4	Gate coordination failure; a timer expired (timer typically in the range of a few seconds)
5	Close initiated by CMTS due to enforced teardown because a higher-priority call requires the reserved resources
6	Close initiated by CMTS due to mismatched reservations
129	Illegal Gate-ID
130	Calculated value of Message Authenticator does not match value contained in message
255	Unspecified error

GATE-OPEN

```
RADIUS Common Header
Gate-ID
[T-spec]
[Reverse-T-spec]
```

The Gate-ID is the value of the Gate *at the far end* of this call. This enables the recipient of this message to know which gate to open at its own end. (It also allows the recipient to retrieve the correct key to authenticate the message.)

If the GATE-OPEN is generated by a CMTS, both the T-spec and Reverse-T-spec objects must be present. The T-spec object contains the values of the resources committed in the upstream direction (from the MTA). The Reverse-T-spec contains the values of resources committed in the downstream direction (toward the MTA).

GATE-OPEN-ACK

The GATE-OPEN-ACK contains only a RADIUS Common Header. The value of the Transaction-ID in the header serves to allow the recipient to match the GATE-OPEN which is being acknowledged by this message.

GATE-OPEN-ERR

```
RADIUS Common Header
Error-Code
```

The value of the Transaction-ID in the header serves to allow the recipient to match the GATE-OPEN which is being acknowledged by this message. The Error-code is one of the values taken from Table 6-11.

If the Error-code is either 129 (Illegal Gate-ID) or 130 (Invalid Message Authenticator), then the value of the Message Authenticator contained in the GATE-OPEN-ERR is a copy of the Message Authenticator in the offending GATE-OPEN message (that is, a new Message Authenticator is *not* calculated for the GATE-OPEN-ERR).

GATE-CLOSE

```
Radius Common Header
Gate-ID
[Error-code]
```

An Error-code is included if the GATE-CLOSE is generated for any reason other than a normal request to release resources by an MTA at the end of a call.

GATE-CLOSE-ACK

The GATE-CLOSE-ACK contains only a RADIUS Common Header. The value of the Transaction-ID in the header serves to allow the recipient to match the GATE-CLOSE which is being acknowledged by this message.

GATE-CLOSE-ERR

```
RADIUS Common Header
Error-Code
```

The value of the Transaction-ID in the header serves to allow the recipient to match the GATE-OPEN that is being acknowledged by this message. The Error-code is one of the values taken from Table 6-11.

The Message Authenticator contained in the GATE-CLOSE-ERR is a copy of the Message Authenticator in the offending GATE-CLOSE message (that is, a new Message Authenticator is *not* calculated for the GATE-CLOSE-ERR).

Example Gate Coordination Message

We can quite easily see what an example Gate Coordination message might look like. In this chapter we have not described the details of the RADIUS format that will be used in the following example. These details may be found in Chapter 7 of this book, or in the RADIUS specification, RFC 2138.

For our example, we will assume that we are sending a GATE-OPEN message.

Octet 1	Octet 2	Octet 3 Octet 4	Description
Message Type: 48	Transaction ID:1234	Message Length:	RADIUS header
Message Authenticator: xxxx			
Type: 224	Length: 8	0	Gate ID of the
Gate:ID 0x12345678			far-end gate
Type: 225	Length: 36	0	T-spec
0 0		7	
1	0 0	6	
127	0	5	
Token Bucket Rate (IEEE floating point): 120.0			
Token Bucket Size (IEEE floating point): 12000.0			

Octet 1	Octet 2	Octet 3	Octet 4	Description
Peak Data Rate (IEEE floating point): 12000.0				
Minimum Policed Unit: 120				
Maximum Packet Size: 120				
Type: 225	Length: 36	0		Reverse T-spec
0	0	7		
1	0	0	6	
127	0	5		
Token Bucket Rate (IEEE floating point): 120.0				
Token Bucket Size (IEEE floating point): 12000.0				
Peak Data Rate (IEEE floating point): 12000.0				
Minimum Policed Unit: 120				
Maximum Packet Size: 120				

Use of Gate Coordination Messages

The Dynamic Quality of Service mechanisms are one of the most complicated aspects of PacketCable Networks. To try to help understand them, we will walk through the way Gate Coordination actually occurs. Afterwards, we shall look at some detailed examples of realistic scenarios that might occur in a PacketCable Network. As part of these examples, we shall examine in detail the contents of the various DQoS messages since, as we have seen, the format is rather complex.

As we saw earlier, PacketCable networks employ a two-phase commit mechanism in which resources are first reserved, and then, and only if both ends successfully reserve the necessary resources, the far-end phone begins to ring. In this way, resources are immediately available to be committed when the answering party picks up the phone.

Reserving resources requires that a gate (or more, likely, a gate pair) be created. Committing resources is logically equivalent to opening the corresponding gate(s). We have already seen how to create a (closed) gate: The GC sends a GATE-SET command to the CMTS. Now we come to the question of how to open a gate.

When the phone at the destination MTA goes off-hook, the system must commit resources (at both ends of the conversation) as quickly as possible. There are several mechanisms by which this can be easily accomplished. Just a note: The DQoS specification also lists other possibilities that rely on a special COMMIT message to be sent from the MTA to the CMTS. These alternative mechanisms, however, require that the network implement the Resource Reservation Protocol, RSVP, which, although included in the PacketCable 1.0 specifications (see Chapter 3 of the DQoS specification) is not generally included in vendor implementations of the 1.0 specification set and is not included by the testing procedures used by CableLabs to determine compliance with the published specification. We therefore assume that no RSVP features are available for use. The mechanisms that do use the RSVP COMMIT message allow for a more symmetrical, and considerably more elegant, procedure for opening the gates. The reader is referred to the DQoS specification for more details.

One mechanism, shown in Figure 6-20, is typically used by DCS.

1. MTA_T (the destination MTA, which has just gone off-hook) sends a Dynamic Service Change Request to $CMTS_T$. This DSC causes the Service Flow to go from the DOCSIS Admitted State to the DOCSIS Active State, which allows the flow to be used. This also logically causes the associated gate to go from the closed to the open state.

2. There is a general rule that when a gate opens on a CMTS, *unless it does so in response to the receipt of a GATE-OPEN message,* it sends a GATE-OPEN message containing both upstream and downstream flowspecs to its twin at the far end of the call.[22] Following this rule, CMTST sends a GATE-OPEN message to $CMTS_O$.

3. When $CMTS_O$ receives the GATE-OPEN, it opens the corresponding gates under its control (using a DOCSIS DSC command to set the flow to the Active state). This commits the resources, making them available for use at the origination end of the call.

4. There is a second rule that when a CMTS opens a gate in response to a GATE-OPEN, it returns a GATE-OPEN-ACK to the originator of the original GATE-OPEN. In obedience to this rule, $CMTS_O$ therefore sends $CMTS_T$ a GATE-OPEN-ACK, informing it that its resources are also available.

A quite different mechanism, shown in Figure 6-21, is typically used by NCS. For simplicity, only one CMS is shown in the figure.

5. MTA_T (the destination MTA, which has just gone off-hook) signals the fact to CMS_T. CMS_T now sends to $CMTS_T$ a GATE-OPEN and a MDCX to MTA_T. It also forwards the fact that the phone is off-hook to CMS_O, which likewise sends a GATE-OPEN to $CMTS_O$ and an MDCX to MTA_O.

---

22. This rule may be modified by setting the No-Gate-Open flag with a GATE-SET message.

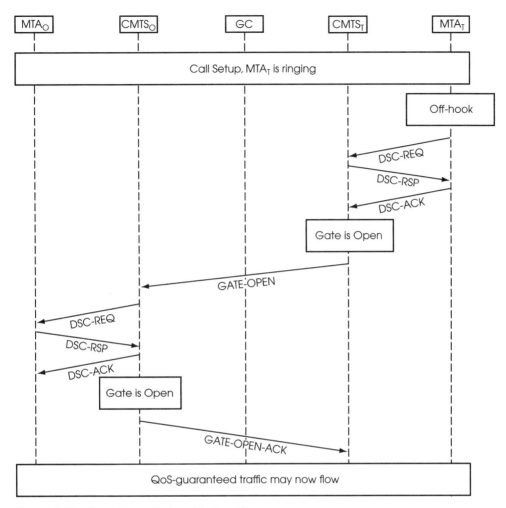

Figure 6-20 Opening a Gate—Method 1

6. At both ends, the same thing happens: The CMTS opens its gate in response to the GATE-OPEN. However, unless it receives a confirming DSC Request from the local MTA (in response to the MDCX) in a short period of time, it will close the gate once more.

Note that the GATE-OPEN has come from the CMS, not from the remote CMTS.

7. Since each CMTS has opened a gate in response to a GATE-OPEN message, following the rules given above it does not send a GATE-OPEN of its own but rather sends a GATE-OPEN-ACK to the local CMS.

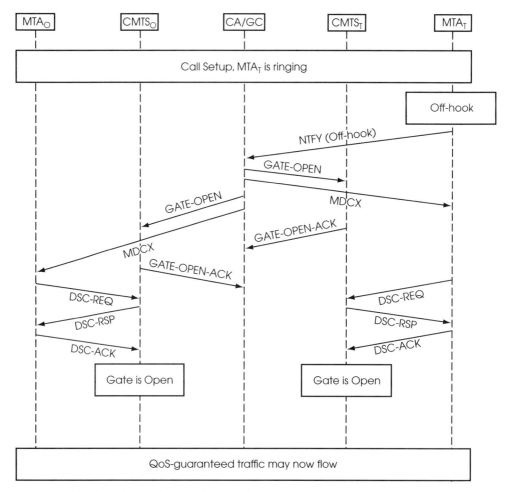

Figure 6-21 Opening a Gate—Method 2

An MTA signals the end of a call by sending a DOCSIS DSD-REQ message to delete the service flow associated with the call. The DSD will cause the gates associated with the call to be closed (and automatically deleted).

As before, exactly what happens depends on whether the CMTSes communicate with one another directly (as in DCS) or only via their CMSes (as in NCS). We'll look at DCS first.

1. When it receives the DSD message, the CMTS, as well as deleting the service flow, also sends a GATE-CLOSE message to its twin. (Note that there are also other ways that the CMTS might detect that the call is no longer in progress: For example, it might detect that there are no longer any packets

being produced by the MTA, or the low-level DOCSIS maintenance commands might cease to operate correctly.)

2. When a CMTS receives a GATE-CLOSE from its opposite number, it must close the local gate associated with the call. It also sends a GATE-CLOSE-ACK, confirming that it has received and acted on the GATE-CLOSE. This flow is shown in Figure 6-22.

In NCS, the MTA sends an NTFY(On-hook) to its CMS, which causes a DLCX to be sent to both MTAs. Both ends then do the same thing.

3. The MTA sends a DSD, which causes the gates to be closed and deleted. After closing the gate, the CMTS sends a GATE-CLOSE to its CMS, which responds as if it were a CMTS by sending a GATE-CLOSE-ACK (see Figure 6-23).

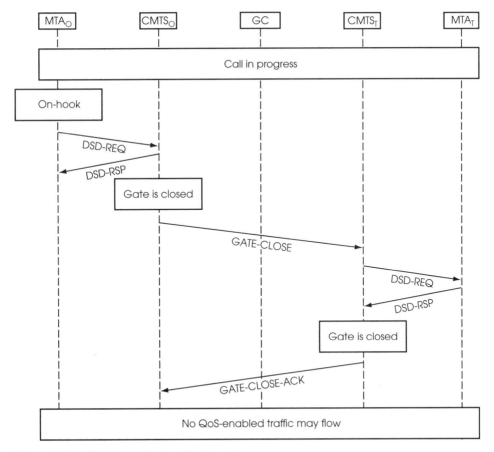

Figure 6-22 Closing a Gate—Method 1

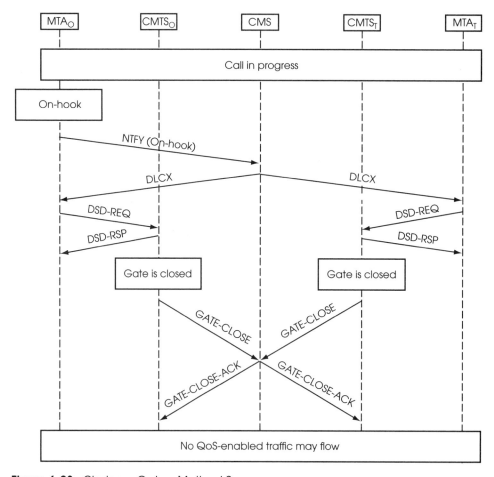

Figure 6-23 Closing a Gate—Method 2

Example Call Flow

DQoS messaging is one of the most complicated aspects of PacketCable. Consequently, it is worthwhile to spend some time studying Figure 6-24 and the corresponding Table 6-12, which show a simple(!) on-net call flow for an NCS network, emphasizing the DQoS signaling messages, which are explained in more detail below. Extraneous messages, such as the Event Messages used for billing purposes, are not included in this call flow.

Message #4—GATE-ALLOC

Contains a Transaction-ID (for example, 1234) and a Subscriber-ID identifying MTA_O (for example, 192.10.20.1).

Message #5—GATE-ALLOC-ACK

Contains the Transaction-ID (1234) and Subscriber-ID (192.10.20.1). Also contains a Gate-ID (for example, 55555) and an Activity Count indicating the number of gates currently in use by this MTA (for example, 0).

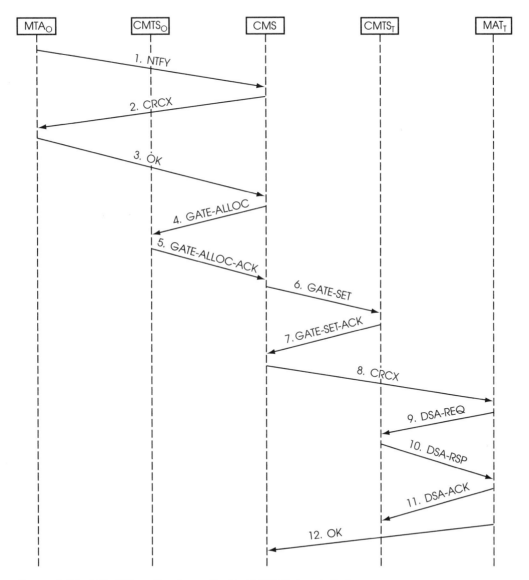

Figure 6-24 DQoS Signaling in an On-Net NCS Network Call

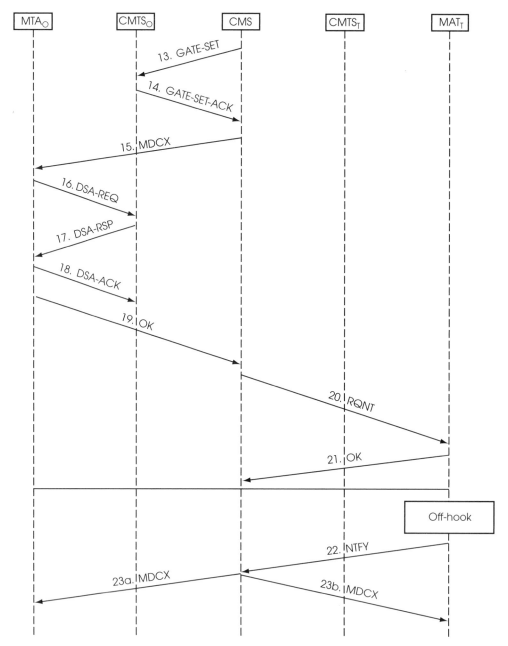

Figure 6-24 DQoS Signaling in an On-Net NCS Network Call (cont.)

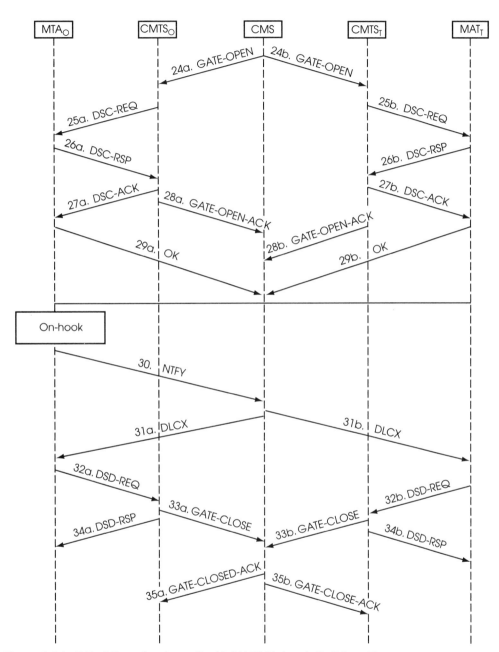

Figure 6-24 DQoS Signaling in an On-Net NCS Network Call (cont.)

Table 6-12   Table Relating Message Number to Explanation

Message #	Explanation
1	NCS NTFY contains dialed digits
2	NCS CRCX creates an inactive connection
3	NCS 200 OK
4	**DQoS GATE-ALLOC**
5	**DQoS GATE-ALLOC-ACK**
6	**DQoS GATE-SET**
7	**DQoS GATE-SET-ACK**
8	NCS CRCX creates an inactive connection; reserves resources
9	DOCSIS DSA-REQ Dynamic Service Flow Add
10	DOCSIS DSA-RSP
11	DOCSIS DSA-ACK
12	NCS 200 OK Response to CRCX
13	**DQoS GATE-SET**
14	**DQoS GATE-SET-ACK**
15	NCS MDCX modifies the existing connection; set the connection to sendrecv and reserve the resources
16	DOCSIS DSA-REQ Dynamic Service Flow Add
17	DOCSIS DSA-RSP
18	DOCSIS DSA-ACK
19	NCS 200 OK Response to MDCX
20	NCS RQNT tells MTA to ring the phone, and to notify the CMS when the phone goes off-hook.
21	NCS 200 OK Response to RQNT
The phone is now ringing. (Ringback is supplied by an RQNT—not shown—to MTA_O.)	
22	NCS NTFY notifies that the phone has gone off-hook
23a, 23b	NCS MDCX modifies the connection to sendrecv, commits the rsources
24a, 24b	**Gate-Coordination GATE-OPEN**
25a, 25b	DOCSIS DSC-REQ Dynamic Service Change *(continued)*

Table 6-12 Table Relating Message Number to Explanation (cont.)

Message #	Explanation
26a, 26b	DOCSIS DSC-RSP
27a, 27b	DOCSIS DSC-ACK
28a, 28b	**GATE-OPEN-ACK**
29a, 29b	NCS 200 OK Response to MDCX
The call is now in progress.	
30	NCS NTFY tells CMS that the originator has gone on-hook
31a, 31b	NCS DLCX Delete the connection
32a, 32b	DOCSIS DSD-REQ Dynamic Service Delete
33a, 33b	**Gate-Coordination GATE-CLOSE**
34a, 34b	DOCSIS DSD-RSP
35a, 35b	**GATE-CLOSE-ACK**
The call is now torn down.	

Message #13—GATE-SET

Contains the following information.

Field	Subfield	Example Value	Explanation
Transaction-ID		1235	A new transaction
Subscriber-ID		192.10.20.1 (in binary)	IP address of MTA_O
Gate-ID		55555	Identifies the gate to be set by this command
Remote-Gate-Info	Remote CMTS Address	IP address of CMS_O; for example, 192.100.200.1	*This is not a misprint.* CMS_O identifies itself as the remote CMTS. The CMTS is to be fooled into thinking that CMS_O is actually $CMTS_T$.
	Remote CMTS Port	2222	Port for Gate-Coordination messages
	Remote Gate-ID	4000	Identifies a proxy gate that is unique on the CMS

Field	Subfield	Example Value	Explanation
	Security Key	Key for Gate-Coordination messages	Used as the "shared secret" to authenticate the RADIUS Gate-Coordination messages
	Flag	No-gate-open	Do not open the gate.
Event-Generation-Info	RKS-Addr	IP address of RKS	For the sake of brevity, we do not include event messages that would normally be sent to the RKS later in the call flow.
	RKS-Port	Port on RKS	
	Billing Correlation ID	16-octet BCID	Used for billing purposes
Gate-Spec	Direction	up	Specifies that these values are for the upstream flow
	Protocol	UDP	The protocol and the source and destination addresses may be used on the CMTS to classify packets so as to assign them to the correct Service Flow.
	Source address	MTA_O; 192.10.20.1	
	Destination address	MTA_T; 192.10.20.2	
	Source port	100	
	Destination port	5000	
	r Token Bucket Rate	12000	
	b Token Bucket Size	120	
	p Peak Data Rate	12000	
	m Minimum Policed Unit	120	
	M Maximum Packet Size	120	
	R Rate	12000	
	S Slack Term	0	*(continued)*

Field	Subfield	Example Value	Explanation
Gate-Spec	Direction	down	Specifies that these values are for the downstream flow
	Flag	Auto-commit	The network operator *might* choose to have the downstream resources automatically committed, so that incoming "early" RTP packets can be passed to the MTA.
	Protocol	UDP	The protocol and the source and destination addresses may be used on the CMTS to classify packets so as to assign them to the correct Service Flow
	Source address	MTA_T; 192.10.20.2	
	Destination address	MTA_O; 192.10.20.1	
	Source port	100	
	Destination port	5500	
	r Token Bucket Rate	12000	
	b Token Bucket Size	120	
	p Peak Data Rate	12000	
	m Minimum Policed Unit	120	
	M Maximum Packet Size	120	
	R Rate	12000	
	S Slack Term	0	

Message #14—GATE-SET-ACK

Contains the Transaction-ID (1235) and Subscriber-ID (192.10.20.1). Also contains the Gate-ID (55555) and the Activity Count for this MTA (now 1).

Message #24a, 24b—GATE-OPEN

The gates are opened more or less simultaneously on the two ends of the call. (Remember that opening a gate is the same as committing resources.) Each GATE-OPEN contains a Transaction-ID and a Gate-ID. Since these are Gate Coordination messages, they do not travel over IPsec (even though they are traveling between a CMS and a CMTS). Instead, they include a RADIUS authenticator.

Message #28a, 28b—GATE-OPEN-ACK

The GATE-OPEN-ACK messages contain only a Transaction-ID equal to the value in the GATE-OPEN.

Message #33a, 33b—GATE-CLOSE

The GATE-CLOSE messages are sent to the opposite CMTS to inform it that the gate has been closed. The GATE-CLOSE messages contain a Transaction-ID and a Gate-ID. Like all Gate Coordination messages, they do not travel over IPsec but instead contain a RADIUS authenticator.

Message #35a, 35b—GATE-CLOSE-ACK

The GATE-CLOSE-ACK messages contain only a Transaction-ID equal to the value in the GATE-CLOSE.

The complexity of this chapter unfortunately reflects the complexity of the Dynamic Quality of Service specification. As is so often the case, what begins as an elegant design to solve a particular problem in a particular environment becomes incresingly complex as it is adapted to a wider range of operating conditions and modified to account for the possible errors that may occur. Even so, the basic principles of DQoS are still fairly easy to understand.

- A Gate Controller provides policy to a CMTS, so that the CMTS knows how to handle incoming requests for bandwidth.

- The two CMTSes at the ends of a call try to remain coordinated by communicating state changes to the far end.

- Any lack of coordination results in the gates associated with a call being closed and deleted, which in turn causes the call to be torn down.

All the rest, as they say, is details.

Now that we have covered the core mechanisms by which PacketCable networks function, we will turn to some of the necessary features that, although they are often overlooked, are of equal importance to network operators.

Provisioning, Back Office and Electronic Surveillance

*Note in the flow details below that certain steps may appear to be a
loop in the event of a failure. In other words, the step to proceed to if a given
step fails is to retry that step again.*

PKT-SP-PROV-I01-991201

Provisioning refers to the process of adding a device to the network in such a way that it becomes a usable device on the network. We use the term *back office* to refer to the operations associated with billing and keeping the correct records about calls.

Provisioning on the PSTN is deceptively simple. If I am a new customer, the local phone company typically takes some details (name, address, credit rating and so forth) and sets up a new account. Part of the account information is my new telephone number. Some time later, a technician appears in my yard and performs some magic, after which he tells me that I have service.

If I now go down to my local discount store, I can choose any one of a hundred telephones that line the shelves, buy it and bring it home. As soon as I plug it into a phone jack, I can place a call anywhere in the world. If this doesn't seem like magic, read on. What is simple in the circuit-switched world turns out to be a couple of orders of magnitude more difficult on a packetized network (perhaps this comes as no surprise to anyone who has ever tried to manage a computer network—which is, after all, exactly what a PacketCable network is).

The goal of the provisioning mechanisms on the PacketCable network is to allow the end-user an experience similar to the one he or she has come to expect with traditional circuit-switched telephony networks. Whether any given network operator will choose to allow users to purchase MTAs at a retail store, take them home, and expect them to work is a decision for the individual operator. Some may prefer, at least initially, to adopt the model that served the phone company for so long. Ownership of the MTA is retained by the network operator; the end-user merely rents it on a monthly basis. Whether such a model can long survive is an issue that is really beyond the scope of this book but that reappears in our final chapter anyway.

We can divide the provisioning process into two distinct phases: customer provisioning and device provisioning. Customer provisioning is the process of setting up an account and generally involves direct person-to-person interaction between a prospective customer and a customer support person. Device provisioning is the process of adding a device to the network in such a way that it functions as expected. This chapter is mostly concerned with device provisioning.

At its most simple, the following is an adequate description of the device provisioning process: The MTA obtains its IP address and other IP configuration information needed for basic network connectivity; it then announces itself to the network and downloads necessary provisioning information from a provisioning server. From that point on, the MTA is ready to originate and receive phone calls.

Much of what follows in this chapter is a detailed examination of these steps. In this chapter, however, we have modified our modus operandi somewhat. In prior chapters, we have been concerned with details at the heart of cable-based telephony, and we have covered issues such as call signaling and security in considerable depth. Partly this was to further this book's aim of providing a "one-stop" description of PacketCable, and partly it was because detailed explanations were generally unavailable elsewhere than in the PacketCable specifications themselves, and often not even there.

In the next couple of chapters, we will be examining parts of the network that, while vital to its correct functioning, are not at the core of the network's purpose. In addition, protocols that we will be discussing such as DHCP and SNMP are complicated, general-purpose protocols about which many books are available (and that, in any case, need entire books of their own to describe them properly).

So for these reasons, although we will look in some depth at how these protocols are used and give a high-level overview of how they work, we will blur over the details of the protocols in a way that we have tried to refrain from doing until now. Having said that, let's have a quick look at SNMP before we move to what happens to an MTA when it is first powered on.[1]

---

1. The MTA is the only device for which provisioning is defined in PacketCable 1.0. Other network devices must also be provisioned, but the way in which this is done varies from vendor to vendor.

Simple Network Management Protocol (SNMP)

Version 3 of the **Simple Network Management Protocol** (**SNMPv3**) is fully described in RFCs 2571 through 2575. SNMP is a protocol suite designed to provide the ability for a centralized manager to interrogate, configure and perform other management actions on devices connected to the network. The "manager" is a computer, not a person, although when something goes wrong, the manager will usually feed the information to a human who can ensure that corrective action is taken.

As you may imagine, a protocol suite that requires multiple RFCs to describe it cannot be examined in depth in a book such as this, especially where, as in this case, the protocols are relatively peripheral to our purpose. However, since all PacketCable equipment is managed using SNMP—and in particular the registration and provisioning of MTAs uses SNMP—it is worthwhile to make a brief digression to discuss the essential features of SNMP.

The Need for Network Management

First of all, we need to be clear exactly what is encompassed by the term *Network Management*. Network Management refers to the control and management of devices attached to the network, not to the control and management of the network itself. The latter is the domain of routing and control protocols such as RSVP and ICMP, and it will not be discussed here. Typically, Network Management can be divided into several lower-level kinds of management.

Fault Management   Network operators need to be able to determine quickly that a device on the network is failing to operate properly. Once a faulty device has been located, it must either be made to operate correctly (if possible, by remote command) or, as a last resort (especially if the failed device is affecting the rest of the network detrimentally), the operator should be able to cause the device either to reboot or even to take itself offline so that manual remedial action may be taken. If this is not possible, then perhaps the network itself can be reconfigured so as to minimize the effects of the failed device.

Resource Management   Devices may be misconfigured (either accidentally or as a result of a successful attack) so that they abuse their privileges, burdening the network at others' expense. The network manager should be able to prevent this from occurring.

Identity Management   A network generally must have at least one, and perhaps several, ways of identifying each individual device attached to the network. For example, the IP address and the **Fully Qualified Domain Name** (**FQDN**) are two common mechanisms used to identify devices. The network manager should be able to ensure that all devices attached to the network can be uniquely identified and communicated with.

Configuration Management   Typically, the network manager is in a much better position to know how a device should be configured so as to operate correctly with the rest of the network than is the device itself. Therefore some means has to exist for the manager to be able to provide the correct configuration to managed entities.

Performance Management   The network manager should typically gather statistics continuously so that it is aware at all times of how the network is performing. If a problem arises, the manager should be able to take action to try to correct it or at least prevent its spread (possibly using network control protocols such as RSVP and ICMP).

Security Management   Although security per se is likely to be independent of the general issues of network management, any errors or warnings in the security modules should be brought to the attention of the network manager, since they may indicate an attack on the network.

SNMP Architecture

A simpified version of the SNMP architecture is shown in Figure 7-1. At least one device on the network is designated the *manager*. The manager collects information from the managed devices, either by polling or by being informed unilaterally of interesting events as they occur. The manager issues commands as necessary to *agents,* which are typically (but not always) processes running on the managed devices themselves.

Managers and agents are allowed access to one or more databases of device information maintained on the device in order to help them manage the device. Such a database is known as a **Management Information Base**, or **MIB**. The device may control the level of access any particular agent or manager has to items in its MIB through a View-based Access Control Model, or VACM. In other words, different managers (or the same manager acting in different capacities) may be presented with two different views of the MIB, containing different variables, and perhaps different permissions associated with the variables. This is shown diagrammatically in Figure 7-2. The PacketCable specifications describe exactly the contents of the MTA device MIB. Different managers see different portions of the MIB, through the VACM mechanism.

Currently, three different portions of the complete MTA device MIB are specified; these are the portions relating to provisioning, security and NCS call signaling. It is expected that the MIB will be expanded in future versions of PacketCable to support DCS call signaling, QoS, primary line requirements, voice interfaces

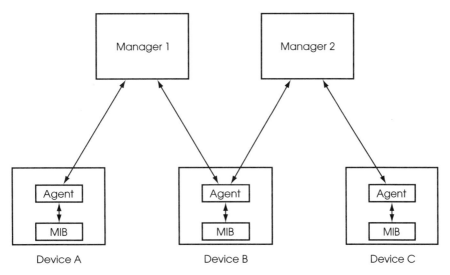

Figure 7-1 The SNMP Architecture

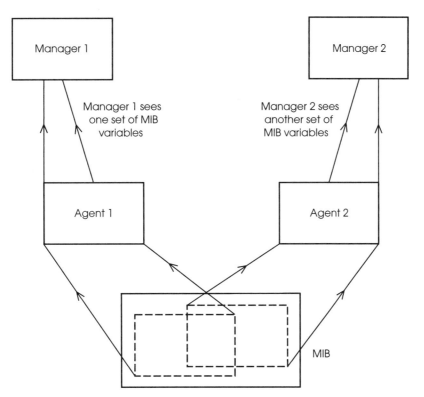

Figure 7-2 The View-Based Access Control Model

(descriptions of the various voice ports supported by the MTA), packet voice transport, fault management, performance management and probably other features that no one has yet thought of.

Table 7-1 lists all the attributes in the MTA Device MIB. For full details about each attribute, and the access allowed to the attributes, see the various PacketCable

Table 7-1   MTA Device MIB Variables

Name of MIB Variable	Meaning or Effect
pktcMtaDevResetNow	Causes MTA to reset
pktcMtaDevSerialNumber	Serial number
pktcMtaDevHardwareVersion	Manufacturer's hardware version
pktcMtaDevMacAddress	Telephony MAC address of MTA
pktcMtaDevFQDN	MTA's FQDN
pktcMtaDevEndPntCount	Number of endpoints supported by MTA
pktcMtaDevEnabled	1 if telephony is enabled
pktcMtaDevTypeIdentifier	Device Type Identifier used in option 60 exchange with DHCP server
pktcMtaDevProvisioningState	Pass, Fail or InProgress
pktcMtaDevHttpAccess	Whether HTTP supported for config file
pktcMtaDevManufacturerCertificate	Manufacturer's X.509 certificate
pktcMtaDevCertificate	X.509 certificate of this MTA
pktcMtaDevSignature	Signature created on-the-fly for SNMP messages prior to establishment of SNMPv3 security
pktcMtaDevCorrelationId	Random value used in registration (*not* a nonce; the nonce is in pktcMtaDevSignature)
pktcMtaDevSecurityTable	Per-endpoint local security information; for details see the MIB specification
pktcMtaDevServProviderCertificate	X.509 certificate of the service provider
pktcMtaDevTelephonyCertificate	X.509 certificate allowing access to telephony
pktcMtaDevKerberosRealm	Name of MTA's Kerberos realm
pktcMtaDevKerbPrincipalName	Kerberos Principal Name of the MTA's CMS
pktcMtaDevServGracePeriod	MTA must obtain new Kerberos ticket this many minutes before the prior ticket expires

Name of MIB Variable	Meaning or Effect
pktcMtaDevTgsTable	Per-endpoint TGS information; for details see the MIB specification
pktcMtaDevServerBootState	One of: operational, disabled, waitingforDhcpOffer, waitingforDhcpResponse, waitingforConfig, refusedbyCmts, other, unknown.
pktcMtaDevServerDhcp	IP address or FQDN of DHCP server
pktcMtaDevServerDns1	IP address or FQDN of primary DNS server
pktcMtaDevServerDns2	IP address or FQDN of secondary DNS server[2]
pktcMtaDevConfigFile	URL of the config file on the server
pktcMtaDevSnmpEntity	IP address or FQDN of SNMP entity for trap handling
pktcMtaDevEvControl	Either resetLog or useDefaultReporting
pktcMtaDevEvSyslog	IP address or FQDN of the Syslog server
pktcMtaDevEvThrottleAdminStatus	One of: unconstrained, maintainBelowThreshold, stopAtThreshold, inhibited.
	Writing to this object resets the threshold state.
pktcMtaDevEvThrottleInhibited	If true, event reporting is currently throttled.
pktcMtaDevEvThrottleThreshold	Number of trap/syslog events transmitted per pktcMtaDevEvThrottleInterval before throttling occurs.
pktcMtaDevEvThrottleInterval	Interval in seconds over which threshold is measured
pktcMtaDevControlTable	Allows control of reporting of event classes; for details see the MIB specification.
pktcMtaDevEventTable	Log of events to assist in troubleshooting; for details see the MIB specification
pktcMtaProvisioningEnrollment	Contains the following objects: *(continued)*

---

2. There is a typographical error in the PacketCable specification. It has been corrected here.

Table 7-1 MTA Device MIB Variables (cont.)

Name of MIB Variable	Meaning or Effect
	pktcMtaDevHardwareVersion, docDevSwCurrentVers, pktcMtaDevTypeIdentifier, pktcMtaDevMacAddress, pktcMtaDevCorrelationId, pktcMtaDevSignature
pktcMtaProvisioningStatus	Contains the following objects:
	pktcMtaDevMacAddress, pktcMtaDevCorrelationId, pktcMtaDevSignature, pktcMtaDevProvisioningState

MIB specifications. The purpose of including this table is to help the reader understand the kinds of parameters that an MTA can report to the network and also to demonstrate the kind of control that the network has over the MTA.

Table 7-2 shows the entries in the MTA's so-called NCS MIB, which is a MIB containing data pertaining to the requirements of Network-based Call Signaling. As yet, no similar MIB has been specified for DCS.

Table 7-2 MTA NCS MIB Variables

Name	Meaning
pktcNcsDevCodecTable	List of supported codecs; for details see the NCS MIB specification
pktcNcsDevEchoCancellation	Is the MTA capable of echo cancellation?
pktcNcsDevSilenceSupression	Is the MTA capable of silence suppression?
pktcNcsDevConnectionMode	Specifies whether the MTA can support voice and/or fax and/or analog modem
pktcNcsDevR0Cadence	Ring 0 cadence
pktcNcsDevR6Cadence	Ring 6 cadence
pktcNcsDevR7Cadence	Ring 7 cadence

Name	Meaning
pktcNcsDefCallSigTos	The TOS bits in the IP header for NCS call signaling packets
pktcNcsDefMediaStreamTos	The TOS bits in the IP header for bearer channel packets
pktcNcsTosFormatSelector	Either ipv4TOSOctet or dscpCodepoint
pktcNcsEndPntConfigTable	Table of pktcNcsEndPntConfigEntry
pktcNcsEndPntConfigCallAgentID	FQDN or IPv4 address of the CA for this MTA
pktcNcsEndPntConfigCallAgentUdpPort	Port on the Call Agent for NCS signaling
pktcNcsEndPntConfigPartialDialTO	Maximum value of the partial-dial time-out, in seconds
pktcNcsEndPntConfigCriticalDialTO	Maximum value of the critical dial time-out, in seconds
pktcNcsEndPntConfigBusyToneTO	Busy tone time-out, in seconds
pktcNcsEndPntConfigDialToneTO	Dial tone time-out, in seconds
pktcNcsEndPntConfigMessageWaitingTO	Message waiting indicator time-out, in seconds
pktcNcsEndPntConfigOffHookWarnToneTO	Time-out for off-hook warning tone, in seconds
pktcNcsEndPntConfigRingingTO	Time-out for alerting the user, in seconds
pktcNcsEndPntConfigRingbackTO	Time-out for local ringback, in seconds
pktcNcsEndPntConfigReorderToneTO	Time-out for reorder tone, in seconds
pktcNcsEndPntConfigStutterDialToneTO	Time-out for stutter tone, in seconds
pktcNcsEndPntConfigTSMax	Time in seconds since sending the initial datagram of a message
pktcNcsEndPntConfigMax1	Number of signaling errors to receive before notifying network operator of a possible problem
pktcNcsEndPntConfigMax2	Number of signaling errors to receive before disconnecting
pktcNcsEndPntConfigMax1QEnable	Enables/Disables querying DNS when the pktcNcsEndPntConfigMax1 threshold is passed *(continued)*

Table 7-2 MTA NCS MIB Variables (cont.)

Name	Meaning
pktcNcsEndPntConfigMax2QEnable	Enables/Disables querying DNS when the pktcNcsEndPntConfigMax2 threshold is passed
pktcNcsEndPntConfigMWD	Seconds to wait after a restart
pktcNcsEndPntConfigTdinit	Seconds to wait after a disconnect
pktcNcsEndPntConfigTdmin	Minimum allowed number of seconds to wait after a disconnect
pktcNcsEndPntConfigTdmax	Maximum allowed number of seconds to wait after a disconnect
pktcNcsEndPntConfigRtoMax	Maximum number of seconds for the retransmission timer
pktcNcsEndPntConfigRtoInit	Currently configured number of seconds for the retransmission timer
pktcNcsEndPntConfigLongDurationKeepAlive	Timeout, in minutes, between sending long-duration call notification messages
pktcNcsEndPntConfigThist	Timeout, in seconds, before MTA assumes that no further response will be received to a message
pktcNcsEndPntConfigStatus	A specialized SNMP variable containing the "Row Status" associated with the variable pktcNcsEndPntConfigTable

The MIBs in Table 7-1 and 7-2 are designed to allow an SNMP manager to fully manage every MTA in the network. The configuration file that the MTA downloads as part of the provisioning process causes the MTA to populate its MIBs with provisioned values that should permit it to function correctly on the service provider's network. Remember, though, that an MTA is untrusted. Although PacketCable 1.0 MTAs are by definition "embedded" with the cable modem and are therefore relatively immune from hacking, this will not be true in later versions of the network, where an MTA might well be a personal computer or some other kind of multipurpose device running MTA software. Such a device might be hacked in such a way that the MIBs contain values other than those provisioned (or, more subtly, the MTA might maintain the provisioned values in the MIB but actually use quite different values). The network operator must be aware of these possibilities and ensure that rogue MTAs cannot disrupt network operations whatever values they happen to report to the management system.

Most of the entries in the MIBs are simple objects. These are known as **leaf** objects. Some, however, are tables containing multiple leaf objects. SNMP does not provide the capability for managing such tables implicitly. SNMP allows access only to leaf objects within a MIB. To manage a table, therefore, the manager must explicitly manage the individual leaf objects in the table.

SNMP Messages

SNMP contains a relatively sparse message set. Messages travel between managers or between a manager and an agent, which is typically a program running on the managed device. Messages that originate at the manager require a response from the agent. SNMP refers to the different message types as Protocol Data Units, or PDUs (just as in DOCSIS). Typical exchanges are shown in Figure 7-3.

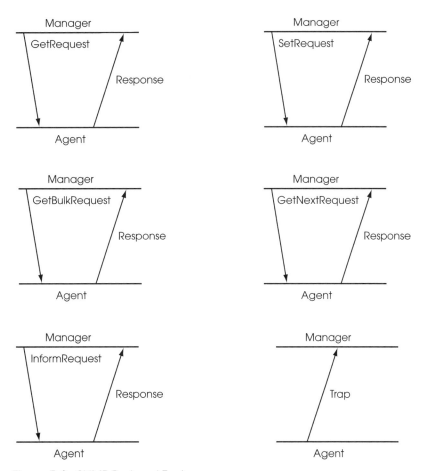

Figure 7-3 SNMP Protocol Exchanges

In general, the manager uses the GET messages to obtain MIB information from an agent and the SET messages to write information to a device MIB (which may cause an ancillary action to occur—for example, writing a particular MIB variable might cause the device to reboot[3]). A TRAP is an asynchronous message sent by an agent to inform a manager of an unexpected event. INFORMs are usually used to pass information between managers. PacketCable, however, uses an INFORM in the MTA initialization sequence to send information to the manager.

SNMP allows three different kinds of message format, as shown in Figure 7-4. The meanings of the fields are as follows.

version

> Version of SNMP.

community

> An SNMP community is a logical concept defined on the managed device that allows multiple managers to control the agent. In PacketCable, each managed device, especially when the device is an MTA, will have only a single manager and therefore only a single community. During startup, the MTA gives the name of its community to the SNMP manager, and the manager must use this name when it attempts to perform certain operations. In a sense, a community name is a kind of password that a manager must present before it is allowed access to the device MIBs.

1. GetRequest, GetNextRequest, SetRequest, Trap, InformRequest

Version	Community	PDU type	Request-id	0	0	Variable-bindings

2. Response

Version	Community	PDU type	Request-id	Error-status	Error-index	Variable-bindings

3. GetBulkRequest

Version	Community	PDU type	Request-id	Non-repeaters	Max-repetitions	Variable-bindings

Figure 7-4 SNMP Message Formats

---

3. On an MTA, this is exactly what happens when the pktcMtaDevResetNow variable is written.

Table 7-3 SNMP PDU Types

Type of Message	PDU Type
GetRequest	0
GetNextRequest	1
Response	2
SetRequest	3
GetBulkRequest	5
InformRequest	6
Trap	7
Report*	8
*The format and usage of the Report Message is implementation dependent.	

PDU type

Defines the type of the information contained in the rest of the message, as in Table 7-3. (*Note:* There is no PDU Type 4.)

request-id

An identifier used to distinguish among multiple outstanding requests and responses.

error-status

Used to indicate the status of the processing that was performed in response to a request. Allowed values are in Table 7-4. The values should be self-explanatory, except for code 1, tooBig. This error occurs when the information to be transmitted is too large to fit within a single PDU.

The response code readOnly is never used.

error-index

Used to indicate which variable within a list caused an error, when the error-status is non-zero.

non-repeaters, max-definitions

See the discussion of the GetBulkRequest message below.

Table 7-4 SNMP Error Values

Value of Error-Status	*Meaning*
0	noError
1	tooBig
2	noSuchName
3	badValue
4	readOnly
5	genErr
6	noAccess
7	wrongType
8	wrongLength
9	wrongEncoding
10	wrongValue
11	noCreation
12	inconsistentValue
13	resourceUnavailable
14	commitFailed
15	undoFailed
16	authorizationError
17	notWriteable
18	inconsistentName

variable-bindings

A list of variable names, along with their associated values (which may be null if the values are unknown, for example in a GetRequest). If the manager wishes to manage an entire table of objects, each leaf object in the table must be explicitly included in the list of variable-bindings. Note that SNMP can only manage leaf objects. If a table consists of multiple entries, each of which is itself a table, the tree must be recursed to the leaf objects, and these must be explicitly listed in the variable-bindings field.[4]

---

4. In such a recursive case, however, it is unlikely that all the responses for all the leaf objects would fit within a single response PDU. Therefore the recursive table of values would normally be constructed piecemeal, using several requests and their responses.

The defined messages that are of interest to us are the following.

GetRequest

The manager uses the GetRequest to query an agent about the value of one or more MIB variables. The variables being queried are contained in the variable-bindings portion of the PDU.

GetResponse

Contains the response to a GetRequest, GetNextRequest or SetRequest PDU. When responding to a GetRequest, three possible errors may occur.

1. The size of the PDU may exceed that allowed by the transmission mechanism. In PacketCable networks, the PDU must be less than 1,500 octets in size. If the response is larger than this, the error-status in the GetResponse is set to the value tooBig.

2. The agent may not be able to provide a valid value for one or more of the objects in the variable list. The GetResponse then contains the error code genErr. The position in the list of the first object for which it could not provide a value is contained in the error-index field.

3. One or more named object in the variable-bindings list may not exist. In this case, the GetResponse contains an error code of noSuchName, and the position in the list of the first object that it could not identify is contained in the error-index field.

If either of the last two errors occurs, the response variable-bindings list contains values for those objects for which a valid value is known. For those values for which no valid value can be provided, an indication of the error is provided rather than a value.

GetNextRequest

This PDU is an interesting twist on the GetRequest PDU. Instead of returning the values of the variables in the variable list, the agent is asked to return the value of the next variable in lexicographical order. This allows a manager to uncover the structure of a MIB without knowing it beforehand. In addition it allows a manager to search a table whose entries are unknown to it.

GetBulkRequest

This is an extension of the GetNextRequest PDU that allows for the return of multiple "next" variables. The GetBulkRequest PDU includes a value called non-repeaters, for which the command is to be interpreted exactly as if it were a GetNextRequest. It also includes a value called max-repetitions, which specifies the number of iterated "next" functions that is to be applied to the remaining variables in the variable-bindings list.

If the total number of variables in the variable-bindings list is N and the value of non-repeaters is M (M < N), then for the first M variables in the list, the GetBulkRequest will be interpreted exactly as if it were a GetNextRequest. For the remaining N-M values in the list, then the command is interpreted as if a series of GetNextRequest PDUs had been issued sequentially, for the values in the list, then their successors, then *their* successors and so on, until either the response PDU reaches its maximum size or until the iteration has proceeded max-repetitions times.

Note that, strictly speaking, max-repetitions is misnamed. Max-repetitions does not count the number of repetitions but the equivalent number of GetNextRequest PDUs that would return the same information as the single GetBulkRequest. This is actually the number of repetitions – 1. For example, if max-repetitions were 1, then there are *no* repetitions, and the agent acts as if only a single GetNextRequest was transmitted.

Suppose that the variables-bindings list comprises the values $V_1, V_2, V_3, \ldots,$ $V_M, \ldots, V_N$. Let non-repeaters have the value M, and max-repetitions = K. Denote the MIB variables lexicographically following the variable alpha by $\mathcal{F}(\alpha)\, \mathcal{F}^2(\alpha), \mathcal{F}^3(\alpha)$ and so on.

Then the agent returns the variables as follows.

1. For V_1 through V_M, the lexicographically next variable in the MIB is returned.

2. For each of $V_{(M+1)}$ through V_N, in order, the lexicographically next K MIB variables are returned, $\mathcal{F}(V_{(M+1)}), \mathcal{F}^2(V_{(M+1)}), \ldots, \mathcal{F}^K(V_{(M+1)}), \mathcal{F}(V_{(M+2)}),$ $\mathcal{F}^2(V_{(M+1)}), \ldots, \mathcal{F}^2(V_{(M+1)}), \mathcal{F}^K(V_{(N)})$

Figure 7-5 shows this diagrammatically.

SetRequest

A SetRequest functions much like a GetRequest, except that it is used to change the value of MIB variables rather than merely to read them. The variable-bindings list here contains the value to assign to each variable, as well as the name of the variable. The response, assuming there is no error, contains the same list of objects, with the same values.

The actual setting of MIB variables is atomic. If an attempt to set any of the variables fails, then any of the variables set to that point is restored to its original value and an appropriate error code is returned in the response.

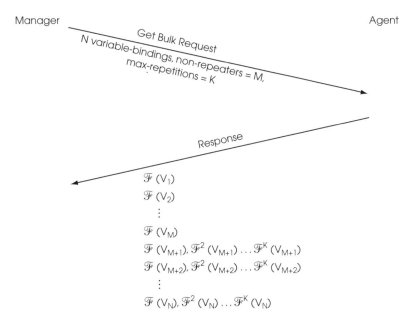

Figure 7-5 Response to a GetBulkRequest

Trap

> A trap is an unrequested message sent from an agent to a manager to inform the manager that an "unusual" event has occurred. There is no mandatory response (by the manager) to receipt of a trap.

InformRequest

> The InformRequest PDU is used to transfer management information among SNMP entities. Like a trap, it is an asynchronous, unrequested message. Unlike a trap, the recipient manager returns a response to the InformRequest. An InformRequest can be thought of as a kind of application-driven trap designed simply to ensure that a manager is told about information that it needs to do its job properly, rather than as an indication that something may be wrong on the sending device.

Power-On Initialization

Power-On initialization begins with the MTA's embedded cable modem initializing itself. The details of this process are beyond the scope of this document. Refer to the current version of the DOCSIS Radio Frequency Interface specification, obtainable at *www.cablemodem.com* for explicit detailed information. Briefly, the CM initialization process is as shown in Figure 7-6.

1. The CM sends a DHCP (Dynamic Host Configuration Protocol) Broadcast Discover containing a device identifier (option code 60).[5] The CMTS acts as a proxy and retransmits this request on to the network.

2. A DHCP server responds with a DHCP Offer.

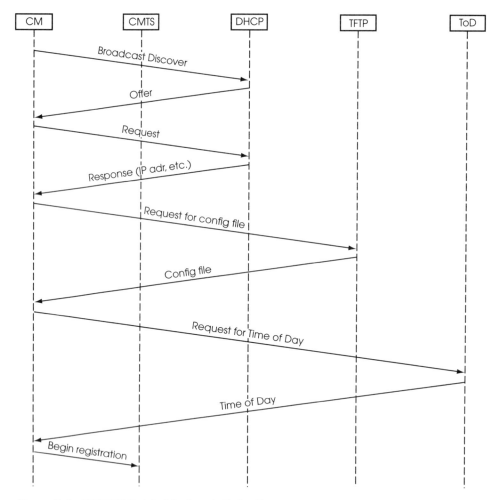

Figure 7-6 DOCSIS Cable Modem Initialization

---

5. See RFC 1531 for an explanation of DHCP options, and the PacketCable Provisioning specification for details of how options are defined for use in PacketCable.

3. The CM sends a DHCP Request to the server.

4. The DHCP server acknowledges the information in the Request, and provides the CM with an IP address, the address of a TFTP file server and the name of a CM configuration file to be downloaded from the file server.

5. The CM obtains the configuration file from the TFTP server.

6. The CM obtains the Time of Day from a Time of Day (ToD) server.

7. The CM registers with its CMTS.

The Cable Modem initialization provides link-layer access to allow the MTA access to the network. Once the CM is properly initialized, the MTA may begin the process of initializing itself.

The MTA initialization sequence can be divided into several logical steps.

1. Obtaining IP connectivity information from a DHCP server

2. Informing the network of the MTA's existence and obtaining a valid configuration file

3. Notifying the network operator that the MTA has configured itself

4. Obtaining a Kerberos ticket to allow the MTA access to a CMS

5. Setting up a Security Association with a CMS

We will examine each of these in turn.

Obtaining IP Connectivity Information

The Dynamic Host Configuration Protocol (DHCP), which is specified in RFC 1531, provides a mechanism by which a device can bootstrap itself onto an IP network. The details of the formats of DHCP messages are beyond our scope, but the essential mechanism is shown in Figure 7-7.

1. The MTA transmits a DHCPDISCOVER message. The message includes a device identifier (DHCP option code 60), which identifies the transmitting device as a DOCSIS device with an embedded MTA. The only allowed value of the identifier is the 30-octet string: EMTA:PKTC1.0:DOCSIS1.1:xxxxxx

   The DHCPDISCOVER is transmitted to the DHCP server address obtained from the DOCSIS DHCPOFFER message.

2. The DHCP server to which the DHCPDISCOVER was transmitted responds with a DHCPOFFER message. The offer contains a temporary IP address for

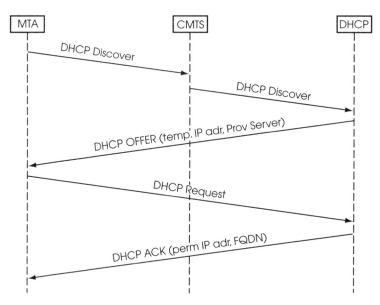

Figure 7-7 Obtaining IP Connectivity Information

the MTA. It also includes the IP address of a provisional SNMPv3 server in the PROV_SNMP_ENTITY field.

3. The MTA accepts the offer. It transmits a DHCPREQUEST to notify the server that it has done so.

4. The DHCP server responds with a DHCP ACK, which includes the permanent IP address of the MTA and (usually) the Fully Qualified Domain Name (FQDN) by which the MTA will be known to the network.

Becoming Part of the Network

Now that the MTA knows its address and name, it begins the process of informing the network management system of its presence on the network. As part of this operation, it will obtain configuration parameters that will allow it to be managed remotely by the network management system.

In order to be allowed to become part of the network, an MTA must identify itself unambiguously. Neither the MTA nor the network have, a priori, any reason to trust incoming messages purporting to come from the other. The initial DHCP exchange is unsecured because relatively little damage can occur if the exchange is intentionally corrupted or interfered with. Once the MTA attempts to become part of the network, however, security assumes an important role. During manufacture, an

X.509 certificate (the MTA device certificate) is placed inside the MTA. The contents of the certificate are specified in Chapter 2.

Inside the DHCPOFFER message that the MTA received was the address of an SNMPv3 server in the PROV_SNMP_ENTITY field of the DHCPOFFER. The MTA now sends to this address an SNMP INFORM message. Included in the SNMP INFORM is an object known as PktcMtaProvisioningEnrollment, which contains the following.

- The hardware version of the MTA
- The software version of the MTA
- The Device Identifier String (EMTA:PKTC1.0:DOCSIS1.1:xxxxxx)
- The MAC address of the MTA
- A so-called Telephony Provisioning Correlation ID, which is simply a number that is used to allow the response to be matched with this INFORM
- The MTA Device certificate
- A nonce (a random value that will be used to validate the response)

Depending on how the operator has configured the network, the SNMP manager may require more information than is provided in the InformRequest that the MTA has sent it. In this case, the SNMP manager sends one or more GetRequests (or a GetBulkRequest) to retrieve the additional MIB objects that it needs from the MTA.

Once it has enough information, the SNMP manager creates a configuration file appropriate for the MTA and stores the file on a TFTP or HTTP server (which may physically be the same device as the SNMP manager). In order to prevent the MTA from accepting a configuration file from a malicious third party, the configuration file contains the same nonce that was transmitted by the MTA in the SNMP Inform-Request. The configuration file is signed by the SNMP manager's private key and encrypted with the MTA's public key, which the SNMP manager obtained from the MTA's Device Certificate.

Once the configuration file has been created and stored, the SNMP Manager sends a SetRequest to set the value of the MIB variable pktcMtaDevConfigFile to the MTA. The variable contains the full URL of the configuration file. For example, if the configuration file `MTAconfigfile.subscriber.3034567891` resides on the TFTP server `tftp.mynetwork.com`, the SetRequest would set the contents of the MIB variable pktcMtaDevConfigFile to the value `tftp://tftp.mynetwork.com/` `MTAconfigfile.subscriber3034567891`. The URL may identify the server either by FQDN or by IP address. If it uses the FQDN, the MTA will use a DNS server to convert the FQDN to an IP address. Now the MTA is in a position to obtain its configuration file by the specified method (either TFTP or HTTP) from the correct server.[6]

MTA Configuration File Format

The MTA configuration file contains a series of TLV encoded values. Some, but not all, of the values in the file are reflected in the MTA MIB. The values that are not reflected in the MIB contain a simple TLV encoding similar to that used in DOCSIS. The values with MIB access are somewhat more complicated.

Values with MIB access are encoded as Type 11. The length is simply the length of the object. The value encoding, however, is the VarBind type encoding specified in RFC 1157:

```
VarBind ::=
        SEQUENCE {
            name
                ObjectName,

            value
                ObjectSyntax
        }
```

where ObjectName and ObjectSyntax are as defined in RFC 1155 (the ObjectSyntax type is a container that can hold different kinds of objects, such as integers and strings). The Value field of the TLV encoding thus contains both the name and the value of those variables that have MIB access.

Suppose, for example, that the configuration file contains a value of 0x12345678 for the PacketCable Telephony Provisioning Correlation ID. Then to construct the entry for this parameter in the configuration file, the following steps are performed.

1. The name ("PacketCable Telephony Provisioning Correlation ID") is encoded as an ObjectName

2. The value (0x12345678) is encoded as an ObjectSyntax

3. The resulting ObjectName and ObjectSyntax are combined into a single VarBind. This VarBind is a collection of N octets.

4. The parameter is placed into the configuration file with TLV encoding, where the Type = 11; Length = N; Value = the collection of N octets that represents the VarBind object.

---

6. Since the configuration file is encrypted with the MTA's public key, there is no need to protect it further (by, for example, using a secure protocol).

Table 7-5 lists all the information that must be in an MTA configuration file.[7] The first entry in the file must be the "telephony configuration file start", and the last entry must be the "telephony configuration file end". Before it attempts to use the entries in the configuration file, the MTA must first decrypt it (using its private key) and must also check that the value of the nonce in the file matches the value that it

Table 7-5 Contents of MTA Configuration File

Name	Type of Variable	SNMP Access	Meaning
Telephony Configuration File Start	Integer	None	T = 254; L = 1; V = 1
Telephony Configuration File End	Integer	None	T = 254; L = 1; V = 255
MTA Authentication Key	String	None	A 16-octet string created by the provisioning server; used for SNMPv3 security
MTA Device Certificate	String	Read Only	The MTA X.509 certificate embedded by the manufacturer
MTA Device Signature	String	Read/Write	Signature from the InformRequest that caused this configuration file to be generated
MTA Manufacturer Certificate	String	Read Only	The MTA X.509 Manufacturer certificate (The current version of the specifications do not explain why this value is present, what its purpose is, or how the Provisioning Server could be expected to know the correct value to place in the file. The author expects that this value is likely to be removed in future versions of the specification.)
MTA Privacy Key	String	None	A 16-octet string created by the provisioning server; used for SNMPv3 security

(continue)

7. Several of these values are redundant (for example, the specification calls for the configuration file to include the MTA Device Certificate—which is silly, because the device already knows its certificate). The redundancies will likely be removed in a later version of PacketCable, but for now the specifications require them.

Table 7-5 Contents of MTA Configuration File (cont.)

Name	Type of Variable	SNMP Access	Meaning
PacketCable MTA Device FQDN	String	Read/Write	The FQDN of this MTA
PacketCable Telephony Provisioning Correlation ID	4-octet integer	Read Only	Arbitrary 32-bit value created by MTA and used only during initialization
Telephony MTA Admin State	ENUM	Read/Write	Globally turns all the telephony ports on this device on/off. The value 1 enables telephony; the value 2 disables it.
Telephony Provider Syslog Server	Read/Write	String	FQDN or IP address of a syslog server. If 0.0.0.0 then syslog logging is turned off; if NULL then the embedded MTA must use the same address as the DOCSIS CM syslog server.
Telephony Service Provider DHCP Server	String	Read/Write	FQDN or IP address of the DHCP server. If the value is NULL, then the value obtained during DOCSIS registration of the CM is used.
Telephony Service Provider SNMP Entity	String	Read/Write	FQDN or IP address of the SNMP manager. If the value is NULL, then the value obtained during DOCSIS registration is used.
USM User Authentication Protocol	ENUM	Read/Write	The authentication protocol used in SNMPv3. Allowed values are specified as follows in RFC 2274: 1: No authentication 2: HMAC-MD5-96 3: HMAC-SHA-96
USM User Name	String	None	The name of the user. This object is an index into a MIB table.
USM User Privacy Protocol	ENUM	Read/Write	The privacy protocol used in SNMPv3. Allowed values are specified as follows in RFC 2274: No privacy CBC-DES

sent to the SNMP Manager in the prior InformRequest. The file is encoded using the EnvelopedData type as defined by the Cryptographic Message Syntax, RFC 2630. The contentType is SignedData, also defined by RFC 2630, which includes a certificate hierarchy that will allow the MTA to authenticate the public key of the provisioning server. This in turn allows the MTA to check the validity of the Provisioning Server's signature on the file.

As well as the mandatory MTA-specific configuration information, the network operator may choose to download MIB information related to NCS or for per-endpoint configuration in the configuration file. If the operator chooses not to download this information in the configuration file, it must be provided by explicit SNMP SetRequest messages to the MTA before the end-user can place a call. In general, it is simpler for the operator to arrange that this information is downloaded in the configuration file.

The following mandatory information must be passed to the MTA, either in the configuration file or via SNMP, before it can utilize NCS telephony services.

- NCS Default Signaling TOS value (value used in the TOS field of the IP header for NCS signaling)
- NCS Default Media Stream TOS value (value used in the TOS field of the IP header for bearer channel traffic)
- NCS TOS Format Selector (selects whether the TOS field is to be interpreted as TOS (RFC 760) or DSCP (RFC 2274) format)
- R0 cadence (A "cadence" is a specific pattern of ringing; for example, in the United States the basic alerting cadence is a two-second ring followed by four seconds of silence.)
- R6 cadence
- R7 cadence

In addition, before a particular endpoint may use telephony service, it must be provided with the following information.

- Port Administration State (used to enable/disable services to the particular port on the MTA)
- CMS name
- Telephony Service Provider (TSP) Kerberos Realm (string used to identify a suite of CMS and TGS devices)[8]

---

8. We have tried to avoid a discussion of Kerberos Realms. Essentially, a Kerberos Realm is the same as an "administrative domain"—that is, all the devices in a single Kerberos Realm are administered by a single entity. PacketCable 1.0 assumes that all the devices on a PacketCable network lie in a single Kerberos Realm.

- TSP Certificate (X.509 certificate of the TSP)

- MTA Telephony Certificate (X.509 certificate that allows the MTA to register with any TGS in any realm operated by the TSP)

- CMS Kerberos Principal Name (identifies one or more CMSes that share a single TGS)

- TGS name list (list of one or more TGSes)

- PKINIT Grace Period (number of minutes prior to expiration of a Kerberos ticket that the endpoint is expected to obtain a new ticket)

Included in the configuration file are explicit keying and protocol information that allows the MTA to turn on SNMPv3 security as specified in RFC 2274 as soon as it has downloaded and authenticated the configuration file. The network management systems use standard SNMPv3 security from this point on.

The MTA now sends a message to the SYSLOG server identified in the configuration file. The message informs the server that provisioning has been completed for this device. The detailed format of the message is contained in the DOCSIS Cable Modem MIB specification. As well as the message to the SYSLOG server, the MTA sends an InformRequest containing its pktcMtaProvisioningStatus object to its SNMP Manager.

At this point the MTA has configured itself so that it has the basic capability to place a call. In addition, the network knows that the MTA is on the network. What it does not know is the identity of the subscriber to whom the MTA belongs. This mapping (subscriber ↔ MTA) is performed out-of-band, typically by a placing a phone call to a Customer Service Representative.

There is one more thing left to do before a call can actually be placed. It is a basic PacketCable requirement that all call signaling must be secured by IPsec. Therefore the MTA must be able to set up a Security Association with its CMS.

Creating an IPsec Security Association with a CMS

The per-endpoint configuration given to the MTA, either in the configuration file or in separate SNMP SetRequest messages, includes the identity of one or more Ticket Granting Servers (TGSes). PacketCable uses an abbreviated version of Kerberos to create security associations between endpoints and their Call Management Servers. Instead of a full-blown Kerberos Key Distribution Center (KDC), PacketCable uses a TGS to manage security between MTAs and CMSes.

MTAs use the PKINIT mechanism (described in Chapter 2) to authenticate themselves to the TGS and to obtain a ticket that allows them to authenticate themselves to the CMS. Figure 7-8 shows a high-level overview of the process.

1. The MTA identifies itself to the TGS, presenting the MTA telephony certificate so that the TGS can authenticate it.[9] The certificate is carried inside a PKINIT Request message, which is itself embedded in a Kerberos KRB_AS_REQ message.

2. The TGS then sends to the MTA a Kerberos ticket valid for use on its CMS. This step betrays an essential difference between a TGS and a KDC. A KDC would return a Ticket Granting Ticket (TGT), which the MTA would present to the same or another KDC to obtain a service ticket. The TGS does not issue TGTs; instead it directly issues the service ticket to the MTA. This is carried in a PKINIT Reply message, which is embedded in a Kerberos KRB_AS_REP message. The ticket includes a session key used during the process of securing communications between the CMS and the MTA.

3. The MTA then forwards the ticket to its CMS in an AP Request message.

4. The CMS authenticates the ticket. Now both the MTA and the CMS can configure the security association between them, beginning with an AP Reply. Inside the AP Reply the CMS embeds a 46-octet (368-bit) secret that it will share with this particular MTA.

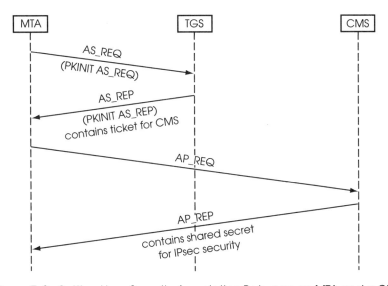

Figure 7-8 Setting Up a Security Association Between an MTA and a CMS

---

9. It may present instead the device certificate, but the telephony certificate is the preferred method. Both certificates contain the MTA's public key, which is the important piece of information that needs to be passed to the TGS.

We have already seen, in Chapter 2, how the first half of this process works. Let's look in a little more detail at the last two steps (see Figure 7-9).

The AP Request is an extended version of the KRB_AP_REQ as specified in the Kerberos RFC, number 1510. It contains the concatenation of the following fields.

Key Management Message ID

A 1-octet field with the value 0x02

KRB_AP_REQ

The DER encoding of the KRB_AP_REQ as specified in *http://www.ietf.org/ internet-drafts/draft-ietf-cat-kerberos-revisions-04.txt*. This is one of several places where PacketCable specifications refer to an Internet Draft. This is usually regarded as poor practice, since Internet Drafts have a strictly limited life span and are also subject to frequent change. An implementor attempting to write code that is intended to conform with the specification should probably attempt to locate the most current version of the Internet

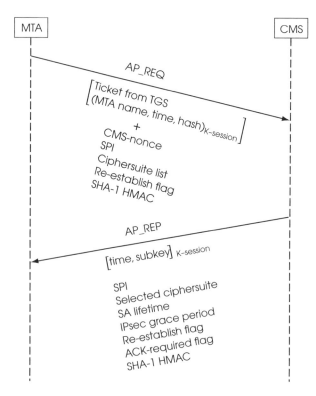

Figure 7-9 The AP_REQ / AP_REP Exchange

Draft (or its resultant RFC) and implement the DER encoding contained therein, since the text of this Internet Draft is not explicitly included in the PacketCable specification.

CMS-nonce

A 4-octet binary string composed of all zeros[10]

SPI

A 4-octet value that specifies the value of the Security Parameters Index for messages received by the MTA (see Chapter 2 for a discussion of SPIs)

Ciphersuite list

This is the list of IPsec ciphersuites that can be supported; it contains these subfields.

- *Number of entries*

  A 1-octet field giving the number of entries in the list

Then, for each ciphersuite:

- *Authentication Algorithm*

  A 1-octet field identifying an algorithm to be used for authentication. The possible values are listed in Table 4-14.

- *Encryption Algorithm*

  A 1-octet field identifying an algorithm to be used for encryption. The possible values are listed in Table 4-15.

Reestablish flag

A 1-octet field with either the value 0x01 or 0x00. If the value is 0x01, then the MTA is attempting to establish a new SA before the existing SA expires; otherwise the value is 0x00.

SHA-1 HMAC

A 20-octet (160-bit) field containing the SHA-1 HMAC of this message, excluding this field. The key for this HMAC is the SHA-1 hash of the session key that the TGS returned in the PKINIT Reply.

The AP Reply is a similarly extended version of a Kerberos KRB_AP_REP message, containing the concatenation of the following fields.

---

10. When we look at the Wake-Up message, we'll see why this field is included.

Key Management Message ID

A 1-octet field with the value 0x03

KRB_AP_REP

The DER encoding of the KRB_AP_REP as specified in *http://www.ietf.org/ internet-drafts/draft-ietf-cat-kerberos-revisions-04.txt.*[11] This field includes the 46-octet MTA-CMS secret from which the IPsec keys are derived as below.

SPI

A 4-octet value that specifies the value of the Security Parameters Index for messages received by the CMS.

Selected Ciphersuite

A list containing exactly one ciphersuite from the list that was presented to the CMS in the AP Request message. Note that both the unidirectional IPsec security associations must use the same ciphersuite.

Security Association Lifetime

A 4-octet value, MSB to LSB, that gives the lifetime of the security association in seconds. The security association is deemed to come into existence (and hence the remaining lifetime begins to decrease) at the time that this AP Reply is sent and received.

IPsec Grace Period

A 4-octet value, MSB to LSB, containing a value in seconds. When the remaining lifetime in the security association reaches this value, the MTA should send a new AP Request to begin creation of a new security association with the CMS (depending on the value of the Re-establishment flag).

Reestablishment Flag

A 1-octet value with either the value 0x01 or the value 0x00. If the value is 0x01, then the MTA should establish a new security association as soon as the remaining lifetime of the current security association reaches the value in the IPsec Grace Period field. If the value is 0x00, then the current security association is permitted to expire.

This flag, along with the Lifetime and Grace Period values, allows the network operator to maintain a degree of control over the number of security

---

11. See the footnote relating to KRB-AP-REQ.

associations that the CMS must maintain at any one time. Some vendors may prefer to maintain security associations "forever"; others may prefer to let them expire relatively quickly, especially if an MTA is infrequently used. See below for further discussion.

The expiration of a Security Association at the MTA and the CMS occurs in the following manner (if the MTA is instructed not to renew an SA): At the expiration time, both the outbound SAs expire. Both inbound SAs expire at a time equal to the expiration time plus the grace period.

ACK-Required Flag

A 1-octet value with either the value 0x01 or 0x00. If the value is 0x01, then the MTA must send an SA Recovered message when it receives this AP Reply. If the value is 0x00, then no SA Recovered message is sent. As a general rule, this flag has the value 0x00 except in some error-recovery scenarios discussed in the PacketCable Security specification. If a Security Association is unexpectedly lost, use of the ACK-Required Flag allows the CMS to determine more quickly whether the Security Association has been correctly recovered.

SHA-1 HMAC

A 20-octet (160-bit) field containing the SHA-1 HMAC of this message, excluding this field. The key for this HMAC is the SHA-1 hash of the session key that the CMS shares with the MTA. (Note that the session key is used, not the 46-octet shared secret contained in the KRB_AP_REP field.)

Although not generally required, if the AP Reply has the ACK-Required Flag set, then the MTA sends an SA Recovered message in response to the AP Reply. The SA Recovered message is simply the concatenation of two fields.

Key Management Message ID

A 1-octet field with the value 0x04

SHA-1 HMAC

A 20-octet (160-bit) field containing the SHA-1 HMAC of the received AP Reply message, as received (that is, including *all* fields). The key used is the authentication key for the outgoing IPsec Security Association. (The first key derived from the 46-octet MTA-CMS secret; see below.)

As soon as it receives an AP Reply, the MTA derives four IPsec-related keys, in order, from the 46-octet MTA-CMS shared secret. The same keys are also derived, in the same order, by the CMS.

1. The authentication key for messages traveling from MTA to CMS

2. The encryption/decryption key for messages traveling from MTA to CMS

3. The authentication key for messages traveling from CMS to MTA

4. The encryption/decryption key for messages traveling from CMS to MTA

The mechanism used to generate these keys from the shared secret is as described in Chapter 2, where, for this security association, the key-generating function $\mathscr{F}$ is defined as $\mathscr{F}$ (S, "MTA-CMS Signaling Security Association").

These IPsec Security Associations do not come for free. In particular, they consume resources on the CMS (to maintain the keying material). For a CMS that is responsible for several tens of thousands of MTAs, many of which may be idle for long periods, the network operator may choose to allow the IPsec security associations to time out after some period of inactivity. Since all call signaling must be protected by IPsec, a network configured to operate in this way must ensure that a security association exists before it attempts to send call signaling between an MTA and a CMS. If no such security association exists, one must be created before the signaling message(s) can be sent.

Two methods exist for creating these security associations "on-the-fly". The first, the Wake-Up message, is used to allow a CMS to force creation of a MTA-CMS security association. The second, the Rekey message, is used only for the situation in which a CMS has been implemented as a cluster of cooperating computers with multiple IP addresses.

Wake-Up

In a network configured so that the security associations between MTAs and CMSes are allowed to expire, there is the possibility that signaling for an incoming call will arrive at a CMS and the CMS will discover that it has no current Security Association with the destination MTA.

Kerberos-based key management suffers the disadvantage that it is inherently asymmetric: The client (the MTA) is expected to initiate the exchange by supplying the server (the CMS) with a ticket. If the CMS has received an incoming call for the MTA, an additional mechanism has to be supplied to allow the CMS, in effect, to bootstrap the generation of a Security Association with the MTA.

In PacketCable, the mechanism used is a special Wake-Up message, whose sole purpose is to instruct the MTA to start the process of establishing a Security Association by sending the CMS a valid Kerberos ticket. The format of the Wake-Up message is simple. It is the concatenation of the following three fields.

Key Management Message ID

A 1-octet field with the value 0x01

CMS-nonce

> A 4-octet binary string containing some random value that is *not* all zeros

CMS Kerberos Principal Name

> A null-terminated ASCII string containing the fully qualified Kerberos Principal Name of the CMS[12]

The Wake-Up includes no authentication protocol. This opens the way to a minor attack, in which an MTA is flooded by bogus Wake-Up messages. There is currently no specific protection against this attack.

Upon receipt of a Wake-Up, the MTA checks to make sure that it has a valid Kerberos ticket for the named CMS (to partially protect against the attack mentioned above, it should also check that named CMS is actually known to it). If it has no such ticket, it obtains one from the TGS using the same mechanism as is used during initialization. Once it has a valid ticket, it sends an AP Request to the CMS. The only difference between this and an ordinary AP Request is that the value of the CMS-nonce field is set to the value received in the Wake-Up message. This allows the CMS to correlate the incoming AP Request with the recently transmitted Wake-Up.

The rest of the sequence is as we have already described: The AP Request triggers an AP Reply from the CMS. If the ACK-required flag is set in the AP Reply, then the MTA transmits an SA Recovered to the CMS, to act as an acknowledgement of the AP Reply.

Rekey

There is one other situation that may give rise to a CMS desiring to contact an MTA for which no security association exists, and it is specific to vendors who choose to implement a CMS as a cluster of several machines. Such a CMS might be configured so that a single logical CMS has several IP addresses (corresponding to the several distinct "mini-CMSes" in the cluster). In such a configuration, there may be no guarantee that the mini-CMS that responds to a message from the MTA has the same IP address as the one to which the message was sent (see Figure 7-10). For this one situation, a special message, the Rekey message, was invented.

The Rekey message uses the fact that each mini-CMS should be configured to share a single Server Authentication Key, which allows it to establish a security association more efficiently than is possible with an ordinary Wake-Up.

---

12. As of this writing, the definition of a fully qualified Kerberos Principal Name is given in *http://www.ietf.org/internet-drafts/draft-ietf-cat-kerberos-revisions-04.txt*. This draft is intended to become an RFC that will replace RFC 1510.

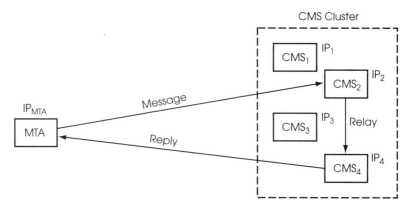

The Reply comes from a different IPaddress
than the one to which the message was sent

Figure 7-10 A CMS Cluster Responding to an MTA Message

The problem with using a Wake-Up in this scenario (although it would work) is one of delay. The message that the mini-CMS is attempting to send is likely to be directly in the flow of messages needed to set up or otherwise manipulate a call, and extra delay should be avoided in those circumstances. The situation is exacerbated if the cluster is configured so that each message might come from a different machine in the cluster, so that simply setting up a call might cause numerous Wake-Ups to be transmitted from the various machines in the cluster.

A Wake-Up spawns a minimum of two further messages that have to travel between the MTA and the CMS (AP Request and AP Reply). The Rekey message is designed to remove the need for the AP Reply.

A Rekey message is the concatenation of the following fields.

Key Management Message ID

A 1-octet field with the value 0x05

CMS Kerberos Principal Name

A null-terminated ASCII string containing the fully qualified Kerberos Principal Name of the CMS

Timestamp

An 11-octet string of ASCII characters, *not* null terminated, representing the UTC time of the message. The message encodes the time in the format YYMMDDhhmmssZ.

SPI

A four-octet value, MSB to LSB, to act as the SPI for the about-to-be-created Security Association.

Ciphersuite list

A list of ciphersuites available for use by IPsec. The format is the same as that used in AP Request messages.

Security Association Lifetime

A 4-octet value, MSB to LSB, that gives the lifetime of the security association in seconds. The security association is deemed to come into existence (and hence the remaining lifetime begins to decrease) at the time that this Rekey message is sent and received.

IPsec Grace Period

A 4-octet value, MSB to LSB, containing a value in seconds. When the remaining lifetime in the security association reaches this value, the MTA should send a new AP Request to begin creation of a new security association with this particular mini-CMS (depending on the value of the Reestablishment flag).

Reestablishment Flag

A 1-octet value with either the value 0x01 or the value 0x00. If the value is 0x01, then the MTA should establish a new security association as soon as the remaining lifetime of the current security association reaches the value in the IPsec Grace Period field. If the value is 0x00, then the current security association is permitted to expire.

SHA-1 HMAC

A 20-octet (160-bit) field containing the SHA-1 HMAC of the rest of the message. The key used is called the Server Authentication Key. The Server Authentication Key is defined as the SHA-1 hash of the session key used in the most recently transmitted AP Reply. (Remember that the session key is the key provided by the TGS; it is not the 46-octet MTA-CMS secret returned in an AP Reply.)

This probably bears repeating in different words. When the MTA last presented a Kerberos ticket to the CMS cluster, the ticket included a session key. The Server Authentication Key is the 160-bit SHA-1 hash of this session key. The Server Authentication Key is then used to key the SHA-1 HMAC over all the prior fields in the Rekey message.

When the MTA receives a Rekey message, it first checks that the HMAC corresponds to the value that it independently calculates. Assuming that the message passes this check (it silently discards the message if the HMAC calculation does not match), the MTA then checks to see whether there are any current SAs with the IP address that transmitted the Rekey message. Any existing SAs are torn down.

The MTA then proceeds to send an AP Request to the IP address from which it received the Rekey. This AP Request is slightly different from the usual form used by the MTA.

1. It contains the 46-octet shared secret, inside the KRB_AP_REQ ASN.1 structure. This allows the mini-CMS to derive the correct keying material for the IPsec Security Association.

2. It sets the Kerberos flag inside the KRB_AP_REQ structure, indicating that no AP_REP is requested.

3. Only a single ciphersuite is included (which must be one of the list presented to it in the Rekey message).

When the mini-CMS receives this AP Request, it immediately generates the inbound and outbound SAs but sends no response. Since the IPsec security associations now exist between the MTA and the mini-CMS, the mini-CMS can now send the message that caused the Rekey to be sent.

Event Messages

As a call proceeds, there are generally several events that occur about which the network operator has an interest. These events may vary from operator to operator, but often they are closely related to the method by which the operator chooses to bill for calls.

PacketCable networks contain a Record Keeping Server (RKS), which is a logical entity that is informed of these events as they occur. PacketCable specifies a number of Event Messages that devices may send to the RKS. The RKS then processes these in accordance with the operator's policy. Often, the result is a line-item on a subscriber's bill.

Typically, for example, an operator will bill a customer only for calls for which QoS is granted. PacketCable provides QoS-Start and QoS-End messages that allow the RKS to determine exactly the period for which QoS was granted in a given call and to bill the customer accordingly.

Event messages may be transmitted in real time, or they may be stored locally on a network device and only transmitted to the RKS later, presumably at a time at which the operator expects the load on his network to be light. Whether real-time or batch transmission is used is a decision left to individual network operators. Real-time transmission may allow for more responsive action, especially if fraudulent calls are being placed. On the other hand, it consumes network resources that may not be readily available. Batched transmissions require that the event messages be stored somewhere for later transmission, and it may not be cost-effective or practical to require access to storage for all network devices. In addition, there are some event messages that must, for legal reasons, be transmitted in real time (see the section "Electronic Surveillance").

In PacketCable 1.0, the only devices that communicate with the RKS are the CMS, the CMTS and the MGC. All of the event messages use the RADIUS protocol, secured by IPsec. The RKS might be configured to perform certain backoffice functions itself. More commonly, it acts as a single point-of-contact between the "main" PacketCable network and the backoffice infrastructure, as depicted in Figure 7-11.

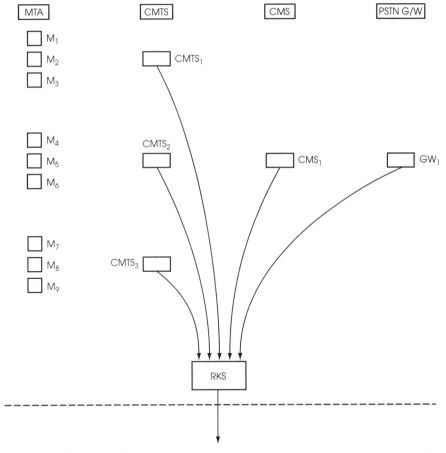

Figure 7-11 The PacketCable Calling Network, the RKS and the Backoffice Network

This architecture allows the backoffice systems to operate relatively independently of the network that is responsible for handling calls. This in turn allows individual network operators to choose a backoffice system that meets their needs, rather than having a particular design forced on them simply because they have chosen to deploy a PacketCable network.

Billing Correlation ID

The fundamental construct used to collate and process Event Messages is the Billing Correlation ID (BCID). The Billing Correlation ID can be thought of as a unique value that identifies a particular call. It is a 16-octet structure formed from the concatenation of three values.

1. Four octets, being the high-order 32-bits of the time in the NTP format specified in RFC 1129. In essence, this is the number of seconds since zero hours UTC on January 1, 1900.

2. Eight octets containing a right-justified, space-padded ASCII string used to uniquely identify the CMS within the provider's network

3. Four octets, representing a counter that should increment by one for each call handled by the originating CMS

For example, a call placed in January 2002 through a CMS with the identifier "NYC#4", might be given a BCID of 0xBFDF30802020204E59432334000004D2, where:

0xBFDF3080 ≡ 3219075200, the number of seconds since zero hours UTC, January 1, 1900;

0x2020204E59432334 ≡ " NYC#4"

0x000004D2 ≡ Call number 1,234.

Types of Event Messages

PacketCable 1.0 defines 17 different event messages, as shown in Table 7-6. Each event message is identified by an Event Message ID, as shown in the table. However, event messages are usually referred to by name, so that one talks of, say, the "QoS_Start" event message, rather than "Event Message number 7". Note that there are no messages corresponding to Event Message ID number 11 or 12.

Table 7-6 PacketCable Event Messages

Event Message ID	Name	Brief Description
0	Reserved	Unused
1	Signaling_Start	Signals that a call leg is being created
2	Signaling_Stop	Signals that no more signaling is expected on a call leg
3	Database_Query	A query is being made to an externable database
4	Intelligent_Peripheral_Usage_Start	Unused
5	Intelligent_Peripheral_Usage_Stop	Unused
6	Service_Instance	Signals that a service is being used
7	QoS_Start	Signals that QoS resources have been committed
8	QoS_Stop	Signals that QoS resources are no longer committed
9	Service_Activation	Signals that a subscriber has activated a service
10	Service_Deactivation	Signals that a subscriber has deactivated a service
13	Interconnect_(Signaling)_Start	Signals the start of call signaling between a PacketCable network and the PSTN
14	Interconnect_(Signaling)_Stop	Signals the end of call signaling between a PacketCable network and the PSTN
15	Call_Answer	Signals that a call has been answered
16	Call_Disconnect	Signals that a call has ended
17	Time_Change	Signals that a network device has changed its notion of the time abruptly
18	QoS_Change	Signals a change in QoS resources

Event Message Format

Event messages share a simple structure: a header followed by one or more fields known as attributes. Attributes are described below. The structure of the Event Message header is fixed, so that recourse to a TLV-encoding is unnecessary. The fields in the 60-octet header are as follows.

Version Identifier

> An unsigned 2-octet integer, MSB to LSB, identifying the PacketCable version of the message. Currently, this must have the value 0x0001.

Billing Correlation Identifier

> A 16-octet structure as defined above, in Billing Correlation ID

Event Message Identifier

> An unsigned 2-octet integer, MSB to LSB, containing the Event Message ID as given in Table 7-5. For example, a QoS_Start message would contain a value of 0x0007 in this field.

Element Type

> A 2-octet integer, MSB to LSB, that identifies the type of device that originated the message. The defined types are shown in Table 7-7.

Element Identifier

> An 8-octet ASCII string, right-justified and padded with spaces, used to identify the actual device that originated the message. The identifier used in PacketCable 1.0 is expected to be the MAC address of the device, rendered in hexadecimal without the usual colons separating the fields. Typically, then, the identifier requires no padding. Any letter-codes in the hexadecimal string may be either uppercase or lowercase.

Table 7-7   PacketCable Device Types

Element Type	Name of Device
0	Reserved
1	CMS
2	CMTS
3	MGC

Sequence Number

An unsigned 4-octet integer, MSB to LSB. Every device keeps track of the number of event messages it has transmitted to each RKS. According to the PacketCable specifications, this field should contain merely a "unique and monotonically increasing integer for each event message sent to a given RKS". However, since this field is used by an RKS to determine whether it has failed to receive any messages from a particular device, this should be regarded as an error in the specification, and the actual contents of this field should be a sequence number that increases by one for each event message sent to a given RKS.

Event Time

An 18-octet ASCII string, which gives the time of the event message. The string has the format YYYYMMDDHHMMSS.TTT, containing the time to a precision of one millisecond. Timestamps must have an accuracy of ±100 milliseconds. Any network device that issues event messages must synchronize its clock at least once per hour with a network clock source. The maximum drift rate from the reference clock must be less than 100 milliseconds per hour.

The actual mechanism by which synchronization occurs is not prescribed by the PacketCable specifications; *neither is the security that must be applied to this synchronization*. However, it is important that there must be no practical probability that an infiltrator in the network be able to cause a network device to obtain an incorrect notion of the time. An incorrectly synchronized device would produce event messages that could confuse the RKS and the various backoffice systems that reside behind it.[13]

Status

A 32-bit mask, with bit 0 as the least significant bit. The meaning of the bits is given in Table 7-8.

Priority

A 1-octet unsigned integer. The use of this field is left to the network operator. Its intent is to signal a measure of the importance of this message "relative to other network traffic". However, this field is generally unused.

Attribute Count

A 2-octet unsigned integer, MSB to LSB, that identifies the number of attributes that follow this header.

---

13. The author regards this as a substantial weakness in the PacketCable security specification.

Table 7-8 Event Message Status Bits

Bits	Description
1,0	Error Indicator:
	0 = No error
	1 = Possible error
	2 = Known error
	3 = Reserved
	If the error code is 2, then attribute #31 is included in the event message (see below)
2	Event Origin:
	0 = trusted device
	1 = untrusted device
3	Event Message Is Proxied:
	0 = unproxied; all data verified by transmitting element;
	1 = proxied; data sent on behalf of another element (which may be untrusted)
31–4	Reserved; all bits set to 0

Event Object

A 1-octet unsigned integer that has the value zero. Non-zero values of this field will be used in future versions of PacketCable.

Attributes

Following the header, an event message contains one or more attributes. An attribute can be thought of simply as a field within an event message, describing the value of some particular parameter whose value is being passed to the RKS. Different event messages contain different sets of mandatory and optional attributes, as we will see shortly.

A large number of attributes are defined. We will first look at the definition of each attribute and then see how the various attributes are used within the different PacketCable event messages.

Each attribute has an Event Message Attribute ID that is used to uniquely identify the attribute. The following are the defined attributes, listed in order of Attribute ID. Note that attributes with identifiers 2, 8, 10, 12, 19, 20, 21, 27, 28 and 29 are undefined.

EM Attribute ID = 0

A reserved attribute that is currently unused

EM Attribute ID = 1; EM_Header

The event message header is defined to be an attribute with the ID number 1. The details of the event message header format are provided above.

EM Attribute ID = 2

Undefined

EM Attribute ID = 3; MTA_Endpoint_Name

This is a variable-length string of ASCII printable characters, with a maximum size of 255 octets, giving the name of the endpoint on the MTA. In NCS, this has the format "aaln/#", as discussed in Chapter 4.

EM Attribute ID = 4; Calling_Party_Number

A 20-octet field containing the E.164 number of the calling party. The field is right-justified and padded on the left with spaces.

EM Attribute ID = 5; Called_Party_Number

A 20-octet field containing the E.164 number of the called party. The field is right-justified and padded on the left with spaces.

EM Attribute ID = 6; Database_ID

A variable-length string of ASCII printable characters, with a maximum size of 255 octets, giving a name that uniquely identifies the database being referenced.

EM Attribute ID = 7; Query_Type

A 2-octet unsigned integer, MSB to LSB, that describes the type of database lookup. These are the allowed values.

0: Reserved

1: Toll Free Number Lookup

2: LNP Number Lookup

EM Attribute ID = 8

Undefined

EM Attribute ID = 9

A 20-octet field containing the E.164 number returned by a database query. The field is right-justified and padded on the left with spaces.

EM Attribute ID = 10

Undefined

EM Attribute ID = 11

A 6-octet field that gives the reason why a call was terminated. The field can be subdivied into two subfields.

- *Source_Document*

  A 2-octet field containing an unsigned integer, MSB to LSB, that identifies the document that maps a Cause Code to its meaning. The only allowed value is 1, which corresponds to the document *Telcordia GR-1100-CORE Bellcore Automatic Message Accounting Format (BAF) Requirements*.

- *Cause_Code*

  A 4-octet field containing an unsigned integer, MSB to LSB, which contains the actual code for the reason that the call was terminated. The Cause Code is interpreted by the document referenced in Source_ Document to determine the actual cause for the call termination.

EM Attribute ID = 12

Undefined

EM Attribute ID = 13; Related_Call_Billing_Correlation_ID

A 16-octet field containing a Billing Correlation ID that might be used if the service provider offers additional (and undefined) "value added" services. In general this attribute is unused.

EM Attribute ID = 14; First_Call_Calling_Party_Number

A 20-octet field containing the E.164 number of the calling party of the first call in a three-way call. For example, if Alice calls Bob and then places a second call to Carol, who is conferenced into the first call, this field would contain Alice's phone number. The field is right-justified and padded on the left with spaces.

EM Attribute ID = 15; Second_Call_Calling_Party_Number

A 20-octet field containing the E.164 number of the calling party of the second call in a three-way call. For example, if Alice calls Bob and then places a second call to Carol, who is conferenced into the first call, this field would contain Alice's phone number. The field is right-justified and padded on the left with spaces.

EM Attribute ID = 16; Charge_Number

A 20-octet field containing the E.164 number of the billable party. The field is right-justified and padded on the left with spaces.

EM Attribute ID = 17; Forwarded_Number

A 20-octet field containing the E.164 number that is being forwarded. (For example, if a call is being forwarded from the number 303-538-0145, that number would be contained in this attribute.) The field is right-justified and padded on the left with spaces.

EM Attribute ID = 18; Service_Name

A 32-octet field containing the name, in ASCII printable format, of the service being invoked. The name is one of the following.

- Call_Block
- Call_Foward
- Call_Waiting
- Repeat_Call
- Return_Call

The name is right-justified and padded on the left with spaces.

EM Attribute ID = 19

Undefined

EM Attribute ID = 20

Undefined

EM Attribute ID = 21

Undefined

EM Attribute ID = 22; Location_Routing_Number

A 20-octet field containing the E.164 number of the terminating party. The field is right-justified and padded on the left with spaces.

EM Attribute ID = 23; Carrier_Identification_Code

An 8-octet field containing a string in ASCII printable format. The string contains the Carrier Identification Code (CIC) of the telecommunications operator, which may be a code for the MSO, or for another entity for which the MSO is providing the telecommunications service.

EM Attribute ID = 24; Trunk_Group_ID

A 6-octet field used to identify the number and type of a trunk group (a trunk group is a particular kind of line used between switches in the PSTN; in a purely PacketCable environment, this field is unused). The field may be divided into two subfields.

- *Trunk_Type*

  A 2-octet subfield containing an unsigned integer, MSB to LSB. Allowed values and their associated meanings are the following.

  3: SS7 direct trunk group number[14]

  4: SS7 from IC to AT and SS7 from AT to EO

  6: SS7 from IC to AT and non-SS7 from AT to EO

  9: signaling type is unspecified

- *Trunk_number*

  A 4-octet string of ASCII printable characters in the numeric range 0000 to 9999 that identifies the number of the trunk.

EM Attribute ID = 25; Routing_Number

A 20-octet field containing the E.164 number of the terminating party. The field is right-justified and padded on the left with spaces.

EM Attribute ID = 26; MTA-UDP_PortNum

A 4-octet field containing an unsigned integer, MSB to LSB, that identifies the UDP port number being used on an MTA for which a start or change in QoS has been detected.

EM Attribute ID = 27

Undefined

EM Attribute ID = 28

Undefined

EM Attribute ID = 29

Undefined

---

14. There is some discussion of SS7 in the next chapter; however, the subject is really beyond the scope of this book.

EM Attribute ID = 30; SF_ID

A 4-octet field containing an unsigned integer, MSB to LSB. This field contains a 32-bit Service Flow ID (see Chapter 3) assigned by the CMTS.

EM Attribute ID = 31; Error_Description

A 32-octet field containing a right-justified string of ASCII printable characters, padded on the left with spaces. The contents of this string are user-defined and are intended to describe an error condition. The presence of an error is signaled by the Error Indicator bits in the Status field of the header. If the value of those bits corresponds to a Known Error, then attribute 31 must be present in the message; if the value of the bits corresponds to a possible error, then attribute 31 may be present but is not required.

EM Attribute ID = 32; QoS_Descriptor

A variable-length field containing a minimum of 8 octets. Like most things to do with QoS, the contents of this field are fairly complex. The field may be divided into three subfields.

- *Status_Bitmask*

  A 4-octet field containing a mask that describes the contents of this QoS_Descriptor attribute. The possible masked parameters are contained in Table 7-6. The presence of a particular parameter is indicated by a 1 in the corresponding position in the mask. The rightmost bit (LSB) is bit number 0. These are low-level DOCSIS flow parameters, and the order in which they occur within the QoS_Descriptor matches the order in which they appear in Table 7-9.

- *Service_Class_Name*

  A 4-octet field containing an ASCII printable string, right-justified and padded with spaces on the left. This is the name of the particular type of service that the CMTS has granted for this service flow. DOCSIS does not require Service Flows to have a class name, nor does it require that a class name be limited to four characters. The intention of this subfield is that it should, where possible, uniquely identify the kind of service flow that has been assigned to this call. This may not always be possible.

- *QoS_Parameter_Array*

  This is the array of values specified by the bitmask in the Status_Bitmask subfield. Each value in the array occupies exactly 4 octets. The complete definition and encoding of the fields is given in Appendix C of the DOCSIS RF specification.

Table 7-9 QoS_Descriptor Status_Bitmask

Bits	Meaning
1, 0	Resource state; 1: Reserved only 2: Activated 3: Reserved and Activated
2	Service Flow Scheduling Type
3	Nominal Grant Interval
4	Tolerated Grant Jitter
5	Grants per Interval
6	Unsolicited Grant Size
7	Traffic Priority
8	Maximum Sustained Rate
9	Sustained Traffic Rate
10	Maximum Traffic Burst
11	Minimum Reserved Traffic Rate
12	Maximum Concatenated Burst
13	Request/Transmission Policy
14	Nominal Polling Interval
15	Tolerated Poll Jitter
16	IP ToS override
17	Maximum Downstream Latency

EM Attribute ID = 37; Direction_Indicator

A 2-octet field containing an unsigned integer, MSB to LSB. This specifies whether the device issuing the event message is acting as an originating or a terminating device at the time that the event message was generated. A single device in a call may issue both originating and terminating event messages as the call proceeds; for example, if both parties use the same CMTS, that CMTS will issue some event messages as originator and some as destination. These are the allowed values.

- 1: originating
- 2: terminating

EM Attribute ID = 38; Time_Adjustment

An 8-octet field containing a *signed* integer, MSB to LSB, giving the amount of the clock adjustment in milliseconds.

EM Attribute ID = 39; SDP_Upstream

A variable-length field containing an ASCII character string containing the SDP description of the upstream packet flow.

EM Attribute ID = 40; SDP_Downstream

A variable-length field containing an ASCII character string containing the SDP description of the downstream packet flow.

EM Attribute ID = 41; User_Input

A variable-length field containing an ASCII character string containing the sequence of digits dialed by a user.

EM Attribute ID = 42; Translation_Input

A 20-octet field containing the E.164 number used as input to a query of an external database. The field is right-justified and padded on the left with spaces.

EM Attribute ID = 43; Redirected_From_Info

A 42-octet field containing information about prior redirections of this call. The structure of this field is shown in Table 7-10.

Table 7-10 Redirection Information

Name of Field	Contents	Type
Last-Redirecting-Party	E.164 phone number of most recent redirecting party	20-octet ASCII string, right-justified, padded on the left with spaces
Original-Called-Party	E.164 phone number of the original destination party	20-octet ASCII string, right-justified, padded on the left with spaces
Number-of-Redirections	Number of times that this call has been redirected	2-octet integer, MSB first

EM Attribute ID = 44; Electronic_Surveillance_Indication

A variable-length data structure that provides information about an electronic surveillance Delivery Function (DF). See the section "Electronic Surveillance" for more information about electronic surveillance. The format of the structure is shown in Table 7-11.

EM Attribute ID = 45; Redirected_From_Party_Number

A 20-octet field containing the E.164 number of the party initiating a redirection. The field is right-justified and padded on the left with spaces.

EM Attribute ID = 46; Redirected_To_Party_Number

A 20-octet field containing the E.164 number of the party to which a call is being redirected. The field is right-justified and padded on the left with spaces.

EM Attribute ID = 47; Electronic_Surveillance_DF_Security

A variable-length binary string containing a key used to authenticate an IKE exchange to initialize a security association between DFs

EM Attribute ID = 48; CCC_ID

A 4-octet integer, MSB first, used to identify an individual call that is subject to surveillance.

Table 7-11   Electronic Surveillance Information

Name of Field	Contents	Type
DF-Address	IP address of the DF of the forwarding party	4-octet binary representation of the IP address, MSB first
CDC-Port	Port number on the DF for signaling messages	2-octet integer, MSB first
CCC-Port	Port number on the DF for content (bearer) packets	2-octet integer, MSB first
DF-DF-Key	A key to be shared between DFs; the destination DF receives the same key in an Electronic_Surveillance_DF_Security attribute	Binary octets, variable length

This concludes the list of attributes that are currently defined. As we have mentioned, each event message contains a header and one or more of these attributes. Most event messages contain some attributes that are mandatory and some that are optional. We shall now look at each of the defined event messages in turn.

Contents of Individual Event Messages

In this section we shall examine each of the PacketCable event messages. We shall discuss the circumstances under which each message is typically used, as well as the attributes that it contains.

Note that, apart from the mandatory header attribute, which must be the first attribute in an event message, the remaining attributes may be present in any order.

Message #1: Signaling_Start

Typically, this message is used to indicate the start of signaling associated with a new call. The message is generated as soon as a CMS (or MGC, in the case of an off-net to on-net call) recognizes that it is about to process signaling messages associated with a new call. For every Signaling_Start message there is a corresponding Signaling_Stop that is issued at the end of the call by the same network device as the one that issued the Signaling_Start.

Depending on the network configuration, there may be more than one Signaling_ Start issued per call. It is mandatory for the originating CMS/MGC to issue a Signaling_Start, but it is also permitted for a terminating CMS/MGC to issue one. If the terminating CMS/MGC issues a Signaling_Start, it must also issue a Signaling_ Stop at the appropriate time.

The timestamp contained in the Signaling_Start message reflects the time at which the very first notification was received by the issuing entity that a call is being placed. Table 7-12 describes the attributes contained in a Signaling_Start.

Note that attributes described as optional in this and subsequent tables (for example, the Trunk_Group_ID, when a Signaling_Start is issued by a CMS) may actually be unknown by the issuer in most PacketCable configurations.

Message #2: Signaling_Stop

This message is issued when a device that issued a Signaling_Start detects that the signaling associated with a call has ceased. Typically, if the device is a CMS, the event that causes a Signaling_Stop to be sent is one of the following.

- Receipt of an acknowledgement from an NCS DLCX message
- Transmitting an acknowledgement for a DLCX message issued by an MTA
- The receipt or transmission of the last signaling message to a peer CMS/MGC

Table 7-12   Signaling_Start Event Message

Attribute Name	Attribute Number	Mandatory/Optional
Header	1	M
Direction_Indicator	37	M
MTA_Endpoint_Name	3	M if source is CMS; O if source is MGC
Calling_Party_Number	4	M
Called_Party_Number	5	M
Carrier_Identification_Code	23	M if source is MGC; O if source is CMS
Trunk_Group_ID	24	M if source is MGC; O if source is CMS

There is a problem with the Signaling_Stop message. The current version of the specifications, since it does not fully support DCS, does not define the events that might cause a Signaling_Stop to be transmitted from a DCS Proxy. This is a problematical message for DCS, since the DCS Proxy withdraws from a call after setup. Therefore the DP receives no indication of when a call is complete. At present, different DCS vendors manage this issue in any way that seems reasonable to them (there are several plausible ways to handle this). However, a future version of the PacketCable specifications will have to carefully define the correct Event Message behavior for DCS networks. A similar lack of DCS-compatible specification applies to several other Event Messages. Vendor-specific schemes can certainly be made to work; however, they undermine the interoperability that lies at the heart of PacketCable. This omission will doubtless be addressed in a future PacketCable release.

If the device is an MGC, one of the following events typically marks the end of signaling for a call.

- Transmission or reception of an SS7 RLC ("Release Complete") to/from a Signaling Gateway

- Receipt of an acknowledgement from a TGCP DLCX issued by this MGC

- Transmitting an acknowledgement for a DLCX message issued by a Media Gateway

- The receipt or transmission of the last signaling message to a peer CMS

Table 7-13 describes the attributes contained in a Signaling_Stop.

Table 7-13 Signaling_Stop Event Message

Attribute Name	Attribute Number	Mandatory/Optional
Header	1	M
Direction_Indicator	37	M
MTA_Endpoint_Name	3	M if source is CMS; O if source is MGC

Message #3: Database_Query

This event message is used to inform the RKS that a database query (or any equivalent action such as an out-of-band request and response) has occurred. The event message is issued *immediately after completion of the query*. The message does not indicate the status (success or failure) of the query. Table 7-14 describes the attributes contained in a Database_Query.

A single database query might result in multiple numbers being returned. In this case, a separate Returned_Number attribute is present for every number returned by the query.

Message #6: Service_Instance

A "service" in this context is a feature supplied by the network. Typically, a subscriber's use of a service is billable, either on a pay-as-you-go basis or by a monthly subscription fee applied to the subscriber's bill. In either case, the network operator would normally wish to be able to track which services are used, either so that each service invocation is billed correctly or so as to check the number of times that a service is being used. The services currently recognized by PacketCable networks are: Call Blocking; Call Forwarding; Call Waiting; Repeat Call and Return Call.

Table 7-14 Database_Query Event Message

Attribute Name	Attribute Number	Mandatory/Optional
Header	1	M
Database_ID	6	M
Query_Type	7	M
Called_Party_Number	5	M
Returned_Number	9	M

Other features provided by the network (for example, Caller ID) do not result in a Service_Instance message being issued. Such features are typically available only by subscription on a month-by-month basis. Table 7-15 describes the attributes contained in a Service_Instance.

Table 7-15   Service_Instance Event Message

Attribute Name	Attribute Number	Mandatory/ Optional	Comment
Header	1	M	
Service_Name	18	M	One of: Call_Block; Call_Forward; Call_Waiting; Repeat_Call; Return_Call
Call_Termination_Cause	11	M if Call_Block; O otherwise	
Related_Call_Billing_ Correlation_ID	13	M if Call_Forward or Call_Waiting; O otherwise	
Charge_Number	16	M if Call_Forward, Call_Waiting, Repeat_Call or Return_Call; O otherwise	
First_Call_Calling_ Party_Number	14	M if Call_Waiting; O otherwise	
Second_Call_Calling_ Party_Number	15	M if Call_Waiting; O otherwise	
Called_Party_Number	5	M if Call_Waiting; O otherwise	
Routing_Number	25	M if Repeat_Call or Return_Call; O otherwise	
Calling_Party_Number	4	M if Repeat_Call or Return_Call; O otherwise	

Message #7: QoS_Start

This message is used to indicate the time at which the CMTS committed bandwidth for the call on the cable access network. Typically, this message is used to mark the time at which billing starts for a call. Table 7-16 describes the attributes contained in a QoS_Start.

Table 7-16 QoS_Start Event Message

Attribute Name	Attribute Number	Mandatory/Optional
Header	1	M
Direction_Indicator	37	O
QoS_Descriptor	32	O
MTA_UDP_Portnum	26	M

Message #8: QoS_Stop

This message is used to indicate the time at which the CMTS released bandwidth for the call on the cable access network. Typically, this message is used to mark the time at which billing ceases for a call. Table 7-17 describes the attributes contained in a QoS_Stop.

Table 7-17 QoS_Stop Event Message

Attribute Name	Attribute Number	Mandatory/Optional
Header	1	M
Direction_Indicator	37	O
QoS_Descriptor	32	O
SF_ID	30	M

Message #9: Service_Activation

Telephony service providers typically allow per-call activation of some services. Usually these services are activated by the end-user pressing a three-digit string commencing with "*". For example, in many areas, "*69" activates a Call Return service.

The Service_Activation message is used to indicate that the user has activated one of these services. The CMS always generates a new BCID for this event

Table 7-18 Service_Activation Event Message

Attribute Name	Attribute Number	Mandatory/Optional
Header	1	M
Service_Name	18	
Forwarded_Number	17	M if Call_Forward; O otherwise

message, even if it pertains to a service that has been activated mid-call. Table 7-18 describes the attributes contained in a Service_Activation.

Message #10: Service_Deactivation

Some services may be deactivated by explicit user action (typically, as for service activation, by entering a "*xx" string on the keypad). For example, in many areas, "*70" deactivates the Call Waiting service.

Whenever a service is deactivated by an explicit user action, the CMS issues a Service_Deactivation message. The CMS always generates a new BCID for this event message, even if it pertains to a service that has been activated mid-call. Table 7-19 describes the attributes contained in a Service_Deactivation.

Table 7-19 Service_Deactivation Event Message

Attribute Name	Attribute Number	Mandatory/Optional
Header	1	M
Service_Name	18	M

Message #13: Interconnect_(Signaling)_Start

This message can only be issued by an MGC, which does so as soon as bandwidth is committed between the PacketCable network and the PSTN. Table 7-20 describes the attributes contained in an Interconnect_(Signaling)_Start.

Message #14: Interconnect_(Signaling)_Stop

This message can only be issued by an MGC, which does so as soon as bandwidth is released between the PacketCable network and the PSTN. Table 7-21 describes the attributes contained in an Interconnect_(Signaling)_Stop.

Table 7-20 Interconnect_(Signaling)_Start Event Message

Attribute Name	Attribute Number	Mandatory/ Optional	Comment
Header	1	M	
Carrier_Identification_Code	23	M	CIC of other provider
Trunk_Group_ID	24	M	Identifier for the trunk over which the interconnection is occurring
Routing_Number	25	M	

Table 7-21 Interconnect_(Signaling)_Stop Event Message

Attribute Name	Attribute Number	Mandatory/ Optional	Comment
Header	1	M	
Carrier_Identification_Code	23	M	CIC of other provider
Trunk_Group_ID	24	M	Identifier for the trunk over which the interconnection is occurring

Message #15: Call_Answer

This message is issued by the terminating CMS or MGC, and indicates that the destination party has gone off-hook.[15] In the most common mode of operation, the off-hook state will also cause resources to be committed, which results in a QoS_Start message being issued, which in turn causes billing to commence. However, an operator might choose to configure his network differently from the norm; a particularly miserly operator might choose to start billing from the moment that the recipient goes off-hook rather than the moment at which useful communication can take place. Table 7-22 describes the attributes contained in a Call_Answer.

---

15. This is another of the event messages that is problematical for DCS because normally the terminating CMS is out of the signaling loop before the destination MTA goes off-hook.

Table 7-22 Call_Answer Event Message

Attribute Name	Attribute Number	Mandatory/Optional
Header	1	M
Called_Party_Number	5	M
Routing_Number	25	M
Charge_Number	16	M
Location_Routing_Number	22	M

Message #16: Call_Disconnect

This message is issued by either the originating or the terminating CMS or MGC, and indicates that the call has been terminated, either because the originating party has gone on-hook or because the destination party has gone on-hook and the call has not been resumed. There is an asymmetry in the way that an on-hook is usually handled in the PSTN. If the originating party goes on-hook, then the call is terminated immediately. If the destination party goes on-hook, the call remains up and a timer, usually set at around ten seconds, begins to run. If the destination party goes off-hook again before the timer has expired, then the call continues. Only if the timer expires without the destination party going off-hook does the call terminate. This behavior allows the destination party time to put a telephone down and to move to another extension located in another room to continue the call without the call being dropped. Generally, PacketCable networks are designed to mimic this feature. Table 7-23 describes the attributes contained in a Call_Disconnect.

Table 7-23 Call_Disconnect Event Message

Attribute Name	Attribute Number	Mandatory/Optional
Header	1	M
Direction_Indicator	37	O
Call_Termination_Cause	11	M

Message #17: Time_Change

This message may be issued by any network element that has experienced a sudden and discontinuous change in its notion of time. The precise meaning of "sudden

Table 7-24 Time_Change Event Message

Attribute Name	Attribute Number	Mandatory / Optional
Header	1	M
Time_Adjustment	38	M

and discontinuous" is left undefined by the specifications. The message contains the amount by which the element's clock changed, in milliseconds. Table 7-24 describes the attributes contained in a Time_Change.

Message #18: QoS_Change

This message is issued by a CMTS whenever an MTA successfully changes the bandwidth reservation associated with a call. Note that this message, according to the specifications, informs the RKS of a change in *reserved* bandwidth, not the committed bandwidth. However, this appears to be an error in the specification, since the operator should bill based only on committed resources. Most likely, a future release of the specification will detail a series of distinct messages relating to changes in the status of QoS resources. Thus there may be a QoS_Reserve and a separate QoS_Commit message.

Bandwidth changes do not occur in an "ordinary" call. However, changes may occur, for example, when a user begins a call with a low-bit-rate codec and then must switch to one with a higher bandwidth requirement in order to send a fax. Similarly, a call may begin with a relatively high bit-rate codec and then switch to a call between TTY or similar devices for the hearing-impaired, at least in one direction. Such a call might signal a change to a lower codec in order to make upstream bandwidth available for other users of the access network. Table 7-25 describes the attributes contained in a QoS_Change.

Table 7-25 QoS_Change Event Message

Attribute Name	Attribute Number	Mandatory / Optional
Header	1	M
Direction_Indicator	37	O
QoS_Descriptor	32	O
MTA_UDP_Portnum	26	M

RADIUS

The various event messages are transported by a subset of the RADIUS protocol, defined in RFC 2139. RADIUS uses a client/server model. In a PacketCable network the RKS is a RADIUS server and the entities transmitting the event messages are RADIUS clients.

The RKS listens for incoming RADIUS messages on port 1813. RADIUS messages travel over UDP; consequently the protocol defines an explicit Request/Response sequence using Accounting-Request and Accounting-Response messages. If a client transmits a Request and does not receive a response within some reasonable period of time (which is a provisionable value), the client retransmits the Request. The retransmission may be either to the same RKS or to an alternative, if the client has been configured with a list of servers to which it may send event messages.

RADIUS and Security

RADIUS defines a security mechanism that allows authentication of its messages by use of a 16-octet secret that is shared between client and server. However, in PacketCable networks, event messages are transmitted over channels secured by IPsec. Therefore the RADIUS authentication mechanism is unnecessary. However, the RFC defines the authentication mechanism to be mandatory. In PacketCable networks, therefore, the shared secret is defined to be always set to the value equal to 16 null octets (that is, 16 octets, all with the value zero).

The way in which the authentication checksum is calculated in PacketCable is exactly as in RFC 2139 (which is also described below). The only difference between PacketCable and ordinary RADIUS is that the shared secret is always set to 16 null octets.

The IPsec connections into the RKS are generated using IKE with pair-wise shared keys between the RKS and each entity that will be sending event messages. IKE runs asynchronously to the calls occurring on the network and ensures that there is always a valid IPsec security association between the RKS and the entity wishing to send an event message.

RADIUS Message Header

Every RADIUS message begins with a 20-octet header as shown in Figure 7-12. The header fields are the following.

Code

A 1-octet field. For an Accounting-Request, this field has the value 4; for an Accounting-Response, the field has the value 5. No other values are used by PacketCable.

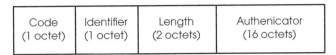

Code (1 octet)	Identifier (1 octet)	Length (2 octets)	Authenicator (16 octets)

Figure 7-12 RADIUS Header Format

Identifier

A 1-octet field. This field is used to match replies to the request that generated them.

Length

A 1-octet field. This is the total length of the message in octets, MSB first. The minimum allowed value is 20, indicating a null message. The maximum permitted value is 4096.

Authenticator

A 16-octet field. This field is used by ordinary RADIUS clients and servers to authenticate the message. In PacketCable this is not necessary, since the RADIUS messages travel over IPsec. However, the field can still be used as an integrity check.

The authenticator is an MD5 checksum. For an Accounting-Request it is calculated over the concatenation of Code, Identifier, Length, 16 zero octets, Request Attributes, 16 zero octets. For an Accounting-Response it is calculated over the concatenation of Code, Identifier, Length, the Authenticator from the Accounting-Request, the Response Attributes (if any), 16 zero octets.

These procedures are equivalent to the algorithms given in RFC 2139, with the shared secret set to 16 null octets.

RADIUS Accounting-Request Format

In an Accounting-Request message, the header is followed by an Acct_Status_Type attribute that is TLV formatted as in Figure 7-13.

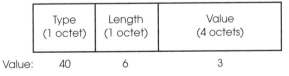

Type (1 octet)	Length (1 octet)	Value (4 octets)
Value: 40	6	3

Figure 7-13 RADIUS Acct_Status_Type Format

The fields of the Acct_Status_Type are the following.

Type

A 1-octet field with the value 40

Length

A 1-octet field with the value 6

Value

A 4-octet field, MSB first, with the value 3

These values never change.

All RADIUS attributes are carried in a similar TLV-encoded format. The Acct_Status_Type attribute is the only standard RADIUS attribute used in PacketCable event messaging. All other attributes are carried over directly from the description of event message attributes provided earlier in this chapter.

Within an event message, each attribute is transmitted as a separate RADIUS Vendor-specific attribute (VSA), with the format shown in Figure 7-14. The VSA always carries a so-called "Vendor ID" that acts as a tag so that the rest of the structure

Type (1 octet)	Length (1 octet)	Vendor ID (4 octets)	Vendor Attribute Type (1 octet)	Vendor Attribute Length (1 octet)	Vendor Attribute Value (n octets)
Value: 26	n + 8	4,491	From section "Attributes" in this chapter	From section "Attributes" in this chapter	

Figure 7-14 RADIUS VSA Format

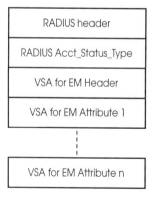

Figure 7-15 RADIUS Format of PacketCable
Event Messages

can be parsed correctly. All PacketCable VSAs carry a Vendor ID value of 4,491, which corresponds to CableLabs, Inc., the manager of the PacketCable project. The Vendor Attribute Type corresponds to the Event Message Attribute ID given for each Event Message in the "Attributes" section of this chapter; the Vendor Attribute Length corresponds to the length, in octets, of the particular Event Message Attribute, to be found in the same place.

The first portion is always the event message header; the second and any other portions are the remainder of the event message attributes. From a RADIUS perspective, then, each transmitted event message comprises a minimum of four fields: the RADIUS header; the RADIUS Acct-Status-Type attribute; a Vendor-specific attribute (VSA) for the event message header; a VSA for the each attribute in the event message. This format is depicted in Figure 7-15.

In order to improve the efficiency of the system, a network device is permitted to batch several event messages within a single RADIUS message. This is done simply by concatenating the VSAs representing the header and other attributes of the second message on to the end of the VSAs for the first message, as in Figure 7-16.

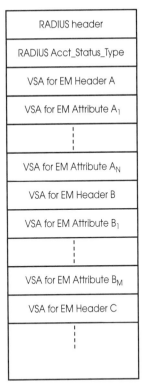

Figure 7-16 Multiple Event Messages Carried Within a Single RADIUS Message

Example RADIUS Message

We will conclude with an example to see how this works in practice. Suppose that an originating CMS wishes to transmit a Signaling_Start event message. The Signaling_Start is wrapped in a RADIUS Accounting_Request message. Therefore the message begins with a standard RADIUS header (where the first octet in the message is octet number 0).

Start Position	Name	Length	Value	Comment
0	Code	1	4	Marks as Accounting_Request
1	Identifier	1	123	Arbitrary value
2	Length	1	<length>	Length of complete message
3	Authenticator	16	<authenticator>	MD5 calculated per RFC 2139

This is followed by the RADIUS Acct_Status_Type object.

Start Position	Name	Length	Value	Comment
4	Type	1	40	Identifies Acct_Status_Type
5	Length	1	6	Length of this object
6	Value	4	3	"Interim-Update", used for all PacketCable Event Messages

The Event Message itself is placed inside a RADIUS VSA. The first attribute is the Event Message Header Attribute.

Start Position	Name	Length	Value	Comment
10	Type	1	26	Identifies Vendor Specific Attribute
11	Length	1	68	Total Attribute Length
12	Vendor ID	4	0x0000118b	Vendor is CableLabs
16	Vendor Attribute Type	1	1	Identifies EM_Header
				(continue)

Start Position	Name	Length	Value	Comment
17	Vendor Attribute Length	1	60 (The specification claims that Event Message headers are 59 octets in length; this is an error.)	Length of EM_Header
18	Vendor Attribute Value	60	<EM_Header>	The 60 octets of an EM_Header Attribute

A Signaling_Start Event Message contains a further six Attributes, as shown in Table 7-9. Each is encoded similarly to the EM_Header Attribute. For example, the Direction_Indicator, which has the value "1" for an originating CMTS is encoded like this.

Start Position	Name	Length	Value	Comment
78	Type	1	26	Identifies Vendor Specific Attribute
79	Length	1	10	Total Attribute Length
80	Vendor ID	4	0x0000118b	Vendor is CableLabs
84	Vendor Attribute Type	1	37	Identifies Direction_indicator
85	Vendor Attribute Length	1	2	Length of Direction_indicator
86	Vendor Attribute Value	2	0x01	Originating CMTS

There is no disputing the fact that Event Messages appear complicated. However, they all follow the same basic structure as outlined above and can actually be constructed (and parsed) with relatively simple code.

Electronic Surveillance

PacketCable is designed specifically for the North American market. Although there is little doubt that the same, or at least closely similar, networks will eventually be used in other countries,[16] the member MSOs in the CableLabs consortium are, with few exceptions, North American companies. Therefore, the interests and needs of the North American markets—and especially the U.S. market—were paramount in the design of the PacketCable system.

Most of the time, this bias had little practical impact on the detailed design of the network. In one area, however, U.S. needs were dominant: the area of electronic surveillance. In this section we will discuss some of the legal requirements pertaining to the U.S. governmental need for electronic surveillance of telephony, and we will then see how these needs translated themselves into devices and protocols within the PacketCable network. Note that although support for electronic surveillance was driven by U.S. needs, many western countries are in the process of adopting quite similar requirements—in fact, the entire issue of electronic surveillance these days is so complex that many countries simply do not have a sufficiently large pool of law enforcement technicians who are sufficiently competant in this area to do otherwise than to follow the U.S. lead.

CALEA

Historically, surveillance of telephone conversations[17] was a relatively well-defined process. A Law Enforcement Agency (LEA) applied to a court of competent jurisdiction[18] for an order to tap a particular phone number. Once the court issued the order, the LEA then served it on the provider of telephony service to the number in question. The provider was then under a legal obligation to provide information pertaining to calls in which that number participated for as long as the order remained in force. The basic mechanism generally used in the conventional case is depicted in Figure 7-17.

At the central office switch serving the suspect's phone, a tap is placed on the circuit, so that all the necessary information can be extracted and sent to the LEA. As we shall see, the situation is considerably more complicated in an IP telephony network. In the following sections we use some terms specific to wiretapping.

Subject

A subject is a phone number for which a court has ordered a wiretap

---

16. In fact, as of this writing, it seems likely that large-scale deployment of PacketCable networks will occur in Europe even before it occurs in the United States.

17. Colloquially referred to as "wiretapping". We will use this term interchangeably with "electronic surveillance"—even though in PacketCable there is neither a wire nor a physical tap.

18. A legal term for a court that has power to act in a particular area. A New York City municipal court, for example, would not normally have competent jurisdiction to order a wiretap for a telephone in Nevada.

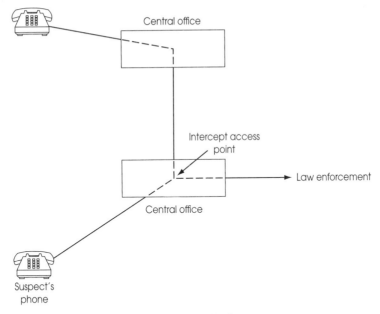

Figure 7-17 A Conventional PSTN Wiretap

Call under interception

A call is said to be "under interception" if the court order mandates that call content (the actual conversation) is to be delivered to an LEA.

Call under surveillance

A call is "under surveillance" if the origination or destination is to a subject.

Types of Wiretap

Generally, a court order allows an LEA to prosecute one or more of the following three kinds of wiretap.

- Pen Register
- Trap and Trace
- Call Content

Theoretically, these three types of tap are independent of one another. However, the first two almost always are ordered concurrently.[19] A tap of the third kind

---

19. We will refer to a combined Pen Register/Trap and Trace tap as a "signaling" tap.

.almost always includes both the first two kinds. The three kinds of taps may be loosely defined as follows.

Pen Register

A tap in which signaling information pertaining to calls originated by the suspect's phone is transmitted to the LEA

Trap and Trace

A tap in which signaling information pertaining to calls received by the suspect's phone is transmitted to the LEA

Call Content

A tap in which the actual contents of a call in which the suspect's phone participates (the actual conversation) are transmitted to the LEA.

Note: Throughout this section, we are specifically talking about surveillance by a third party. Some states allow recording of calls by one of the parties in the call without the knowledge and/or consent of the other party or parties in the call; that is not what we are discussing here. There are several legal and technical issues that are important here.

1. No wiretap is permitted without a court order. In the United States, telephone conversations are generally assumed to be immune from surveillance unless a court has specifically ordered otherwise. This requirement, of course, is not necessarily true in other countries.

2. A suspect may be tapped simultaneously by several LEAs. In this case, each tap is physically separate (in other words, the circuit is tapped once for each court order). In general, no LEA may be informed of taps already placed by other LEAs on a suspect's phone.

3. If the suspect is multiply tapped, not all taps need be of the same kind. It is perfectly possible for different LEAs to require different kinds of taps on a particular suspect. The Customs Service, for example, might require only a Pen Register/Trap and Trace tap on a particular phone; the same phone may be tapped simultaneously for Call Content by the FBI.

4. It is the phone number that is tapped, not the suspect. If the FBI has a Call Content tap placed against a particular phone number, all conversations in which the phone is a party are tapped, regardless of whether the participant using the phone is the suspect.

5. The suspect must not be able to detect that the tap is taking place. The tap must not be detectable by any change in timing, feature availability or

operation and so forth. For example, if the suspect habitually uses call forwarding, then the presence of the tap must not disable the call forwarding feature. Nor may it introduce any additional systematic, detectable delay in the time the service provider takes to implement a particular feature.

6. Courts generally emplace a much higher bar for Call Content taps (sometimes called *intercept taps*) than for signaling taps. As a result, approximately 90% of court-ordered wiretaps are for signaling taps.[20]

7. In a different vein, it is worth noting that CALEA places the cost burden on to the service provider for delivering the surveillance content to a well-defined demarcation point at the edge of their network. Beyond that point, the law enforcement agency must pay for further transport to their own system.

This relatively simple system works well enough in the circuit-switched world of the PSTN of just a few years ago. However, as we are all aware, the simple circuit-switched PSTN is no longer the only telephony game in town. To the circuit-switched PSTN, we now have to add a veritable plethora of telephony and telephony-like services. Even discounting PacketCable digital telephony over cable, we now have wireless, broadband PCS, paging, Short Messaging System and other services carrying information that an LEA might believe it has the right to intercept.

In order to try to meet the brave new world of digital communications networks, Congress enacted the **Communications Assistance for Law Enforcement Act** in 1994. This statute is generally referred to by an acronym formed from its initials: **CALEA**, pronounced "ku-lee´-a".

The CALEA Framework

CALEA is an interesting law.[21] In some ways, it is a unique law that demonstrates remarkable percipience on the part of lawmakers. On the other hand, it contains minefields that will generate plenty of work for lawyers and successor Congresses over the course of the next few years.

Let's start by looking at what Congress did right. Legislatures (at any level) are not a good place to create laws that affect a fast-moving industry. Perhaps the only worse place to make such laws is the courts, which have proved themselves generally inept at understanding fundamental technical issues surrounding much

---

20. As a matter of interest, the FBI estimates that there were in 1998 roughly 53,000 tap-days (a single tap active for one day is one tap-day) of intercept taps. Approximately half of these delivered data to federal LEAs and half to state and local LEAs.

21. No, seriously, it really is—not its words, perhaps, but the concepts it contains are worthy of a few moments' serious consideration. If nothing else, they define the field for a battle between individual privacy rights and the needs of LEAs that Congress will have to address sometime in the next few years.

of current technology. (Courts, of course, do not, strictly speaking *make* laws; they merely interpret them. The difference, however, is often only theoretical.)

To give one trivial example, suppose that you physically sign a piece of paper and later renege on the promises made on that paper. If I then take you to court, there is at least some chance that you will be able to convince a judge that your signature was a forgery, since we all know that ordinary signatures are easy to fake. Suppose, however, that you had digitally signed an electronic document. The fact that digital signatures are (essentially) unforgeable is not yet generally recognized or understood by courts, although Congress recently passed an "e-commerce" bill that, at least in theory, will motivate courts to become more technically competent in this area. However, in the real world, an unknowledgeable judge is still reasonably likely to agree with your contention that the signature was a forgery, despite the fact that such a forgery is impossible. One hopes that this situation will change in the coming years. For some real-world displays of technical naïveté by courts, a good place to start is *www.eff.org*.

Faced with these unpalatable alternatives, Congress chose the sensible third possibility: let a technically competent agency provide the mechanism for interpreting CALEA.[22]

Congress devolved to the Federal Communications Commission (FCC) the power and responsibility to interpret CALEA, and it has done so on several occasions—although doubtless there will be many more occasions for it to do so in the next few years. Let's look at a couple of specific requirements that CALEA emplaces.

1. Section 103: "... a telecommunications carrier shall ensure that *its* equipment, facilities, or services that provide a customer or subscriber with the ability to originate, terminate, or direct communications are capable of ... [prosecuting a wiretap]" (emphasis added).

Note that this emplaces a condition on the "telecommunications carrier". Avoiding the question (for now) of what constitutes a "telecommunications carrier", the requirement is placed *directly on the carrier that provides the subscriber with service*. The provider cannot point to some other entity in the network and suggest to an LEA that the entity is the one responsible for prosecuting the tap. In these days of multiparty networks where calls may be routed through devices belonging to several corporate entities, this requirement defines the entity responsible for performing the wiretap.

There are realistic examples of when this requirement comes into force. Suppose that an MSO deploys a quasi-PacketCable network, in which the CMS is actually

---

22. At least in the first instance. A party disagreeing with the agency's interpretation may still force the issue in court, but there is a strong presumption by the court that the agency acted correctly.

implemented as a front-end to a conventional PSTN switch that, because of the cost of a switch, is owned by a separate entity that interfaces the switch to several different networks, as in Figure 7-16. The language in CALEA places responsibility for prosecuting wiretaps squarely on the shoulders of the MSO, not on the owner of the switch.

2. The Safe Harbor provision.

The precise manner in which the requirements of CALEA should be implemented will vary from technology to technology. For example, what is easy to do in the PSTN may be very hard, or even impossible, in a network that uses some other kind of technology. Conversely, a digital network may contain call information that has no corollary in the circuit-switched PSTN (for example, encryption keys—a subject to which we shall return shortly).

Therefore each industry segment is expected to produce a standard or specification that defines the technical manner in which that segment will meet the requirements emplaced by CALEA. There is no implication in the statute that these various standards and specifications will be related to one another in any particular manner.

In general, if a provider is unable to prosecute a court-ordered wiretap, then that provider (and its vendor) is subject to a fine of $10,000 per day per unprosecuted tap. However, if the provider has deployed equipment designed to perform in accordance with an industry standard or specification, then both the provider and the vendor are provided with a "Safe Harbor" that causes the fine to be waived. Therefore it is important to both providers and vendors to ensure that industry specifications and standards are written and that their equipment meets those standards and specifications.

The first industry standard was J-STD-025, written by the Telecommunications Industry Association (TIA), and covering the "wireline, wireless and broadband PCS" segments.[23] The history of J-STD-025 following its release illuminates the manner in which CALEA operates.

Shortly after its release, the FBI and Department of Justice (DoJ) challenged J-STD-025 before the FCC. Note that, in the absence of such a challenge, the FCC *cannot* make changes to a standard or specification. However, once a challenge has been made, the FCC is free to order changes in the standard or specification, *on the issues that have been brought before it*. In other words, the FCC acts much like a conventional court.

Almost simultaneously, various privacy-advocate groups (the Center for Democracy and Technology, the Electronic Frontier Foundation, the Electronic Privacy

---

23. The presence of one standard covering these segments does not preclude the issuance of some other competing standard covering one or more of the same segments. To date, however, no such competing standard has been issued.

Information Center, and the American Civil Liberties Union) also challenged the standard. We will not go into the technical details of the challenges. In essence, the FBI/DoJ challenged the standard on the ground that insufficient material was being provided to the LEAs. The privacy advocates challenged it on the ground that too much material was being provided.

The FCC released its decision on the challenges in its Third Report and Order, dated August 26, 1999. The FCC granted the FBI/DoJ six of nine requested changes; it also agreed with the privacy advocates that, when packet-mode communications were being monitored, the standard was deficient in that it provided for the possibility of call content to be delivered to an LEA that was authorized only to receive call signaling.

As of this writing, the ordered changes are being made to J-STD-025. However, the privacy advocate groups have challenged the FCC's Third Report and Order before the U.S. Court of Appeals.[24] So where does PacketCable fit in with all this?

First, J-STD-025 *does not apply* to PacketCable networks. The FCC-ordered revisions to the standard emplace requirements that are technically very difficult (and perhaps impossible) to meet in a PacketCable network. Perhaps more importantly, an LEA should reasonably have access to some signaling information that occurs in a PacketCable network but for which J-STD-025 does not provide.

For example, telephony calls on PacketCable networks may use any one of a number of codecs (at least, the possibility exists for this in the future). Therefore the details of the codec should reasonably be available to an LEA; otherwise it will find it difficult, if not impossible, to decode received packets correctly.

More fundamentally, all bearer traffic on a PacketCable network is stream-encrypted. Without the encryption key, call content is useless to an LEA. CALEA specifically requires that, when a provider is in possession of an encryption key, that key must be handed to the LEA as part of the tapped signaling stream.

To address these and other concerns, the PacketCable project produced a separate specification, specifically designed to meet the requirements of CALEA in PacketCable networks. As of this writing, the specification is complete and released. No entity has yet come forward to challenge it before the FCC. However, it would be naïve to assume that no one will do so. It is highly likely that one or more challenges will occur in the upcoming months. In the author's opinion it is less likely, but certainly possible, that such a challenge will succeed to the extent that the challenges against J-STD-025 did so. However, a realist would have to conclude that at least some changes to the PacketCable Electronic Surveillance specification will be required in the course of the next year or so.

---

24. Note added in proof: The Court of Appeals has ruled, and in so doing has added to the confusion. The text of the ruling is available at: *http://pacer.cadc.uscourts.gov/common/opinions/200008/99-1442a.txt*.

Compliance with CALEA

Most of this book is concerned with technical issues. When we come to the issue of call surveillance, however, there are several legal issues that must be addressed before we can reach the technical concerns involved with actually performing a wiretap. The first question is Who must comply with CALEA?

The short answer is that no one knows for sure. CALEA does not go into force until the end of June 2000, which is in the recent past as this section of the book is being written. There have (as yet) been no lawsuits designed to determine exactly which entities are required to provide wiretaps, and this and other similar issues are ones that will be decided in the courts rather than on technical grounds.

You might be wondering why this is even an issue. Just a few paragraphs ago, didn't we say that the statute says: ". . . a telecommunications carrier shall ensure that its equipment, facilities, or services that provide a customer or subscriber with the ability to originate, terminate, or direct communications are capable of . . . [prosecuting a wiretap]"? We did indeed say that—but we never defined what is meant by the seemingly innocuous words "a telecommunications carrier"(!).

It may seem obvious to nonlawyers that an MSO providing a telephony service is automatically a "telecommunications carrier", but lawyers make a very good living by arguing against the obvious.

However, at least on this issue, the FCC has come to our rescue. In its Second Report and Order, adopted August 26, 1999, it discusses what constitutes a "telecommunications carrier". It essentially endorses the obvious interpretation, which the FCC itself had promulgated in a Notice of Proposed Rulemaking: "Those we tentatively concluded would be subject to CALEA include, for example, . . . in general any entity that holds itself out to serve the public indiscriminately in the provision of any telecommunications service".

The FCC also reiterates wording contained in CALEA itself: "The term telecommunications carrier" . . . includes . . . a person or entity engaged in providing wire or electronic communication switching or transmission service to the extent that the [FCC] finds that such service is a replacement for a substantial portion of the local telephone exchange service and that it is in the public interest to deem such a person or entity to be a telecommunications carrier for purposes of this title".

In other words, until the FCC changes its mind, or a court overrules it, it is reasonable to conclude that an MSO offering a PacketCable-based telephony service automatically becomes subject to CALEA.

What May Be Tapped?

The CALEA statute does not specify exactly what communications may be tapped. For example, while a court order may specify that voice communications to or from a particular phone number may be tapped, what about nonvoice communications such as, for example, electronic mail?

In the PSTN, the issue is to some extent moot. Most people use ordinary dial-up lines for communication with their Internet Service Provider. Since the modem signals are simply another form of analog traffic on the line, it is reasonable to expect that, if a line is tapped, the LEA is entitled to the analog signal that contains the contents of (for example) e-mail.

But the situation is different in a PacketCable network. All signals are digital, and voice (RTP) packets are easily separable from other traffic such as SMTP. The PacketCable specification addresses this issue by making a clear separation between "calls" (which are tappable) and other traffic (which in general is not tappable).[25] The PacketCable specification defines a "call" as follows.

Call

> A telecommunication originated by or terminated to a customer that enters or leaves the PacketCable network at a PC/TSP [PacketCable Telecommunications Service Provider] PSTN gateway, or a telecommunication that originates or terminates at a PC/TSP customer's MTA that (1) makes a request to the proper Call Management System for that endpoint, which then authorizes enhanced QoS facilities; (2) is granted the request for enhanced QoS facilities; and (3) uses those enhanced QoS facilities for transfer of packetized information.

In other words, only communications over PacketCable networks that use PacketCable QoS services are subject to tapping.

Wiretapping Architecture in PacketCable Networks

The addition of wiretap capability to the basic PacketCable architecture was designed to occur with minimal disruption to the existing architecture. The PacketCable specification defines several Intercept Access Points (IAPs), which are places in the network where a tap may occur. These occur at the following devices.

- CMS
- CMTS
- MGC
- MG

---

25. There is a rare form of court order that permits an LEA to have access to *all* communication into and out of a residence. Such orders are not included in the discussions in this section.

In order to minimize changes in these devices, their additional function is limited to duplicating information already present and transmitting the information to a new device, the PacketCable **Delivery Function** (**DF**), which is responsible for implementing most of the logic associated with prosecuting a wiretap. Figure 7-18 presents an overview of the architecture.

Streams of signaling and content information are transmitted from the IAPs to a DF, which then collates and manages these streams. The DF reformats the information and sends it to a *demarcation point,* which is defined to be an RJ-45 (Ethernet) port that is physically attached to the DF. The demarcation point represents the edge of the PacketCable network. The MSO has no responsibility (either legal or technical) for anything that occurs on the far side of the demarcation point.

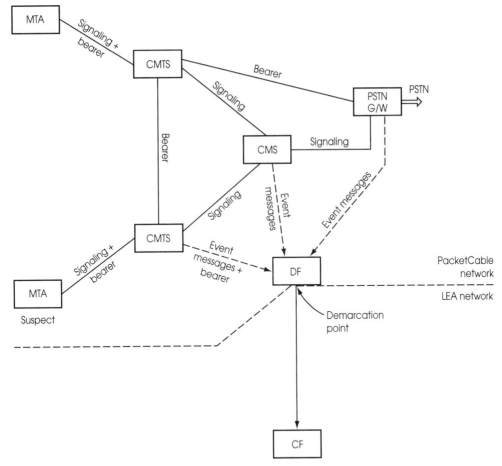

Figure 7-18 PacketCable CALEA Architecture

In practice, one of several mechanisms is used to transfer the packets that arrive at the demarcation point to a device known as a **Collection Function** (**CF**) that lies on the LEA's network. Note that it is the responsibility of the LEA, not of the service provider, to transfer the information from the demarcation point to the LEA's CF. Since everything beyond the demarcation point is "outside" the PacketCable network, we will not address the various means by which an LEA might transport and manipulate the streams arriving for it at the demarcation point.

Call Signaling

In order to support signaling taps, there has to be a mechanism that allows the signaling information to be passed to a DF. Such a mechanism already exists in the network: It is the event message mechanism used to transport information between network devices and the RKS. The wiretap mechanism reuses the mechanism (and indeed the very same messages) to allow signaling information to be passed to the LEA.

The essential process is as follows: When a CMS receives notification of a call (either inbound or outbound), it checks in a database of wiretap information to determine whether the call is subject to surveillance. This database contains information about all the current court orders served against the provider for customers within the area served by the CMS.

In the normal circumstance, the call will not be subject to surveillance, and everything proceeds as normal. Thus in the vast majority of cases, the only additional cost associated with adding wiretap capability to the network is a database query (actually two queries—one for the originating number and one for the terminating number).

Suppose, however, that the call is being placed to a number that does appear in the database. Now the network must pass the signaling information to the LEA, and it must do so in a timely manner: The PacketCable specification requires that the delay between arrival of signaling traffic at an IAP and its delivery to the CF must be no more than eight seconds 95% of the time.

The CMS internally marks the call as being subject to wiretap. From this point on, all event messages associated with the call will be duplicated. As well as being sent to the RKS, they will also be sent to the DF designated in the wiretap database as the one responsible for serving this phone number.

Event messages transmitted to a DF behave slightly differently from those transmitted to an RKS.

1. The CMS is permitted to store locally event messages destined for the RKS and to send them in batch mode at a later time, when the network might be less busy. Because of the strict timing requirements emplaced by CALEA, this

is not possible for the messages destined for the DF. Although the message for the DF is an exact copy of the one to the RKS, it must be transmitted immediately, even if the message for the RKS is stored for later transmission.

2. The additional message transmitted to the DF is a clone of the message sent to the RKS; *it is not a new message.* The difference is vital, since the RKS uses the sequence number contained in the RADIUS messages to determine whether it has missed any event messages. Messages sent to the DF *never* cause the RADIUS sequence number to increment.

3. A PacketCable operator has a great deal of latitude as to exactly what kinds of event messages he transmits to the RKS. One could imagine a scenario in which a particular operator might choose not to send certain messages if he does not base his billing on the events they represent. However, certain messages must be transmitted to the DF at the appropriate time, regardless of whether the operator chooses to send the same message to the RKS. Therefore it is possible that in some configurations, some of the messages transmitted to the DF will not merely be clones of those sent to the RKS but are entirely original messages, generated solely for the purpose of prosecuting a wiretap. As before, such messages must not cause the RADIUS sequence number of messages sent to the RKS to increment.

4. Since the transport mechanism between the CMS and the DF is RADIUS over UDP, a retry mechanism must operate between the devices. Typically this will be the same retry mechanism as that used between the CMS and the RKS.

5. The DF makes no use of the RADIUS sequence number. Since the sequence number is based on the traffic flowing to the RKS, there is no expectation that it will increase in the ordinary "increment by one" manner.

Changes to Event Messages

To support the needs of the DF, some additional fields are necessary in some of the event messages. A CMS vendor may, for the most part, choose to include these fields in the event message transmitted to the RKS (in which case the messages traveling to the RKS and the DF are identical) except in the case that the Electronic_ Surveillance_Indication attribute is present. This attribute is sent only to the DF and never to the RKS.[26] In the alternative, the CMS vendor may choose to generate distinct event messages to send to the DF.

---

26. Otherwise the fact that a call was placed under electronic surveillance would be known to the billing system.

Message #1: Signaling_Start

Table 7-26 describes the additional fields in the Signaling_Start message.

Table 7-26   Signaling_Start Event Message for Electronic Surveillance

Attribute Name	Attribute Number	Mandatory/ Optional	Comment
User_Input	41	O	M if call origination; contains dialed digits as received from MTA or PSTN gateway
Translation_Input	42	O	M if the number was translated through a query to a database
Carrier_Identification_ Code	23	O	M if call origination and the destination is a PSTN gateway
Redirected_From_Info	43	O	M if call termination and information is available to show that this is a redirected call
Electronic_Surveillance_ Indication	44	O	M if this message goes to a DF and this call has been redirected by a subject MUST NOT be present in any messages to a RKS

Message #6: Service_Instance

This message must be sent to the DF if a call under surveillance is redirected. If the redirection is as a result of an action by a suspect, then the message must include an Electronic_Surveillance_DF_Security attribute. Table 7-27 describes the additional fields in the Service_Instance message.

Table 7-27   Service_Instance Event Message for Electronic Surveillance

Attribute Name	Attribute Number	Mandatory/Optional
Redirected_From_Party_Number	45	M if Call_Forward; O otherwise
Redirected_To_Party_Number	46	M if Call_Forward; O otherwise

Attribute Name	Attribute Number	Mandatory/Optional
Carrier_Identification_Code	23	M if Call_Forward and a transit carrier is used for the redirected call
Electronic_Surveillance_DF_Security	47	M if Call_Forward for calls redirected by subject MUST NOT be present in messages sent to RKS

Message #7: QoS_Start

This message is used to indicate to the DF that QoS has been granted. It is transmitted if the Gate-Set message received by the CMTS for this call contained an Electronic-Surveillance-Parameters object and the dup-event flag was set. If the Session-Description-Parameters object was included in the received Gate-Set, then the message includes the known SDP descriptions.

The message is also sent by an MGC when it creates or modifies a connection on an MG, such that the connection becomes sendonly or sendrecv, since this is the equivalent action (at the PSTN gateway) to granting QoS at a CMTS. Table 7-28 describes the additional fields in the QoS_Start message.

Table 7-28 QoS_Start Event Message for Electronic Surveillance

Attribute Name	Attribute Number	Mandatory/Optional
SDP_Upstream	39	M for a message sent to a DF; O otherwise
SDP_Downstream	40	M for a message sent to a DF; O otherwise
CCC_ID	48	M for a message sent to a DF; O otherwise. Contains the Gate-ID if the message comes from a CMTS.

Message #8: QoS_Stop

This message is used to indicate to the DF that QoS resources associated with the call have been released. Like the QoS_Start message, it may be transmitted either by a CMTS or an MGC. Table 7-29 describes the one additional field in the QoS_Stop message.

Table 7-29 QoS_Stop Event Message for Electronic Surveillance

Attribute Name	Attribute Number	Mandatory/Optional
CCC_ID	48	M for a message sent to a DF; O otherwise. Contains the Gate-ID if the message comes from a CMTS.

Message #15: Call_Answer

If a call is subject to surveillance, this message must be sent to the DF, either by the CMS/MGC or by establishing a gate in the CMTS in such a manner that the CMTS transmits this message to the DF.

The CMS can force the CMTS to issue a Call_Answer by including a Media-Connection-Info-Object in the Gate-Set message. This tells the CMTS to generate the Call_Answer immediately when the QoS resources associated with the call are committed.

The presence of an Electronic-Surveillance-Parameters object in the Gate-Set forces the CMTS to send the message to the DF (as well as to the RKS). Note that, as we discussed earlier, a Call_Answer is often generated along with a QoS_Start message. Although both messages are triggered by the same event (resources being committed), the messages are conceptually different: As their names indicate, one is intended to signal that the destination party has answered the call; the other signals that QoS resources have been made available for the call. Unusual implementations of QoS allocation (for example, one in which QoS is automatically granted before a call is answered) are legal implementations of PacketCable networks, and in such implementations it is possible that the Call_Answer and QoS_Start messages would be triggered off separate events. Table 7-30 describes the one additional field in the Call_Answer message.

Table 7-30 Call_Answer Event Message for Electronic Surveillance

Attribute Name	Attribute Number	Mandatory/Optional
Direction_Indicator		M for a message sent to a DF; O otherwise.

Message #16: Call_Disconnect

There are no changes to the content of this message, but the network must ensure that the Call_Disconnect is sent to the DF if a call is under surveillance. The message may be transmitted either by the CMS or by the CMTS. The CMS can force the

CMTS to generate the message for the DF by including a Media-Connection-Event-Info and Electronic-Surveillance-Parameters objects in the Gate-Set message. The CMTS will generate and send the message when QoS resources associated with the call are released *if a Call_Answer was previously transmitted*. If a call is not answered, there is no need to send a specific Call_Disconnect message, since no tappable conversation occurred between the parties.

CDC Connection Between DF and CF

Each DF has five physical RJ-45 ports (a number that is derived from historical wiretap requirements), and each port is generally associated with a different LEA. When an LEA serves a network operator with a court order requiring the operator to perform a tap, the operator ensures that a DF port is made available to the LEA.

Some LEAs may serve an operator with multiple court orders that are simultaneously valid; the operator generally does not provide a separate port for each order. Rather, the information from all the wiretaps pertaining to a single LEA are transmitted to a single DF port. Every packet is marked with an identifier that allows the LEA to identify the "Case ID" with which the packet is associated. This permits filters operating on the LEA's network to route packets correctly, so that each packet reaches the correct device (which may be a tape recorder, a computer, a fax machine or any other appropriate device) for that particular wiretap.

Each ongoing wiretap has either one (in the case of a signaling tap) or two (in the case of a content tap) logical connections to the LEA's Collection Function (CF). We will look at these logical connections in turn.

The PacketCable Electronic Surveillance specification defines a PacketCable Electronic Surveillance Protocol (PCESP) that includes a Call Data Connection (CDC) interface between a DF and the corresponding CF. The CDC interface is designed to pass the signaling and Call Content control information from the PacketCable network to the LEA. Across the CDC interface, flow CDC messages that encapsulate the signaling information reported to the DF by the various event messages flowing from the Intercept Access Points (IAPs) within the PacketCable network.

In addition to the CDC interface, there is a second interface between the DF and the CF. A separate Call Content Connection (CCC) interface is used to deliver the audio stream associated with a call.

It is an important function of the DF that at all times it must ensure that an LEA is given only information to which it is legally entitled. If, for some reason, it receives event messages for which it cannot positively confirm the fact that the LEA is entitled to the content, it must not deliver the content to the LEA. However, the DF should immediately alert the network operator if any unexpected event occurs, since it might indicate a corrupted wiretap database. Other possible reasons for unexpected messages arriving at the DF are equally unpalatable: They might represent an attempt by an unscrupulous attacker to transport private information off-net, or a malfunctioning CMS or CMTS.

To transport signaling and content-control information across the DF-to-CF CDC interface, the following eight CDC messages are defined.

Answer

Indicates that the destination party has answered, allowing two-way communication to begin

CCChange

Indicates that Call Content is being delivered but that a change has occurred in the details of the delivery

CCClose

Indicates that no further call content will be delivered (widely interpreted by LEAs as a signal to "stop the tape recorder"—sometimes literally)

CCOpen

Indicates the commencement of call content flow (widely interpreted by LEAs as a signal to "start the tape recorder"—sometimes literally)

Origination

Indicates that a subject is attempting (or has attempted) to place a call

Redirection

Indicates that a call under surveillance has been redirected

Release

Indicates that the QoS resources associated with a call have been released

TerminationAttempt

Indicates that a suspect has received an incoming call

CDC Message Formats

Unlike most other message formats in the PacketCable network, the format of CDC messages are given in **ASN.1** notation. ASN.1 describes the fields and records of a message at a high level; it does not specify the detailed octet-by-octet structure of the messages.

The conversion from ASN.1 to a stream of octets occurs as a result of transforming the ASN.1 to a set of rules for encoding the message (typically by transforming the ASN.1 code to C code by running the ASN.1 message descriptions through an

ASN.1 compiler). There exist several different methods (called *Encoding Rules*) for producing a stream of octets from an ASN.1 description. Depending on the encoding rules, there may exist multiple ways of converting a particular ASN.1 description to a stream of octets.[27] The definitions of ASN.1 and the various encoding rules are such that whatever stream of octets is produced by the transmitting entity will be correctly decoded into the same high-level message by the decoding entity. Figure 7-19 depicts the encoding, transport and decoding operations.

Let's look at a brief example of how a trivial piece of information might be handled by ASN.1. Suppose that we have a message containing a single field that is a string of octets. ASN.1 has a defined type, OCTET STRING, for such a field. We can write a simple description of the message in ASN.1 notation.

```
dummy DEFINITIONS ::=
BEGIN
value ::= OCTET STRING
END
```

We now compile the ASN.1 description into C code for a particular platform. (The details of the C code will in general depend on details of the hardware on which the code will run—for example, the allowed length of integers, and whether multi-octet values are stored in big-endian or little-endian format.) The C code is then incorporated into a

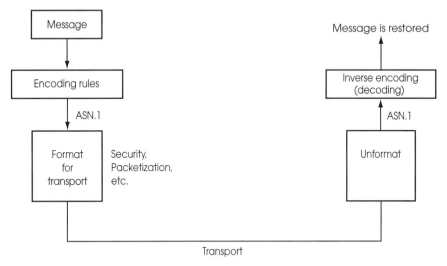

Figure 7-19 Information Transport Using ASN.1

27. Some encoding rules, such as the Distinguished Encoding Rules (DER), allow only one way to encode variables. However, the Basic Encoding Rules (BER) used in the PacketCable Electronic Surveillance specification permit multiple encodings.

program that actually places a value into the variable "value" for transmission, or reads the value of the variable "value" upon reception, as in Figure 7-20.

Suppose, however, that we could examine the actual stream of octets flowing between the transmitter and receiver. What would it look like? The short answer is "It depends".

Suppose that we place the four hexadecimal octets 09 87 65 43 into the variable "value". These may be encoded, for example, as 04 04 09 87 65 43. The recipient of this octet stream would correctly interpret this as a 4-octet OCTET STRING containing the values 09 87 65 43.

However, the transmitter could equally well have encoded the variable "value" as 24 08 04 02 09 87 04 02 65 43. The recipient of this (quite different) octet stream would also interpret this as a 4-octet OCTET STRING containing the values 09 87 65 43.

Consequently, because the CDC messages are specified in ASN.1 with Basic Encoding Rules, it is not useful to try to describe the messages in the more usual

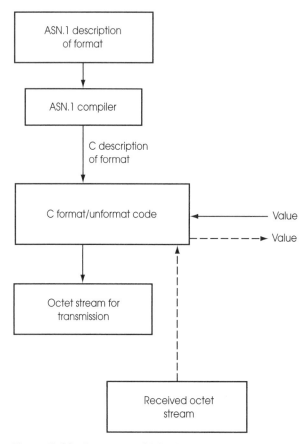

Figure 7-20 Example of ASN.1 and Message Flow

"this octet goes here" manner used for most of the messages in the various PacketCable protocols.

We give the complete ASN.1 description of these CDC messages, followed by a more detailed description of each message.

```
PCESP DEFINITIONS IMPLICIT TAGS ::=
BEGIN


Message ::=  CHOICE {
 answer                          [1]  Answer,
 ccclose                         [2]  CCClose,
 ccopen                          [3]  CCOpen,
                                 [4]  NULL,
 origination                     [5]  Origination,
                                 [6]  NULL,
 redirection                     [7]  Redirection,
 release                         [8]  Release,
                                 [9]  NULL,
 terminationattempt              [10] TerminationAttempt,
                                 [11] NULL,
 ccchange                        [12] CCChange
}


Answer ::= SEQUENCE {
                                 [0]  CaseId,
                                 [1]  AccessingElementId,
                                 [2]  EventTime,
                                 [3]  CallId,
 answering                       [4]  PartyId              OPTIONAL
}


CCChange ::= SEQUENCE {
                                 [0]  CaseId,
                                 [1]  AccessingElementId,
                                 [2]  EventTime,
                                 [3]  CallId,
                                 [4]  EXPLICIT CCCId       OPTIONAL,
 originating                     [5]  SDP                  OPTIONAL,
 terminating                     [6]  SDP                  OPTIONAL
}


CCClose ::= SEQUENCE {
                                 [0]  CaseId,
                                 [1]  AccessingElementId,
```

```
                                          [2] EventTime,
                                          [3] EXPLICIT CCCId
        }

        CCOpen ::= SEQUENCE {
                                          [0] CaseId,
                                          [1] AccessingElementId,
                                          [2] EventTime,
                                          CHOICE {
                                                  [3] SEQUENCE OF CallId,
                                                  [4] NULL
                                          } ,
                                          [5] EXPLICIT CCCId,
         originating                      [6] SDP,
         terminating                      [7] SDP
        }

        Origination ::= SEQUENCE {
                                          [0] CaseId,
                                          [1] AccessingElementId,
                                          [2] EventTime,
                                          [3] CallId,
         calling                          [4] PartyId,
         called                           [5] PartyId                    OPTIONAL,
         input
                                          CHOICE {
         userinput                                [6] VisibleString (SIZE (1..32)),
         translationinput                         [7] VisibleString (SIZE (1..32))
                                          } ,
                                          [8] NULL,
                                          [9] TransitCarrierId           OPTIONAL
        }

        Redirection ::= SEQUENCE {
                                          [0] CaseId,
                                          [1] AccessingElementId,
                                          [2] EventTime,
         old                              [3] CallId,
         redirectedto                     [4] PartyId,
                                          [5] TransitCarrierId           OPTIONAL,
                                          [6] NULL,
                                          [7] NULL,
         new                              [8] CallId                     OPTIONAL,
         redirectedfrom                   [9] PartyId                    OPTIONAL
        }
```

```
Release ::= SEQUENCE {
                              [0] CaseId,
                              [1] AccessingElementId,
                              [2] EventTime,
                              [3] CallId
}


TerminationAttempt ::= SEQUENCE {
                              [0] CaseId,
                              [1] AccessingElementId,
                              [2] EventTime,
                              [3] CallId,
 calling                      [4] PartyId,
 called                       [5] PartyId                OPTIONAL,
                              [6] NULL,
                              [7] RedirectedFromInfo      OPTIONAL
}


AccessingElementId ::= VisibleString (SIZE(1..15))


--   This is a copy of the Element ID present in the
--   Event Message specification [PKT-SP-EM]
CallId ::= SEQUENCE {
 sequencenumber               [0] VisibleString (SIZE(1..25)),
 systemidentity               [1] VisibleString (SIZE(1..15))
}


-- The Delivery Function generates this structure from the
-- CallID contained in the Event Messages by converting
-- the timestamp (32 bits) and eventcounter (32 bits) into
-- ASCII strings, separating them with a comma, and
-- placing the resulting string in the sequencenumber above


CaseId ::= VisibleString (SIZE(1..25))


CCCId ::= CHOICE {
 combCCC                      [0] VisibleString (SIZE(1..20)),
                              [1] NULL
}


-- The Delivery Function generates this structure from the
-- CCCId contained in the Event Messages by converting
-- the 32-bit value into an ASCII string.
EventTime ::= GeneralizedTime
```

```
PartyId ::= SEQUENCE {
                                    [0]  NULL                     OPTIONAL,
                                    [1]  NULL                     OPTIONAL,
                                    [2]  NULL                     OPTIONAL,
                                    [3]  NULL                     OPTIONAL,
                                    [4]  NULL                     OPTIONAL,
                                    [5]  NULL                     OPTIONAL,
     dn                             [6]  VisibleString (SIZE(1..15))  OPTIONAL,
                                    [7]  NULL                     OPTIONAL,
                                    [8]  NULL                     OPTIONAL,
                                    [9]  NULL                     OPTIONAL,
                                    [10] NULL                     OPTIONAL,
                                    [11] NULL                     OPTIONAL,
     trunkId                        [12] VisibleString (SIZE(1..32))  OPTIONAL
}


RedirectedFromInfo ::= SEQUENCE {
     lastRedirecting                [0]  PartyId              OPTIONAL,
     originalCalled                 [1]  PartyId              OPTIONAL,
     numRedirections                [2]  INTEGER (1..100)     OPTIONAL
}


SDP ::= VisibleString (SIZE(1..2048))


TransitCarrierId ::= VisibleString (SIZE(3..7))


END
```

Answer

The Answer message is used (perhaps not surprisingly) to report that a call under surveillance has been answered. The DF will typically receive two event messages when a user goes off-hook. First it will receive an Answer message, followed almost immediately by a QoS_Start message as soon as QoS resources are committed (which is equivalent to cut-through in the PSTN). The DF should transmit a PCESP Answer to the CF at the first indication that a call has been answered (see Table 7-31). The meaning of the word "Optional (in the Table 7-31 column heading)" in this specification is not its common one. In other words, it does not mean "may or may not be included at the implementor's disgression". Rather, it has the rather tortuous reading "this must be included if known, but there may be circumstances in which it is unknown, in which case it may be omitted". We follow the convention used in the specification, perhaps unwisely.

Table 7-31 PCESP Answer Message

Attribute Name	Mandatory/ Optional	Comment
Case_ID	M	Used to identify the court order under which this tap is being prosecuted
Accessing_Element_ID	M	Identifies the IAP
Event_Time	M	The date and time at which the event occurred
Call_ID	M	Uniquely identifies a call within a system. This is the same Call_ID as appears in the related Origination or TerminationAttempt message.
Answering_Party_ID	O	Include to identify the destination of the call, when known, if it is different from the called party identifier. If the call terminated within the originator's PacketCable network, this is the number of the answering party. If the call terminated at a PSTN gateway, this is the identity of the last known destination for this call.

CCChange

When a change in SDP associated with a call under interception occurs, the LEA must be informed of the fact; otherwise it may not be possible for the LEA to correctly convert the incoming RTP packets correctly. The CCChange message is used to signal the change to the LEA (see Table 7-32).

Table 7-32 PCESP CCChange Message

Attribute Name	Mandatory/ Optional	Comment
Case_ID	M	Used to identify the court order under which this tap is being prosecuted
Accessing_Element_ID	M	Identifies the IAP
Event_Time	M	The date and time at which the signaling change became effective
		(continue)

Table 7-32 PCESP CCChange Message (cont.)

Attribute Name	Mandatory/ Optional	Comment
Call_ID	M	Uniquely identifies a call within a system. This is the same Call_ID as appears in the related Origination or TerminationAttempt message.
Originating_SDP	O	The SDP information for the originating endpoint if that SDP has been changed
Terminating_SDP	O	The SDP information for the terminating endpoint if that SDP has been changed
CCC_ID	M if CCC-ID value for this call is changing; O otherwise	The CCC-ID value that will appear in all intercepted packets for this call.

CCClose

The CCClose message is used to inform the LEA that it should expect no more content packets for a call under interception. It is transmitted to the LEA when resources associated with a call are released (see Table 7-33).

Table 7-33 PCESP CCClose Message

Attribute Name	Mandatory/ Optional	Comment
Case_ID	M	Used to identify the court order under which this tap is being prosecuted
Accessing_Element_ID	M	Identifies the IAP
Event_Time	M	The date and time at which the event occurred
CCC_ID	M	The CCC-ID value that appeared in the intercepted packets associated with this call. (Usually this value does not change throughout the call, but if it does change— for example, in a CCChange message—then the CCClose message reflects the most recent value.)

CCOpen

The CCOpen message is used to indicate that a call under interception has committed QoS resources in at least one direction. It contains enough information for the LEA to be able to decode the voice traffic in both directions. There is a slight subtlety here. There will typically be a very brief period in which the QoS resources are open in only one direction. Suppose that resources are committed in the direction AB but not yet in the direction BA. Now if B sends a packet to A *during this brief interval,* it will be traveling over a path without guaranteed QOS. Theoretically, therefore, that packet should not be tapped. It is up to the IAP *not* to forward the packet to the DF, since the DF will otherwise forward the packet to the LEA. See Table 7-34.

Table 7-34 PCESP CCOpen Message

Attribute Name	Mandatory/ Optional	Comment
Case_ID	M	Used to identify the court order under which this tap is being prosecuted
Accessing_Element_ID	M	Identifies the IAP
Event_Time	M	Identifies the date and time that the first voice packet utilizing QoS resources was detected
Call_ID	M	Uniquely identifies a call within a system. This is the same Call_ID as appears in the related Origination or TerminationAttempt message.
Originating_SDP	M	The SDP information for the originating endpoint
Terminating_SDP	M	The SDP information for the terminating endpoint
CCC_ID	M	The CCC-ID value that will appear in all intercepted packets for this call

Origination

The Origination message is used to signal to the LEA any of the following events.

1. The subject is attempting to place a call, and the network has determined either that the destination is a valid on-net number or that the destination lies off-net. If the network has translated the digits input by the subject (for

example, an 800-number translation or a speed dial service), that information is included in the message.

2. The subject is attempting the place a call, and the network has determined that the dialed number does not represent a valid destination.

3. The subject attempted to place a call but then caused the call to be abandoned (for example, by going on-hook) before the call routing could be completed.

Depending on the way that the network is configured, the network may not always know when situation number 3 arises. For example, in a DCS network, or in certain kinds of NCS networks, the MTA stores dialed strings locally until the complete string matches an internal digit map. Only when the MTA determines that the subscriber has dialed a valid digit sequence is the network notified that a call is under way. On the PSTN, Law Enforcement Agencies receive digits from partially dialed calls. On a PacketCable network, this may not always be possible, depending on how the network is configured.

Since the MTA is not an Intercept Access Point (because it is untrusted) the fact that a partial string was dialed cannot always be reported to the DF—and hence to the LEA (see Table 7-35).

Table 7-35 PCESP Origination Message

Attribute Name	Mandatory/ Optional	Comment
Case_ID	M	Used to identify the court order under which this tap is being prosecuted
Accessing_Element_ID	M	Identifies the IAP
Event_Time	M	Identifies the date and time that the translation was completed
Call_ID	M	Uniquely identifies a call within a system. The unique Call_ID included in the Origination message is used to correlate other messages.
Calling_Party_ID	M	The phone number of originating party
Called_Party_ID	O	Must be included when the identity of the called party is known. This is not present for calls that were partially dialed or could not be completed by the network.

Attribute Name	Mandatory/ Optional	Comment
		Note that under some network configurations, the fact that the subject goes off-hook, dials a partial string then goes on-hook will not be transmitted to any IAP. In this circumstance, no record of the subjects actions exists within the network, and so cannot be forwarded to an LEA.
User_Input	O	The digits dialed by the subject
Translation_Input	O	Identifies input to a translation process (for example, 800 number, network-based speed dial input). One of the fields User_Input and Translation_Input must be present.
Transit_Carrier_ID	O	Must be included when a transit carrier is used to transport the call (the call goes off-net).

Redirection

The Redirection message is used to indicate that a call under surveillance has been redirected by either the direct action of the subject or by the network operating on the subject's behalf. In general, this means that one of the following events has occurred.

1. An incoming call to the subject has been automatically forwarded to another destination.

2. An incoming call to the subject has been forwarded by the subject's direct intervention.

3. A call originated by the subject has been transferred by the subject to another destination.

Although it is not mandatory, a Redirection message may also be sent if a call under surveillance is redirected by a party other than the subject (see Table 7-36).

Table 7-36 PCESP Redirection Message

Attribute Name	Mandatory/ Optional	Comment
Case_ID	M	Used to identify the court order under which this tap is being prosecuted
Accessing_System_ID	M	Identifies the IAP
Event_Time	M	The date and time at which the event occurred
Call_ID	M	Uniquely identifies a call within a system. The unique Call_ID included in the Origination message is used to correlate other messages.
New_Call_ID	O	Included when the redirected call will be identified by a different Call-ID in future CDC messages
Redirected_from_Party_ID	O	Identifies the phone number which is no longer an endpoint of this call
Redirected_to_Party_ID	M	Identifies the phone number to which the call is being redirected
Transit_Carrier_ID	O	Must be included when a transit carrier is used to transport the call (the call goes off-net)

Release

The Release message signals the end of a call for which a prior Answer message has been sent (see Table 7-37).

Table 7-37 PCESP Release Message

Attribute Name	Mandatory/ Optional	Comment
Case_ID	M	Used to identify the court order under which this tap is being prosecuted
Accessing_System_ID	M	Identifies the IAP
Event_Time	M	The date and time at which the event occurred
Call_ID	M	Uniquely identifies a call within a system. The unique Call_ID included in the Origination message is used to correlate other messages.

TerminationAttempt

This message signals that an incoming call is being made to the subject (see Table 7-38).

Table 7-38 PCESP TerminationAttempt Message

Attribute Name	Mandatory/ Optional	Comment
Case_ID	M	Used to identify the court order under which this tap is being prosecuted
Accessing_Sytem_ID	M	Identifies the IAP
Event_Time	M	The date and time at which the event occurred
Call_ID	M	Uniquely identifies a call within a system. The unique Call_ID included in the TerminationAttempt message is used to correlate the other messages.
Calling_Party_ID	M	Identifies the originating party
Called_Party_ID	O	Included if this information is more specific than the surveillance subject identity associated with the Case_ID
Redirected_From_Info	O	Included if information about previous redirections for the incoming call is available to the IAP

CCC Message Format

The actual voice content of a call is transported in messages delivered across the logical Call Content Connection (CCC) interface. These messages are very simple. The DF receives incoming intercept packets from a CMTS. These packets are identical to the audio packets sent to and from the MTA under surveillance, with the addition of an extra IP header that allows the packets to be routed by the network to the DF instead of to their original destination. Note that the original IP header is retained, as part of the data in the packet.

When it receives such a packet, the DF strips the extraneous header, replacing it with the four-octet CCC-ID for this call. It then adds a new IP header that directs the packet to the CF and transmits it to the demarcation point. This is shown in Figure 7-21.

Example Call Flow

Most call flows that make use of PCESP messaging are quite simple. There are occasions, however, when calls flows can become remarkably complex. These typically

Original IP packet:

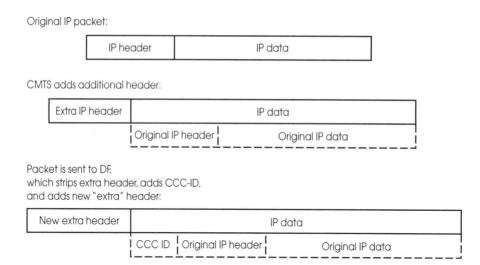

Figure 7-21   CCC Message Format

occur when the phones of major underground figures are being tapped and the subject suspects that this is the case. Such calls may be routed through a tortuous path of forwardings and transfers through several metropolitan areas, perhaps even crossing the country one or more times, simply in an attempt to thwart the attempt to surveil the call.[28] The PacketCable specification is designed to work correctly even in these cases. However, to protect what remains of both your and our sanity, we will look only at the simple case where a suspect is making an on-net to on-net call.

One basic call flow for the case when a suspect originates an on-net call on an NCS network is shown in Figure 7-22 (from which much of the irrelevant messaging has been removed). As usual, there is the caveat that this is only one flow of many that might be used in practice.

1. When the first NTFY reaches the CMS, the CMS sends a Signaling_Start Event Message to the DF.

2. The DF looks up the case number contained in the received Event Message and correlates it with an output port to which PCESP messages will be sent. It sends a PCESP Originate message to this port (and hence to the Law Enforcement Agency's CF).

---

28. Yes, the word "surveil" is in my dictionary. According to the *Oxford English Dictionary,* the etymology is somewhat interesting: "surveil" was back-formed from "surveillance".

3. In the GATE-SET that the CMS sends to the originating CMTS, it includes an Electronic-Surveillance-Parameters object that advises the CMTS that this call is under surveillance and the identity of the DF to which messages should be sent.

4. When the CMS is notified that the destination party has answered, it sends a Call_Answer Event Message to the DF.

5. The DF translates this into an Answer message and sends it to the CF.

6. As soon as the resources are committed for this call, the CMTS sends to the DF a QoS_Start Event Message.

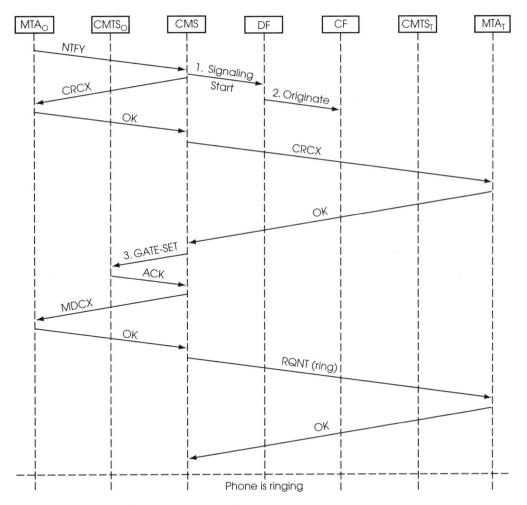

Figure 7-22 Electronic Surveillance Call Flow (continued)

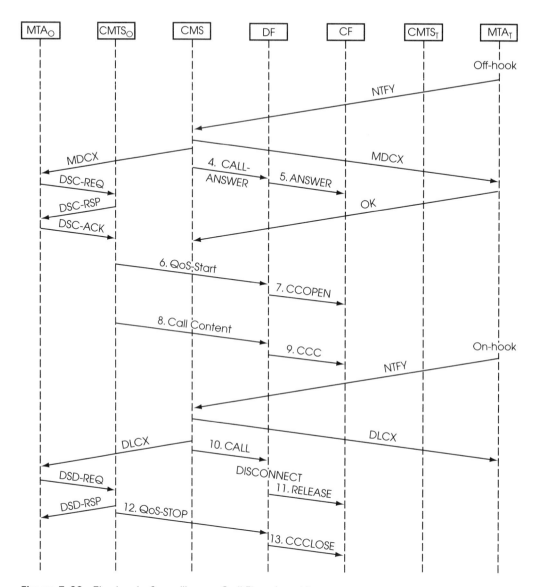

Figure 7-22 Electronic Surveillance Call Flow (cont.)

7. The DF sends a CCOpen message to the CF, indicating that bearer-channel traffic is now beginning to flow.

8. During the call, the CMTS clones the bearer traffic and forwards it to the DF.

9. The DF packages it in CCC messages and forwards the traffic to the CF. The DF does not attempt to decrypt the traffic (which will be RC4 encrypted). The

Law Enforcement Agency has been handed the key for the traffic, since it was included in the QoS_Start Event Message and hence the CCOpen.

10. When the destination party hangs up, a Call_Disconnect Event Message is sent to the DF.

11. The DF sends a RELEASE to the CF.

12. When the DOCSIS dynamic service flow is deleted, the CMTS sends a QoS_Stop to the DF to indicate that there will be no more bearer traffic.

13. The DF sends a CCClose to the CF, allowing it to "stop the tape recorder".

Complications

Although the PCESP specification was written in such a way that electronic surveillance functioned "properly" in all the cases that the authors imagined, the basic premise of the architecture is that the network must provide the correct input to the Delivery Function. This is not always as simple as it might seem, and it does mean that some devices need to implement functionality in ways that perhaps are not obvious.

A prime example is to consider what happens in the case where an off-net subscriber, Agnes, places a call to an on-net suspect, Bernard, who has his phone set to automatically forward all calls off-net to Charlie's number. Since Bernard is a suspect (we will assume that his calls are subject to a call-content wiretap order), even though the call is forwarded back off-net, the signaling and content of the call must be passed to Law Enforcement, even though the end result of the call-forwarding process is that a call is taking place between Agnes and Charlie.

We shall see in the next chapter that calls to and from the PSTN pass through a device known as a PSTN gateway. In the example we have just cited, ordinarily one might choose to design the PSTN gateway in such a way that the voice traffic, which enters on one PSTN trunk, would simply be shunted straight back out again on another trunk. That is, it would never enter the PacketCable network. However, this content now has to be delivered to a DF. As a consequence, the traffic must be digitized and encrypted. (This in turn means that the "inbound" side of the gateway must communicate with the "outbound" side of the same gateway as if they were a pair of MTAs. In particular, they must agree on a shared secret from which the RC4 encryption key can be generated. This key is then forwarded to the DF in a QoS_Start Event Message that is generated when Charlie goes off-hook.) The encrypted traffic is forwarded to the DF as usual (see Figure 7-23).

This example serves to illustrate that the design of all devices designated as Intercept Access Points in the network must be carefully thought out so that the devices can properly deliver the necessary event messaging and bearer traffic to the DF.

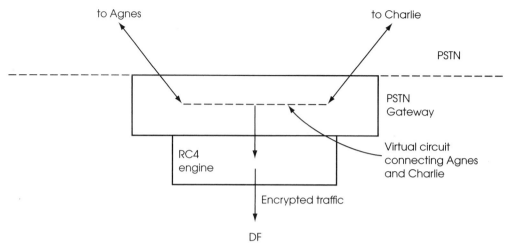

Figure 7-23 Intercepting an Off-Net to Off-Net Call That Passes Through a PSTN Gateway

8

Interworking with the PSTN

*The gateway . . . becomes a simple device, without any call state,
that receives general instructions from the Media Gateway Controller
without any need to know about or even understand the concept of calls,
call states, features, or feature interactions.*

PKT-SP-TGCP-I01-991201

In this chapter we will examine how a PacketCable network interfaces seamlessly to the PSTN, allowing subscribers on a PacketCable network to transparently place calls to, and receive calls from, users located on the PSTN or on other networks that themselves connect to the PSTN.

In a way, the need to interwork correctly with the PSTN, although naturally vital for a PacketCable network, is not part of its core functionality. Accordingly, and since some of the details can be quite complex without adding much to one's understanding of the process, we shall not cover this topic to the same depth as we have covered the rest of the PacketCable network. For a fuller treatment of the issues discussed here, the reader is referred to the PacketCable specifications themselves.

Figure 8-1 shows the basic topology. Any general-purpose telephony network attached to the PSTN (including other PacketCable networks) can be reached by using the PSTN as an intermediate carrier of the signaling and bearer channel information.

It is important to note that the PSTN is fundamentally a *telephony* network. While PacketCable networks have been designed with the goal of initially emulating many of the features of the PSTN, the fact that they are inherently packet-based means that they are not subject to many of the limitations of the PSTN. As PacketCable operators begin to deploy advanced services that rely on features available only to packet networks, there will be an increasing divergence between

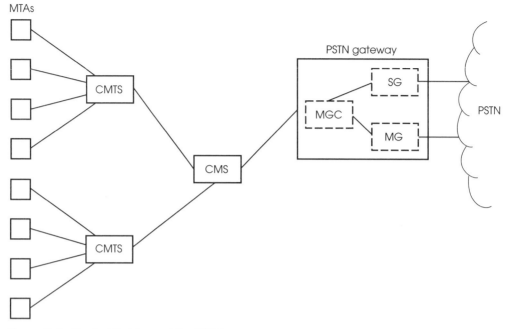

Figure 8-1   PacketCable and the PSTN

PacketCable and the PSTN, although basic PSTN emulation will likely always remain as one "feature" of PacketCable networks. Increasingly, however, on-net to on-net calls will have access to a wider range of services than those that traverse any segment off-net.

Architecture

Figure 8-2 is an expanded view of part of Figure 8-1, and it shows the basic PacketCable architecture for interworking with the PSTN ("interworking" is the telephony term for "interoperating").

Calls to or from the PSTN pass through a **PSTN gateway** at the point where the two networks touch. The PSTN can be broken down into three conceptual components: a **Media Gateway (MG)** that acts as the intermediary between the two networks for media; a **Signaling Gateway (SG)** that acts as the intermediary between the two networks for signaling; and a **Media Gateway Controller (MGC)** that (unsurprisingly) controls the Media Gateway.

Fundamentally, the PSTN gateway appears like a proxy-MTA to the PacketCable network. When an MTA places a call that will go off-net, the MTA will in general be unaware of the fact that the call is going off-net. For almost all purposes, the traffic

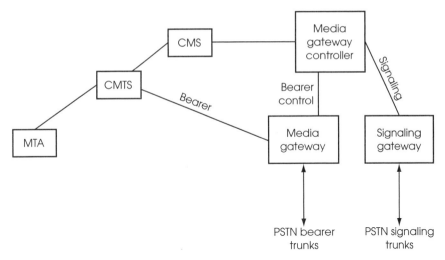

Figure 8-2 PSTN Interworking Architecture

to and from the originating MTA is exactly as if it were talking to another on-net MTA. The same is true for an incoming call from the PSTN: The on-net MTA is generally unaware that it is communicating with a PSTN gateway instead of another MTA.

Because the gateway must act as if it were an MTA, it must have many of the features of an MTA. For example, it must be able to signal its preference of codecs and encryption schemes. It must also be able to derive encryption and authentication keys, and (most importantly) it must be able to encrypt and decrypt the bearer traffic as it passes on to and off the PacketCable network. Since the PSTN has no concept of encrypted bearer traffic, all traffic must be decrypted before being placed into the PSTN or encrypted on arrival from the PSTN. Even though the RC4 encryption engine is very lightweight, since every RTP stream is encrypted, encryption and decryption can place a significant burden on a large PSTN gateway that may be carrying many hundreds of conversations simultaneously.

As well as handling the actual bearer-channel traffic, the PSTN gateway is responsible for converting signaling from the Signaling System Number 7 (SS7) protocol used on the PSTN to whichever signaling protocol is in use on the PacketCable network. This allows the PacketCable network to offer common telephony features such as Caller-ID even when one party is on-net and the other is off-net.

In the modern PSTN, media and signaling are segregated. It was not always thus. Until quite recently, signaling traveled in-band along the same physical circuits as those used to carry media. The signaling was tone-based, which allowed sophisticated thefts of service to occur by unscrupulous people equipped with tone-generators (or even whistles) placed near the microphone of the handset.

To combat these attacks, the PSTN evolved into a dual-network system in which the signaling and the media became segregated.[1] Thus the need for two gateways on the PacketCable network—one for signaling and one for media—to convert correctly between the single IP-based PacketCable network and the dual networks on the PSTN.

Signaling

We will look first at the conversion of call signaling information between a PacketCable network and the PSTN. The PSTN uses a signaling architecture and protocol suite called SS7 (Signaling System Number 7). The protocol used to transport PSTN-related signaling information on the PacketCable network is the **Internet Signaling Transport Protocol (ISTP)**. ISTP is designed to act as a bridge between basic IP transport mechanisms and application-level signaling. It implements analogs of many of the operations and interfaces used by various SS7 protocols, allowing the PacketCable network to carry a rich mix of signaling information.

In the protocol stack, ISTP sits directly above TCP and below protocols such as TCAP and ISUP, which are discussed in this chapter. TCP is used because signaling has to travel over a reliable transport. However, TCP, because of its inherent delays, is not ideal for transporting real-time signaling information, and work is currently under way in the IETF to define a so-called Stream Control Transmission Protocol (SCTP) that is designed to provide a better transport mechanism for real-time events in a reliable manner. When SCTP becomes stable, it is expected that it will supplant TCP as the transport protocol of choice for carrying ISTP on PacketCable networks.

ISTP is a generic protocol, designed to support a wide variety of network configurations. Network elements that use ISTP are known as ISTP-Users. In PacketCable, the ISTP-Users are the CMS, the MGC and the SG. Figure 8-3 shows typical protocol stacks on the ISTP-Users in a PacketCable network. Note that the SG contains dual stacks, one for the PacketCable side and one for the SS7 side.

ISTP contains functions for the following.

- Initialization
- Registration of circuit IDs with the SG
- Mapping addresses between SS7 and IP domains

---

1. A few attacks are still possible, typically from pay phones as many of these still use in-band tone-signaling to signal when coins are deposited.

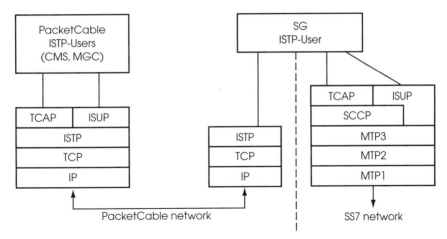

Figure 8-3 Protocol Stacks in PacketCable ISTP-Users

- ISUP maps based on Point Code and Circuit Identification Code

- TCAP maps based on Point Code and Transaction ID

- Reliable ISUP/TCAP message delivery

- Maintenance

- Activation and deactivation of Circuit IDs in the SG

- Error recovery from faults and from congestion

  — SS7 Signaling Point Inaccessible

  — SS7 Signaling Network Inaccessible

  — MGC Inaccessible

  — CMS Inaccessible

  — Signaling Point Congested

  — Signaling Link Congested

  — MGC Congested

  — CMS Congested

Two different protocols use the services of ISTP in PacketCable networks. The first of these is the **Integrated Services Digital Networks User Part**, **ISUP**. ISUP is used to carry out-of-band signaling information between the SG and the MGC, which in turn uses these signals to control the MG, as in Figure 8-4.

The second protocol that uses the services of ISTP is **TCAP**, the **Transaction Capabilities Application Protocol**, which is another of the SS7 suite of protocols.

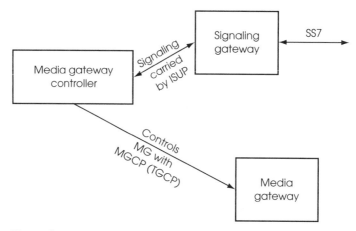

Figure 8-4 ISUP Between the SG and the MGC

TCAP is used to allow network devices to query external databases on the PSTN for information such as 800-number lookup[2] and **Local Number Portability (LNP)** routing. Local Number Portability databases provide a mapping between a number and the provider responsible for servicing that number. This allows a subscriber to keep the same number when he changes service providers. The only devices currently permitted to perform such lookups are the CMS and the MGC. Consequently the only interfaces permitted to carry TCAP are those between these two devices and the SG (see Figure 8-5).

The SG lies at the interface of the PSTN SS7 and the PacketCable networks. To the SS7 network, it appears as a "signaling endpoint", understanding and responding

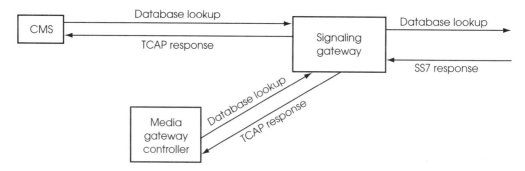

Figure 8-5 TCAP on a PacketCable Network

---

2. When the user dials a toll-free number, the network resolves the dialed number into a "real" phone number, which is the actual destination of the call.

correctly to the complex, low-level signaling protocols such as SCCP, MTP3, MTP2 and MTP1 (whose details are beyond the scope of this book).

The SG converts the low-level SS7 messages to the relatively high-level ISUP and TCAP equivalents, which the PacketCable devices can interpret and implement relatively easily. The SG must manage all aspects of this conversion, including ensuring that the correct PacketCable device receives the particular message.

Mapping

It is the responsibility of the SG to manage correctly a large number of addresses and identifiers of various kinds so that the correct conversions take place as messages travel between the two networks. This is a far from trivial task. Since this book concerns itself with the PacketCable network, which is basically a simple IP network, it would be inappropriate to spend too much time discussing the intricacies of addresses and identifiers on the SS7 network. Unfortunately, we cannot avoid the task completely, since at least some understanding of the complexity is necessary to understand properly the job of the Signaling Gateway. (For a thorough discussion of SS7, see *Signaling System #7* by Travis Russell, published by McGraw-Hill; ISBN 0-0-07-058032-4.)

SS7 uses several numbering schemes to identify elements on the network. Here are the important ones for our purposes.

Point Code

> This is essentially the address of a particular logical device on the SS7 network. The Point Code may be divided into three fields, representing the network number, the number of the cluster within a network, and the number of the member within a particular cluster. In ANSI, each of the three components is a single (binary) octet. The ITU has a similar scheme, but with fields of size 3 bits, 8 bits and 3 bits, respectively.

Circuit Identification Code (CIC)

> This 2-octet value identifies a particular trunk circuit used by a particular voice path.

ISTP adds a further value, the **Circuit Identity** (**CID**, pronounced "kid"), which is a combination of a Point Code and a CIC. A CID may be thought of as an identifier for a particular (single) network resource. When used to identify trunks (connections) within an MG, the CID is a "fixed" value, in the sense that once a trunk has been identified by a particular CID during initialization, the identity does not change. The Signaling Gateway maintains a mapping between CIDs and IP addresses that is used in the following manner.

When the SG receives an incoming SS7 ISUP message, the message contains in its header the following elements.

- CIC

- **Signaling Link Selection (SLS) code**, which is unused by PacketCable

- Origination and Destination Point Codes (OPC and DPC, respectively)

The Signaling Gateway merges the Destination Point Code and the Circuit Identification Code to produce a Circuit Identity, which it can then map to the IP address of the particular Media Gateway Controller responsible for managing the CID (which, remember, identifies the trunk on a particular MG), to which it can route the message. The SG does not need to be aware of the fact that the MGC does not directly manage the trunk and that the MGC is acting merely as a proxy for the MG.

The detailed initialization, administration and management of the databases used to allow the SG to perform address translation are undefined by the PacketCable specifications and are left to each individual equipment vendor to implement as that vendor sees fit.

In the PacketCable network, the SG is considered to be an ISTP server. The MGC and CMS act as clients, which means that during initialization of their ISTP stacks, a long-lived connection is constructed to the SG. This connection is assumed to exist permanently as long as the client device is operational. PacketCable and other specifications define the procedure to be followed in the event that one of the devices at the end of an ISTP connection goes down. Essentially, the procedure is that the failure should be quickly detected and failover to a backup device must occur.

Media Control

The Media Gateway (MG)[3] is responsible for managing the transfer of media between the PacketCable network and the PSTN. As we have mentioned earlier, it is controlled by a Media Gateway Controller (MGC). The protocol used to manage the MG is the **Trunking Gateway Control Protocol (TGCP)**.

TGCP is, like NCS, a profile of MGCP. Therefore TGCP shares many features with NCS. Much of what follows is covered in more detail in the chapter on NCS. Also, it's worth emphasizing that TGCP is used to manage the Media Gateway even in a DCS network.

---

3. The Media Gateway is occasionally referred to as the **Trunking Gateway (TGW)**. We will use only the former term.

A Media Gateway has characteristics that differ from those of an MTA, and therefore a different profile of basic MGCP is needed to allow for the correct control of the facilities provided by an MG compared to those provided by an MTA.

The most fundamental difference between an MTA and an MG is that the endpoints associated with an MTA are physical handsets (or their surrogate—for example, a personal computer), whereas the endpoints associated with an MG are trunks within the PSTN. These are the major differences between NCS and TGCP.

Connection Modes

NCS supports connection modes "conference" and "replicate"; TGCP supports neither of these.

TGCP supports the connection modes "continuity test" and "loopback"; NCS supports neither of these.

The remaining connection modes are common to both NCS and TGCP.

Digit Maps

TGCP contains no support for digit maps; NCS does contain such support.

DQoS

TGCP contains no support for PacketCable Dynamic Quality of Service signaling; since the PSTN gateway lies within the core IP network, it does not need to support this signaling.

Event Packages

The defined event packages for the two protocols are different.

Protocol Name

The protocol name and version are carried in the first line of the header; for NCS this is MGCP 1.0 NCS 1.0; for TGCP it is MGCP 1.0 TGCP 1.0.

Naming Scheme

The naming schemes for endpoints in the two protocols are slightly different.

Provisional Responses

NCS supports provisional responses ("temporary" responses with 1xx reason codes). TGCP does not (yet) do so.

Every endpoint must have a name. As currently defined, all endpoints connected to a Media Gateway are of type "ds", and the name of every endpoint must begin with the string "ds/".

The general naming convention is that an endpoint name looks like this.

```
ds/<unit-type1>-<unit #>/<unit-type2>-<unit #>/ ... /<channel #>
```

This somewhat opaque definition is interpreted as follows.

- The first term (ds) defines the endpoint naming scheme and the type of the endpoint (in this case, a PSTN DS-0 trunk)

- The last term (<channel #>) is a decimal value representing the number of the channel on the trunk used by the endpoint (each trunk contains a number of logically separate channels)

- Intermediate terms contain two values, a unit-type and a unit-number, separated by a hyphen.

  — Currently defined unit-types are s, su, oc3, ds3, e3, ds2, e2, ds1 and e1. s is used to represent a particular slot number and su to represent a subunit within a particular slot.

  — The unit-number is a decimal value representing a particular instance of the unit-type. For example, a particular MG may contain 5 physical slots. Suppose that the third slot contains an OC3 interface, which itself supports a number of DS3 interfaces that support DS1 interfaces. Then the identifier used to identify a particular trunk (in this case the fifth) might look like this.

```
ds/s-3/oc3-1/ds3-1/ds1-2/5
```

Three different packages of events and signals are supported by TGCP. The default package is IT (for "ISUP trunk"). Other supported packages are MO (for "MF OSS") and MT (for "MF Terminating"). A given event within a package is referred to by the name <package-code>/<event-code>, except that the package code may be omitted if it is the default package (that is, "IT").

As in NCS, connections are referred to by a unique 32-bit identifier, and when a signal is to be applied to a particular connection the format used is:

```
<package>/<signal>@<connection>
```

For example, `IT/rt@0A99E2` represents the signal encoded as "rt" within the IT package ("rt" actually represents "ringback tone") that is to be applied to the connection number 0A99E2.

Note that because the endpoints on a Media Gateway are trunks, audible signals that are sent to an MG (by an MGC) are placed on the PSTN trunk and are therefore heard by the party on the PSTN side of the connection, not by the party on the

PacketCable side. Thus, for example, for an incoming call that originated on the PSTN, the MGC would typically signal the MG to play the rt signal as soon as the connection to the destination (that is, PacketCable) endpoint has been established but before the phone has gone off-hook.

Packages

In this section, we describe the events and signals supported by the three packages used to control MGs. The following legend describes the abbreviations used in the tables that appear in the subsections.

Event

> R: the event may be requested by the MGC (that is, the MGC may send an RQNT such that when the event occurs, a NTFY is sent to the MGC)

> P: the event is persistent

> S: the event is a state that may be audited

> C: the event may be detected on, or the signal may be applied to, a connection

Signal

> If the event can be signaled on command by the MGC, the kind of the signal is identified by one of:

> OO: an on/off signal; the signal remains in the state commanded by the MGC until such time as the device receives a command to change state from the MGC

> TO: a time-out signal; the signal remains on for a particular duration, unless it is superceded by a new signal.

> BR: a "brief" signal; the event has a known duration (either because it uses a default duration or because it has been provisioned to a particular value normally it is expected that the duration is at most a few seconds.)

IT—The ISUP Trunk Package

Table 8-1 defines the events and signals in the IT package.

co1

> A 2010 Hz tone, which may be either an event or a signal. When co1 is signaled, the tone lasts for a specific period of time. The default duration is 3 seconds, but this may be changed by provisioning. The event is generated when the tone ceases.

Table 8-1 Events and Signals in the IT Package

Code	Description	Event	Signal
co1	Continuity tone #1	R	TO
co2	Continuity tone #2	R	TO
ft	Fax tone	R	
ld	Long duration connection	C	
ma	Media start	C	
mt	Modem tone	R	
oc	Operation complete (successful)	R	
of	Operation failure	R	
ro	Reorder tone		TO
rt	Ringback tone		C, TO
TDD	TDD tones	R	

co2

A 1,780 Hz tone, which may be either an event or a signal. When co1 is signaled, the tone lasts for a specific period of time. The default duration is 3 seconds, but this may be changed by provisioning. The event is generated when the tone ceases.

ft

This event is generated when the gateway detects a fax tone. (This is sometimes called a "CNG tone" and is a series of brief 1,100 Hz tones that indicates that the initiator of the call is a fax machine.)

ld

This event is generated when a connection has been maintained for a "long" time. By default, the definition of "long" is one hour, but this value may be changed by the provisioning process. No specific changes are made to the connection when this event is detected. The event is designed merely to inform the controlling entity that the connection has been maintained for an extended period.

If no connection is specified during the request for this event, then it is generated whenever any single connection on the endpoint becomes "long" (although it is unclear what the purpose of such a "wildcard" ld event might be).

ma

> This signals the receipt of the first valid RTP packet on a connection. If no connection is specified during the request for this event, then it is generated whenever any single connection on the endpoint receives a valid RTP packet.

mt

> This event is generated when the gateway detects a modem tone (for modem communication at any speed).

oc

> This event is generated when a gateway applies a signal of type TO (time-out) and the signal completes without being interrupted by the detection of another requested event.

> The message may (but is not required to) report the identity of the signal that completed. For example, if a co1 event completes, then the SDP could look like this.

```
O: IT/oc(IT/co1)
```

> If the signal was applied to a particular connection, then the name of the connection may be included in the report.

```
O: IT/oc(IT/oc1@88AE32)
```

> These two syntaxes may be used only when reporting an oc event. They may not be used when an oc is Requested.

of

> This event is generated when a gateway applies a signal of type TO (time-out) and the signal fails before time-out. Note that failure is not the same as interruption by another event or signal. As in the case of the oc event, the message may report the identity of the signal that failed.

ro

> The reorder tone is sometimes called "fast busy" or "network busy" and is typically used to indicate that an end-to-end connection could not be generated due to a failure in the network.

rt

> The ringback tone is generated when an end-to-end connection has been made but the destination party has not yet gone off-hook. The precise cadence

of the ringback tone varies from country to country and may be changed through provisioning.

TDD

This event is generated when the gateway detects that a TDD device is in use.

MO—The Operator Services Package

This package is used for signaling and notification of events associated with special operator services. Operator services use special trunks (called "one-way MF Feature Group D trunks"), which are reserved for the purpose. Signaling applied to these trunks is called Operator Services Signaling, or OSS. The operator is sometimes called the OSS Operator.

The MO package is important because, for the foreseeable future, human operators (and the specialized services they provide) will be available only via connections to the PSTN. Eventually, the operators will be able to provide services using devices embedded within the IP network, but for the present all such interactions must pass through a PSTN gateway.

The operator communicates with ordinary subscribers by way of special trunks reserved specifically for the purpose. These trunks can carry specialized signals that only the operator may originate (by way of the operator console). The trunks also have special properties (such as, for example, the fact that only the operator may release them).

Operator signaling in the PSTN is a complex subject, well outside the focus of this book. However, Table 8-2, which defines the events and signals in the MO package, should give some indication of the kinds of signals and events that are important to providing operator services. For more details about exactly how these are to be interpreted, the reader is referred to Section 8 of the PacketCable PSTN Gateway Call Signaling Protocol specification, which contains numerous references to Bellcore documents that describe (in excruciating detail) exactly how operator signaling works within the PSTN.

The MO package is used to support E.911 calls, as well as ordinary operator services.

ans

This event indicates that the signaling indicates that the call has been answered by an operator. Once this occurs, the trunk will remain open until the operator releases it. In other words, the trunk will *not* be released if the non-operator party goes on-hook.

Table 8-2 Events and Signals in the MO Package

Code	Description	Event	Signal
ans	Call answer	P	
ft	Fax tone	R	
ld	Long duration connection	C	
mt	Modem tone	R	
orbk	Operator ringback	R	
rbz	Reverse make busy	P	
rcl	Operator recall		BR
rel	Release call	P	BR
res	Resume call		BR
rlc	Release complete	P, S	BR
sup	Call setup		BR
sus	Suspend call		BR
TDD	TDD tones	R	

ft

This event is generated when the gateway detects a fax tone.

ld

This event is generated when a connection has been maintained for a "long" time. By default, the definition of "long" is one hour, but this value may be changed by the provisioning process. No specific changes are made to the connection when this event is detected. The event is designed merely to inform the controlling entity that the connection has been maintained for an extended period.

If no connection is specified during the request for this event, then it is generated whenever any single connection on the endpoint becomes "long". Normally, however, a connection would be specified during the request.

mt

This event is generated when the gateway detects a modem tone (for modem communication at any speed).

orbk

> This event is generated when the operator requests (via the operator console) that the calling party be alerted. Typically, if the MTA is on-hook, the event will cause the phone to ring; if the MTA is off-hook, the reorder tone will be applied.

rbz

> This event is generated when the operator requests that the trunk be marked as busy.

rcl

> This signal is applied to invoke "operator recall"—for example when a customer performs a hookflash.

rel

> Although Release-Call may be signaled to the MG, the call will not actually be disconnected until the operator releases it. A rel event is generated when the operator actually releases the trunk.

res

> This signal is used to indicate to the MG that a call has been resumed by the non-operator party.

rlc

> This signal and event are used to confirm that the operator trunk has been released and is available for use by another party.

sup

> This sets up a call to the operator system service, using address and identification information provided in the Request. The syntax is:
>
> sup(addr(address_info), id(id_info))
>
> where typically each of address_info and id_info take the form:
>
> K0, comma-separated-list-of-digits, S0.
>
> So, for example, for call setup where the address information is 3034941111 and the identification information is 2021115555, the call setup signal would be:

```
sup(addr(K0, 3, 0, 3, 4, 9, 4, 1, 1, 1, 1, S0), id(K0, 2, 0, 2, 1, 1, 1, 5,
5, 5, 5, S0))
```

sus

> This signal indicates that the non-operator party has suspended the call (typically by going on-hook). However, the trunk is not released by this action, since only the operator may release the trunk.

TDD

> This event is generated when the gateway detects that a TDD device is in use.

MT—The MF Terminating Protocol Package

This package is designed to support two specialized services: **Busy Line Verify (BLV)** and **Operator Interrupt (OI)**.

BLV is used by an operator to determine that a line that is apparently in use is actually carrying traffic. Typically, if the line is carrying traffic, the console provides a garbled version of the traffic to the operator so that the operator is able to determine whether the line is in use and possibly the type of traffic being carried (for example, ordinary voice or data), but the operator cannot hear the plaintext traffic.

The OI (sometimes called **Emergency Interrupt**, or **EI**) service allows the operator to interrupt an existing conversation. These services use special trunks allocated solely for this purpose. These trunks are separate from those used for most other operator services. The MT package may be used only on these special BLV/OI trunks. Table 8-3 defines the events and signals in the MT package.

ans

> This signal informs the trunk that the verified party has gone off-hook (this includes the case where the party was off-hook initially).

bz

> The busy tone signal

hf

> Indicates that the verified party has performed a hookflash.

oc

> This event is generated when a gateway applies a signal of type TO (timeout) and the signal completes without being interrupted by the detection of another requested event.

Table 8-3 Events and Signals in the MT Package

Code	Description	Event	Signal
ans	Call answer		BR
bz	Busy tone		TO
hf	Hook flash		BR
oc	Operation complete	R	
of	Operation failure	R	
oi	Operator interrupt	R	
pst	Permanent signal tone		TO
rel	Release call	P	BR
res	Resume call		BR
rlc	Release complete	P, S	BR
ro	Reorder tone		TO
sup	Call setup	P	
sus	Suspend call		BR

of

This event is generated when a gateway applies a signal of type TO (time-out) and the signal fails before time-out. Note that failure is not the same as interruption by another event or signal.

oi

This event is generated when the operator attempts to interrupt an ongoing call. In the PSTN, this is audibly signaled by the presence of a tone on the trunk. However, there is no standard specification that defines the tone used to signal that an operator is interrupting a call. Therefore the MG is expected to detect a transition from background line noise to a significant energy level and to interpret this transition as an attempt by the operator to interrupt the call. When this transition is detected, therefore, the MG should generate the oi event.

This is a one-way transition. Once an Operator Interrupt has been detected, there is no way (short of releasing the trunk) to return to a non-interrupted state.

pst

Places a tone on the trunk.

rel

The MGC may use the rel signal to indicate that the MG should release the trunk. However, normally only the operator is permitted to release the trunk, and so the MG may choose to ignore such signals. When the verified party goes on-hook, typically the sus signal will be used rather than the rel signal.

When the operator releases the trunk, the MG will typically send a rel event to the MGC, informing it of the release.

res

This signal indicates that the verified party has resumed a call by going off-hook.

rlc

This signal and event are used to confirm that the operator trunk has been released and is available for use by another party.

ro

The reorder tone is sometimes called "fast busy" or "network busy" and is typically used to indicate that an end-to-end connection could not be generated due to a failure in the network.

sup

The Call Setup is used to indicate to the MGC that a call should be placed to a particular destination (for the purpose of issuing a subsequent BLV or OI). The format is:

sup(destination_address)

where the destination address is of the form K0, comma-separated-list-of-digits, S0.

For example, if the operator intends to perform a BLV on the number 4175551111, then the sup event would have the form:

sup(K0, 4, 1, 7, 5, 5, 5, 1, 1, 1, 1, S0)

sus

This signal indicates that the verified party has gone on-hook (suspending but not releasing the call, which can be done only by the operator).

Messages

The basic TGCP message set is the same as is used by NCS (and other profiles of MGCP). For details, see Chapter 4.

Example Call Flow

By now it has probably become clear that interworking with the PSTN is a nontrivial matter. This should not be surprising: The PSTN has been evolving for more than a hundred years, and it now spans the globe, performing a vast array of functions and providing an equally large array of features for which it was never designed.

Making the matter more complex is the fact that, like most of PacketCable (and the PSTN), although individual messages are well defined, as is much of the behavior triggered by the messages, the precise manner in which the messages can be put together to construct a functioning system remains unspecified.

We therefore provide an example call flow of an on-net to off-net call, emphasizing the functionality that occurs at the PSTN gateway. This, however, is only one of a large number of ways in which equivalent functionality could be obtained using the protocols as defined. (The PacketCable document PKT-TR-CF-ON-PSTN-V01-991201, for example, gives a rather different call flow that achieves the same result.)

The details of the interactions within the PacketCable network are not described in this call flow, since they are unimportant. The base signaling protocol could be either NCS or DCS (or some as yet unspecified signaling protocol that provides, at a minimum, equivalent functionality). Figure 8-6 is the basic call flow.

In order for the call to reach the PSTN gateway, the originating CMS queries a database with the destination phone number and determines that the call must be routed to the PSTN via a particular PSTN gateway. Typically, each CMS will route off-net calls only to a single PSTN gateway. A single PSTN gateway would typically serve a number of CMSes.

The call is passed to the MGC, which may be responsible for controlling more than one MG. It determines the correct MG for this call, if necessary. For the purpose of the example, the MGC decides to route the call through the MG called mg1.ratco.net. The MGC determines, for this example, that the trunk circuit will be tested for continuity before it is used. The first message is a combined RQNT and CRCX, which travels from the MGC to the MG.

```
CRCX 1051 ds/ds1-2/3@mg1.ratco.net MGCP 1.0 TGCP 1.0
    This is a Create Connection command, to create connection number 1050 on
    channel number three of the second DS1 unit on the MG called
    mg1@ratco.net. The protocol being used is version 1.0 of TGCP, which is
    itself a profile of version 1.0 of MGCP
C: 0123FC4A690EAA61
```

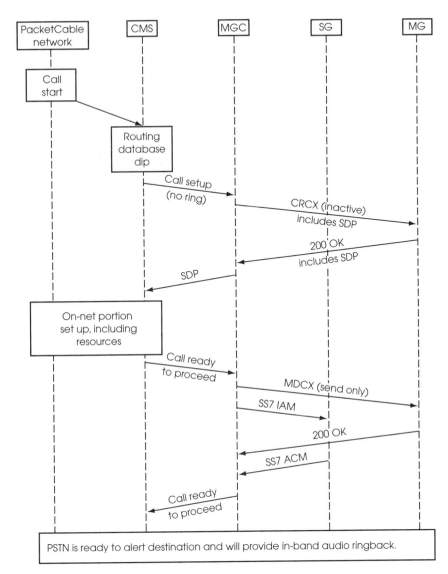

Figure 8-6 Example Flow for an On-Net to Off-Net Call (continued)

```
L: p:10, a:PCMU
M: inactive
X: 0123456789B0
R: co2, oc, of
    The MGC is registering that it wishes to be notified when the gateway
    detects any of the three events co2, oc, or in the default (IT) TGCP
    package.
```

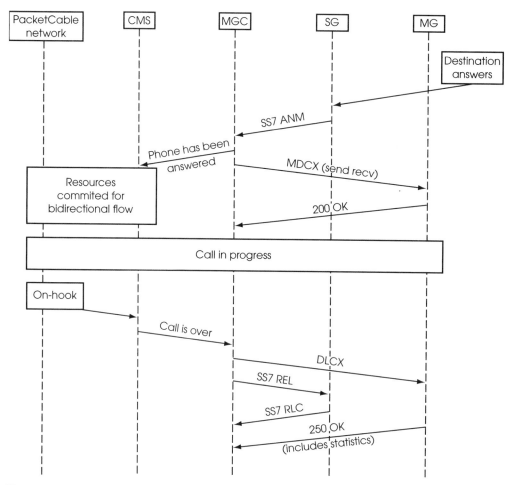

Figure 8-6 Example Flow for an On-Net to Off-Net Call (cont.)

```
S: co1
    The MG is to apply the co1 signal to the connection. If the trunk is
    indeed continuous, applying the co1 signal will result in a co2 event
    being received on the trunk, which will cause the co2 event to occur.
<blank line>
    A blank line separates SDP from the TGCP headers
v=0
o=- 25678 753849 IN IP4 10.96.41.1
s=-
c=IN IP4 10.96.41.1
t=0 0
m=audio 3456 RTP/AVP 0
```

The MG now performs the co1 test, placing a 2010 Hz signal on the trunk. In response (assuming that there is indeed continuity) it will receive a 1,780 Hz tone on the trunk. This causes the MG to detect the co2 event, which causes it to stop the co1 signal and to notify the MGC of the co2 event.

The message also instructs the MG to create a G.711 connection with a packetization interval of 10 milliseconds on the trunk, with the particular properties described by the SDP that follows the blank line.

The MG acknowledges message #1.

```
200 1051 OK
     The command has been received
I: 32F345E2
<blank line>
     A blank line separates SDP from the TGCP headers
v=0
o=- 4723891 7428910 IN IP4 10.96.63.25
s=-
c=IN IP4 10.96.63.25
t=0 0
m=audio 1297 RTP/AVP 0
```

The MGC sends an SS7 message (via the SG) to the switch at the far end of the trunk. This message informs the switch that continuity testing is being performed on the trunk, so that when the incoming 2,010 Hz tone is detected, the switch responds with a 1,780 Hz tone, thus triggering the co2 event on the MG.

When the co2 event occurs, the MG transmits message #3.

```
NTFY 2000 ds/ds1-2/3@mg1.ratco.net MGCP 1.0 TGCP 1.0
     This is a Notify message, number 2000, from this trunk, using TGCP 1.0
X: 0123456789B0
     The message pertains to this connection number
O: co2
     The detected event is co2 in the default (IT) package
```

The MGC informs the remote switch (through the SG) that the continuity test was successful. It also acknowledges Message #3 with Message #4.

```
200 2000 OK
     The MGC is acknowledging message number 2000

MDCX 1055 ds/ds1-2/3@mg1.ratco.net MGCP 1.0 TGCP 1.0
     Modify a connection; this is message number 1055, for the identified
     trunk, using TGCP 1.0
```

```
C: 0123FC4A690EAA61
I: 32F345E2
M: recvonly
   The connection should be permitted only to receive (for now); this
   allows the MTA to receive bearer-chanel information from the destination
X: 0123456789B0
R: ft, mt
   Detect and inform the MGC if fax tones or modem tones are detected; this
   allows the network to take special action if the communication is either
   fax or data
```

The network has now opened a one-way path from the destination party to the originating party. This allows the caller to hear any announcements or other audio that may be produced by the destination.

The MGC will receive a message via the SG that the destination party is being alerted (the phone at the far end is ringing). Typically, the ring cadence will be transmitted along the trunk and will pass through the receive-only connection at the MG and on to the calling party's MTA.

When the destination party goes off-hook, the MGC receives a signal to that effect via the SG. The MGC now modifies the connection so that it shifts into full-duplex mode.

```
MDCX 1101 ds/ds1-2/3@mg1.ratco.net MGCP 1.0 TGCP 1.0
   This is a ModifyConnection message, number 1101, to the identified
   trunk, using TGCP 1.0
C: 0123FC4A690EAA61
I: 32F345E2
M: sendrecv
   Make the connection full-duplex
```

The MG responds with this simple acknowledgement.

```
200 1101 OK
```

The MGC will normally signal the originating MTA (via the originating CMS) that the call has been answered. One or more event messages will be sent to the RKS by the MGC and/or the originating CMS and CMTS indicating that the call has been answered and that QoS has been granted, implying that billing can now begin.

When the conversation is complete, the originating party goes on-hook. This causes event messages to be sent to the RKS, indicating that the call is over and billing should cease, and a signaling message reaches the MGC informing it that the call is to be torn down.

The MGC will check that it is permitted to release this trunk (that is, that the calling party is allowed to release it—some calls involving operators may only be released by the operator). Assuming that this is permitted, the MGC signals both the far-end switch (in an SS7 command sent through the SG) and the local MG (in a DeleteConnection) to release the trunk.

```
DLCX 1229 ds/ds1-2/3@mg1.ratco.net MGCP 1.0 TGCP 1.0
    This is a DeleteConnection message, number 1229, to the identified
    trunk, using TGCP 1.0
C: 0123FC4A690EAA61
I: 32F345E2
```

When the MG has released the trunk, it responds with an acknowledgement that includes the performance parameters for the just-deleted connection.

```
250 1229 OK
    This is a response to message 1229; the connection was deleted properly
P: PS=1245, OS=62345, PR=780, OR=45123, PL=10, JI=27, LA=48
    The statistics relating to the deleted connection:
    1245 packets were transmitted
    62345 octets were transmitted
    780 packets were received
    45123 octets were received
    10 packets were (apparently) lost
    The average inter-packet arrival jitter was 27 milliseconds
    The average latency was 48 milliseconds
```

The MGC will also receive an RLC from the SG, indicating that the release of the trunk has been confirmed.

Chapter

9

The Future

Who is the more foolish: the one who predicts the future
or the one who believes the prediction?

Ancient Chinese proverb—invented for the occasion by the author.

Attempting to divine the future is an operation fraught with peril at the best of times. When one attempts to discern the direction of an industry that is developing at the rate evidenced by the technology we have been discussing in this book, it probably lies somewhere between downright silly and pointless.

That said, it seems impossible to close without at least an attempt to glimpse into a crystal ball—always bearing in mind that, as the chapter epigraph states, the one who pays too much attention to the prognosticator stands condemned at least as much as that prognosticator!

In this chapter, which is purposefully brief, we will look at the possible evolution of PacketCable in three different areas: changes to the current specifications, new specifications and business issues. For the most part, we will not attempt to divine the precise nature of the future. Instead our aim is to raise issues and perhaps share some insights that, at some point, PacketCable will have to address if it is to achieve the widespread acceptance and success hoped for by those responsible for framing the project.

Changes to Current Specifications

The PacketCable 1.0 specifications contain many errors, omissions and areas of confusion (and, quite possibly, internal contradictions). Although the PacketCable project did a superb job to produce in such a short time a number of high-quality specifications covering an extremely complex technology, the organization of the project precluded the in-depth checking and cogitation that accompanies specifications produced by standards bodies such as the IETF and the ITU. Therefore, although the version 1.0 specifications are "published", they should be regarded more in the nature of late-version IETF drafts than as published RFCs.

During the time that this book has been written, numerous changes have been (and continue to be) made to the internal working copies of the specification documents. Most of the changes are in the nature of minor corrections or clarifications, and when possible the text of this book has reflected the interpretation that will eventually be published in revised copies of the various specifications.

In a very few instances, the changes are more substantive. In these cases, the author has been forced to remain silent, since open discussion of these changes is not permitted until they are made public by the release of revised specifications. However, there are fortunately only very few instances where a portion of a specification has been revised in a substantive manner. Such are the perils of attempting to cover in some depth a rapidly evolving technology.

New Specifications

PacketCable version 1.0, which we have been discussing in the preceding pages, is only the first of a series of PacketCable releases.

While the PacketCable architecture was originally designed to meet the short-term goal of providing support for so-called "PSTN toll quality" telephony over a cable access network, the designers were careful to try to ensure that other uses for the network were not precluded.

One can usefully think of PacketCable as providing two basic technologies. The first is a general-purpose QoS-enabled packet network whose access mechanism runs on bidirectional HFC infrastructure. This is essentially the DQoS portion of the specifications, which provides applications access to the low-level DOCSIS flows. The second technology supplied by PacketCable builds on the first: It is the series of specifications describing one way to supply telephony over the QoS-enabled network.

Telephony is only one example of a technology that benefits from a QoS-enabled network. Other technologies that require real-time QoS support include such diverse uses as video conferencing, on-demand video streaming and gaming. PacketCable 1.0 provides a basic mechanism that can be used to implement these and other services, but it gives no guidance as to how any particular vendor might reasonably go about implementing such services in any way that would be interoperable with offerings from other vendors.

In addition, although PacketCable 1.0 does define how to implement basic telephony over the QoS-enabled network, the emphasis is very much on the word "basic". Despite the undoubted complexity of the material we have covered in the preceding pages, readers familiar with how telephony functions in the PSTN will recognize that there are many, many features and issues that PacketCable 1.0 does not address.

The reason for the lack of completeness is simply due to the speed with which the version 1.0 specifications were produced (essentially, in about one year of concerted effort). The PacketCable project is currently working on specifications to cover several of the more important omissions in the version 1.0 specifications. However, it is likely to be several years before PacketCable can reasonably be regarded as "complete" (and by that time, a book such as this will likely run to several volumes).

In this context it is perhaps worth recognizing that it has taken more than a century for the PSTN to develop to its current maturity, and for most of that time it was developed (at least in the United States) by a monopoly with almost absolute power to control the technology and the manner in which features were implemented.

In contrast, PacketCable technical specifications are the product of representatives from several competing companies who sell their equipment to the MSOs. As such, they necessarily are more complex and less coherent than might otherwise be the case. On the other hand, despite the number of difficulties and competing interests that the PacketCable project has had to face, the released specifications, for all their warts, provide an excellent base from which great things are likely to grow.

The author could continue in this sort of vague and rather unhelpful manner, but instead, let's try to be a bit more practical and look at a few of the ways in which, given the current specifications, new features are likely to be added in subsequent releases.

Calls Utilizing More Than One CMS

Figure 9-1 introduces some new nomenclature. A **zone** is a set of MTAs served by a single CMS. A **domain** is a set of MTAs served by a single TGS (that, in general, is likely to include several CMSes).

A gaping hole in the version 1.0 specifications is the lack of official support for call paths in which more than one CMS takes part (that is, interzone communication). The NCS specification includes no mention of how one CMS might pass necessary information to another CMS. In other words, the only calls that are adequately included in the version 1.0 specifications are either those calls that remain on-net and are local to a single CMS (which may serve something of the order of 10,000 subscribers) or those that go off-net to the PSTN.

The DCS specification does describe how to carry information between a pair of CMSes—but that specification, although generated and released under the auspices of the PacketCable project, does not form an official part of the version 1.0 specifications.

Therefore, under PacketCable 1.0, any call whose signaling passes from one CMS to another must do so using some proprietary mechanism, which is antithetical to

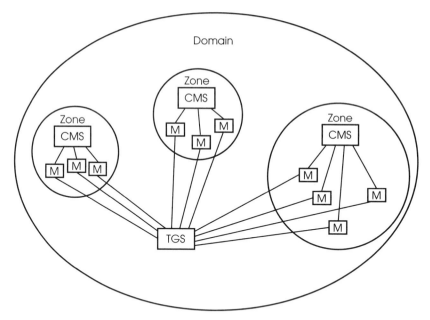

Figure 9-1 Zones and Domains

the fundamental goal of PacketCable of ensuring that equivalent products from different vendors should interoperate. So it is not hard to guess that a CMS-CMS protocol will be defined and released in an early future release.

There are a number of security and architectural issues relating to interzone (but intradomain) communication. For example, when two CMSes communicate, they must do so securely, and so a mechanism must be defined for allowing arbitrary pairs of CMSes out of a (possibly large) number of CMSes to do so in a manner that does not appreciably impact call setup time.

Calls Utilizing More Than One Service Provider

More complex than the interzone, intradomain case is the interdomain scenario one in which different MSOs service the two ends of a call. This complexity is further exacerbated by the possibility that the call may be routed through an IP network belonging to a third party.[1] This raises issues that are not just technical ("How are we going to get the necessary packets and information from A to B?") but also ones pertaining to the degree to which the network operators involved trust one another.

---

1. The complexity may be expanded arbitrarily. For example, the call signaling could be routed along an entirely different path from the bearer packets. Or the routing followed by the bearer packets may change midcall. Or the paths for the bearer packets may be asymmetric. I'm sure you get the idea.

And these cannot be simply solved ("Hey, Mr. Network Provider B. You tell me that you are giving this call from one of my subscribers n kilobits per second of bandwidth, but how do I know that in fact you aren't dropping packets on the ground?"). Other issues involve charge settlement and routing ("You're charging me how much per packet?", and "Here's a packet. Please route it to its destination, but don't you dare send it through Fly-By-Night-Telco's network because we don't trust them not to sell the information to the government of country X").

These are truly complicated issues. The PSTN struggles along with some surprisingly naïve solutions to many of these problems. The PacketCable project will have to decide if the PSTN's simplistic practices[2] will be sufficient or whether more complicated settlement procedures will be necessary.

Automated Security

Although PacketCable 1.0 provides a relatively good security schema, the way in which that security is administered leaves much to be desired. For example, most pairwise interfaces are secured by IPsec, but the IPsec security associations are configured by an Internet Key Exchange (IKE) exchange based on the existence of "preshared" secrets. In plain English, this means that before two devices can communicate, they must somehow be provided, via some out-of-band mechanism, with a secret that they (and only they) share. This is clearly a mechanism whose scalability leaves something to be desired.

Therefore some automatic scheme needs to be designed whereby two devices can set up a security association on the fly without any advance knowledge of one another's existence. The easiest way to do this is to use certificate-based mechanisms, so it is likely that future versions of PacketCable will require that almost all devices in the network carry one or more digital certificates, which will be used in some manner to build security associations as needed. (Certificate-based IKE or a Kerberized IPsec such as is already used during MTA provisioning come to mind as possible mechanisms for implementing this.)

New Codecs

A major weakness of PacketCable 1.0 is in the definition and use of codecs. In version 1.0, only support for G.711 is required. Although other, lower bit-rate codecs may be supported, it is unlikely that vendors will deploy any codecs that are not mandatory. G.711 is, relatively speaking, an inefficient, high-bandwidth codec remarkably ill-suited for an environment in which upstream bandwidth is limited and expensive.

---

2. Which are often more or less along the lines of "Let's see. This month I carried 5 bzillion minutes of your traffic, and you carried 4 bzillion minutes of mine, so you owe me for one bzillion minutes".

So it seems that mandatory support for additional codecs will be included in future versions. In particular, relay codecs will doubtless be added, so that (for example) faxes may be sent without requiring the bandwidth-hungry G.711 codec.[3]

In a similar vein, the codec negotiation mechanism provided in version 1.0 is very naïve. In general, one would desire that the party paying for the call should be the one who ultimately determines which codec or pair of codecs is to be used on the call. Some method for implementing fairer codec negotiation will surely be added.

New Encryption Algorithms

In PacketCable 1.0, the only supported encryption algorithm is RC4. This is a controversial and not altogether wise choice for (at least) two reasons. First, it is a pure stream cipher, which means that for the mechanism defined in PacketCable, it is nontrivial to extend it to the case where multiple packets contain the same timestamp. This does not occur with the PacketCable 1.0 codecs, but it will occur once other codecs, and especially video codecs, become supported.

There is also the issue that RC4 is a privately owned cipher. In theory at least, any company wanting to build any of the PacketCable devices that must encrypt or decrypt audio information must first obtain an RC4 license from RSA Data Security, Inc. This company, however, is under no obligation to grant such a license at any price, fair or otherwise. Thus the PacketCable project, by choosing RC4, effectively placed veto power over who may implement its specs in the hands of a private company that has made no agreement to provide licenses to all-comers.

Some companies may prefer to design a product using the RC4-compatible algorithm known as ARC-FOUR, whose source code is widely available on the Internet. However, this would risk a lawsuit from RSA Data Security, Inc.[4]

The easiest solution to both of these problems would be to replace RC4 as a mandatory-to-support algorithm with a block cipher that is free and reasonably fast. The U.S. government has sponsored a contest to define a replacement for the aging DES standard. The winner of this contest, to be known as AES (the "Advanced Encryption Standard") should meet both these criteria. As of this writing, the tentative winner has been announced, so it is likely that a forthcoming revision of the PacketCable security specification will specify that AES should be used for all bearer channel encryption.

---

3. The recent RFC number 2833 provides a mechanism for sending relay events via RTP. One could reasonably expect PacketCable to adopt some mechanism compliant with this RFC.

4. It is the author's opinion that such a lawsuit would be doomed to failure. However, the author is emphatically not a lawyer, and his opinions have been known to be wrong.

Non-Embedded MTAs

Because there is no defined interface for controlling a cable modem, PacketCable 1.0 MTAs are generally assumed to be "embedded"—that is, combined with a cable modem into a single unit. This restriction will be relaxed in a future version of the specifications, leading to the possibility of so-called "standalone" or "non-embedded" MTAs.

A standalone MTA is merely a device running ordinary computer code and that communicates with a cable modem through some yet to be defined mechanism, probably using Ethernet-based transport. In other words, the MTA could easily be a conventional personal computer. In a few years, one may be able to download MTA software from the Internet (this is especially likely if the DCS signaling protocol becomes dominant), tailoring the user interface and the supported features to whatever the user desires.

Future Services

We have said this before, but it bears repeating: Although PacketCable is presented as a telephony network, what the designers have really done is to produce an architecture for a general-purpose QoS-enabled packet network whose access is via an HFC physical plant. Therefore the PacketCable network can support almost any kind of real-time application, of which telephony is merely the first example.

Future versions of the PacketCable specifications will define exactly how other applications will use the network to implement the needed features and services. Obvious examples of these are real-time video conferencing for businesses and real-time gaming and video streaming on demand for residences.[5]

Some services could be deployed independently of the PacketCable architecture, even though they might run on the same physical network. However, a more likely scenario is that PacketCable will expand to define how such services are to be deployed within a PacketCable context. It would be especially attractive to build these services on the certificate-based security architecture of PacketCable. If designed carefully, a PacketCable Key Distribution Center (KDC) could provide a central authority for deploying new features and services in a secure manner.

Business Issues

Although this is a technical book, it is a truism that technical issues often defer to business ones in determining the direction and ultimate success of a new technology. We began the book with a brief look at the business forces that forged the creation of

---

5. The author will take this opportunity to make the heretical suggestion that MSO revenue from such services may eventually overtake that from telephony.

the PacketCable specifications. We shall end by a similar look at some of the forces that determine the manner in which PacketCable is actually deployed.

It is worthwhile to remember that, while most of the major MSOs were united in supporting the creation of the PacketCable project, they remain competitors and they have no united deployment strategy. Indeed the MSOs generally regard their individual deployment strategies as proprietary information, and different MSOs are likely to solve the same problems in different ways.

The MTA: Where Does It Belong, and Who Owns It?

Some MSOs believe that the MTA, which is a relatively complex and expensive item, should be rented (probably monthly) by the subscriber. If a subscriber merely rents the MTA, then the MSO would generally like to be sure that he has easy access to it for maintenance. These MSOs therefore tend to believe that the proper location for an MTA is outside, on the side of the house (like the interface box that now connects the house telephony wiring to the wiring of the local telephone company).

Placing the MTA on the side of the house has several repercussions. The external environment is much harsher than the environment inside the home, requiring more expensive components and more robust design. If the MTA is to provide primary line service (see next section), the extremes of temperature are likely to preclude the possibility of using batteries to ensure uninterrupted power, which in turn suggests that some form of network powering will be needed.

Other MSOs support a retail model, in which MTAs will be made available through ordinary retail outlets. The disadvantages of this, from an MSO's standpoint, are that subscribers are required to invest a substantial sum (PacketCable 1.0 MTAs, if available through retail outlets, will likely cost between $300 and $400) before they can use the service, that the MSO has essentially no control over the MTA and that provisioning retail MTAs may be considerably more complicated than provisioning a known device.

In the early deployment stages of PacketCable, the most likely scenario is that most subscribers will rent the MTA from the MSO. However, as the technology becomes more entrenched, MTA prices should fall, more vendors will offer competitive and differentiated MTAs, consumers will want to have the freedom to decide which MTA they want to use and the retail model is likely to become prevalent. Eventually, as we mentioned above, there is no reason why general-purpose computers could not function as MTAs.

Primary Line or Secondary Line?

Telephone service may be either so-called primary line or secondary line. A primary line service is intended to be usable under all except the most extreme conditions, including times when normal utility power is unavailable. A primary line service must meet other requirements, such as the ability to place emergency calls even though the line may not be used for other purposes (such as, for example, if the subscriber has not paid his bill). Typical residential telephone service from traditional telephone companies qualifies as primary line service.[6] A secondary line does not need to meet these stringent requirements.

Providing cable-based primary line service is considerably more difficult than providing secondary service. For example, the typical reliability of many cable networks is approximately 99.98%, which corresponds to loss of service for about one and three quarter hours per year. Upgrading the HFC networks to provide for the increased reliability needed to deliver primary line service can be a very expensive proposition for MSOs.

There is also an issue raised above: whether the MTA is located inside or on the side of the house. An MTA located inside the house may be provided with backup batteries that can provide power for several hours, enabling the MTA to deliver phone service even when the utility power is unavailable. An MTA sited on the side of the house, however, cannot be provided with batteries because of the extremes of temperature to which they would be exposed. Consequently, the only way to provide primary line service through such an MTA is if it obtains power from the MSO network (independent of the utility electrical supply). This is also an expensive proposition.

However, it is not clear whether customers will demand primary line service. In the past, when the ordinary wired-in residential telephone was needed in emergencies, it was important that all homes be provided with primary service. With the advent of widespread cell phone use, this need is no longer obvious. A reasonably reliable secondary service, combined with a backup cell phone (in other words, the combination of two independent secondary line services) may well provide sufficient reliability for most people.[7]

So while some MSOs (notably AT&T) are likely to concentrate on offering primary line service via PacketCable networks, others are likely to limit themselves to providing less expensive secondary line service. The marketplace, as usual, will determine which is the most profitable strategy.

Partially Compliant Networks

While we have been careful to discuss only PacketCable-compliant telephony, some MSOs are experimenting with only partially compliant networks. The need for such

---

6. Availability for ordinary phone service is approximately 99.999%, which is equivalent to loss of service for about five minutes per year.

7. One member of a PacketCable focus team once observed that the least expensive way for an MSO to provide primary line service would be to provide each subscriber with a little glass case with the legend "In emergency, break glass". Inside would be a cell phone.

networks has arisen because of the slowness with which vendors have been able to provide fully compliant equipment.

PacketCable networks are relatively complex. The apparent complexity is increased because much of the functionality is distributed into several small boxes rather than being concentrated into a single "switch", as in a conventional PSTN telephony network. While some of the functions can be performed by equipment that is either off-the-shelf or by reasonably simple modifications of off-the-shelf equipment, some functions must be implemented essentially from scratch. In particular, the NCS Call Management System is a device that most vendors have to construct from the ground up.

Competitive business pressures, however, have forced some vendors to deploy, on an interim basis, some form of IP telephony over cable despite the lack of supporting equipment. Figure 9-2 shows a typical installation of a quasi-PacketCable network in which the function of the CMS is handled by a Class 5 telephony switch, such as is used in a conventional telephony Central Office.

Although such a network achieves the objective of allowing an MSO to deploy digital telephony rapidly, it suffers many drawbacks. While good for a short-term,

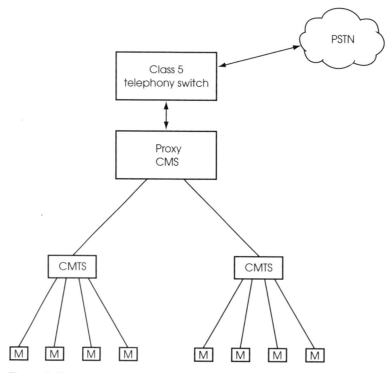

Figure 9-2 Partially Compliant Network

interim solution, several factors indicate that any MSO deploying such a network would be wise to migrate to a fully PacketCable-compliant solution as quickly as possible.

Cost of Switch This solution requires that a Class 5 switch be available. These switches are very expensive, and in general, it would be prohibitive to purchase one merely for this purpose. If, however, the deploying company already owns Class 5 switches (as does, for example, AT&T), then these switches may be usefully pressed into service in a partially compliant network.

Cost of Providing Service The reason that an MSO deploys a telephony service is to make money. In general, to make money the MSO must lure subscribers away from the established telcos. And in order to do this, he must, in most cases, offer equivalent service at a lower cost. However, consider the two halves of Figure 9-3.

The difference in the two networks lies in the method used to access the Class 5 switch. For conventional telephony, access is over ordinary twisted-pair copper wires. For the partially compliant network, access is over bidirectional QoS-enabled HFC and an in-house IP network. The conventional network requires only an ordinary telephone in the house. The partially compliant network requires that an MTA be placed in or on the side of the residence.

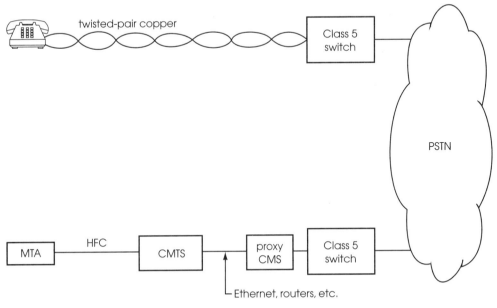

Figure 9-3 Comparison of Partially Compliant PacketCable Network with Conventional Telephony (Simplified)

By comparing the two halves of Figure 9-3, one fact is very clear: The partially compliant solution is much more expensive to deploy than is conventional telephony. It is difficult to see how an MSO deploying such a partially compliant solution can offer service at a price lower than the telco without sustaining losses. It may be true that the initial offering may be at a lower cost than that of the telco but only because the telco may be overpricing its offering. It would surely not take long for the telco to lower its prices to the point where the MSO, to maintain its subscriber base, is forced to sustain considerable losses.

Surveillance Requirements The partially compliant solution suffers another (possibly fatal) flaw. Because it is not a solution endorsed by an accepted industry specification, it does not meet the terms imposed by CALEA for granting the MSO a "Safe Harbor" from the penalties associated with missing a wiretap.

Wiretaps in such networks are performed by the Class 5 switch. This requires that all bearer-channel packets must pass through the switch. Unfortunately, in most of the architectures that the author has seen, this cannot be guaranteed. Briefly, the attacks work like this.

Suppose that MTA1, with IP address IP1, is placing an on-net call to MTA2, with IP address IP2. During call setup, MTA1 is told that MTA2's IP address is actually IP3, which corresponds to the CMS. Similarly MTA2 is told that MTA1's IP address is IP3 (or IP4, which also corresponds to the CMS). Under normal circumstances, bearer traffic from MTA1 to MTA2 flows as in Figure 9-4.

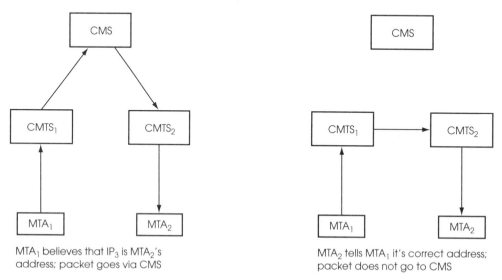

MTA$_1$ believes that IP$_3$ is MTA$_2$'s address; packet goes via CMS

MTA$_2$ tells MTA$_1$ it's correct address; packet does not go to CMS

Figure 9-4 Hacking a Partially Compliant Solution

The packet flows from MTA1 to the CMS (where it may be tapped if necessary by passing through the Class 5 switch), and then it passes from the CMS to MTA2.

However, the MTAs are untrusted. They can do anything they happen to think is to their advantage. In particular, once the call is set up, MTA2 might tell MTA1 its true IP address. Now MTA1 can send a packet directly to MTA2. The packet will be routed through the CMTS directly to MTA2 and the packet can never be tapped by the CMS.

Just a note: There are more complex ways of routing the packets so that this attack does not directly succeed. In addition, the success of this particular attack depends on the way in which the CMTS is implemented. However, other equivalent attacks are usually possible. The fundamental problem is that the architecture violates an important rule of electronic surveillance: Always place the Intercept Access Point as close as is technically possible to the trust boundary between the network and the subject (for this architecture, on the CMTS).

NCS vs DCS

All the planned early deployments of PacketCable are being designed to support NCS signaling. AT&T, now the largest MSO, is, of course, historically a telephone company, and the NCS paradigm in which call features are implemented centrally and the endpoints are controlled via messaging coming from a centralized location is very much familiar territory to a telephone company. In some sense, a telephone company finds it much easier to understand the mechanics of how an NCS system works—and how quality can be controlled and money might be made in such a network—because it so closely resembles the conventional PSTN.

The DCS model, on the other hand, tends to look more anarchic. The network operator is in real danger of being relegated to little more than the entity that provides a pipe over which various services and features may be offered—possibly by third parties—and many of which may even be implemented on the subscriber's device beyond the direct control of any service provider. (This is especially true if the government forces some sort of open-access policy on the operator, so that third parties must be allowed to offer services—including telephony—using the operator's physical plant.) Such a model is not particularly attractive to a company that has historically maintained a tight control on the quality and contents of the feature set made available to consumers and the way in which those features are implemented and paid for.

So for some time there is little doubt that NCS networks will dominate. However, as the risk of entry becomes less, some of the smaller companies who have less to lose by rolling out a more experimental service are much more likely to begin to embrace DCS, whose architecture is much better adapted to offering a wide range of advanced features and services using intelligent endpoints. Once DCS begins to get a foothold, the author sees little chance that NCS will remain a viable competitor unless it is artificially supported in that role by major MSOs. (But remember, this is just the author's opinion. He has been known to be wrong.)

Fiber to the Home (FTTH)

Although there is no serious competitor to the PacketCable architecture for delivering telephony to the home via cable access networks, there are other competitors that provide broadband access to the home and that might in the future be used to deliver telephony and multimedia services.

Although the most frequently cited competitor is xDSL, as currently deployed xDSL is usually marketed as a data-only solution that simultaneously allows one to place ordinary voice calls over the same line. While this is also an effective short-term description of what PacketCable supplies, as we have indicated, telephony is merely the first of many features and services that will be supplied over PacketCable networks. It is not yet at all clear that xDSL technologies will be able to match the level of features and sophistication that will be provided by PacketCable networks a few years from now. Note, however, that there is no reason that PacketCable networks could not operate over a DSL access network. The important long-term difference, though, is that the access bandwidth available to cable networks is substantially greater than that available to DSL, especially in the downstream direction, and that extra bandwidth may allow some services to be deployed over PacketCable/cable that are simply not feasible over PacketCable/DSL.

But there is another competitor that supplies even greater bandwidth than cable: so-called **Fiber to the Home** (**FTTH**) technology. This operates very much like the cable plant, except that the coax is replaced by fiber, so that the ultra-high-bandwidth fiber pipe is taken directly into the home. This is a nascent technology (even more so than PacketCable), and as yet there are no clear indications how telephony and other services might be deployed in a standardized manner such that vendors' equipment might interoperate correctly. It is perfectly possible that this problem will be solved merely by adapting the relevant PacketCable specifications to the FTTH environment.[8] However, the various FTTH carriers may choose a completely different solution, or they may choose no standardised solution at all, relying only on proprietary architectures and equipment, much as in the early days of cable modem technology.

The possibility of ultra-high-bandwidth pipes to the home is even a threat to the MSOs continued existence, at least in their present form, so it will be interesting to see how they respond to FTTH technology as it begins to be deployed.

---

8. Which is certainly what the author would consider doing if he were in charge of an FTTH company.

Putting It All Together

In PacketCable we are privileged to see a new technology being born. Unlike most technological births, this one was planned. It is, however, like births of all kind, still a messy affair.

The PacketCable specifications released to date, along with the underlying DOCSIS specifications, provide an architecture for a QoS-enabled IP network that reaches to the home through the same cable used to deliver television. Vendors are scrambling to produce products that comply with these specifications, but the specifications are complicated—and they spawn complicated devices. Most major telephony vendors, and several of the larger companies providing data networking equipment, are participating in small-scale trials and controlled introductions of PacketCable networks. Barring major unforeseen difficulties, the first medium-scale deployments will occur in the first half of 2001, with wide-scale deployment by national MSOs beginning before the end of the year.

In the meantime, the PacketCable focus teams are still in business, clarifying and expanding the specifications (and also taking them to international standards bodies). The forecasts for how large the PacketCable market will become, and how quickly it will grow, vary widely. Those of us fortunate enough to have been present at the birth have little doubt that there are surprises, both good and bad, in store for the industry. But few of us doubt that we have seen the birth of a major new technology that will become pervasive in the telecommunications world in the next few years.

Appendix
A
Glossary

3DES

Triple DES or Three DES—a variant of DES that, although slower, is much harder to break using an exhaustive search.

ADSI

Analog Display Services Interface. Defined in Bellcore document GR-1273-CORE, this is a mechanism for passing short messages over telephone lines.

ADSL

Asymmetric Digital Subscriber Line. A technology (see xDSL) suited to the home and that allows for much higher downstream bandwidth than upstream bandwidth.

AES

Advanced Encryption Standard. An effort by the U.S. government to replace the Data Encryption Standard.

AK

Authorization Key. A key generated by a CMTS and passed to a CM for the purpose of deriving other keys used in BPI+.

alerting

The process of signaling to a user that a call is incoming. Typically, this consists of ringing a phone.

AM

Amplitude Modulation. A simple modulation scheme wherein information is encoded by changing the strength of a transmitted signal.

ASCII

> American Standard Code for Information Interchange—the coding used by most computers to represent common characters such as those found on typewriter keyboards.

ASN.1

> Abstract Syntax Notation number 1—defined in recommendation X.680 of ITU-T, ASN.1 is a notation that allows for the precise description (at the bit level) of the format of an object.

authentication

> In network parlance, the process of ensuring that a device that claims to be the originator of some piece of information is indeed the true originator.

authorization

> The process of ensuring that the resources requested by a call do not exceed a preprovisioned allocation to which the user is entitled.

backbone

> The innermost portion of a network, where devices are typically linked by high-bandwidth pipes. In a PacketCable network, the term usually refers to the connections between devices located logically "inside" the HFC access networks. This includes CMTSes, CMSes, PSTN gateways and the other core devices in a PacketCable network.

backhaul

> The act of moving packets, typically over long distances, to a separate location for processing.

bandplan

> A map in the frequency domain that shows how various frequencies are allocated to different services or how frequencies are used by a particular service.

BASE64

> An encoding mechanism specified in RFC 1521, used to convert arbitrary strings of binary data into a strictly limited subset of printable ASCII characters.

BCID

> Billing Correlation Identifier. A 16-octet quantity used to identify a particular call within PacketCable event messages.

bearer traffic

> Sometimes simply called "bearer", this is the actual content of a call: the digitized voice or fax information, for example.

BER

Basic Encoding Rules. A set of encoding rules that allows one to encode a stream of objects that have been specified in ASN.1 notation. See also *DER*.

best effort

A communications channel that makes no guarantees concerning available bandwidth nor timeliness (nor even success) of delivery.

Big Endian

A system for placing octets in order, sometimes called "Motorola order", in which the most significant octet appears first. For example, the number 54321 is 0xD431 in hexadecimal Big Endian order. See also *Little Endian*.

block cipher

A method of encrypting a message in blocks of a fixed number of octets.

blocking

A term used to describe the deliberate failure of a network to complete a telephone call because of a lack of the necessary resources to allow the call to proceed with acceptable quality.

BLV

Busy Line Verify. An operator service whereby the operator can determine whether a line that the network believes to be in use is actually carrying traffic.

BNF

Originally Backus Normal Form, a notation useful for defining formal grammars.

BPI+

Baseline Privacy Interface Plus. A mechanism used in DOCSIS for rendering private packets that pass along the access portion of the network.

BPKM

Baseline Privacy Key Management. The portion of BPI+ that provides for the secure distribution of keying material between a cable modem and its CMTS.

bucket

A conceptual device used to control the rate at which packets belonging to a single flow are injected into a QoS network.

CA

Call Agent. In NCS, the part of a CMS responsible for functions related to call control.

CA

Certification Authority. In a digital certificate hierarchy, an entity empowered to sign certificates for entities lower in the hierarchy.

CableLabs®

> Cable Laboratories, Inc.—a consortium of cable operators; responsible for the suite of PacketCable interoperability specifications.

cadence

> A pattern of ringing mixed with silence. In the United States, the basic cadence used for alerting the destination party is a two-second ring followed by four seconds of silence.

CALEA

> Communications Assistance for Law Enforcement Act. A statute enacted by the U.S. Congress in 1994. CALEA defines the responsibilities of telephony service providers to provide wiretap capabilities to law enforcement agencies in possession of a surveillance order from a court of competent jurisdiction.

call signaling

> Information associated with a call that must be passed among various entities in the network in order for the call to proceed correctly.

CBC

> Cipher Block Chaining. A feedback mechanism that functionally converts a block cipher to a stream cipher.

CBR

> Constant Bit Rate. A term used to describe a codec that produces a constant amount of information every second, regardless of input. May also be used to describe a bandwidth allocation designed to pass traffic from such a codec.

CCC

> Call Content Connection. An interface used to transport bearer packets for the purpose of electronic surveillance. Not really a "connection", since UDP is typically used.

CDC

> Call Data Connection. An interface used to transport signaling information for the purpose of electronic surveillance.

central office

> In a conventional circuit-switched network, the place where a subscriber's line initially terminates (often colloquially known as the "telephone exchange"). The line terminates on a *switch,* which allows a physical circuit to be completed so that bearer traffic may flow between subscribers.

CERN

> The European Organization for Nuclear Research; the birthplace of HTML.

certificate

An authenticated document that is signed, typically by some higher authority, and that usually contains useful information in an encapsulated form.

CF

Collection Function. The device used by an LEA to collect information from a service provider's network.

CFNA

Call Forward No Answer—a feature whereby if a call to a number is not answered within a specified number of rings, the call is automatically forwarded to a different number.

CIC

Circuit Identification Code. In SS7, a 2-octet field that identifies a particular trunk circuit.

CID

Circuit Identity. A value used by ISTP that represents a combination of a Point Code and a CIC.

ciphersuite

A grouping consisting of an encryption algorithm, a decryption algorithm (which may be the same as the encryption algorithm) and an authentication algorithm. The particular ciphersuite to use is often a subject of negotiation between devices.

circuit-switched telephony

Classical "wireline" telephony, in which switches are configured in such a way as to provide a physical circuit between the communicating parties.

clipping

An undesired effect often caused by a failure to make resources available for use sufficiently quickly. Clipping results in the loss of the some or all of the typical "Hello" greeting when a person answers the phone. See also *cut through*.

CM

cable modem. The device located on a user's premises and that allows digital communication with the cable company's headend.

CMS

Call Management Server. The entity in a PacketCable network responsible for managing call signaling and related information. In an NCS network, a CMS comprises a CA and a GC; in a DCS network, a CMS comprises a DP and a GC.

CMS

Cryptographic Message Syntax. A syntax geared to the delivery of cryptographic information; specified in RFC 2630. CMS is used by the PKINIT exchange between an MTA and its TGS.

CMTS

Cable Modem Termination System. The device in the MSO headend that communicates with users' cable modems.

CO

See *central office*.

Codec

Coder/Decoder—In general, an algorithm for encoding and decoding information, usually into a form that is more easily transmitted. More specifically, an algorithm for encoding and decoding real-time data for transmission over a packet-based network.

Commitment

The process of marking resources as in-use for a call. It occurs only after the resources have been authorized and committed.

Community

An SNMP term, a community is a logical entity that allows multiple managers to manage a single agent.

Cookie

A (usually short) bitstream stored by a client but used by a server.

COPS

Common Open Policy Service. A mechanism, and also a protocol defined by that mechanism, for implementing policy decisions using a client/server model. Defined in RFC 2748.

CPE

Customer Premise Equipment—devices that are contained within the home and are generally assumed to be accessible to, and operated by, the user.

CRC

Cyclic Redundancy Check. A polynomial-based method for calculating a value from an input bitstream, such that if any of the bits in the stream is changed, then with high probability the value of the CRC is changed. CRC values are frequently appended to packets so that the recipient may check whether the packet has been damaged en route.

CRLF

> A pair of contiguous ASCII characters corresponding to a Carriage Return followed by a Line Feed. These are the characters numbered 0x0D and 0x0A (that is, 13 and 10), respectively.

CSRC

> Contributing Source as defined in RFC 1889, a source that has contributed a stream to the output of a (typically audio) mixer. See also *SSRC*.

cut through

> A telephony term used to describe the existence of a bearer-channel path between two parties. The called party's voice must be cut through sufficiently quickly that the calling party does not miss the first part of the "Hello" greeting.

database dip

> Colloquial term for consulting a database.

DC bias

> The addition of a constant voltage to a varying signal. In a digital circuit (one in which a "1" is represented by one value and a "0" by another), long sequences of ones or zeros can cause the circuit to misinterpret the relatively long-term static voltage caused by the sequence as a DC bias, rendering the circuit. This will attempt to remove the bias before decoding—prone to decode the sequence incorrectly. See *scrambling*.

DCS

> Distributed Call Signaling. A call signaling architecture in which endpoints are treated as relatively intelligent devices and in which no call state is maintained within the CMS.

denial of service

> An attack whose principal goal is to deny services to a legitimate user.

DER

> Distinguished Encoding Rules. A subset of BER, this provides a unique way to encode a stream of objects that have been specified in ASN.1 notation.

DES

> Data Encryption Standard—a 64-bit block cipher with a 56-bit key, authorized for use by U.S. government agencies to protect unclassified material. Described in FIPS PUB 46 and ANSI X3.92.

DF

> Delivery Function. The legal name for the device (colloquially, a "wiretap server") to which an LEA connects in order to obtain call signaling and content information provided by a network operator.

DHCP

Dynamic Host Configuration Protocol. A protocol defined in RFC 1531 that allows a device to obtain a temporary (but possibly long-lived) IP address, as well as other IP connectivity information.

dielectric

A plastic insulating material that separates the inner wire from the outer flexible braid in coaxial cable.

DiffServ

Differentiated Services—a network in which traffic flows are tagged, so that the network has the capability to treat different flows differently.

digital certificate

A method of encapsulating information, typically relating to security. Certificates are usually signed by a trusted party, who guarantees that the information in the certificate is correct.

digital envelope

A message encrypted by a recipient's public key. Only someone holding the corresponding private key can correctly decrypt the message.

digital signature

A number calculated from the contents of a message and a private key and (typically) appended to the message. The recipient can check the validity of the signature using the message contents and the sender's public key.

digit collection

The process of storing digits as they are dialed, accumulating digits until a valid phone number has been dialed.

digit map

An algorithm that determines when a sequence of digits constitutes a complete phone number. Optionally, it is an algorithm that determines the type of phone number (toll-free, long distance, international, and so on) that has been dialed.

Distribution Node

Another term for Fiber Node.

DOCSIS

Data-Over-Cable Service Interface Specifications. The set of specifications that govern the communication between CM and CMTS. Currently at level 1.1.

domain

A set of zones that are administered by a single Key Distribution Center.

DOSA

Distributed Open Systems Architecture. An internal AT&T architecture that provided the foundation of both DQoS and DCS.

downstream

In the direction from the network to the end-user.

DP

DCS Proxy. In DCS, the part of a CMS responsible for functions related to call control.

DPC

Destination Point Code. A value that represents the Point Code of a device that is the destination of an SS7 message.

DQoS

Dynamic Quality of Service. Guaranteed-bandwidth flows administered on a call-by-call basis. DQoS superseded Provisioned Quality of Service, or PQoS, or QoS on a device-by-device basis. PQoS was removed from the PacketCable specifications prior to the release of PacketCable version 1.0.

DSCP

DiffServ Code Point. An interpretation of the IP TOS field specified in RFC 2274, used to identify per-hop behavior in a DiffServ network.

DSP

Digital Signal Processing. Processing digital waveforms. This is a difficult task that typically requires dedicated hardware (DSP chips).

DTMF

Dual Tone Multi-Frequency. The tone pairs that are generated when digits on an ordinary telephone keypad are pressed. Also, pairs of tones used for signaling in a telephony network.

E.164

A recommendation from ITU-T entitled, "The International Public Telecommunication Numbering Plan". In other words, how telephone numbers are assigned and formatted.

ECB

Electronic Codebook. The simplest method of using a block cipher, in which a given plaintext always encodes to the same ciphertext if the key is unchanged.

EDE

Encrypt-Decrypt-Encrypt—a mode of operation for 3DES in which encryption is performed by the sequence encrypt-decrypt-encrypt and decryption is performed by the sequence decrypt-encrypt-decrypt.

egrep

> Extended Global Regular Expression Pattern—a command on UNIX systems for determining whether strings match a predetermined pattern. The syntax of the pattern-matching string used in PacketCable digit maps is based on the syntax used in the egrep command.

EI

> Emergency Interrupt. See *OI*.

Ethernet

> A networking mechanism suitable for local area networks, specified in IEEE standard 802.3.

FCC

> Federal Communications Commission—the agency of the U.S. federal government responsible for regulating telephony.

FEC

> Forward Error Correction. Any one of a number of mechanisms in which a small amount of additional information is added to a packet in such a way that, if some fraction of the data in the packet is lost, the data may be reconstructed without retransmission of the packet.

Fiber Node

> Element in an HFC network where fiber terminates and coax begins. Typically serves around 500 homes.

Flash

> See *Hookflash*.

Flowspec

> A set of parameters, defined in RFC 1363, that are used to define the packetization output of a codec.

FM

> Frequency Modulation. A simple modulation scheme wherein information is encoded by changing the frequency of a transmitted signal.

FQDN

> Fully Qualified Domain Name. An absolute domain name as specified in RFC 1034.

Frame

> A single unit of output from a codec.

FTP

File Transfer Protocol—defined in RFC 959, this is a client/server protocol for transferring files between two network devices.

FTTH

Fiber to the Home. A noncable, ultra-high-bandwidth, bidirectional access network technology in which fiber is taken all the way into the home.

Full-duplex

A connection that permits communication to occur simultaneously in both directions.

Gate

The fundamental construct in DQoS, residing in a CMTS. When a gate is open, resources are available for use in a call. Calls may be completed until two gates are open.

Gate Coordination

The process of ensuring that all the gates in a call open and close together. Gate coordination is necessary to thwart Theft of Service attempts based on placing half-calls.

Gate-ID

A 32-bit quantity used to refer to a gate or to a gate pair.

Gate Pair

A pair of gates, one upstream and one downstream, that share a common value of Gate-ID.

Gate Quartet

A pair of gate pairs, one pair residing on the originating CMTS and one pair residing on the terminating CMTS, which together constitute all the gates controlling QoS within a single call.

GC

Gate Controller. The device in a PacketCable network that controls the creation of gates to allow flows with guaranteed Quality of Service in the access network.

hairpin

In the PSTN, the circuit for a call from A to B that is forwarded by B to C adds a leg between B and C to the original leg between A and B. Such a call is said to be "hairpinned" at B. By contrast, in an IP network, packets would be transferred directly between A and C.

half-call

A call in which a talk path exists from one party to another but no path (or only a path with unacceptable quality) exists in the reverse direction.

half-duplex

A connection that permits communication to occur in only one direction at a time. Note that communication can still occur in both directions; it simply cannot occur *simultaneously* in both directions.

hash

An algorithm for converting a variable-length message into a fixed-length bitstream, especially an algorithm that does so in a manner such that small changes in the message produce a different bitstream.

headend

The "far end" of a digital cable communications link; the MSO facility where programming is injected into the HFC network.

HFC

Hybrid Fiber Coax. A cable distribution system in which the signals travel over both fiber and coax.

HMAC

Hashed Message Authenticity Check. A keyed hash added to a packet to ensure both the integrity of the data and the identity of the sender; described in RFC 2104.

Hook Flash, or Hookflash

The process, starting from the off-hook state, of going briefly on-hook and then back off-hook.

HTML

Hypertext Markup Language. The language used to build pages for the World Wide Web.

IAP

Intercept Access Point. A place in a network where information and/or content is intercepted for the purpose of passing it to a Law Enforcement Agency.

IE

Information Element. A short piece of information used in a DOCSIS MAP message and that maps time (in the form of minislots) to an activity associated with that time.

IEEE

Institute of Electrical and Electronics Engineers, Inc. Usually referred to as the "I-triple-E".

IEEE Floating Point format

A format for representing 32-bit and 64-bit floating point numbers, promulgated by the IEEE in ANSI/IEEE Standard 754-1985, *Standard for Binary Floating Point Arithmetic*. The details of the format are available at many places on the Web—for example, try *http://www.psc.edu/general/software/packages/ieee/ieee.html*. A later standard, number 854, extended the formats.

IETF

Internet Engineering Task Force—the body that oversees the technical aspects of the Internet.

IKE

Internet Key Exchange—a peer-to-peer key management protocol specified in RFC 2409.

IKE-

A form of IKE in which the devices are provided with preshared keys by some out-of-band mechanism.

Intserv

Integrated services—a network in which traffic flows are undifferentiated.

IP

Internet Protocol—a connectionless protocol with no guarantee of delivery. Defined in RFC 760, this is the protocol over which all other Internet protocols run.

IPsec

A secure version of IP, described in RFCs 2401, 2402 and 2406. IPsec can run in two modes: transport mode and tunnel mode. In PacketCable it is used only in transport mode.

ISDN

Integrated Services Digital Network. A relatively high-cost 128 kbps digital service.

ISO

International Standards Organization—oddly enough, an international organization that develops standards.

ISP

Internet Service Provider—a third party who provides Internet services for (usually paying) customers.

ISTP

Internet Signaling Transport Protocol. The protocol used by PacketCable networks to carry PSTN-like signaling.

ISUP

Integrated Services Digital Network User Part. One of the SS7 suite of protocols. Used in PacketCable networks to carry signaling information between the SG and the MGC.

ITU

International Telecommunications Union. An international standards body responsible for many telecommunications-related standards.

ITU-T

The "Telecommunication Standardization Sector" of the ITU.

IUC

Interval Usage Code—a 4-bit code used by a CMTS in a DOCSIS MAP message to indicate the type of an Information Element.

IV

Initialization Vector. A number used to prime a cryptographic algorithm that relies on prior values (such as a block cipher in Cipher Block Chaining mode).

jitter buffer

A buffer designed to smooth the playing of received audio so as to correct for variable transmission delay across the network.

KDC

Key Distribution Center. A centralized authority for managing security, typically by handing out tickets. In PacketCable, the full-blown KDC is replaced by a less-competent TGS, that performs only some of the functions of a KDC.

KEK

Key Encryption Key. A key used to encrypt another key.

Kerberos

Described in RFC 1510, Kerberos is a mechanism involving the granting of tickets that permits servers to authenticate clients requesting use of their services.

key

> A bit-sequence used in accordance with a well-defined algorithm and applied to a message to obtain either ciphertext (if the message was plaintext) or plaintext (if the message was ciphertext).

LAES

> Lawfully Authorized Electronic Surveillance. Copying a subscriber's signaling or content and making it available to an LEA who possesses a court-authorized right to it. Colloquially, "wiretapping".

LEA

> Law Enforcement Agency. A body with the legal standing to obtain a subpoena or other legal device that requires a network operator to make available signaling or content pertaining to a particular subscriber's calls.

Leaf

> An SNMP term, referring to a simple object (not a table) within a MIB.

LF

> The ASCII character corresponding to a Line Feed. This is the character numbered 0x0A (10).

Little Endian

> A system for placing octets in order, sometimes called "Intel order", in which the least significant octet (of a 16-bit quantity) appears first. For example, the number 54321 is 0x31D4 in hexadecimal Little Endian order. See also *Big Endian*.

LLC

> Logical Link Control. A layer in the DOCSIS protocol stack, used to encapsulate MAC management messages.

LNP

> Local Number Portability. The principle that a subscriber may keep his or her phone number even when changing service provider. Also, the database that allows a service provider to determine the provider that serves a particular phone number.

Local Ringback

> Ringback that is generated by the calling party's MTA.

LSB

> Least Significant Bit—the bit in a group of bits corresponding to the lowest power of two contained in the group (generally the 2^0 bit).

MAC

Media Access Control. The layer directly above the PMD layer.

MAC

Message Authentication Check. Additional data added to a packet that allows the recipient to confirm that the sender is indeed who he or she claims to be.

MAP

A DOCSIS MAC management message transmitted periodically by a CMTS to inform its client CMs how an upcoming series of minislots is to be used.

MCNS

Multimedia Cable Network System. The consortium of cable operators responsible for the DOCSIS specification.

MD5

Message Digest Number 5 algorithm—an algorithm that produces a one-way 16-octet hash from a stream of octets.

MG

Media Gateway. That portion of a PSTN Gateway responsible for the media interface between the two networks.

MGC

Media Gateway Controller. That portion of a PSTN Gateway that acts as a surrogate CMS; it also controls the Signaling Gateway and the Media Gateway.

MGCP

Media Gateway Control Protocol. Specified in RFC 2705, MGCP forms the basis of the PacketCable NCS protocol.

MIB

Management Information Base. A view of a database that typically contains device-specific information used to manage a network.

MIC

Message Integrity Check. Additional data added to a packet that allows the recipient to confirm that the data in the packet have not been tampered with during transit.

MIME

Multipurpose Internet Mail Extensions—defined in RFC 1521, this defines the standard Internet mechanism for sending arbitrary information safely through 7-bit channels.

Minislot

The minimum unit of data transmission in a CM/CMTS system.

MIPS

Millions of Instructions Per Second—a (somewhat crude) measure of the power of a processor. Also used to measure the amount of DSP processor power needed to implement codecs.

MMH

Multilinear Modular Hash. As used in PacketCable, a variant of the original published algorithm. The MMH is used as a MAC that is optionally added to audio RTP packets. In PacketCable the output of the hash may be configured to be either 16 or 32 bits.

modulation (demodulation)

The process of adding information to (extracting information from) a carrier signal.

MPEG

Moving Picture Experts Group—also, the name of a format for compressed video originally specified by this group and subsequently adopted by the ITU as recommendation H.222.0.

MSB

Most Significant Bit—the bit in a group of bits corresponding to the highest power of two contained in the group.

MSO

Multiple Systems Operator. A cable company.

MTA

Multimedia Terminal Adapter. A device situated in the residence, with which the user interacts (for example, a "smart phone").

MTA Device Certificate

An X.509 certificate placed in nonvolatile read-only memory by the manufacturer at the time of manufacture. The certificate contains (among other things) the MTA's public key and its MAC address. The certificate is signed by the manufacturer.

MTA Telephony Certificate

An X.509 certificate provided to the MTA during the initialization process by the service provider. The certificate contains the MTA's public key and is signed by the telephony service provider.

NAT

Network Address Translation. A function that changes the network address of a packet as it traverses the route from source to destination. Typically used either to ensure anonymity or to minimize the need for a large address space.

NCS

Network-Based Call Signaling. A call signaling architecture in which endpoints are treated as relatively dumb devices and in which call state is maintained within the CMS for the duration of a call.

network order

Multi-octet values transmitted in the order from most significant octet to least significant octet. When transmitting multi-octet values (for example, a 32-bit integer), unless specified otherwise, all the protocols in this book require that the octets be transmitted in network order.

NID

Network Interface Device. A device that is attached to the side of the house and marks the demarcation point between wires owned by the local telephone company and the in-home telephony wiring. A NID also provides electrical isolation from the telephony network.

NIST

National Institute of Standards and Technology. Successor to the National Bureau of Standards, NIST is the agency responsible for setting standards for the U.S. government.

NIU

Network Interface Unit. A device that acts as the interface between a home network and the cable network.

Nonce

A number, almost always encrypted, that is passed from one device to another and that typically is returned by the second device along with other information. The presence of the nonce in the returned message validates the other information.

NSA

National Security Agency—the American government agency responsible for the development of cryptographic and other security measures. For many years, the agency was so secret that no reference to it could appear in any federal documents. Now it even has its own Web page (*www.nsa.gov*), but even so, it has proved itself highly capable of guarding its secrets.

NTP

Network Time Protocol—specified in RFC 1129, NTP provides a method for synchronizing clocks on physically separated machines.

NULL

An ASCII character corresponding to 8 bits with the value 0.

octet

A group of eight bits—nowadays often used interchangeably with the term "byte", which originally was a hardware term for a group of bits not necessarily eight in number.

OI

Operator Interrupt. An operator service whereby the operator may interrupt an ongoing conversation. Sometimes called an Emergency Interrupt (EI).

one-way super encryption algorithm

A semi-facetious name for an algorithm that performs "encryption" but cannot support decryption. Typically this is used where a specification (an RFC) requires that a field be filled, but a particular implementation (PacketCable DCS) does not want useful information to be revealed. Such an algorithm might be: "for any input, the output is the letter 'a'".

OPC

Origination Point Code. A value that represents the Point Code of a device that originates an SS7 message.

OSS

Operations Support System. The devices and protocols used to manage "backend" aspects of a network such as provisioning and billing; sometimes referred to as the "Backoffice".

out-of-band

Information exchange among devices that rely on some mechanism different from the one that usually connects them—for example, placing a security key on a floppy and physically distributing it to several devices instead of transmitting the key through a network protocol interface.

PacketCable™

The name of the project to define a suite of interoperability specifications to allow for devices within a packetized telephony-over-cable network to function correctly even if provided by many vendors.

PBX

Private Branch Exchange. A system that controls local phone calls among a reasonably small number of users, typically at a company's single location. An intelligent MTA can act as a sort of mini-PBX for the home.

PC

Personal computer—a computer used in the home.

PDP

Policy Decision Point—a COPS server; the entity that makes decisions as to whether flows should be admitted to a network.

PDU

Protocol Data Unit. The data portion of a packet in a particular protocol.

PEP

Policy Enforcement Point—a COPS client; an entity that enforces admission policy for a network.

periodic rekeying

The process of changing keys from time to time to secure a long-lived connection.

persistent event

In NCS, an event on the endpoint whose occurrence is signaled to the Call Agent regardless of whether it is explicitly included in the currently active RequestedEvents list for that endpoint.

PKINIT

A method of using public key cryptography to authenticate a client during its initial exchange with a Kerberos Ticket Granting Server.

PMD

Physical Media Dependent. The sublayer at the bottom of the DOCSIS stack.

port

A numeric logical entity on a device that allows the operating system to direct incoming packets to the correct application.

post dial delay

The period between when a user dials the last digit of a phone number and hears the phone at the other end begin to ring.

post pickup delay

The period between when a user lifts a handset off-hook and hears a dial tone.

preshared keys

Cryptographic keys that are shared by some out-of-band mechanism and that must be shared before communication can be secured.

private key

A key used to decrypt a message encrypted with the owner's public key or to sign a message from the key's owner. Sometimes called a **secret key**.

profile

> A particular implementation or instantiation of a more general protocol. Many protocols are extremely general and allow one to specify a restricted set of messages and their actions for a particular purpose. Such a set is known as a profile. For example, NCS is a profile of MGCP with a few extensions.

protected field

> That portion of a packet that is to be protected by some mechanism, typically either encryption or a cyclic redundancy check.

protocol stack

> A series of protocols, each one running on top of the one below it in the stack.

provisional response

> An "interim" signaling response, used to indicate that a request or command has been received and is currently being processed. Provisional responses are typically used to prevent the original request or command from being unnecessarily retransmitted due to the expiration of a retransmission timer.

PSK

> Phase Shift Keyint. A modulation scheme in which information is encoded by changing the phase of a transmitted signal of constant amplitude and constant frequency.

PSTN

> Public Switched Telephone Network. The ordinary telephone network.

PSTN Gateway

> A device that straddles the boundary between a PacketCable network and the PSTN; it allows signaling and content information to pass between the two networks.

public key

> A cryptographic key that is made public for the purpose of encrypting messages to the key's owner or validating signed messages from him or her.

public key cryptography

> A cryptographic system in which pairs of keys are used: One key is public, and available to everyone, one key is private. Keys are always generated in pairs, and the strength of public key cryptography lies in the presumed mathematical difficulty in deriving the (unknown) private key from the (known) public key.

QAM

> Quadrature Amplitude Modulation. A multistate system of amplitude modulation. The number of states determines efficiency and robustness in the presence of noise. 16-QAM, 64-QAM and 256-QAM are commonly used.

QoS

> Quality of Service. Usually used in a manner that implies a certain guaranteed bandwidth for information flow.

QPSK

> Quadrature Phase Shift Keying. A modulation scheme that is simple to implement, tolerant of noise and relatively inefficient, although more efficient than PSK. Often used by cable modems in the upstream portion of the HFC access network.

RADIUS

> Remote Authentication Dial In User Service—specified in RFCs 2138 and 2139, RADIUS provides a client/server protocol that permits information flow from client to server over UDP in a timely manner.

ranging

> The process by which a CM/CMTS system establishes the correct operating parameters for the CM.

RBOC

> Regional Bell Operating Company. A company that was originally part of AT&T but that was split off as a result of the Modified Final Judgement and owns and operates local telephony lines.

RC4

> A highly efficient stream cipher claimed as a trade secret by RSA Security, although fully-compatible source code is freely available on the Internet.

Reed-Solomon Encoding

> A method of FEC used in DOCSIS modems.

remote ringback

> Ringback that is generated elsewhere than at the calling party's MTA. Remote ringback is rarely used in PacketCable networks, but it is typically used when placing a call from a PacketCable network to a device on the PSTN.

reservation

> The process of setting aside resources for a call. Reserved resources may not be used for any other call, even if they are not currently being used. Reservation occurs after authorization and prior to commitment.

RF

> Radio Frequency—electromagnetic radiation in the "radio" portion of the spectrum (that is, typically between a few megahertz and a few gigahertz).

RFC

Request For Comments—the quirky name by which the standards that define the operation of the Internet are called. RFCs are issued by the IETF; every major Internet protocol is specified in a numbered RFC.

ringback

An indication (usually audible) that the phone at the far end is ringing. Ringing may be either *local* or *remote*.

router

A network device that accepts packets and forwards them appropriately after determining the ultimate destination of the packets.

RSA

Rivest, Shamir, Adleman—a common public key algorithm, named after its three inventors.

R-spec

Resource Flowspec—a flowspec describing the resources required by a flow.

RSVP

Resource Reservation Protocol—defined in RFC 2205, this protocol defines a mechanism for reserving resources for flows in a network.

RTCP

Real-Time Control Protocol. Defined in RFC 1889, this protocol provides a mechanism for controlling and reporting on the flow of real-time data in an IP network. This protocol is of limited utility in PacketCable, since the source of RTCP packets is typically an untusted device.

RTP

Real-Time Transport Protocol. Defined in RFC 1889, this protocol provides a mechanism for encapsulating real-time data for an IP network.

SA

Security association—an interface between two network elements that ensures that traffic passing through the interface is cryptographically secure (typically, through encryption).

SAID

Security Association Identifier. A 14-bit number used to identify security associations in BPI+.

scrambling

The process of encoding binary data so as to remove long sequences of zeros and ones. See *DC bias*.

SCTP

> Stream Control Transmission Protocol. An effort currently under way within the IETF to define a protocol suitable for the reliable delivery of real-time signaling information.

SDP

> Session Description Protocol. Defined in RFC 2327, this is used throughout PacketCable to provide high-level definitions of connections and media streams.

Secret Key—see *Private Key*.

Security Association

> An SA exists between two devices when they have agreed on a mechanism and its associated parameters that will permit them to exchange traffic securely (that is, in such a way that an eavesdropper would not be able to make sense of the traffic).

service class

> A DOCSIS term for a group of service flows with particular QoS parameters.

service flow

> A DOCSIS term for a unidirectional stream of packets that are guaranteed that a particular amount of bandwidth will be available.

SFID

> Service Flow Identifier. A 32-bit number assigned by a CMTS and used to identify a particular DOCSIS Service Flow.

SG

> Signaling Gateway. That portion of a PSTN Gateway responsible for the signaling interface between the two networks.

SHA-1

> Secure Hash Algorithm number 1. A cryptographic hash function originally published by NIST as the "Secure Hash Standard", NIST FIPS PUB 180. SHA-1 has no known weaknesses and produces an output of 160 bits.

shared secret

> In cryptography, something (typically a bitstream known as a *key*) known to two parties who wish to exchange information and that other parties do not know (and cannot easily guess).

SID

> Service Identifier. A 14-bit identifier assigned by a CMTS to a CM. Each SID is unique within the universe of modems managed by a particular CMTS. A CM may have more than one SID.

Signaling Link Selection (SLS) code

An identifier used within SS7 that is unused by PacketCable elements.

SIP

Session Initiation Protocol—defined in RFC 2543, this is the basis of the messaging system used in DCS.

SNMPv3

Version 3 of the Simple Network Management Protocol—defined in RFCs 2571 through 2575. SNMP defines a protocol designed to allow a network operator to manage the individual devices on his network.

SPI

Security Parameter Index. A 32-bit value that identifies which particular ciphersuite and key is to be used on an IPsec connection. The actual ciphersuite and key are not part of the SPI. The SPI merely allows one of the devices on the connection to look up the correct values in a table.

SS7

Signaling System Number 7. A combined architecture and suite of protocols used by the PSTN to perform out-of-band call signaling.

SSRC

Synchronization Source—as defined in RFC 1889, a 32-bit identifier used to identify the source of RTP packets.

state blob

An encrypted representation of call information that is stored on an untrusted MTA in the DCS protocol.

stream cipher

A method of encrypting a stream of octets one at a time.

switch

In a conventional telephony network, a device in the Central Office to which a subscriber's line is connected, and which allows physical circuits to be completed, allowing phone calls to occur.

symmetric key

A key that may be used for either decryption or encryption.

SYNC

DOCSIS message transmitted periodically by a CMTS.

TCAP

Transmission Capabilities Application Protocol. An SS7 protocol used to perform database transactions.

TCP

Transmission Control Protocol. Defined in RFC 793, this is a protocol for the reliable delivery of information.

TDD

Telecommunication Devices for the Deaf. Devices and protocols used to allow hearing-impaired individuals to conduct conversations via telephony.

TDMA

Time Division Multiple Access. A method whereby several transmitters can share a common medium by synchronizing their transmissions according to some agreed-upon clocking mechanism.

TEK

Traffic Encryption Key. A key used in BPI+ to encrypt and decrypt traffic flowing between a cable modem and its CMTS.

TFTP

Trivial File Transfer Protocol—defined in RFC 1350, this protocol provides a very simple mechanism for transferring files between devices.

TGCP

Trunking Gateway Control Protocol. A variant of the Media Gateway Control Protocol used by the Media Gateway Controller to control the Media Gateway.

TGS

Ticket Granting Server. A device that authenticates MTAs and issues tickets that allow them to use other services on the network.

TGT

Ticket Granting Ticket. An intermediate ticket issued by a KDC, allowing a device to obtain a service ticket. In PacketCable, TGTs are not used.

TGW

Trunking Gateway. An alternative term for a Media Gateway.

theft of service

An attack whose principal goal is to use a service without paying for it.

ticket

An encoded string that confirms the identity of the possessor, allowing it access to other services on the network.

TLV

Type-Length-Value—an extensible method of encoding parameters; used by DOCSIS.

TOS

> Type of Service. The second octet of the IP header. The meaning of the TOS field as specified in RFC 760 has been superseded (or perhaps "overloaded" is a better term) by several other interpretations. In particular, RFC 2475 defines a modern interpretation used in DiffServ networks.

trap

> An asynchronous SNMP message in which an agent informs its manager that an unusual condition has occurred.

trunk

> A connection in the PSTN that is used to carry information (either signaling or user content, although a particular trunk is typically used to carry only one kind of information).

TSP

> Telephony Service Provider. The network operator who is providing the telephony service.

T-spec

> Traffic Flowspec—a flowspec describing a transmitted stream.

UCD

> Upstream Channel Descriptor. A DOCSIS MAC management message transmitted periodically by a CMTS to define the characteristics of an upstream channel.

UDP

> User Datagram Protocol. Defined in RFC 768, this protocol provides no guarantee that transmitted information has been received.

UGS

> Unsolicited Grant Service. A DOCSIS Service Flow in which the CMTS automatically and periodically provides a fixed number of minislots for use by a particular CM. Typically used for transmission of CBR information such as G.711 encoded voice.

Upstream

> In the direction from the end-user to the network.

URI

> Uniform Resource Indicator—a string that defines the location of a resource.

URL

> Uniform Resource Locator. A string that defines the location of a resource, as well as the protocol to be used to access the resource.

USM

> User-based Security Model—the security model defined in RFC 2274 for version 3 of SNMP.

VoIP

> Voice over Internet Protocol—a catch-all term for various technologies that transport voice conversations over IP networks. The author finds it useful to distinguish VoIP from "telephony over IP". VoIP in general carries no connotation that quality of service is guaranteed, that the system can interoperate with the PSTN, or that the billing is part of the architecture. True telephony over IP includes all these.

VSA

> Vendor-Specific Attribute. Many protocols allow vendors to extend the basic information passed within a message by permitting them to define VSAs. RADIUS is a good example of such a protocol. It allows for arbitrary information to be carried by the use of VSAs.

X.509

> A specification that governs the format of public key certificates—more fully, *Information Technology—Open Systems Interconnection—The Directory:Authentication Framework*. Part of the ITU-T X.500 standard.

*x*DSL

> Any one of a number of DSL (Digital Subscriber Line) technologies.

XOR

> The Exclusive Or operation—an operation applied to a pair of bits to produce a single output bit. The output bit is 1 unless both input bits are the same.

Zone

> A set of MTAs served by a single CMS.

Appendix
B
Cyclic Redundancy Checks

Packetized data are subject to occasional errors while being transmitted from point to point. These errors may occur for any of a number of reasons: collisions, maladjusted transmitters or receivers and noise in the transmission medium being typical ones. In order to ensure that a received data packet is identical to the packet that was transmitted, short **Cyclic Redundancy Checks** (**CRC**s) are frequently added to the packets.

CRCs have the property that, if any of the bits in the packet are changed, the computed value of the CRC also changes (with a high degree of probability). This means that, if a receiver receives a packet containing a CRC, and the receiver independently calculates the value of the CRC from the contents of the packet and obtains the same result as that contained in the packet, the receiver can be almost certain that the packet has been received undamaged.

CRC calculations are not trivial, and are usually performed in hardware. Consider a packet that we desire to protect with a CRC. We select the bits that we wish to protect and call this the **protected field**. Typically, this is the entire packet, but it is not necessarily so. We wish to protect the protected field with an n-bit CRC. Usually, CRCs are either 16 or 32 bits long; the longer the CRC, the greater the confidence that damaged packets will be correctly detected.

CRCs require a *generating polynomial,* $G(x)$. A typical method of generating a CRC is that described in ISO 8802-3, which is used to protect DOCSIS MAC headers (see Chapter 3, "MAC Header Format"). The procedure, which generates a 32-bit CRC, is as follows.

1. Complement the first 32 bits of the protected field.

2. Consider the n bits of the protected field to be the coefficients of a polynomial, $M(x)$, of degree $(n - 1)$, in order.

3. Multiply M(x) by x^{32}. Call this P(x).

4. Divide P(x) by G(x), where G(x) is given by:

$$G(x) = x^{32} + x^{26} + x^{22} + x^{16} + x^{12} + x^{11} + x^{10} + x^8 + x^7 + x^5 + x^44 + x^2 + x + 1$$

which is equivalent to the 33-bit pattern:

```
100000100010000010001110110110111
```

This procedure gives a remainder polynomial, R(x), of degree <= 31.

5. Consider the coefficients of R(x) as a 32-bit sequence and invert it. The result is the 32-bit CRC.

Let's consider a (comparatively) simple example. Suppose that we are sending a packet with a length of 6 octets, and we wish to protect it with the above 32-bit CRC. For simplicity's sake, we will assume that the bits in the packet alternate, starting with a 1.

The original protected field looks like this:

```
101010101010101010101010101010101010101010101010
```

1. Complement the first 32 bits.

Now the packet looks like this:

```
010101010101010101010101010101011010101010101010
```

2. Consider this pattern to represent the coefficients of a polynomial of degree 47. Call this polynomial M.

3. Multiply M by x^{32} to give P. This is equivalent to left shifting the bit pattern by 32, filling on the right with zeros. Thus, P can be written:

```
010101010101010101010101010101011010101010101010100000000000000000000000000000000
00000
```

4. Divide P by G and note the remainder, R. In our example this is:

```
11010110111101001011011000000111
```

5. Inverting gives the final 32-bit CRC:

```
00101001000010110100100111111000
```

Appendix

C

Standard Encodings

PacketCable networks make use of several more or less standard methods of representing information in encoded formats. This appendix details several of these.

Binary to Hex

Plaintext is limited to using printable ASCII characters. Frequently, however, PacketCable networks need to pass binary values around the network (for example, many of the identifiers are 32-bit binary values). The most common method of representing such values is to convert them to an ASCII representation of the hexadecimal characters that are equivalent to the binary number.

For example, suppose that we wish to encode the value 366609136, which is a 32-bit identifier of some kind within a PacketCable network. The number 366609136 in base 16 is 15DA02F0. To represent the number 366609136, the string "15DA02F0" is transmitted in its ASCII representation. The number 366609136 is therefore encoded as the sequence 31 35 44 41 30 32 46 30. In this encoding, an n-bit number is encoded as a string of $n/4$ octets.

BASE64

BASE64 is a general-purpose encoding mechanism that takes as its input any arbitrary binary string (possibly including the NULL character, character number zero) and produces as its output one or more lines of printable ASCII characters. The encoded data are 33% longer than the unencoded data.

The algorithm is presented in detail in RFC 1521, which is the RFC that defines the Internet MIME mechanism for transmitting arbitrary nontextual information safely inside 7-bit SMTP e-mail messages.[1]

---

1. The alert reader should be able to see why such an algorithm is needed in this RFC.

In PacketCable, BASE64 encoding is used in signaling messages to convert arbitrary strings into ones that can be safely handled by the ASCII-based signaling mechanisms. For example, the shared secrets and keys used to set up secure communication channels may be strings containing arbitrary binary characters. These are converted with the BASE64 algorithm to allow them to be incorporated safely in the signaling messages.

The BASE64 Algorithm

The output character set is limited to 65 characters. Sixty-four of these are used as ordinary output characters (hence, "BASE64"). The 65th character (the "=" sign) is used to indicate the need for special processing.

The algorithm takes input in 24-bit chunks (three contiguous octets), mapping each 24-bit chunk to a four-character output. There is no randomization or encryption in the process: Identical 24-bit input always produces identical 4-character output.

The 24-bit input is divided into four 6-bit pseudocharacters. Each of the 6-bit pseudocharacters is mapped directly to a single output character.[2] Table C-1 shows the mapping used to produce an output character from an input 6-bit pseudocharacter.

At the end of the input stream, there may be insufficient bits to make up a complete 24-bit input block. If this is true, the shortfall may be either 8 or 16 bits. In either case, the input is padded with zero bits on the right until the 24-bit size is reached. The conversion then takes place as just described except that (1) if the shortfall was 16 bits, only the first two output characters are taken, and two octets comprising the ASCII character "=" (ASCII character number 61) are appended; and (2) if the shortfall was 8 bits, only the first three output characters are taken, and a single octet comprising the ASCII character "=" is appended. The addition of "=" padding allows the decoder to correctly recognize that a number of zero bits have been added to the original string before conversion.

As an example, suppose that the phrase "PacketCable is the future" is to be BASE64 encoded. In ASCII, this begins with the sequence with the three-octet series (in decimal): 80, 97, 99.

In 8-bit binary this is:

```
01010000, 01100001, 01100011.
```

Converting this to 6-bit groups:

```
010100, 000110, 000101, 100011,
```
or, in decimal:

```
20, 6, 5, 35
```

---

2. The bitstream is assumed to be ordered monotonically in order from most significant bit to least significant bit.

Table C-1 BASE64 Encoding

In	Out	In	Out	In	Out	In	Out
00	A	16	Q	32	g	48	w
01	B	17	R	33	h	49	x
02	C	18	S	34	i	50	y
03	D	19	T	35	j	51	z
04	E	20	U	36	k	52	0
05	F	21	V	37	l	53	1
06	G	22	W	38	m	54	2
07	H	23	X	39	n	55	3
08	I	24	Y	40	o	56	4
09	J	25	Z	41	p	57	5
10	K	26	a	42	q	58	6
11	L	27	b	43	r	59	7
12	M	28	c	44	s	60	8
13	N	29	d	45	t	61	9
14	O	30	e	46	u	62	+
15	P	31	f	47	v	63	/

which, according to Table C-1, maps to the four printable characters:

```
UGFj
```

A similar operation gives us the following output groups until we reach the end of the phrase. The final complete input group is the sequence "tur". Once this has been encoded, we are left with the single character "e", which has the decimal value 101. To construct a 24-bit group, we pad with zeros:

```
101, 0, 0
```

which in binary is:

```
01100101, 0, 0
```

Splitting this into 6-bit pseudocharacters:

```
011001, 010000, 000000, 000000
```

In decimal:

25, 16, 0, 0

The first two output characters are therefore the pair ZQ. The last two characters are the "=" character, to indicate the fact that the last input group was padded with two NULL characters. The complete BASE64 encoding of the ASCII phrase "PacketCable is the future" is:

"UGFja2V0Q2FibGUgaXMgdGhlIGZldHVyZQ=="

Appendix
D

Bearer-Channel Keying Material

The keying material used to secure bearer-channel traffic (conversations) is derived from a secret that is shared by the two MTAs and that is passed inside the call signaling messages.

The keys are produced from the secret by a Key Derivation Function, $\mathcal{F}$, which is a function of two values: the shared secret, S and a constant bit pattern to act as a seed, most easily represented as an ASCII-encoded string whose value conveys the purpose to which it is being put. This sounds rather obscure, but in fact it is fairly simple. The particular seed used to derive the keying material for end-to-end communication corresponds directly to the ASCII-encoded string "`End-End RTP Security Association`", not including the enclosing quotation marks. When the function is called with the intention of deriving keying material for other purposes, a different bit pattern, but one that is equally descriptive, is used.

Suppose that we denote the seed by the symbol D. Now we define a function A by:

```
A₀ = D
Aᵢ = HMAC_SHA-1(S, Aᵢ₋₁)
```

where HMAC_SHA-1(x, y) is the SHA-1 HMAC of y with the key x.

The HMAC algorithm is described in detail in RFC 2104 and also in the section HMACs of Chapter 2. The mechanism for deriving a key from the HMAC function is given in the section "Key Derivation Function" in Chapter 4.

For the purpose of this example, we will take the value of the shared secret, S, to be the ASCII string "`This is a shared secret`". The seed we will take to be the ASCII string "`This is the seed`".

The key deriviation function, $\mathcal{F}$ (S, Δ), is calculated as:

$$\mathcal{F} \; (S, \; D) = \text{HMAC\_SHA-1}(S, \; A_1 + \Delta) \; +$$
$$\text{HMAC\_SHA-1}(S, \; A_2 + \Delta) \; +$$
$$\text{HMAC\_SHA-1}(S, \; A_3 + \Delta) \; + \; . \; . \; . \; .$$

where "+" implies concatenation, and the algorithm proceeds until a key of the needed length has been derived.

Let us suppose that we wish to derive a 64-bit key. This requires only the first eight octets of output. That is, only the first eight octets of the function $\mathcal{F}$ (S, D) are needed, where:

$$\mathcal{F} \; (S, \; D) = \text{HMAC\_SHA-1}(S, \; A_1 + \Delta)$$

Then (all values are in hexadecimal):

```
A₀ = 54 68 69 7320 69 73 20 74 68 65 20 73 65 65 64 = Δ
A₁ = HMAC_SHA-1("This is a shared secret", A0)
   = ed 5b f2 6a fc 57 c1 bd c2 50 ca fa 33 16 83 46 f8 63 e0 b3
```

So:

```
𝓕 (S, Δ) = HMAC_SHA-1("This is a shared secret", A1 + Δ)
         = a6 a4 ae ac 80 32 5a a4 09 01 0b 3b 6e c2 5f ca ba 61 e3 96
```

The key then has the value:

```
a6 a4 ae ac 80 32 5a a4
```

Index

A NOTE ON THE TYPE

This book was set in New Century Schoolbook, a typeface adapted by A. Chekulaev from Century Schoolbook, which was designed by Morris F. Benton (1872–1948). Century Schoolbook was one of several variations of Century Roman as cut by Linn Boyd Benton (1844–1932) in response to a request by Theodore Low De Vinne for an attractive, easy-to-read typeface to fit the narrow columns of his Century Magazine. Century Schoolbook was specifically designed for school textbooks, but its great legibility quickly earned it popularity in many applications.

Composed by
Stratford Publishing Services
Brattleboro, VT

Printed and bound by
Phoenix Color Corporation
Hagerstown, MD